|Gymnasium Bayern|

access 7

Cornelsen

Access Bayern 7

Im Auftrag des Verlages herausgegeben von
Prof. Dr. Engelbert Thaler, Augsburg
Prof. Jörg Rademacher, Mannheim

Erarbeitet von
Laurence Harger, Nürnberg
Cecile Niemitz-Rossant, Berlin
Jennifer Seidl, München
Eleanor Toal, Liverpool

unter Mitarbeit von
Dr. Annette Leithner-Brauns, Dresden
Birgit Ohmsieder, Berlin
Mervyn Whittaker, Bad Dürkheim
Dominik Eberhard (Vocabulary, Dictionaries), Bonn

in Zusammenarbeit mit der Englischredaktion
Filiz Bahşi (Projektkoordination, verantwortliche Redakteurin), Dr. Philip Devlin, Ursula Fleischhauer, Bonnie Glänzer, Stefan Höhne (Redaktionsleitung), Sophia Schneider

Beratende Mitwirkung
Thomas Bohlen, Traunstein
Gerhard Finster, Dillingen
Ingola Seger, Augsburg
Claudia Vetter, München
Jörg Wunderlich, München

Illustrationen
Tobias Dahmen, Utrecht/NL; Burkhard Schulz, Düsseldorf *sowie* Roland Beier, Berlin

Fotos
Nigel Wilson Photography, Bristol

Umschlaggestaltung
hawemannundmosch, Berlin

Layout und technische Umsetzung
Eric Gira, Ungermeyer, Berlin

www.cornelsen.de

In diesem Werk wird in Form von Symbolen auf Audio-Material verwiesen; dieses enthält – bis auf die Hörverstehensübungen – ausschließlich optionale Unterrichtsmaterialien. Die Audio-Materialien unterliegen nicht dem staatlichen Zulassungsverfahren.

Die Mediencodes enthalten zusätzliche Unterrichtsmaterialien, die der Verlag in eigener Verantwortung zur Verfügung stellt.

Dieses Werk berücksichtigt die Regeln der reformierten Rechtschreibung und Zeichensetzung.

1. Auflage, 1. Druck 2019

Alle Drucke dieser Auflage sind inhaltlich unverändert und können im Unterricht nebeneinander verwendet werden.

Druck: Mohn Media Mohndruck, Gütersloh

ISBN 978-3-06-033491-9

ISBN 978-3-06-034317-1 (E-Book)

PEFC
PEFC/04-31-1033

PEFC zertifiziert
Dieses Produkt stammt aus nachhaltig bewirtschafteten Wäldern und kontrollierten Quellen.

www.pefc.de

Access Bayern 7 enthält folgende Teile:

Units	die fünf Kapitel des Buches
Access to cultures	landeskundliche Informationen
Text File	eine Sammlung englischer und amerikanischer Geschichten und Sachtexte
Skills File	eine Beschreibung wichtiger Lern- und Arbeitstechniken
Grammar File	eine Zusammenfassung der Grammatik jeder Unit
Vocabulary	das Wörterverzeichnis zum Lernen der neuen Wörter jeder Unit
Dictionary	alphabetisches Wörterverzeichnis zum Nachschlagen (Englisch-Deutsch / Deutsch-Englisch)

In den Units findest du diese Überschriften:

Background file	Informationen über Land und Leute
Everyday English	Englisch in Alltagssituationen
Looking at language	Beispiele sammeln und sprachliche Regeln entdecken
Language help	Hilfe in Form von sprachlichen Regeln
Practice	Aufgaben und Übungen
Writing course	englische Texte besser schreiben
The world behind the picture	vom Bild in den Film – Videoclips mit Aufgaben
Thinking about language	Aufgaben zur Sprachreflexion
Text	eine spannende oder lustige Geschichte
Your task	In der Lernaufgabe kannst du in jeder Unit zeigen, was du gelernt hast und dich selbst einschätzen.
Checkpoint	Auf diesen Seiten kannst du den Wortschatz und die Grammatik einer Unit wiederholen und dich auf Schulaufgaben vorbereiten.

Du findest auch diese Symbole:

	Texte, die du dir anhören kannst: *www.cornelsen.de/webcodes* (Webcode: *dozugi*)
	zusätzliche Materialien, die du unter *www.cornelsen.de/webcodes* (Webcode: *nasedi*; Kaleidoscope-Videos: *zopeno*) finden kannst
	Übungssequenz: neue Grammatik intensiv üben und dann anwenden
Early finisher	zusätzliche Aktivitäten und Übungen für Schüler/innen, die früher fertig sind
More help	zusätzliche Hilfen für eine Aufgabe
You choose	eine Aufgabe auswählen
EXTRA	zusätzliche Aktivitäten und Übungen für alle
My Book	schöne und wichtige Arbeiten sammeln
Study skills	Einführung in Lern- und Arbeitstechniken
	Hören Sprechen Lesen Schreiben
	Mediation (zwischen zwei Sprachen vermitteln), Thinking about language (Sprachreflexion)
	Partnerarbeit Partnercheck Gruppenarbeit Kooperative Lernform

	Lerninhalte	Texte
Unit 1 This is London	• Sending messages and holiday postcards • Talking about sights • Making plans • Reading a street map • Reading a Tube map	A Up on the roof B London attractions C Watching the cricket Text The Notting Hill Carnival Parade (p. 24)
Access to cultures: The Tower and the monarchs		
Unit 2 Welcome to Snowdonia	• Town and country • Moving house • Talking about a trip • Volunteer work • Wales and Welsh	A Everything is wrong B Climbing Mount Snowdon Text Snowdonia at night (p. 46)
Access to cultures: Welcome to Wales		
EXTRA · Kaleidoscope · The British Isles and the USA		
Unit 3 My trip to the Southwest	• Planning a trip • Visiting places • Discovering the Southwest • Life on a farm • Texting • Writing a diary	A Monument Valley B Back in Santa Fe C Texting from Taos Background file The Southwest (p. 64) Text The horse ride (p. 76)
Access to cultures: Celebrating in America		

Kompetenzen	Sprache	
Access to cultures Small talk (p. 13) **Writing course** Good sentences (p. 16) **Study skills** Giving feedback on a text (p. 17) **MyBook** Write a text (p. 17) **Viewing** A bus tour of London (p. 23) **Checkpoint** (p. 27)	**Vocabulary** holidays, German *gehen* **Grammar** simple past / present perfect (Revision); present perfect progressive with *for* and *since* **Pronunciation** different stress in German and English (p. 13)	8 Skill in focus: Speaking
		30
Study skills Using an English-German dictionary (p. 38) **Viewing** Adam's video blog (p. 39) **Writing course** Paragraphs and topic sentences (p. 45) **MyBook** A text about a walk in a city or about a film (p. 45) **Checkpoint** (p. 51)	**Vocabulary** jobs **Grammar** *will*-future (Revision); conditional 1 (Revision); conditional 2 *one/ones*	34 Skill in focus: Reading
		54
		56
Viewing A tour guide in Monument Valley(p. 61) **Study skills** Teamwork (p. 69) **Writing course** Using time markers in a story (p. 75) **MyBook** A story (p. 75) **Checkpoint** (p. 79)	**Vocabulary** countries, travelling, describing people and places **Grammar** adjectives and adverbs; past perfect; comparison of adverbs; reflexive forms **Pronunciation** consonants	58 Skill in focus: Writing
		82

Inhaltsverzeichnis

	Lerninhalte	Texte
Unit 4 Inside New York	• Neighbourhoods • Multicultural NYC • High School • 9/11 Memorial • Talking about feelings • Describing people and places	A Rivers, towers and waterfalls B A day at the park C Take a walk on the High Line **Song** An open letter to NYC (Beastie Boys) (p. 85) **Background file** High school in the USA (p. 96) **Text** Underground New York (excerpt) (p. 100)

Access to cultures: In the New World

	Lerninhalte	Texte
Unit 5 New Orleans	• Music • Thanksgiving • Hurricane Katrina • Food • Talking about somebody's life • Making suggestions • Describing objects • Social media	A Tyler in New Orleans B The memory box C Big plans **Background file** American football (p. 119) **Text** A true Fourth of July (p. 126)

Text File	Text 1	Text 2	Text 3
	Underground etiquette	London shapes	*Jerry*
	Cautionary verse	Poems	Excerpt from novel

140 More help
148 Early finisher
151 Partner pages
154 Skills File
169 Grammar File
188 Vocabulary
224 Dictionary English – German
253 Dictionary German – English
276 English sounds · 277 Partner B

Kompetenzen	Sprache	
Viewing New York sights, People and places, Hanging out in Brooklyn (p. 86) **Writing course** Structuring a text (p. 95) **Study skills** A good presentation (p. 99) **Checkpoint** (p. 105)	**Vocabulary** American English / British English **Grammar** reporting what someone said; reflexive pronouns; reciprocal pronouns; reflexive verbs **Pronunciation** British and American English (p. 90)	84 Skill in focus: Listening
		108
MyBook Write a social media post about New Orleans (p. 111) **Writing course** The elements of writing (p. 117) **Study skills** Skimming a text (p. 124) **Viewing** A musician in New Orleans (p. 125) **Checkpoint** (p. 129)	**Vocabulary** the media, climate, food, music describing objects synonyms **Grammar** conditional 1 (Revision); conditional 2 (Revision); conditional 3; adverbial clauses of time; *would have*-form; *wish* + past perfect	110 Skill in focus: Mediation

Text 4	Text 5		
1 WTC… Freedom Tower	*Three teeth*		132
Non-fictional text	Fictional text		

278 Self check
279 List of names
280 Countries and continents
282 Irregular verbs
284 Early Finisher Lösungen
286 Classroom English
287 Instructions
288 Quellenverzeichnis
291 Giving feedback to classmates

This is London

London

8 million people

611 square miles

300 languages

Europe's biggest street festival

…

1 London pictures

Think: Do you recognize any of the places, people, signs … in the pictures? Make notes on what you know.

Pair: Exchange information with a partner.

- I think that's …
- Do you know what that is?
- That must/could be … What do you think?

If you still have questions about any pictures, write them down.

Share: Join another pair and try to find answers to your open questions.

2 London sounds

Listen to these sounds of London. Match as many as you can to the pictures.

3 London and you

Do you know London?
Yes? When were you there? What did you do?

I went to London in …

We visited … and I saw …

The best thing about my trip was …

No? Tell your group what you would like to see and do there.

I'd really like to see …

I've always wanted to see …

One thing that I'd really like to do is …

→ **Workbook** *1 (p. 2)*

F

Your task

Your task for this unit: With your group you'll become an expert on a London sight and give your classmates a tour.

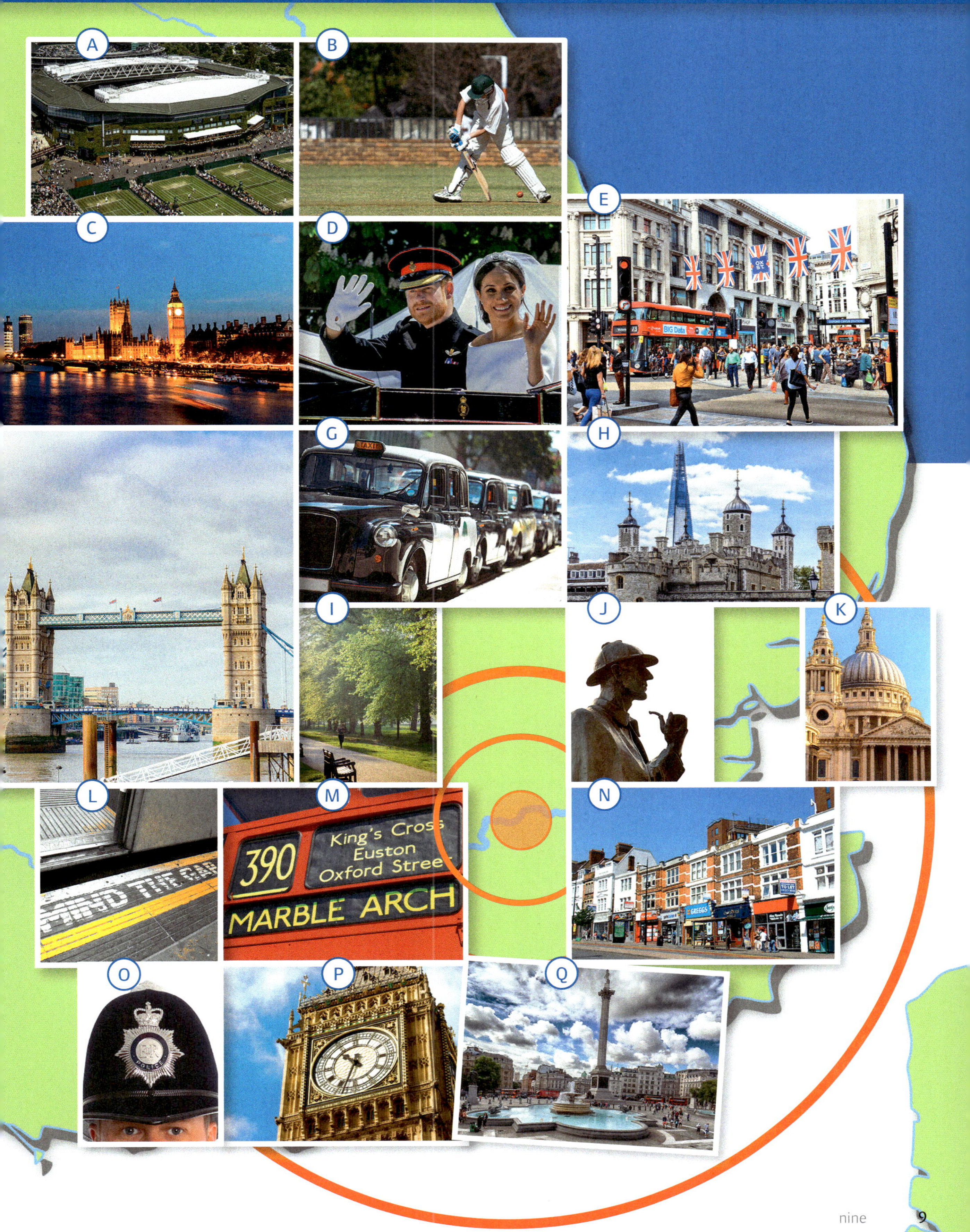
A
B
C
D
E
G
H
I
J
K
L
M
N
O
P
Q
TAXI
390
King's Cross
Euston
MARBLE ARCH
GREGGS

1 Up on the roof

Emily makes some new friends

"Here we are," Mo said to his friend Luke and pointed to a huge glass building.

"You want to take photos of One New Change?" Luke asked. "But why? It's just a shopping centre."

"Oh – have you been here before?" Mo asked.

"Yeah, I came with Dad a few months ago. We bought Mum's birthday present here."

"So, have you been up on the roof too?"

"The roof? No. Why?"

"Well, you'll see. That's where I want to take some photos."

❖

"Just one more photo, Luke," Mo said. "As soon as these people move out of the way."

There were lots of tourists on the roof. Mo and Luke could hear all the different languages.

"St Paul's Cathedral ist mehr als 350 Jahre alt," a man said.

"Hey, that's German!" Mo said to Luke.

"Buckingham Palace'ı görebiliyor musun?"

"And what language is that, Mo?" asked Luke.

Mo didn't know.

"Beth ydi enw yr adeilad yna?" said a woman, and pointed to the Shard.

"Please don't speak Welsh, Mum," a girl replied.

"You have to practise your Welsh for your new school, Emily. I'm only trying to help."

The girl was quiet. A man looked up from a map.

"The building is called the Shard, Emily. It's the tallest building in Europe."

"No, it isn't!" Mo whispered. Then he couldn't stay quiet. "Excuse me. The Shard is only the tallest building in western Europe. There are two taller buildings in Moscow."

"Oh, I see," said the man, and smiled at Mo.

"But," Mo went on, "the Shard is 306 metres high. It has 87 floors, 44 lifts, and amazing views from the top."

"Oh, have you been up there?" the man asked.

Mo shook his head. "It's much too expensive."

"So how do you know all about it?" Emily asked.

"I put a post about it on my blog last weekend," Mo explained. For a moment nobody said anything. Then Luke asked: "Are you here on holiday?"

"Yes, we are," said the man. "But we only arrived yesterday evening, so we haven't seen much yet."

"But we have a lot of plans," the woman said.

"Mum wants to visit lots of museums," Emily said. "But I'd really like to do something different."

"Well," said Luke. "Notting Hill Carnival is this weekend."

"And the England–Australia test match!" Mo went on.

"I'm not into cricket," Emily replied, "but the carnival sounds fun."

"Yes, it is," said Mo. "Well, I hope you enjoy your holiday. And now I must take my photo."

"Er … wait a minute," said Emily. "Your blog – could you give me the address?"

"Sure," said Mo. "Just give me your number and I'll text you. Oh … and I'm Mo, by the way. And this is my friend Luke."

2 Talking about the text

a) Answer the questions.

1 Where are the teens? What are they doing there?
2 How many different languages do the teens hear? Can you name them?
3 Is the Shard the tallest building in the world?

b) Take turns to say who the people are.

This person …

1 has been to One New Change before.
2 wants to take photos.
3 can understand German.
4 says something in Welsh.

c) Write four more sentences like the ones in b).

d) Read your sentences to your partner.

This person doesn't want to speak Welsh.

I think that's …

➔ **Workbook** 2 (p. 3)

3 Mo's blog

SOUTH LONDON BLOGGER

ABOUT ME | CRICKET | LONDON IN FILM

LONDON IN FILM

- Harry Potter
- Into Darkness
- Notting Hill
- James Bond
- Sherlock Holmes

Into Darkness

Year 2016

Director Kathryn Johnson

Story It's the year 2301 and aliens are attacking London. Led by a small group, the people of London fight back.

Guess what city this is. Here's a clue. There is one building in both pictures. What is it? Is this how the skyline will look in 200 years?

Say what this page on Mo's blog is about. Which photo did he take at One New Change, and why? Imagine what information you might find on one of the other pages on Mo's blog and write a few sentences for it.

4 Mo sends a link

Listen to a conversation between Emily Evans and her parents.

a) Listen. Then say which parts of Mo's blog they talk about. What else do you learn about Mo?

b) Listen again and complete the sentences with the correct words in your exercise book.

Was that … …[1]?
No, it … …[2]. Ooh, …[3] a …[4] from Mo. He … … …[5] the link. The link … … …[6]?
Yes. Ooh! … …[7] the …[8] he …[9] from … …[10] of St Paul's Cathedral. Look.

c) Answer the questions.

1. What do they say about Notting Hill?
2. Does Emily like cricket?
3. What does Emily want to see?

www Find out about London in Mo's other films. Find out about cricket.

1 WORDS City holidays

TIP
When you practise vocabulary, it helps to learn verbs and nouns that go together.

a) Write down verb/noun combinations like this:
go by bus, take the bus, wait for the bus, get on …

go by go on take get on wait for	bus · the bus car +Tube · the Tube +underground · the underground a tour · a boat trip

go to +stay at have look at queue at visit walk around	a hotel · a bed & breakfast a map · a website · a +timetable a cathedral · a museum · a +gallery the theatre · the cinema a café · a +restaurant · a carnival a park · a shopping centre lunch · a cup of tea · a drink

More help ➔ p. 140

+ new words

b) What do you do on holiday in a big city? Correct the silly sentences and underline the correct verb/noun combinations.
You don't queue at a cup of tea. You queue at a …

1 You go to a drink.
2 You visit a map.
3 You wait for a park.
4 You stay at the bus.
5 You walk around a tour.
6 You take a gallery.
7 You go on a drink.
8 You look at lunch.
9 You have a café.
10 You go by a hotel.

Early finisher Make three more silly sentences and let a partner correct them.

➔ Workbook 3 (p. 3)

2 REVISION Your holidays (Simple past)

a) Write questions like these for a partner:
Did you stay at home or go away?
Did you go to a city / to the coast / … ?
Where did you stay? What … ?

More help ➔ p. 140

When you're finished, go to a bus stop.

A bus stop is a place in the classroom where you meet a partner to work with.

b) Take turns to ask and answer questions. Take notes on your partner's answers.
A: What did you do in Nürnberg?
B: We walked around the city centre and went to a museum.

c) Go to another bus stop. Tell your new partner about your last partner's holiday.
A: Jan went on a boat trip in Dresden. He …

➔ GF 1.1: Simple past (p. 170) ➔ Workbook 4 (p. 4)

3 REVISION Have you ever …? (Present perfect)

Find out if you have both done the same things.
Each make a window for the answers.

Have you ever been to London?
Have you ever eaten rabbit?
Yes, I have. / No, I haven't.

WE HAVE BOTH … *eaten rabbit.* …	ONLY I HAVE … *visited another country.*
WE HAVEN'T … *played cricket.*	ONLY MY PARTNER HAS … *been to Bamberg.* …

Early finisher ➔ p. 148

➔ GF 1.3: Present perfect (p. 171)

4 REVISION A message from London (Simple past or present perfect?)

Complete Emily's message with the correct tenses: simple past or present perfect.

Hey Amelia,
Hi from London. I 1... (arrive) on Friday evening (with Mum and Dad), so we 2... (already do) a few things. Yesterday morning we 3... (go) up to the roof of a building where we 4... (have) a great view. On the roof we 5... (meet) two boys – Luke and Mo. They 6... (give) us some tips. Luke 7... (tell) us about a carnival at a place called Notting Hill.
After lunch we 8... (visit) St Paul's Cathedral and then we 9... (take) a red London bus to Hyde Park. It 10... (be) beautiful there, and the park is really huge. 11... you 12... (ever be) there?
There are lots of places that we 13... (not be) to yet – like Buckingham Palace, so I 14... (not have) tea with the Queen either (LOL). And we 15... (not visit) any museums yet, but Mum has plans!
16... you 17... (enjoy) your trip to France last week? What 18... (be) the weather like there? In London it 19... (not rain) yet! Hugs, Emily xxx

More help ➜ p. 140 ➜ GF 1.4 Present perfect or simple past? (p. 171)

➜ Workbook 5 (p. 4)

5 THINKING ABOUT LANGUAGE Different stress in German and English

a) Many English and German words look very similar and have the same meaning – but their pronunciation is often different. One reason for that is that the stress is on a different syllable in the words.
Listen to this example: interessiert - interested
In a copy of the table, underline the syllable where the stress comes in the German and English words.

Familie	family	Programm	programme
Kathedrale	cathedral	Tourist	tourist
Moment	moment	traditionell	traditional
Palast	palace		

b) Listen and check.

➜ Workbook 6 (p. 5)

6 Everyday English: Small talk

a) Two people meet at One New Change. Read their dialogue. Put the blue sentences in the right order. Then listen and check.

A: It's a great view of the cathedral, isn't it?
B: Thanks. Have a nice day.
A: Have you been here before?
B: I'm John. Nice to meet you, Sandy.
A: Well, I work near here, so I come here often.
By the way, my name is Sandy.
B: Just for a long weekend.
A: How long are you staying in London?
B: No, this is my first time. I'm a tourist.
A: Well, enjoy the rest of your visit. Bye.
B: Oh, yes, it's amazing.

b) Practise the dialogue.

c) Act out your own dialogue.
Partner A ➜ p. 151 Partner B ➜ p. 277

Access to cultures

In Britain and in other English-speaking countries, people often have short, friendly conversations with people they don't know, for example at a shopping centre or a bus stop. Then they say goodbye and don't expect to meet again.
What about your country? Is it the same there?

➜ Workbook 7 (p. 5)

1 London attractions

Say what the headings and pictures tell you about each of the four attractions.

2 The Evans family's plans

a) Listen to Emily and her parents. Which attraction would each of them like to visit?

b) Listen again. Take notes on:
- Emily and her parents' arguments for and against the attractions.
- what they decide to do today.
- what they are going to do tomorrow.

c) Check with a partner.

d) Why do you think Emily and her parents have chosen "their" attractions? Read texts A–D. Then say what their reasons could be.

I think Emily's mum wants to go to … because …

I'm sure Emily likes … because …

3 Your plans

Make plans for a day in London. Talk about arguments for and against the four attractions. Then agree on two attractions you would like to visit.

→ Workbook 8 (p. 6)

A

LOVELY PLANET ***London*** *and its treasures*

NATURAL HISTORY MUSEUM

This cathedral of science is THE place for everyone who is interested in the history of our planet.

Open every day – 10:00 – 17:50

Entry free

37

B

Inside **Big Ben**

Inside Big Ben

Everyone calls this famous clock tower 'Big Ben', but its real name is the Elizabeth Tower. Big Ben is in fact the name of the largest bell inside it.

The bell rang for the first time on 11th July 1859. Today, not only Londoners hear the clock every hour; around the world millions of people also hear it on BBC radio. Most people who visit London see Big Ben from the outside. Why don't you climb the tower and see the inside too?

Tour times

December–May, Mon–Fri: 9:15, 11:15, 14:15
May–September, Mon–Fri: 9,11,14 and 16
Tours are only for people who live in the UK.
Tours are free, but please reserve your place early.

What will you see?

The tour will take you up 334 stone steps to hear Big Ben ring out the hour. You'll have an amazing view over London – and a chance to walk behind the clock faces and see the clock wheels at work.

C

THE LONDON EYE
FACTS AND FIGURES

1 The London Eye travels at less than 1 km an hour. That's as fast – or slow – as a tortoise. This means that a ride takes about 30 minutes and you have lots of time to enjoy the sights.
2 The London Eye is 135 m high. That is like 64 red telephone boxes on top of each other.
3 From the top of the Eye you can see around 40 km on a clear day. There is a great view of famous sights like Buckingham Palace, the Houses of Parliament, the Shard and St Paul's Cathedral.
4 800 people can travel in the Eye at one time, as many as in 11 big red London buses.

Opening times

The London Eye is open every day except Christmas Day.
The first ride starts at 10:00 am, and the ticket office opens at 9:30 am.
Check the website for more details.
www.londoneye.com

Tickets & Prices	on the day	online
Adult (16+)	£19.95	£17.96
Child (4–15 yrs)	£14.00	£12.60
Child (under 4)	FREE	FREE
Family of four	£67.91	£54.33

London Eye: Conceived and designed by Marks Barfield Architects

D

TOWER OF LONDON
Over 900 years of history.

During its long history, the Tower of London has been a palace, a prison, and even a zoo.
When you take a tour with one of the Beefeaters who guard the Tower, you'll hear many stories and legends from the past. One legend is that six ravens must always live at the Tower. If they leave, the king will fall. The Beefeaters look after the ravens and feed them 'bird biscuits', full of blood!
The Tower is also home to the Crown Jewels.
School classes which visit the Tower education centre can try on a copy of the Crown.

Opens	9 am Tues to Sat 10 am Sun and Mon	**Closes**	17:30 (16:30 Nov to Feb)	**Adult**	£21.45	**Child** (under 16)	£10.75

1 Learn how

Good sentences give your readers a clearer picture of what you want to say.

a) Read the tips on the right.
Think of more examples for each tip.

You can use terrible or awful instead of bad.

Five years ago or during the holidays are examples of time phrases.

TIP

1 Use different adjectives (*bright, fantastic, dark, …*) to describe people, things and places – not just *good, bad* and *nice*.
Use *really, very, a bit,* etc. (*really slow, very quiet, a bit dark*) to be more exact.
2 Use time phrases (*last week, tomorrow, …*) to tell your reader when things happened.
3 Use linking words (*and, but, because, …*) and relative clauses to link short sentences.

b) Read the first draft of Leon's text. Then look at his corrections.
Say how he has followed the tips.
Suggest other ways to make his text better.

My trip to London — Leon Schmidt

My family and I were in London from Friday night to Saturday. We stayed at a hotel. It was near London Bridge. I had a nice view of the River Thames from my window.

We visited the Natural History Museum. The exhibits were very good. There were also lots of people there. The queue for the dinosaurs was long. We waited over an hour. It was worth it! There was a big model of T. Rex. It moved and roared. We also went to the Tower of London. We went on a tour there. I didn't like it. The tour guide spoke too fast. His jokes weren't funny.

We had dinner at an Indian restaurant. I had vegetable curry. It was good. I ate too much. I felt sick.

London is a nice city. Two days aren't enough. There are so many places to visit.

My trip to London — Leon Schmidt

My family and I were in London *for the weekend* ~~from Friday night to Saturday~~. We stayed at a hotel ~~It was~~ near Lo[ndon] Bridge. I had a *fantastic* ~~nice~~ view of the River Tham[es …] window.

On Saturday ~~We~~ we visited the Natural History Museum. The [exhibits] were *really amazing. It was also very crowded.* ~~very good. There were also lots of people there.~~ The queue for the dinosaurs was *really* long. We waited over an hour*, but* ~~It~~ it was worth it! There was a *huge* (big) model of T. Rex *which* ~~It~~ moved and roared. We also went ~~to~~ *of* the Tower of London. We went (on a tour) there. I didn't *enjoy* ~~like~~ it *because* ~~The~~ the tour guide spoke too fast*, and* ~~His~~ his jokes weren't funny.

On Sunday ~~We~~ we had dinner at an Indian restaurant. I had vegetable curry. It was good*, but* I ate too much. I felt *a bit* sick *in the evening*.

London is a *great* ~~nice~~ city*, but* ~~Two~~ two days aren't enough. There are so many *exciting* places to visit.

adjectives:
+ beautiful, great, fantastic, amazing
– silly, boring

SF 3: Good sentences (p. 156) Workbook 9 (p. 6)

2 Now write …

You choose Choose a), b) or c).

a) Describe a place that you visited in the summer holidays.
b) Write a short story about a person that you met in London.
c) Describe the loudest/quietest/strangest / most dangerous / … place in your hometown.

Workbook Wordbank 1, 2, 8 (pp. 70, 71, 77)

1 STUDY SKILLS Giving feedback on a text

With good feedback, you can improve your writing. On this page you will learn to
- check another student's text.
- give good feedback to another student.
- react to the feedback that you get.

a) Checking a text

Give your partner the text you wrote for 2 on p. 16.
Look back at the writing tips on p. 16.
Read your partner's text and enter your feedback in a copy of the checklist on p. 291.

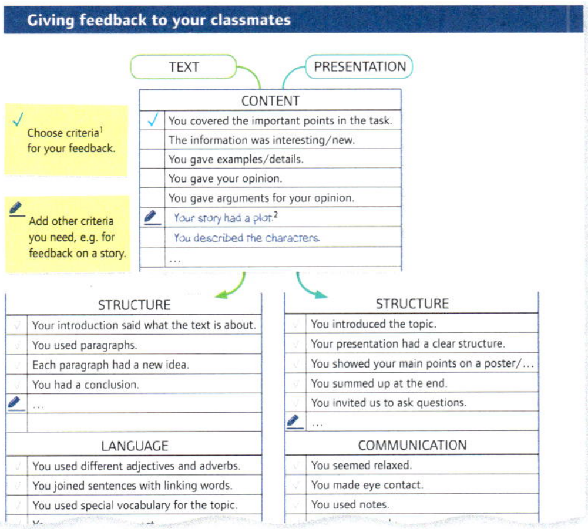

Giving feedback to your classmates

TEXT — PRESENTATION

✓ Choose criteria[1] for your feedback.

Add other criteria you need, e.g. for feedback on a story.

CONTENT
✓ You covered the important points in the task.
The information was interesting/new.
You gave examples/details.
You gave your opinion.
You gave arguments for your opinion.
Your story had a plot.[2]
You described the characters.
…

STRUCTURE (TEXT)
Your introduction said what the text is about.
You used paragraphs.
Each paragraph had a new idea.
You had a conclusion.
…

LANGUAGE
You used different adjectives and adverbs.
You joined sentences with linking words.
You used special vocabulary for the topic.

STRUCTURE (PRESENTATION)
You introduced the topic.
Your presentation had a clear structure.
You showed your main points on a poster/…
You summed up at the end.
You invited us to ask questions.
…

COMMUNICATION
You seemed relaxed.
You made eye contact.
You used notes.

Make notes on how your partner can improve his/her text. Check spelling and grammar too.

b) Giving feedback

Make comments, suggestions and corrections on your partner's text. Follow these steps:

1 Tell your partner what he/she did well:
- I really liked what you wrote here because …
- The details were interesting and …
- I liked it when you used the word …
- My favourite part was … because …

2 Say what you think your partner didn't do well. Say what he/she could do better.
- Your sentences are really short. Maybe you could link these two sentences with …
- It's hard to understand *when* something happens. Why don't you use …?
- You use the same adjective more than once. You could use a different adjective here.

3 Point out grammar and spelling mistakes.

4 Finish with something nice if you can.
- I really enjoyed what you wrote.
- This was really fun to read because …

c) Revising your text

Think about what your partner has said.
Decide what to change.

My Book Write your final text.

➜ **Workbook** *10–11 (p. 7)*

Study skills

Giving feedback on a text

Wenn ich jemandem eine Rückmeldung zu einem Text gebe, …
- sollte ich zuerst sagen, was …
- dann sollte ich erklären, was …
- …

Vergleiche deine Ideen mit dem Abschnitt im Skills File:

➜ *SF 7: Giving feedback on a text (p. 158)*
➜ *pp. 291–292*

2 REVISION How can I get there?

a) Find these places on the map of London on the front inside cover of your book:

- the British Museum
- the Millennium Bridge
- the London Eye
- Piccadilly Circus

Then explain where they are. Take turns.

It's in … Street/Road · It's near … <name of tube station> · It's on the corner of … Street and … · It's between … <names of tube stations/ roads/other places>

b) You're at Russell Square tube station. Ask the way to other places on the map.

Excuse me, please. How can I get to the British Museum?

Oh, the museum. Well, walk along Southampton Row. Then turn right into …

More help ➜ p. 141

Early finisher Find a partner. Give directions to places in your town.

➜ Workbook 12 (p. 8)

3 Go by tube

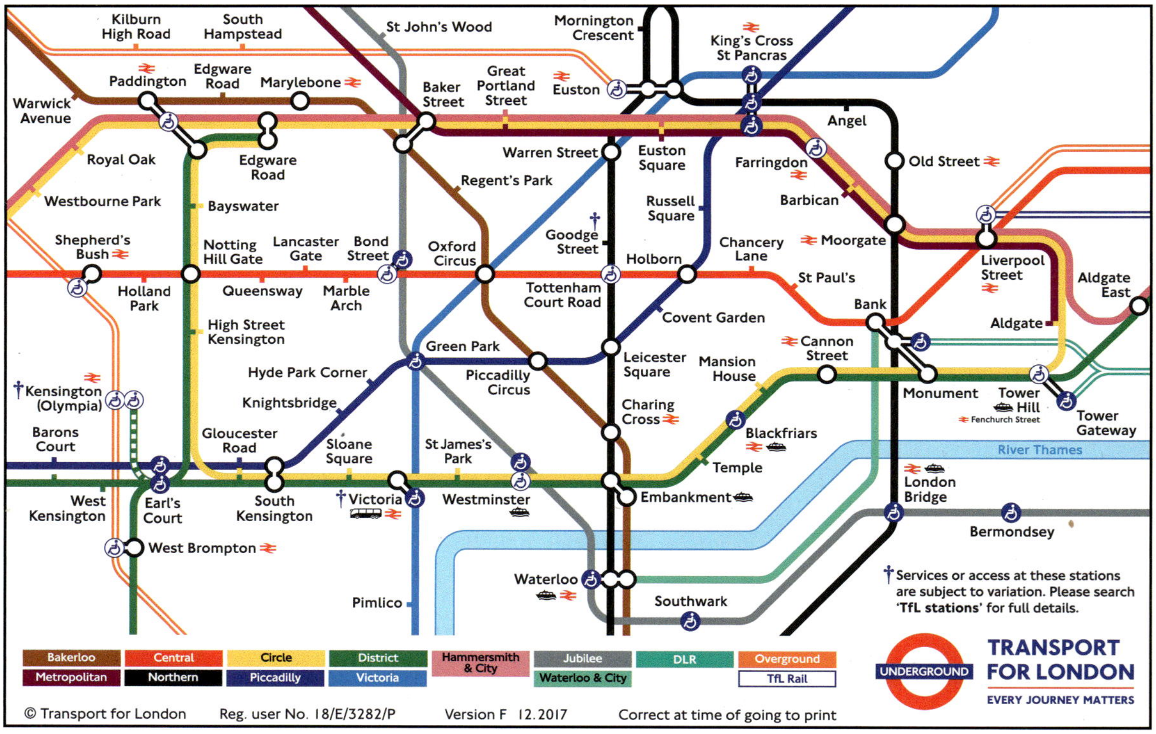

a) You're staying near Marble Arch. You want to go by tube to Big Ben. Practise this dialogue. Take turns.

A: How do we get from here to Big Ben?

B: Big Ben? That's Westminster tube station. We take the Central line eastbound from Marble Arch to Bond Street. And then we change to the Jubilee line southbound.

take the … line · change to the … line · northbound · southbound · eastbound · westbound

b) Choose other sights from the map on the inside cover. Find the nearest tube station. Act out more dialogues like the one in a).

➜ Text File 1 (p. 132) ➜ Workbook 13 (p. 8)

4 WORDS German *gehen*

Some German words like *gehen* have lots of different meanings in English.
Choose eight sentences that match the pictures. Translate them into German. Use a form of *gehen*.

1 They're going for a walk.
2 I don't feel well.
3 The clock is slow.
4 How are you?
5 Can you answer the phone?
6 We've missed it! Let's walk.
7 I'm fine, thank you.
8 It's too cold to go swimming.
9 This torch doesn't work.
10 You can't do that!
11 What's the book about?
12 Just head for the church.

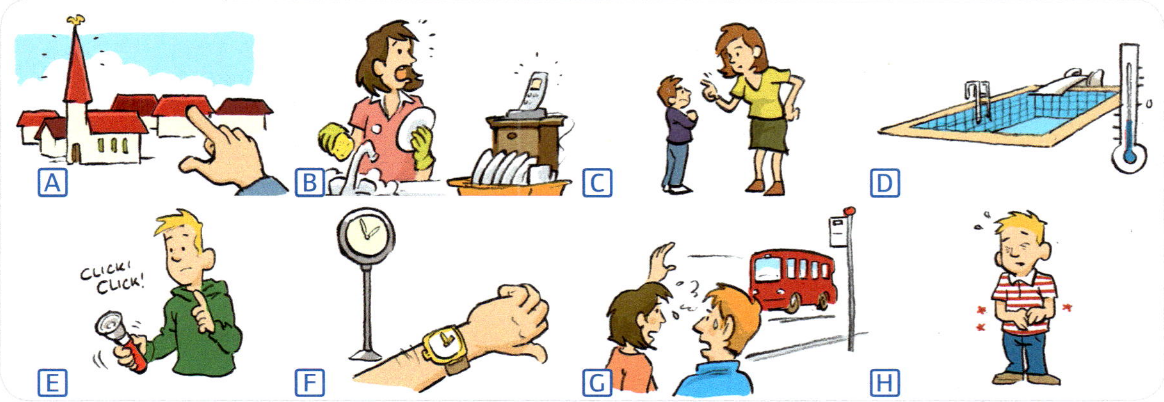

Early finisher Look at the four sentences that didn't go with a picture. Translate them into German.

5 A station announcement

a) Du bist auf dem Bahnhof und befindest dich gerade auf dem Weg nach Bonn. Du hörst eine Ansage. Höre zu.

b) Eine britische Familie hat Schwierigkeiten, die Ansage zu verstehen. Spielt eine Situation nach und beantwortet ihre Fragen. Wechselt euch mit der Rolle des/der britischen Sprechers/Sprecherin ab.

1 We're going to Bonn.
Was that announcement for our train?
2 What's the problem?
3 When and where does it leave from now?

TIP

The most important thing about mediation is the *message*. You don't have to translate every word. If you don't know *Gleis* in English, try to explain it.

➔ Workbook *14–15 (pp. 8–9)*

The adventures of Morph

1 Watching the cricket

On Sunday morning Luke rang Mo's doorbell. When Mo opened the door, Luke said, "It's 10:30, Mo. The cricket is on TV."

In the living room, Mo's big sister Mishal was on the sofa. She was watching a music show. The music was so loud she didn't notice the two boys.

"Can we watch the cricket, Mishal?" asked Mo, but Mishal didn't answer. So Mo shouted, "Mishal! The cricket is on. Can we watch the test match?"

Mishal looked over at the two boys: "No way!"

"You've been watching TV for hours," Mo said.

"No, I haven't," his sister said. "I've been watching since 10, when Mum went out. Remember? And anyway, the cricket lasts all day. You can watch it later."

"But we're going to Notting Hill Carnival later, Mishal," Luke said and smiled at her. "Please, can we watch the cricket before we go? Please?"

"Nice try, Luke," Mishal said, "but no."

Then she picked up the remote and turned the volume up even louder.

Luke and Mo looked at each other. Mo made a face at his sister, then he said, "OK, Luke, let's just go to the carnival."

Five minutes later the two boys were walking towards the tube station when they passed a pub. Luke pointed through the door to a big TV screen. "Look, the cricket is on. Let's watch it for a while."

"But we can't go into a pub," Mo said. "We're not old enough."

"But we *can* watch through the door."

The boys stood at the door of the pub and looked in. After a while, Mo felt a tap on his shoulder. He turned round. A man shook his head at them.

"I've been waiting here for five minutes, boys. Do you think I can go in now?"

"Sorry," Mo and Luke both said. They moved to the side and the man went in.

The match was getting very exciting and the boys moved a bit closer to the TV. In a few minutes, they were just inside the door of the pub. They could hear the TV now too: **"The English team has been playing much better since the break," the commentator's voice said.**

When England made a breakthrough, Mo shouted "Yes!" and Luke clapped his hands and sang, "England! England!"

Suddenly they heard another voice.

"All right, you two," said the barman. **"I've been watching you since you came in. You**'re too young to be in here, you know that. Off you go now."

Luke and Mo turned round and left the pub.

"Notting Hill, here we come!" Mo shouted and they ran off together towards the tube station.

2 Follow the story

Take turns to explain:

1 why Luke goes to Mo's house.
2 what Mo and Luke's plans for the day are.
3 why they can't do what they want to at home.
4 where they decide to go.
5 where they stop on the way.
6 what they do there.
7 who speaks to them and why they leave.

3 Have a go

Say how long you have been doing these things:

sit in this room
*I've been sitting in this room for **25** minutes.*
go to this school
learn English
use this book
work on this page

for

… minutes
… hours
… days
… weeks
… months
… years

Looking at language

Look at these sentences from p. 20.
Then complete the explanation.

You've been watching TV for hours.
I've been waiting here for five minutes.
The English team has been playing much better since the break.

The **present perfect progressive** has three parts:
have/has + ________ + _____-form

We use this tense to say that something started in the past and is still going on now.
I've been watching TV since 3 o'clock.
= I started at 3:00 and I am still watching TV now.

In German we use
1 the ... tense in situations like this.
2 ... for the English for and since.

➜ *GF 1.5: Present perfect progressive (p. 172)*

1 I've been waiting for the bus ...

(Present perfect progressive) ■

Complete each sentence in two ways: with for and since.

1 I ... (wait) for the bus ...
I've been waiting for the bus for 20 minutes. / since nine o'clock.
2 You ... (watch) TV ...
3 It ... (rain) ...
4 She ... (feel) ill ...
5 I ... (learn) maths at school ...
6 We ... (prepare) our presentation ...

for	since
20/45/... minutes a few hours two/three/... days a year/two years/... ...	8:30/nine o'clock/... yesterday evening last week/January/... 2016/2017/... ...

➜ Workbook *16 (p. 9)*

2 I've been living here ...

(Present perfect progressive) ■■

Complete Mo's sentences.

I'm a Londoner.
I've been living here ...

Use the verb in brackets and for and since.

1 I'm a Londoner. I ... (live) here ... I was three.
2 I like languages. I ... (learn) German at school ... three years.
3 My sister Mishal loves music. She ... (sing) in a band ... over a year.
4 I have a blog. I ... (write) posts ... last March.
5 My friend Luke and I love cricket. We ... (play) in the same team ... a long time.
6 Luke is a big fan of the Notting Hill Carnival. He ... (go) there ... he was twelve.

More help ➜ *p. 141*
➜ Workbook *17 (p. 10)*

3 How long ...? ■■■

a) Make a profile like this about yourself.

Name:	Daniel		
Hometown:	Passau	Languages:	English/...
Address:	...straße 14	Sports:	football/...
School:	... Gymnasium	Hobbies:	choir/...

b) Meet a partner at a bus stop.
Swap profiles. Then ask and answer like this:

How long have you been living in Passau?
I've been living in Passau for thirteen years.
How long have you been going to ... Gymnasium?

More help ➜ *p. 141*

c) Go to another bus stop. Tell your new partner about your last partner.
Daniel has been singing in a choir since last May.

Early finisher ➜ *p. 148*

Language help

Use the present perfect simple to say that something has happened but not when:
I've written five emails.

Use the present perfect progressive to say that something began in the past and is still going on. Use *since* and *for* to show the length of the action:
I've been writing emails for an hour/ since 10 o'clock.

You can use the present perfect progressive with verbs for "actions" like *do, learn, play, rain, read, wait, watch, work, write* but not verbs for "states" like *be, know, love, hate, seem, understand,* for example:
I've known my best friend for six years.

4 Luke and Mo (Simple or progressive?)

Complete the sentences with the present perfect simple or progressive.

1 Luke ... (know) Mo for a long time.
2 Mo ... (learn) German at school for three years, but he ... (not be) to Germany yet.
3 Mo writes a blog too. Do you know how long he ... (do) it?
4 The boys ... (always love) cricket and they ... (play) in the same cricket team for a few years.
5 Today they want to watch cricket on TV, but Mo's sister ... (watch) a music show since 10 o'clock.
6 On the way to the carnival, the boys watch TV through a pub door. But oh dear! The barman ... (watch) the boys since they arrived. So off they go to the Carnival.

➔ *GF 1.5–1.6 (pp. 172–173)*

5 London for free

Du hast eine/n amerikanische/n Austauschschüler/in als Gast. Deine Eltern wollen in den nächsten Ferien mit euch beiden nach London reisen. Ihr habt nicht viel Geld zur Verfügung.
Deswegen sucht ihr nach günstigen Aktivitäten dort. Du findest die folgende Seite im Internet.
Erkläre deinem amerikanischen Gast auf Englisch, was ihr in London umsonst unternehmen könnt.

Weltstädte können teuer sein, aber in London kannst du viel unternehmen, ohne einen Cent auszugeben!

Die meisten staatlichen Museen verlangen keinen Eintritt, so dass man in der National Gallery Van Goghs *Sunflowers* umsonst anschauen kann, wie auch den berühmten Rosettastein im British Museum, mit dem man ägyptische Hieroglyphen entziffern konnte.

Rosetta Stone

Von den Brücken über der Themse kannst du das Leben am Fluss und die beeindrückenden Gebäude der Stadt betrachten. Man kann 27 der 34 Brücken zu Fuß überqueren.

Millennium Bridge

Willst du die wichtigsten Personen des Königreichs mal sehen, lohnt es sich in der Downing Street (Sitz des Premierministers) oder im Buckingham Palace (Wohnsitz der Königin) vorbeizuschauen. Das kostet nichts.

London is eine grüne Stadt mit Hunderten von Parks. Entkomme dem Lärm des Verkehrs bei der Gedenkstätte für Princess Di im Hyde Park, oder beobachte die Rehe in Richmond Park, dem größten Park Londons.

Richmond Park

Die besten Aussichten bekommst du auch umsonst. Wenn dir die Shard zu teuer ist, genieße die kostenlose Aussicht in One New Change oder am Parliament Hill in Hampstead Heath.

Parliament Hill

➔ Workbook *18–19 (pp. 10–11)*

1 A bus tour of London

The number 11 bus passes lots of famous sights. You can get on and off as often as you like and walk to sights near the route too.

a) Look at the London map on your inside cover.
Make a list of sights like the one below.
Put a star beside *your* five favourites.

On the bus route	Near the bus route
St Paul's Cathedral	The Tower of London ✶
...	...

b) Watch the film.
Tick (✓) the places on your list that you see.

c) Watch again and listen for information about your favourites.
Write captions for each one that you see.
1 The royal family lives here.
2 ...

d) Read your captions to your partner.
Can he/she say what your favourites are?

The royal family lives here.

That's easy! Buckingham Palace.

2 Making the film: Time

a) Watch the film again. Think about *time*.
How long was the film?

How long do you think the tour really was?
Give reasons for your opinion.
You can check the distances on the map.

b) Think about *speed*.
The film-maker often speeds up the film.

Where in the film does he do this?
What could his reasons be?
Do you think it's a good idea?

c) Say which statement you agree with.

I liked the film because I had the feeling I was sitting on the bus.

It was a pity that we didn't see the person who was speaking.

What else did you like/not like about the film?

➜ Text File 2 (p. 134)

The Notting Hill Carnival Parade

Look at the picture. What do you think might happen in the story?

"Hurry," said Emily, "or I'll miss Mo and Luke."

"Don't be silly, Emily," her mum replied, "There'll be thousands of people at the carnival. There's no way you'll see those two boys there."

The platform at the tube station was full. When the train came in, everyone moved to the doors.

"Dad!" said Emily and pointed to two free seats. "You and Mum sit there. I can stand."

But more and more people got onto the train at each station, and they pushed Emily further and further away from her parents.

At Notting Hill Gate, everyone got off. Emily tried to wait for her parents, but the crowd pushed her along the platform and up the stairs. Out in the street, she held onto a lamppost. She scanned the sea of faces, but her parents didn't appear.

❖

Dancers in bright costumes moved along the street. Caribbean music filled the air. On the crowded pavement, Mo held his camera high and took as many photos as he could. Luke tried to move to the front of the crowd.

"Where are you going?" Mo shouted.

"I want to see my cousins. They're in the parade with my Uncle Ray. They're drummers!"

❖

Emily tried to call her parents.

"The number you are calling is not available at the moment. Please try again later."

All around Emily, it was getting louder. The sound of drums filled her ears. People were shouting and blowing whistles. The crowd danced to the music and everyone was pushing against her. She started to panic. Then she took out her phone again. "Just do it!" she said to herself. A moment later she tapped 'Call Mo'.

❖

"Who?" said Mo. "Oh, right, Emily – I remember. ... You're at Notting Hill Carnival? Cool, I'm here too, with Luke. ... Oh! ... Don't worry. Tell us where you are! We'll come and find you. ... Well, can you see a street sign? ... Westbourne Grove? Where? ... Emily? Oh no, ... I've lost her."

He called back, but Emily didn't answer.

"Maybe she's in trouble, Luke," he said. "We have to find her. She's in Westbourne Grove."

❖

Emily bent down between someone's dancing legs and picked up her phone.

"Oh no!" she cried. "It doesn't work." She decided to go back to the tube station, but it was impossible to move on the crowded pavement.

"I'll have to walk with the parade," she thought.

She climbed under the rope onto the road. Suddenly she was in the middle of a group of dancers. On their backs were huge wings in all the colours of the rainbow. They turned in circles, faster and faster, and sang:

"Chiga-lee-a-chiga-lee-chiga-lee-bom!"

Emily started to feel dizzy. Suddenly she felt a pair of hands on her waist.

"Come and dance with me," said a voice. Emily turned and looked into a strange painted face.

"Aaaaaah," she screamed. "Don't touch me!"

❖

"It's too crowded here," said Mo. "If we want to find her, we'll have to join the parade."

"But we're not wearing costumes," Luke replied.

"We just have to dance to the music – like this."

Mo started to move his hips in a little circle.

"That's not how you dance, Mo!" Luke laughed. "You have to have rhythm, man. Watch me!"

And the two boys danced their way towards Westbourne Grove as fast as they could.

❖

"Sorry if I scared you," said the man with the painted face. "When I saw you with the dancers, I thought you wanted to take part."
"No," said Emily. "I was looking for my parents. I've lost them. And …"
Suddenly, a loud voice filled the air.
"Hello, Notting Hill! How are you feeling?"
The crowds in the street clapped and roared.
Emily looked up and saw a red bus. On the open roof was a man with a loudspeaker, and drummers and dancers in bright orange costumes.
"Come on," said the man with the painted face. "Let's take that bus. Ray won't mind. You can sit downstairs and rest for a bit. And then we'll look for your mum and dad."

❖

There was no sign of Emily in Westbourne Grove.
"Man, my eyes are tired," said Luke. "I can't look at any more faces!"
"And my legs are tired," Mo replied.
"Hello, Notting Hill! Do you want to dance?" said a voice over a loudspeaker.
"No, thanks," said Mo under his breath.
Luke looked up. "Mo! That's Uncle Ray's bus."
"Your uncle has a bus?" asked Mo.
"That's him with the loudspeaker. And my cousins are playing the drums."
Luke took Mo's arm and ran towards the bus.
"Come on," he said. "Let's go up to the top. I'm sure we'll see Emily from there."

❖

"Are you feeling better now?" asked the man with the painted face.
"Yes," smiled Emily. "I'm sorry I screamed at you."
"Don't worry," said the man. "Let's go to Ray."
Upstairs, the dancers were dancing to the drums. Emily started tapping her foot to the rhythm. The man with the painted face went over to Ray and whispered in his ear. Then Ray took his loudspeaker and spoke:
"Hello, Notting Hill! Hello, Mr and Mrs Evans from Cardiff. Can you hear me? Your daughter Emily is waiting for you here, so please come up!"
"What?" said Mo. The two boys looked around. And there was Emily behind them.
"Mo! Luke!" she said. "How did you get here?"
"The question is: How did *you* get here?" Mo replied. "And who is that man?"

1 How did they feel?

a) How many parts does the story have? Give the lines.
What happens in each part? Write a few sentences for each part in your exercise book.

b) Say how Emily, Mo and Luke feel at different points in the story. You can use these words:

angry · excited · lonely · happy · scared · shocked · surprised · unhappy · worried

I think Emily feels excited when she is on the train.

I think Mo is … when …

2 The end of the story

How does Emily find her parents?
What happens when they meet?

You choose Choose a), b) or c).

a) Write an ending of about 10 to 15 lines.

b) Make a cartoon.
One partner can draw pictures.
The other can write the speech bubbles.

c) Write a dialogue and act it out.

→ *Workbook 20 (p. 11)*

Workbook Checkpoint 1 (pp. 12–15)

London tourists and tour guides

Become an expert on a London sight and give your classmates a tour.
Visit your classmates' sights and take their tours.

STEP 1 Work in groups of four.
Go to one of the learning stations and choose one of the sights.
Read through. Listen to the information pack for your sight several times until you think you are an expert on it.
Test each other on what you know.
Research more information if you like.

STEP 2 Together, work out what you will tell your classmates about your sight when they come for their 'tour'. You will only have 3-4 minutes for each tour.

STEP 3 Two from your group will be tour guides. They should practise giving their tour. The other two will be tourists and visit the London sights at the other learning stations. Look at the list of sights and try to think of questions you would like to ask about them.

STEP 4 Pair 1: Give your tour to the classmates who come to visit your sight.
Pair 2: Walk round to other sights in the classroom and go on the tours there. Don't forget to ask any questions you have.
Then swap roles so that Pair 1 walks round and Pair 2 presents.

Wie gut warst du?

Wie schätzt du dich selbst ein? Schreibe *Words & Content*, *Grammar* und *Speaking* in dein Heft und ordne dir für jede Frage eine Ampelfarbe zu.

- Das lief nicht gut, ich muss mehr üben.
- Das war OK, aber ich könnte besser werden.
- Das habe ich gut geschafft.

Words & Content
Fielen dir passsende Wörter zur Beschreibung deiner Londoner Sehenswürdigkeit ein? Konntest du die Fragen deiner Mitschüler/innen beantworten?

Grammar
Warst du sicher bei der Verwendung von *present perfect* und *simple past* in deinen Ausführungen oder Fragen?

Speaking
Hast du flüssig gesprochen und gut auf Fragen oder Kommentare reagiert?

Wie kannst du besser werden?

Dort, wo du dich rot oder gelb eingeschätzt hast, helfen dir folgende Tipps:

Words & Content
Schau dir die Materialien in deiner Lernstation oder die Texte der Unit wieder an. Versuche, die Fragen, die man dir gestellt hat, noch einmal richtig zu beantworten.

Grammar
Nimm deine Rede über deine Sehenswürdigkeit auf dein Smartphone auf. Hör sie dir an und achte auf die Verwendung der Verbzeiten, vor allem *simple past* und *present perfect*.

➜ *GF 1.1: Simple past (S. 170); 1.3 Present perfect (S. 171)*
➜ *Workbook 4-5 (S. 4), 17 (S. 10)*

Speaking
Hör dir deine Rede noch einmal an. Wie könntest du sie verbessern? Finde Tipps im Skills File.

➜ *SF 11: Speaking (S. 162); 16 Giving a good presentation (S.165)*

A

1 London places

a) Write down the names of these places in London, then match the right ones to sentences 1–3.

A

B

C

D

E

F

1 Watch it go up and down to let ships pass.
2 Even if you're not in London, you can hear it on the BBC.
3 It looks like the top is broken but it's still the highest building in the city.

b) Write similar sentences about the places in the other pictures.

2 In the city

a) Find the city words that match these paraphrases.

1 A very big, beautiful house for a king or queen.
2 A large and important church.
3 This is where you go to look at art.
4 Trains that run through tunnels.
5 The part of a road that people walk on.
6 This is where you wait for a train.

b) Write paraphrases for these city words.

bridge · hospital · park · restaurant · shopping centre · post office

3 Getting around in the city

a) Which words/phrases in B can go with which verbs in A? Some can go with more than one verb.

A · cross · go · take · travel · visit

B
- a boat ride
- a bridge
- a church/cathedral
- a gallery
- a museum
- a road
- around town
- by bus/taxi/…
- for a walk
- on a tour
- shopping
- the bus/the underground/…
- the sights
- to a restaurant

b) Now imagine you have just been to London. Write a short email to an English-speaking friend about your trip.
Use at least five collocations with verbs and phrases from A and B.

4 At the bus stop

You're waiting for a bus in London. A Londoner speaks to you. Here is what she says. What do you say? Write down the dialogue.
Have you been waiting long? · Where are you off to? · How long have you been in London? · Are you staying in a hotel? · Enjoy your weekend.

5 Greetings from London (Simple past or present perfect)

Gareth is writing about his London trip for his friends in Wales. Complete his blog with the correct form of the verbs in brackets (statement, negative, question) in the simple past or present perfect.

Hey everyone!
We ...[1] (be) in London for five days now. Yesterday was one of the nicest days we ...[2] (have). ...[3] (know) that London is full of parks? We ...[4] (find) that out when we ...[5] (take) the train from Stratford to Hampstead Heath.
We ...[6] (go) straight to the park from the station. It's a huge, wild park. I ...[7] always ...[8] (love) great views, and the views on Hampstead Heath are fantastic, as fantastic as the weather we ...[9] (have) since we ...[10] (arrive). You can see that from the photo. I ...[11] (put) a lot more photos on my gallery page. ...[12] (see) them yet?
After that we just ...[13] (wander) around for miles until we ...[14] (arrive) at Highgate Village. They call it a village, but it ...[15] (not be) like our village in Wales. We ...[16] (enjoy) a cold drink in a café there before our next stop: Highgate Cemetery. Wow! It ...[17] (be) huge and wild. We ...[18] (walk) around for over an hour there before we ...[19] (find) the most famous grave: Karl Marx! I ...[20] (not know) he ...[21] (die) in London, but I ...[22] (see) his grave now. Really it ...[23] (be) a beautiful day in London!

6 How long? (Present perfect progressive)

Use the notes and write sentences about how long these people have been doing these things. Use the present perfect progressive and *since* or *for*.

 Ethan	ride his bike to school	a year
	write stories	last month
 Amelia	live with her grandparents	last December
	learn to ride	her birthday
 Lily	drive to work	she got a new job
	live in Wales	just a few weeks
 Muhammed	play in a band	six months
	wear glasses	years and years
 Isla	play the guitar	she was 16
	work in London	two weeks

7 MIXED BAG Polly's message

Gareth's friend Polly sent him a message. Fill in the missing words and phrases.

Hi Gareth,
I'm happy you ...[1] London for the last few days. It sounds like you ...[2] a great time. We ...[3] away last weekend too. You know I'm really ...[4] mountain-biking and we found ...[5] great tracks[1]. But on the second track we ...[6] left ...[7] right and didn't know where to go for a while. But that was fun too.
It's a pity that you ... ...[8] with us.
We ...[9] in a nice hostel[2] where they ...[10] the elecricity[3] in the evening so then we ...[11] candles ...[12] lights and we ...[13] a camp fire at night too. I ...[14] so much fun ...[15] a long time!
My big sister took my favourite CD while I ...[16] away and now she ...[17] it! We ...[18] it for days, but there is ...[19] it anywhere. She probably ...[20] it to one of her friends. Well, at least I have it on my phone.
It's school again next week. ...[21] the maths homework ...[22]? It's hard. I need ...[23] help.
So call ... ...[24] you get back.
Polly XXXXXX

1 **track** [træk] Weg, Pfad · 2 **hostel** ['hɒstl] (Jugend-)Herberge · 3 **electricity** [ɪˌlek'trɪsəti] Elektrizität, Strom

B

8 Somewhere in London 1

a) Listen and find out:
   1 who the people are.
   2 what London sight they are visiting.

b) Look at the pictures on the right. Put them in the order that the people talk about them.

c) Read the questions. Then listen again. Take notes so that you can give short answers.
   1 Who first notices the exhibition[1] about snakes, spiders[2] and other dangerous animals?
   2 Why does the girl decide she doesn't want to see it?
   3 Why doesn't her father want to see it?
   4 What is free at this place, what costs money?
   5 Who notices the exhibition about catching a killer?
   6 What are the three reasons they do not go to it?
   7 Who wants to see the whales, who doesn't?
   8 What do they decide to do first?
   9 The girl is not interested in dinosaurs, so why does she agree to see them?
   10 How does the girl feel about the dinosaur exhibition at the end?

A

B

C

D

1 **exhibition** [ˌeksɪˈbɪʃn] Ausstellung · 2 **spider** [ˈspaɪdə] Spinne

C

9 Somewhere in London 2

Prepare and then give a two-minute talk about a place in London. The phrases on the right might help you.

1 Choose a place you have visited/are going to visit/would like to visit.
2 Make notes about the place (where it is, how to get there, how much it costs, when it is open, what you can do there, why you are interested in it, why it is a good place to visit, …).
3 Give your talk to your group.

The place I am going to talk about is …

It's in the West End, near … Tube station.

I have only been there once, but I'd really like to go again.

It's cheaper than most things to do in London because it's free.

So you can get there on the … Line. Or if you're staying in the West End, you can walk.

We had such a great time there. We … and …

If I go to London again, I'll certainly go there again.

It's best to go at the weekend because …

The Tower and the monarchs

Today, the Tower of London is a tourist sight where you can see the Beefeaters in their colourful uniforms, the ravens and, of course, the Crown Jewels. But the Tower has also often played an important role in British history and in the lives of many kings and queens.

1 Normans and Anglo-Saxons

After the Romans invaded Britain in 43 CE, the island became a part of the Roman Empire for over 400 years. But tribes from Europe, like the Angles and Saxons, began invading Britain towards the end of that time. When the Romans left Britain in the 5th century, these tribes moved in and stayed. They pushed the Celtic Britons west into Wales and Cornwall, and for the next 500 years the Anglo-Saxons ruled the country.

The Anglo-Saxons were farmers and they lived in small kingdoms that often fought each other. After a few hundred years there was only one kingdom left, which they called England, "the land of the Angles".

Then in 1066, William of Normandy in northern France decided he wanted to take over England too. He beat the Anglo-Saxons at the Battle of Hastings and became **King William I (1066 – 1087)** – or William the Conqueror.

The Normans built castles all over England to show the Anglo-Saxons who the country now belonged to. William built the biggest and strongest castle in London: the Tower of London. The White Tower at the centre gives the whole castle its name. It was a royal palace where Norman kings and lords lived, but it was also a prison and it reminded Anglo-Saxon Londoners that the Normans ruled the country now.

During the next hundred years or more, the Norman kings of England still often spent more time in France than England. After King John lost Normandy to the French in 1204 this changed. Now even Norman lords started to think of themselves as English rather than Norman or French.

William I on a coin, 1073-76

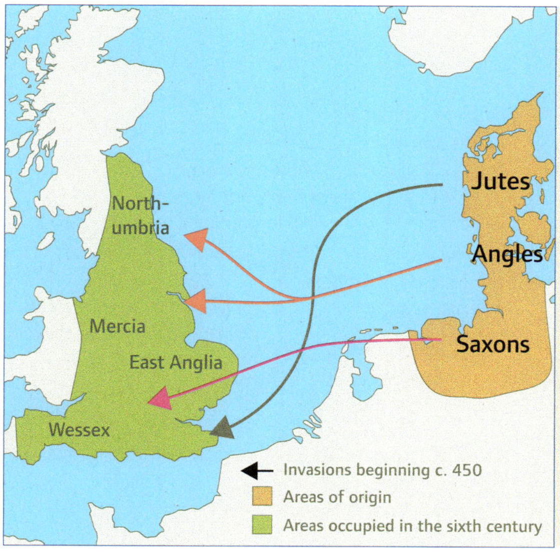

Tribes from Europe invade Britain in the 5th century

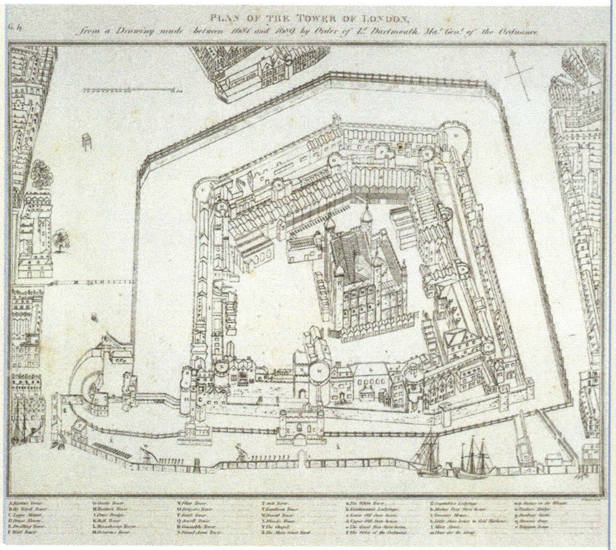

The Tower c. 1200

a) Read about the Normans and Anglo-Saxons and find out:

1 where the Anglo-Saxons came from.
2 who ruled Britain before them.
3 where the Celtic Britons went when the Anglo-Saxons came.
4 how England got its name.
5 who built the Tower of London and why.
6 when the Normans began to become "English".

b) Make a timeline which shows who ruled England at different times from 43 CE to 1200 CE.

2 The English language

When the Normans came to England in 1066, they also brought their language, French, with them. It remained the first language of all English monarchs till the middle of the 14th century. **Henry IV (1399-1413)** was the first king of England whose mother tongue was English.

About 10,000 French words came into the Old English language that the Anglo-Saxons spoke. People still use three quarters of these words in English today. As French-speaking Normans now ruled the country, it is not surprising that many words in the areas of government, the law, education, the good life have come into English from French.

Although the most common words and the structure of English still come from Old English, the French that the Normans brought had a big influence on the English language. During the 12th, 13th and 14th centuries English slowly changed into the beginnings of the language we know today - but it was still quite different from modern English of course.

a) Agree why modern English is a mixture of words that have come from Old English and French. Then explain this to another pair.

b) Which language do you think these modern English words have come from: Old English or French? Explain why you think so.

beef/cow · house/mansion · king/monarch

c) Knowing one language often helps you understand another language. Imagine you are on holiday in France. You are talking in English to some French kids and they use these French words because they don't know the English for them. Can you help them out?

automne · château · délicieux · ennemi · introduire · promesse · tente

government	*gouvernement*
prison	*prison*
college	*collège*
flower	*fleur*
judge	*juge*
language	*langage*
lesson	*leçon*
royal	*royal*
parliament	*parlement*
painter	*peintre*

English words from Norman French

Modern	Old
the	*þe*
be	*beon*
to	*to*
of	*of, æf*
and	*and, ond*
a	*an*
in	*in, innan*
that	*þæt*
have	*habban*
I	*ic*

The ten most common words in English today all come from Old English

Henry VIII
by Hans Holbein the Younger

Anne Boleyn
c. 1533 –1536

Elizabeth I, c.1575

3 The Tudors

The Tudor family ruled England for almost 120 years, from 1485 to 1603. When Henry Tudor defeated **King Richard III (1483-1485)** at the Battle of Bosworth Field, he became **King Henry VII (1485-1509)**. Five more Tudor monarchs followed, including two of the most famous English kings and queens ever: Henry VIII and Elizabeth I.

London was the largest and most important city in the country. During Tudor times its population grew from about 50,000 to 200,000. It was the centre of government and trade, which made it the richest place in the kingdom too. The Tower of London, now over 400 years old, still had an important part to play, for example in the life of Anne Boleyn. "Who was she?" you ask. She was the second wife of **King Henry VIII (1509 – 1547)**.

His first wife was Catherine of Aragon, but she only gave him a daughter and Henry wanted a son. So he asked for a divorce. When the Pope in Rome said no, Henry started his own church, the Church of England. It is still the official state church of Britain today, and the monarch is the head of the church.

Anne Boleyn and Henry had a great party at the Tower the night before their wedding.
Anne stayed there in the luxurious Queen's apartments before she travelled through London to Westminster Abbey the next day. But Anne also only gave Henry a daughter and three years later, she was back in the same apartments at the Tower, this time as a prisoner. She was killed there in 1536 for treason.
Henry had four more wives after Anne.

Like her mother before her, **Queen Elizabeth I (1558-1603)** was a prisoner in the Tower of London. She was the daughter of Henry VIII and Anne Boleyn. When her half-sister **Mary**, a Catholic, was queen **(1553-1558)**, she sent Elizabeth, a Protestant, to the Tower. Elizabeth was only 20 years old. She lived in nice apartments there, but the young girl was probably scared. Her mother and her cousin Catherine Howard, another of Henry VIII's wives, were both killed there.
But Queen Mary let Elizabeth go again, and when Mary died, Elizabeth became queen herself.
During Elizabeth's time as queen, England became one of the most powerful countries in Europe.

The Elizabethan Age

- 1558: Elizabeth becomes queen – France, Spain and Portugal are the great powers of Europe
- Elizabeth supports sea captains like Francis Drake who attack Spanish gold ships on their way from South America to Spain. Spain calls them pirates, England heroes.
- 1580: Drake becomes one of the first men to sail around the world. On his return to England his ship, the *Golden Hind*, is full of Spanish gold.
- 1588: the Spanish king, Philip II, sends 130 ships to attack England. His plan: overthrow Elizabeth and make England Catholic again. Francis Drake and the English ships destroy the Spanish Armada.
- England's sea power begins to grow and is the key factor for the huge British Empire of the 18th and 19th centuries.
- The Elizabethan Age is a great time for literature. Audiences love William Shakespeare's plays – you can still see them all over the world today.
- Elizabeth I never marries and is known as the Virgin Queen. England's first colony in America is called Virginia after her.
- 1603: Elizabeth dies on March 24. She is 69 years old.

a) Read about the Tudors and find out:
   1 how many Tudor kings and queens there were.
   2 who were the most famous two of them.
   3 who started the Church of England and why.
   4 who made England into a great sea power.

b) Find three interesting facts about the Tudors and England. Write questions about the facts and ask your group. Can the others answer them?

Full-size replica of Drake's Golden HInd in Brixham, Devon

The colony of Jamestown, Virginia, 1607

4 Tour guides

a) Work in groups. Each student works on one of the monarchs you have read about. Imagine you are a tour guide at the Tower of London. Use what you have read here. You can also do more research.

Tell the others about your monarch's connection to the Tower. Answer any questions the others have about your monarch.

b) When you have all talked about your monarchs, give each other feedback.

➜ *SF 17: Peer feedback (p. 165)*

5 In your area

Choose an important historical site or building you know in your area.
In English, write a short text (about eight sentences) for a brochure about the site.

You could explain:
- where it is/how old it is
- why it is famous
- what happened there
- what you can find out there
- when to visit
- …

➜ **Workbook** *1–4 (p. I–II)*

Welcome to Snowdonia

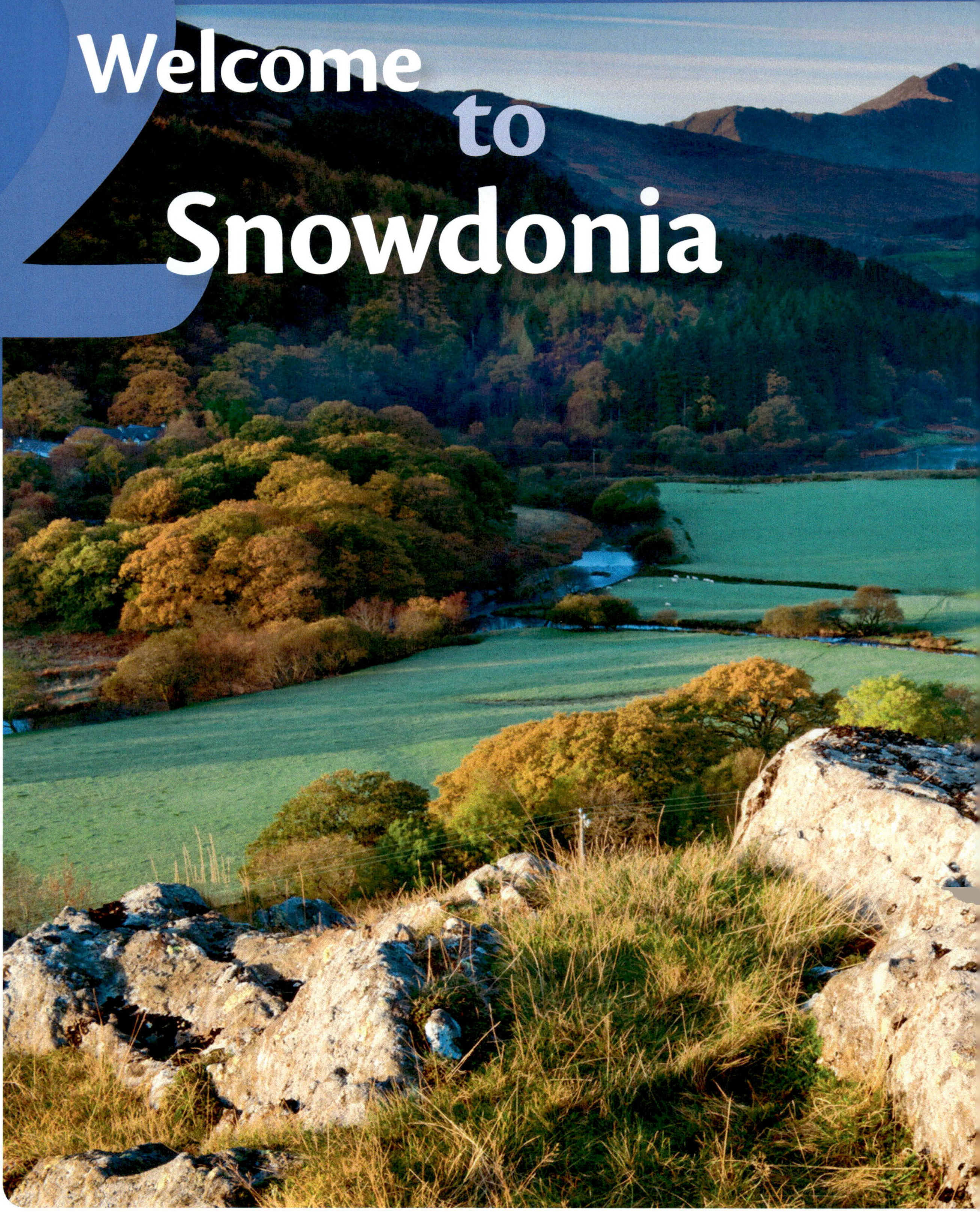

1 Welsh countryside

a) Make a list of words to describe the picture.

b) Compare your lists and add words.

c) Take turns to describe the picture.

In the background, I can see mountains with shadows on them.

On the left, there's a …

d) Imagine you're in the picture.
Choose a place and describe what you can see, hear, smell or feel there.
Can your partner guess where you are?

I can see some birds in a tree and hear a river behind it.

OK … are you in the field in the middle of the photo?

→ *SF 14: Describing and presenting pictures (p. 164)*

→ **Workbook** *1 (p. 16)*

2 A long journey

a) → *p. 56* Look at the map and find Cardiff and Caernarfon. Describe a possible route between them (mountains? big cities? …?).

b) Listen and find out who the people are and the reason for their journey.

c) Listen again. Say how the girl feels and how she shows her feelings.

More help → *p. 142* → **Text File 3** *(p. 135)*

EXTRA Imagine the family's arrival in Caernarfon. Write a text (about 80-100 words) in your exercise book.

You choose a) or b).
a) Draw a picture story about it.
b) Write a mail from the girl to a friend in Cardiff.

Your task

At the end of this unit: Imagine you're moving to Wales. You'll write about how your life would change.

1 Everything is wrong

As Emily walked down the long path to her new home, her legs felt heavy and tired. The house was dark and empty. Then she remembered that her mum was out at sea. Mrs Evans was a scientist who studied sea animals and plants.

Emily walked across the garden to her dad's workshop. There was music in the air – someone was singing a Welsh song. She walked through the workshop door and turned the radio off with a groan. "If I hear one more word of Welsh, I'll scream!" she said.

Emily's dad was building a table. He was a carpenter and made all kinds of beautiful furniture. His workshop smelled of wood and special oils.

"Someone has had a bad day," he said.

"I just don't like that music – that's all," said Emily. She picked up a hammer from the table.

"What's happened?" Mr Evans asked.

"I don't want to talk about it." Emily started hitting an old piece of wood with the hammer.

"And put that hammer down! It's making me nervous. You have to be careful with a hammer."

"Sorry!"

"So, tell me what's wrong?"

"What's wrong? Everything is wrong! Seven hours of school and then Welsh lessons at the learning centre. I have to work harder than all the others! And my Welsh still sounds funny – kids laugh when I speak. *And* it's hard to understand the teachers – they speak so fast!"

"Which language do your classmates speak at the breaks: English or Welsh?"

"Breaks are the worst! Today at lunch, we were talking about the class trip to Snowdon. Then this boy came over. Dylan. He *never* stops telling jokes. He said something in Welsh and everybody laughed except me. I asked a girl what was so funny, and she said, 'Oh forget it, you probably don't want to know.' You see, Welsh is their language, not mine. I know that boy was making fun of me."

"Well, if you laugh with the others, you won't feel so bad."

"That's silly, Dad. How can I laugh at their jokes if I don't understand them?"

"Give it more time. Your Welsh will be as good as theirs soon ... if you don't give up."

"Yeah, right, Dad," said Emily. She picked up the hammer again, but this time she was more careful. "When will Mum be back?"

"She won't be back till tomorrow. So I'll make my famous vegetable curry for dinner."

"Hmm ... well, I'll cook tonight," said Emily, "I'm *really* hungry, and ..."

"You don't like my curry?" he said. "It's better than yours!" Then he laughed. "Just a little joke. Let's have pizza instead then."

2 Understanding the story

a) Look at lines 1–23 again. Find places which describe Emily's feelings. How does she show them? Write down the words that describe her feelings. What kind of words are they? Use your exercise book.

b) Read lines 25–48 again. Then describe Emily's relationship with her classmates.

c) Have a look at the title of the text. What does it tell you about the content?

d) Which part of the text does the picture show? Give the lines and reasons for your answer.

3 An email to Mo

Imagine you're Emily. Write an email (about 100-150 words) to Mo in London and tell him about your new school in Wales.

1 WORDS Jobs

a) Complete the sentences about jobs with the right words.

actor · +architect · artist · +astronaut · carpenter · dentist · farmer · +hairdresser · +musician · +painter · scientist

1 Astronauts travelled to the moon in the last century.
2 ... study plants, animals or other things in the natural world.
3 ... paint pictures or people's houses.
4 ... play an instrument.
5 ... draw plans for new buildings.
6 ... cut other people's hair.

b) Write sentences for the other jobs in the box.
1 ... in films or plays or TV shows.

More help → p. 142

c) Write down the jobs from a) in a list.
Add other jobs that you know.

d) Act out a job from your list. The others say what you're doing and guess the job.
A: You're playing an instrument.
B: Yes, right!
C: You're a musician.

→ Workbook 2 (p. 16)

2 REVISION Tom thinks he'll be an astronaut (*will*-future)

a) What do you think you'll be or do in the future? Copy the chart and add ideas.
Then make appointments with three classmates and interview them.

What we will be/do	Me	Partner A	Partner B	Partner C
in 5 years				
in 10 years				
in 20 years				

More help → p. 142

b) Report interesting ideas to the class.
- Tom thinks he'll be an astronaut in 20 years.
- Dilek thinks she'll work in Hollywood in …

c) Write sentences about what you *won't* do.
I'm sure I won't be in Germany in 10 years.
I'm sure I won't play for Chelsea in …

→ *GF 3.1: will-future (p. 175)* → Workbook 3 (p. 17)

3 REVISION If I don't go to bed now, … (Conditional sentences 1)

a) **Chain Game:** Look at the sentences in the game. Think of endings for the last sentence.

A *If I don't go to bed now, I won't get enough sleep.*
B *If I don't get enough sleep, I'll be tired tomorrow.*
C *If I'm tired tomorrow, I'll be bad in the match.*
D *If I'm bad in the match, our team won't win.*
E *If our team doesn't win …*

b) Play the if-sentence game. You can use these ideas:

If we work hard for the English test, …
If you eat too much, …
If the weather is nice tomorrow, …
If you don't wear warm gloves, …

Early finisher → p. 149 → *GF 4.1: Conditional 1 (p. 176)* → Workbook 4–5 (pp. 17–18)

4 STUDY SKILLS Using an English-German dictionary

When you read English texts, try first to understand a new word from the context.
Thinking about what kind of word it is (noun, verb, adjective, etc.) can help you to understand it.
If you really need to check the meaning, you can use a dictionary.

a) Write down what you think the underlined words mean.

1 That's not your pen, it's mine!
2 My grandfather worked in a coal mine.
3 They mine the gold deep underground.
4 The navy dropped mines in the enemy harbour.

Compare your answers, then check on the right.

headword · part of speech · example · translation · context

mine[1] [maɪn] *Pronomen*
1 meine(r, -s): ***Your bike is newer than mine.*** Dein Rad ist neuer als meins. • ***It's mine.*** Es gehört mir. • ***some friends of mine*** ein paar Freunde von mir
2 at mine *umg* bei mir zu Hause

mine[2] [maɪn] *Substantiv*
1 ≈ *Zeche* Bergwerk, Mine
2 MILITÄR Mine

mine[3] [maɪn] *Verb* (**mining**): *auch* **mine for** *Bodenschätze* abbauen

b) Say what the underlined words mean. Use a dictionary if you need to.

1 He didn't want to sit on the ground because it was wet.
2 My parents will ground me if I'm late.
3 Welsh is one of the country's two official languages.
4 He works as a city official.

c) Words like for, on, up, away, ... can change the meaning of a verb.
Say what the underlined verbs mean in German. Use a dictionary if you need to.

1 Let's look for a good place to have lunch.
2 I look after my baby sister every Sunday.
3 He looked around the room to see if he knew anyone.
4 Please look up the meaning of that word.
5 We're looking forward to your visit next week.
6 The police are looking into the fire at the hotel.

d) Translate these sentences into German. Use a dictionary if you need to.

1 Nicholas came up with a new idea.
2 He came down the stairs at 9 am.
3 Her aunt came down with malaria.
4 Can you come over to my house tomorrow?
5 We came across an old church on the moor.
6 Chelsea came back well in the second half.

Study skills

Working with an English-German dictionary: ➜ *SF 19: English-German dictionaries (p. 166)*

➜ **Workbook** *6 (p. 18)*

1 Adam's video blog

Watch the video blog.
Say what you learn about Adam.

One thing I've learned is that Adam speaks …

Another thing is that he …

2 Adam and Welsh

Watch the video blog again. Choose the right answer for each question: a) or b).

1 Adam says the number of Welsh speakers is
a) 500,000. b) 3,000,000.

2 He says his first school was
a) English-speaking. b) Welsh-speaking.

3 He says that, for him, changing from one language to the other is
a) sometimes difficult. b) always easy.

4 In English, the Welsh word for *goodbye* means
a) big carrot. b) big fun.

3 Making a video

a) Adam is a video blogger who talks about his everyday life.
Tell your partner about other video bloggers you know.
Say what you think about them.

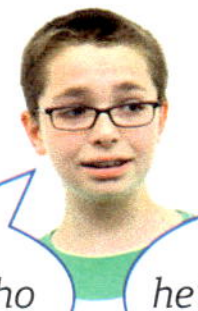

I've seen a video blogger who talks about …

I think he's really funny because …

b) Plan a video blog like Adam's.
Complete the table with ideas from the box.
Add more ideas of your own.

things I need	before I start	while I'm filming
a good place to film	think of a good topic	…
…	…	

a good place to film · computer · look at the camera · look friendly/angry … · make notes · smile · speak in a clear voice · think of a good topic · use captions · use music/sounds/… · wear something interesting

c) Choose a topic and make your video blog.

Access to cultures

Who speaks Welsh? – facts and figures

- About 19% of the population of Wales speak Welsh – so about 81% do NOT.
- The majority of the population in some parts of North-West Wales speak Welsh (Anglesey 57%, Gwynedd 65%). In many parts of South Wales only about 10% or even less speak Welsh.
- Of Welsh speakers, 21% are more comfortable with Welsh than English, 52% are more comfortable with English than Welsh, 27% are equally comfortable in both languages.
- EVERYONE in Wales speaks English.

1 Climbing Mount Snowdon

On Friday morning, Emily's class travelled by bus to Snowdonia National Park. When they arrived, their teacher, Mrs Grant, spoke to the group, first in Welsh, then in English. "Before we start, please choose a partner. You should know where he or she is all the time. The walk to the top of Mount Snowdon isn't an easy one, and I don't want any accidents or lost children." Mrs Grant scanned the students' faces to make sure they were listening. She went on: "We'll stop for lunch in about two hours, when we get to the waterfalls. Altogether, the walk will take eight hours, so we won't be back here at the hostel till 6 pm. OK?"

"OK, Miss!" the students shouted, and hurried around to find their partners.

"Will anyone choose me?" Emily wondered. She studied the ground and wished she could disappear into it. Then someone tapped her on the shoulder. It was Dylan. "He wants to make fun of me again," she thought.

"Wyt ti wedi dewis partner?"

Emily pretended not to understand.

"Sorry?" she asked.

"Have you chosen a partner, Emily?" he repeated.

"Not really," she answered.

"Good, me neither. Is this your first time here?"

Emily nodded.

"Well, I've been here lots of times."

"Really?" said Emily in a bored voice.

"Yes. If you gave me a pound for every trip, I would be rich." Dylan started talking about his last trip, but Emily wasn't listening any more. "Why did it have to be him?" she thought.

They started walking. Everyone was excited. Some of the boys climbed and jumped off the big rocks along the path, until Mrs Grant stopped them. Soon they were at the waterfalls.

"See that waterfall?" Dylan said. "If I had a kayak, I'd paddle right down from the top to this pool."

"That's a stupid idea, Dylan," said a boy called Philip. "If you did that, you would die. If I were you, I'd go down inside a great big beach ball. That way, you wouldn't hit the rocks!"

"Let's test your idea, then," said Dylan. "See this water bottle? I'm going to write a note and put it inside. Then I'm going to run to the top, and drop it into the water. I need a pen. Does anyone have one?"

Emily gave Dylan hers. He wrote something on a piece of paper and put it into the bottle.

"You wait here at the pool and catch the bottle before it goes downstream," Dylan said, and started to climb up the side of the waterfall. Emily looked nervous. "I hope Mrs Grant doesn't see," she whispered.

"Ready?" Dylan shouted down from the top of the waterfall. He held up the bottle with the note inside. Then he threw it into the waterfall. The bottle sailed down, crashed against a rock, flew up in the air again, and then dropped back into the water. Emily and the others waited by the pool. As the bottle came nearer, Emily tried to fish it out, but it was too far from the edge. Mrs Grant blew her whistle. The break was over and it was time to go on. Emily tried to reach the bottle with a stick, but she only pushed it towards Philip.

"I've got it!" he shouted. Dylan ran over to Philip, grabbed the bottle, and gave it to Emily.

"This is for you," he smiled. "If Philip read it, he could get the wrong idea."

Then Mrs Grant blew her whistle again. The others

were already on their way. "I'll read it later," Emily said under her breath, and put the bottle into her rucksack.
As they went on up the mountain, the path became steeper.
"How much further is it to the top?" asked Philip. "We've been walking for hours!"
"Let's sing a song," said Dylan. "An English one that Emily knows." Emily went bright red. Dylan thought for a moment. "What about *If I had a hammer?*"

Emily knew the song. "If I had a hammer, I'd hammer in the morning …" She and her dad often sang it together. Dylan started singing, then Emily and the others joined in. They sang song after song, all ones that Emily liked. Before long, they were at the top of Mount Snowdon.
"Wow, what a view!" Philip shouted. "Amazing!"
Emily looked across the countryside. Yes, the view was amazing. But she was only thinking one thing: what was the message in the bottle?

2 On the walk

a) Choose the correct answer to the questions about Mrs Grant, Dylan and Emily: a, b or c. Write in your exercise book.

1 Before the walk, Mrs Grant tells the students not to
   a) lose their partners.
   b) be late for lunch.
   c) get back to the hostel too early.

2 When Dylan asks Emily about her partner, she
   a) doesn't understand him.
   b) says that she already has one.
   c) doesn't give a clear answer.

3 Dylan tells Emily that
   a) he always gets money for climbing Snowdon.
   b) she should give him some money.
   c) he has climbed Snowdon many times before.

b) Answer the questions about Dylan and Emily.
1 How does Dylan want to go down the waterfall?
2 Who should get the message in the bottle?
3 Why does Emily put the bottle in her rucksack?

c) Explain how you know that some of the group are getting tired before the end of the walk.

d) Describe how Emily feels when:
– Dylan says they should all sing an English song.
– he suggests *If I had a hammer*.
– they sing a lot of other songs together.

e) What do you think Dylan's message in a bottle says? Write your idea down on a piece of paper. Collect all the ideas in class and read them out. Vote for your favourite.

f) **EXTRA** What could Emily write to Dylan? Write a text message (about 60-80 words).

3 Have a go

Say what you would do if you were alone on a small island.

If I were alone on a small island, I would …

Looking at language

a) Complete these sentences from p. 40.

if-clause	main clause
If you ... me a pound for every trip,	I ... be rich.
If I ... a kayak,	I... paddle right down ...
If I ... you,	I... go down inside a ...
If Philip ... it,	he ... get the wrong idea.

b) Say how we form conditional 2 sentences.

- In the ***if*-clause**, the verb is in the ... **past**.
  With the verb *be*, we often say *If I ...* instead of *If I was*.
- In the **main clause**, we use ... or ... + infinitive.

c) Look at this German sentence.
Wenn du weniger reden würdest, könnte ich meine Hausaufgaben machen.

Which translation is correct?
If you would talk less, I could do my homework.
If you talked less, I could do my homework.
Now make a rule to help you to form *if*-clauses in the correct way.

→ *GF 4.2: Conditional 2 (p. 176)*

1 If I had ... (Conditional sentences 2)

a) Dylan and Philip are talking in the break. Finish five of the sentences with an idea from the box. Use *would* or *could*.

do more at weekends · have more fun in the breaks · not know the time · often visit them · paddle across the lake

1 If I had a kayak ...
If I had a kayak, I could ...
2 If we had a climbing wall at school ...
3 If I had friends in Wales ...
4 If we had a sofa in our classroom ...
5 If we didn't have clocks or watches ...
6 If we didn't have school on Mondays ...
7 If I had eyes in the back of my head ...

Early finisher Think of as many endings as you can for the other two sentences.

b) Read the first verse of the song the students sang on the trip. Then listen. What else do the singers say they would do?

If I had a hammer (Hays & Seeger)

If I had a hammer,
I'd hammer in the morning,
I'd hammer in the evening,
All over this land.
I'd hammer out danger,
I'd hammer out a warning,
I'd hammer out love between
my brothers and my sisters,
All over this land.

EXTRA Use these ideas to write another verse.

dance · drum · flag · torch · pen · poem

dance · fly · light · play · say · write

If I had a drum, I'd play it in the morning.

2 If I were a police officer ... (Conditional sentences 2)

Think of six jobs. Write a sentence about what you could or would do in each job.
If I were a police officer, I'd catch lots of thieves.
If I became a cameraman, I could film action movies.

More help → *p. 143*

EXTRA Read your sentences.
Say which job would be best for you, and why.

→ **Workbook** *7 (p. 18)*

3 What would happen if ...? (Conditional sentences 2)

a) Emily doesn't feel at home in North Wales. Sometimes she wants to ...

- run away to London
- shout at Dylan
- walk alone in the hills
- invite classmates home
- stop speaking Welsh
- ask a teacher for help

Are Emily's ideas good or bad? Make notes like this:

Idea	+	–
run away to London:	see Mo and Luke	no place to live
...		

More help ➜ p. 143

b) Say what would happen.

If Emily ran away to London, she could see Mo and Luke.

Yes, but if she ran away, she wouldn't have a place to live. So that's not a good idea.

➜ Workbook 8–9 (p. 19)

4 If this was our garden, we would ... (Conditional sentences 2)

a) Think: How would you clean up this garden if it was yours? Write three sentences that begin like this:
- If this was our garden, we would ...

b) Pair: Compare your ideas with a partner and choose the best four.

c) Share: Compare your ideas with another pair's. Choose five and present them to the class.

More help ➜ p. 143

5 If I were the head teacher ...

a) Which of these things would you do if you were the head teacher? Make a list. Then add more ideas.

- buy more laptops
- allow mobiles in class
- have a school uniform
- start dancing lessons
- send students that fight home
- give students free sweets

Yes	No
– more laptops	– ...
– ...	

- more laptops: students would learn more.
- mobile phones: ...

b) On a different piece of paper, make notes about your reasons.

c) You're a reporter. Interview the head teacher. Use your partner's list from a) to ask questions. Then swap roles.

You say you would buy more laptops. Why?

Well, students would learn more if we had more laptops.

➜ Workbook 10 (p. 19)

6 Text messages (Prop-word *one/ones*)

Which words can you replace with *one* or *ones* in these text messages? Write in your exercise book.

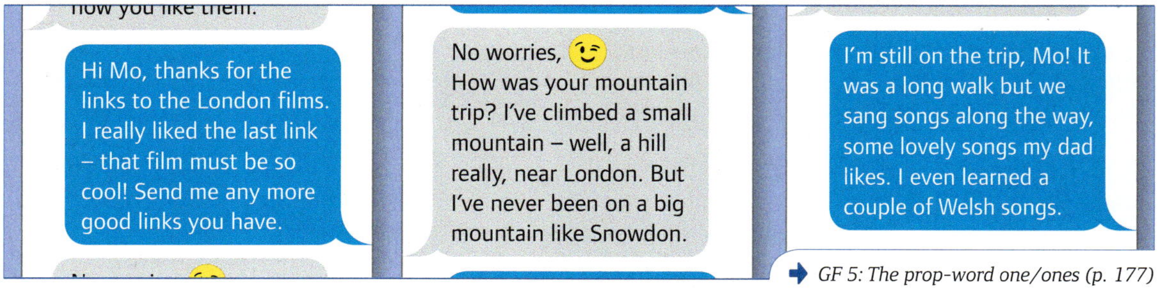

➔ *GF 5: The prop-word one/ones (p. 177)*

7 THINKING ABOUT LANGUAGE Similar words

a) The word *partner* is the same in Welsh, English and German.
Find other English words in 1 *Climbing Mount Snowdon* (p. 40) that are very similar to words you know in German or another language, e.g. *waterfall*.
Compare with a partner.

b) Think of a language that you speak at home or at school, or a language that you are learning (Latin, German, Turkish, French, ...).
Write down five words that are similar to English words and mean the same.
But be careful – similar words can have different meanings, e.g.
English: *map* – German: *Landkarte* (not *Mappe*!).

8 A conservation project

a) Du möchtest für ein Projekt in Wales arbeiten. Du bist dir nicht sicher, ob deine Eltern dir das erlauben werden. Mache dir Notizen über das Projekt auf Deutsch.

TIP
Give only key information when you mediate.
The Skills File can help you to take good notes.
➔ *SF 9: Mediation (p. 160); SF 22: Taking notes (p. 169)*

b) Deine Eltern wollen wissen, was du machen und brauchen wirst und warum die Teilnahme für dich eine gute Idee ist. Verwende deine Notizen und schreibe einen Text auf Deutsch,um sie darüber aufzuklären.

Volunteer for a conservation project in Wales!
The Snowdonia Project needs you!

"This was the best week in our whole college course. It was a real honour to work at the hostel and on the footpaths on Snowdon!"
Gemima, 16

We are working so that future generations can enjoy Snowdonia's beautiful countryside and amazing wildlife. When we do practical conservation work, we invite local people and visitors to take part in our workdays. Join us. Remember: It's your Snowdonia.

Why volunteer?
You can see more of Snowdonia, meet new friends, keep fit and active, get training and experience and feel that you have done something special.

General information
The work involves: removing problematic, non-native plants and repairing and maintaining footpaths.
You will need warm work clothes, waterproofs and strong boots or wellies. Trainers are not acceptable.
We provide tools, gloves, training, insurance, first-aid kit.
We do a full risk assessment before each activity and a First Aider is always present.

➔ **Workbook** *11–14* (pp. 20–22)

1 Learn how

People don't think in paragraphs.
When you write, ideas often come all at once.
But paragraphs and topic sentences help you to organize ideas for your reader.

A paragraph is a group of sentences that are all connected to one main idea.

A topic sentence tells your reader what the main idea of a paragraph is. Try to start each paragraph with a topic sentence.

A trip to the top of Snowdon
by Philip Nash

On Friday our class walked to the top of Mount Snowdon. It's 13 km and a 1,085-metre climb to the summit. It was a long, hard walk up and back down again, but all 24 kids in our class managed it.

At 10 am, we started walking on the Watkin Path. The first part of our walk was easy. We walked for two hours through a beautiful forest and stopped at some amazing waterfalls for lunch. We stayed there until it was time to continue our walk. The second part of our walk was hard. The path was rocky and steep. Sometimes we had to use our hands – like real mountain climbers. We reached the summit at 2 pm. At the top of Snowdon the sky was clear, so we had a great view of Snowdonia National Park. We saw a great big lake and mountain after mountain. The trip back was fun because it was all downhill. We even ran down some parts of the path. But we still needed energy: our class ate a total of 59 chocolate bars on the way down! We reached our hostel at 6 pm. We were really tired, but we all felt like heroes!

a) Read Philip's report. On a copy, mark where other paragraphs should start. Underline the topic sentence for each paragraph.

b) Compare *where* you marked paragraphs. Did you choose the same first sentences? Explain your reasons.

- I started the paragraph here because …
- I think this is the topic sentence and these sentences go with it.
- I think this sentence goes in the next paragraph.

2 Now write …

You choose a) or b).
Write at least four paragraphs about:

a) a walk through a big city, a forest, in the mountains, or by the sea.
b) a film you have seen.

➔ Workbook *Wordbank 1, 8*

TIP

1 Before you start writing, make a mind map or table to collect and organize your memories and ideas.
2 The 5 ***Ws*** (When? Where? What? Who? Why?) can help you to find ideas.
3 Start a new paragraph for every new idea.
4 Use a topic sentence in each paragraph. In the other sentences add details or examples.

3 … and revise

a) Give feedback. Read your partner's text and make notes to answer these questions:

- Does it have clear paragraphs?
- What is the topic sentence in each paragraph?
- Do you get information about the 5 Ws?

Take turns to make comments, suggestions and corrections.

b) Think about what your partner has said. Decide what to change and write a second draft.

➔ *SF 5: Paragraphs (p. 157)*
SF 7: Giving feedback on a text (p. 158); ➔ *pp. 291 – 292*
SF 8: Revising your text (p. 159)

➔ *Unit 1 (p. 17): Feedback*

➔ Workbook *15 (p. 22)*

Snowdonia at night

Look at the pictures in the story. Where are Dylan and Emily? Who are the other people in the pictures and what are they doing?
Make notes what you think the story is about. Then tell your group.

When the class got back to the hostel, Emily ran to the toilet and closed the door behind her. She pulled the bottle out of her rucksack and tried to shake out the note, but the neck of the bottle was too narrow. With a pencil, she pressed hard against the note and tried again and again to pull it towards her. Finally, she had the note in her hand and was able to read the message:
Meet me at the last door on the 2nd floor at 8 pm. I want to show you something! Dylan.
Emily put the note back into her rucksack and hurried downstairs. The kitchen and dining room were noisy and crowded. A large choir group from Bangor was staying at the hostel too. Emily entered the kitchen, where the kids from her class were preparing the evening meal.
During dinner, Emily kept checking the time on the big clock over the dining room door. At five to eight, she looked across the table at Dylan. He nodded, pointed to the stairs, pressed his finger against his chest, and mouthed: "I'll go first." Then he left the table and disappeared up the stairs.
A few minutes later, Emily stood up to follow him.
"Where are you going, Emily?" said Mrs Grant. "We haven't had dessert yet."
"I'm really tired, Miss," replied Emily. "I think I'll go to bed early."
"All right. Good night, then."

❖

Emily ran up the stairs. It was dark on the first floor, but she didn't turn on the lights. She walked to the end of the corridor and almost screamed as a hand touched her shoulder.
"Shshsh ... it's only me!" said Dylan. "Come, it's this way – Look! These stairs go to the roof!"
"The roof? Are you sure we can go up there? I mean, won't Mrs Grant be angry?"
"Don't worry, Emily. It's all right. I've done this before," said Dylan. "Come on!"

Emily followed him up. At the top of the stairs, there was another door. Dylan pushed it open. They walked out onto the roof and looked out. The trees were full of dark shadows, and behind the trees, a large lake shimmered in the moon-light. The night sky was clear and full of stars.
"Welcome to Snowdonia!" Dylan said.
"It's magical," whispered Emily.
"Come on," Dylan said. "We can lie down here and look up at the stars."
"Lie down?" she asked, "but ..."
"Don't worry. It's all right. No one will find us."

❖

Back downstairs it was as busy and noisy as before. Emily's classmates were clearing dishes from the table. In the living room area, the choir group were sitting in a circle, laughing and talking. One of the girls whispered to her neighbour.
"Morgan, let's go upstairs and get our guitars."
"Good idea, Gwen. I want to play a new song for you. Gareth and I wrote it together."
At the top of the stairs, they felt a cool breeze.
"Brrr ... it's cold up here!" said Gwen.

"Of course it's cold! Someone has left the door to the roof open," said Morgan. "Look!"

"Hey, can you really go up to the roof?" Gwen asked. "Let's go and have a look, then!"

"But what if someone finds out? We'll get into trouble, I'm sure," said Morgan.

"Oh, come on. We'll just say that we went through the wrong door," said Gwen, and pushed Morgan up the stairs.

❖

"What was that sound?" Emily whispered to Dylan.

"What sound?"

"I heard something."

"It's probably just the trees. You always hear those kinds of sounds in the country," said Dylan.

"Wow!" Emily whispered. "A shooting star!"

"I think you *were* right," whispered Dylan.

"What do you mean?"

"Someone *is* coming up the stairs," he said.

Emily sat up like a wooden puppet, her eyes wide open in the dark. Two figures appeared on the roof. A girl spoke: "Look, Morgan. We're not alone. Hey, can we join you?" she asked, and walked towards Emily and Dylan. "My name's Gwen, and this is Morgan."

"Hi! I'm Dylan and this is Emily."

❖

"What a great place," said Morgan. "So many stars! You can even see the Milky Way."

Dylan pointed up at the sky. "See that bright light there?" he said. "That's the planet Venus. If you lie down and look up, the view is amazing."

"Right! Good idea," Gwen said, and they all lay on their backs.

"Wow! It's so beautiful!" said Gwen. "I'm sure if we stayed here long enough, we'd see a shooting star."

"I've already seen one," Emily told her.

Then Gwen took out her harmonica and played a few notes. Morgan started to sing a song:

Cold star, you're such a cold star.
Why are you so far, cold star, cold star?
Why are you so far away-ay-ay-ay?
Never calling me, never touching me. Cold star.

❖

"Wow, you sing really well! What's the name of that song?" Emily asked. "It's really nice."

"The name?" Morgan asked. "Oh, I don't know. I've just made it up. Let's try again. This time, all of us join in, OK? One, two, three: Cold star …"

The four kids sang the song again and again. They changed the words and sang louder each time. And then, as they looked up into the night, a shadow moved over their heads. There was something behind them.

"What, may I ask, are you doing up here?" asked a voice that Emily and Dylan knew very well.

"We're looking at the stars, Mrs Grant," said Dylan. "We've learned a lot about stars this year in science and we thought if we watched …"

"That's enough, Dylan. The party is over. Go downstairs, please. It's very dangerous up here and it's against the rules."

"But, Mrs Grant …" started Dylan.

"Don't argue, Dylan," Mrs Grant said.

They stood up and walked back down the stairs. Nobody said another word.

"Please go to your rooms," said Mrs Grant.

"Are we going to be in trouble, Miss?" asked Emily.

"We'll talk about that tomorrow. It's been a long day and now it's time to get some sleep."

❖

Emily and Dylan didn't sit together at breakfast, but more than once their eyes met between spoonfuls of cornflakes and bites of toast. Mrs Grant wasn't there yet.

"I hope she won't come," Emily thought.

But Mrs Grant did come. "Follow me," she said, and went towards the hostel director's office.

"What you both did last night is not only against the rules, it's very dangerous!" Mrs Grant began. "We've given Mr Smart, the hostel director, a very bad picture of our school. He could send the whole class back home. Do you understand that?"

Emily and Dylan nodded.

"He isn't going to do that," Mrs Grant went on. "But we have to show him that our students know how to behave. It will be your job, Emily and Dylan, to wash the floors in the corridors, in the toilets and in the living room each day for the rest of our weekend. Mr Smart will show you where the mops are. Any questions?"

"No, Mrs Grant," said Emily and Dylan.

"Good. Then you can start work now."

❖

"Careful," laughed Emily as Dylan mopped the corridor floor like a madman. "You're splashing me!"

"Oops!" said Dylan. Then he started to sing: "Have you seen the mopping man, the mopping man, the mopping man …?"

"Good song," said Emily, "but I know a better one." In a quiet voice, she began to sing: "Cold star, you're such a cold star …"

Dylan put his mop down and joined in: "Why are you so far, cold star … "

1 The story

a) Look at the notes you made before you read the story. Were your ideas about the story and the people in it correct?

b) Match these headings to the right part of the story.

1 We aren't alone
2 Door to the roof
3 Looking up at the stars
4 The note in the bottle
5 Singing while you work
6 The dark shadow
7 You've broken the rules
8 Welcome to Snowdonia

c) Make groups of four.
Each student chooses two parts of the story and sums up each part in one or two sentences. Then put all the sentences together to tell the story.

2 A fair punishment?

a) What do you think about Dylan and Emily's punishment? Make notes like this:

fair because	not fair because
roof dangerous	kids only wanted to see stars
...	

More help → p. 144

b) Discuss your ideas in a double circle.

EXTRA If your teacher found you on the roof of your hostel on a class trip, how would you explain why you were there?

3 Points of view

You choose a) or b)

a) Imagine you're Emily or Dylan.
In four or five sentences, write about what you think about the other person.

b) Imagine you're Dylan, Mrs Grant or Mr Smart.
Write one part of the story again from that person's point of view.

EXTRA Find other classmates who chose the same task. Compare your ideas.

→ *Writing course, p. 45*
→ *SF 5: Paragraphs (p. 157)*

→ Workbook *16–17 (p. 23)*

Workbook Checkpoint 2 (pp. 24–27)

2 Your task

Imagine you had to move to Wales with your family. Follow Steps 1–5 and write a text (about 150-200 words, or more) for an online magazine about how your life would change.

STEP 1 Look through Unit 2 again and note down the important things that you have learned. Think about topics, vocabulary, skills, …

STEP 2 Discuss which things you have learned in Unit 2 will help you with your text.

STEP 3 Think about why you could have to move. One student writes down *one* idea on a piece of paper. Then another student adds an idea. Go on like this for two minutes. Present your group's ideas to the class.

STEP 4 Decide where you would move to. Make notes on how your life would change and what you would miss about Germany.

STEP 5 Structure your ideas. Write your text, with a paragraph for each idea.

STEP 6 Swap texts. Your teacher will give you a checklist. Use it to give your partner feedback.

STEP 7 Think about the feedback from your partner. Then revise your text.

➜ *SF 8: Revising your text (p. 159)* ➜ **Workbook** *Wordbank 8*

Wie gut warst du?

Wie schätzt du dich selbst ein? Schreibe *Words & Content*, *Grammar* und *Writing* in dein Heft und ordne dir für jede Frage eine Ampelfarbe zu.

🔴	Das lief nicht gut, ich muss mehr üben.
🟡	Das war OK, aber ich könnte besser werden.
🟢	Das habe ich gut geschafft.

Words & Content
Fielen dir passende Wörter zur Beschreibung deines Lebens in Wales ein?

Grammar
Fiel es dir leicht, *Conditional sentences* zu verwenden, um über deine Möglichkeiten zu schreiben?

Writing
Hast du deinen Text gut strukturiert?

Wie kannst du besser werden?

Dort, wo du dich rot oder gelb eingeschätzt hast, helfen dir folgende Tipps:

Words & Content
Schaue dir die Texte der Unit mit Infos über Wales wieder an. Notiere Wörter und Wendungen, um Landschaften oder Städte zu beschreiben.

Grammar
Schaue deinen Text durch und überprüfe die Richtigkeit der Konditionalsätze. Wiederhole die Übungen auf Seite 42/43.

➜ *GF 4.2: Conditional sentences 2 (S. 176);*
➜ *Workbook 7-10 (S. 18-19)*

Writing
Überprüfe deinen Text mithilfe der Tip Box auf Seite 45.

➜ *SF 5: Paragraphs and topic sentences (S. 157)*

A

1 The world of work

a) In a copy of the table, put the words from the box under the right heading.

Jobs	Workplaces
…	…

actor · architect · artist · author · barman/barmaid · cameraman/camera woman · carpenter · comedian · dancer · director · doctor · drummer · farm · farmer · football pitch · hairdresser · head teacher · hospital · musician · office · painter · pub · referee · sailor · school · ship · shop · shop assistant · singer · studio · teacher · theatre · workshop

b) Match as many jobs as you can to each workplace.

c) Choose five jobs and write a sentence about each. The verbs in the box might help.

act · build · cut · dance · feed · film · grow · hammer · make · manage · organize · paint · play · record · sell · sing · study · teach · tell · test · train · travel · write

2 What's my job?

a) Write down what jobs these people do.

1 I work in the evenings and sell drinks to people.
2 I help people when they're not feeling well.
3 I organize and manage a big school.
4 I help people choose clothes in our shop.
5 I play different people on TV.
6 I cut people's hair so they look nice.

b) Write paraphrases like the ones in a) for the following jobs.

1 farmer
2 author
3 artist
4 comedian
5 referee
6 sailor
7 musician
8 singer

3 The meaning changes

Complete the sentences about Emily and Dylan with the correct form of the correct verb in brackets.

1 (make · make fun of · make up)
Mum … a really scary story for my birthday party.
My big brother … me because I was scared.
My father … me a cake.

2 (give · give up)
Dad … me a ticket for the rugby match.
Our team lost but they never …

3 (come · come across · come over)
My family … to Caernarfon last year.
The neighbours soon … to meet us.
We … an old bike at the end of the garden.

4 (look · look after · look for · look forward to · look like)
Mum … the tomatoes she bought yesterday.
She … making a salad for dinner.
I … in the kitchen.
Dad … our dog, Ben.
Ben … a large mop.

5 (go · go by · go red)
I … when I couldn't answer a question in Welsh.
I … to the canteen for lunch.
My lunch break … in a flash.

4 What will happen if …?

a) For each picture, write two sentences about what will happen if …, e.g.:
If the cat catches the mouse, … / If the mouse reaches …

b) Answer these questions for yourself in complete sentences.
1 What will you do if it rains at break?
2 What will you say if the bell doesn't ring at the end of this lesson?
3 How will you react if you get all the answers to this exercise right?

5 If pigs could fly …

Use the following ideas and make funny sentences.

1 If pigs could fly, *we would have …*
2 I'd ask for lots of money …
3 If I was Santa Claus, …
4 I could be the first person on Mars …
5 If T-Rex was still alive, …

a) become/astronaut.
b) have/anything I wanted.
c) nobody/get/any Christmas presents.
d) be/dinosaur dinner.
e) have/pork wings/lunch.

6 What would you do …?

Imagine the following situations and answer the questions in complete sentences.

1 What would you do if it rained for six weeks?
If it rained for six weeks, …
2 Who would you invite if your parents said you could stay up late?
3 Where would you go if you won a free train ticket for all of Bavaria?
4 What would you say if the President phoned you?
5 How would you react if someone gave you 50 euros?
6 What would you do if you saw a ghost?

7 MIXED BAG A new home?

Emily's classmate Lisa wrote the following text.
Complete it with the correct form of the verbs or other words.

I don't know what I *would do* (do) if I had to *move* to another place to live. I …[1] (miss) all my friends, of course. I know I could **p**…[2] them or **t**…[3] them but I …[4] (be able to) **s**…[5] them. It …[6] (be) different if I …[7] (work) already …[8]. If I …[9] (be) a **s**…[10] I …[11] (have to) work in Antarctica. Or if I …[12] (be) an **a**…[13] my work …[14] (take) me millions of miles into space. If I …[15] in a different part of the country, the people there …[16] (speak) another dialect. Maybe I …[17] (be able to) understand them and they …[18] (laugh) when I talked. That …[19] terrible. I …[20] (hear) some people from Scotland on the radio yesterday and I …[21] (understand) a word they said. But kids do have to **m**…[22] sometimes when their **p**…[23] get new **j**…[24] in a **d**…[25] town. I had a **f**…[26] when I was 10 and she …[27] (leave) with her family. They …[28] in London now. I wonder what she …[29] (do) now. If she …[30] on facebook, maybe I can **f**…[31] her. I'm sure that …[32] too hard. I …[33] (try) this evening. Now I …[34] (have to) work for a test at school next week. I **s**…[35] (can) at the weekend, because my parents …[36] (take) me on a long walk up a big hill in the park. They're so full of **e**…[37]. I don't have this much **e**…[38]. Oh well, at least when we're at the top, it …[39] (be) all **d**…[40] after that!

B

8 In Snowdonia National Park

a) Scan the text below for *volunteers* and write down what they do in two minutes.

Would you take a job 3,000 feet up in the mountains if you had the chance? Seren Jones and Rhys Lewis did and now they're working as summer rangers in Snowdonia National Park. Our reporter, Jessica Davies asked them what they needed for the job.

"Well, you have to be very fit," Seren said. "I do a lot of sport – mountain-biking, running, swimming, so the job was perfect for me. I just love being outside."

"They wanted Welsh speakers, too," said Rhys. "Well, we are in Wales and this part of the country has the most Welsh speakers. Welsh is our first language, so that was no problem for us. If you could just speak a little Welsh, that would be fine too."

Rhys and Seren's work changes all the time – no two days are the same. They are the face of the national park for the walkers who use the area – more than 500,000 walkers a year, so they meet a lot of these visitors and talk to them about the mountain paths.

They also have to manage the volunteers[1] who work on the paths and stone walls. That's a very big job in the mountains. A helicopter brings in the stones that they need.

"It's a really exciting part of the work when the helicopter comes," Rhys says. "It's just amazing when it flies in and drops the stones."

Seren likes the mountains better when they are quiet, so she is happier when she's looking for invasive[2] plants like rhododendron.

"If we don't do anything about them," she tells me, "they can grow everywhere in no time. When we find them, volunteers come and take them out."

On other days, Rhys and Seren plant trees or count birds and wild animals. They will both be a bit sad when their time up in the mountains comes to an end.

"If I had the chance, I'd come back next year," Seren tells me as I start the long walk back.

"Me too," Rhys agrees. They watch me for a while and then turn to start another busy day as summer rangers in Snowdonia.

b) Read the text carefully. Are the following statements right or wrong?

1 Seren and Rhys work 3,000 metres high up in the mountains.
2 You need to do a lot of sport for their job.
3 Rhys doesn't speak much Welsh.
4 They do different things every day.
5 They manage the park volunteers.

c) Answer these questions.

1 What does Rhys like most about the job?
2 How is Seren different from Rhys?
3 What jobs do they have to do?

d) Read the text and then choose the best title for it from this list of four:

A summer job in Wales | *Walkers in Snowdonia* | *Volunteers and helicopters* | **You have to be fit**

e) Explain in one or two sentences why you would or would not want to work in Snowdonia as a summer ranger.

1 **volunteer** [ˌvɒlənˈtɪə] Freiwillige/r 2 **invasive** [ɪnˈveɪzɪv] invasiv, in fremden Lebensraum eindringend

C

9 A day out

Write an email (about 200 words) to an English-speaking friend about a day out.
It could be a day you experienced or you could make up a story.
Remember what you have learned about using paragraphs with topic sentences.

Welcome to Wales

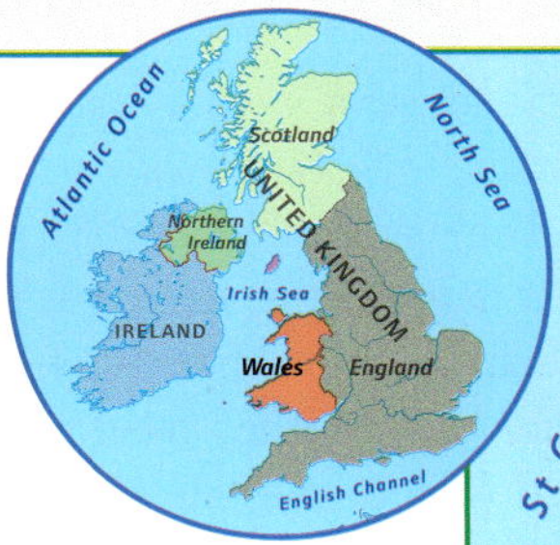

Facts about Wales

- *A country in the UK*
- *Population (2016): 3.12 m*
- *Area: 20,779 square km*
- *Capital: Cardiff (Caerdydd)*
- *Languages: English, Welsh*
- *Highest point: Snowdon, 1085 m*

The capital city

Cardiff, the capital, is Wales's largest city (346,000). With over 300,000 tourists a year, it is one of Britain's favourite cities. People go there to see its old castle or watch the Welsh Parliament at work. Or they visit the Welsh National Museum or the famous Doctor Who Experience.

Cardiff Castle

Steel, coal and rugby: the Valleys

Wales was once a land of steel and coal. In 1945, 30 per cent of all Welsh men worked in these industries in the valleys of south Wales. But today, steel and coal are no longer important. The last coal mine closed in 2008. One million people still live in the Valleys, but today they work in manufacturing or health and social services. The Valleys are still a centre of Welsh culture, and rugby, the "national sport" of Wales, is very popular. There are rugby grounds in most of the towns and villages.

Town in the Welsh valleys

The National Parks

Wales is a small country but it has three national parks. Brecon Beacons is a great place for adventures above and below the ground. Start with a visit to Dan-yr-Ogof National Showcaves. Then you can go rock climbing. Finish at night and gaze at the Milky Way – the Brecon Beacons is an international Dark Sky Reserve. Snowdonia is the place for mountain-biking and

Brecon Beacons National Park

whitewater rafting. You can enjoy the waterfalls and forests and walk or take the steam train to the top of the highest mountain in England and Wales, Mount Snowdon.
If beautiful beaches are more your style, then go to Pembrokeshire Coast and relax by the water, go sea kayaking or just enjoy the nice walks.

Two languages
Welsh and English are official languages in Wales. That's why road signs are bilingual. Everyone in Wales speaks English, but about 20 per cent of the population also speak Welsh, the country's original Celtic language. In the north-west, the number of Welsh speakers is higher. There, many people use Welsh in everyday life and at school.

The National Eisteddfod (Eisteddfod Genedlaethol Cymru)
The Eisteddfod is the biggest festival in Wales and takes place in a different town every year. 150,000 visitors come for a mix of music, dance and theatre. There are competitions for everything from disco dancing to large choirs, many of them for young kids and teens.
The Eisteddfod goes back to 1176. It promotes Welsh language and culture and all official events are in Welsh.
But everyone is welcome, even if they can't speak Welsh.

Beach in Pembrokeshire Coast National Park

Road sign in Wales.

At the Eisteddfod

1 More Wales

a) Watch the video and find out even more about Wales.

b) Write six questions for a quiz on Wales. Ask your partner your questions.

➜ **Workbook** *5–6 (p. II–III)*

2 Wales and Bavaria

a) Compare Wales with Bavaria. Think about size, population, languages, sport, culture, festivals, the capital, …
Make notes in your exercise book.

b) Work in groups of five. Agree on five interesting places or things that a visitor should do or see in Bavaria. Write short texts in English about them. Hang them up for a gallery walk. Give the other groups feedback.

1 A first look: The British Isles

a) Look at map 1 and the key. What do they tell you about the British Isles? Find countries, cities, mountains, water, …

b) Watch the first video clip.
Talk about what you've learned about the British Isles.

2 A first look: The USA

a) Look at map 2 and the key. What do they tell you about the USA? Find states, cities, mountains, water, …

b) Watch the second video clip.
Talk about what you've learned about the USA.

3 The British Isles and the USA

a) Look at the six captions. Say what you already know about the topics.

The British Isles

1 Land and water

2 Sports

3 Music

The USA

4 National parks

5 Sports

6 Music

b) Watch the other video clips.
Note down the two topics you liked most.
What would you like to know more about?
Compare your ideas. Give reasons why you are interested in a topic.

MAP 1

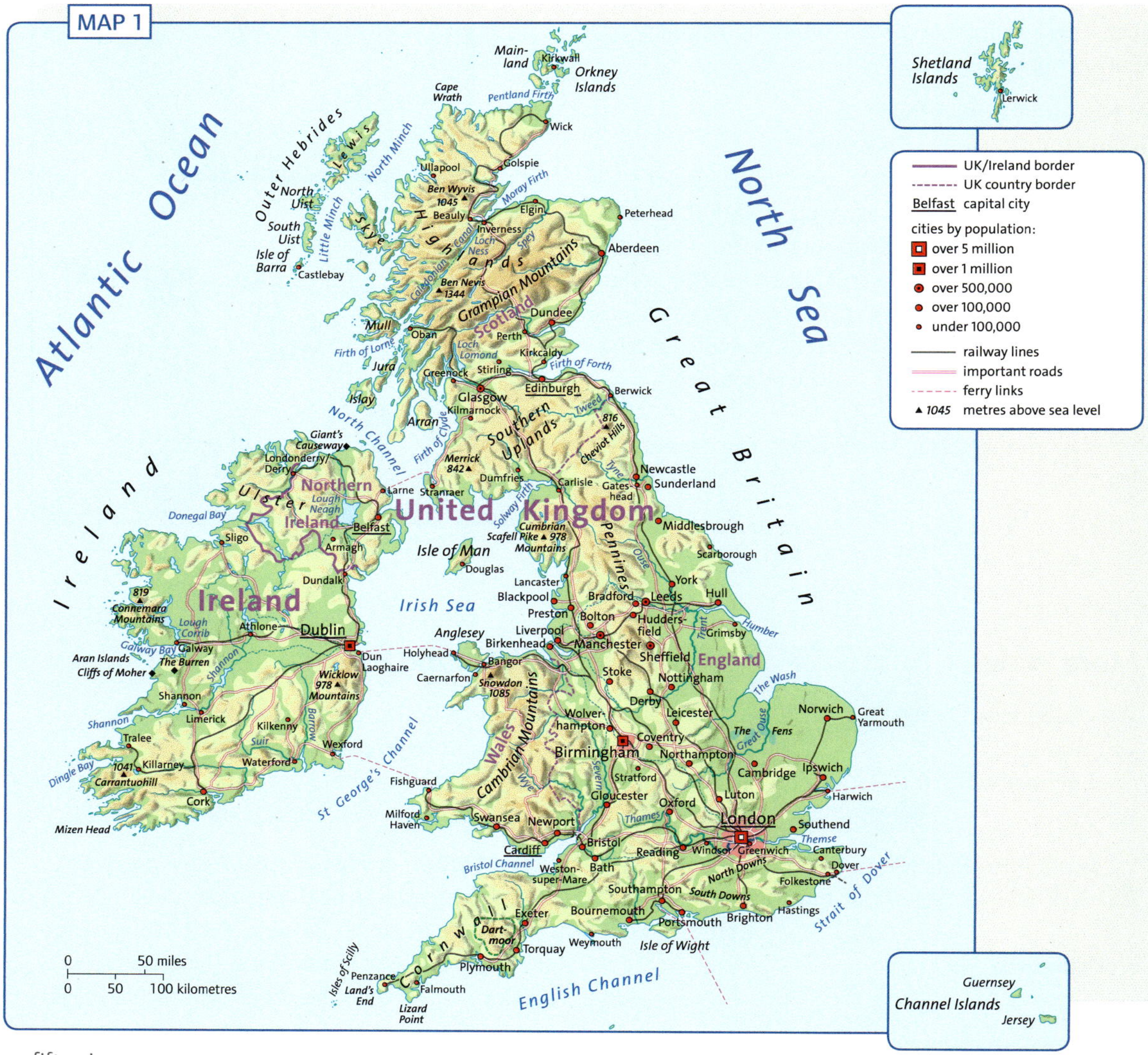

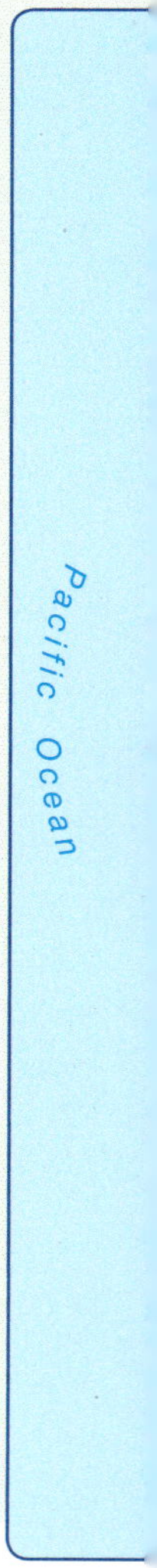

4 EXTRA The British Isles and the USA: a poster project

a) Choose one topic from the list below and make notes for a poster about the British Isles and the USA.

1 Land, water and national parks in the British Isles and the USA
2 Sport in the British Isles and the USA
3 Music in the British Isles and the USA

www You can watch the video clips again to get ideas.

b) Now follow these steps:

- Decide what the main focus of your poster will be (e.g. lakes and mountains/famous sports teams/musical festivals in the British Isles and the USA, …).
- Find the information you need and collect pictures of places, people, events, stories, etc.
- Write your texts.
- Make your poster with your texts and pictures.

My trip to the Southwest

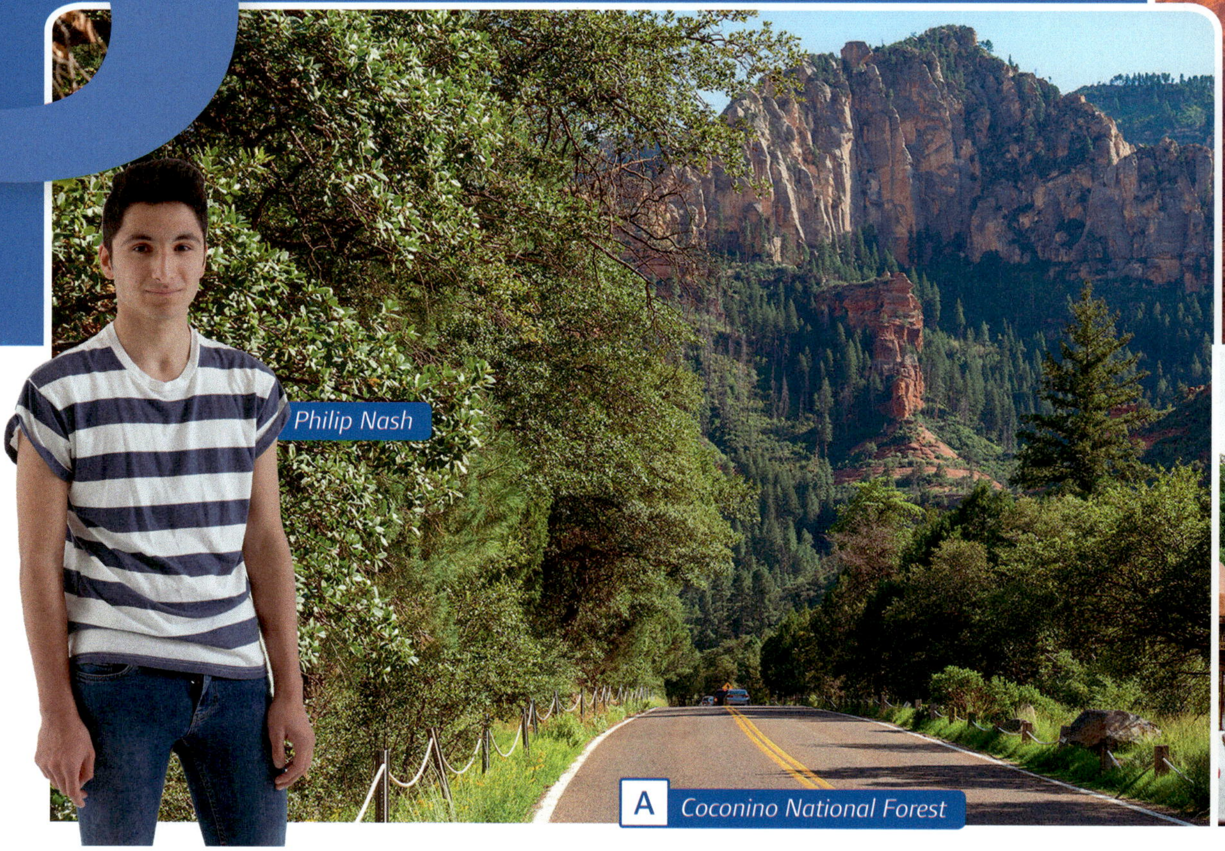

A Coconino National Forest

1 First impressions

a) Look at the photos. In what way do they seem similar or different to your part of the world?

b) In which of the four places would you most like to be? Where would you least like to be? Discuss your ideas.

A: I'd quite like to be in … It looks …
B: The place I'd most like to be in is …
I can imagine that it's …

2 Head southwest!

a) Listen to a radio advertisement for a vacation in the Southwest. Note down the names of the places you hear.

b) Listen again. Then say how the advertisement describes the Southwest.

→ p. 57 Look at the United States on the map. Find the Southwest. Which places that you heard about in the advertisement can you see?

B Monument Valley

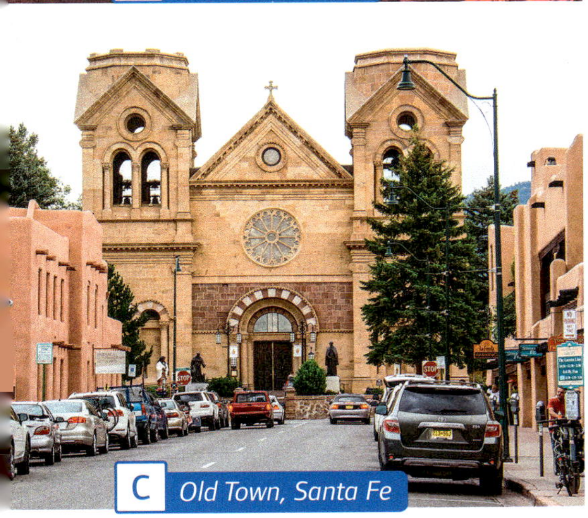

C Old Town, Santa Fe

D The oldest skyscraper (right) in Downtown Albuquerque

3 Planning Philip's trip

a) Philip from Caernarfon is going to stay with his aunt and uncle in Santa Fe. Listen as the two of them discuss his visit. Take notes on Taos, Albuquerque, Coconino National Forest and Monument Valley.

b) Listen again. Say when they plan to visit these places. When will they be in Santa Fe?

→ *p. 57* Look again at the map. How many miles do you think the road trip will be?

c) Say which part of Philip's trip you would find most interesting and why. Have you changed your mind about the photos you talked about in 1? Explain why.

Your task

Your task for this unit: In a team, you'll make a brochure with practical tips for US students who want to visit Germany.

→ Workbook *1 (p. 28)*

1 Monument Valley

Philip is with his Aunt Gwen and Uncle Dave.

Uncle D.: Can you pass the coffee?
Aunt G.: Here you are. I hope there's still enough.
Philip: May I have some more too, please?
Aunt G.: You drink a lot of coffee for a boy of your age. Is your mum OK with that?
Philip: She doesn't mind.
Aunt G.: Well, I'm not sure it's good for you. Anyway, let's hurry and get ready to leave.
Philip: Where are we going today?
Uncle D.: To Monument Valley – it's less than an hour and a half in the car from the B&B. An hour for your aunt. She's a fast driver. Anyway, it might as well be the other side of the moon.
Philip: I don't understand.
Uncle D.: You will. Now go and get your backpack!

❖

Uncle D.: Don't drive so fast, Gwen. I want to read this to Philip. "The deep red stone forms huge rocky towers and columns that rise up 1,000 feet from the valley floor."
Philip: Only 1,000 feet? We have much higher mountains than that in Wales.
Uncle D.: 1,000 feet above the valley floor, Philip! That's over 5,000 feet above the sea.

❖

Philip: That rock is like a huge gravestone! You could bury a giant here. And this place is like the moon! Who built it?
Uncle D.: There are quite a few Navajo legends about the geography of the area.
Philip: Navajo?
Aunt G.: The Navajo are a Native American tribe from this part of the Southwest.
Uncle D.: Some of their legends say that the mountains here were the home of the gods. And there's also a legend about a tribe of white giants who lived here long ago. They ruled the land wisely for many years. No challenge was too great for them. They were strong and fought their enemies fiercely. But in the end they went back to the heavens and all that is left today are the mountains where they once lived.
Aunt G.: I'm glad that legend ends quite happily.

Uncle D.: Actually, there's another, less happy ending. Shall I tell you, Philip?
Philip: Yes, please!
Uncle D.: After many years the giants became too proud and the gods were angry. And so in a short time, the tribe of giants died out. None of them were left. What we see now are the mountains where they lived.
Philip: Are there many Native American legends?
Uncle D.: Oh, yes. All the different tribes have their special legends. There's one about …
Aunt G.: Later, Dave. We can't stand here all day.
Philip: Are we going to explore now?
Uncle D.: We're going on a tour, Philip. Our guide is a member of the Navajo tribe.

2 Talking about the text

Where do Philip's aunt and uncle take him? Describe how his thoughts on the place change.

3 Describing Philip

Say which adjectives best describe Philip. Find lines in the text which show this.

careful · curious · excited · impolite · nervous · polite · proud · shocked · shy

Early finisher Describe Philip's aunt and uncle. Say why you would('nt) enjoy a trip with them.

4 Legends

Say which ending to the legend of Monument Valley you prefer, and why.

1 A tour guide in Monument Valley

a) You will see a short video in which a Native American tour guide talks about the Navajo Reservation in Monument Valley.
Look at five stills from the video.

Write down what you think the topic of each still will be.

b) Now watch the video. Take notes on the topics the guide talks about.

Together, discuss your first ideas about the five stills and your notes on the whole video.

c) Say what you have already learned about:
- the name of the valley.
- the Navajo language.
- schools on the Reservation.
- getting food and water.
- why the hogan is important.

Then watch and listen carefully one more time and note down any more information you hear.

d) Does the film make you more or less interested in visiting Monument Valley? Explain why.

1

2

3

4

5

2 Making the film: Story-telling in a documentary

a) There are different techniques for telling a story in a documentary. Read definitions of three techniques and say which one this video uses:
i) Narration: You do not see the narrator – you only hear his/her voice.
ii) Host: You see one person who guides you through the story and gives his/her view.
iii) Talking heads: There are interviews with different people with different opinions.

b) Say if you think the film-maker used the best technique for this topic. Or would one of the other techniques be better? Give reasons for your opinion.

1 WORDS Countries

Choose one way to order these words: a), or b). Then choose 25 words and try it out.

battle · beautiful · +border · capital · +change money · city · county · crown · culture · +currency · defend · +dollar · +emigrate · enemy · +EU · +euro · Europe · +exports · fierce · flag · +governor · +ID card · +independent · island · king · land · language · mayor · +nation · navy · parliament · passport · +peace · peaceful · police officer · +police station · population · pound · president · queen · +republic · royal · state · traditional · travel · United Kingdom (UK) · +United States (US) · village · +visa · visit

a) Copy the table and add nouns from the box. Then add verbs/adjectives that go with them.

noun	verb	adjective
battle		
border		

Think of more words for each noun, e.g. *passport + show*

b) Write the words in a mind map.

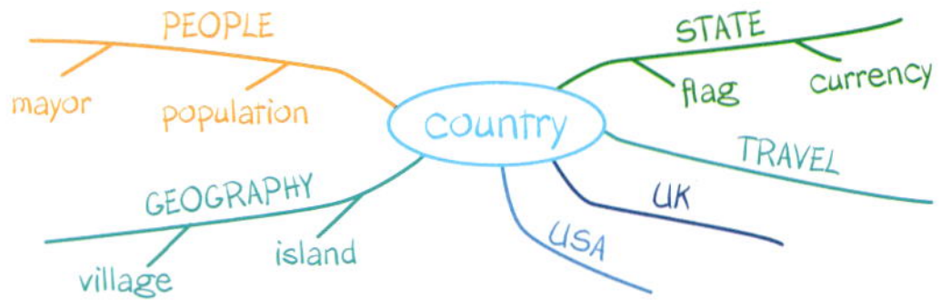

Compare your mind maps. Make changes to yours if you get new ideas.

c) Choose one of the topics from your mind map (e.g. people, geography, etc.). Then, for the topic you chose, compare the United Kingdom and the United States. Write a short text (about 100–150 words).
The United States has a much bigger population than the United Kingdom. ...

➔ Workbook *2–3 (pp. 28–29)*

2 WORDS Describing people and places

a) Copy the Venn diagram into your exercise book and add the adjectives from the box in the right sections: adjectives that:
- describe people.
- describe places/things.
- describe both.

American · beautiful · blue · British · cloudy · different · fantastic · fast · golden · good · green · high · hilly · narrow · nice · northern · peaceful · proud · +public · quick · rocky · royal · scared · special · tall · traditional · wide

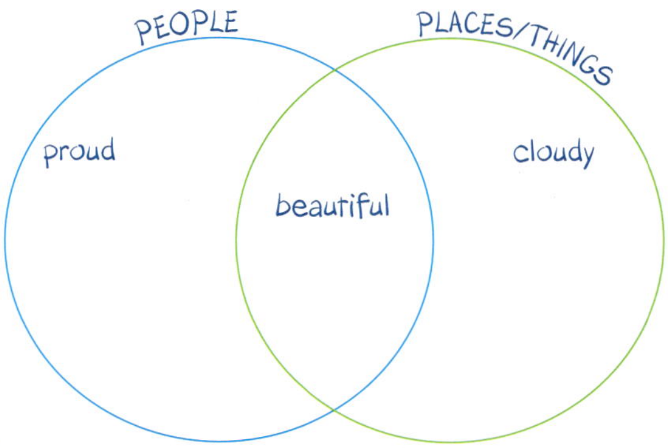

b) Add more adjectives that you know to the diagram.

c) Choose two adjectives from each section and write a sentence with each. Or use them to write a short story or description. Write about 100–120 words.

➔ Workbook *Wordbank 1, 2, 4 (pp. 70, 71, 73)*

Looking at language

Adjectives describe a **person** or a **thing**. Adverbs describe **how somebody does something.**

a) Find the missing words from these sentences on p. 60. Are they adjectives or adverbs?
She's a ... driver.
They ruled the land ...
That legend ends quite ...

b) Finish this sentence:
To make an adverb, you usually add ... to the adjective.

c) Scan 1 on p. 60 and find more adverbs.

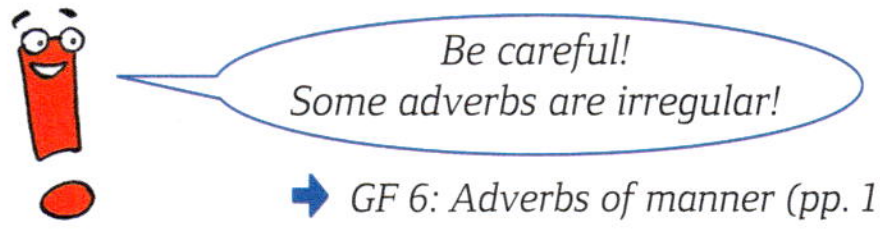

➜ *GF 6: Adverbs of manner (pp. 178 – 180)*

1 A video for Emily (Adjectives and adverbs)

At a market in Santa Fe, Philip makes a video to send to Emily back in Caernarfon. Finish the text of his commentary with adverbs.

Hi, Emily! This is a great market. You can get here ... [1] from my aunt's house – it's very near. What an atmosphere! People are talking quite ... [2], so I hope you can hear me ... [3]. Hey! Here's a boy on a bike. He isn't riding very ... [4]. Oops! He almost hit a fruit stall. But some people are relaxing too. This mother is reading ... [5] at a table outside a café and her two kids are playing ... [6] next to her. Oh dear! Not everyone is so happy. These two teenagers are shouting ... [7]! I think they're having an argument.

2 An email from Santa Fe (Adjective or adverb)

Philip emails his mum about his holiday. Finish the text with one of these adjectives or with the adverb:
amazing · bad · busy · colourful · easy · fast · friendly · good · nervous · safe · slow · tired

We got back safely [1] to Santa Fe last night. The Southwest is bigger than Wales, but the roads aren't so ... [2] and you can get to places very ... [3]. Aunt Gwen drives ... [4] too, and Uncle Dave looked quite ... [5]. The road trip was just ... [6], especially Monument Valley, where our ... [7] guide explained everything very ... [8].
It was hot last night, and I slept ... [9]. I felt ... [10] when I got up, so I just walked very ... [11] to a ... [12] market nearby and made a video for Emily.

3 GAME Are you playing the drums quietly?

a) Write 15 activities and 10 adverbs on separate cards.

b) Mix the activity cards. Put them on a desk, face down. Put the adverb cards around them.

c) Take a card and act out the activity with one of the adverbs. Can the others say what you are doing? Take turns.

➜ Workbook 4 –6 *(pp. 29 –30)*

The region called the Southwest is made up of five states in the southwest corner of the United States – Nevada, Utah, Colorado, New Mexico and Arizona – and of parts of California and Texas.

Hot

Much of the Southwest is desert and is often hot and dry, like Death Valley, which recorded the hottest ever US temperature: 134°F, 56.7°C.

Death Valley, California

Aspen, Colorado

… and cold

But the region is also full of high mountains and plateaus, so it can get very cold in winter with lots of snow in the USA's most popular ski resorts, like Aspen, Colorado.

Drought

Drought is already a problem in the Southwest, and scientists fear that, with climate change, droughts will become longer in the future and may even go on for decades.

Drought in New Mexico

Hoover Dam, Colorado River on the Nevada-Arizona border

… and water

Tens of millions of people live in the Southwest, and people cannot live without water.
Dams on the Colorado, Rio Grande and other major rivers help to supply the population with the water they need.
The water is also used by power plants which supply the region with electricity.

Old

Native Americans have lived in the Southwest for thousands of years, and there are many reservations there today.
The ruins of the ancient Pueblo Indian cultures can still be seen in the region. Their buildings and cities were the largest in North America before the 19th century. People still live in the Taos Pueblo adobe houses in New Mexico. They are over 1,000 years old.

Taos Pueblo, Taos, New Mexico

Phoenix, Arizona

… and new

The states in the Southwest are some of the youngest in the US: Arizona and New Mexico only became states in 1912.
Most of the big, modern cities are young too. Phoenix is less than 150 years old. Las Vegas, which was founded in 1912, is even younger. But there are some older cities. The city of Santa Fe, the state capital of New Mexico, is over 400 years old. Spanish settlers founded it in the year 1610.

English … and Spanish

Look at the names of the states (Nevada, Colorado, …), cities (Las Vegas, Santa Fe, …) or rivers (Rio Grande, …), and you see the Southwest's Hispanic heritage. For centuries, most of the region belonged to the Spanish colony of New Spain, and to Mexico after it became independent from Spain. It became part of the United States after the Mexican-American War (1846–1848).
This region has a long border with Mexico. Many immigrants from Latin America cross it to enter the USA. All over the Southwest you'll hear people speaking Spanish and see lots of Spanish advertisements and signs. The Latino population is especially high in big cities (Los Angeles 48.3%, Phoenix 40.8%).

a) Look at the pictures. Say what they tell you about the Southwest.

b) Read the texts. Then find as many of the places as you can on the map on p. 57. Say what you find most interesting/surprising/exciting/… about the region.

c) My Book Prepare a quiz on the Southwest (on cities, rivers, mountains, climate, languages, Native Americans, …).
Do more research if you need to.
Swap and do your partner's quiz.
www Find out more about sights in the region.

→ Workbook 7 (p. 31)

1 Back in Santa Fe

WHAT HAPPENED

Saturday

After breakfast, Philip got his bags and hurried to the car, where his aunt and uncle were waiting. He felt sad as he thought back to all he had seen in the last week: Albuquerque, the Grand Canyon, Monument Valley. It had been a great trip and now it was almost over.
It was 400 miles back to Sante Fe and they stopped only once, for gas. Finally, after over six hours on the road, they arrived. Philip began to feel excited again. He didn't know the city yet because they had started the road trip just after his arrival in the US. But now he was looking forward to exploring it.

Sunday

Next day Uncle Dave and his nephew did a tour of Santa Fe. Philip took photo after photo as they walked along. He had never seen such buildings. Uncle Dave told him their history. In the 1920s, architects had started to copy the traditional Native American adobe style, and it soon became the typical style of the city. After 20 minutes, they reached the 150-year-old cathedral. They couldn't walk around because a service had started. Before long they came to the Palace of the Governors. Philip learned that the Spanish had built it and that it was one of the oldest buildings in the United States. They then came to the New Mexico Museum of Art, where Uncle Dave suggested that they check out the section with paintings by artists from the Southwest.

POSTS AND PHOTOS

Philip Nash We stopped here for petrol on the way back to Santa Fe.

Dylan Davis Don't they call it gas over there?

Emily Evans Looks like they're invading Earth. Are they from Mars?

Philip Nash This whole place is like Mars. Red stone everywhere! Incredible!

Philip Nash Even the houses are kind of red.

Dylan Davis Cool buildings!

Philip Nash It's the local style. You see it everywhere.

Philip Nash Here's another one. I was here yesterday with Uncle Dave.

Emily Evans What is it?

Philip Nash A museum – right in the centre of Santa Fe.

Dylan Davis You're spending your time in museums?

Philip Nash But I'm spending my money at the markets!

Dylan Davis Hey, big spender! What have you bought?

Philip Nash One of these skulls. :-))

Emily Evans You bought a cow's skull? Are you crazy?

Philip Nash Hey, you're just like my Aunt Gwen. I walked in with it and she was like: "So why did you buy that, Philip? You must have too much money in the bank."

Emily Evans She sounds kind of strict.

Philip Nash No! She's an angel – in her own special way.I'm going to miss her when I go back ;-)

Dylan Davis And why did you buy a cow's skull?

Philip Nash Because they're cool. Everyone here has one. It's a present for my dad.

Emily Evans And what have you got for your mum?

Philip Nash Either one of those smiling suns – or one of these pots. She'd like the pot – it's a Native American design.

Monday

On Monday morning, Aunt Gwen and Uncle Dave went back to work. Philip was free to explore Santa Fe on his own. He knew what he wanted to do. On Sunday, he had seen so many stores that were full of things you couldn't get in Britain: colorful Native American clothes, jewelry, peace pipes and traditional pots, smiling suns and white cows' skulls. He had wanted to go inside but his uncle had said no. Stores like those were just for tourists. But now he was on his own and could be a tourist as much as he liked. Before long he was walking into a big souvenir shop in downtown Sante Fe. On the wall inside, there was a line of white cows' skulls, just like the ones he had seen on houses everywhere in the Southwest. "I wonder how much they cost," he thought. "I could get one of those for Dad – it would certainly make an awesome present." "Ouch," he thought a few moments later as he left the shop with a cow's skull under his arm and $99 less in his pocket. "I hope I have enough to buy one of those pretty pots for Mum."

2 From Saturday to Monday

a) Sum up what Philip did from Saturday to Monday. Write just one sentence for each day.

b) Say how Philip felt about what he did or saw. Which parts of the texts support your view?

c) Compare the content and style of the posts and the structured texts. What is similar? What is different?
Which of the two texts gives you a clearer idea of what Philip did and felt?
Give reasons for your view.

3 Have a go

Read this sentence from the text:

They couldn't walk around because a service had started.

Now give similar explanations for these situations:

1 I – take a photo – leave my phone at home
2 I – write any postcards – hurt my right hand
3 I – go into the club – forget my ID
4 I – do the homework – miss the last lesson
5 I – learn the song – lose the words

Looking at language

a) Look at these sentences from p. 66.
Say which action came before the other(s).
He felt sad as he thought back to all he had seen in the last week.
Philip learned that the Spanish had built the Palace of Governors.

b) The tense we use for the action that came first in the past is called the past perfect. Explain how you form it.

➜ GF 1.7: Past perfect (pp. 173–174)

1 After the trip to Taos (Past perfect)

Some students from Santa Fe were on a class trip to Taos.
Say how they felt when they got back. Use the past perfect for the earlier action.

1 Susan ... (be) happy to be back because she ... (miss) her parents.
Susan was happy to be back because she had missed her parents.
2 Dan ... (be) unhappy because he ... (lose) his mobile.
3 Sam ... (feel) tired because he ... (not sleep) very well.
4 Peter ... (feel) sick because he ... (eat) too many biscuits.
5 Jill ... (look) worried because her boyfriend ... (not phone) her.
6 Tom ... (be) all red because he ... (stay) in the sun too long.
7 Ben ... (look) excited because he ... (meet) a nice girl at the hostel.

2 In Santa Fe (Past perfect)

A teenage tourist writes a blog about his visit to Santa Fe. Read and complete the text.
Choose the correct form of the verbs in brackets: simple past or past perfect.

I ... [1] (arrive) in Santa Fe on Friday afternoon. Downtown ... [2] (be) smaller than I ... [3] (expect), so I ... [4] (be able to) go everywhere on foot. I ... [5] (already look) at photos of the city on the internet, so I ... [6] (know) quite a few of the buildings. After I ... [7] (finish) my walk, I ... [8] (sit) down at one of the cafés on the Plaza and ... [9] (order) a cool drink. The atmosphere ... [10] (be) amazing. Lots of other young people were using skates to get around and I ... [11] (be) really sorry that I ... [12] (not bring) mine with me.

On Saturday, downtown ... [13] (seem) even busier that it ... [14] (be) the day before. I ... [15] (go) back to the Plaza and ... [16] (head) for the Palace of the Governors. I ... [17] (read) that it's the oldest public building in the United States, so I ... [18] (want) to see it. We ... [19] (have) a great guide who ... [20] (tell) us a lot about the city, so after the tour I ... [21] (decide) to check out some of the places he ... [22] (tell) us about.

Early finisher ➜ p. 150

3 I had never been to ... before

a) Write 80–100 words on your first trip to a place you know. Use at least five past perfect forms.
Begin like this: *I had never been to ... before ...*

b) Swap with a partner. Give each other feedback.

➜ Workbook 8–11 (pp. 31–33)

4 STUDY SKILLS Teamwork

This page will show you how to work in a team.

a) When you work in a team, everyone has a special job. Match these four jobs to the speech bubbles.

1 coordinator

2 writer

3 picture and layout editor

4 language watchdog

A *I do research. When I find the information we need, I write the texts.*

B *I look for pictures, or I draw them. Then I put the pictures and the texts together so that our results look good.*

C *I check all the texts and make sure there are no mistakes. I also suggest how we can improve our texts and make sure we speak English in our discussions.*

D *I plan our discussions and take notes on our decisions. I also check that everyone does their job at the right time.*

b) Work in teams of four.
Choose one of these topics and make a brochure on it.

1 Taos
2 Great buildings in Santa Fe
3 Writers in the Southwest
4 Horse riding in the Southwest
5 Native American legends
6 New Mexico

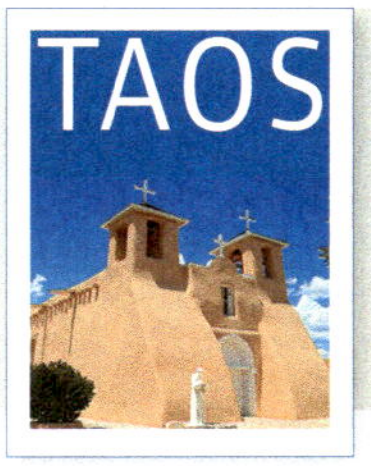

Decide who will do what job and make a timetable for all the work. Then make your brochure.

c) Swap brochures with another team. In your team, say what you think about the other brochure.

d) **Think**: Think of at least two reasons why teamwork helped you, and write them down.
Pair: Compare your reasons. Number them 1 *(most important)*, 2, 3, etc.
Share: Join two other pairs and agree on the four most important reasons.

e) In your team, talk about your teamwork. Did each member of the team have the right job? Did the team do the task successfully?

Study skills

Teamwork
Wenn wir im Team arbeiten, kann ich folgende Aufgaben übernehmen: ...
Ein Team kann ...

→ *SF 12: Teamwork (p. 163)*

→ **Workbook** *12 (p. 33)*

1 Texting from Taos

Emily Evans Still in Santa Fe?

Philip Nash No, we left when Aunt Gwen finished work this afternoon.

Emily Evans Left for where?

Philip Nash For a place called Taos. We're at a riding centre. The owner's daughter has just shown us our cottage. She's weird.

Emily Evans What do you mean?

Philip Nash She looks like a VAMPIRE. Black hair, black clothes and a very white face!

Emily Evans Sounds cool to me.

Philip Nash Cool? She's scary! She didn't even smile when she gave us the key. I tried to chat to her, but she didn't react.

Emily Evans Hey, you'll have to try harder next time.

Philip Nash No way. She just stared right through me. She should behave more politely to guests.

Emily Evans You're just imagining it all. Anyway, where exactly is Taos?

Philip Nash 70 miles north of Santa Fe.

Emily Evans How long are you staying there?

Philip Nash For the weekend. Uncle Dave says it's a great place for outdoor activities.

Emily Evans Outdoor activities? You? Make sure you don't hurt yourself ; -)

Philip Nash Thanks! Actually, I'm going on an 8-hour tour tomorrow – on a horse.

Emily Evans With your aunt and uncle?

Philip Nash No, just me and a guide. We leave at 8 am. Uncle Dave organized it. He thinks I'll enjoy it.

Emily Evans When were you last on a horse?

Philip Nash When I was 10.

Emily Evans Well, I hope you have a great time tomorrow ;-)

Philip Nash Love your sense of humour, Emily. Actually, I'll be happy if I survive.

Emily Evans Don't worry – you'll be OK. Probably ;-)

Philip Nash Hope you're right. I'll send you some photos if I'm still alive.

2 At a new place

a) Read through the posts and say:
- where Philip is and how long he is staying.
- what his plans are for tomorrow and how he feels about them.

Say which posts give you key information on each point.

b) Say what Philip thinks about the owner's daughter at the riding centre.
How does Emily react to his opinion?

3 A closer look at the text

a) Philip and Emily do not always use full sentences, e.g. *Still in Santa Fe?* instead of *Are you still in Santa Fe?*
Find other examples. Explain why people write like this in text messages.

b) In his second to last text Philip writes *Love your sense of humour, Emily*. Do you think he means this here? Explain why or why not.

Do you think there is humour in the posts? Give examples to support your opinion.

4 Tiffany's diary

FRIDAY APRIL 15

I had a big argument with Mom today. She wants me to take a guest on a horse ride tomorrow. But she knows I don't want to. He's a young guy who's with some folk from Santa Fe, but I don't think he's from round here. I don't dislike him, but he speaks kind of funny. He tried to introduce himself when I showed them their cottage, but I just said goodnight and left them to unpack. I probably seemed rude, I couldn't stop myself.

Mom just doesn't understand. "You have to think of the guests, Tiffany," she said. "They're here to have fun. They don't want to look after themselves." Yeah, Mom, right. But don't you care about me? I need to look after myself. And I'm not having fun! Not since Oreo's accident. I loved that horse so much. I may be difficult but I just don't feel like being with people now. I'm too sad to enjoy myself.

Today I rode out with Pearl. She's a fine horse, but she's just not Oreo. She doesn't understand me yet and she's still quite nervous. We went out on my favorite trail, the one I used to take with Oreo. It was so beautiful out there. But when we came to the stream, my eyes filled with tears. I just couldn't stop crying. It seems like only yesterday that we threw Oreo's ashes into the water there. But it's almost a month now and I still miss him so much. Nothing has changed.
Mom says I'm the only one who can do the tour tomorrow. All the other guides are busy. She thinks I'm being unfair. But I don't see myself like that. I always used to help with the guests. And I never complained – although I didn't always get paid. So, OK, I guess I'll have to take that boy on the trail. We meet tomorrow at 8. But I'm not looking forward to it. I don't want to have to talk to anyone for eight hours.

5 Tiffany and Philip

a) Read the text and make notes on:
   1 Tiffany's feelings about Philip, her mother, and helping at the riding centre.
   2 what you learn about Oreo.

b) Use your notes to compare your ideas about the points in a). Add notes where your partner's view is different from yours. At the end, discuss any differences.
   → *SF 22: Making and taking notes (p. 169)*

c) Imagine the first few minutes of Tiffany's meeting with Philip tomorrow. What might they say? Write a short dialogue.

6 Writing a diary

a) Explain in what way a diary is a different kind of text from a text message.

b) Say why you think Tiffany keeps a diary. What other reasons might people have for writing a diary?

Early finisher Imagine you are Tiffany's mother. Write a short diary entry about your argument with Tiffany.
Then find another early finisher and share your texts.

→ **Workbook** *13–14 (p. 34)*

1 THINKING ABOUT LANGUAGE Reflexive forms

a) Partner A: Work with box A.
Partner B: Work with box B-
The sentences are from the texts on pp. 70–71. Translate them into German.
Then read the statements a–d below. Look carefully at your English sentences and German translations and decide if the statements are true or false.

A
1 Make sure you don't hurt yourself.
2 You're just imagining it all.
3 Nothing has changed.
4 Don't worry – you'll be OK.
5 I couldn't stop myself.
6 They don't want to look after themselves.

B
1 Sounds cool to me.
2 He tried to introduce himself.
3 I need to look after myself.
4 I don't see myself like that.
5 I never complained.
6 We meet tomorrow at 8.

a English reflexive pronouns are words like myself, yourself, etc.
b You use reflexive pronouns in English when a verb has the same subject and object.
c Verbs that take a reflexive pronoun in German always take one in English.
d Verbs that take a reflexive pronoun in German don't always take one in English.

b) Compare your answers for statements a–d.
Support your answers with examples from your English sentences and German translations.

c) Partner A: Translate the sentences in box A into German.
Partner B: Translate the sentences in box B into German.
Then compare your sentences. Say what you notice about the reflexive pronouns.

A
1 Suddenly I saw myself in the mirror.
2 Have you introduced yourself yet?
3 You'll enjoy yourself there!

B
1 I made myself some coffee.
2 Did you buy yourself a new jacket?
3 You need to give yourself more time.

Which sentence could you rewrite using the preposition for: A1 or B1? Rewrite it.
Complete this rule:
In German, some reflexive pronouns have two forms, e.g. mich (direct object) and …
In English …

d) A young blogger spent a few days in Taos with his mother. Read his blog about the first day.
Add reflexive pronouns in the gaps wherever possible or necessary.

When we got to our hotel, Justin, the owner, introduced …[1] and showed us our rooms. After we had unpacked, we went downtown. It's hard to imagine …[2] that such a small city can have so many museums. The Kit Carson Museum sounded …[3] really cool, so we agreed …[4] to go there. It's the home of the pioneer who made a name for …[5] in the Southwest in the 19th century. After the museum, we walked to the plaza, where we got …[6] some food. There are lots of stores nearby, so Mom *had* to go shopping. I just walked around. There's a lot to see, and I really enjoyed …[7]. Mom and I met …[8] an hour later. She had bought …[9] some jewelry of course. Some things never change …[10]! Before long, I felt …[11] hungry again. We went to a Mexican restaurant. The food was tasty and I can only complain …[12] about one thing: there wasn't enough ;-)

→ *GF 7: The -self/-selves-pronouns (pp. 180–181)*

2 Pronunciation (Consonants)

a) Look at the word pairs below. Then listen. For each pair, write down the word you hear.
Compare your answers.

1 white – wide
2 feed – feet
3 God – got
4 side – sight
5 bang – bank
6 docks – dogs
7 cheap – jeep
8 pick – pig
9 card – cart
10 nod – not
11 choose – juice
12 thing – think

b) Listen and write down the missing word in your exercise book.

1 the red ...
2 with a red ...
3 a lovely ... beach
4 lots of lovely ... beaches
5 all the different ... in Dublin
6 on different ... in the match
7 put it in the ... of the car
8 put your ... in the car
9 on your own two ...
10 time to ... her
11 and then it went ...
12 we went to the ...

More help ➜ p. 144

➜ Workbook 15 (p. 34)

3 Can you do it differently, please? (Comparison of adverbs)

Language help

Use *more* or *most* to make the comparative and superlative forms of adverbs that end in *-ly*.
Be careful with irregular adverbs like *well, badly, fast* or *hard*.

➜ *GF 6: Adverbs (pp. 178–179)*

Adverb	Comparative	Superlative
slowly	more slowly	most slowly
easily	more easily	most easily
well	better	best

Read the situations. What are the people doing the wrong way? Ask them to do it differently.
Use a verb from box 1 and the comparative adverb form of an adjective from box 2.

1 behave · drive · listen · play · ride · speak · write

2 careful · clear · good · loud · quick · quiet · slow

1 Your guide in Taos has a quiet voice. You can't hear him.
Can you speak more loudly, please?
2 You and your dad are on your bikes. He's much too slow.
3 You see that your mum is driving too fast.
4 Your partner's handwriting is very difficult to read.
5 Your neighbour is playing the piano too loudly.
6 Your friend didn't hear what you just told him.
7 Your little sister is throwing litter on the ground.

4 How to travel around Santa Fe (Comparison of adverbs)

Read this information about how you can travel when you're in Santa Fe.
Finish the text with the comparative adverb form of the adjectives in brackets.

There's a lot to see in Santa Fe, but how should you travel around – by bike or by car? Of course, you get to some places ... [1] (quick) by car, but you get there ... [2] (cheap) by bike. And if you're on holiday, it's nice to go a bit ... [3] (slow) and to look ... [4] (close) at everything you pass. There are also places you can visit ... [5] (easy) on a bike, like downtown Santa Fe and the historic quarters.

On Santa Fe's bigger roads, cars move ... [6] (fast) than in quieter streets, so you will need to ride ... [7] (careful) there. If possible, use a bike route, where you can travel ... [8] (safe) than on the roads. Just remember, bikes are a fun way to move around and you will see the sights ... [9] (good) than from a car. For more information, buy a good guide. It will explain everything much ... [10] (clear).

5 THINKING ABOUT LANGUAGE The future

a) In English, we use many different tenses and verb forms when we talk about something in the future. Look at these examples from p. 70. Which can you match to one of the descriptions on the right? Which do not match?

1 How long are you staying there?
2 We leave at 8 am.
3 I'll send you some photos if I'm still alive.
4 I hope you have a great time tomorrow.
5 Don't worry. You'll be OK. Probably.

a) In conditional sentences, the *will*-future is often used in the main clause when the *if*-clause is in the simple present.
b) We make predictions with the *will*-future.
c) We use the present progressive to talk about dates/appointments in the future, things we may have in our diary or calendar.
d) The simple present has a future meaning in timetables and programmes for events.

b) How would you say the sentences in a) in German? What tenses do you use there?

c) Do you know any other ways of talking about the future in English? Write descriptions like the ones above. Rewrite one of the sentences in a) with this tense/verb form.

➜ *GF 3: The future (p. 175)*

6 A holiday flat

Ein Amerikaner versteht diese Ferienwohnungsanzeige nicht. Findet die Informationen, die er braucht, und gebt sie an ihn weiter. Nehmt abwechselnd die Rolle des Amerikaners ein.

a) Partner A spielt den Amerikaner:
1 We need a flat for two adults and one child.
2 Will I be able to use the internet?
3 I'd like to experience everyday life in Günzburg.
4 And we'd like to see some nice countryside.

b) Partner B spielt den Amerikaner:
1 We'd also like to go on some bike tours.
2 Are there any special attractions for children?
3 Are there any special events in the summer?
4 Are there other interesting towns we could visit?

Ihre Ferienwohnung in Günzburg – eine Perle im bayerischen Schwabenland

Altstadt, Unteres Tor

Die Wohnungen
Zwei helle, freundliche Ferienwohnungen nah am historischen Marktplatz
- Wohnung 1 „Waldrebe": *1 – 4 Personen, EUR 95 pro Nacht*
- Wohnung 2 „Sonnenblume": *1 – 6 Personen, EUR 145 pro Nacht*

Ausstattungsmerkmale
- Kinderbetten auf Wunsch möglich
- Bettwäsche / Handtücher inklusive
- Haustiere willkommen
- Nichtraucher
- Kabel-TV und W-LAN
- Sonnige Terrasse
- Parkplätze vorhanden
- Fahrräder zu mieten (EUR 5 pro Rad/Tag)

Stadt und Umgebung
- Besuchen Sie die Altstadt mit ihren Wochen- und Bauernmärkten, ihrem 10-tägigen Volksfest (um den 15. August) und traditionellem Weihnachtsmarkt.
- Genießen Sie die Natur am Donauradweg oder im nahgelegenen Allgäu.
- Fahren Sie mit den Kindern zum Legoland (nur 9 Autominuten entfernt).
- Gönnen Sie sich eine Tagestour nach München, Augsburg oder Ulm (schnell über die Autobahn oder ohne Umsteigen mit der Bahn zu erreichen).

➜ **Workbook** *16 – 18 (pp. 35 – 36)*

1 Learn how

a) Make a table like this. On a copy of the story, underline all the time markers. Then put them in the correct column of your table.

when sth. happened	what happened first, second, etc.	how much time passed
the Easter holidays	First	for about five minutes
…	…	…

b) Add these time phrases to your table too.

after that · next · last Monday · for two weeks · at the beginning · a few hours ago · for a while · two weeks later · later

c) Now look at these two sentences:
Philip went horse riding.
His aunt and uncle walked around Taos.

Link the sentences in as many ways as you can with phrases from the box. Change the tense of the verbs if necessary.

before · after · as soon as · while · shortly after that · earlier · First … then

- While Philip went horse riding, his aunt and uncle walked around Taos.
- After Philip had been horse riding …

TIP

1 Use time markers to help your reader to see:
- when something happened.
- what happened first, second, etc.
- how much time passed.

2 Use time markers to link sentences.

The view from my window

It was the Easter holidays and I had nothing to do because all of my friends had gone away. Early one morning, I was watching TV, but the show was silly and I soon got bored. So I sat by the window to watch the people go by.

Our flat is on the fifth floor of a corner building at a busy junction, so there are always lots of cars and pedestrians.

First I watched a woman I had often seen before. She was walking three little dogs. They had very short legs which moved very quickly and it looked like they were taking her for a walk instead.

Then I watched a little boy and his father. The boy didn't want to walk any more and sat down on the pavement. At first his father waited, but then he became angry and started shouting. This continued for about five minutes. Finally the father picked up the boy and carried him like a baby. The boy kicked and screamed.

Suddenly a white sports car raced down the street. It was going really fast! The traffic light turned red as the car reached the junction and BAM! It drove into a green van. The white car spun around, while the green van hit a parked car. Glass flew everywhere.

Seconds later, I saw a man in a black hat jump out of the white car and run away. I called the police immediately. Five minutes later I heard the siren and ran down to the street. But it was too late – the man in the black hat had disappeared. I had to wait for an hour while they cleared the road. Finally I had the chance to tell a policeman what I had seen.

2 Now write …

Write a short story in your exercise book (about 200 words or more). Use time markers to show the order of events. Remember to start a new paragraph for every new idea.

➜ *SF 5: Paragraphs and topic sentences (p. 157)*
➜ **Workbook** *19 (p. 37) Wordbank 8 (p. 77)*

3 … and revise

a) Give feedback. Read your partner's text and make notes where it is clear/unclear to you when things happened.

Take turns to make comments and corrections.

b) MY Book Think about your partner's feedback and what you've learned on this page. Decide what to change and write a final draft of your story.

➜ *SF 6: Using time markers (p. 158); SF 7: Giving feedback on a text (pp. 158, 291–292); SF 8: Revising your text (p. 159)*

The horse ride

Part 1

As he left the cottage, Philip saw that the owner's daughter was standing just outside.

"Are you ready for the tour?" she asked.

"Yes," said Philip. "Actually, I'm on my way to meet the guide. He's waiting at the main building."

"She's waiting here," said the girl. "I'm Tiffany O'Shea and I'm the guide on your tour today."

"Er … hi!" said Philip and introduced himself.

"Your accent is kind of weird," said Tiffany. "Are you from England?"

"From Wales, actually."

"Isn't that in England?"

"Not *in* England," Philip explained. "Next to it. Wales is a different country."

"I thought you were all one country."

"We are. It's just that … er …"

"Just what?"

"It's not important," Philip sighed. "People over here don't seem to know so much about Britain."

❖

"Have you ridden much before?" asked Tiffany.

"I'm almost a beginner," said Philip.

"So why did you choose the eight-hour trail?"

"It wasn't my idea. My uncle chose the tour."

"Don't hold the reins like that!" shouted Tiffany suddenly. "Watch me and try to do the same."

They rode off together. As they were leaving the village, they came towards a ditch.

"Faster!" cried Tiffany. "We have to jump."

"Phew!" said Philip as his horse landed on the other side. "That was exciting."

Tiffany said nothing. Philip wondered how he could make conversation.

"Er … did your family come here from Ireland?"

"Why do you ask?"

"O'Shea is an Irish name, isn't it?"

"You're right. My people emigrated from Ireland long ago. There was a famine. They were starving."

"We learned about that at school," said Philip. "There was a potato disease in Ireland in the 1840s. Poor people had nothing to eat. A million people died, and another million left the country."

Tiffany was silent again.

"Did your family come straight to New Mexico?" Philip asked.

"No," said Tiffany. "They went to New York first. They came here much later. New Mexico didn't join the United States until 1912."

"Really?" said Philip. "I didn't know that."

"It's not important," said Tiffany. "People from Britain don't seem to know so much about the US."

Part 2

"We don't have to go quite so slowly," said Philip. "I feel surer now that I've practised a bit."

"OK," said Tiffany. "But be careful! Yesterday it rained. These trails can be slippery if they're wet."

"But the ground is dry," Philip protested.

"You're the boss," said Tiffany and pressed against the side of her horse. "Good girl, Pearl," she said as her horse moved off quickly.

"Wait!" cried Philip and rode after her.

Tiffany stopped and Philip rode up to her.

"I didn't mean as fast as that!" he said. "What's up, Tiffany? You weren't very friendly yesterday, and today you're being just as rude."

For a moment, Tiffany just stared at Philip. Then she spoke: "There are some things you just don't understand." And with that, she turned and rode fast towards the forest at the edge of the field.

Part 3

Inside the forest, Tiffany followed a narrow trail with shrubs and young trees at each side. She was close to tears. "Why did I do that?" she thought. "Should I go back? What could I say to him? And what will Mom say to me?" Then suddenly, there was a sound from below. It was a sound that she knew, and it meant danger. But a moment or two passed before she realized exactly what it was.

"No!" she thought, and quickly tightened the reins to stop Pearl. But it was too late. Without any warning, Pearl jumped up and lifted her front legs high into the air.

"I mustn't fall!" thought Tiffany. "I mustn't fall!" Quietly, she spoke to her horse. "You'll be OK. Stay calm, Pearl." And Pearl stood still and was calm again. On the ground below, a large, yellow rattlesnake disappeared into the shrubs.

"I'll have to check your legs for snakebites, Pearl," said Tiffany and climbed down to the ground.

"That's deep," she thought as she saw the bite on

Pearl's right front leg. "I'll have to get help fast." She pulled out her phone and pressed. Nothing happened. Then all was clear. The battery was empty. She had forgotten to charge it.

Part 4

"I'll just go at my own speed," Philip thought, and followed the route he thought Tiffany had taken.
"I can't believe I'm doing this," he smiled to himself after a short time. "Maybe this will even be fun."
Then, as he went round a corner, a few hundred metres in front of him he saw a horse on the ground. Suddenly, the rider appeared. It was Tiffany.
"Help!" she called as she came closer. "I need your phone!" Excitedly, she told him what had happened.
"Do you know a vet's number?" Philip asked. Tiffany nodded as she took his mobile. Then a moment later she gave an angry shout: "No! There's no signal! Philip – what am I going to do?"
"Listen," said Philip. "Why don't I stay here with Pearl? You can take my horse and go to get help."
"Philip," said Tiffany. "Can we do it the other way? You get help and I'll stay here with Pearl."
"But why?" Philip asked. "You ride so much faster."
"I can't leave Pearl," said Tiffany. "I have to stay with her. Don't ask me to explain. It's hard for me."
"You're the boss," said Philip.
"It's best to take the route we came," said Tiffany.
"And you aren't worried I'll get lost?"
Tiffany gave a little smile. "No," she said. "I'm not."

Part 5

Tiffany sat down next to Pearl and whispered softly in her ear. "Maybe this had to happen," she said. "Not to you, but to me. Because now I know how much you mean to me."
A tear ran down Tiffany's face. "You'll be OK, Pearl – Philip will be back soon. And *I'll* have to say sorry. It shouldn't be so hard, because I *am* sorry. But it's easier to *be* sorry than to *say* sorry. Will I have to explain why I behaved like that – even tell him about Oreo's death? What will he think?"
And then, as the thoughts passed through her head, she heard the sound of a motor. The vet's truck was arriving. Help would soon be there.
"Here!" cried Philip as he led the vet towards Pearl.
"Everything OK, Tiffany?" he asked.
"Yes, Philip," she smiled. "Everything OK."

1 The main events

a) Make notes on the main events in the story.
Use your notes to say what happened.
More help → *p. 144*

b) Describe the picture above.
Then discuss which other scene from the story would make a good illustration.

2 The characters

Work in groups of three. Each student reads *one* of these sections of the story again:
Part 1 · Parts 2–3 · Parts 4–5

Choose a few lines from your section that express well how the characters feel. Explain your choice. Describe how their feelings change.

3 Continue the story

You choose Choose a) or b). Write:

a) a text (100–150 words) about Philip from the time he leaves Tiffany to the time he gets back with the vet.

b) a dialogue between Tiffany and Philip back at the riding centre.

→ **Workbook** *20 (p. 37)*

Workbook Checkpoint 3 (pp.38–41)

A brochure for students from the Southwest

Students from the Southwest of the United States want to visit your area.
Work in a team of four students.
Make a brochure with tips for the visit.

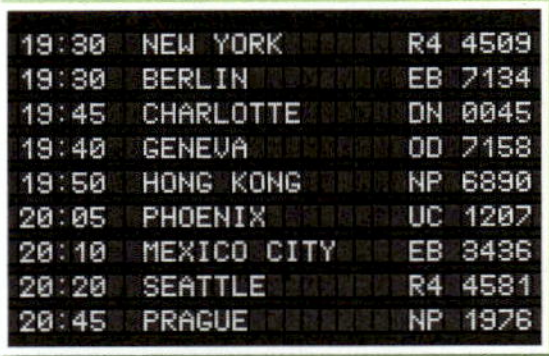

STEP 1 Make a checklist with the main points. Think of what you could say about each point. You can get ideas from the list on the right:

Attractions/Activities in your area
- The countryside around … is very beautiful.
- Our local chocolate museum is a big attraction.
- The games café near the market place is fun.

What your guests can see/do/…
- Why not pack some strong boots? Then you'll be able to …
- You can relax peacefully at …

Tips on travel
- Most /Some flights from the US land in …
- After you land at … you can …
- You'll only need a visa if …

Where to stay
- There's a very good hostel in …
- But you'll like staying in the old town best.

STEP 2 Choose your team roles: writer, language watchdog, picture and layout editor, and coordinator.
- writer: get information and write the texts
- language watchdog: check the language
- picture and layout editor: find good pictures that go with the brochures
- coordinator: suggest the best order for the jobs and set deadlines for them

➜ *SF 12: Teamwork (p. 163)*

STEP 3 Before the meeting, check your work.

STEP 4 At the team meeting, the coordinator leads the discussion.
The team agrees on the final steps, who does what, and when the brochure must be ready.
When your brochure is finished, swap with another group and read theirs.

EXTRA Give feedback to the other group about their brochure.

➜ *Giving feedback: pp. 291–292*
➜ **Workbook** *Wordbank 1, 3, 4, 8 (pp. 70, 72, 73, 77)*

A

1 Countries and nations

a) Complete the sentences about the USA, UK and Germany with the correct words.

1 The United States became ... from Great Britain in 1776. The first ... was George Washington. At that time, there were only 13 ... , all of them along the east ... .

2 To enter the United Kingdom from Germany, you must show a ... or an ... . However, to enter the United States an ... is not enough. You will also need a ... if you want to stay for more than 90 days.

3 When we crossed the ... from Arizona into Utah, we saw a big ... with the words "Welcome to Utah".

b) Write English paraphrases of these words.

1 emigrate

This is what you do when you move ...

2 dollar 3 government 4 president 5 governor 6 population

c) What do these letters stand for? Write out their full names.

1 UK 2 EU 3 GB 4 USA 5 UN

2 Word families

Fill in as many of the gaps in these word families as you can. Write in your exercise book.

Nouns	Verbs	Adjectives
death	...	...
...	...	practical
argument	...	X
sleep	...	...
...	arrive	X
...	edit	X
...	paint	...
...	X	beautiful
...	begin	X

3 Collocations

Make collocations with the words in the boxes and use the correct ones to complete the sentences below. You can use some words more than once. Be careful with verb tenses.

be · care · check · look · spin · stare · turn · welcome

about · around · at · left · out · red · to

1 She ... the German boy for some time before she spoke.
2 When she told him he looked pretty, he ... .
3 "I don't ... how I look," he answered.
4 "... Santa Fe! Have you been here before?"
5 He heard a noise behind him so he ... quickly.
6 Another tourist ... his phone and said, "You should ... this new Santa Fe app. It's great!
7 The hostel was almost empty. Most people had already ...
8 Everyone had gone home. Only two boys ...

4 What's the opposite?

a) Find words that mean the opposite of these:

1 polite 2 wet 3 day 4 dead 5 (to) like 6 (to) start 7 before 8 wide

b) Choose six words from the word pairs in a) and use them to write a 100-150-word story.

5 Nanabush and the first rainbow: A Native American legend (Adverbs of manner)

Complete the text about the first rainbow with the correct adjectives or their adverb forms.

amazing · angry · beautiful · different · excited · good · happy · loud · noisy · quiet· quick · sudden

One day, Nanabush stood at the waterfall near his house. As he looked at the white flowers in the fields, an idea came to him …[1]. "Why are flowers always white?" he whispered …[2] . "They'd look so …[3] if they weren't all the same color." So he hurried home and came back with his paints. Then he began to paint the flowers …[4] colors: red for roses, orange for lilies, purple for lavender, and so on. "That's much better!" he said, and smiled …[5].
Nearby, some bluebirds were playing. "Here's a new game," said one of them. "Watch this." Then he flew …[6] towards Nanabush, stuck his wing into the orange paint, and flew back again. "Didn't I do that …[7]?" he cried …[8]. One by one, the other birds did the same. Each came back with a different colour on their wings. "Stop!" shouted Nanabush …[9]. "This paint is for the flowers, not for you bluebirds!"
"Oops!" said a bluebird. "Nanabush is getting …[10]. Let's go." With that, he flew to the top of the waterfall. There, as he passed through the mist above the …[11] waters, an orange stripe appeared in the sky. As the other birds followed, more stripes appeared. Nanabush looked up. The sun shone on the watery mist and a semi-circle of colored lines had formed in the sky. "…[12] !" he thought. "I have painted the flowers, but the bluebirds have painted the sky."

6 The right order (Adverbs: comparison)

Use the verbs and adverbs and write comparisons like this:
Dave sings more beautifully than Lucy, but a bird sings most beautifully.

7 Philip's horse ride with Tiffany (Past perfect)

Complete the text about Philip's horse ride with the simple past or past perfect form of the verbs.

When Philip …[1] (arrive) in Taos, he …[2] (not ride) a horse for several years, so he …[3] (feel) a bit nervous when he …[4] (get up) on the morning of the ride. He …[5] (be) surprised when he saw Tiffany outside the cottage because he …[6] (not imagine) that she would be his guide on the trail. At the start of the ride, Tiffany …[7] (not be) very happy either. She …[8] (be) rude to Philip the evening before and even worse: she …[9] (have) a big argument with her mother. The tour …[10] (go) badly at first. Tiffany …[11] (get) angry with Philip and …[12] (leave) him on his own. Then, after she …[13] (ride) a few miles through the forest, a rattlesnake …[14] (bite) her horse. Tiffany …[15] (need) Philip's help now. She …[16] (be) sorry that she …[17] (not be) more friendly. Luckily, everything …[18] (end) happily, and before long the two …[19] (become) friends.

8 MIXED BAG Philip talks about his trip to the Southwest

Complete Philip's sentences with the right words. Be careful with the verb tenses.

I ...[1] in Santa Fe on Friday evening. The next day I ...[2] for Albuquerque with my ...[3] and uncle. The ...[4] there only took about an hour. Albuquerque is the ...[5] city in New Mexico, but it isn't actually the ...[6]. That's ...[7], which is ... ...[8] I expected – the Spanish built the first houses there in the early 17th ...[9].
Uncle Dave grew ...[10] in Albuquerque, ...[11] he knew it very ...[12] and showed us ... ...[13] places. I ...[14] liked the American International Rattlesnake ...[15], where I saw so ...[16] cool snakes. We ...[17] two nights altogether in Albuquerque and then ...[18] along Route 40 and crossed the ...[19] into Arizona. We headed ...[20] the Coconino National Forest, which my uncle says is one of the ... ...[21] in the US. From there we travelled to Monument ...[22] in Utah. We did a tour with a ...[23] American ...[24] who told us all about the traditions of the ...[25] tribe. Back in Santa Fe, I was free to explore on my ...[26] because my aunt and uncle ...[27] work.
I bought a cool ...[28] for my dad – a white cow's ...[29].
At the weekend, we drove to a riding centre in ...[30], where I went on a horse ...[31] with the ...[32] daughter, Tiffany. ...[33] Tiffany ...[34] through a forest, a rattlesnake bit her horse and I ...[35] to go ...[36] to Taos to find the ...[37]. Believe me, I rode ...[38] than I ...[39] ever ...[40] before. Luckily, I got there on time and the story ended ...[41].

B

9 The Shoshone tribe and Death Valley

a) Listen to the first part of a talk about the Shoshone tribe. Then answer these questions.

1 How long have the Shoshone lived in Death Valley?
2 How did the Shoshone survive in winter?
3 Where did the Shoshone move to in summer, and why?
4 What does the Shoshone name Tumpisa mean?
5 Why did pioneers go to the Southwest?
6 Explain how Death Valley got its name?
7 Why did the Shoshone way of life change after 1849?
8 What is the situation of the Shoshone today?

Tumpisa or Death Valley.

b) Listen again. Complete the sentences in your exercise book.

1 There wasn't much water, ...
2 In the very hot summer months ...
3 Life wasn't easy in ...
4 Without water ...

c) Listen to the rest of the talk. Write down the missing words in your exercise book.

The legend is about a ...[1] who wanted to ...[2] a big and beautiful ... [3]. At first, her people ...[4] the plan. They worked for many ...[5], and the building grew and ...[6]. But it was never ... ...[7] for the Queen. One day a woman complained. She said the palace was ...[8] enough for everyone ... ...[9]. Then she fell down and ...[10]. The Queen realized that she had ...[11] a ...[12]. But it was ... ...[13]. Her ...[14] were now against her and nature was ...[15] her too. It became very ...[16] and dry, and most of the ...[17] in the area died.

C

10 Your blog

You choose a) or b).

a) Write a blog post (about 200 words) on your last visit to another town, region or country.

b) Write the story of a legend you know from your area or country.

Celebrating in America

1 Federal holidays in the United States

There are ten federal holidays a year in the United States. Two of them, Christmas Day and New Year's Day, are public holidays in several countries around the world. But the other eight holidays remember people or events that have played a key role in the history of the United States.

The federal holiday that is best known outside of the US is probably Independence Day, also called the Fourth of July, the date on which the celebration takes place.

Three other holidays – Christmas, New Year's and Veterans' Day – also have fixed dates. If they fall at a weekend, there is a holiday on the Friday before or Monday after, so that nobody loses a free day. Thanksgiving, when families come together for a traditional meal of roast turkey, is always on the 4th Thursday in November. In over half of the 50 states, the Friday that week – 'Black Friday' – is also free so many people can enjoy a long, four-day weekend.

Since 1971, the other five holidays have been on the Monday closest to the actual date. Columbus Day, for example, which used to be on October 12th every year, is now on the second Monday of the month. Not everyone liked this change. Critics said that people would no longer think of the meaning of the day if it wasn't on the real date.

Supporters of the Monday holiday wanted to give people a longer weekend break so that they could spend more time with their families. And long weekends also mean that people have more time to go shopping. On federal holidays, most of the big stores and shopping malls are open for business. Only government offices, banks, post offices, schools and public libraries, etc. are closed.

FEDERAL HOLIDAYS

Holiday	Date
New Year's Day	*January 1st*
M. Luther King, Jr. Day	*January: 3rd Monday*
Presidents' Day	*February: 3rd Monday*
Memorial Day	*May: last Monday*
Independence Day	*July 4th*
Labor Day	*September: 1st Monday*
Columbus Day	*October: 2nd Monday*
Veterans' Day	*November 11th*
Thanksgiving Day	*November: 4th Thursday*
Christmas Day	*December 25th*

For big stores and online traders, federal holidays are important dates with big sales and lots of lower prices. The most famous is 'Black Friday' – the day after Thanksgiving – which marks the beginning of the Christmas shopping season. Shopping, however, is not the only activity on a federal holiday. Each day has its own special theme, and there may also be speeches, concerts, parades, picnics, barbecues or fireworks.

a) Look at the list of American federal holidays. What are the reasons for the celebrations? What are the origins of the public holidays in your country? How similar are the reasons for celebrating in the two different countries?

b) Compare federal holidays in the US and public holidays in your country. Which do you think is better: celebrating a holiday on the exact date or having a long weekend? Explain your opinion.

2 Two federal holidays

Columbus Day

Columbus Day marks the arrival of Christopher Columbus, the 15th century Italian explorer, in the Americas. The date was October 12th, 1492, and the first known celebration was in 1792, three hundred years later. In the 19th and 20th centuries, the day became very popular, especially among Italian immigrants, who saw him as a figure they could identify with. As Catholics in a country with a strong Protestant tradition, they felt they needed a symbol like Columbus.

A statue of Columbus with a model of his ship, the Santa Maria, at the parade in New York's Fifth Avenue.

Columbus Day became a federal holiday in 1937. Today it celebrates Italian-American culture, with huge parades and other events. Many people wear traditional Italian costumes or carry Italian flags. And, of course, there is Italian food and music too. For many people Columbus stands for positive ideas. He was a great explorer, someone who never gave up when things got difficult. Other people are more critical. They see Columbus as a cruel adventurer who did not respect the rights of the Native American population. In four US states – Alaska, Hawaii, Oregon and South Dakota – the holiday is now an official celebration of the native population, not of Columbus.

Presidents' Day

The official name of this holiday is *George Washington's Birthday*. Washington, who was born on February 22nd, 1732, played a key role in the battle for American independence from Britain and was the first president of the US (1789–1797). February 22nd became a federal holiday in 1885, although people had celebrated it long before. Today, *Presidents' Day* is the more common name for the holiday. One reason is the popular wish tc remember other great presidents, especially Abraham Lincoln, who was president during the American Civil War. Lincoln was born on February 12th, 1809, so both birthdays are close.

Soldiers in historical costumes at a Presidents' Day ceremony at Mount Vernon, George Washinton's home.

Celebrations on *Presidents' Day* have a strong focus on history. There are ceremonies and parades at federal monuments, and people often dress up in historical costumes. Sometimes they act in plays about important events during the life of the presidents.

a) Compare Columbus Day with Presidents' Day. In what ways are they similar or different?

Decide which of the two holidays you would prefer to take part in and explain why.

b) Which public holiday in your country is most similar to Columbus Day or Presidents' Day? Explain why.

➜ **Workbook** *7 (p. III, Wordbank 6 (p. 75))*

4 Unit

Inside New York

1 New Yorkers

a) Describe the photo. Say
- where the people are.
- what they're doing.
- what they might be thinking about.

b) Now listen to the people's thoughts. Match each voice to a person in the photo. Compare your results.

c) Listen again. Take notes on what the people are thinking about, how they feel, and why. Compare your ideas.

The man on the left is thinking about …

I don't think he feels very happy because …

2 You and New York

a) The people in the subway also had thoughts about New York City. Match one item from this list to each person.

- Empire State Building
- taxis
- five boroughs
- Central Park
- Statue of Liberty
- Upper East Side
- New York Yankees
- Times Square
- JFK
- Chinatown
- Harlem
- Coney Island

b) Use the map on the back inside cover of your book to show your partners where the places are. Say what you know about these places or things. Take turns.

3 An open letter to NYC

a) Read these lines from the song. Then find Manhattan and the other four boroughs on the map on the front inside cover.

An Open Letter To NYC (Beastie Boys)

Brooklyn, Bronx, Queens and Staten
From the Battery to the top of Manhattan
Asian, Middle Eastern and Latin
Black, white, New York you make it happen

Brownstones, water towers, trees, skyscrapers
Writers, prize fighters, and Wall Street traders
We come together on the subway cars
Diversity unified, whoever you are

b) Watch the video. Say what impression it gives you of New York.

c) In class, say what connections you see between the song and the New Yorkers on the subway.

Your task

Your task for this unit: Imagine you're an exchange student in a New York high school. You'll present yourself to your American class.

→ Workbook *1 (p. 42)*

1 New York sights

Everybody knows something about New York from films, TV, books or holidays.
Look at these New York places. Say which ones you recognize and what you could do there.

A

B

C

Find each place on the New York map on the back inside cover. How far are they from each other?

2 People and places

a) You will see a film about four people. Each person is in a different neighbourhood of New York. Watch the film without sound. Take notes about the different areas you see.
Use your notes to describe what you saw.

In the first part, there were narrow streets with old buildings.

Yes, and there were metal steps on the outside of the buildings.

b) Watch the film with sound. Take notes on what each person is thinking.
Then say how they feel about the city. Take turns.

3 Making the film: Music

Each part of the film has different music. Watch the whole film again. Then describe the music and say how well it matches the feelings of the four people.

D

E

4 Hanging out in Brooklyn

a) In the first part of the film about free-time activities, some friends from Brooklyn meet on a stoop.
Watch and say what they're wearing, doing, eating, and talking about.

b) Now watch the next three parts and take notes on the friends' activities.
Check with a partner.

In the first part they …

Yes, that's right. Then they …

c) Watch the whole film again. Each group concentrates on one part.
Write five questions for your part and give them to another group.

d) Answer the other group's questions. Then watch again and check your answers. Add more information if you can.

EXTRA Say what impression of New York the people and places have given you.

→ **Workbook** *2 (pp. 42–43)*

1 Rivers, towers and waterfalls

Look at the photo at the bottom. What do you think the people are saying? Then read the text.

❖

3:30 pm. The school bell rang.
"Finally!" Jasmine whispered to Tyler and the two teenagers smiled at each other. After a quick stop at their lockers, they left Stuyvesant High School and walked to their favorite place in Hudson River Park. Tyler went over to the railing. Out on the river, boats and yachts sailed slowly past. He held up his camera and took several shots. Then Jasmine came over with her phone and the two took some photos with the Jersey City skyline in the background.
"Hey, where's Alex?" Jasmine asked.
"He said he had to go home – he has a chess competition in a few weeks."
"Oh, yeah, chess," Jasmine said. "I played him once but he's way too good for me. Made me nervous."
"He's nervous about the competition himself – he gets a lot of pressure from his parents. But I think he's very excited too."
The late afternoon sun disappeared behind a cloud. Jasmine threw back her long black hair and took off her sunglasses. "Why don't we just chill for a while? I'll draw and you can take photos."
"Sounds nice, but …"
"I know, you have too much homework, right?"
"No, I want to go and take some photos of the 9/11 Memorial," said Tyler.
"You mean those huge pools? Are you interested in them?"
"Yes, it's for the school newspaper. They want to see some of my photos before I join their team."
"And how are you getting there?"
"I'm going to walk. It's only four blocks away!"
Jasmine grabbed her backpack. "Wait, I'm coming!"

❖

"What a sound!" said Jasmine, as they listened to water which roared below them.
"It's the largest man-made waterfall in the US," Tyler explained. "Each pool covers the area where one of the World Trade Center Towers used to be."
"The way the water just disappears into that dark hole is scary!" Jasmine walked along the edge of the memorial. Her fingers moved across the names in its metal surface. Someone had left a white rose next to one of them.

"I wonder if anyone has ever climbed down there." Tyler shouted to Jasmine.
"That's impossible! How could you get down? It must be 30 feet deep!"
"You could throw a rope down and then climb."
"You'd probably get arrested! This is a memorial for people who died in the attack."
"Yeah, but it's also really awesome."
Tyler leaned over the edge and watched the water disappear into the dark hole. Suddenly they heard a voice say: "If you lean over one more inch, I'll have to arrest you." It was a policeman. Tyler and Jasmine looked at one another in fright. Tyler felt hot. He wanted to explain, but no words came out. The policeman's face broke into a big smile. "Just joking! You kids probably never even saw the towers yourselves – am I right?"
Jasmine replied that they hadn't even been born.
"Well, they used to stand right in this spot. The fastest elevators could carry you up to the Top of the World! And that view: it was just beautiful!"
"Yeah," said Tyler quietly. "I'm sure it was."
"But now lots of people are buried down there – some of my friends too. I see this place like a cemetery, myself."
Jasmine and Tyler didn't know what to say.
They looked at the dark hole again. "It's getting late, Jasmine. I'd better get home."
Jasmine said she would go home too.
They said goodbye and walked away.
"That was heavy ..." whispered Tyler. "Why did he tell us that?"
"I guess he thought we should know what we were looking at."

2 Three kids from NYC

a) How close to reality were your ideas about what Tyler, Jasmine and the policeman were saying?

b) Collect information about Jasmine, Alex and Tyler in a table. Include a column for their hobbies, their school, their personalities and their feelings.

Then look at ll. 51-77 and find sentences that give information about Jasmine and Tyler's feelings. What kind of words express the feelings? Write them in your table too.

Then exchange your ideas and talk about the three teenagers.

c) Look at the text again. How is it written?
- Who tells the story?
- How do you get to know what Jasmine and Tyler think?

Find lines in the text and make notes in your exercise book. Then exchange what you have found out with your partner.

3 The past and the present

a) Read the information about the Twin Towers. Close your books and tell each other what you can remember.

You choose b) or c).

b) Talk with a partner. Compare how Tyler and the policeman see the memorial. Do you think Tyler's view changes? Give reasons for your answer.

c) Write a diary or blog entry (about 200 words) for the policeman, Jasmine or Tyler about what happened at the memorial.

→ **Text File 4** *(p. 137)* → **Workbook** *3 (p. 43)*

THE TWIN TOWERS

In 1973, when they first rose above New York, the 110-story World Trade Center towers were the tallest buildings in the world. Most of them were offices, where 50,000 people worked. The South Tower also had indoor and outdoor observation decks. They were called 'Top of the World' and, at 400 and 420 meters, they gave visitors amazing views of New York and New Jersey. On September 11, 2001, in a terrorist attack, two planes crashed into the Twin Towers. Less than two hours later, the famous skyscrapers collapsed. 2,753 people died, including 366 fire and police officers and 147 people on the planes.

1 THINKING ABOUT LANGUAGE British and American words and spelling

a) Look back at the word elevator on p. 59 (l. 63). This an American English (AE) word. Do you know the British English (BE) word?
Now decide which word is BE and which is AE. Make two lists. Use a dictionary if you need help.

apartment : flat	garbage : rubbish	pavement : sidewalk
biscuit : cookie	holiday : vacation	shop : store
cell phone : mobile	line : queue	subway : underground
chips : French fries	pants : trousers	

flat ⟷ apartment
biscuit ⟷ …

b) Look at the lists from a) and write five sentences each.
Partner A: Use a BE word in each sentence.
Partner B: Use an AE word in each sentence.

Read your sentences to each other.
Partner A: Say the correct BE word for your partner's AE word.
Partner B: Say the correct AE word for your partner's BE word.

c) The same words are sometimes written differently in BE and AE. Complete the table.

BE	AE
centre	…
theatre	…
…	color
favourite	…
…	

Early finisher ➜ p. 150 More help ➜ p. 145

2 THINKING ABOUT LANGUAGE British and American pronunciation

a) Listen to a British and an American speaker. Say how they pronounce the blue words.

The city was so hot on Tuesday.
We went to see my aunt on her farm.

LISTENING TIP
American English pronunciation of some words is different from what you have learned. Knowing the differences will help you to understand more easily.

b) Decide if the people in the five dialogues speak British or American English. The way they say the words in the box will help you.

city · dirty · pity · pretty · stop · problem · project · topic · rock · pop · stupid · new · student · studio · glasses · can't · basket · danced · father · here · later · armchair · over there · corner

c) **EXTRA** Take six words from the box in b) and write a dialogue (about 60 words). Then read the dialogue first with BE pronunciation and a second time with AE pronunciation.

➜ Workbook 4–6 (pp. 44–45)

3 THINKING ABOUT LANGUAGE Reporting what someone said

a) Have a look at the speech bubbles.

I have to go home. — *We weren't even born then.* — *I'll go home too.*

b) Here's how the text on pages 88-89 reports what the teens said:
He said he had to go home. Jasmine replied that they hadn't even been born then. Jasmine said she would go home too.

TIP Notice what happens to the tenses of the verbs when you report what someone said or thought in English: *simple present* ▶ *simple past*, *simple past* ▶ *past perfect*, *will-future* ▶ *conditional*

c) What happens to the verbs when you report what someone said or thought in German? Give examples.

4 Do it yourself (Reflexive pronouns)

Complete the sentences about Jasmine and her friends with a reflexive pronoun for emphasis.

1 Alex's parents didn't help him. He learned how to play chess …
2 Jasmine and Tyler never saw the Twin Towers …
3 "I thought what the policeman said was a bit weird, …" Tyler told Jasmine.
4 "He probably doesn't see it like that …," Jasmine said.
5 Jasmine's not a chess player … . She draws.
6 "Wow, that looks great, Jaz!" Alex said. "Did you draw it …?"
7 "Our school is close to the memorial, so we can go there by …"

➜ GF 7 (p. 180) ➜ Workbook 7 (p. 45)

Language help

Copy and complete the table. Look for the missing reflexive pronouns on pages 88/89.

…	ourselves
yourself	…
…	…
herself	…
itself	…

You can use reflexive pronouns for emphasis - like the German *selbst/selber*.

5 Jasmine and Tyler are friends (Reciprocal pronouns)

Jasmine and Tyler are good friends. Show that this is true. Make sentences with *each other* and *one another*.

argue with · give · help · invite · meet · miss · sit next to · text · work with	homework · in class · many times a day · most weekends · on vacation · parties · presents · projects

1 Jasmine and Tyler never argue with …
2 They always give … on …
3 …

TIP

They looked at …

themselves.

each other.
one another.

➜ GF 7.4 (p. 182) ➜ Workbook 8 (p. 45)

6 The 9/11 Memorial

a) Du bist auf einem Schulaustausch in New York. In Manhattan hast du die Aufgabe, Schülerinnen und Schülern aus anderen europäischen Ländern Informationen über das 9/11 Memorial zu geben. Sie haben ein paar Fragen:

1 Wo genau ist das 9/11 Memorial? Ist es ein Museum?
2 Seit wann gibt es die Gedenkstätte?
3 Was können wir dort sehen und machen?
4 Wie lange wird der Besuch dauern?
5 Können wir dort etwas essen und trinken?

Scan die Broschüre und schreibe die Antworten auf die Fragen auf Englisch auf.

b) Spiele die Unterhaltung zwischen dir und den anderen Schülern/Schülerinnen mit deinem/deiner Partner/in auf Englisch nach. Wechselt euch ab.

➜ Workbook 9 (p. 46)

Das 9/11 Memorial

Zehn Jahre nach dem Angriff auf das Word Trade Center wurde das 9/11 Memorial eingeweiht. Es gedenkt der fast 3.000 Opfer der Anschläge.
Die beiden Pools des 9/11 Memorial sind genau an der Stelle, wo ursprünglich die Twin Tower standen. Auf großen bronzenen Flächen sind die Namen aller Opfer eingraviert. Diese Flächen erstrecken sich um die beiden Pools. Im dazugehörigen Museum erfährt man was vor, während und nach den Angriffen passierte und auch viel vom Leben der Menschen, die dort starben. Es gibt Geräte im Museum, an denen man Informationen über die Opfer erhält. Die letzte Säule eines der ursprünglichen Türme ist auch zu sehen.
Da dieser Ort eine Gedenkstätte ist, sollte man sich respektvoll verhalten und nur für den Notfall eine kleine Flasche mit einem Getränk und einen Snack mitnehmen. Es ist empfehlenswert, sich mindestens zwei Stunden Zeit für den Besuch zu lassen. Ein längerer Aufenthalt ist aber auch möglich.

1 A day at the park

2 Washington Square Park

Form a buzz group. In two minutes, say all you can about the atmosphere in the park and say what Tyler, Alex and Jasmine do there.

3 The end of the game

a) Say who you think wins the chess game. Give a reason for your opinion.

b) Listen to the end of the story and complete the sentences in your exercise book.

1 Tyler: I told you, ...
2 Alex: They don't let you ...
3 Tyler: Last time I ...

c) Say how Tyler and Alex feel about the game.

4 Have a go

a) Say when these people enjoy themselves.
Tyler · Jasmine · Birdman · Alex · Cornbread

Alex enjoys himself …

Jasmine enjoys herself when she's …

b) Make comments like Alex's.

1 The park itself is nice enough, but it's full of weirdos!
2 The town ... was OK, but ...
3 The hotel rooms ... were nice, but the beds were ...
4 The dentist ... was friendly, but ...
5 The princess ...

Looking at language

a) Which of these sentences from the text on p. 92 uses a reflexive pronoun for emphasis?

1 Yeah, we really can enjoy ourselves here.
2 The park itself is nice enough, but ...

Translate the sentences.

b) Find two more examples of each kind of reflexive pronoun on pp. 92–93.

Compare your examples with a partner's.

➜ *GF 7: The -self/-selves-pronouns (p. 180)*

1 Did you make it yourself? (The *-self/-selves*-pronouns)

Complete the sentence pairs with the correct reflexive pronoun.
Say which reflexive pronoun (a or b) means ***selber/selbst*** and which means ***sich+Verb***.

1 a) This cake is good. Did you make it ... ?
b) Dad's in the kitchen. He's making ... a cup of tea.
2 a) Careful! You'll cut ... with that knife!
b) Most people don't cut their hair ... .
3 a) The author ... will introduce her new book.
b) A girl came over to me and introduced ... .
4 a) Look at ... in the mirror. Your face is dirty!
b) Mum has seen a great bike in the bike shop. but I want to look at it ... before we buy it.
5 a) I didn't buy this hat ... . Dad gave it to me.
b) If we're hungry, we can buy ... a takeaway.
6 a) I didn't enjoy the film ..., but maybe you will.
b) Justin enjoyed ... a lot at the hotel in Miami.

2 REVISION Chess game (The *-self/-selves*-pronouns)

In English, not as many verbs need a reflexive pronoun as in German.
Read the dialogue between Jasmine and her mother and add reflexive pronouns where you need them.
Check the Grammar file if you are not sure.

Mother: Hi Jaz, have you been enjoying ...[1]?
Jasmine: Hi Mom. Yes, I was with Alex and Tyler. We met ...[2] in Washington Square Park.
Mother: Yes. I remember ...[3] now. You told me.
Jasmine: Just imagine ...[4] what Alex did!
Mother: Tell me.
Jasmine: He challenged one of those guys who play chess there.
Mother: Alex? Well, he's changed ...[5] then. Did he win?
Jasmine: No, he didn't ...[6]. In fact, he really enjoyed ...[7].
Mother: Then I'm sure he felt ...[8] good after that. I wonder ...[9] if he'll play there again.

➜ *GF 7: The -self/-selves-pronouns (p. 180)*

3 Meeting A, J and T

Imagine you were on holiday in New York and you met Alex, Jasmine and Tyler and spent some time with them.
Write an email (about 180 words) to another American friend about what you did. Use six verbs from the box and reflexive pronouns where you need them.

behave · buy · change · decide · enjoy · feel · get lost · help · hurt · introduce · meet · relax · wonder

➜ **Workbook** *10–12 (p. 47)*

1 Learn how

A text is easier to follow when it has an introduction, a body and a conclusion.

- In the **introduction**, you tell your reader what your text is about.
- In the **body**, you go into detail about your topic. You usually use several paragraphs.
- In the **conclusion**, you can give your opinion, or end with an interesting or a funny fact about the topic.

a) Read these five paragraphs about the game of chess. On a copy, label the paragraphs **introduction**, **body** and **conclusion**. Decide on the right order.

A Today, computers can play chess better than the strongest human players. In 1997, the chess computer Deep Blue became the first computer to beat a world champion, Garry Kasparov.

B It is important to checkmate the other player's king. Checkmate means the king can't move to escape capture. Often, nobody is able to win a game and it ends in a draw.

C Chess is one of the most popular games in the world, and millions of people play it every day. It probably started in India in the 7th century, but today's standard rules date only from the 19th century. Today, chess is also a popular online game.

D Does chess have a future in our modern world? The answer must be yes, as many children still learn the game at school. Chess often plays a role in literature, like Alice in Wonderland or Harry Potter, and films like Blade Runner and X-Men.

E Chess is a board game for two players. The board has 64 squares, 32 in each of two colours in an 8x8 grid. Each player begins with one king, one queen, two rooks, two knights, two bishops, and eight pawns. These pieces all move differently across the board. The queen is the most powerful while the pawn is the weakest.

b) Compare your labels. Did you label the text in the same way? Do you agree on the right order? Explain your reasons.

2 Now write ...

Write a text (about 200-250 words) for social media about one of your favourite games.

TIP
1 Organize your ideas and plan your paragraphs.
2 Write your text. Use a dictionary to look up words you need. Remember:
  - say what the text is about (first paragraph).
  - use topic sentences in the body of the text.
  - find a good way to end your text.
3 Read your text. Check your topic sentences. Check your paragraphs are in the right order.
4 Change the order of the paragraphs if you need to.

3 ... and revise

a) Give feedback. Read your partner's text and make notes to answer these questions:
- Is there a good introduction to the topic?
- Do the paragraphs in the body of the text give more information about the topic? Are they in a good order?
- Do you understand how the game works?
- Does the conclusion end the text in a funny or an interesting way?

Take turns. Make comments and suggestions.

b) Think about your partner's feedback. Decide what to change and write a second draft.

→ *SF 3: Good sentences (p. 156); SF 7: Giving feedback on a text (pp. 158, 291-292)*
→ **Workbook** *Wordbank 8 (p. 77)*

→ **Workbook** *13 (p. 48)*

High school in the USA

Big and small

Like almost everything about American high schools, the size and the number of students in a school varies greatly. Schools in big cities like New York, Boston and Philadelphia are usually smaller, with 400 to 1000 students. Schools in rural areas also have around this number of students. But in suburban parts of the country, there are schools with over 4000 students. This difference has much to do with available space. Urban school buildings are usually taller and part of the city block. In the suburbs and small towns, schools can occupy a large area or campus and have several buildings, separate sports facilities, sports fields and even their own stadium.

Sports in high school

The size of the campus influences the sports that schools can offer. In city schools, students usually do indoor sports like basketball, volleyball, wrestling, gymnastics, judo and swimming. In rural and suburban schools, students do indoor *and* outdoor sports like American football, soccer, baseball, and track and field. Larger schools in suburban areas also have marching bands and cheerleading teams, which are not common in urban schools.

Getting to school

In the US, the legal age to get your driver's license varies from state to state. In some states, you can start learning to drive at 14 and have a driver's license at 15! In other states, you can get a driver's license at 16 or 17. In suburban and rural areas, many high school students drive to school or take the school bus. Having a car often means more freedom and a certain status. Kids who go to city high schools usually walk, ride a bike or take public transport to school. In a city, having a driver's license isn't as important as it is in suburban and rural areas.

The school day

High school is for grades 9 through 12. A typical school day usually starts at 8 am and ends at about 3 pm, but many clubs and sports take place after school. Teachers take attendence twice a day. In the first period and after lunch, teachers read out all the names to make sure every student is at school. At most schools, students take courses in language, writing and literature, math, science, social studies and physical education (PE). They can also choose other subjects like Spanish, and learn practical skills like building, cooking and computer programing. Students are given regular assignments which they have to pass (grades A, B, C or D). If they fail a course (grade F), they must take the course again.

Special events

Important events in the school year can also vary, depending on whether you attend school in a small town or a big city. A very important event in the school year in rural and suburban areas is Homecoming, a week of parades and dress-up days (e.g. hippy day, pajama day), and a football game and Homecoming dance. The Homecoming Queen and King are chosen by students and crowned at the dance. They're usually very popular kids, and often great sport stars.

In small towns all over the USA, people give strong support to their local schools. The whole town comes out to support the school teams – especially at football and baseball games. Not many city schools celebrate Homecoming, and usually, only parents and classmates attend school sports events.

However, students in city schools are often involved in local events which celebrate the cultural diversity of their neighborhood.

High school students and their communities across the country have been in the headlines for their important role in political protests and demonstrations. High school students have demanded stricter gun laws, especially after tragic school shootings. High school students have also led protests to demand government action to slow climate change and to protect the rights of LGBTQ+ people.

As you can see, there is no single 'typical high school experience' in the US.

About 10% of students in the US attend private schools, and about 3.4% of students are homeschooled – that is, they don't attend school. Instead, their parents teach them, and they take classes online. Homeschooled students take tests to make sure they have learned the required material and to show that they are ready to enter the next grade. Homeschooling is illegal in Germany and in many other EU countries.

If you plan to study in the US for a year, there are many choices you can make that will affect your experience.

a) Find the sentences in the text that connect to the photos and read them carefully. Then write your own caption for each photo.

b) Compare your captions in your group. Agree about which are the best.
Share your results with the class.

c) Make a chart with these three headings: small town school / city school / our school

d) Each group member chooses one section of the text. Re-read your section and make notes about the differences between city and small town schools.

e) Add your notes to the chart in clear bullet points.

f) Together review your group's chart. Discuss and agree what to write under the heading 'our school'.

g) Imagine you are going to do a year at a school in the US.
Write a paragraph that explains what type of American high school you would like to attend.
Give reasons for your choice.

h) Watch a short film about a typical American high school and take notes.

i) Tell the class what you found most interesting or most surprising.

→ **Workbook** *14–15 (p. 49)*

1 An article in the school newspaper

Listen and say who takes a walk on the High Line and why they go there.
Name one place in the park that they visit. Then read the newspaper article.

Take a walk on the High Line

Tracks from the past
25 feet above the ground and one and a half miles long, the High Line is one of New York's most unusual parks. It started life as a railroad in 1934. At that time, the High Line's trains carried goods to and from the many factories in Manhattan. The railroad tracks cut through the middle of the blocks and right into the factory buildings. It was a quick way to move goods, but in the 1960s and 70s, they began to use trucks instead of trains. In 1980, a train full of frozen turkeys made the last journey down the High Line's tracks.

Imagining the future
New York city leaders wanted to tear down the High Line. But two New Yorkers, whose homes were nearby, had a different idea. They wanted to make the old railroad into a park, not tear it down. In 2003, they organized an 'Open Ideas Competition' in which 720 people from all over the world took part. There were some brilliant ideas. One saw the High Line as a 2,500-meter swimming pool, another as a country field with real cows, while a third imagined a long roller coaster.

Growing in the present
And so, between 2006 and 2014, the High Line became a park – with tall grasses, wild flowers and local shrubs. These plants bloom at different times of the year and their seeds spread on the wind. The park has a green lawn and a sun deck. There is also an open theater with a view of 10th Avenue through its great windows. As you walk down the High Line, you'll pass many works of art, and cafés with delicious food. If you're lucky, you might see a dance or music performance.
There are also activities for teens. Young people work with the park's gardeners and learn how to look after its many plants. Or they can join the Teen Arts Council and help to organize art and performance events on the High Line in summer.

2 A special park

a) Find the High Line on the map of NYC (back inside cover).

b) Scan the article for these numbers and words and explain what you find out about them.

2003 · seeds · 1980 · 2,500 · activities for teens · 1934 · city leaders

c) Compare your results with your partner and talk about the High Line. Is it possible to build such a park in your town or area?

EXTRA Imagine your hometown has a competition:

How to make our town a better place to live.

Come up with ideas and make a poster as your entry for the competition.

→ **Workbook** *Wordbank 1, 3, 4 (pp. 70, 72, 73)*
→ **Workbook** *16–17 (p. 50)*

1 STUDY SKILLS A good presentation

The High Line park made Manhattan a better place to live. Choose a place or an event or activity that makes your area a better place to live.
This page will help you to prepare and give a good presentation about your idea.

Preparing and giving your presentation

1 Do your research.
- Find out more about your place/event/…
- Make notes on the points you want to talk about.

2 Look up words you need in a *German-English dictionary*.
- Explain the meaning of important words in your presentation on a handout – or write them on a transparency or the board.
- Don't just use the first translation you find.
- Make sure you find the right translation for your context. For example, what English word do you need for Griff in this sentence: *Zweimal in der Woche schrauben wir Griffe raus und dann wieder rein, um neue Parcours zu bauen.*

➜ *SF 20: Using a German–English dictionary (p. 167)*

3 Write down your presentation and make notes on cards with numbers.

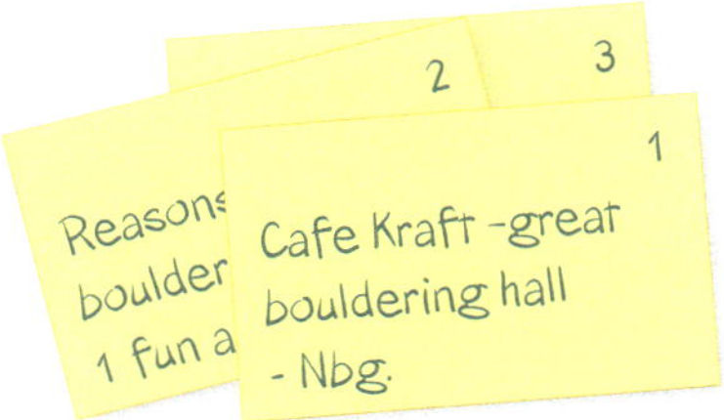

4 Practise your presentation in front of a mirror, your family, a friend, …

5 Give your presentation.
- before you begin, make sure you have everything ready (cards, handout, photos, drawings, …)
- wait till your classmates are quiet then tell them what your presentation is about
- use your cards, but look at your classmates when you speak, not at your notes
- speak slowly, loudly and clearly
- finish your talk and ask for questions

➜ **Workbook** *18 (p. 51)*

Griff
1. *(von Tür usw.)* handle **2.** *(Handgriff)* grip **3.** *(Klettern)* hold

KEY VOCABULARY
bouldering - Klettern
altitude - Höhe
rope - Seil
? - Griff
improvement - Verbesserung

Children's climbing wall at Café Kraft

Study skills

A good presentation
Für eine gute Präsentation muss ich Folgendes beachten:
- …
- …

➜ *SF 16: Giving a good presentation (p. 165)*

Underground New York *from the novel by Cecile Rossant*

Describe graffiti you know in your town and the places you find it. Say if you think it is art. Is it OK to spray graffiti anywhere? Discuss.

Sister and brother Zoe and Basti from Darmstadt are visiting their cousins Rick and Debby, who live in NYC. Rick is 16 and along with his friends Moog and Raul wants to show Zoe and Basti the Freedom Tunnel – a sight you won't find in any travel guide. But is the adventure worth the risk?

"Next stop: 125th Street – Martin Luther King Boulevard," said the voice over the speakers. It had been a long slow ride on the Uptown local train and they were all standing in front of the doors, ready to get off when the train pulled into the station.
"Moog, Raul! Hey, man!" yelled Rick to the two boys who walked towards them. Rick came up to a chubby[1] but tall boy and they gave each other a soul shake: they touched forearms[2] then slid[3] down to their hands, ending in a hook[4] action with three of their fingers. Rick's friend was wearing a big white T-shirt and long, baggy cargo shorts. He was smiling as if he was ready to tell a joke. The other boy was wearing a black woolen hat and was even taller and skinnier[5] than Basti. He walked up to Rick and performed the same greeting, adding a shoulder bump to the mix.
"These are my cousins, Basti and Zoe," said Rick.
"Hi, I'm Moog and this is Raul," he said and put out his hand. "You guys live in Germany, right?"
"Yes, we live in Darmstadt – it's close to Frankfurt. You know Frankfurt?" asked Basti.
"I know frankfurters – you know the kind you can eat – hot dogs," said Moog and laughed.
"Well, we are Frankfurters … but not that kind. We call hot dogs *Wiener Würstchen* – have you ever heard of them?" asked Basti.
"Yeah, yeah – we sometimes call hot dogs wieners, but I've never heard that other word, what was it … worstchain?"
"Yes, something like that," said Basti laughing.

"OK, we can continue with the language lesson later. I think we should head out now while the sun is still high," said Raul and started to walk towards the stairs. […]

"That's the tunnel entrance," said Moog pointing to a dark, square opening with grass and even small trees growing on top. They walked along a gravel[6] path next to the tracks until they reached the tunnel opening.
"I think we should wait here for a train to go by," said Rick.

[1] **chubby** ['tʃʌbi] pummelig, mollig [2] **forearm** ['fɔːrɑːm] Unterarm [3] (to) **slide, slid, slid** [slaɪd, slɪd] gleiten [4] **hook** [hʊk] Haken [5] **skinny** ['skɪni] mager, dünn, dürr [6] **gravel** ['grævl] Kies, Schotter

"Really, man?" said Raul, shaking his head.
"Yeah, come on, Rick. If one just passed by, we might have to wait here another half an hour," added Moog, kicking a few bits of gravel towards the metal tracks.
"Well, I don't think one just went by. We would have heard it. We weren't that far away. And besides[1], this is Basti and Zoe's first time down here and their second day in New York!
If anything happens, man, it will be my fault[2]. I want to make it as safe as possible," said Rick, kicking a few more pebbles[3] at the tracks.
"Rick – you, Zoe and I could also wait here. Moog and Raul should go ahead if they want," suggested Basti.
"I don't …" – whatever Rick was going to say, the thundering[4] sound of an approaching[5] train was cutting him off. The five kids jumped back into the green area just as the train raced by, kicking gravel and dust[6] into the air. It blew its horn[7] as if to say: I know you kids are there. As soon as the train passed, Moog started running into the tunnel screaming like a madman.
"Stop! Wait!" shouted Rick, but Moog didn't turn back.
"We should all check our watches. It's 11:05 now. That means the next train will be at 11:45. OK?"
"OK, OK … now, let's get going!" said Raul impatiently[8], shifting[9] his backpack on his back and taking a few wide strides[10] into the tunnel.
"Wow!" he screamed, "look at that light!" The tunnel was about 6 meters high and 18 meters wide. Although it was bright and sunny outside, the tunnel was very dark. About every 20 meters, sunlight from openings above cut into the tunnel's thick darkness. You could almost touch the light with your fingers.
"Oooh eeee!" That was Moog and the tunnel echoed back and made funny changes to his voice.
Raul tried out his voice with a loud "Hellooooo, hellooo …," then Zoe echoed him, "Haaaaallo, haaaallo …" […]

Crunch, crunch, crunch was the sound of the stones under their feet as they went deeper into the tunnel. Gravel and dirt[11] mixed with all kinds of garbage that covered the ground next to the tracks. There were empty cans[12] of spray paint, old clothes, shoes, blankets[13], and plastic dolls[14] with dirty faces. The air became cooler and had a strange smell of rusty[15] metal, machine oil, old garbage and earth. The colors that had filled their eyes that morning were gone: the green of the trees, the blue sky, and the bright sunlight. Now there were the grays, browns and blacks of this underworld. Color appeared only in the explosion of graffiti on the tunnel walls. […]
When Raul and Moog found an empty section of wall, they set down their bags, took out their paints and started shaking the cans. Rick, Basti and Zoe stopped to watch. Soon the two boys were doing a kind of hip hop dance in front of the wall while spraying on their names. Moog wasn't Moog's real name. He shared it with the rabbit robot character that Zoe had seen on some of Rick's stickers. As the rabbit's ears and face began to appear on the tunnel wall, Rick, Zoe and Basti walked on into the darkness of the tunnel. To the left and to the right colorful graffiti burst[16] out from the walls. "Man, this is great stuff!" said Rick. "There should also be real paintings down here. Here! Look at this!" Rick jumped in front of a long wall painting that was over three meters high and about 30 meters long. […]

"This is a painting by a guy who called himself 'Freedom'," explained Rick. "The tunnel is named after him. I've read about him on the Internet. His real name is Chris Pape and he even lived down here for a while. There are a lot more of his paintings further down in the tunnel," said Rick. He realized that he sounded like a museum guide who explains the artwork to a small group of tourists. So he quickly said, "Now I need to find a good place to do my own work." The best places directly under the light from above were all taken.

[1]**besides** [bɪ'saɪdz] außerdem [2]**fault** [fɔːlt] Schuld, Fehler [3]**pebble** ['pebl] Kieselstein [4]**thundering** ['θʌndərɪŋ] donnernd [5]**approaching** [ə'prəʊtʃɪŋ] sich nähernd [6]**dust** [dʌst] Staub [7](to) **blow the horn** [hɔːn] hupen [8]**impatiently** [ɪm'peɪʃntli] ungeduldig [9](to) **shift** [ʃɪft] verschieben [10]**stride** [straɪd] Schritt [11]**dirt** [dɜːt] Schmutz [12]**can** [kæn] Dose [13]**blanket** ['blæŋkɪt] Decke [14]**doll** [dɒl] Puppe [15]**rusty** ['rʌsti] rostig [16](to) **burst out, burst, burst** [bɜːst] hervorbrechen

"How about here?" suggested Basti and stopped. He pointed to an area where somebody had started a graffiti but not finished it. The wall was white in some places, but there was still a large area that was untouched.
"That's great, Basti," said Rick excitedly. He dropped his bag and took out all of his spray cans. "Can you start shaking some of these? You can also use them if you want. You could even just write 'Basti the Frankfurter, 2009'!"
"I'll just start with the shaking," said Basti.
"I'm going to walk on and take some more pictures," said Zoe.
"Do you want me to come with you?" asked Basti vigorously[1] shaking one of the cans.
"No, that's all right. I'll be back very soon, don't worry."
Zoe took a sip of water from her bottle and headed out. [...]

At each spot where light entered, the wall below was washed in light. It was just like an art gallery or a museum, where strong spot lights light up the paintings on the walls. And there were paintings here, too – real paintings. [...]

Copies of Leonardo da Vinci, or was it Michelangelo? One had the face of an angel. Another was just the body of a woman and a man like those old Greek statues with no arms and no heads. She reached 107th Street – she knew because the sign on the wall told her. Below the little sign was the strangest painting she had seen yet. It was a picture of a figure in a black sweat jacket with a spray paint can for a head.
"*Wow, komisch* ..." she heard herself say out loud. [...]

Zoe checked her watch. 11:35! She had been wandering alone for over 20 minutes so there must be another train soon. The others were blocks away. What did Rick say? Get as far away from the tracks as possible. Get out of sight of the train driver. Find a niche in the wall. Press yourself against the wall before the train comes. That means NOW! Zoe was scared – her hands were shaking. "I've got about eight minutes." She ran over the tracks to the wall. She tried to get around a pile of garbage, but by mistake[2] she stepped on a soft and very dirty teddy bear that lay in her path. She saw an opening or door on the other side. Zoe ran over. There was a door. There were even a few steps leading up to it. Painted on the wall next to the door were the words 'Home Sweet Home'. No train can come up here, she thought and hopped up the steps. She pushed open the door and stepped in. It was totally dark inside the room. My flashlight![3] she thought happily and reached[4] inside her backpack. Flick went the switch[5]. She heard a sound. Movement[6]. A little snort[7]. With the light illuminating the little room, Zoe met eye to eye with an old man. He was sitting at a large metal desk and looked at her with a surprised look.
"*Entschuldigung! Ich* ... I ... I'm sorry ..."
"German! You're German?!" said the man in a gruff[8] voice. "Who are you?"
"My name is Zoe. I was just ..."
"And you're German, right?"

[1]**vigorously** ['vɪgərəsli] kräftig [2]**by mistake** [mɪ'steɪk] aus Versehen [3]**flashlight** ['flæʃlaɪt] *(AE)* Taschenlampe [4](to) **reach** [riːtʃ] greifen [5]**switch** [swɪtʃ] Schalter [6]**movement** ['muːvmənt] Bewegung [7]**snort** [snɔːt] Schnauben, Prusten [8]**in a gruff voice** [grʌf] barsch, schroff

1 Did you get it?

a) Choose the correct answer for each question, a, b, or c and write it in your exercise book.

1 Zoe and Basti are visiting
a) Moog. b) Raul. c) Rick.

2 They get off the subway train at
a) Freedom Tunnel.
b) Uptown.
c) 125th Street.

3 Rick and his friends greet each other with a
a) handshake.
b) smile.
c) soul shake.

4 Moog and Basti share a joke about
a) Frankfurt. b) hot dogs. c) Vienna.

5 When they reach the tunnel entrance, they
a) all agree to wait for a train to pass first.
b) discusse whether to go in or wait.
c) go straight into the tunnel.

6 After a train passes, Moog
a) makes everybody check their watches.
b) runs straight into the tunnel screaming.
c) shouts, "Stop! Wait!"

7 Who shouts and hears the echo of their voices in the tunnel?
a) Basti, Raul and Rick.
b) Rick, Raul and Zoe.
c) Moog, Raul and Zoe.

b) Answer the questions in your exercise book.

1 What do Moog and Raul do when they reach an empty section of wall?
2 What does Zoe do when Rick begins to spray?
3 What does Zoe find when she is on her own in the tunnel?
4 What does the man in the tunnel want to know?

2 Thinking about the text

a) Talk about the title and the pictures. Find text parts that match the title and the pictures. Give the lines.

b) Who is telling the story? Find sentences in the text for your answer. Give the lines.

c) How does the text show when the kids are speaking? Give examples from the text.

d) How many parts does the text have? Give the lines for each part and write in one to two sentences what happens in each part.

e) How does the text describe the graffiti sprayers? Find sentences and give the lines. List adjectives and nouns that are used.

3 The Freedom Tunnel

Work in groups and talk about the following:

a) Describe the Freedom Tunnel. Name the risks of walking through it.

b) Explain why the Freedom Tunnel attracts graffiti artists.

c) Say if you would walk through this tunnel. Give reasons why or why not.

4 The man in the tunnel

Who is the man Zoe meets? Give him a name and create a short biography.

Explain why he is down there and why he is so interested in the fact that Zoe is German.

Continue to tell the story. Write about 200-250 words in your exercise book.

➜ **Workbook** *19 (p. 51)*

Workbook Checkpoint 4 (pp.52–55)

A presentation for your American class

You are on a school exchange in New York. Give a presentation to your American class where you introduce yourself and your neighbourhood, your likes and dislikes and give your first impressions of New York.

STEP 1 Make notes on the information you would like to present. You can use a mind map, lists, tables, …

Me and my interests
- your name/age/where you come from
- your family/home
- your likes/interests
- …

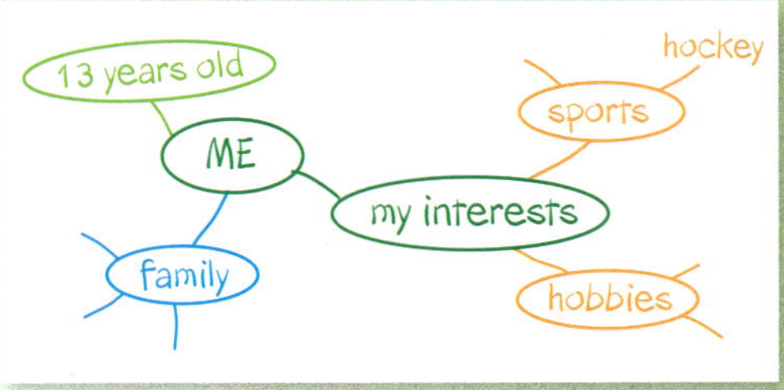

My neighbourhood
- location of hometown in Germany
- what your neighbourhood/area is like - e.g.: city/countryside/in the mountains/by the sea/on a river or lake
- local monuments/interesting sights
- busy/interesting/exciting/quiet/boring/…
- activities you can do
- what you like or dislike about your neighbourhood.
- …

New York
- first impressions
- neighbourhoods you have visited
- foods or restaurants you have tried
- sights you have seen
- …

STEP 2 Prepare your presentation.
- Write down ideas for a good introduction and ending to your presentation.
- Write key words/notes about what you want to say on index cards. Number the cards and use them during your presentation.
- Find images to go with your presentation, e.g. a map of Germany with your hometown, photos of your home area, sights in NYC, …

STEP 3 Practise your presentation.
➜ *SF 16: Giving a good presentation (p. 165)*

STEP 4 In groups of four, take turns, give your presentations and give each other feedback.
➜ *SF 17: Peer feedback (pp. 165, 291–292)*

A

1 Out and about in Manhattan

An exchange student in New York: complete the text with the correct words.

I'm an exchange student at a … …[1] in Manhattan, which is one of the five …[2] of New York City. It's an …[3] place to go to school. After classes, my friends and I often … …[4] in Hudson River Park – that's … …[5] our school. You can stand at the …[6] and see boats on the water. Once, we went to Washington Square Park. To get there, we took the …[7] and then walked a few …[8]. It was full of kids, …[9] and …[10] playing chess. I had taken my camera with me, and I got some great …[11]. But I didn't like the birds – I was a bit … …[12] them.
The 9/11 Memorial is also near my school. There … …[13] be two towers there, but they …[14] in 2001 in a …[15] attack. Two planes …[16] into them and many people died. I wasn't really … …[17] a visit to the memorial. It was my host family's …[18]. But I didn't want them to feel …[19], so I went with them. I'm happy that I did, because the …[20] waterfall was amazing, and the memorial was sad but interesting.

2 Cities, buildings and transport

a) Find the words that match these paraphrases.

1 a kind of plant, smaller than a tree
2 something that an artist makes
3 a place at the top of a tower where you can look at the view
4 Use this if you don't want to walk up/down all the steps inside a building.
5 a place – often near a church – full of people who have died
6 very famous

b) Write English paraphrases of these words.

1 statue *This looks like a person and can be made of stone, wood or metal.*
2 central 3 truck 4 lawn 5 performance 6 railroad

3 Comparing BE and AE words

Tyler's friend Jayden is spending a month in London with a host family.
Read the paragraph from his email and complete the sentences with the correct words.

… We all know that British people use some different words, but man, it's like a whole new language sometimes! I already knew that a movie is a …[1] here in the UK, but I was surprised about some of the other differences.
The Robertsons call their apartment a …[2], and their elevator is a …[3]. We use it to take out the 'rubbish' that's …[4] to you and me. Last night we had burgers and 'chips' …[5] and this afternoon we had 'biscuits'…[6] with our tea. The roads here have …[7], not sidewalks, and people travel on the 'underground' that's like the New York …[8].
In 'shops' …[9], people stand in a …[10], not a line, and look at their mobile phones …[11] while they're waiting. It's funny how weird the language is here! But I like London and I don't want this …[12] or should I say 'holiday'? to end…

4 Talking about people and places

a) Which words in A go with which words in B? Write them in your exercise book.

A awful · excited · famous · good · happy · interested · perfect · proud · scared · worried

B about (x3) · at (x2) · for (x2) · in (x1) · of (x2)

b) Use the words in a) to write a text (about 80 words) about people and places you know. *My mum is awful at English.*

5 Visiting New York (Reflexive pronouns for emphasis)

myself · yourself · himself · herself · itself · ourselves · yourselves · themselves

Some tourists and a New Yorker talk about New York.
Write each sentence with the correct reflexive pronoun for emphasis.

1 We've never been to the High Line, but our son has – and he loved it.
2 Manhattan's great for tourists, but I think Brooklyn's more interesting.
3 New York is always so busy: sometimes it feels like the city is alive.
4 You'll never guess who we saw near Central Park: the President!
5 They didn't realize how huge the Statue of Liberty was until they saw it.
6 Everyone's seen photos of Times Square, but it looks different when you go there.
7 She watched Birdman with the pigeons, but she didn't want to touch them.
8 You tourists probably don't think you're making much noise, but you're very loud!

6 Jasmine and Kayla (Reciprocal pronouns)

always buy · often call · sometimes show · usually see · sometimes make fun of

at Grandma's house at Christmas · but only as a joke · presents on their birthdays · to talk about their day · their drawings

Jasmine and Kayla are cousins who live in different cities. Write at least five sentences about them using the words and phrases in the boxes and each other/one another.

They always buy one another presents on their birthdays.

7 Kayla's trip to Ellis Island (Reflexive verbs)

Kayla was on Ellis Island. Which of the verbs below need a reflexive pronoun in English? Add reflexive pronouns where you need them.

Last week our class enjoyed ...[1] a trip to the immigration museum on Ellis Island. We met ...[2] at the ferry. When we arrived at the museum, our guide, David, introduced ...[3] and told us about the history of Ellis Island. Some of the kids complained ...[4] because they wanted to visit Liberty Island instead, but our teacher told them to behave ...[5]. Inside the museum, I wondered ...[6] if my great-grandmother's name was in the digital flag of faces. I felt ...[7] very excited when her photo came up on the screen! I told the class her story: Aileen O'Hara decided ...[8] to leave her home in Ireland because she couldn't find a job and her parents couldn't give her money. She only spoke Gaelic, but she quickly taught ...[9] English. Aileen and my great-grandfather, Jack, met ...[10] in Queens a year later: she got lost ...[11] one day and he helped her. They visited Ireland some years after they had married ...[12], but everything had changed ...[13] and Aileen decided ...[14] that New York was her real home. Everyone liked my story. Before we left, we bought ...[15] a snack at the museum café and talked about our families. I really enjoyed ...[16] on Ellis Island.

8 MIXED BAG The game café

Complete the text about Alex and his friends with the right words.

In the winter, Alex and his friends often ... ...[1] at the board game café in Manhattan, ...[2] blocks from Alex's home. The café has ... ...[3] 100 different games, and visitors ... ...[4] chess or watch other ...[5] games and learn ...[6] new ...[7]. Alex loves chess, ...[8], but he's ... ...[9] most other board games too – and there's ... ...[10] at the café ...[11] at a chess competition! Jasmine is also ... ...[12] board games, and when she and Alex play against ... ...[13], she often ...[14]. Alex ... ...[15] games online and is very ... ...[16] how much he knows, but he sometimes has to watch ...[17], because Jasmine also learns the rules very ...[18]. Tyler is ...[19] at ...[20] board games, but he likes the café because he ... ...[21] a drink, turn on his camera and take ... ...[22] of people as they play and enjoy ...[23].

B

9 The falcons of New York

a) Scan the article from a young people's magazine and name the famous NYC sight where a pair of falcons lives.

Everyone knows that the streets of New York City are full of cars and pedestrians, but if you think the skies above it are empty, you're wrong. We talked to sixteen-year-old Blake Simpson to find out about the city's birds, how and why falcons came to live there, and how New Yorkers look after them.

"I've been interested in birds since I was three years old. New York is an awesome place for this, because a lot of birds come through the city when they fly south for the winter. You can see all kinds of unusual birds from the tall buildings. But nothing beats seeing a falcon.

Falcons nearly disappeared in the east of the USA in the 1960s – and it was a man-made problem. Farmers were using something called DDT on their plants to kill insects, and the falcons had terrible problems with it. But in the 1970s, a team of scientists brought some falcons to the countryside near New York. They fed the young birds and helped them learn to fly. In 1974, they started to let the birds fly away to live in the countryside. But they were surprised when the falcons didn't all stay there: in 1983, some of the birds flew to New York City. There are more than 30 in the five boroughs now. Two even live in a box on Brooklyn Bridge!

Why did these falcons come here? Well, New York City is a good home for these birds. They like to sit up high and look down to find food – pigeons and other birds – and they can do that here, with all the tall buildings. And the lights on buildings like the Empire State Building help the falcons to see even better.

There are falcons in other cities around the world, too, but people there don't always look after them like they do in New York. Here, people have started groups to help falcons. And we don't try to feed or catch them. We understand that they are wild animals, not pets.

I've been in a group for a year, now. If someone finds a falcon that has hurt itself, they can call us. We know what to do. I once found one in the street myself. I put it in a box and took it to an animal rescue center. It nearly died, but in the end it survived."

b) Are the following statements right or wrong? Correct the wrong sentences in your exercise book.

1 In the 1960s, there were hardly any falcons in the west of the USA.
2 In the 1970s, scientists brought young falcons to New York City.
3 New York City offers falcons a good home.
4 The lights on tall buildings are bad for falcons.
5 People in New York don't give food to the falcons.

c) Answer these tasks in your exercise book.

1 Name two things that make New York a good place to watch birds.
2 Name three things that people in New York can do to help the falcons.
3 Describe what a team of scientists did in 1970 in your own words.

d) Explain in about 60-80 words in your exercise book why you would or would not like to be a member of a club that watches birds.

C

10 Where to go in Manhattan

You are an exchange student at a high school in Manhattan. Your teacher has asked you to give a presentation about local sights to two new exchange students from Portugal and Italy. Prepare and give a two-minute talk about interesting places in or near Manhattan and what you can do there. The ideas in the box can help you.

- Ellis Island is where people arrived in the USA …
- The 9/11 Memorial is where the Twin Towers used to …
- At Washington Square Park you can …
- The High Line used to be a railroad, but now it's …

Hi, and welcome to Manhattan!
I'm going to tell you about some cool places to visit. One interesting place is…

In the New World

1 The same place, six years apart

1615

Wampanoag Indians working in a field of corn, squash and beans in the village of Patuxet, population about 2,000.

1621

Colonists in the English colony of Plymouth, population 52

a) Describe what is going on in the two pictures.

b) The map of part of Massachusetts shows that the two villages were in the same place at dfferent times. What do you think happened between 1615 and 1621?

c) Listen to Tapenum and Sarah. Explain who they are and where they live. Take notes on their lives.
Check with a partner

d) Now answer question 1b again.

2 The colony of Massachusetts – a timeline

Read though the timeline. Explain what it tells you about the relationship between the colonists and the Native Americans.

1620 – 101 men, women and children arrive from Plymouth, England, on a ship called the *Mayflower* at the empty Wampanoag village of Patuxet.
They call their colony Plymouth. Today, Americans know them as the *Pilgrims*.

1621 – The Pilgrims and some Wampanoag celebrate the colonists' first harvest together.

1630 – Puritans found the *Massachusetts Bay Colony*.
It grows quickly, governs itself and is almost like an independent state.

1675/1676 – British colonists win "Metacom's War" against the Wampanoag and other Native Americans. Settlers begin to move into Native American lands.

1750 – In the next 75 years, more and more settlers arrive. In 1750, there are 12 other British colonies in North America. Virginia, the first colony, is the richest and most important. Massachusetts is the most important colony in the area known as New England.

The Mayflower *in Plymouth Harbour*

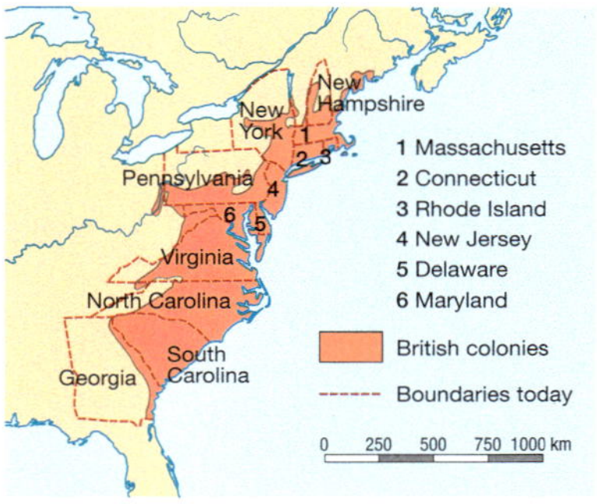

British colonies in America, 1750

3 Harvest celebration, 1621 – what really happened?

Every year, on the fourth Thursday in November, Americans everywhere celebrate the first harvest of the Pilgrims in Plymouth, MA in 1621. They call it *Thanksgiving*.
The usual story is that this harvest was the first Thanksgiving in America. But the Wampanoag lived there long before the Pilgrims arrived and they also had a tradition of giving thanks.
The usual story says that the colonists invited the Native Americans to the celebration, but really nobody knows if the Wampanoag got an invitation. We do know that many Wampanoag came. In fact, there were about 90 Wamanoag at the harvest celebration but only 50 colonists.

According to the usual story, the colonists and the Indians had just one dinner together, a dinner the colonists cooked. Actually, the Wampanoag brought food with them, five deer, and stayed for three days. They built their own shelters, played games, talked politics and generally had a good time.

People sometimes celebrate events that have little to do with reality. Are there any examples similar to Thanksgiving in your country?

www Find out more about the harvest celebration of 1621.

➔ **Workbook** *8–9 (p. IV)*

New Orleans

A

B

D

E

1 Your first impressions

a) You will hear sounds of New Orleans. Listen to them while you look at the photos. Now imagine you are in two of the photos. Say what you can see, hear and smell.

b) Look at the photos again. Note down:
- three things that seem different from your home area.
- two things that seem similar to your home area.
- one thing you would like to know more about.

c) Discuss your ideas in class.

2 Tyler's first impressions

a) Listen to Tyler and his parents as they arrive in New Orleans. Note down what Tyler learns about the city. You can use these words.

Mississippi River · Hurricane Katrina · brass band · French Quarter · colony · Mardi Gras · swamp · alligator · palm tree

b) Compare your notes. You can refer to the pictures above when you exchange ideas.

c) Listen again. Then say if you think Tyler will enjoy his stay in New Orleans. Give reasons.

3 New Orleans here I come!

→ p. 57 Look at the map and say what it tells you about New Orleans (where it is, how big it is, etc.).

EXTRA My Book Write a short social media post (about 200 words). Say:

- what you know about New Orleans.
- why you would/wouldn't like to go there.

You can use your notes from 1 and 2.

Read out your texts and give feedback.

→ **Workbook** *1-2 (p. 56)*

Your task

At the end of this unit:
You'll give a three-minute talk about objects/ photos/… that are important to you and/or your family and their history.

1 Tyler in New Orleans

Look at the pictures Tyler sent for a chat with his friends. Describe what you can see.

Hey guys! Here I am in N'Awlins! 9:27 pm

Jasmine
Hey, palm trees! 9:29 pm

Right in front of Grandma Betty's house. It's kind of tropical here. 9:30 pm

And look at this … 9:30 pm

Alex
What's that? 9:32 pm

A gourd banjo. It's very old. Dad saw it in the living room. Of course he had to play it. 9:32 pm

It sounded awful. If he plays that thing again, I'll go crazy! 9:33 pm

Jasmine
So what are you doing down there in N'Awlins? 9:34 pm

We walked around the French Quarter this morning. 9:35 pm

I wanted to go to Bourbon Street to PARTY. But my Aunt D'Avila said Bourbon Street was just for tourists. 9:36 pm

Jasmine
You are a tourist ;-). 9:36 pm

If I ever come back, I'll head straight for Bourbon Street. LOL 9:37 pm

Alex
A jazz band! Cool. 9:39 pm

So cool that Mom and Dad started dancing right in the middle of the sidewalk. Embarrassing! 9:40 pm

Check this out!. 9:41 pm

Alex
You ate that? No way. Disgusting. 9:43 pm

Jasmine
I wouldn't eat alligator if you gave me a hundred bucks. 9:44 pm

If you give me one hundred dollars, I'll eat it again. 9:44 pm

It was delicious … like chicken. 9:45 pm

Jasmine
So what's happening down south for July 4th? 9:47 pm

Fireworks on the Mississippi River!!! And a big barbecue!!!! I'll tell you all about it tomorrow … 9:48 pm

2 My first day

a) Read through the chat on p. 112 and make notes on what you find out about New Orleans.

b) Write an entry (about 80-100 words) for Tyler's diary about his day in New Orleans.

c) Read your entry to your partner.

3 A friend of yours?

Hey guys! Can you believe what this dude posted!? 9:05 am

MeanManhattanMan
Eating alligator, Tyler? That sucks! So typical of you people. Keep your Deep South habits outta NYC!

Jasmine
Wow! Who is he? You should block him. 9:48 am

I don't even know the guy! And how did he find out about my New Orleans trip? 9:49 am

Alex
That's Dean Sims. What a jerk! OMG, maybe he saw the photos of your trip on my timeline. 9:52 am

This guy's a friend of yours? 9:54 am

a) Explain what you think Dean Sims' post really means and why Tyler is upset about it.

b) THINK: How should Tyler and Alex react to the post? Note down ideas.

PAIR: Compare your ideas with a partner and agree on the best ones.

SHARE: Discuss your ideas in a group and agree on the best ones to present to the class.

4 Stop using social media ??!!

Social media – are you safe?

Kaylee Lopez, 14, NYC

My parents often tell me to be careful about what I post on social media. But they're from a different generation – social media is the theater of our lives!
Seriously, the first thing I do when I wake up is reach for my phone and check my messages. At breakfast, I'm already texting my friends. We all post lots of photos. I don't usually ask my friends if I can post a photo that they're in – and they never ask me. Maybe we should. Sometimes I wonder who is looking at that photo of me dancing with my friend in her bedroom.
This was our homework assignment for our English class: *Compare the ads on your newsfeeds with those of your parents. Are the ads the same?* Of course, they were totally different! My mom had ads for jewelry and summer dresses, while mine were all for video games.
Our teacher told us that companies start collecting information about us the moment we're on social media. Their advertising matches our profile. I get that, but what can I do about it?
Stop using social media ????… WHAT??!!
Anyway, I don't even look at the ads. What I post online is not the real me – it's an image – something that I create. That's why I feel safe. I know what I want to buy, and I know who I want to spend time with.

a) In a two-column table take notes on Kaylee's and your own social media use. How are they similar or different?

b) Choose what you think is the most important pro and the most important con of social media use. Make notes to support your opinion. **More help** → (p. 145)

c) In a double circle exchange your opinions with several partners and discuss how you can protect yourself in social media.

1 WORDS The media

a) Make a four-column table with these headings:

Social media

TV/Radio | Magazines/Newspapers

Other media (streaming, ...)

Then put the words/phrases from the box on the right where you think they go best.

> block sb. · buy · chat · check my/your/… … +account · +cyberbullying · +download sth. · +enter a password · friend · internet meme · be/go online · like · listen to · +log in/out · message · +on demand · post · read an article · +stream · text · timeline · turn on/off · +update your profile · +upload sth. · visit a website · watch a film/video

b) Add other words/phrases to do with the media that you know. In a German-English dictionary, look up words/phrases you would like to know and add these too.

c) Compare your table with a partner and make any changes you think are necessary.

2 You and the media: a class survey

a) Answer the questions on a copy of the questionnaire. You do not need to write your name on it.

Which media do you use?	How often? (daily, weekly, ...)	How long per day?	Main activities (e.g. check messages, watch news, ...)
Social media			
Blogs			
Streaming sites			
TV			
Radio			
Newspaper			
Magazine			
Other (name)			

b) Split the class into three groups.
Group 1: Find out how many people use which type of media and how often.
Group 2: Find out on average how long people spend on each media type per day.
Group 3: Find out the two most popular activities for each media type.

Collect and cut all the questionnaires so that each group has the right information to work with.

c) Report your findings to the class. Then discuss the topic.

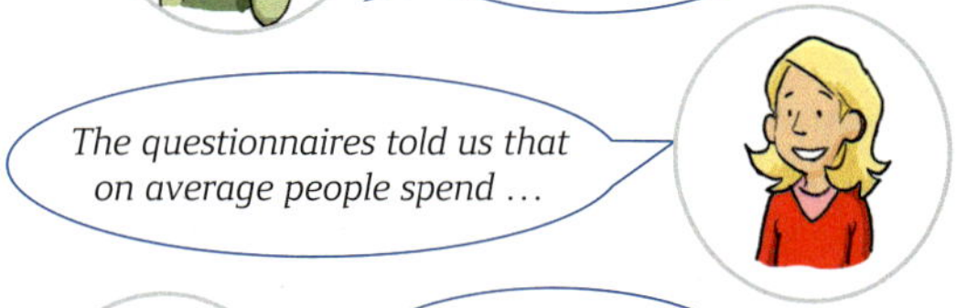

3 A post is forever

An American school gives this advice about posting on social media. Think about which points you agree with and which you disagree with. Then exchange your ideas in a group.

Think hard before you post

You cannot delete a comment you have posted. It may seem funny or harmless when you post it, but it could hurt someone. You may feel angry when you post something, but people might then think you're angry all the time. So think hard about each post before you put it online. Make sure it is something you can live with forever because that post will never disappear again.

➔ **Workbook** 3-4 (p. 57)

4 Escape room

Deine zwei amerikanischen Freunde/Freundinnen besuchen dich in Bayern.
Ihr wollt zusammen zu einem Escape Room gehen. Lies dir die Online-Rezensionen durch und erzähle deinen Freunden/Freundinnen auf Englisch, was an dem Ort gut und was nicht so gut ist.

Genialer Spaß vom Feinsten! ★★★★★
Wir haben zwei der aktuell drei Räume getestet und sind absolut begeistert. Die Geschichten sind super aufgebaut, jedes Rätsel ist anders, bei der Ausstattung merkt man die Liebe zum Detail, und es bleibt bis zuletzt spannend. Beide Male wurden wir sehr nett eingeführt, und auch die Hinweise während des Spiels waren immer passend, ohne zu viel zu verraten.

Online keine Schwierigkeitsangaben ★★☆☆☆
Daher erfuhren wir erst vor Ort, dass wir den leichtesten Raum gewählt hatten. Die Story fing erst mit Verspätung an und war über die Lautsprecher schwer zu verstehen. Außerdem erhielten wir aus Versehen einen Tipp, der für eine andere Gruppe bestimmt war, und die Technik funktionierte nicht einwandfrei. Alles in allem etwas unorganisiert und chaotisch.

➜ Workbook 5 (p. 57)

5 REVISION I'll go for a walk if it doesn't rain (Conditional 1)

Complete the sentences about things you do and say every day with the correct form of verbs from the box.

be (2 x) · break · drop · eat · get · get back · go (2 x) · not leave · need · not rain · not taste · remember · use · watch

1 The weather seems OK. I ... for a walk later if it ...
2 Yes, and if you ... before seven, we ... that film on TV.
3 Please hurry up! We ... late for the party if we ... now.
4 If you ... anything from the shops, just say, and I ... it for you.
5 If I ... to the market, I ... that you love strawberries.
6 Careful! If you ... too much salt, the soup ... very nice.
7 Haven't you had enough? You ... sick if you ... so much!
8 Be careful with that plate. It ... if you ... it.

More help ➜ p. 146
➜ GF 4.1: Conditional 1 (p. 176)
➜ Workbook 6 (p. 58)

6 REVISION If I went fishing in New Orleans, ... (Conditional 2)

Say what you would do if you were one of the people or animals in the pictures.
Think of different ways to react to each situation.

1

2

3

1 If I went fishing in New Orleans, I'd watch out for alligators.
If I saw an alligator, I would ...
If the alligator ..., I would/could ...
If I were the alligator, I would/could ...

More help ➜ p. 146
Early finisher ➜ p. 150
➜ GF 4.2: Conditional 2 (p. 176)
➜ Workbook 7 (p. 58)

7 Help! My kids want to become vegetarians

a) The letter below has several words you haven't learned yet in this book.

Read it paragraph by paragraph.
With a partner, discuss the meaning of words you don't know.
Only use a dictionary if you are still not sure what they mean.

TIP
When you read, you can often understand new words without looking them up.
For example, they may be similar to a German word or an English word you already know.
Or the meaning may be clear from the context.
➜ *SF 18: Understanding new words (p. 166)*

Dear Mara,

We've always been a family of meat-eaters, especially on festive days like Thanksgiving and Christmas. Even on normal days we enjoy a juicy steak or a meaty stew. Or at least until last week. That was when my two kids broke the news that they want to become vegetarians.

My daughter, who has just turned 12, says there are countless health reasons why we shouldn't eat meat, but I disagree with that. We humans evolved because we ate meat. It's against nature to go without it completely. My daughter says your body gets all the protein it needs from things like cheese, eggs, lentils, tofu, etc. But I feel that a totally meat-free lifestyle is a big health risk, especially for adolescents.

My daughter also says she is against animal cruelty. The kind of factory farming we have in this country today disgusts her. I kind of agree with that, but it's just one of those things we have to accept. I'd offer to buy organic meat, but we aren't made of money and we couldn't afford it.

My son, who is 14, also goes on about health and animal cruelty, but he mainly wants to change his diet because of the environment. His biggest worry is the destruction of the rainforest. Do I know, he keeps asking me, that we destroy an area equal to the state of Florida every year, just so that we can grow food for factory-farmed animals. And what kind of future will our planet have if we go on like this? Of course I know this, and I worry about it too, so it isn't so easy for me to convince him that it's risky to do without meat at his age.

What can I say to my kids to make them see sense? I wouldn't mind eating less meat, but no meat at all would be a major mistake.

Worried mom, Louisiana

b) Answer the questions about the text.
Try to use your own words.
1 Who wrote the letter?
2 What is the main topic of the letter?
3 Who does the writer speak of?
4 What worries the writer?
5 Who do you think Mara is?

c) In a two-column table, list all the pros and cons you can find in the letter for a vegetarian diet for teenagers.
Write down the lines where you can find the arguments in the text.

d) Check your table with a partner. Then together add any other arguments you might know.
Then discuss the arguments with your partner. Which arguments do you agree with? Give reasons.

e) Write a reply to the worried mom. Use the arguments from c) and d) and write about 150-200 words.

EXTRA Imagine a conversation at the dinner table between the mother and one of her children. Write the conversation (about 200-250 words) and act it out for the class.

1 Learn how

You've learned different writing skills in this school year. Here you will learn how to choose which skills you need and how to combine them when you write a longer text.

2 Now write ...

a) Decide what you're going to write about: you can write about a film, a game or a book. Or you can write a story.

b) Read the tips and choose the ones that might help you. Then write a first draft of your text (about 200-250 words).

➜ **Workbook** *Wordbank 8 (p. 77)*

3 ... and revise

a) Read your text again carefully. Look at the tips you wrote down. Can you use them to improve your text more? Correct any grammar or spelling mistakes.

b) Give feedback. Read your partner's text and make notes. Take turns to make comments and corrections.

c) Think about your partner's feedback and what you've learned on this page. Decide what to change and write a second draft.

EXTRA Put together a class magazine with all the texts for each member of your class.

➜ *SF 3: Good sentences (p. 156); SF 4: Structuring a text (p. 157); SF 5: Paragraphs and topic sentences (p. 157); SF 8: Revising your text (p. 159)*

➜ **Workbook** *8 (p. 59)*

TIPS – UNIT 2

1 Before you start writing, make a mind map or table to collect and organize your memories and ideas.
2 The *5* ***Ws*** (When? Where? What? Who? Why?) can help you to find ideas.
3 Start a new paragraph for every new idea.
4 Use a topic sentence in each paragraph. In the other sentences add details or examples.

TIPS – UNIT 3

1 Organize your ideas and plan your paragraphs. (See the TIPS on p. 43.)
2 Write your text. Remember:
   - say what the text is about (first paragraph)
   - use topic sentences in the body of the text
   - find a good way to end your text.
3 Read your text. Check your topic sentences and decide if the paragraphs are in a good order.
4 Change the order of the paragraphs if necessary.

TIPS – UNIT 1

1 Use different adjectives (*bright, fantastic, dark, …*) to describe people, things and places – not just *good, bad* and *nice*.
   Use *really, very, a bit,* etc. (*really slowly, very quietly, a bit dark*) to be more exact.
2 Use time phrases (*last week, tomorrow, …*) to tell your reader when things happened.
3 Use linking words (*and, but, because, …*) and relative clauses to link short sentences.

TIPS – UNIT 4

1 Use time markers to help your reader to see
   – when something happened
   – what happened first, second, etc.
   – how much time passed.
2 Use time markers to link sentences.

1 The memory box

Say what you think a memory box is.
What kind of things would you put in it?

After dinner, Tyler's dad picked up the old banjo again and started to play.

"Ooh … that old thing needs some tuning," said Grandma Betty. "It's hurting my ears."

D'Avila reached over. "Give it to me."

She tightened its strings and started playing.

"Ah, that sounds better," said Grandma Betty.

"Where is it from?" Tyler asked.

"I found it in the upstairs' closet," said Aunt D'Avila.

Grandma Betty laughed. "I remember that day! D'Avila ran into the room. She was screaming 'Mama! Mama! Do you know what this is?' I thought she had found gold!"

"Well, to me it *was* like finding gold!" said D'Avila "A gourd banjo! In my own house!"

"What's so special about it?" Tyler asked.

"It's a link to our ancestors in West Africa," replied Aunt D'Avila. "They played instruments that are a lot like the gourd banjo."

Tyler's grandmother took the banjo in her arms. "And it belonged to my daddy, your great-grandfather. He used to sit out on the porch and play. There was one song, how did it go?" Grandma Betty began to hum an old tune.

"I wish I had known him, Grandma," said Tyler.

"I wish you had too. I know you would have liked him, Tyler. He was a good man."

"Do you have a picture of him?"

"D'Avila, honey, go to my room and bring down my box – you know which one."

❖

"Tyler fished something out of the box. "What are these?" he asked.

Grandma Betty laughed and held them up to her ears. "They're earrings – alligator teeth earrings. They were a present from a boy I knew in high school. He told me he had killed the alligator himself. I guess he thought that I'd like that - can you imagine?" She laughed again.

"What was his name?" asked Tyler. "You must have liked him. I mean you wouldn't have kept these if you hadn't liked him."

Grandma seemed not to hear his question. She was looking through the other things in the box.

"Here they are!" she cried and pulled out a pile of old photos. "Tyler, this is your great-grandfather. His name was Ray. And here is your grandpa when he was not much older than you. Wasn't he handsome!"

"He played football?" Tyler asked.

"He sure did. He was the star quarterback for his high school team," said Grandma Betty.

"Come on, honey," she said, and patted Tyler's leg. "I think we have to look for something for you too in that old upstairs' closet."

"Here it is! Number 7!"

Grandma Betty handed Tyler a carefully folded football jersey. I'm sure he would have wanted you to have it."

"Oh, and look! Here's his old football!"

2 What is in the memory box?

a) Name the objects that D'Avila, Grandma Betty and Tyler find in the box and the upstairs' closet. Write one or two sentences for each object that describe the memories they trigger.

b) Share your sentences in class.

EXTRA Background file

American football, known in the US as 'football', is a lot like rugby and soccer and began as a game that college students played at university. Today, 150 years later, it is the nation's most popular sport. Its games have the highest average attendance of any professional sport in the world.

There are three forms of the game:

- **Professional football:** The most popular league is the NFL or National Football League. The NFL's championship - the Super Bowl - is one of the most watched sporting events in the world. Professional football is also big business. The NFL earns about US$10 billion every year through advertising, ticket and merchandise sales. Top entertainment stars like Beyoncé perform in high-tech shows at the Super Bowl.
- **College football:** Teams from different colleges and universities compete with one another. College coaches often visit high schools to recruit players for their teams. They offer the young players scholarships and promises of a great sports career.
- **High school and youth football:** 1.1 million high school students play the sport each year. At the professional level, American football is mostly a male sport.

a) Tell the class what you know about American football. Have you ever played or watched a game?

b) Contrast the importance of American football in the US with ***Fußball*** **in Germany.**

www Find out more about American football.

3 I wish I had known him

Say how do you think Tyler feels when his Grandma gives him his grandfather's football jersey and old football.

4 Have a go

Imagine Tyler had met his grandfather or great-grandfather. Say what Tyler would have or wouldn't have *done* with him.
Tyler/They would have / wouldn't have …

played football · learned how to play the banjo · sung old songs · heard stories about the past · hunted alligator · …

➜ **Workbook** *9 (p. 60)*

Looking at language

a) Look at these sentences from p. 118. Are the people talking about the past **or** about something that could happen now or in the future?
"I wish I had known him, Grandma," said Tyler. (l. 25)
"You wouldn't have kept these if you hadn't liked him." (ll. 40–41)
"I'm sure he would have wanted you to have it." (ll. 58–60)

b) Choose the correct answers to complete the rules.
You use the *would have*-form with the simple past / past participle form of a verb.
When you wish something about the past / the future, use the past perfect after *wish*.
In an *if*-clause about the past, you use the simple past / past perfect.

➜ *GF 8.2 Conditional 3 (p. 183)*

1 I would have stayed inside (*would have*-form)

What would you have done differently? Act out short dialogues. Use sentences with *I would have ...* Take turns to play A and B. You can also use your own ideas for B.

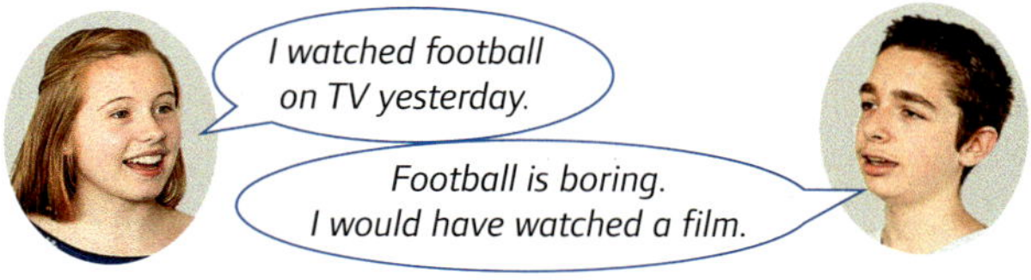

1 A: We went for a walk in the rain yesterday.
B: In the rain? (stay at home)
I would have stayed at home.

2 A: Eva was late again yesterday. So I waited ten minutes and then I went home.
B: Only ten minutes? (wait a bit longer)

3 A: Our host family in France gave us frogs' legs for dinner.
B: The poor frogs. (ask for other/different food)

4 A: I didn't really enjoy Kim's party, but I stayed till the end.
B: Really? (leave early)

5 A: I bought a pair of pink trainers yesterday.
B: Pink! (buy a different colour)

6 A: I gave my dad a pair of socks for his birthday.
B: Socks aren't so interesting! (give him a book or a DVD)

2 Would've, could've, ...

a) Look at these phrases with short verb forms:

1 it couldn't've been
2 I'd've helped
3 they shouldn't've told
4 I could've given
5 we wouldn't've come
6 she'd've texted

Listen and match phrases 1–6 to the sentence you hear them in (a-f). You will hear each sentence twice.
Write in your exercise book.

b) Write down the full form of the phrases in a).
It could not have been ...
Listen again to the short forms and pay attention to the difference.

c) Write short forms of the phrases in blue.
Then write two more sentences like these in your exercise book.
1 *He would have helped* you if you'd asked him.
2 If he hadn't helped, *we could not have done* it.

Read out the sentences with the short forms.

LISTENING TIP In spoken English, native speakers usually use short forms of conditional 3 verbs. Instead of *I would have done ...*, they say *I would've done ...* or *I'd've done ...*, etc. Knowing such pronunciation patterns will help you to understand native speakers.

➜ **Workbook** *10 (p. 61)*

3 I wish I had been more careful (*wish* + past perfect)

a) Look at the pictures. Think about what might have happened.
Then imagine you are the person in the picture and make a sentence like this for each situation:
- I wish I had been more careful when I climbed the tree.
- I wish I hadn't run down the stairs so quickly.

More help → p. 147

A
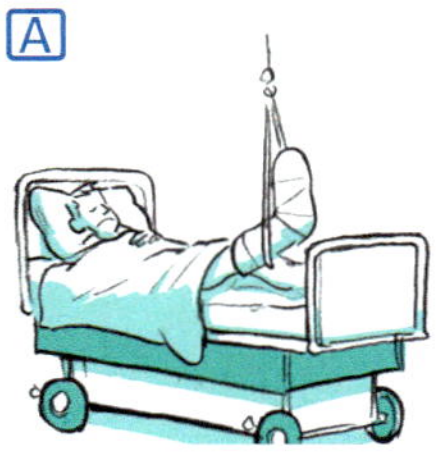
B

C

D

E

b) Now imagine that you are speaking to the people in the pictures.
Show that you feel sorry about their situation. Make comments like
- You poor thing. I bet you wish you hadn't run down the stairs so quickly.

4 ... if you had been more careful (Conditional 3)

a) Imagine you are talking to the person in picture A above. Make six more *if*-clauses for this sentence.

You wouldn't have fallen …

if you ... (be) more careful.
if you had been more careful.
if you ... (not climb) that tree.
if you ... (not run) down the stairs so quickly.
if you ...

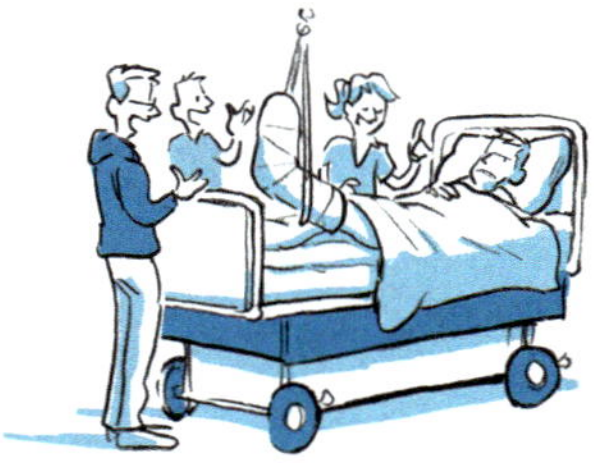

b) What do the people in pictures B–E say? Complete their sentences.

1 If I ... (not drive) so fast, I ... (not crash) into the tree.
2 If I ... (take off) my backpack, I ... (not break) the lamp.
3 If I ... (not forget) my umbrella, I ... (not get) so wet.
4 If I ... (leave) home earlier, I ... (be) in time for the bus.

→ *GF 8.3 Conditional 3 (p. 183)*

c) Write a short dialogue with a person from one the pictures in 3. Use one conditional 3 sentence. Act out your dialogue together.

A: Did you hear that I crashed Mum's car?
B: Yes. I bet you wish you hadn't driven so fast.
A: Right. If I hadn't ...

More help → p. 147 → **Workbook** *11–12 (pp. 61–62)*

5 Something went wrong

You will read a story about something that went wrong. Tell your partner about it.
Partner A: Go to p. 151.
Partner B: Go to p. 277.

TIP
When you report about something that went wrong, you can use phrases like:
I wish I had/hadn't done that.
When you comment on something that went wrong, you can use phrases like:
I wouldn't have done that. / I would have …

1 Big plans

What sort of information would you expect to find on the website 'Experience New Orleans'?

On July 4th, Independence Day, – Tyler's family had big plans. There were so many events taking place in New Orleans, and everyone wanted to do something different. One thing was sure, Tyler wasn't going to miss the fireworks display.
"Sorry, Ty – if we hadn't bought tickets to this great concert, we would go with you." said Dad.
"Don't worry, honey, if your mom and dad can't take you, I'll call my friend Eugene. He'll drive us," offered Grandma Betty. "It will be just fine. We'll have a true 4th of July barbecue picnic in Crescent Park: barbecue chicken, hamburgers, hot dogs and …"
"Corn!" shouted Tyler.
"Yes, of course! Lots of corn! I'll call Eugene right now."
"Tyler, is that all right?" Mom asked. "If you don't want us to go, we'll stay."
Grandma Betty put her arm around Tyler, "Aw, come on, he's not a baby! Tyler, Eugene and I will be just fine; actually, we want you to go!"
Tyler wondered who this Eugene-guy was. "And what about the fireworks?" he asked. "Are you going to miss them too?"
"No, we promise … we'll be there," replied his parents. But they already had that look in their eye of 'Ooh-wee! We're free!'

❖

During the next few hours, it was chaos. Everyone was getting ready for the big night out. Grandma Betty was packing up the food, Mom and Aunt D'Avila were trying on different dresses, and Dad was playing 'The Star Spangled Banner' – the national anthem – on the banjo.
When the doorbell rang, Tyler raced to answer it. Before him stood a big man with a safari hat. He wore cowboy boots, and a long alligator tooth hung around his neck. He held out a large hand.
"Hi, I'm Eugene," he said. "You must be Tyler."
Grandma Betty called out from the kitchen – "Is that Eugene!?" She ran to the door and gave him a big hug. "Happy Fourth of July, honey!" she said.
"Tyler … Eugene lives out in Slidell. He knows the backwaters better than anyone. Ah, Tyler, you should've seen his old house," she sighed. "It was on the edge of the bayou in the Honey Island Swamp. The porch was right on the water."
"That's right," said Eugene. "But if we hadn't left then, I wouldn't be here today. Hardest decision in my life, to leave that old house … my family had lived there for generations until Hurricane Katrina carried it away."
"Hey, why are we all standing at the doorway? Come on in!" Grandma Betty took Eugene and led him by the hand to the kitchen. "I tell you, we are going to have the best barbecue tonight. But we'd better hurry. If we don't leave soon, we won't get a place at the park. Have you moved into your new house yet?" asked Grandma Betty.
"Yup, I finally have a roof over my head again. It has a wide wooden porch and a round window with colored glass …" Their voices became softer as they disappeared into the kitchen.
"Eugene has some great stories," Aunt D'Avila whispered to Tyler. "About swamps and hunting alligators. Don't forget to ask him about it."

★ *Experience* New Orleans ★

What next

Things to do on Fourth of July in New Orleans

Categories | **Highlights** | News | Party | Links

2 We want you to go!

a) Describe what each member of Tyler's family plans to do on the Fourth of July.

b) Imagine you're Tyler. Write a post (about 100 words) to Alex and Jaz. In your post:
- Explain your plans for the Fourth of July and how you feel about them.
- Describe your first impressions of Eugene.
- Speculate about Eugene and Grandma Betty's relationship.

1 WORDS It's round and made of glass (Describing objects)

a) Copy the table. Add the headings material, shape, size. Then add words from the box.

...	colour	...	...
big	black	round	glass
small	white	oval	plastic
...	...	...	...

+cotton · dark blue · +leather · +light brown · +medium · metal · paper · pink · purple · square · +tiny · +triangular · wooden · xx +centimetres long

Compare your tables and correct them if necessary. Then add other words you know.

b) Write a description of an object in the room or in your bag, but don't say what it is. Swap descriptions. Try to guess what your partner has described.

➜ Workbook 13 (p. 62), Wordbank 1 (p.70)

2 THINKING ABOUT LANGUAGE Conditional: mixed forms

a) Name the tenses which you usually find in conditional sentences:

Conditional sentences type 1	
***If*-clause**	**Main clause**
If your mom and dad can't take you,	I'll call my friend Eugene.
Conditional sentences type 2	
***If*-clause**	**Main clause**
If I was in New Orleans,	I'd try alligator on a stick.
Conditional sentences type 3	
***If*-clause**	**Main clause**
If we hadn't left then ,	I would have died.

b) Describe what's different about the tenses in these sentences from 1 on page 122:

1 If we hadn't bought tickets to this great concert, we would go with you.
2 If we hadn't left then, I wouldn't be here today.

TIP
As in German, the tenses in conditional sentences can vary. It depends on the actual situation. In the sentences above, something that happened/didn't happen in the past has consequences in the present. We are talking about them now.

➜ GF 4, 8: Conditional (p. 176, pp. 183-184) ➜ Workbook 14 (p. 63)

3 July 4th in New Orleans (Adverbial clauses of time)

Use the conjunctions in the box and connect the sentences.

after · before · until · when · while

1 The party had finished. They went to see the fireworks.
2 They were driving into town. Tyler asked Eugene about life in the swamps.
3 They arrived in the French Quarter. The fireworks began.
4 They stayed in town. The fireworks were over.
5 Grandma Betty got tired. Eugene took her home.

b) Finish the sentences below in a way that makes sense to you.

1 As soon as I started at this school, I …
2 I read through all the new posts on my timeline before …
3 I'll be happy with myself when …
4 I won't be happy with myself until …
5 After I finish this exercise, I …

➜ GF 9: Adverbial clauses of time (p. 185)
➜ Workbook 15–16 (p. 63)

4 STUDY SKILLS Skimming a text

Skimming is a reading skill that can help you to check if a text has the information you need. It is different from *scanning*, which you have already learned about.

➔ *SF 1: Skimming and scanning (p. 154)*

a) Scan the text on the right to find out when the Fourth of July became a federal holiday. Then say what you look for when you scan: general information or specific details.

b) You skim a text to find out what it's about. Then you can decide if you want to read it in detail. You skim like this:

1 Read the **title** or **heading**.
2 Read the **sub-headings**.
3 Look at the **pictures**, **photos** or **graphics** and read their **captions**.
4 Read the **first sentence** of **every paragraph**, not the whole text.

Now in one minute skim the text on the Fourth of July and say what you find out.

c) Work in groups of three.
Imagine you have to give a presentation. Each of you has a different topic:

Partner A: Wildlife in the Louisiana swamps
Partner B: New Orleans swamp tours
Partner C: The people of the swamps

Go to pp. 152–153. Skim the three texts there and decide which one you should read. Then say which text you chose and why.

Study skills

Skimming

Skimming hilft mir, wenn ich
- …

Wenn ich einen Text überfliege, sollte ich
- die Überschrift lesen
- …

➔ *SF 1: Skimming and scanning (p. 154)*

➔ **Workbook** *17–19 (pp. 64–65)*

Fourth of July – Independence Day

America's national holiday

On the fourth of July every year, Americans celebrate their country's independence.

What happened?

13 British colonies on the east coast of North America declared that they were independent states and no longer part of the British Empire. They waged a war against Britain and won. Although that war went on till 1783, people still think of July 4th, 1776, the day the new states signed the Declaration of Independence, as the birthday of the United States of America.

Celebration

The Fourth of July has been a federal holiday since 1870, but Americans have been celebrating the day for much longer than that. The town of Bristol, Rhode Island, held its first celebration in 1777 and still holds one every year today.

Millions of Americans look forward to a host of traditional activities on July 4th. The red white and blue of the flag are everywhere, in decorations, people's clothes, even the cakes they bake. Cities often put on parades where people celebrate the traditions, history and government of the USA. In the afternoons, families and friends come together for barbecues and picnics, or to watch a baseball game.

Lighting up the night

Fireworks above Brooklyn Bridge, New York

Little by little, as the sun goes down, first on the east coast and hours later in California, the night skies come to life with great fireworks displays in cities and towns across the nation. As the national day comes to an end, many Americans of course party on into the night.

1 A musician in New Orleans

a) Watch the film. Does it make you want to visit New Orleans and/or meet Ado? Explain why/why not.

b) Make a table with these headings.
- The city
- The narrator

Watch the film again and note down what you learn about the city of New Orleans and the narrator Ado.

Think of two alternative titles for the film and write them down.

c) Discuss your alternative titles. Choose the best one and tell your class.

2 Making the film: Sound and atmosphere

a) Look at these four stills from the film and describe the atmosphere. Say what kind of sound (words, music, sound effects) you would expect to hear.

1

2

3

4

b) Watch the film again and check the sound for each still. Is it as you expected? Say how the sound influences the atmosphere in a film.

3 Making the film: Picture material

Watch part of the film again and say what times in Ado's life it shows. What materials does the film-maker use for the different times?

The film shows Ado when he was a young child. The film-maker uses …

Yes, and then it shows …

A true Fourth of July

Tyler, Eugene and Grandma Betty said their goodbyes and drove into the city. They rode in Eugene's car with a boat attached to the back. The city streets were packed with people. Many waved little American flags while others had painted their faces red, white and blue. Flags also hung from balconies in the old French Quarter. Music was everywhere.

The park ran along the Mississippi River, and Grandma Betty was right: it was hard to find a free spot. Families and friends sat around big picnic tables covered with dishes of food. The smell and smoke of grilling meat hung in the air. Tyler's stomach growled.

Grandma Betty finally found a place to sit and they set up their table and garden chairs. Eugene lit the coals and Grandma Betty laid out the meat and corn and bowls of salad. They chatted away as the meat sizzled.

Tyler wandered through the park. He felt like he was watching a movie: he passed people dancing on stilts, painting each other's faces, playing frisbee, and eating hamburgers and corn. His stomach growled again.

"Tyler! Food's ready! Come and get it!" Grandma called out.

Tyler ate a hamburger, two hot dogs and three grilled corns. Grandma Betty was laying out some more corn on the coals when an older lady in a big purple hat came to their table.

"Oh my god! Betty!" she shouted.

"Lana! It's been ages! Pull up a chair, honey! We have to catch up on everything!"

The two women spoke excitedly and kept on hugging each other. Eugene leaned back in his lawn chair.

"Son," he said, "I think it's time we bring the boat out on the river. It'll be dark in about an hour and we'll want to get the best view of the big show."

Eugene led Tyler back to the car, drove to a landing and pushed the boat into the river. Eugene grinned. "Hop in, boy," he said.

Eugene started up the motor and they were soon humming along, slithering through the river like a water snake. Eugene pointed out important sights, but Tyler wasn't really listening: he couldn't stop thinking about that alligator tooth.

"When did you kill your first gator?" he asked suddenly. Eugene smiled and three gold teeth shone in the light. "I guess I was about your age. It was me and my daddy. Hunting gator is like fishing: you move through the water real quiet and when you see a gator, you stay calm, throw out a line and hook him. But remember: your hook needs to be big and sharp."

"And then what?" asked Tyler impatiently.

"Well, as soon as you get the gator close to your boat, you shoot him." He pointed his finger in the air. "Make sure he's dead before you pull him into your boat, or he'll pull you right into the water."

"Did you get that tooth on the chain from an alligator you killed?" Tyler asked.

"I sure did ... Hey, Tyler, how about you steer the boat for a while?"

Tyler's face lit up and he quickly jumped over to the back seat by the motor.

"Hey! Not so fast … quick jumps like that make this old boat rock."

With his calm, deep voice, Eugene showed Tyler what to do. "Just keep your hand on the tiller. If you turn it left, the boat will go left – if you turn it right, it will go right. It's that simple. You just need to keep her steady. Keep your eyes open for boats … and let's enjoy the ride."

Eugene took a harmonica from his pocket and played a few notes. A few minutes later, an orange and white buoy appeared in their path. Tyler carefully steered the boat around it.

"Well done, son. You're getting the hang of it."

Tyler felt good. It was both peaceful and exciting out on the river. A heavy orange sun was setting over the city, and the sky turned a beautiful, deep blue. Tyler's hand buzzed with the motor's vibrations. Eugene was playing a sweet tune on his harmonica.

Suddenly, a bright spot of light trailed through the sky and exploded in red.

Eugene put down his harmonica. "Looks like the show is starting up," he said.

Tyler had never seen such a display. Huge balls of light exploded in the sky, one after the other: red, white, blue and green. It was mesmerizing …

❖

"Go left! Left!" Eugene shouted. Tyler had been too busy staring up at the sky to notice that the river was suddenly full of boats. Shocked and surprised, Tyler had steered the boat the wrong way. They

were headed straight for a riverboat! Eugene rushed over, and Tyler felt his large, rough hand grab his own. Eugene turned the tiller sharply left and they were able to pass the boat safely. Passengers waved at them from the riverboat and cheered. Fireworks were still bursting in the sky.

"Gee! We sure have a good story to tell your folks!" said Eugene and once again flashed his gold tooth smile at Tyler.

1 Before the fireworks

a) Note down the activities at Crescent Park on Fourth of July.

b) Compare your notes with a partner.

2 On the Mississippi River

In your own words, explain what happened to Tyler when the fireworks display began.

3 You won't believe this!

a) Compose the dialogue that Tyler and his parents have when they meet Tyler and Eugene back on shore.

b) Form groups of three or four students. Make a copy of your dialogue for each member of your group. Take turns reading each dialogue out loud.

➜ **Workbook** *20 (p. 65)*

Workbook Checkpoint 5 (pp. 66–69)

Your memory box

In this unit you have read about people who kept things that were special to them in some way. Your task now is to "fill" your own memory box.

Then you will give a three-minute talk to your group about the things in it and why they are important to you or your family.

STEP 1
Decide what objects you want to put in your memory box. They can be:

- old or new
- worth a lot of money or no money
- things for special days
- everyday things
- things you can wear, play with, use for work, read, look at, listen to, …

Looking around your room or home will give you some ideas.

STEP 2
Think about what to tell your group. When you give your talk you should:

- show each object (if it is possible to take it with you to school) or a photo of it
- describe each object (colour, material, shape, size, …), especially if you cannot show it at school
- explain who owns it, how old it is, where it comes from, how long you have had it/known about it, what you can do with it, …
- say why it is important to you or your family.

Use keywords to make notes on a piece of paper or on cards. ➜ **Workbook** *Wordbank 1, 2, 7 (pp. 70-71, 76)*

STEP 3
Practise your talk. While you're practising, make changes to your notes if necessary.
Here are some phrases you could use.

- My objects are …
- The first thing I'd like to talk about is …
- As you can see, it's red. It's made of …
- I couldn't bring this to school, so I'll describe it as well as I can.
- It belongs/belonged to …
- I've had it since …
- It's been in my family since …
- It's at least 50 years old.
- It comes from …
- It's worth quite a lot of money.
- It isn't worth much/anything, but …
- I/We/… use/used it to …
- It's special to me/my mum/… because …
- If I/she/… had/hadn't bought/gone to/…, then I/she/… would/wouldn't have …

STEP 4
Give your talk to your group and answer their questions.

STEP 5
Go to page 278 and have a look at some tips on how to do better.

A

1 Social media

a) Match the words/phrases in A and B. You can use some words/phrases more than once.

A	B
block · chat · delete · enter · log out · stream · update · upload	a comment · a password · a photo · TV programmes · (of) your account · somebody · with friends · your profile

b) Use the phrases in a) to write at least six sentences.

2 Paraphrases

a) Find the words that match these paraphrases. Write them in your exercise book.

1 Something that tastes so bad that you feel sick is ...
2 A place in the home where you keep clothes or other things ...
3 If an object has an edge that can cut you, it is ...
4 A soft, wet area of land with trees ...
5 The part of a person that makes it possible to speak, think, feel and understand ...
6 An idea that someone gives you about what you could/should do ...

b) Write English paraphrases for these words.

1 documentary 2 to hunt 3 jewellery 4 tiny 5 great-grandfather 6 wildlife

c) Choose six words from a) and b) and write a story of about 100-150 words.

3 At Grandma's house

Tyler is at his grandmother's house. Make collocations with the words in the boxes and use the correct ones to complete the sentences in your exercise book.
You can use some words more than once.
Be careful with verb tenses.

belong · catch · head straight · link · log · look · put · speak · try · turn	against · for · off · on · out · through · to · up

1 When we arrive at Grandma's house, I always ... the kitchen to find her.
2 You have to be careful with that guitar – it ... my grandfather.
3 We told Grandma that she should ... when she has finished with a website.
4 Sometimes it's good to just ... your laptop and read a book.
5 Grandma ... the box to find an old photo of Grandpa.
6 D'Avila sees the gourd banjo as a ... to her family's ancestors in West Africa.
7 I can't wait to ... on your latest news.
8 Do you always ... clothes before you buy them?
9 We're going to ... a parade to celebrate Independence Day.

4 If only …

a) You sometimes wish you had or hadn't done something.
Read about the following situations and add a comment with *If only I/Tyler …*

1 Tyler: I ate too much gumbo. My stomach hurt.
2 Tyler: There wasn't enough time. We didn't do a swamp tour.
3 Jaz forgot her homework. Mr Lopez was angry.
4 Alex didn't listen in class. He didn't do well in the geography test.

b) Write about four thing(s) that you did or didn't do, like the sentences in a).

5 A trip to New Orleans (*would have*-form)

What would you have done differently on a trip to New Orleans? Write sentences with *I would have …*

1 A: We went there in the summer. B: In the summer? (go for Mardi Gras)
2 A: I lost my mobile on the swamp tour. B: You took it on the swamp tour? (leave it at the hotel)
3 A: After the tour, we tried alligator on a stick. B: Alligator? Disgusting! (not eat that)
4 A: We went to a musical. B: A musical? (go to a jazz concert)
5 A: I loved the art museum. B: The art museum? (not find it very interesting)
6 A: We had lunch at a Spanish restaurant. B: A Spanish restaurant? (go to French Market)
7 A: My dad went alligator hunting. B: The poor alligators. (ask him not to go)
8 A: My brother bought a gourd banjo. B: A banjo? (not spend money on that)

6 *Before, after, while…* (Adverbial phrases of time)

a) Read the sentences about things that happened in this unit. Make pairs of sentences from the two lists. Then use a conjunction to make one sentence for each pair.

1 Tyler's dad saw the gourd banjo.
2 Tyler took photos of the sights.
3 Tyler didn't know what alligator tasted like.
4 Tyler got angry.
5 Tyler met Eugene.

A He was exploring the city.
B They all sat down for a July 4th lunch.
C He had read Dean Sims' post.
D They went into Grandma Betty's living room.
E He tried 'gator on a stick'.

b) Finish the sentences below in a way that makes sense to you. Use your exercise book.

1 As soon as I wake up, …
2 Before I write a comment online, …
3 When I started to learn English, …
4 I can't wait until …
5 After I leave school, …
6 While I am doing my homework, …

7 MIXED BAG The swamp tour

Complete the sentences with the right words.

…[1] we … …[2] New Orleans, we went on a swamp tour. We'd seen posters for it … …[3] the city. We took a bus from …[4] New Orleans. …[5] the tour began, Captain Cody told us to keep our arms …[6] the boat, away from hungry …[7] and other …[8]. …[9] the boat … …[10] to move, he held …[11] food above the water on a stick. Then a gator jumped up … …[12] and ate the food. Cody stayed calm, but I … …[13] screamed! I didn't know that I had lost my cell …[14] the end of the tour. …[15] only I … …[16] it at the hotel! I wish I … …[17] so stupid. …[18] I hadn't lost it, I … …[19] sent …[20] really …[21] photos to my friends. My advice … …[22] : don't take your cell …[23] a boat!

B

8 An interesting place in New Orleans

a) Listen to the podcast. What is it about? Write the correct answer in your exercise book.
1 A school for young people in New Orleans who want to learn to cook.
2 A museum about food and drink from the southern states of the USA.
3 A restaurant that was rebuilt after Hurricane Katrina.

b) Listen again and finish the sentences in your exercise book.
1 There are just hundreds of …
2 If you're interested in …
3 SoFAB's website describes it as a place …
4 Tony says the people …
5 SoFAB smells good …

c) Answer the questions in your exercise book.
1 How many people know SoFAB?
2 When did SoFAB open?
3 What kind of event was there around 2006?
4 How can you get to SoFAB?
5 How much is a ticket for adults?
6 What is the "Gallery of the South"?

d) Explain in about 50 words why you would or would not like to visit SoFAB. Write in your exercise book.

C

9 Restaurant reviews

Eine Schülergruppe aus New Orleans wird nächste Woche deine Schule besuchen. Am letzten Abend wollt ihr alle in ein Restaurant gehen. Lauren, eine Schülerin aus der Austauschgruppe, hat einige Online-Rezensionen über ein Restaurant in eurer Stadt gefunden. Sie versteht aber vieles nicht. Lauren lässt dich auch wissen, dass Matt, ein anderer Schüler aus der Austauschgruppe, kein Fleisch isst. Lies die Rezensionen durch und schreibe Lauren eine E-Mail auf Englisch, in der du auf das Essen, den Service und die Preise eingehst. Gib auch an, ob sich das Restaurant für eine große Gruppe eignet. Gib Gründe an.

★★★★ **Empfehlenswert**
Die Lage ist top: direkt gegenüber vom Rathaus. Das Restaurant ist groß mit langen Tischen und sehr schön gestaltet. Unserem Wunsch, zwei Tische für die Gruppe zusammenzustellen, wurde freundlich entsprochen. Die Bedienung war sehr zuvorkommend. Das bestellte Essen wurde in angemessener Zeit serviert. Zwar keine besonders große Auswahl an vegetarischen Speisen, aber das, was wir gegessen haben, war lecker. Fazit: super nettes Restaurant mit guter bayerischer Küche. Preis-Leistung: in Ordnung.

★★★★½ **Traditionell bayerische Küche**
Wir waren 22 Personen mit Reservierung und es hat alles super geklappt. Das Essen dauerte nicht lange und alles kam ziemlich zeitgleich. Der Service war flink und freundlich. Die Preise waren etwas höher als wir erwartet hätten, dafür sind die Portionen sehr groß! Die Essensqualität war super. Vor allem das Dunkelbiergulasch und der Schweinebraten waren sehr gut. Das Ambiente war sehr schön. Wunderschöne Location, man kann im Sommer draußen sitzen.

★★★★★ **Sehr lecker**
Sehr einladendes Ambiente! Es gibt kleine, aber auch sehr lange Tische. Da wir das erste Mal in Bayern sind, haben mein Mann und ich deftige bayerische Gerichte wie Krustenbraten mit Dunkelbiersoße, Semmelknödel und bayerisches Kraut bestellt. Wir mussten nicht lange auf unser Essen warten. Der Geschmack war hervorragend. Meine Tochter, die Vegetarierin ist, hat es leider nicht so gefallen, weil die Auswahl an Gerichten ohne Fleisch eher dürftig ist. Alles in allem aber herrlich bayerisch, sollte jeder besuchen, der das Ursprüngliche und Natürliche mag. Fünf Sterne!!!.

Hi Lauren, I read …

Text 1

Underground etiquette

a) Look at the illustrations in each tip.
Describe the situation in each one.
Then listen to the rhymes.
For each rhyme, sum up the tip in one short sentence.

b) Choose your favourite rhyme.
Say why you like it.
Learn it by heart and say it to the class, or read it aloud.

[1] **yet** [jet] aber

c) Tips No. 2 and No. 5 are missing.
Say what you think they could be.
Think of as many tips as you can about how to behave on trains or buses.

d) Is it a good idea to use rhyme to give people tips about how to behave?
Give reasons for your opinion.
Write a rhyme for another tip.

[1] **destination** [ˌdestɪˈneɪʃn] Ziel [2] **plain** [pleɪn] deutlich, offensichtlich [3] **delay** [dɪˈleɪ] Verspätung [4] **rather** [ˈrɑːðə] ziemlich
[5] **please sb.** [pliːz] jm. eine Freude machen

Text 2

London shapes

a) Listen to the poems. Then read them aloud.

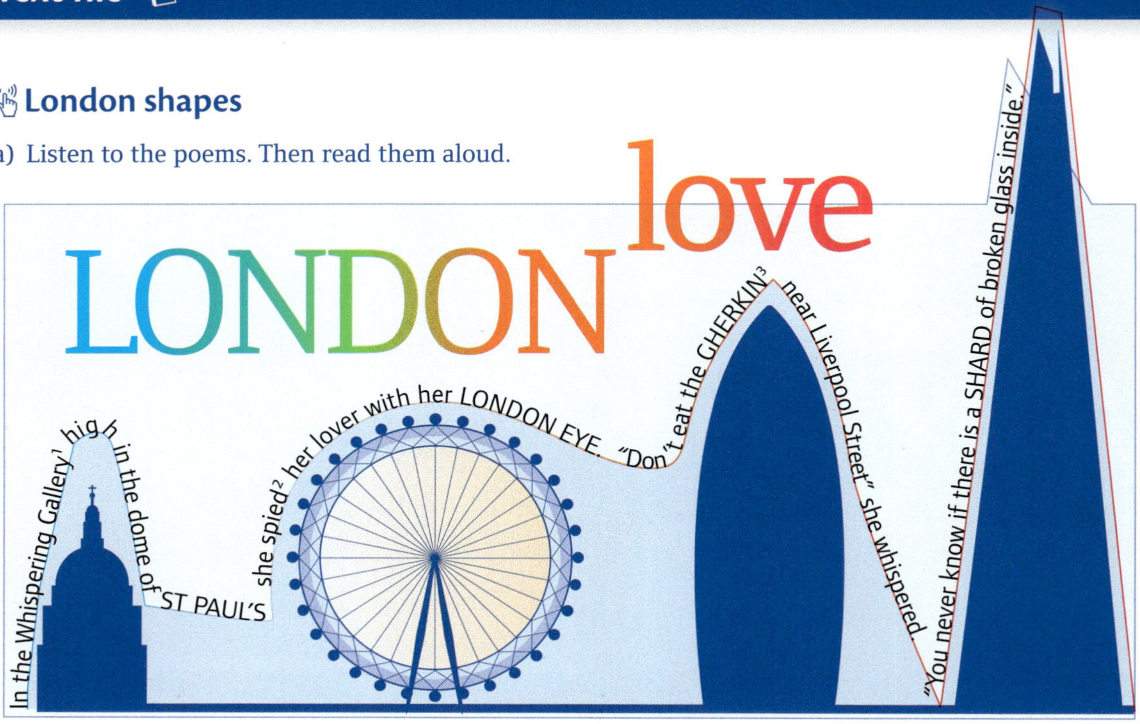

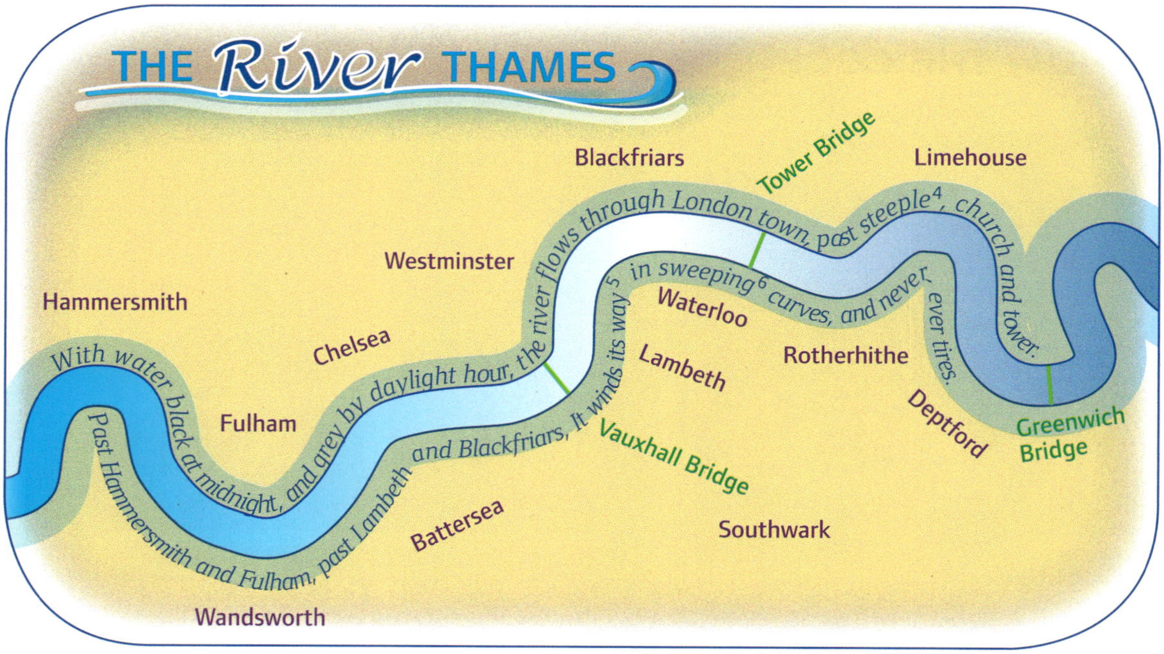

b) Think of London shapes you could write a poem about.

Tower Bridge! | *A policeman's helmet.* | …

c) MY BOOK Choose one shape. Then write a shape poem.

[1] **whispering gallery** *ein Ort, an dem sich Personen über eine große Entfernung in normaler Lautstärke unterhalten können*
[2] **spy** [spaɪ] erspähen [3] **gherkin** ['gɜːkɪn] Gewürzgurke [4] **steeple** ['stiːpl] Kirchturm [5] **wind its way** [waɪnd] sich schlängeln
[6] **sweeping** ['swiːpɪŋ] weit ausholend

Text 3

Jerry

by Laurence Harger and Cecile Rossant

Chapter 5 The magic hit

Paige walked along to the big COMPANY shop and set up her table in front of the shop window with all its adverts. ONE PHONE FOR THE WHOLE WORLD. NO MORE LONELY DAYS OR NIGHTS – WITH PERFECT PAL, YOU'LL ALWAYS HAVE COMPANY.

She put her sign on the table: Matches' Magic Show. Then she placed her hat for money in front of it and got everything else that she needed out of her bag: the cards, the coins, the small cups and larger boxes.

When she started on her magic routine, a few people stopped to watch: an old man with a walking stick, a young boy with his mother.

"Look, Mummy. She's doing magic like on TV!"

Soon five or six people, a small crowd, stood in front of her table. At the end of every trick the little boy clapped, the old man smiled kindly and a teenage boy in a bright blue jacket, with a COMPANY phone in his hand, shook his head and rolled his eyes.

"OK," Paige thought and gave him a hard look. "I know I'm not very good yet, you tosser[1], so why don't you just …"

Suddenly Paige felt that someone was standing behind her. She turned round quickly to see Knuckles. He was dressed as usual in an army pullover and trousers. He moved his face towards her and gave her a horrible smile. She saw the big gap in his front teeth and felt his hot breath on her face.

Knuckles pulled a five-pound note out of his trouser pocket and held it up.

"See this?" he said.

"Yes," Paige nodded at him. "It's a five-pound note."

"Right," Knuckles agreed. "I bet you a fiver[2] I can work out how you do your next trick. If I'm right, I win a fiver from you. If you win, you get this."

He waved the money around for everyone to see.

Paige looked at the coins in her hat and said, "All right."

She took a pack of cards and spread them across her table so that everyone could see they were normal playing cards. She picked them up and began to shuffle[3] them. Then she held them out to Knuckles. "Pick a card," she said to him, "any card."

Knuckles picked a card from the pack.

"Now, don't let me see the card, but show it to everyone else, so they can see what it is."

As Paige went on with her trick she thought, "This is the easiest trick in the world, but I don't think Knuckles will get it …"

At the end of the trick, Paige placed one card after another on the table. "Not that one," she said. "Not that one. Not that one …"

Finally she looked up at Knuckles as she placed the Queen of Spades[4] on the table for everyone to see. "Was that your card?" she asked. "The Queen of Spades?"

Everyone in the crowd began to clap and Paige smiled at the big boy in his army clothes.

Knuckles didn't smile back.

---

[1] **tosser** ['tɒsə] *(infml)* Vollidiot/in [2] **I bet you a fiver.** [bet], ['faɪvə] Ich wette mit dir um 5 Pfund. [3] **shuffle** ['ʃʌfl] *(Kartenspiel)* mischen [4] **Spades** [speɪdz] *(Kartenspiel)* Pik

"No," he said. "That wasn't my card."
The crowd booed him. "Don't be a cheat[1]," the old man said. "Give the young lady her fiver."
"Don't you call me a cheat," Knuckles threatened[2]. "She's the only cheat here."
"Cheat, cheat, cheat," the crowd began to chant and Knuckles went wild. He put his hands under Paige's table and threw it into the air. Her cards, her hat, coins and boxes flew everywhere. Suddenly everyone was shouting. The noise was so loud that all the customers[3], the shop assistants and a security guard[4] came out of the COMPANY shop to find out what was happening.
"Oi!" the guard shouted at Knuckles as he stood over Paige, who was picking her things up off the ground. "Get lost, will you! You're scaring our customers away."
"You get lost!" Knuckles shouted. He walked over, grabbed the guard's hat and ran off along the street. The security guard started to run after him but soon stopped. He turned back to Paige.
"Hurry up," he told her. "Pack up and get out of here. And don't let me catch you here again, or I'll call the police."
Then he spoke to the big crowd of customers outside the shop.
"Sorry about that, ladies and gents, but the show's over now, so if you'd like to go back inside …"
Slowly, the crowd of COMPANY customers started to move into the shop again. The security guard followed them, and as he entered the shop his hand flew up to his mouth.
"What the …? Who did that?"
Paige had all her things together again now and went to look in the shop too. Across the walls, and the counters, she could see slogans in big, bright red letters: "EVERY TEXT YOU SEND, EVERY CALL YOU MAKE, WE'LL BE WATCHING YOU! THE COMPANY" the slogans said. "YOUR PERFECT PAL IS THE COMPANY'S PERFECT SPY[5]!" And "DUMP[6] YOUR COMPANY PHONE! DO IT TODAY! THE GROUP"
A big smile spread across Paige's face. "Yes!" she said under her breath, clenched her fist[7] and started to walk away. She stopped when the teenager in the bright blue jacket stood in her way. He held out a five-pound note to her. She took it automatically.
"Here," the boy said, "you won this. That kid had no idea how you did that trick."
Then he turned round and walked quickly away before Paige could say a word. She just stood there and watched him with her mouth open. When he disappeared round a corner she looked down at the note in her hands. Next to the picture of the Queen was a telephone number and a smiley face.

❖

a) Say …
   – how Knuckles behaves towards Paige.
   – what Paige thinks when she sees the slogans on the walls of COMPANY.

b) You've read one chapter of *Jerry*.
   Say what you think the book is about.

---

[1] **cheat** [tʃiːt] Mogler/in [2] **threaten sb.** ['θretn] jm. drohen [3] **customer** ['kʌstəmə] Kunde/Kundin [4] **security guard** [sɪ'kjʊərətɪ ˌɡɑːd] Wachmann [5] **spy** [spaɪ] Spion/in [6] **dump sth.** [dʌmp] etwas wegwerfen [7] **clench your fist** [klentʃ] die Faust ballen

Text 4

1 WTC... Freedom Tower

1 *1 World Trade Center* opened in 2014. New Yorkers often call it "Freedom Tower". To get an idea why, look at the building's dimensions. It is 196 by 196 feet, the same area as each of the twin towers which collapsed on September 11, 2001, after two hijacked airplanes flew into them. While we're still at ground level: The base[1] of the building is like a box with concrete[2] walls,186 feet high. These walls are covered in glass panels[3] which light up at night. They have no windows.

Can you guess why not?

To protect the building from truck bombs and other attacks at ground level.

2 54 high-speed elevators travel up to the top of the building. Let's take one of the express elevators that go non-stop to the restaurant and observation deck and reach a speed of 2,000 feet a minute.
The observation deck is 1,362 feet above ground – exactly the height of the old World Trade Center 2 building. To the top of the glass parapet[4] it is 1,368 feet – the height of the old World Trade Center 1 tower.

How long do you think it takes to go the top?

It takes about 45 seconds to reach the top. That's really fast!

3 Although you can't climb to the top of the antenna (unless you're King Kong!), its height of 1,776 feet above ground is important too.

What is important about that number?

1776 is the year that the United States declared[5] its independence[6] from Britain.

4 Now, after you have enjoyed all the incredible[7] views of Manhattan and all five boroughs of New York City, you can take the elevator back down … and in less than a minute you are back on the street, not far from from the 9/11 Memorial – those two deep fountains where the old twin towers once stood. One more thing: when you are walking around Manhattan at night, don't forget to watch out for the Freedom Tower antenna which lights up the night sky like a gigantic lighthouse.[8]

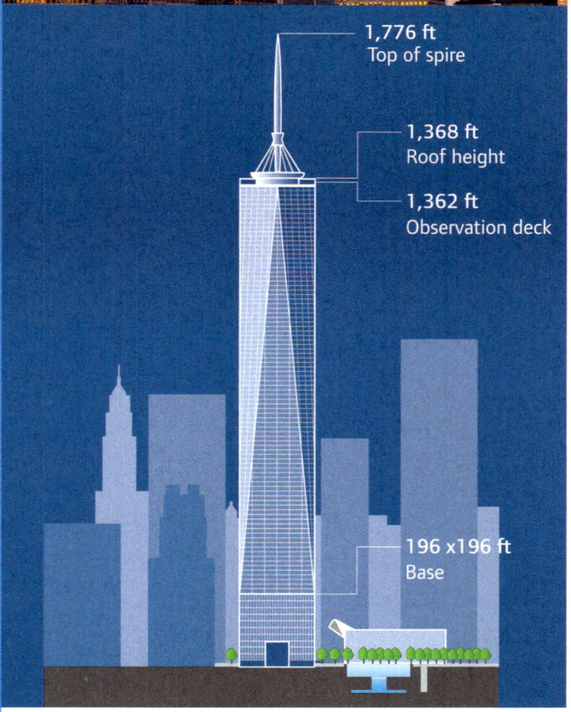

a) Say what connections you see between the dimensions of *1 World Trade Center* and the and the name *Freedom Tower*.

b) Explain why *1 WTC* is a popular tourist attraction.
Would you visit it too? Give reasons.

[1] **base** [beɪs] Sockel [2] **concrete** ['kɒnkriːt] Beton [3] **panel** ['pænəl] Platte [4] **parapet** ['pærəpet] Brüstung [5] (to) **declare** [dɪ'kleə] **erklären** [6] **independence** Unabhängigkeit [7] **incredible** [ɪn'kredəbl] unglaublich [8] **lighthouse** Leuchtturm

Text 5

Three teeth

The boy sat on his porch and looked out at the Honey Island Swamp. This house in Slidell had been in his family for years, and like his daddy and his grand-daddy before him, the boy would be a fisherman. In a way, he already was. Since the age of eight he had spent hours on the water. No one was better at catching fish and shrimp.

It was late afternoon in the last week of the summer vacation and the boy wanted to spend as much time out on the water as he could before school began again. He stood up and jumped into his canoe. He had packed all he needed: his fishing pole and line, his knife, and his lucky lure[1], the one he had used when he had caught one of his biggest fish.

He paddled his canoe silently through the old cypress trees. When he reached his favorite fishing spot, he threw out his line from the back of his canoe, put his pole between his knees, sat back and waited.

An hour or so later, when he felt a pull on the line, the boy opened his eyes. The sun was sinking behind the trees.

"Must have fallen asleep," he said to himself as he calmly held his line and waited for the next pull. But nothing happened – the line was still.

"Must have slipped away," he thought and began to pull in his line. But he soon found it was stuck[2]. He tried shaking his pole, and then lifting it, but it didn't move. Sweat began to run down the sides of his face. The last thing he wanted was to lose his lucky lure. He pulled off his shirt, jumped in and swam towards the cypress roots that stood in the water. He followed his fishing line to its end, took a deep breath and dived down. He opened his eyes underwater – but it was too dark to see where his lure was caught[3].

"I'll jump on those old roots and shake it out," he thought and jumped up and down on the underwater roots. But they were slippery, and with the last jump his foot slipped between two thick[4] ones and trapped his ankle[5].

"Ow! … Damn!" he shouted out loud. He felt around with his hand in the muddy water and tried to get his ankle free but he couldn't move it. He was trapped.

"Damn ankle's as big as a football now …" he whispered to himself.

In the distance he heard the sound of a small boat, but it was too far away to call for help.

"They won't hear me," he thought, "and anyway, it's probably old René LaPlace and he would never let me forget this."

He could just imagine René at all the parties and dances in Slidell for years to come: "Did I ever tell you how I rescued Lash Landry's boy that time? If I hadn't heard him, …"

No, the boy couldn't stand the thought.

Suddenly something slipped past his leg. He held his breath and slowly turned his head to watch a long snake move onto an old log[6] on the water, where it waited quietly for a fish or a frog.

As night fell on the swamp, the night-time animals began to wake. He could hear frogs and an owl[7] and, although[8] there was no wind, strange sighs and whisperings in the leaves[9] of the trees. Mosquitoes flew round his face, a fish came up to the surface next to him and disappeared with a splash.

[1] **lucky lure** [lʊə], [ljʊə] Glücksköder [2] (to) **be stuck** stecken bleiben, festsitzen [3] (to) **be caught** sich verfangen [4] **thick** [θɪk] dick [5] **ankle** [ˈæŋkl] Knöchel [6] **log** [lɒg] Holzscheit, Baumstamm [7] **owl** [aʊl] Eule [8] **although** [ɔːlˈðəʊ] obwohl [9] **leaf,** *pl* **leaves** [liːf, liːvz] Blatt

He felt cold. With the mist that slowly rose over the water, his canoe was almost invisible now.

“If I just had that knife in my hand, I could …”

Suddenly a smile lit up his face as he thought of a plan. He took hold of his fishing line. The pole was still in the canoe so he could pull the boat towards him, get the knife, cut the roots and get free.

Carefully, he began to pull on the line and felt the canoe start to move. Then, just as he started to hope that his plan might be working, he heard a quiet splash as his fishing pole fell out of the canoe into the water. The canoe stopped moving. “Damn,” he said quietly. “Maybe I should shout for help – but who’s going to hear me at night in the swamp? There must be another way.”

As he tried to think of another idea, the moon began to rise. In its light, the boy could see the cypress trees that rose like ghosts through the low mist. Seconds later, he saw something else in the light of the moon – two eyes glowed just above the surface of the water, two eyes behind the long snout of an alligator that was looking right at him! He remembered a story his daddy once told about watching an old gator eat a wild pig. The gator just stuck that pig between the cypress roots and bit off one piece and then another.

The boy waved his arms and kicked his free leg in fear,[1] but the alligator slowly moved a little closer. He waved his arms again. His arm hit the small log and the snake slipped into the swamp and disappeared in the night.

The boy, scared for his life now, picked up the log and held it in front of him as the alligator suddenly surged forward[2]. The gator hit the log hard with its open mouth, then, with a swipe[3] of its tail[4], swam slowly away.

The boy took a deep breath and sighed. As the water became calm again and he was sure that the gator was really gone, something touched his back. He screamed out loud and jumped round, hurting his ankle even more, but the tears he soon felt on his face were tears of joy[5], not pain[6]. While he had watched the alligator, his canoe had drifted up behind him and hit him in the back.

He grabbed the canoe, quickly found the knife and in a few minutes he was able to cut his ankle free and climb back into the canoe.

He lay there for a short while before he got up to go home. As he lifted his paddle, he suddenly saw in the moonlight the log that had saved him. Something shone[7] white on it. He pulled the log out of the water. Stuck in it were three alligator teeth. As he cut them out with his knife, he wondered, “Now, Eugene, what’ll you do with these?”

[1] **fear** [fɪə] Angst [2] (to) **surge forward** [sɜːdʒ] *etwa:* vorschießen, nach vorn schießen [3] **swipe** [swaɪp] Schlag [4] **tail** [teɪl] Schwanz [5] **joy** [dʒɔɪ] Freude [6] **pain** [peɪn] Schmerz [7] (to) **shine** [ʃaɪn], shone, shone [ʃɒn], *AE* [ʃəʊn] leuchten, glänzen

1 New words

Look at these new words from the story and explain how you could understand them.

pole *(l. 13)*	pull off *(l. 32)*	invisible *(l. 70)*
cypress *(l. 17)*	root *(l. 33)*	rise *(ll. 85, 86)*
sink *(l. 22)*	trap *(l. 46)*	glow *(l. 88)*
sweat *(l. 30)*	distance *(l. 49)*	drift *(l. 111)*

- … is like the German word …
- I understood … from the context because …
- …

2 Understanding the story

You choose a) or b).

a Summarize the story in sentences that answer the five Ws (who, where, etc.). Start like this: *A boy goes out fishing …*

b) When and why do the boy’s feelings change? Note down line numbers where this happens.

3 Dramatic reading

a) Listen to lines 63–70 of the story. Comment on the reader’s speed, where he pauses, and which words he stresses.

b) Look at another 6 or 7 lines. Think about where to pause and which words to stress. Then read aloud to your partner.

Part A Practice

1 WORDS City holidays

p. 12

Can you find the verb-noun combinations in the snakes?

2 REVISION Your holidays (Simple past)

p. 12

Make questions for a partner.

Did you	stay at home / go away? make new friends? do any sports? visit friends/family?

What did you	do/see/play there?
Where did you	go/stay?
How did you	travel/get there?

Go back to b) on p. 12.

4 REVISION A message from London (Simple past or present perfect?)

p. 13

Complete Emily's message with the correct tenses. Look closely at the signal words for the simple past or the present perfect. They can help you to choose the right tense.

Hey Amelia,
Hi from London. I [1]… (arrive) on Friday evening (with Mum and Dad), so we [2]… (already do) a few things. Yesterday morning we [3]… (go) up to the roof of a building where we [4]… (have) a great view. On the roof we [5]… (meet) two boys – Luke and Mo. They [6]… (give) us some tips. Luke [7]… (tell) us about a carnival at a place called Notting Hill.
After lunch we [8]… (visit) St Paul's Cathedral and then we [9]… (take) a red London bus to Hyde Park. It [10]… (be) beautiful there, and the park is really huge. [11]… you [12]… (ever be) there?
There are lots of places that we [13]… (not be) to yet – like Buckingham Palace, so I [14]… (not have) tea with the Queen yet! (LOL) And we [15]… (not visit) any museums yet, but Mum has plans!
[16]… you [17]… (enjoy) your trip to France last week? What [18]… (be) the weather like there? In London it [19]… (not rain) yet! Hugs, Emily xxx

Part B Practice

1 REVISION How can I get there?

p. 18

b) You're at Leicester Square Tube station.
Ask the way to other places on the map.
You can use these phrases to answer your partner's questions.

Go along … Street.
Cross … Road near the … .
Turn left between the … and the … .
Turn right behind the church/… .
Go past the hotel/… .
Go straight on until you get to …

How can I get to Covent Garden Market, please?

Walk along Cranbourn Street. Then turn right into …

Part C Practice

2 I've been living here … (Present perfect progressive)

p. 21

Complete Mo's sentences with *for* or *since*.

I'm a Londoner. I've been living here …

1 I'm a Londoner. I've been living here ... I was three.
2 I like languages. I've been learning German at school ... three years.
3 My sister Mishal loves music. She's been singing in a band ... over a year.
4 I have a blog. I've been writing posts ... last March.
5 My friend Luke and I love cricket. We've been playing in the same team ... a long time.
6 Luke is a big fan of Notting Hill Carnival. He's been going there ... he was twelve.

3 How long … ?

p. 21

b) Swap profiles.
Ask and answer like this:

How long have you been living in Berlin?

I've been living in Berlin for thirteen years.

How long have you been going to … Gymnasium?

Here are some example answers to questions about hobbies and sport.

I've been

learning the piano
playing the drums
playing computer games
playing football
going swimming
doing judo
collecting comics
taking photos

for
ten months.
a long time.
three years.
my whole life.

since
April.
Year 5.
last summer.
I was little.

Lead-in

2 A long journey

p. 35

c) Listen again. Say how the girl feels and how she shows her feelings when:

- her parents speak about her when they think she's asleep.
- her mother asks her if she wants to stop for lunch.
- her mother wants to listen to the weather report.
- her father asks her to explain some Welsh words.
- her father asks if she'd like to go on a train.
- her mother asks her the name of a lake.

You can find ideas in the box.

- She feels angry/bored/sad/unhappy.
- She speaks loudly / in an angry voice.
- She shouts.
- She makes a funny sound.
- She says she doesn't want to …
- She says her mother/father can/can't/should …

Part A Practice

1 WORDS Jobs

p. 37

b) Write sentences for the other jobs in the box.

1 ... in films or plays or TV shows.
2 ... draw or paint pictures.
3 ... work on a farm.
4 ... are doctors for people's teeth.
5 ... make furniture.

actor · +architect · artist · +astronaut · carpenter · dentist · farmer · +hairdresser · +musician · +painter · scientist

2 REVISION Tom thinks he'll be an astronaut (*will*-future)

p. 37

a) What do you think you'll be or do in the future? Copy the chart and add ideas.
Then make appointments with three classmates and interview them.

You can use these ideas about your future.

live in another town/country · be a star · have a family · become a farmer/teacher/… · go on a bike tour across the Sahara · travel to Mars … · be rich and famous

What we will be/do	Me	Partner A	Partner B	Partner C
in 5 years				
in 10 years				
in 20 years				

Part B Practice

2 If I were a police officer, … (Conditional 2)

p. 42

Think of six jobs. Write a sentence about what you could or would do in each job.
If I were a police officer, I'd catch lots of thieves.
If I became a cameraman, I could film action movies.

Match the ideas in the boxes to make more sentences.

If …	I would / I could …
architect	be nice to my students.
artist	grow vegetables in my fields.
carpenter	paint pictures of famous people.
designer	build the highest building in the world.
hairdresser	play songs in the pedestrian zone.
farmer	make a desk for my room.
musician	make beautiful clothes.
teacher	cut my friends' hair for free.

Workbook 7–9 (pp. 18–19)

3 What would happen if …? (Conditional 2)

p. 43

a) Make notes like this. You can use the ideas from the list.

Idea	+	–
run away to London	see Mo and Luke	no place to live
shout at Dylan		
walk alone in the hills		
invite classmates home		
stop speaking Welsh		
ask a teacher for help		

- laugh at her
- shout back
- feel sad
- lose her way
- be more friendly
- become her friends
- give her some good tips
- have time to think
- not learn the language
- not feel at home in North Wales

4 If this was our garden, we would … (Conditional 2)

p. 43

a) Think: How would you clean up the garden if it was yours? Write three sentences that begin:
– If this was our garden, we would …
These nouns and verbs might be useful:

Nouns

fence · flowers · grass · tree · tyre · weed

Verbs

cut · repair · plant · water · weed

2 More help

Text

2 A fair punishment

p. 49

a) What do you think about Dylan and Emily's punishment?
Read the statements below. Choose the five that you agree with most and write them down.

FAIR BECAUSE …
- It's very dangerous on the roof.
- They knew that they weren't allowed to go up.
- They're lucky that they didn't fall.
- Mrs Grant was right to be angry. She's responsible for a lot of students.
- Mrs Grant didn't send Dylan and Emily home. They only had to wash the floors.

NOT FAIR BECAUSE …
- The kids only looked at the stars and sang.
- They didn't do anything dangerous.
- The door to the roof was open.
- Mrs Grant didn't listen when Dylan tried to explain why they were on the roof.
- It isn't right to tell children to clean toilets.
- It would be enough to wash the corridor floors.

3 More help

Part C Practice

2 Pronunciation (Consonants)

p. 73

b) Listen. Which of the words in brackets do you hear? Write it down.

1 the red … (card/cart)
2 with a red … (card/cart)
3 a lovely … beach (white/wide)
4 lots of … beaches (white/wide)
5 all the different … in Dublin (sides/sights)
6 on different … in the match (sides/sights)
7 put it in the … of the car (back/bag)
8 put your … in the car (back/bag)
9 on your own two … (feed/feet)
10 time to … her (feed/feet)
11 then it went … (bang/bank)
12 we went to the … (bang/bank)

Text

1 The horse ride

p. 77

Find these key words in parts of the story:

PEOPLE AND ANIMALS

Tiffany, Pearl, Oreo
Philip, a vet

TOPICS

country, phone
famine, help
rattlesnake

Use the words in sentences when you talk to your partner.

Part A Practice

1 BE and AE (British and American English)

p. 90

biscuit · chips · flat · holiday · lift · mobile · pavement · queue · rubbish · shop · trousers · underground

apartment · cell phone · cookie · elevator · French fries · garbage · line · pants · sidewalk · store · subway · vacation

b) Complete these sentences with words from the lists you made in a).

Partner A: Use a BE word in these sentences:

1 We don't live in a house – we live in a/an …
2 I need to call my dad. Where's my …?
3 I don't want to wait – the … is much too long.
4 It's faster to use the … than to go up the stairs.
5 I'm hungry. Let's get a hamburger and some …

Partner B: Use an AE word in these sentences.

6 Our last … was wonderful: we went to Rügen.
7 Do you know a good … where you can buy CDs?
8 It isn't far, so take the bus, not the …
9 Can I have a glass of milk and a …, please?
10 Their front garden is terrible – it's full of …

Read your sentences to each other.
Partner B: Say the correct AE word for your partner's BE word.
Partner A: Say the correct BE word for your partner's AE word.

Part A

4 Stop using social media ??!!

p. 113

b) Choose what you think is the most important pro and the most important con of social media use. Make notes to support your opinion.

Possible pros:
- good for education (working with partners, help with research, …)
- personal life (connect with friends, networking, express own identity, …)
- creative life (taking photos, making films, writing, …)
- finding good advice (on health, relationships, …)

Possible cons:
- personal life (online bullying, feeling unliked, fake information about you, …)
- time (too much time spent, no time for other stuff, …)
- personal data (putting too much online, hacking, …)
- too much time alone (as too much time online, harder to talk to people in real life, …)
- research: hard to know if information is real or fake

Part A Practice

5 REVISION I'll go for a walk if it doesn't rain (Conditional 1)

p. 115

Complete the sentences with the correct form of the verbs.

1 The weather seems OK. I (go) for a walk later if it (not rain).
2 Yes, and if you (get back) in time, we (watch) that film on TV.
3 Please hurry up! We (be) late for the party if we (not leave) now.
4 If you (need) anything from the shops, just say, and I (get) it for you.
5 If I (go) to the market, I (remember) that you love strawberries.
6 Careful! If you (use) too much salt, the soup (not taste) very nice.
7 Haven't you had enough? You (be) sick if you (eat) so much!
8 Be careful with that plate. It (break) if you (drop) it.

6 REVISION If I went fishing in New Orleans ... (Conditional 2)

p. 115

Say what you would do if you were one of the people or animals in the pictures.
Make as many conditional 2 sentences as you can. Use the ideas to help you.

1

If I went fishing in New Orleans, I'd watch out for alligators.
If I saw an alligator, I would ...
If the alligator ... , I would ...
If I were the alligator, I could ...

- run away as fast as possible
- leave the fish in the water
- try to speak nicely to the alligator
- smile at the boy
- ask for some fish

2

If I were the boy, ...
If I were the girl, ...
If I were the little dog, ...
If I were the big dog, ...

- take my dog and walk away
- laugh
- ask the little dog to stop barking
- bite the other dog
- call for help

3

If I were the woman, ...
If I were the boy, ...
If I were the girl, ...
If I were the monkey, ...

- give the ice cream to the monkey
- shout at the boy
- give the woman money to clean her clothes
- move away
- move to Africa
- try to get the ice cream

Part B Practice

3 I wish I had been more careful (*wish* + past perfect)

← p. 121

a) Look at the pictures. Think about what might have happened.
Then imagine you are the person in the picture and make a sentence like these for each situation.

I wish *I had been more careful when I climbed the tree*. I wish *I hadn't run down the stairs so quickly*.

Use the ideas below or your own ideas.

A

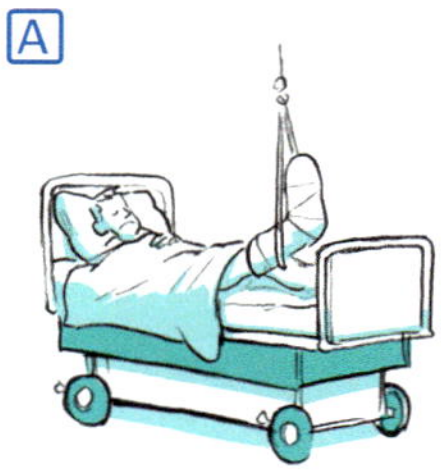

- be more careful
- not run down stairs so quickly
- kick ball, not goal
- not go to ski resort

B

- not drive fast
- not use mobile
- ask Mum to drive
- see tree

C

- not go into shop
- take off backpack
- see lamp on table
- not take so much stuff

D

- not go outside
- read weather forecast
- take umbrella
- wear coat

E

- wake up earlier
- run faster
- not go to bed so late
- do more sport

4 ... if you had been more careful (Conditional 3)

← p. 121

c) Write a short dialogue with a person from one the pictures in 3. Use one conditional 3 sentence. Act out your dialogue together. Use the ideas below, or your own ideas.

A
A: Hi, I'm in hospital. My leg is broken.
B: I bet you wish you (not go) on holiday.
A: Right, if I (not go), I (not break) my leg.

C
A: I had an accident in a shop with a lamp.
B: Do you wish you (not take) your backpack?
A: Yes, if I (take off) my backpack, I (not break) the lamp.

D
A: I got very wet yesterday.
B: I bet you wish you (not go) outside.
A: Well, if I (wear) a coat, I (not get) wet.

E
A: I missed the bus this morning.
B: I guess you wish you (run) faster.
A: Or if I (wake up) earlier, I (not be) late.

Unit 1

Hidden words

p. 12, 3 REVISION Have you ever ...?

a) Copy the grid.

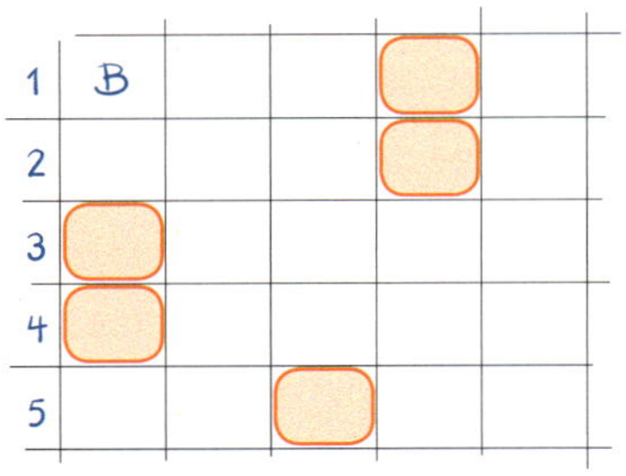

Write in the simple past of these verbs.

1 BEGIN
2 CHOOSE
3 DRIVE
4 HEAR
5 THROW

Use the letters in the orange boxes to make the name of a famous London building.

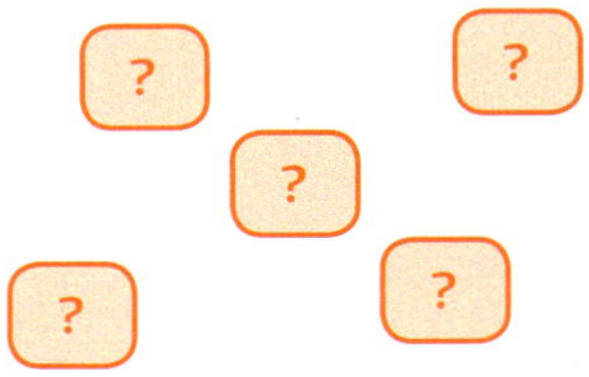

b) Copy the grid.

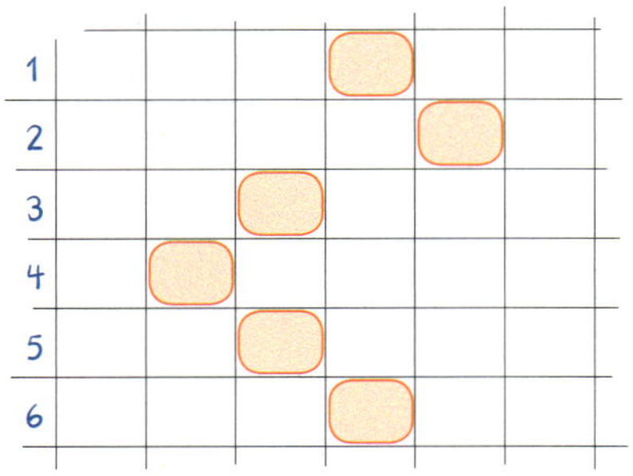

Write in the past participle of these verbs.

1 AGREE
2 BECOME
3 CHOOSE
4 DRIVE
5 JUMP
6 PLAY

Use the letters in the orange boxes to make the name of a game.

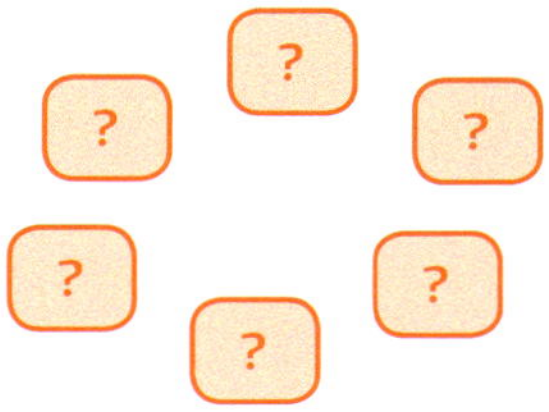

True or false?

p. 21, 3 How long ...?

Read the black sentences. Then decide if the green sentences are true or false. Correct the false sentences.

1 We moved here in 2010. Our neighbours moved here one year after us.
a) Our neighbours have been living here since 2009.
b) We have been living here longer than our neighbours.
c) Our neighbours have been living here for two years.

2 I got up at 7 o'clock and had breakfast at 8. It started raining during breakfast. It's 3 o'clock in the afternoon now and it is still raining.
a) It has been raining for 8 hours.
b) It has been raining since 7 o'clock.
c) It has been raining since breakfast.

3 Mrs Adams got to the bus stop at 10:10. Mrs Bell got there 5 minutes before Mrs Adams. When Mrs Crown got to the bus stop, nobody was waiting there. After 10 minutes Mrs Bell came. It is now 10:15.
a) Mrs Crown has been waiting the longest.
b) Mrs Bell has been waiting for the bus since 10 o'clock.
c) Mrs Crown has been waiting for 15 minutes.

Word games

p. 37, 3 REVISION If I don't go to bed …

Do a) or b).

a) Find the fourth word

1

music	musician
science	???

2

guitar	instrument
table	???

3

cloud	cloudy
???	rocky

4

farmer	farm
teacher	???

5

drive	car
???	plane

6

carpenter	furniture
???	pictures

7

hairdresser	hair
???	teeth

8

April	spring
October	???

9

shoe	foot
???	hand

b) Words from a Welsh village

A village in Wales has the longest place name in Europe:
Llanfairpwllgwyngyllgogerychwyrndrobwllllantysiliogogogoch.
It also has a shorter name: *Llanfairpwll.*
Make as many words as you can from the shorter name.

Unit 3 When is Tina's birthday?

p. 68, 2 Three tourists in Santa Fe

Complete this text with the correct prepositions and you will find out when Tina's birthday is.
Use *at*, *in* or *on*.

Tina's birthday isn't in the shortest month of the year. It isn't in one of the longest either. That means it must be [1]... April, June, September or November. But when is it? Her birthday isn't [2]... the autumn, so it must be [3]... the spring or the summer. When Tina was 'sweet sixteen' she had a big party. She didn't have one the year before because her 15th birthday was [4]... a Thursday, and [5]... Friday morning she had a test at school. She couldn't have a party [6]... the weekend because her father had planned dinner in a restaurant [7]... Friday evening to celebrate her mother's 40th birthday. And her mother had already organized a big party for her friends [8]... Saturday. But this year Tina started planning very early. She decided to have a garden party because the weather is usually good [9]... her birthday. And it doesn't get dark very early. The party started [10]... 5 o'clock [11]... the afternoon and finished late [12]... night. The last friends left [13]... 4 o'clock [14]... the morning! Now you should know the month, but what date is Tina's birthday? Is it [15]... the 5th, 6th, 7th or 8th? Count how many times you used the preposition ***on*** and you will know! And if you need a bit more help, the month and the date are the same!

Unit 4 Guess the AE word

p. 90, 1 BE and AE

You have learned the BE words on the left. But you haven't learned most of the AE words.
For each orange word, guess the correct American English word: a), b) or c).

1 Please put that plastic bag in the litter bin.	a) trash hole	b) trash can	c) trash box
2 The tram stops right outside our house.	a) streetcar	b) street train	c) rail bus
3 It's a nice flat, but the street is very loud.	a) living	b) apartment	c) parterre
4 We love playing football in our garden.	a) green	b) park	c) yard
5 The lights have gone out. Do you have a torch?	a) lightthrower	b) flasher	c) flashlight
6 I've made a mistake. Where's my rubber?	a) eraser	b) paper cleaner	c) correcter

Unit 5 Good guy, bad guy

p. 115, 6 REVISION If I went fishing in New Orleans, ...

Copy and complete this quiz. Write two answers for each question.
A is the "good guy" answer. B is the "bad guy" answer.
When you're finished, swap quizzes with another early finisher and answer the questions.

What would you do ...

1 if someone in front of you dropped (drop) €50?
A: I'd pick it up and give it back to them. B: I'd pick it up and put it in my pocket.

2 if an old woman ... (get on) the bus and there were no free seats?
A: I'd ... B: I'd stay in my seat. Old people can stand too.

3 if you ... (break) a neighbour's window while you were playing ball?

4 if you ... (not like) the birthday present your best friend gave you?

5 if you ... (see) a friend stealing something in a shop?

Unit 1

6 Everyday English: Small talk

p. 13

c) Partner A:
You're at a tourist sight in London (choose your sight).
You want a photo of yourself at the sight and ask a person who is standing there.
He/She takes the photo and starts to talk to you.
Have a nice conversation with him/her.

Unit 5

5 Something went wrong

p. 121

Partner A:
Read the text and make notes on the key points.
Use your notes to tell your partner what happened.

"My text is about someone who ..."
...
"I bet they wish they had/hadn't ..."

A few years ago, when I was younger, there was snow late on Christmas Day. We don't get much snow here, so it's always very special when we do. My sister and I were bored, so we decided to go out. Our street was on a hill, so we took the sledge[1]. At the bottom of the hill there was a main road. We went down the sidewalk on our sledge, got faster and faster, and tried to stop at the end before the big road. But we were still too fast, and when we got to the bottom of the hill, we flew off the sidewalk. We crashed right into Mrs Brown's car and broke its mirror. We both hurt our shoulders but were laughing, because we were glad to be alive. Then Mrs Brown came out of her house, saw us, saw the broken mirror, and looked very, very angry.

[1] **sledge** [sledʒ] Schlitten

4 STUDY SKILLS Skimming a text

p. 124

c) Work in groups of three. Imagine you have to give a presentation. Each of you has a different topic:

Partner A: Wildlife in the Louisiana swamps
Partner B: New Orleans swamp tours
Partner C: The people of the swamps

Skim the three texts on these pages and decide which one you should read. Then say which text you chose and why.

1 Where no one else goes

What should you expect from kayaking in a swamp?

A perfect day
Imagine this: it's a perfect day, 79 degrees and sunny. The cypress trees rise like monuments to nature from the Pearl River where we start. Two guides start you on an easy tour, down river, so that you can learn how to paddle. Yes, the river isn't slow everywhere. And watch out for the bushes because there are poisonous snakes ... But isn't that why you're out here? For nature – beautiful and dangerous?

Meet the locals
As you paddle down river you see some of Louisiana's culture – swamp houses and boats are hidden in the trees or are on the river itself. If you run into other paddlers, they're wonderfully friendly.

Almost religious
As the trip goes on, you begin to paddle in and out of trees and go where other tours wouldn't take you. You find yourself in the middle of a swamp forest of cypresses and old oaks. The beauty of this view is almost religious: the sun streams through trees, and vines and Spanish moss hang from branches high and low. Nature is quietly buzzing around you, and if you can take a moment to be quiet and just watch, you might see alligators or other animals around the river.

2 Animals of the wetlands

Mammals

There are many wild mammals in the Louisiana wetlands. Examples are the coyote, muskrat, Norway rat and red fox. Armadillos also live in the wetlands as well as large mammals like the black bear.

Reptiles

Maybe the most famous of swamp animals, the American alligator is quite common. But it is still in danger. Several kinds of snakes make their home in the Louisiana wetlands. America's largest freshwater turtle, the alligator snapping turtle, shares the habitat with its cousin, the common snapping turtle.

Birds

Some of America's tallest birds love the fish in the Louisiana wetlands. Brown pelicans, which are endangered, also take advantage of the plentiful fish. Raptors live in the marshes of southern Louisiana. Migratory water birds and songbirds often make stopovers or actually spend the winter in these wetlands.

The Honey Island Swamp is home to snowy white egrets.

3 What is Cajun?

In America's largest swamp, the bayous and wetlands of Louisiana, lives a people like no other – the Cajuns.

Where their name comes from

After Britain beat France in the Seven Years' War in the late 18th century, French settlers from a part of Canada they called Acadia moved to Louisana's swamp country. The French called them "les Acadiens" or "les 'Cadiens". Later came the Americans, who could not pronounce "Acadien" or "Cadien". Instead they said "Cajun" and in this way gave the people of the swamps their name.

Cajuns still hunt gators in the swamps

Way of life

The Cajuns today still continue many of the traditions of the first Acadiens who came to live in the swamps, like hunting alligators. They are a thrifty, hard-working and religious folk. But they are also known for their "joie de vivre" and this expresses itself in the community festivals, dancing and food of bayou life. With their herbs, spices and other ingredients they make some of the most tasty dishes in North America.

Cajun music

Cajun music is known as Zydeco. Its traditions go back to the music of the French settlers of Canada. It is sometimes sad, sometimes happy, and sometimes both at the same time. In the past, the fiddle was the main instrument, but the accordion has become important too. Cajun music became more famous in 2007 when the Grammy Award for Best Zydeco Album was created.

Skills File – Inhalt

			Seite
READING SKILLS	SF 1	Skimming and scanning	154
	SF 2	Marking up a text REVISION	155
WRITING SKILLS	SF 3	Good sentences	156
	SF 4	Structuring a text	157
	SF 5	Paragraphs and topic sentences	157
	SF 6	Using time markers in a story	158
	SF 7	Giving feedback on a text	158
	SF 8	Revising your text	159
LANGUAGE SKILLS	SF 9	Mediation REVISION	160
	SF 10	Listening REVISION	161
	SF 11	Speaking REVISION	162
PROJECT AND PRESENTATION SKILLS	SF 12	Teamwork	163
	SF 13	Finding information online (Internet research)	163
	SF 14	Describing and presenting pictures REVISION	164
	SF 15	Putting a page together REVISION	164
	SF 16	Giving a good presentation REVISION	165
	SF 17	Peer feedback REVISION	165
STUDY SKILLS	SF 18	Understanding new words REVISION	166
	SF 19	Working with an English–German dictionary REVISION	166
	SF 20	Using a German–English dictionary	167
	SF 21	Study posters REVISION	167
	SF 22	Making and taking notes REVISION	168

In diesem **Skills File** findest du **Lernhilfen und Methoden,** die dir z.B. den Umgang mit Texten erleichtern, beim Schreiben von eigenen Texten und bei der Sprachmittlung helfen oder Tipps zum Vorbereiten von Präsentationen geben.

Alles, was du auf den *Study skills*- und *Writing course*-Seiten in den Units gelernt hast, wird hier noch einmal aufgenommen und erläutert.

Einige der Einträge wie z.B. **Study posters** kennst du schon aus Band 1 oder 2. Sie sollen dich an das schon Gelernte erinnern. Du erkennst sie am Zusatz REVISION.

READING SKILLS

SF 1 Skimming and scanning (Media skills)

➜ *p. 124*

Skimming *(reading for gist)* und Scanning *(reading for specific information)* sind Lesetechniken, die viel Zeit sparen, v. a. beim Lesen von langen Texten.

SKIMMING

Angenommen, du suchst Informationen zu einem bestimmten Thema, z. B. für ein Referat oder als Antwort für eine Hausaufgabe. Deine Suche im Internet liefert eine Vielzahl an Ergebnissen, die für dein Thema relevant sein könnten. Die alle gründlich zu lesen, würde zu viel Zeit kosten. Hier hilft das Skimming.

Step 1: Siehe dir die folgenden Textteile an, um zu sehen, worum es im Text geht:

- Überschrift und Unterüberschriften
- Bilder und Bildunterschriften
- den ersten Satz jedes Absatzes – dieser Satz ist meist der *topic sentence*, der die Hauptidee des Absatzes nennt
- den letzten Absatz des Textes, der oft eine Zusammenfassung des Textes enthält

Step 2: Fasse für dich selbst den Text in ein paar Worten zusammen. Wenn dir das ohne Probleme gelingt, dann weißt du, um was es in dem Text geht – und dass dein Skimming erfolgreich war.

TIPP
Mache dir um unbekannten Wortschatz erstmal keine Gedanken – dafür ist Zeit, wenn du feststellst, dass der Text für dich geeignet ist.

SCANNING

Wenn du in einem Text nach Informationen oder Antworten auf eine Frage suchst, aber nicht den ganzen Text lesen willst, reicht es oft, wenn du den Text nach Schlüsselwörtern *(keywords)* absuchst und nur dort genauer liest, wo du sie findest.

Step 1: Überlege dir *keywords*, die für dein Thema oder deine Frage relevant sind. Wenn du z. B. nach den Öffnungszeiten eines Museums usw. suchst, dann könnten das Wörter (oder Symbole) sein wie *open, (opening) hours, days,* oder Zahlen wie *8am–5pm*.

Step 2: Gehe mit deinen Augen sehr schnell durch den Text und suche nach deinen *keywords*. Du kannst auch mit dem Finger in breiten Bewegungen wie bei einem „S" von oben bis unten durch den Text gehen, bis du eines oder mehrere deiner *keywords* gefunden hast.

Step 3: Lies die Textstelle, die dein *keyword* enthält, um zu sehen, ob sie die gewünschten Informationen enthält. Wenn nicht, scanne weiter.

TIPP
Wenn du mit Texten im Internet arbeitest, kann dein Browser dir viel Arbeit abnehmen.
Mit Strg+F (Cmd+F am Mac) kannst du nach deinen *keywords* suchen und nur die Textstellen lesen, in denen ein *keyword* markiert ist.

SF 2 Marking up a text REVISION

Wenn du mit Kopien von Texten arbeitest, kannst du wichtige Informationen darin markieren, um sie einfacher wiederzufinden oder als Grundlage für die Weiterarbeit zu verwenden, z. B. wenn du eine Zusammenfassung schreiben oder mit Hilfe des Textes eine inhaltliche Frage beantworten sollst.

Step 1: Lies dir die Aufgabe genau durch und überlege, welche Informationen du zur Beantwortung brauchst. Behalte dies im Kopf, während du den Text liest.

Step 2: Lies den Text und markiere nur Informationen, die wichtig sind. Nicht jeder Satz enthält Wichtiges, und oft reicht es aus, nur ein oder zwei Wörter in einem Satz zu markieren. Hebe wichtige Informationen hervor, z. B. durch Unterstreichen, Einkreisen oder Markieren mit einem Textmarker.

Step 3: Mach dir kurze Notizen am Rand – z. B. kurze Überschriften oder Stichwörter –, die den Inhalt kurz zusammenfassen. (➔ *SF 22*)

TIPP
1. Verwende unterschiedliche Farben für unterschiedliche Aufgaben/Fragestellungen.
2. Markiere wirklich nur Stichwörter, sonst wird es unübersichtlich.

Fifty years ago today, Rudy Lombard, who is black, and his friend Lanny Goldfinch, who is white, walked into a diner in downtown New Orleans. With two other black friends, they took seats at a whites-only counter. Immediately they were asked to leave. They didn't. Instead they sat Many of those who took part were students, both white and black. Through their protests, they put themselves in great danger. People were arrested, beaten up and murdered. Some spent time in prison. Some lost their jobs. But they never gave up and finally, after two years, the city ended segregation

WRITING SKILLS

SF 3 Good sentences

➔ p. 16

Gut formulierte Sätze machen deine Texte interessanter und anschaulicher. Um gute Sätze zu schreiben, solltest du folgenden Dinge beachten.

Wie kann ich meine Texte lebendiger und besser gestalten?

Die folgenden Techniken helfen dir, dich gut und abwechslungsreich auszudrücken und damit den Stil deiner Texte zu verbessern.

Verwende …

- ***Adjektive***, wenn du Dinge, Orte und Menschen näher beschreiben möchtest:
  - a bright face
  - a fantastic trip
- aber die Adjektive good, bad and nice nicht zu häufig in deinem Text. Ersetze sie durch andere Adjektive mit einer ähnlichen bzw. genaueren Bedeutung:
  - a nice teacher: a friendly teacher, a helpful teacher, …
  - a good book: an interesting book, a funny book, …
- ***Adverbien***, um Handlungen näher zu beschreiben:
  - They walked home slowly.
  - She talked quietly.
- Ausdrücke wie really, very, a bit etc., um Aussagen zu verdeutlichen oder zu verstärken:
  - It was a really sad story.
  - The houses are very high.
- adverbiale Bestimmungen der Zeit ***(time markers)***, um zeitliche Abfolgen oder Zeitpunkte zu verdeutlichen:
  - I am going to London next month.
  - He came home yesterday at 5 o'clock.

  (➔ *SF 6*)
- ***Konjunktionen*** wie and, but oder because, um deine Sätze zu verbinden und ihnen eine klare, gut nachvollziehbare Struktur zu geben:
  - We went to the London Eye, but it was very expensive.
- ***Relativsätze***, um Sätze zu verbinden oder eine Sache oder eine Person näher zu erklären:
  - This is the shop which sells the best ice cream in Passau.

SF 4 Structuring a text

Media skills

→ p. 95

Welche Struktur braucht mein Text?

Ein guter Text besteht in der Regel aus den folgenden drei Teilen:

- eine ***Einleitung*** (introduction): hier sagst du, worum es in dem gesamten Text geht. Manchmal formulierst du hier auch ein Problem, das in dem Text erörtert werden soll.
- ein ***Haupt- oder Mittelteil*** (body): dieser Teil ist in mehrere Absätze gegliedert und präsentiert die Details zu deinem Thema.
- ein ***Schluss*** (conclusion): hier gibst du deinem Text ein passendes, interessantes Ende.

My Trip to Wales

Last summer I wanted to go to Wales because I like the mountains.

First I had to find some information on Wales. So I went to the library and looked for books about Wales. I found a book with some interesting information on hiking tours and I also found a camping guide for Wales. I went home with three books under my arm.

At home I started to plan for my trip. I read all the books and took notes on hiking trails, the weather and the equipment I would need for camping and hiking. After a few days I knew where I wanted to go and what I wanted to do there.

I did not want to go to Wales alone, so I had to find someone to go with me. I called most of my friends and told them about my plan. Some of them did not want to go hiking and others had no money for the trip. But my friend Judith agreed to go with me. We decided to go in late August.

Judith and I spent two lovely weeks in Wales. We went to Snowdonia and enjoyed the fantastic mountains. We stayed in a lovely bed and breakfast and met lots of really nice people. Before we went home we spent two very interesting days in Cardiff.

This was one of the best summer holidays I ever had. Go to Wales - it's fantastic!

SF 5 Paragraphs and topic sentences

→ p. 45

Wozu brauche ich Absätze?

Man kann einen längeren Text einfacher lesen und schneller verstehen, wenn dieser in Absätze eingeteilt ist.

Was sollte ich bei Absätzen beachten?

- Beginne mit einem interessanten *topic sentence*.
- Fange für jeden neuen Aspekt einen neuen Absatz an.
- Beende deinen Text im letzten Absatz/in den letzten Absätzen mit einer Zusammenfassung oder etwas Persönlichem.

Was sind topic sentences?

Jeder Absatz sollte mit einem Einleitungssatz beginnen. Dieser *topic sentence* beschreibt, worum es in dem Absatz geht.

Wichtige Dinge, die du in einem *topic sentence* ansprechen kannst, sind z.B.

- ***Orte:*** *My trip to Berlin was exciting.*
- ***Personen:*** *The Beatles are one of the most famous bands in the world.*
- ***Aktivitäten:*** *Lots of people ride their bike every day.*

SF 6 Using time markers in a story

➜ p. 75

Zeitangaben ***(time marker)*** helfen den Lesenden, sich in einem Text oder einer Geschichte zeitlich zurechtzufinden. Dazu machen sie einen Text anschaulicher.

Welche Zeitangaben sollte ich machen?

Verwende *time markers*, um …

- die Reihenfolge von Ereignissen zu verdeutlichen:
  at first, next, finally, …
- zu zeigen, wie viel Zeit zwischen einzelnen Ereignissen vergeht:
  for half an hour, just three minutes later, I counted thirty seconds, …
- zu verdeutlichen, wie langsam oder schnell etwas passiert:
  immediately, it took hours, faster than I could look, …
- zu sagen, wenn etwas zeitgleich passiert:
  while I was waiting, during the lesson, as we came round the corner, …
- die Ereignisse eines Textes/einer Geschichte zeitlich einzuordnen:
  two summers ago, last Halloween, on my way home from school yesterday, …

SF 7 Giving feedback on a text

➜ p. 17

Warum ist Feedback zu Texten wichtig?

Wenn du einen Text geschrieben hast, ist es oft schwierig, deine Fehler oder Schwächen des Textes zu entdecken. Deshalb kann es sehr hilfreich sein, eine Rückmeldung von einem Partner/einer Partnerin zu bekommen.

Was muss ich bei Feedback zu Texten beachten?

Wenn du jemandem eine Rückmeldung zu einem Text geben sollst, gelten dafür grundsätzlich die gleichen Regeln wie bei jeder anderen Art von Feedback auch. (➜ *SF 17)*

Folgende Schritte helfen, wenn du eine Rückmeldung geben sollst:

1. Lies den Text sorgfältig durch, um dir einen ersten, allgemeinen Eindruck zu verschaffen.
2. Beim zweiten Lesen achte besonders auf die Punkte, zu denen du eine Rückmeldung geben sollst. Bei geschriebenen Texten gehören dazu in der Regel
   - Inhalt,
   - Struktur,
   - Wortwahl und abwechslungsreiche Sätze,
   - Grammatik und Rechtschreibung.
3. Streiche Fehler oder weniger gelungene Teile im Text an und mache dir Notizen zu wichtigen Punkten. Wenn du einen Feedbackbogen hast, benutze ihn und trage dort dein Feedback ein.

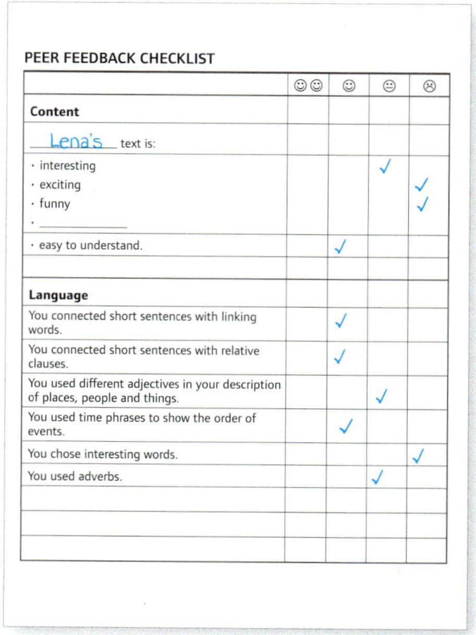

PEER FEEDBACK CHECKLIST

	☺☺	☺	😐	☹
Content				
Lena's text is:				
· interesting			✓	
· exciting				✓
· funny				✓
· ___________				
· easy to understand.		✓		
Language				
You connected short sentences with linking words.		✓		
You connected short sentences with relative clauses.		✓		
You used different adjectives in your description of places, people and things.			✓	
You used time phrases to show the order of events.		✓		
You chose interesting words.				✓
You used adverbs.			✓	

4. Beginne deine Rückmeldung mit einer Aufzählung der gelungenen Teile/Aspekte des Textes. Es ist immer gut, positiv anzufangen.
5. Erläutere deine kritischen Anmerkungen und mache Verbesserungsvorschläge. Gib Hinweise, wie dein Partner/deine Partnerin bei der Überarbeitung des Textes vorgehen könnte.

SF 8 Revising your text

Egal, ob du eine Rückmeldung von einem Partner/einer Partnerin bekommen hast oder nicht – einen Text solltest du auf jeden Fall noch einmal gut prüfen, bevor du ihn z.B. abgibst.

Worauf muss ich achten?

1. **Stimmt die *Gliederung*?**
   Jeder Text braucht
   - eine Einleitung, die in das Thema einführt,
   - einen Hauptteil, der das Thema ausführt,
   - einen Schluss, der alles auf den Punkt bringt.

   (➡ *SF 4)*

2. **Stimmt der *Aufbau* der Absätze?**
   Jeder Absatz
   - befasst sich mit einem zusammenhängenden Gedanken,
   - beginnt mit einem ***topic sentence***, der diesen Gedanken einführt.

   (➡ *SF 5)*

3. **Stimmen die *Verknüpfungen*?**
   Gute *linking words*
   - schaffen Verbindungen zwischen Sätzen oder Satzteilen,
   - helfen, Zusammenhänge besser darzustellen und verständlich zu machen.

   (➡ *SF 3)*

4. **Sind die *Zeitangaben* richtig gesetzt?**
   Time markers
   - helfen, sich z.B. in einer Geschichte zurechtzufinden,
   - machen das Geschehen anschaulicher.

   (➡ *SF 6)*

5. **Enthält der Text *Adjektive* und *Adverbien*?**
   Adjektive und Adverbien
   - erlauben nähere Beschreibungen von Personen und Dingen
   - machen Texte anschaulicher.

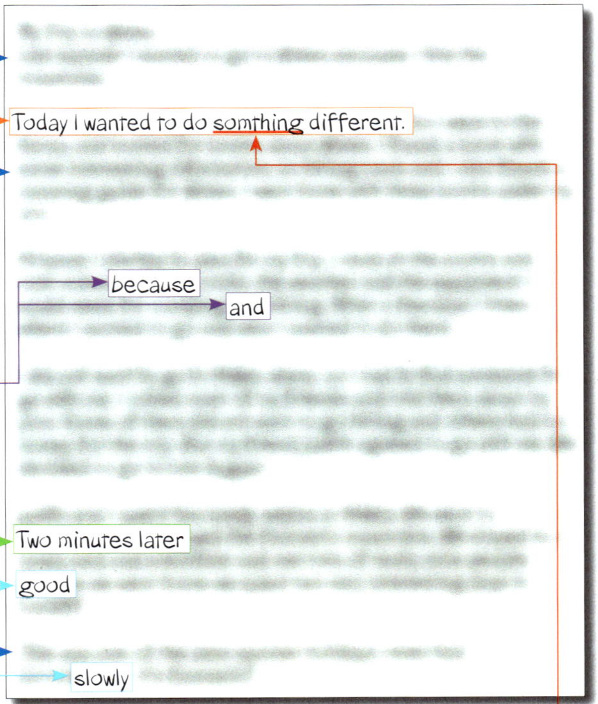

6. **Hat der Text sprachliche/grammatikalische *Fehler*?**
   Überprüfe deinen Text
   - auf Rechtschreibung,
   - grammatischen Formen, z.B. die Verbformen,
   - Satzbau *(word order)* usw.

LANGUAGE SKILLS

SF 9 Mediation REVISION

Manchmal musst du zwischen zwei Sprachen vermitteln. Das nennt man ***mediation***.

Wann brauche ich Mediation?

Hier sind einige Situationen, in denen es sein kann, dass du zwischen Deutsch und Englisch vermitteln musst:

- Du gibst englische Informationen auf deutsch wieder:
  Du fährst z.B. mit deiner Familie nach Großbritannien und deine Großeltern, Eltern oder Geschwister wollen wissen, was jemand gesagt hat oder was auf einer Informationstafel steht.
- Du gibst deutsche Informationen auf englisch wieder:
  Wenn du eine/n Austauschschüler/in aus England (oder einem anderen Land) bei dir zu Hause zu Gast hast, kann es sein, dass er/sie wenig Deutsch spricht und deine Hilfe braucht.
- In schriftlichen Prüfungen musst du manchmal in einem englischen Text gezielt nach Informationen suchen und diese auf Deutsch wiedergeben. Oder du sollst Informationen aus einem deutschen Text auf Englisch wiedergeben.

Worauf muss ich bei Mediation achten?

Übersetze nicht alles wörtlich, sondern gib nur das für die gegebene Situation Wesentliche wieder. Du kannst Unwichtiges weglassen und Sätze umformulieren.

Was kann ich tun, wenn ich ein bestimmtes Wort nicht kenne?

Vielleicht findest du es manchmal schwer, mündliche Aussagen oder schriftliche Textvorlagen in die andere Sprache zu übertragen, z. B. weil

- dein Wortschatz nicht ausreicht
- dir bekannte Wörter „im Stress" nicht einfallen
- spezielle Fachbegriffe auftauchen.

Viele Wörter kannst du umschreiben, z. B. mithilfe von Relativsätzen wie:

It's somebody/a person who ...
It's something that you use to ...
It's an animal that ...
It's a place that/where ...

SF 10 Listening REVISION

Manchmal ist es schwer, einem Hörtext zu folgen, weil du die Sprechenden nicht sehen kannst und du dich auch noch auf die Aufgaben zum Hörtext konzentrieren musst. Die folgenden Tipps können dir beim Hörverstehen helfen.

Was kann ich vor dem Hören tun?

- Sieh dir die Aufgabenstellung genau an. Was sollst du heraushören?
- Schau nach Überschriften und Bildern zum Text. Sie können oft schon einige Fragen beantworten helfen: Wer spricht mit wem, wo sind sie, worüber reden sie?
- Überlege, was du selbst zum Thema schon weißt und welche englischen Begriffe daher im Gespräch fallen könnten.

Worauf kann ich während des Hörens achten?

- Lass dich nicht verwirren, wenn es mehrere Sprecher oder Sprecherinnen gibt. Versuche, die unterschiedlichen Stimmen Personen zuzuordnen. Das macht es einfacher, dem Gespräch zu folgen.
- Wenn es um generelles Hörverstehen geht, höre gezielt auf die Hintergrundgeräusche. So kannst du herausfinden, ob das Gespräch z.B. am Strand, auf der Straße oder in der Schule stattfindet.
- Sicher wirst du einiges nicht verstehen. Das ist nicht schlimm – versuche aus dem, was du alles verstanden hast, das Fehlende zu erschließen.

Worauf kann ich beim Hören achten, wenn es um Details geht?

- Gerate nicht in Panik, wenn du denkst, du hättest etwas Wichtiges verpasst. Konzentriere dich auf die nächste wichtige Information.
- Ignoriere Hintergrundgeräusche. Wenn du bestimmte Details heraushören sollst, sind sie unwichtig und lenken nur ab.
- Mach nur kurze Notizen, z.B. Anfangsbuchstaben, Symbole und Stichworte (➔ *SF 22*)
- Je nachdem, welche Details du heraushören sollst, können Signalwörter helfen, dem Hörtext zu folgen und dich auf die Details zu konzentrieren:
  - Aufzählungen: *and, another, too, …*
  - Gegensätze: *although, but, …*
  - Gründe, Folgen: *because, so, so that, …*
  - Vergleiche: *larger/older/… than, as … as, more, most, …*
  - Reihenfolge: *before, after, then, next, later, …*

Was kann ich nach dem Hören tun?

- Vervollständige deine Notizen sofort.
- Wenn möglich, vergleiche mit einem Partner/einer Partnerin, was ihr verstanden habt.
- Wenn dir die Beantwortung einer Frage noch Schwierigkeiten macht, versuche schlau zu kombinieren.

SF 11 Speaking REVISION

Lies die beiden Dialoge. Welche Unterschiede erkennst du?
Wodurch entstehen sie?

Jen: Hi.
Ben: Hi.
Jen: It's a great parade.
Ben: Yeah.
Jen: Do you like the bands?
Ben: No.
Jen: The food smells good.
Ben: Yeah.
Jen: Do you want some too?
Ben: All right.
Jen: Do you live in Plymouth?
Ben: No.
Jen: …

Ed: Hi there, great parade, isn't it?
Jo: Yeah, I didn't know it was this big.
Ed: Is it your first time here, then?
Jo: That's right, I'm new in Plymouth.
Ed: Okay, so did you come here for the day?
Jo: Yeah, we arrived early this morning … Wow, that food smells good.
Ed: Are you hungry? Look, my friends have this pasties stall over there. Do you want to try one?
Jo: Okay, yes please.
Ed: My name's Ed, by the way.
Jo: Hello Ed, I'm Jo.

Wie kann ich freundlich ein Gespräch führen?

Wenn du dich mit jemandem auf Englisch unterhalten willst, können dir diese Hinweise helfen:

1 Eröffne das Gespräch mit einer freundlichen Anrede oder Frage.

2 Antworte nicht nur mit einem Wort, wenn dich dein Gesprächspartner/deine Gesprächspartnerin etwas fragt.

3 Zeige Interesse an deinem Gesprächspartner/deiner Gesprächspartnerin, indem du auch ein paar Fragen stellst.

4 Erzähle auch etwas von dir, um das Gespräch am Laufen zu halten.

5 Verabschiede dich am Ende freundlich.

1 *Hi, can I sit here?*
Hello, how are you?
Hi there, are you from Plymouth?

2 *Fine, thanks. / Yeah, sure.*
Yes, I am. / No, not really.

3 *What about you?*
I'm Nick and you are …?
Do you like …?
So what do you think …?

4 *I'm new here in …*
I'm with my friends over there.
I love these …
And I really like …

5 *Bye then.*
See you.
Have a good time!

PROJECT AND PRESENTATION SKILLS

SF 12 Teamwork

➜ p. 65

Bei Projekten arbeitet ihr oft im Team. Dabei solltet ihr eure unterschiedlichen Fähigkeiten und Talente einbringen und bestimmte Regeln beachten.

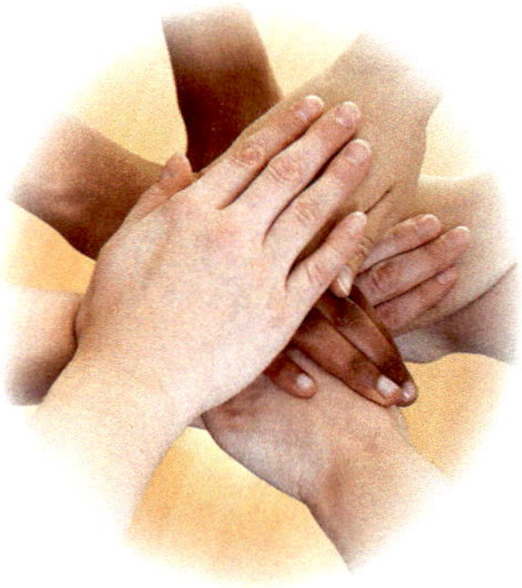

Was ist wichtig für gutes Teamwork?

Folgende Schritte können helfen, die Arbeit zu organisieren:

1. Legt ***Regeln*** für die Arbeit in der Gruppe fest, z.B. gegenseitige Unterstützung, pünktliches und zügiges Arbeiten, einander zuhören oder verschiedene Lösungen diskutieren usw.
2. Sammelt Ideen für die Bearbeitung eures Themas (z.B. in einer Mindmap). Wählt gemeinsam Unterthemen aus und legt die ***Arbeitsschritte*** fest, die für die Bearbeitung nötig sind.
3. ***Verteilt Rollen*** und Aufgaben nach euren Interessen und Fähigkeiten. Wenn ihr euch nicht einigen könnt, hilft Auslosen oder Würfeln.
   Folgende Rollen solltet ihr auf jeden Fall verteilen:
   - coordinator
   - writer/researcher
   - picture and layout editor
   - language watchdog
4. Macht einen ***Zeitplan*** für eure Arbeiten, an den sich alle halten sollten.
5. Am Ende der Arbeit sollte ein ***Rückblick*** stehen: Besprecht, was gelungen war und wo ihr Verbesserungsmöglichkeiten seht.

SF 13 Finding information online (Internet research)

Media skills

Das Internet ist voller Informationen und es ist nicht einfach, genau die Informationen zu finden, die du benötigst

Wie finde ich die Informationen, die ich brauche?

- Überlege, was die wichtigsten ***Stichwörter*** für dein Thema sind. Für das Thema "The Beatles in Hamburg" wären *Beatles* und *Hamburg* ein guter Start.
- Gib deine Stichwörter in eine ***Suchmaschine*** ein. Je mehr gute Stichwörter du eingibst, desto genauer sind die Ergebnisse. In der Infografik rechts kannst du sehen, wie du an ganz spezielle Informationen kommen kannst.
- Sieh dir mehrere ***Suchergebnisse*** an, um zu sehen, ob sie passen. Wenn du schnell ein bestimmtes Wort wie z.B. *Hamburg* finden willst, dann kannst du mit der Tastenkombination ***Strg + F*** danach suchen. Das Wort wird dann auf der Seite markiert und du kannst schnell sehen, ob die Information relevant ist.
- Achte darauf, wer die Webseite erstellt hat, um die ***Qualität*** der Suchergebnisse einzuschätzen. Sind sie eher zuverlässig (Online-Lexikon, bekannte Medien, …) oder eher persönliche Meinungen (Forum, Fan-Seite, …)?

Internet research
Tipps und Tricks

Wenn du ganz spezifische Informationen suchst, helfen diese Tricks:

Was du suchst: Artikel aus dem *Guardian* von 2016–2018 über den FC Liverpool in der Champions League.

Wie du danach suchst:

site:theguardian.com "FC Liverpool" "champions league" 2016..2018

site:	" "	..
sucht nur auf der genannten Seite	sucht den exakten Begriff	zeigt nur Ergebnisse aus diesem Zeitraum

Was du suchst: Einen englischsprachigen Bericht, am liebsten als PDF, über den Lebensraum von Füchsen.

Wie du danach suchst:

filetype:pdf intitle:habitat of *fox

filetype:	intitle:	*
sucht nur diesen Dateityp (pdf, doc, jpg usw.)	zeigt nur Ergebnisse, in denen dieses Wort im Titel auftaucht	sucht auch Worte wie Red Fox, Black Fox, Desert Fox usw.

- Kopiere nicht einfach ganze Artikel aus dem Internet. Mach dir Notizen und verwende deine eigenen Worte, um die Inhalte wiederzugeben.
- Setze dir ein Zeitlimit für deine Recherche und ordne dann dein Material. Prüfe, ob dir etwas fehlt und suche ggf. gezielt nach nur noch diesen Informationen.
- Lege alle interessanten Materialien zu deinem Thema in einem eigenen Ordner ab. Dann kannst du sie dir später genauer ansehen und auswählen, was du nutzen möchtest.

Was die Suchmaschine auch noch kann:

Definitionen: Wenn du schnell eine Definition für ein Wort suchst, kannst du das mit **define:** tun.

define:prejudice

Konvertieren: Tippe einfach die Einheit, die du schon hast und die, die du wissen möchtest.

50 kilograms in pounds

SF 14 Describing and presenting pictures REVISION Media skills

Manchmal sollst du ein Foto vor der Klasse vorstellen. Hier sind ein paar Hilfen.

Wie stelle ich ein Foto vor?

1 Stelle das Foto vor und sage, woher es kommt.

2 Beschreibe das Foto:
   - Sage, was wo zu sehen ist: *at the top/bottom* • *in the foreground/background* • *in the middle* • *on the left/right*
   - Diese Präpositionen sind auch hilfreich: *behind* • *between* • *in front of* • *next to* • *under* • *over*
   - Gehe bei der Beschreibung in einer bestimmten Reihenfolge vor, z.B. von links nach rechts oder von oben nach unten.

3 Sage, was dir an dem Foto gefällt oder nicht.

4 Wenn du mit der Vorstellung des Fotos fertig bist, bedanke dich fürs Zuhören und frage, ob noch jemand Fragen hat.

1 *I'd like to talk about this photo of … I found it on the internet/in a magazine/…*

2 *In the foreground you can see … I think the people in the photo are talking about …/having fun/celebrating/…*

3 *I really like/don't like the photo because … It's interesting/boring/exciting/ … because …*

4 *Thank you for listening. Do you have any questions?*

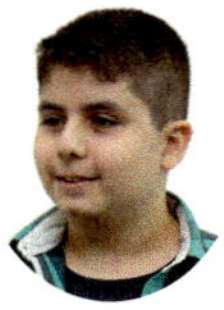

SF 15 Putting a page together REVISION Media skills

Wenn du eine Bildseite gestalten sollst, z.B. einen Artikel für eine Schülerzeitung, helfen dir die folgenden Hinweise.

Wie gehe ich am besten vor?

- Sammle und sortiere die Informationen, die auf der Seite stehen sollen.
- Schreibe deinen Text und gib ihm eine klare Struktur. (→ *SF 4*)
- Beginne einen neuen Absatz für jeden neuen Gedanken. (→ *SF 5*)
- Wähle eine passende Überschrift: sie verdeutlicht, worum es in deinem Text geht und macht die Lesenden neugierig auf deinen Text.
- Wenn es in deinem Text um mehrere Themen geht, dann kannst Du für einzelne Abschnitte auch Zwischenüberschriften verwenden. Das gibt deinem Text eine klare Struktur und hilft den Lesenden, sich schnell zu orientieren.

SF 16 Giving a good presentation REVISION Media skills

➜ p. 99

Wie bereite ich eine Präsentation vor?

- Trage Informationen zu deinem Thema zusammen. (➜ *SF 13)*
- Wähle eine Form der Präsentation aus, die das Thema gut veranschaulicht (Poster, Folie, Tafel, …).
- Schlage Wortschatz nach, den du brauchst. (➜ *SF 20)*
- Mache dir Notizen für deinen Vortrag, z.B. auf nummerierten Karteikarten.
- Bereite deine Medien vor (Poster, Folie, Tafelanschrieb, …). Schreibe groß und für alle gut lesbar.
- Übe deine Präsentation zu Hause vor einem Spiegel oder vor einem kleinen Publikum (Eltern, Großeltern, Freunde). Sprich laut, deutlich und langsam.

My presentation is about …
First I'd like to talk about …

Here's a new word. It is … in German.

That's the end of my presentation. Do you have any questions?

On my poster you can see a photo of …
The mind map shows …

Wie halte ich eine gute Präsentation?

- Warte, bis es ruhig ist. Schau die Zuhörer/innen an.
- Erkläre, worüber du sprechen wirst und wie deine Präsentation aufgebaut ist.
- Lies nicht von deinen Karten ab, sondern sprich möglichst frei.
- Bedanke dich fürs Zuhören und frage, ob jemand Fragen hat.

SF 17 Peer feedback REVISION

Gegenseitige Rückmeldungen sind für dich und deine Mitschüler/innen wichtig. Du kannst darin jemanden loben für etwas, das er/sie gut gemacht hat, oder Hinweise geben, wo sie noch Probleme haben. Du selbst erfährst, was du schon gut kannst und was du anders machen könntest.

Was muss ich beachten?

Bei deiner Rückmeldung solltest du drei Dinge beachten:

- Halte dich an die Punkte, zu denen du Rückmeldung geben sollst, z.B. die Aussprache, Betonung und Verständlichkeit bei einem Dialog, die Rechtschreibfehler in einem Text, das Einhalten eines roten Fadens in einer Geschichte usw. Begründe deine Einschätzungen.
- Gib deine Rückmeldung mit Respekt – niemand soll sich angegriffen fühlen. Nenne zuerst Gelungenes und mache dann Verbesserungsvorschläge zu Punkten, die aus deiner Sicht noch nicht so gelungen sind.
- Wenn du eine Rückmeldung bekommst, überdenke die Vorschläge gut. Korrigiere die Fehler, die andere gefunden haben, und arbeite an den Stellen nach, wo du eventuell Probleme hattest.

What I liked	What you could do better
You chose a great photo. ☺ You spoke clearly and looked at us. …	Next time, say what is happening in the photo. Sometimes you stood in front of the photo. …

STUDY SKILLS

SF 18 Understanding new words REVISION Media skills

Das Nachschlagen unbekannter Wörter kostet Zeit und ist auch nicht immer nötig. Oft geht es auch ohne den Einsatz eines Wörterbuches.

Immer gleich im Wörterbuch nachschlagen?

- Viele englische Wörter werden ähnlich wie im Deutschen geschrieben oder klingen ähnlich (z.B. *brochure, statue, insect*). Manche sehen auch einem Wort aus anderen Sprachen ähnlich, z.B. *voice (French: voix; Latin: vox)*.
- In manchen Wörtern stecken bekannte Teile, z.B. *bottle opener, snowshoe*.
- Präfixe und Suffixe wie *un-, re-* und *-er* helfen beim Erschließen: *listen**er** (sb. who listens), **un**happy <> happy, **re**pay (pay sb. back)*.
- Bilder zum Text zeigen oft Dinge, die du im Text vielleicht nicht verstehst.
- Der Kontext, also die Wörter und Sätze um das Wort herum, kann beim Verstehen helfen, z.B. *Let's hurry. The train **departs** in ten minutes.*

SF 19 Working with an English-German dictionary REVISION Media skills

➜ p. 38

Wenn du unbekannte Wörter nicht selbst erschließen kannst, nutze ein englisch-deutsches Wörterbuch, entweder in Buchform oder im Internet.

Wie benutze ich ein englisch-deutsches Wörterbuch?

Die Leitwörter *(running heads)* oben auf der Seite helfen dir, schnell zu finden, was du suchst. Auf der linken Seite steht das erste Stichwort, auf der rechten Seite das letzte Stichwort der Doppelseite.

- *resign* ist das **Stichwort** *(headword)*. Stichwörter sind alphabetisch geordnet: *r* vor *s*, *ra* vor *re*, *rhe* vor *rhi* usw.
- Die ***kursiv* gedruckten** Hinweise helfen dir, die für deinen Text passende Bedeutung zu finden.
- Die **Ziffern 1, 2** usw. zeigen, dass ein Stichwort unterschiedliche Bedeutungen haben oder unterschiedlichen Wortarten angehören kann (z.B. Adjektiv, Nomen, Verb).
- **Beispielsätze und Redewendungen** sind dem Stichwort zugeordnet.
- **Unregelmäßige Verbformen**, **besondere Pluralformen**, die **Steigerungsformen der Adjektive** und ähnliche Hinweise stehen oft in Klammern oder sind kursiv gedruckt.
- Die **Lautschrift** zeigt, wie das Wort ausgesprochen und betont wird.

resort

resign /rɪˈzaɪn/
1 BERUF • *als Vorsitzender usw* zurücktreten: ***He resigned from the company.*** Er verließ das Unternehmen.
2 *(job, post)* aufgeben *(Stelle, Posten)*
3 **resign oneself to something** sich mit etwas abfinden
resignation /ˌrezɪɡˈneɪʃn/
1 BERUF • *bei Unternehmen* Kündigung; *von Minister usw* Rücktritt
2 **hand in one's resignation** *von Angestelltem* kündigen; *von Minister usw* sein Amt niederlegen
3 *Gemütszustand* Resignation
resigned /rɪˈzaɪnd/ *(look, sigh)* resigniert *(Blick, Seufzer)*

resit¹ /ˌriːˈsɪt/ *Verb* (→ *sit*) *BE (exam)* wiederholen *(Prüfung)*
resit² /ˈriːsɪt/ *Substantiv* • *BE* Wiederholungsprüfung
resolution /ˌrezəˈluːʃn/
1 POLITIK Beschluss, Resolution
2 *bei Problem, Streit* Lösung
3 ≈ *Entschiedenheit* Entschlossenheit

TIPP

Wenn du ein Online-Wörterbuch verwenden möchtest, erkundige dich vorher bei deinem Lehrer/deiner Lehrerin, welche zu empfehlen sind, denn nicht alle sind gleich gut. Fast alle funktionieren aber nach den gleichen Prinzipien wie gedruckte Wörterbücher, sodass du sie problemlos ebenso verwenden kannst.

SF 20 Using a German–English dictionary

Media skills

Wann brauche ich ein deutsch-englisches Wörterbuch?

Stell dir vor, du sollst einen Text über deine Lieblingsband/deinen Lieblingsverein schreiben und du möchtest sagen, wie schwer die Band/der Verein kämpfen musste, um Erfolg zu haben. Aber was heißt in diesem Fall „schwer"? In diesem Fall hilft dir ein deutsch-englisches Wörterbuch.

Wie benutze ich ein deutsch-englisches Wörterbuch?

Vieles kennst du von der Arbeit mit einem englisch-deutschen Wörterbuch:

- **Leitwörter** *(running heads)* oben auf den Seiten helfen dir, das gesuchte Wort zu finden.
- Die **Stichwörter** *(headwords)* sind alphabetisch geordnet. Beispielsätze und Redewendungen sind den Stichwörtern zugeordnet.
- Die ***kursiv*** gedruckten Hinweise helfen dir, die für deinen Text passende Bedeutung zu finden.
- Die **Ziffern 1, 2** usw. zeigen, dass ein Stichwort unterschiedlichen Wortarten angehören kann (z.B. Adjektiv, Nomen, Verb).
- Bei **schwierig auszusprechenden Wörtern** stehen auch Hinweise zu Aussprache und Betonung.
- Bei Wörtern mit vielen Bedeutungen gibt es oft weitere Hilfen und Hinweise.

Schwede

schwer
1 ↔ *leicht* • *im Gewicht* heavy /'hevi/
2 *(Essen, Parfüm etc)* heavy /'hevi/ *(meal, scent etc)*
3 ≈ *mühevoll* hard /hɑːd/: ***Sie muss schwer arbeiten.*** She has to work hard.
4 ≈ *schwierig* difficult /'dɪfɪkəlt/, hard /hɑːd/
5 es jemandem schwer machen make* it difficult for someone
6 sich mit etwas schwer tun find* something difficult, have* difficulty with something
7 ≈ *hart* difficult /'dɪfɪkəlt/: ***Sie hatte eine schwere Kindheit.*** She had a difficult childhood.
8 ≈ *schlimm, heftig* serious /'sɪəriəs/: ***ein schwer kranker Patient*** a seriously ill patient
9 schwer verletzt sein be* seriously injured

schwer
Das deutsche ***schwer*** hat zwei Hauptbedeutungen:
– *schwer* in Bezug auf das Gewicht: *heavy*, im übertragenen Sinn auch *serious, bad*:
ein schwerer Koffer — *a heavy suitcase*

TIPP
Nimm nicht einfach die erste Übersetzung, die dir angeboten wird!
Lies immer erst den gesamten Wörterbucheintrag, bevor du dich für eine bestimmte Übersetzung entscheidest.

SF 21 Study posters REVISION

Lernplakate sind ein gutes Hilfsmittel, um Informationen darzustellen, die du dir merken möchtest wie z.B. Grammatikregeln.

Was muss ich beachten, wenn ich ein Lernposter erstelle?

- Sammle und notiere alle Informationen zum Thema, die du auf dem Poster darstellen willst.
- Überlege, wie du das, was du dir merken willst, am besten darstellen kannst. Du kannst z.B. Kästen oder Tabellen verwenden, aber auch kleine Zeichnungen.
- Finde einen guten Titel für dein Plakat.

- Gestalte dein Plakat. Schreibe groß und gut leserlich.
- Hebe wichtige Punkte hervor, z.B. durch Unterstreichen oder durch unterschiedliche Farben. Verwende aber nicht zu viele verschiedene Farben, denn sonst wird dein Lernposter unübersichtlich.
- Wenn du ein Lernposter zu einer Grammatikregel machst, kannst du auch ein paar Beispielsätze aufschreiben. Am Besten kannst du dir die Regel merken, wenn du dir zwei oder drei eigene Beispielsätze ausdenkst.
- Häng dein Poster zu Hause oder in der Schule an einer Stelle auf, an der du es häufig siehst, so dass sich dir der Inhalt ganz automatisch einprägen kann.

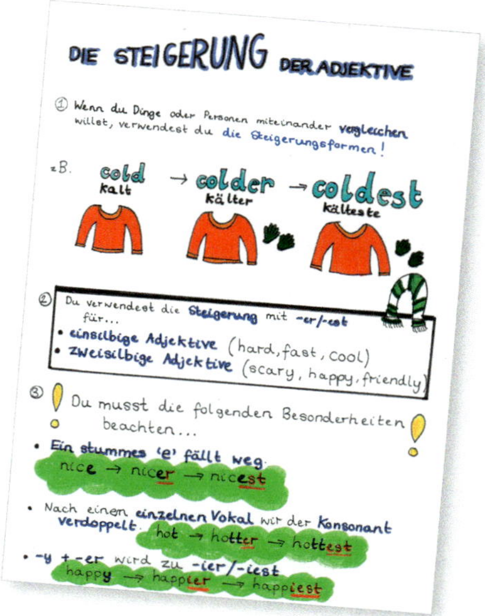

SF 22 Making and taking notes REVISION Media skills

Wenn du Informationen oder eigene Gedanken kurz für dich notierst – z.B. als Vorbereitung auf einen eigenen Vortrag oder eine Präsentation –, heißt das im Englischen making notes. Wenn du dir Notizen beim Lesen oder Zuhören machst, heißt das taking notes. Für beide Varianten gelten aber die gleichen Grundsätze.

Step 1: Achte auf keywords, die die wichtigsten Informationen enthalten, um deine Frage/Aufgabe zu beantworten oder den Inhalt eines Textes grob zu verstehen.

Step 2: Notiere nur die wichtigsten Informationen. Verwende Abkürzungen und Symbole, aber achte darauf,
dass du ein System hast und immer dieselben verwendest, damit du deine Notizen auch später noch verstehst.
Markiere offene Fragen.

Step 3: Gehe im Anschluss an das Lesen oder Hören nochmal durch deine Notizen und ergänze evtl. noch fehlende Informationen.

TIPP

Wenn du kein eigenes System von Abkürzungen hast, kannst du z. B. auch diese verwenden:

the same as	=	for example	e.g.
not the same as	≠	important	!
about the same as	≈	not	x
and	+	with	w/
becomes/will be	->	without	w/o
between	b/w	open question	??

Grammar File – Inhalt

Seite

GF 1 **The past** Die Vergangenheit ... 170
- 1.1 REVISION **The simple past** Die einfache Form der Vergangenheit ... 170
- 1.2 REVISION **The past progressive** Die Verlaufsform der Vergangenheit ... 170
- 1.3 REVISION **The present perfect** Das *present perfect* ... 171
- 1.4 REVISION **Present perfect or simple past?** *Present perfect* oder *simple past*? ... 171
- 1.5 **The present perfect progressive** Die Verlaufsform des *present perfect* ... 172
- 1.6 **Present perfect simple or present perfect progressive?** *Present perfect simple* oder *present perfect progressive?* ... 173
- 1.7 **The past perfect** Das *past perfect* ... 173

GF 2 **The possessive pronouns** Die Possessivpronomen ... 174

GF 3 **The future** Die Zukunft ... 175
- 3.1 REVISION **The *will*-future** Das Futur mit *will* ... 175
- 3.2 REVISION **The *going to*-future** Das Futur mit *going to* ... 175
- 3.3 REVISION **The present progressive** Das *present progressive* ... 175
- 3.4 REVISION **The simple present** Das *simple present* ... 175

GF 4 **Conditional sentences (I)** Bedingungssätze (I) ... 176
- 4.1 REVISION **Conditional sentences, type 1** Bedingungssätze, Typ 1 ... 176
- 4.2 **Conditional sentences, type 2** Bedingungssätze, Typ 2 ... 176

GF 5 **The prop-word *one/ones*** Das Stützword *one/ones* ... 177

GF 6 **Adverbs of manner** Adverbien der Art und Weise ... 178
- 6.1 **Use** Gebrauch ... 178
- 6.2 **Regular forms** Regelmäßige Formen ... 178
- 6.3 **Irregular forms** Unregelmäßige Formen ... 179
- 6.4 **Comparison** Steigerung ... 179
- 6.5 **Adjective or adverb after certain verbs?** Adjektiv oder Adverb nach bestimmten Verben? ... 179

GF 7 **The *-self/-selves* pronouns** Die *-self/-selves*-Pronomen ... 180
- 7.1 **The *-self/-selves* pronouns as emphasizing pronouns** Die *-self/-selves*-Pronomen als verstärkende Pronomen ... 180
- 7.2 **The *-self/-selves* pronouns as reflexive pronouns** Die *-self/-selves*-Pronomen als Reflexivpronomen ... 181
- 7.3 **"sich" in German – no reflexive pronoun in English** „sich" im Deutschen – kein Reflexivpronomen im Englischen ... 181
- 7.4 ***themselves* or *each other/one another*?** *themselves* oder *each other/one another*? ... 182

GF 8 **Conditional sentences (II)** Bedingungssätze (II) ... 183
- 8.1 REVISION **Conditional sentences, types 1 and 2** Bedingungssätze, Typ 1 und 2 ... 183
- 8.2 **Conditional sentences, type 3** Bedingungssätze, Typ 3 ... 183
- 8.3 **Conditional sentences, other types** Bedingungssätze, andere Typen ... 184

GF 9 **Clauses of time** Nebensätze der Zeit ... 185

Grammatical terms (Grammatische Fachbegriffe) ... 186

Lösungen der Grammar-File-Aufgaben ... 187

Das **Grammar File** (S. 169–187) fasst die in diesem Buch behandelten grammatischen Themen zusammen.

In English: The simple past

In English-Abschnitte enthalten kurze Zusammenfassungen der wichtigsten grammatischen Regeln auf Englisch.

Verweise wie ➔ *Unit 1: p. 12, exercise 2* zeigen dir, welche **Übungen** zum gerade behandelten Thema gehören.

Die **grammatischen Fachbegriffe** *(grammatical terms)* kannst du auf den Seiten 186–187 nachschlagen.

Hier stehen kleine **Aufgaben** zur **Selbstkontrolle**. Damit kannst du überprüfen, ob du das behandelte Thema verstanden hast. Auf S. 187 kannst du nachsehen, ob deine Lösungen richtig sind.

GF 1 The past Die Vergangenheit

1.1 REVISION The simple past — Die einfache Form der Vergangenheit

*Last Saturday, Mo and Luke **went** to One New Change. They **didn't want** to go shopping there, they **wanted** to go up on the roof.*

*On the roof, they **saw** lots of tourists and **heard** lots of different languages. Later, they **talked** to a girl called Emily and her parents. Mo **told** them about the Shard … and about his blog.*

Wenn du über **Vergangenes** berichtest – z.B., wenn du eine Geschichte erzählst –, benutzt du überwiegend das ***simple past***.
Das *simple past* drückt aus, dass etwas **zu einem bestimmten Zeitpunkt** oder **in einem bestimmten Zeitraum** in der Vergangenheit stattfand.

Das *simple past* steht häufig mit Zeitangaben wie ***last Saturday, yesterday, two years ago, in 2010***.

want* → *wanted ***arrive* → *arrived***
stop* → *stopped ***try* → *tried***

◄ Bei **regelmäßigen** Verben hängst du ***-ed*** an den Infinitiv, um das *simple past* zu bilden.

go* → *went ***meet* → *met***
hear* → *heard ***tell* → *told***

◄ **Unregelmäßige** Verben haben eine eigene Form für das *simple past*, die du einzeln lernen musst.

➔ *Liste der unregelmäßigen Verben, S. 282–283*

*Mo and Luke **didn't meet** their friends at the shopping centre.*
*– Who **did** they **meet**? **Did** they **meet** their parents?*
*No, they **didn't**. They met Emily.*

◄ **Verneinte Aussagesätze** im *simple past* werden mit ***didn't*** gebildet, **Fragen** mit ***did***.

(**Ausnahme**: Verneinungen und Fragen mit dem Verb ***be*** werden nicht mit ***did*** gebildet:
Was it expensive? – No, it wasn't.)

➔ *Unit 1: p. 12, exercise 2*

Die einfache Form der Vergangenheit

Bejahte Aussagen	Verneinte Aussagen	Fragen
I/You/He/She/It talk**ed** …	I/You/He/She/It **didn't** talk …	**Did** I/you/he/she/it talk …?
We/They talk**ed** …	We/They **didn't** talk …	**Did** we/they talk …?

1.2 REVISION The past progressive — Die Verlaufsform der Vergangenheit

Police officer: *Mr Clarke, what **were** you **doing** between 8 and 10 o'clock yesterday morning?*

Mr Clarke: *I **was working** in the garden.*

Mit dem ***past progressive*** drückt man aus, dass **zu einer bestimmten Zeit in der Vergangenheit** etwas **gerade im Gange** und **noch nicht abgeschlossen** war.

Es wird mit ***was/were* + *-ing*-Form** des Verbs gebildet:
*I **was working** … / You **were working** … /*
*He **was working** … / They **were working** …*

past progressive	*simple past*
was gerade vor sich ging,	**als …**
*He **was making** tea*	*when the phone **rang**.*
Er kochte gerade Tee,	als das Telefon klingelte.

◄ Das *past progressive* wird oft verwendet, um zu beschreiben, was gerade vor sich ging, als etwas anderes passierte. (Das neu einsetzende Ereignis steht im *simple past*.)

In English: The simple past
You use the **simple past**
- when you want to say or ask when something happened
- when you talk about things in the past (e.g. when you tell a story).

The past progressive
You use the **past progressive**
- when an action or event was in progress at a particular time in the past.

1.3 REVISION The present perfect

Das *present perfect*

Luke ***has been*** *at the shopping centre before.*
*But he****'s*** *never* ***been*** *up on the roof.*
Luke ist schon einmal im Einkaufszentrum gewesen.
Aber er war noch nie auf dem Dach.

Auch das ***present perfect*** wird verwendet, um über etwas zu sprechen, das in der Vergangenheit geschehen ist. Aber es ist nicht wichtig oder nicht bekannt, wann das war – ein genauer Zeitpunkt wird nicht genannt.

Mo ***hasn't been*** *up the Shard yet. It's too expensive.*
Have *you ever* ***visited*** *the Shard?*

Das *present perfect* steht oft mit Adverbien wie ***just, already, often, never, not … yet, before***.

Emily ***has given*** *Mo her number. Now he can text her.*

◂ Das ***present perfect*** wird oft verwendet, wenn man betonen will, dass ein vergangenes Geschehen wichtig für die Gegenwart oder die Zukunft ist: Emily hat Mo ihre Nummer gegeben; jetzt kann Mo ihr Mails schicken.

Das ***present perfect*** wird mit ***have/has*** **+ 3. Form des Verbs** (Partizip Perfekt; englisch: *past participle*) gebildet.

visit → visited   ***phone → phoned***
plan → planned   ***copy → copied***

◂ Bei **regelmäßigen** Verben hängst du ***-ed*** an den Infinitiv, um das *past participle* zu bilden.

be → been   ***take → taken***
give → given   ***see → seen***

◂ **Unregelmäßige** Verben haben eigene *past participle*-Formen, die du lernen musst.

➔ *Unit 1: p. 12, exercise 3*

➔ *Liste der unregelmäßigen Verben, S. 282–283*

Das *present perfect*

Bejahte Aussagen	Verneinte Aussagen	Fragen
I've visited …	I haven't visited …	Have I/you/we/they visited …?
You've visited …	You haven't visited …	
He**'s**/She**'s**/It**'s** visited … (= He/She/It **has** visited …)	He/She/It hasn't visited …	Has he/she/it visited …
We've/They've visited …	We/They haven't visited …	

In English: The present perfect
You use the **present perfect**
- to say that something has happened (not when it happened).

1.4 REVISION Present perfect or simple past?

Present perfect oder *simple past*?

Mo: ***Have*** *you* ***been*** *here before?*

Luke: *Yeah, I* ***came*** *with Dad* ***a few months ago****.*
We ***bought*** *mum's birthday present here.*

Mo: *So,* ***have*** *you* ***been*** *up on the roof too?*

"We only ***arrived yesterday evening****, so we* ***haven't seen*** *much yet."*

➔ *Unit 1: p. 13, exercise 4*

- ***Present perfect:***
Wenn du sagen willst, **dass etwas (irgendwann) geschehen ist** oder wenn du fragen willst, **ob etwas geschehen ist**.
Ein Zeitpunkt wird nicht genannt.
- ***Simple past:***
Wenn du sagen oder fragen willst, **wann etwas geschehen ist**.

Vervollständige jetzt diese beiden kurzen Dialoge. Wo muss es *simple past* sein, wo *present perfect*?

1 Katie: *Hannah and I … (decide) to go to that rock concert in Bath. Do you want to come with us?*
Daniel: *No, thanks. I … (see) both bands on TV last month, and I … (not like) them.*

2 Thomas: *Hi Jessica. … (you/just arrive)?*
Jessica: *Yes, I'm a bit late. … (the meeting/start yet)?*
Thomas: *I think so. Mr Carter … (go in) a few minutes ago.*

1.5 The present perfect progressive

Die Verlaufsform des *present perfect*

*You've **been watching** TV for hours.*
Du siehst (schon) seit Stunden fern.

***Have** you **been waiting** long?*
Wartest du schon lange?

*How long **has** she **been going** to this school?*
Wie lange/Seit wann geht sie (schon) auf diese Schule?

Mit dem ***present perfect progressive*** kannst du ausdrücken, dass etwas in der Vergangenheit begonnen hat und bis jetzt andauert.

! Im **Deutschen** benutzen wir meist das Präsens:
*Ich **warte** hier seit fünf Minuten.*
Im **Englischen** steht das *present perfect progressive*:
*I**'ve been waiting** here for five minutes.*

Das *present perfect progressive*

I've been waiting …	Have you been waiting long?
You've been waiting …	Has he/she/it been waiting long?
He's/She's/It's been waiting …	How long have they been waiting?
(= He/She/It **has** been waiting …)	How long has he/she/it been waiting?
We've/They've been waiting …	

Das ***present perfect progressive*** wird mit ***have/has been*** + ***ing*-Form** gebildet.

! Im **Englischen** gibt es zwei Worte für das deutsche **„seit"**:

1 *I**'ve been watching** TV **since** 10 o'clock.*
Ich sehe seit 10 Uhr fern.
*England **has been playing** better **since** the break.*
England spielt besser seit der Halbzeitpause.

◄ 1 Mit ***since*** gibt man einen **Zeitpunkt** an: *since 2012; since 10 o'clock; since Friday evening; since I was born.*
since **+ *Zeitpunkt*** drückt aus, **seit wann** etwas bereits andauert.

2 *I**'ve been waiting** here **for** five minutes, boys.*
Ich warte hier (schon) seit fünf Minuten, Jungs.
*We**'ve been living** here **for** 14 years now.*
Wir wohnen jetzt (schon) seit 14 Jahren hier.

◄ 2 Mit ***for*** gibt man einen **Zeitraum** an: *for hours; for 14 years; for five minutes; for a long time.*
for **+ *Zeitraum*** drückt aus, **wie lange** etwas bereits andauert.

since **+ Zeitpunkt – *for* + Zeitraum**

It's **4 o'clock**. Hannah and Declan are in the kitchen.

They've been working in the kitchen …

… **since 3:30**.	seit 15 Uhr 30
… **for half an hour**.	seit einer halben Stunde

➔ *Unit 1: p. 21, exercises 1–3*

In English: The present perfect progressive
You use the **present perfect progressive**
- to say that something began in the past and is still going on now.

Sieh dir die Bilder an und schreib die dazu passenden Sätze in dein Heft.

1 
They – wait – a long time

2 
She – read – lunchtime

3 
He – play – an hour

1.6 Present perfect simple or present perfect progressive?

Present perfect simple oder *present perfect progressive?*

Ella wants to invite her friends to her birthday party. She ***has written*** *three invitations already.*
… Sie hat schon drei Einladungen geschrieben.

She ***has been writing*** *invitations all morning.*
Sie schreibt schon den ganzen Morgen Einladungen.

- ***Present perfect simple:***
  Wenn es darum geht, **dass etwas geschehen ist** (es liegt ein **Ergebnis** vor; es gibt **Auswirkungen** auf Gegenwart oder Zukunft).
- ***Present perfect progressive:***
  Wenn es darum geht, dass eine Tätigkeit noch **andauert**, noch **nicht abgeschlossen** ist.

*They****'ve been*** *in London since last month.*
Sie sind seit letztem Monat in London.

*We****'ve had*** *our dog for more than three years now.*
Wir haben unseren Hund jetzt seit mehr als drei Jahren.

How long ***have*** *you* ***known*** *your boyfriend?*
Wie lange kennst du deinen Freund (schon)?

Would you like to visit me in Sydney?
*– I'd love to. I****'ve*** *always* ***wanted*** *to go to Australia.*
… Ich wollte schon immer nach Australien reisen.

➜ *Unit 1: p. 22, exercise 4*

! Beachte:
Verben, die nicht Tätigkeiten, sondern **Zustände** beschreiben, werden in der Regel **nicht in der Verlaufsform** verwendet (siehe die Beispiele links).

Wichtige Zustandsverben sind

- ***be*** („sein"), ***have*** („haben, besitzen"), ***own*** („besitzen"), ***seem*** („scheinen");
- ***believe*** („glauben"), ***know*** („wissen, kennen"), ***think*** („meinen, glauben"), ***understand*** („verstehen");
- ***like*** („mögen"), ***love*** („lieben"), ***hate*** („hassen, nicht mögen"), ***want*** („wollen, haben wollen").

Present perfect simple oder *present perfect progressive?* Vervollständige die folgenden Sätze.

1 *Hannah … (draw) all afternoon, but she still … (not finish) her art homework.*
2 *Jonathan still … (find) a present for his father although he … (look) around the mall for hours.*
3 *Oh no, we … (go) around in circles! This is the second time we … (see) this sign.*
4 *Oliver … (try on) boots all morning. He … (try on) six pairs but can't decide which ones he likes.*

1.7 The past perfect

Das *past perfect*

Philip ***packed*** *his backpack and* ***got*** *into the car. He* ***went*** *to Monument Valley with his aunt and uncle. On the way, his uncle* ***told*** *him about the rocky towers and columns.*

◄ Wie du weißt, gebraucht man überwiegend das *simple past*, wenn man über Vergangenes redet.

After they ***had spent*** *over six hours on the road, they arrived back in Santa Fe. It* ***had been*** *a great trip.*
Nachdem sie mehr als sechs Stunden auf der Straße verbracht hatten, trafen sie wieder in Santa Fe ein. …

The service ***had started*** *when they* ***reached*** *the cathedral.*
Der Gottesdienst hatte begonnen, als sie die Kathedrale erreichten.

◄ Wenn du sagen willst, dass etwas **noch vor einer anderen Handlung** oder **vor einem bestimmten Zeitpunkt in der Vergangenheit** stattgefunden hatte, verwendest du das ***past perfect*** (Vorvergangenheit, Plusquamperfekt).

Handlung 1 *(past perfect)* geschah vor **Handlung 2** *(simple past)*:
The service ***had started*** **(1)** *when they* ***reached*** **(2)** *the cathedral.*

The service ***started*** *when they arrived.*
Der Gottesdienst begann, als sie ankamen.
(sie kamen an, und der Gottesdienst begann)

The service ***had started*** *when they arrived.*
Der Gottesdienst hatte begonnen, als sie ankamen.
(er hatte schon begonnen, ***bevor*** *sie ankamen)*

! Beachte die Bedeutungsunterschiede, je nachdem, ob du das ***simple past*** oder das ***past perfect*** verwendest.

Das *past perfect*

Bejahte Aussagen	Verneinte Aussagen	Fragen
I had visited …	I hadn't seen …	Had I closed …?
You had visited …	You hadn't seen …	Had you closed …?
He/She/It had visited …	He/She/It hadn't seen …	Had he/she/it closed …?
We/They had visited …	We/They hadn't seen …	Had we/they closed …?

Das ***past perfect*** wird mit ***had*** (Kurzform: ***'d***) und der **3. Form des Verbs** (Partizip Perfekt; englisch: *past participle*) gebildet.

Philip ***had*** *never* ***seen*** *such buildings.*
Philip **hatte** nie zuvor solche Gebäude **gesehen**.

He ***had*** *never* ***been*** *to Monument Valley before.*
Er **war** nie zuvor im Monument Valley **gewesen**.

! Das ***past perfect*** wird immer mit ***had*** gebildet, egal ob im Deutschen **„hatte"** oder **„war"** steht.

➜ *Unit 3: p. 68, exercises 1–3*

In English: The past perfect
You use the **past perfect**
- for actions that finished before a time in the past.

Sieh dir die Bilder genau an und vervollständige die Sätze.
Wo muss es *simple past* sein, wo *past perfect*?

Holly didn't go to the cinema because …

1 *she … (leave) her money at home.*
2 *the queue … (be) too long.*

Matthew bought lots of apples because …

3 *they … (be) very cheap.*
4 *his mother … (ask) him to get some fruit.*

GF 2 The possessive pronouns Die Possessivpronomen

my cat	– **mine**	*meiner, meine, meins*
your cat	– **yours**	*deiner, deine, deins; Ihrer, Ihre, Ihrs*
his cat	– **his**	*seiner, seine, seins*
her cat	– **hers**	*ihrer, ihre, ihrs*
our dog	– **ours**	*unserer, unsere, unseres*
your dog	– **yours**	*eurer, eure, eures; Ihrer, Ihre, Ihrs*
their dog	– **theirs**	*ihrer, ihre, ihrs*

Die **Possessivpronomen** ***mine, yours, his, hers, ours, yours, theirs*** drücken **Besitz** oder Zugehörigkeit aus und werden daher manchmal auch **besitzanzeigende Pronomen** genannt.

Anders als die Possessivbegleiter *my, your, his, her, our* usw. stehen sie **allein, ohne Nomen**.

Man verwendet ein Possessivpronomen, wenn man ein schon genanntes Nomen nicht noch einmal wiederholen will:

This is my ***T-shirt****, not* ***yours****.*
(= This is my T-Shirt, not your T-shirt.)

GF 3 The future Die Zukunft

3.1 REVISION The *will*-future — Das Futur mit *will*

*When **will** Mum **be** back? – She **won't be** back till tomorrow.*

Mit ***will/won't* + Infinitiv** sagst du, was in der Zukunft geschehen bzw. nicht geschehen wird.

*I'm sure you'**ll** soon **speak** Welsh as well as the others.*

◄ Wenn **Vermutungen** geäußert werden, steht häufig *I (don't) think, I'm (not) sure, maybe* oder *probably*.

*Wales **will get** a lot of rain tomorrow, and it **will be** very windy in Scotland.*

◄ Oft geht es um Dinge, die man nicht beeinflussen kann, z.B. **Vorhersagen** über das Wetter.

*Laugh with the others, then you'**ll feel** better.*
Lach mit den anderen, dann **fühlst** du dich besser.

! Im Deutschen benutzen wir oft das Präsens, wenn wir Vermutungen äußern oder Vorhersagen machen. Im Englischen steht das *will-future*.

➜ *Unit 2: p. 37, exercise 2*

3.2 REVISION The *going to*-future — Das Futur mit *going to*

*The Evans family **is going to move** to Wales. Mrs Evans is happy that they **are going to live** in the country.*

Wenn es um **Vorhaben, Pläne, Absichten** für die Zukunft geht, verwendet man ***am/are/is going to* + Infinitiv**.

3.3 REVISION The present progressive — Das *present progressive*

*Emily and her new class **are climbing** Mt Snowdon next weekend.*

*What **are** you **doing** on Sunday? **Are** you **going** skiing again?*

Wenn etwas für die Zukunft **fest verabredet** ist, kannst du auch das ***present progressive*** benutzen. Es muss aber deutlich sein, dass es sich um etwas Zukünftiges handelt, z.B. durch eine Zeitangabe *(next weekend, tomorrow, on Sunday)* oder aus dem Zusammenhang. (Man spricht hier manchmal vom ***diary future***, weil es oft um Verabredungen geht, die schon im Terminkalender stehen.)

3.4 REVISION The simple present — Das *simple present*

*The next train to Cardiff **leaves** at 8:25.*

*Our French classes **start** on Monday.*

Auch das ***simple present*** kann futurische Bedeutung haben. Es wird verwendet, wenn ein zukünftiges Geschehen durch einen **Fahrplan**, ein **Programm** oder Ähnliches genau festgelegt ist. Verben wie ***arrive, leave, go, open, close, start, stop*** werden häufig so verwendet. (Diese Verwendung nennt man ***timetable future***.)

In English: Talking about the future

You often use the **will-future** to talk about the future.
But …

- you use the **going to-future** for intentions and plans for the future;
- you can use the **present progressive** to talk about what you have arranged to do in the future;
- you can use the **simple present** for future events that are listed in a timetable or programme.

Schreibe die Sätze mit der passenden Futurform in dein Heft.

1 *Do you think it … tomorrow?* *(will rain / is raining)*
2 *Have you got any plans for this summer? – Yes, we … to Spain.* *('ll fly / 're going to fly)*
3 *Do you like your new flat? – Well, it's too small, really. We … out again. We've already started looking.* *('ll move / 're going to move)*
4 *Are you free next Friday? – No, I … Julian.* *('ll meet / 'm meeting)*

GF 4 Conditional sentences (I) Bedingungssätze (I)

4.1 REVISION Conditional sentences, type 1 — Bedingungssätze, Typ 1

Emily: ***If** I **hear** one more word of Welsh, **I'll scream**!*
Wenn ich noch ein walisisches Wort höre, dann schreie ich!

Dad: ***If** you **laugh** with the others, you **won't feel** so bad.*
Wenn du mit den anderen lachst, fühlst du dich nicht so schlecht.

Emily: *I **can't laugh** with them if I don't understand them.*

Dad: *If they speak too fast, **ask** them to slow down.*

➔ *Unit 2: p. 35, exercise 3*

Bedingungssätze vom Typ 1 sind **„Was ist, wenn …"**-Sätze: Sie beschreiben, was unter bestimmten Bedingungen geschieht oder nicht geschieht.

Die Bedingung steht im *if*-Satz. Der Hauptsatz sagt aus, was passiert, wenn die Bedingung erfüllt wird.

Im *if*-Satz steht das *simple present*. Im Hauptsatz steht meist das *will-future*.

◄ Im Hauptsatz können auch *can, must, could, should* + Infinitiv oder ein Imperativ stehen.

4.2 Conditional sentences, type 2 — Bedingungssätze, Typ 2

Dylan: ***If** you **gave** me a pound for every trip, I **would be** rich.*
Wenn du mir für jeden Ausflug ein Pfund geben würdest, dann wäre ich reich.

! Kein *would* im *if*-Satz! Nicht: *If you ~~would give~~ me …*

Dylan: ***If** I **had** a kayak, **I'd paddle** right down from the top to this pool.*
Wenn ich ein Kajak hätte, würde ich geradewegs … hinunterpaddeln.

*Emily **wouldn't feel** so bad **if** her Welsh **was** better.*
Emily würde sich nicht so schlecht fühlen, wenn ihr Walisisch besser wäre.

Bedingungssätze vom Typ 2 sind **„Was wäre, wenn …"**-Sätze: Sie drücken aus, dass etwas nicht sehr wahrscheinlich oder sogar unmöglich ist:

1 ***If** we **met** Emily in Wales, we **would go** climbing together.*

2 *"**If** I **were** you, **I'd go** down the waterfall inside a beach ball", said Philip.*

Es ist unwahrscheinlich, dass wir Emily in Wales treffen (Satz 1), und Philip ist nun einmal nicht Dylan (Satz 2). Die Sprecher/innen drücken nur aus, was geschehen würde oder der Fall wäre, wenn …

Bedingung	Folge für die Zukunft
***If** you **did** that,*	*you **would die**.*
simple past	***would + infinitive***

Im *if*-Satz steht das *simple past*. Im Hauptsatz steht meist *would* + Infinitiv (Kurzform: *'d*).

*If Philip read the message, he **could get** the wrong idea.*
… könnte er das missverstehen.

◄ Im Hauptsatz kann auch *could* („könnte") + Infinitiv stehen.

! Beachte, dass nach ***I*** im *if*-Satz oft ***were*** statt ***was*** steht:
If I were a cat …
(*If I was* … ist aber ebenfalls möglich.)

➔ *Unit 2: pp. 42–43, exercises 1–5*

In English: Conditional sentences

- **Type 1:**

simple present	will-future or can/must/should + infinitive
*If she **wins** the competition,*	*she **will be** the star of the whole school.*

The speaker thinks there is a good chance that she will win the competition.

- **Type 2:**

simple past	would + infinitive or could + infinitive
*If she **won** the competition,*	*she **would be** the star of the whole school.*

The speaker thinks it is less probable that she will win the competition.

Vervollständige die Sätze in deinem Heft. Achte auf die richtige Form der Verben.

1 *If the weather **is** nice, we … (have) a picnic in the park.*
2 ***Would** you **change** anything if you … (be) the head teacher at your school?*
3 *What **would** you **do** if your classmates … (make) fun of you?*
4 *If we really **go** to Wales this summer, I … (try) to climb Mount Snowdon.*
5 *If I **had** more money, I … (travel) all over Europe in the summer.*
6 *If you … (not hurry up) now, you'**ll be** late for school.*

GF 5 The prop-word *one/ones* Das Stützwort *one/ones*

*Dylan wanted to write a note. He asked for a **pen**, and Emily gave him **one**.*
… Er bat um einen Stift, und Emily gab ihm einen.

*They sang **song** after **song**, all **ones** that Emily liked.*
Sie sangen ein Lied nach dem anderen, alles welche, die Emily mochte.

*Let's sing a **song**. An English **one** that Emily knows.*
Lasst uns ein Lied singen. Ein englisches, das Emily kennt.

*These **T-shirts** are nice. What about a green **one**?*
*– I like the blue **ones** better.*
… Wie wäre es mit einem grünen? – Mir gefallen die blauen besser.

➔ *Unit 2: p. 44, exercise 6*

Wenn man ein schon genanntes (zählbares) Nomen (z. B. *pen, song, T-shirts*) nicht wiederholen will, verwendet man anstelle des Nomens das sogenannte **Stützwort *one*** (Plural: ***ones***).
Im Deutschen hat *one(s)* in der Regel keine Entsprechung.

! Beachte, dass im Englischen – anders als im Deutschen – Adjektive nicht allein stehen können.

In English: The prop-word *one/ones*

- If you don't want to repeat a (countable) noun, you can use the **prop-word *one*** (plural: ***ones***) instead.
- In contrast to German, English adjectives cannot stand on their own. You have to use them with ***one*** or ***ones***.

GF 6 Adverbs of manner Adverbien der Art und Weise

6.1 Use — Gebrauch

Adjectives *My grandfather is a careful* ***driver****.*

Grandpa *is always careful.*

◀ **Adjektive** beziehen sich auf ein **Nomen**. Man verwendet sie, um Personen, Dinge oder Ideen näher zu beschreiben – sie drücken aus, wie etwas oder jemand **ist**.

Adverbs *My Grandfather always* ***drives carefully****.*

Walk carefully *down the stairs, Grandpa.*

◀ **Adverbien der Art und Weise** *(adverbs of manner)* beziehen sich auf ein **Verb**. Man verwendet sie, um Handlungen oder Vorgänge näher zu beschreiben – sie drücken aus, wie jemand etwas tut oder wie etwas geschieht.

1 *She* ***shook her head slowly****.*

Sie **schüttelte** langsam **den Kopf**.

2 *He* ***carefully*** *opened the door.*

3 ***Slowly****, the room filled with people.*

! Im Deutschen können Adverbien der Art und Weise zwischen Verb und Objekt stehen.
Englische *adverbs of manner* stehen **nie zwischen Verb und Objekt**. Sie stehen gewöhnlich am Ende des Satzes (1), manchmal aber auch direkt vor dem Verb (2) oder am Satzanfang (3).

➡ *Unit 3: p. 63, exercises 1 – 3*

In English: Adverbs of manner (I)
You use **adjectives** to describe people, things or ideas (“what something or somebody is like”).
You use **adverbs** to describe actions or events (“how something happens or how somebody does something”).

6.2 Regular forms — Regelmäßige Formen

Adjective → **Adverb**

quick → *quickly*
nice → *nicely*
fierce → *fiercely*

Die meisten Adverbien der Art und Weise werden gebildet, indem *-ly* an das Adjektiv angehängt wird.

! Beachte folgende Besonderheiten:

This legend ends quite ***happily****.*

1 *-y* + *-ly* wird zu *-ily*:
happy → ***happily***

We should use water ***responsibly****.*
(verantwortungsvoll,-bewusst)

2 *-le* wird zu *-ly*:
responsible → ***responsibly***

Thank you very much. You did that job ***fantastically****.*

3 Nach *-ic* wird *-ally* angehängt:
fantastic → ***fantastically***

Adverb *We always ride our bikes* ***carefully****.*
Wir fahren immer **vorsichtig**.

Adjective *We're always* ***careful****.*
Wir sind immer **vorsichtig**.

◀ Im Deutschen haben Adverbien der Art und Weise und Adjektive dieselbe Form, im Englischen in der Regel nicht.

➡ *Unit 3: p. 63, exercises 1 – 3*

Morph waited nervously on the shelf till the cat walked away.

6.3 Irregular forms

Unregelmäßige Formen

Einige Adverbien der Art und Weise haben eine unregelmäßige Form, die du einzeln lernen musst:

*My sister is a **good** swimmer. She can swim very **well**.*

◄ Das Adverb zum Adjektiv ***good*** heißt ***well***.

*Aunt Gwen is a **fast** driver. She usually drives quite **fast**.*

*The job of a teacher can be **hard** sometimes. Teachers often have to work very **hard**.*

◄ Bei ***fast*** und ***hard*** haben Adjektiv und Adverb dieselbe Form.

➜ *Unit 3: p. 63, exercises 1 – 3*

6.4 Comparison

Steigerung

Auch Adverbien der Art und Weise können gesteigert werden. Die Superlativformen werden allerdings nur sehr selten verwendet.

*Can't you run a bit **faster**?*

- Einsilbige Adverbien werden mit ***-er/-est*** gesteigert.

*My grandpa drives **more carefully** than my dad.*

- Adverbien auf ***-ly*** werden mit ***more/most*** gesteigert.

*My sister sings a lot **better** than me.*
*Today our team played a lot **worse** than last weekend.*

- Die Adverbien ***well*** und ***badly*** haben **unregelmäßige Steigerungsformen**.

Die Steigerung der Adverbien der Art und Weise

Einsilbige Adverbien: *-er / -est*	Adverbien auf *-ly*: *more / most*	unregelmäßig:
fast – faster – fastest	*slowly – more slowly – most slowly*	*well – better – best*
hard – harder – hardest	*clearly – more clearly – most clearly*	*badly – worse – worst*

➜ *Unit 3: p. 73, exercises 3 – 4*

6.5 Adjective or adverb after certain verbs?

Adjektiv oder Adverb nach bestimmten Verben?

*She **shouted angrily** at me.* … schrie mich wütend an.
*He **greeted** us **nervously**.* … begrüßte uns nervös.

◄ Wie du weißt, drücken **Adverbien der Art und Weise** aus, **wie** – auf welche Art und Weise – **jemand etwas tut**.

*She **looked** very **angry**.* … sah sehr wütend aus.

*He **felt** a bit **nervous** when the guests arrived.*
Er war ein bisschen nervös, als die Gäste eintrafen.

*She **seemed** very **happy**. What happened?*
*The soup **smelled wonderful** and **tasted great**.*
*Fresh strawberries? **Sounds nice**!*

◄ Bei manchen Verben geht es aber nicht darum, wie jemand etwas tut, sondern darum, **wie jemand oder etwas ist** – sie beschreiben einen **Zustand** oder eine **Eigenschaft**.
Nach solchen Verben steht nicht ein Adverb, sondern ein **Adjektiv**. Beispiele:

(to) ***feel*** (sich fühlen), *(to)* ***look*** (aussehen), *(to)* ***sound*** (klingen), *(to)* ***seem*** (scheinen), *(to)* ***smell*** (riechen), *(to)* ***taste*** (schmecken)

! Bei den Verben ***feel, look, smell, taste*** kann – je nach Bedeutung – ein **Adverb** oder ein **Adjektiv** stehen:

1 *The doctor **felt** my arm **carefully**.*
*He **looked nervously** at his watch.*
*The dog **smelled** the shoe **carefully**.*
*She **tasted** the meat **slowly**.*

1 Ein **Adverb** steht, wenn eine **Tätigkeit** beschrieben wird.

2 *My arm **felt heavy** and a bit **sore**.*
*He **looked scared**.*
*The shoe **smelled awful**.*
*The meat **tasted delicious**.*

2 Ein **Adjektiv** steht, wenn ein **Zustand** oder eine **Eigenschaft** beschrieben wird.

In English: Adverbs of manner (II)

- Most adverbs of manner are **formed from adjectives** by adding ***-ly***.
- **Adverbs ending in *-ly*** form the comparative and superlative with ***more/most***.
- **One-syllable adverbs** form the comparative and superlative with ***-er/-est***.
- After a verb which describes a **state** or a **quality** – e.g. *feel, look, sound, seem, smell, taste* –, we use an **adjective**, not an adverb.

Welches Wort ist richtig, das Adjektiv oder das Adverb?
Vervollständige die Sätze in deinem Übungsheft.

1 *We sailed … down the river.* (***slow / slowly***)
2 *The match got more … after a very … start.* (***interesting / interestingly – slow / slowly***)
3 *Suddenly there was a … BANG and the lights went out.* (***loud / loudly***)
4 *Suddenly somebody sneezed very … .* (***loud / loudly***)
5 *She looked … at her watch. It was almost too late now.* (***nervous / nervously***)
6 *She always plays with her hair when she's … .* (***nervous / nervously***)
7 *I slept very … last night.* (***bad / badly***)
8 *I always take an umbrella in … weather.* (***bad / badly***)
9 *She smelled … at the flowers and smiled.* (***happy / happily***)
10 *The flowers smelled …* (***wonderful / wonderfully***)
11 *The man on the phone sounded very … .* (***excited / excitedly***)
12 *My new loudspeakers sound really … .* (***brilliant / brilliantly***)

GF 7 The *-self/-selves*-pronouns Die *-self/-selves*-Pronomen

7.1 The *-self/-selves*-pronouns as emphasizing pronouns — Die *-self/-selves*-Pronomen als verstärkende Pronomen

*The **hotel itself** was OK, but the view was awful.*
Das **Hotel selbst** war OK, …

*You'll be able to talk to the **actors themselves**.*
Sie werden mit den **Schauspielern und Schauspielerinnen selbst** sprechen können.

*The cake tastes great. Did **you** make it **yourself**?*
… Hast **du** ihn **selbst** gemacht?

*It'll be a lot cheaper if **we** paint the room **ourselves**.*
Es ist viel billiger, wenn **wir** das Zimmer **selbst** streichen.

The *-self/-selves* pronouns

Singular		Plural	
I	– **myself**	we	– **ourselves**
you	– **yourself**	you	– **yourselves**
he	– **himself**	they	– **themselves**
she	– **herself**		
it	– **itself**		

Unit 4: p. 91, exercise 4

Die Pronomen auf ***-self/-selves*** werden als **verstärkende Pronomen** verwendet, um ein Nomen oder Pronomen hervorzuheben oder um zu betonen, dass jemand etwas allein, ohne Hilfe getan hat.

Im Deutschen verwendet man „selbst" oder „selber".

! Die Betonung liegt auf der zweiten Silbe:
myself [maɪ'self] *usw.*
ourselves [aʊə'selvz] *usw.*

7.2 The *-self/-selves*-pronouns as reflexive pronouns

Die *-self/-selves*-Pronomen als Reflexivpronomen

John *went home and made* ***himself*** *a cup of tea.*
John ging heim und machte **sich** eine Tasse Tee.

My mother *cut* ***herself*** *with the bread knife.*
Meine Mutter hat **sich** mit dem Brotmesser geschnitten.

Is ***he*** *talking to* ***himself*** *or is he speaking on his mobile?*
Redet **er** mit **sich selbst** oder telefoniert er mit dem Handy?

You *should be old enough to look after* ***yourselves****.*
Ihr solltet alt genug sein, um auf **euch (selbst)** aufzupassen.

My brother *hurt* ***him****.*	… ihn verletzt
My brother *hurt* ***himself****.*	… sich verletzt

Behave yourself *– and don't be late.*
Benimm dich anständig – und komm nicht zu spät.

Did they ***enjoy themselves*** *in the park?*
Haben sie sich im Park gut amüsiert?

There are some biscuits on the table. ***Help yourselves****.*
Auf dem Tisch stehen Plätzchen. Bedient euch./Greift zu.

Watch yourself*. She's really good at chess.*
Sieh dich vor. Sie ist wirklich gut im Schachspielen.

➔ *Unit 4: p. 91, exercise 4*

Die Pronomen auf ***-self/-selves*** werden auch als **Reflexivpronomen** („rückbezügliche Fürwörter") verwendet. Sie bezeichnen dann dieselbe Person oder Sache wie das Subjekt des Satzes:

Im ersten Beispiel links bezieht sich das Reflexivpronomen ***himself*** zurück auf das Subjekt ***John***.

! Verwechsle nicht **Personal-** und **Reflexivpronomen**.

Merke dir auch diese Wendungen:

behave yourself	sich (gut/anständig) benehmen
enjoy yourself	Spaß haben, sich (gut) amüsieren
help yourself	sich bedienen, zugreifen
watch yourself	sich vorsehen, vorsichtig sein

Morph is enjoying himself by the sea.

7.3 "sich" in German – no reflexive pronoun in English

„sich" im Deutschen – kein Reflexivpronomen im Englischen

I can't ***imagine*** *living in the country.*
Ich kann **mir** nicht **vorstellen**, auf dem Land zu leben.

My two brothers often ***argue****.*
Meine beiden Brüder **streiten sich** oft.

Mr Ash always ***complains*** *about the noise in our garden.*
Mr Ash **beschwert sich** immer über den Lärm …

My little brother ***got lost*** *in the shopping mall last week.*
… **hat sich** letzte Woche im Einkaufszentrum **verirrt**.

Morph often ***hides*** *behind the books.*
Morph **versteckt sich** oft hinter den Büchern.

➔ *Unit 4: p. 91, exercise 4*

! Es gibt eine Reihe von Verben, die **im Deutschen mit „sich"** gebraucht werden, aber **im Englischen ohne Reflexivpronomen** stehen. Zu diesen Verben gehören:

(to) ***argue***	sich streiten
(to) ***behave***	sich benehmen
(to) ***change***	sich (ver)ändern
(to) ***complain***	sich beschweren
(to) ***decide***	sich entscheiden
(to) ***feel***	sich fühlen
(to) ***get lost***	sich verirren, sich verlaufen
(to) ***hide***	sich verstecken
(to) ***hurry (up)***	sich beeilen
(to) ***imagine sth.***	sich etwas vorstellen
(to) ***improve***	sich verbessern
(to) ***meet***	sich treffen
(to) ***move***	sich bewegen
(to) ***relax***	sich entspannen
(to) ***remember sth.***	sich an etwas erinnern
(to) ***sit down***	sich hinsetzen
(to) ***wash***	sich waschen
(to) ***wonder***	sich fragen
(to) ***worry***	sich Sorgen machen

7.4 *themselves* or *each other/one another*?

themselves oder *each other/one another*?

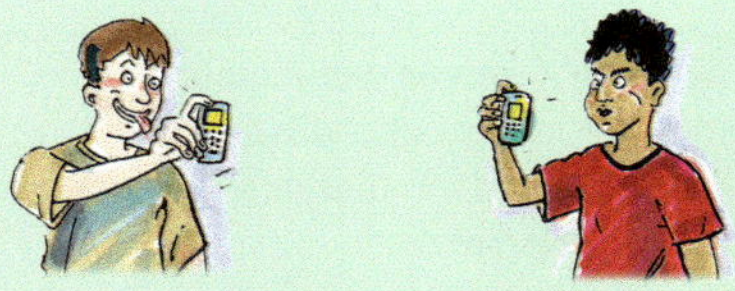

Finn and Asif are taking photos of ***themselves****.*
Finn und Asif machen Fotos von **sich (selbst)**.

Das Reflexivpronomen ***themselves*** steht für **„sich"** im Sinne von **„sich selbst"**.

Now they are taking photos of ***each other/one another****.*
Jetzt fotografieren sie **sich gegenseitig**.

➜ *Unit 4: p. 91, exercise 5*

Wenn **„sich gegenseitig"**, **„einander"** gemeint ist, verwendet man ***each other*** oder ***one another***. (***each other*** und ***one another*** werden **reziproke Pronomen** – englisch: *reciprocal pronouns* – genannt.)

In English: The *-self/-selves* pronouns

You can use the *-self/-selves* pronouns (e.g. ***myself, themselves***)
- to **emphasize** a noun or pronoun (= German „selbst" or „selber"): *We spoke to the president* ***himself****.*
- as **reflexive pronouns**; reflexive pronouns refer back to the subject of the sentence: *She hurt* ***herself****.*

There are many reflexive verbs in German whose **English equivalents are not reflexive**, e.g. *(to) argue, (to) change, (to) complain, (to) decide, (to) feel, …*

You use ***each other*** or ***one another*** (not: *themselves*) to express a two-way relationship between two or more people: *Tyler and Alex looked at* ***each other/one another****.* (= Tyler looked at Alex, and Alex looked at Tyler.)

Sieh dir die Bilder an und vervollständige die Sätze. Brauchst du *themselves* oder *each other*?

1 *They're laughing at …*

2 *They might hurt …*

3 *They're teaching … German.*

4 *They're talking to … on the phone.*

1

2

3

4

GF 8 Conditional sentences (II) Bedingungssätze (II)

8.1 REVISION Conditional sentences, types 1 and 2

Bedingungssätze, Typ 1 und 2

Die Bedingungssätze vom Typ 1 und 2 kennst du bereits. Sie beziehen sich auf die **Gegenwart** oder **Zukunft**.

If *Dad* ***plays*** *that banjo again,* ***I'll go*** *crazy!*
Wenn Dad noch mal auf diesem Banjo spielt, werde ich verrückt!

If *you* ***visit*** *New Orleans, you* ***can try*** *alligator meat.*
Try *alligator meat* ***if*** *you* ***visit*** *New Orleans.*

➜ *Unit 5: p. 115, exercise 5*

◂ **Bedingungssätze vom Typ 1** sind **„Was ist, wenn ...“**-Sätze:
Sie beschreiben, was unter bestimmten Bedingungen geschieht oder nicht geschieht.

Im *if*-Satz steht das *simple present*. Im Hauptsatz steht das *will-future*, ein Modalverb oder ein Imperativ.

➜ *GF 4.1, S. 176*

Would *you* ***eat*** *alligator meat* ***if*** *I* ***gave*** *you 100 dollars?*
Würdest du Alligatorfleisch essen, wenn ich dir 100 Dollar geben würde?

I ***might try*** *alligator meat* ***if*** *you* ***gave*** *me 100 dollars.*
If *I* ***were*** *you, I* ***would visit*** *New Orleans.*

➜ *Unit 5: p. 115, exercise 6*

◂ **Bedingungssätze vom Typ 2** sind **„Was wäre, wenn ...“**-Sätze:
Sie drücken aus, was geschehen würde oder der Fall wäre, wenn ... (aber es ist nicht sehr wahrscheinlich oder sogar unmöglich).

Im *if*-Satz steht das *simple past*. Im Hauptsatz steht *would/could/might* + Infinitiv.

➜ *GF 4.2, S. 176*

8.2 Conditional sentences, type 3

Bedingungssätze, Typ 3

1 *Grandma Betty* ***wouldn't have kept*** *the earrings* ***if*** *she* ***hadn't liked*** *the boy.*
Grandma Betty hätte die Ohrringe nicht behalten, wenn sie den Jungen nicht gemocht hätte.

2 ***If*** *Tyler* ***had known*** *his great-grandfather, he* ***would have liked*** *him.*
Wenn Tyler seinen Urgroßvater gekannt hätte, dann hätte er ihn gemocht.

◂ **Bedingungssätze vom Typ 3** sind **„Was wäre gewesen, wenn ...“**-Sätze.
Sie beziehen sich auf die **Vergangenheit**.

Sie drücken aus, was unter bestimmten Bedingungen geschehen oder nicht geschehen **wäre**:

- Der ***if*-Satz** nennt eine **nicht** erfüllte Bedingung. (Satz 2: Tyler hat seinen Urgroßvater nicht gekannt.)
- Der **Hauptsatz** drückt aus, was der Fall gewesen wäre, wenn er ihn gekannt hätte. (Satz 2: Dann hätte er ihn gemocht.)

Bedingung	Folge
If *he* ***had known*** *him,*	*he* ***would have liked*** *him.*
past perfect	**would have-*form*: (would have + *past participle*)**

*If she'****d asked*** *me,* *I'****d have helped*** *her.*
If she ***had*** *asked me,* *I* ***would*** *have helped her.*

If it hadn't rained, we ***could have gone*** *swimming/ we* ***might have gone*** *swimming.*
..., hätten wir schwimmen gehen können / wären wir vielleicht schwimmen gegangen.

➜ *Unit 5: p. 121, exercise 4*

◂ Beachte: Die Kurzform *'d* steht im ***if***-Satz für *had*, im Hauptsatz aber für *would*.

◂ Im Hauptsatz können auch ***could have*** + **past participle** oder ***might have*** + **past participle** stehen.

In English: Conditional sentences

- **Type 1** (about the present or the future):

  simple present — will-future or can/must/could/should + infinitive

  *If they **score** another goal, they **will win**.*

  The speaker thinks there is a good chance that they will score another goal. (The match has just begun.)

- **Type 2** (about the present or the future):

  simple past — would/could/might + infinitive

  *If they **scored** another goal, they **would win**.*

  The speaker thinks it is less probable that they will score another goal. (The match is nearly over.)

- **Type 3** (about the past):

  past perfect — would/could/might + have + past participle

  *If they **had scored** another goal, they **would have won**.*

  The match is over. They didn't score another goal, so they didn't win.

a) Was trifft zu, **A** oder **B**?

1	*If it wasn't raining, we could go surfing.*	**A** *it's raining*	**B** *it might rain*
2	*If he arrives late, John will be in trouble.*	**A** *he arrives late*	**B** *he might arrive late*
3	*Can you close the windows if it rains?*	**A** *it's raining*	**B** *it might rain*
4	*If the lights were on, we'd know he's in.*	**A** *the lights aren't on*	**B** *the lights might be on*
5	*He'd be so happy if he had a dog.*	**A** *he doesn't have a dog*	**B** *he might have a dog*
6	*Call Mum if she doesn't text you.*	**A** *Mum won't text you*	**B** *Mum might text you*

b) Sieh dir Beispiel 1 an. Bilde dann Bedingungssätze vom Typ 3 für die Sätze 2 bis 4.

1	*We couldn't go shopping. The shops were all closed.*	If the shops hadn't been closed, we could have gone shopping.
2	*Claire didn't turn off her computer, so it was on all night.*	If Claire had turned off ...
3	*The weather wasn't good enough, so we couldn't go swimming.*	If the weather ...
4	*I found out about the fire when I turned on the radio.*	If I hadn't turned on ...

8.3 Conditional sentences, other types

Bedingungssätze: andere Typen

Die **Abschnitte 8.1 und 8.2** beschreiben die häufig vorkommenden **Grundtypen** der Bedingungssätze. Aber ähnlich wie im Deutschen werden auch andere Zeitformen in Bedingungssätzen verwendet – je nach Situation. Hier einige Beispiele:

1 *If it's very cold, water **turns** to ice.*
Wenn es sehr kalt ist, wird Wasser zu Eis.

*If you **add** blue to yellow, you **get** green.*
Wenn du Blau zu Gelb hinzufügst, erhältst du Grün.

◄ **Sätze 1**: Wenn etwas immer der Fall ist, kann im Hauptsatz auch das *simple present* stehen (***if*** heißt hier so viel wie „immer wenn" oder „jedes Mal wenn").

2 Grandma: *We'**d be** outside for a barbecue if it **hadn't started** to rain.*
Wir wären jetzt draußen zum Grillen, wenn es nicht angefangen hätte zu regnen.

*If Eugene **hadn't left** New Orleans very fast, he **wouldn't be** here today.*
Wenn Eugene New Orleans nicht sehr schnell verlassen hätte, wäre er heute nicht hier.

◄ **Sätze 2**: Diese Sätze beschreiben, was jetzt oder in Zukunft der Fall wäre, wenn eine bestimmte Bedingung in der Vergangenheit erfüllt worden wäre.

3 *If you've **been** to New Orleans before, you'**ll know** Bourbon Street.*
Wenn du schon mal in New Orleans warst, dann wirst du Bourbon Street (ja) kennen.

*If she **has missed** her train, we'**ll have** to start without her.*
Wenn sie ihren Zug verpasst hat, müssen wir ohne sie anfangen.

*If you **knew** him better, you **wouldn't have invited** him.*
Wenn du ihn besser kennen würdest, hättest du ihn nicht eingeladen.

➜ *Unit 5: p. 123, exercise 2*

◄ Sieh dir auch die **Sätze 3** und ihre Übersetzungen an.

GF 9 Clauses of time Nebensätze der Zeit

*She got a job in a bank **after** she left school.*
Sie bekam eine Stelle in einer Bank, nachdem sie die Schule verließ.

***Before** the tour began, our guide told us to be careful.*
Bevor die Tour begann, forderte unser Reiseleiter uns auf, vorsichtig zu sein.

***When** they had packed the car, they got in and drove off.*
Als sie das Auto gepackt hatten, stiegen sie ein und fuhren los.

Nebensätze der Zeit werden durch **Konjunktionen** wie ***after, before, when, while, as, as soon as, until*** eingeleitet.

*He bought a paper **while** he was waiting for his train.*
Er kaufte eine Zeitung, während er auf seinen Zug wartete.

***As** I was getting on the bus, I saw my class teacher.*
Als ich in den Bus einstieg, sah ich meine Klassenlehrerin.

◄ Die Konjunktionen ***while*** („während") und ***as*** („als", „während") drücken aus, dass zwei Handlungen oder Ereignisse gleichzeitig stattfinden bzw. stattfanden.

*I'**ll call** you as soon as **I've checked** in.*
Ich rufe dich an/Ich werde dich anrufen, sobald ich eingecheckt habe.

*We'**re going to wait** here until you **get** back.*
Wir warten hier/Wir werden hier warten, bis du zurückkommst.

➜ *Unit 5: p. 123, exercise 3*

! Auch wenn eine **zukünftige** Handlung beschrieben wird, darf in Nebensätzen der Zeit **nicht das *will-future* oder das *going to-future*** stehen.
Der Zukunftsbezug wird durch den Hauptsatz ausgedrückt. (In den Beispielen: *I'll call* bzw. *We're going to wait*.)

Grammatical terms (Grammatische Fachbegriffe)

active ['æktɪv]	Aktiv	*A heavy storm* ***destroyed*** *twelve houses.*
adjective ['ædʒɪktɪv]	Adjektiv (Eigenschaftswort)	*good, new, green, interesting, …*
adverb ['ædvɜːb]	Adverb	*today, there, outside, very, …*
adverb of frequency ['friːkwənsi]	Häufigkeitsadverb	*always, usually, often, sometimes, never*
adverb of indefinite time [ɪn'defɪnət]	Adverb der unbestimmten Zeit	*already, ever, just, never, before, yet, …*
adverb of manner ['mænə]	Adverb der Art und Weise	*nicely, happily, quietly, slowly, well, fast, …*
article ['ɑːtɪkl]	Artikel	*the, a, an*
backshift of tenses ['bækʃɪft]	Rückverschiebung der Zeitformen	*"I'****m*** *tired." ⟶ She said (that) she* ***was*** *tired.*
comparative [kəm'pærətɪv]	Komparativ (1. Steigerungsform)	*older; more expensive*
comparison [kəm'pærɪsn]	Steigerung	*old – older – oldest;* *expensive – more expensive – most expensive*
compound ['kɒmpaʊnd]	Zusammensetzung	*somebody, anyone, something, …*
conditional sentence [kən'dɪʃənl]	Bedingungssatz	*If I see Sam, I'll tell him.*
conjunction [kən'dʒʌŋkʃn]	Konjunktion	*and, but, …; because, when, …*
direct speech [ˌdaɪrekt 'spiːtʃ]	direkte Rede	***"I'm tired."***
going to**-future** ['fjuːtʃə]	Futur mit *going to*	***I'm going to watch*** *TV tonight.*
imperative [ɪm'perətɪv]	Imperativ (Befehlsform)	*Open your books. Don't talk.*
indirect speech [ˌɪndərekt 'spiːtʃ]	indirekte Rede	*She said (that)* ***she was tired****.*
infinitive [ɪn'fɪnətɪv]	Infinitiv (Grundform des Verbs)	*(to) open, (to) go, …*
irregular verb [ɪ'regjələ]	unregelmäßiges Verb	*(to) go – went – gone,* *(to) see – saw – seen, …*
modal auxiliary [ˌməʊdl‿ɔːg'zɪliəri]	modales Hilfsverb, Modalverb	*can, may, might, needn't, should, must, …*
negative statement ['negətɪv]	verneinter Aussagesatz	*I don't like oranges.*
noun [naʊn]	Nomen, Substantiv	*Justin, girl, man, time, name, …*
object ['ɒbdʒɪkt]	Objekt	*Justin has* ***a new camera****.*
object question	Objektfrage, Frage nach dem Objekt	***Who did*** *Mrs Pascoe* ***invite*** *to tea?*
past participle [ˌpɑːst 'pɑːtɪsɪpl]	Partizip Perfekt	*checked, phoned, tried, gone, eaten, …*
past perfect [ˌpɑːst 'pɜːfɪkt]	*past perfect* (Vorvergangenheit, Plusquamperfekt)	*I* ***had*** *already* ***gone*** *to bed when they arrived.*
past progressive [ˌpɑːst prə'gresɪv]	Verlaufsform der Vergangenheit	*Olivia* ***was playing*** *cards.*
personal pronoun [ˌpɜːsənl 'prəʊnaʊn]	Personalpronomen (persönliches Fürwort)	*I, you, he, she, it, we, they;* *me, you, him, her, it, us, them*
plural ['plʊərəl]	Plural, Mehrzahl	
positive statement ['pɒzətɪv]	bejahter Aussagesatz	*I like oranges.*
possessive determiner [pəˌzesɪv dɪ'tɜːmɪnə]	Possessivbegleiter (besitzanzeigender Begleiter)	*my, your, his, her, its, our, their*
possessive form [pəˌzesɪv 'fɔːm]	s-Genitiv	*Sam's sister, the Blackwells' house, …*
possessive pronoun [pəˌzesɪv 'prəʊnaʊn]	Possessivpronomen	*mine, yours, his, hers, ours, theirs*
preposition [ˌprepə'zɪʃn]	Präposition	*after, at, in, into, near, next to, …*
present perfect [ˌpreznt 'pɜːfɪkt]	*present perfect*	*We****'ve made*** *some scones for you.*
present perfect progressive [ˌpreznt ˌpɜːfɪkt prə'gresɪv]	Verlaufsform des *present perfect*	*He****'s been watching*** *TV for hours.*
present progressive [ˌpreznt prə'gresɪv]	Verlaufsform der Gegenwart	*Olivia* ***is playing*** *cards.*
pronoun ['prəʊnaʊn]	Pronomen (Fürwort)	
prop-word ['prɒp wɜːd]	Stützwort	*one, ones*
question tag ['kwestʃn tæg]	Frageanhängsel	*isn't he?, are you?, can't we?, …*
question word ['kwestʃn wɜːd]	Fragewort	*who?, what?, when?, where?, how?, …*
reciprocal pronoun [rɪˌsɪprəkl 'prəʊnaʊn]	reziprokes Pronomen	*each other, one another*
reflexive pronoun [rɪˌfleksɪv 'prəʊnaʊn]	Reflexivpronomen	*myself, yourself, themselves, …*
regular verb ['regjələ]	regelmäßiges Verb	*(to) help – helped, (to) look – looked, …*
relative clause [ˌrelətɪv 'klɔːz]	Relativsatz	*I like teachers* ***who laugh a lot****.*
relative pronoun [ˌrelətɪv 'prəʊnaʊn]	Relativpronomen	*who – which – that*
short answer [ˌʃɔːt‿'ɑːnsə]	Kurzantwort	*Yes, I am. / No, we don't. / …*
simple past [ˌsɪmpl 'pɑːst]	einfache Form der Vergangenheit	*Olivia* ***played*** *cards last Friday.*
simple present [ˌsɪmpl 'preznt]	einfache Form der Gegenwart	*Olivia* ***plays*** *cards every Friday evening.*

singular ['sɪŋgjələ]	Singular, Einzahl	
statement ['steɪtmənt]	Aussage(satz)	
sub-clause ['sʌbklɔːz]	Nebensatz	*I like Plymouth* ***because I like the sea****.*
subject ['sʌbdʒɪkt]	Subjekt	***Justin/He*** *has a new camera.*
subject question	Subjektfrage, Frage nach dem Subjekt	***Who invited*** *the Coopers to tea?*
substitute ['sʌbstɪtjuːt]	Ersatzverb (eines Modalverbs)	*be able to, be allowed to, have to*
superlative [su'pɜːlətɪv]	Superlativ (2. Steigerungsform)	*(the) oldest; (the) most expensive*
verb [vɜːb]	1. Verb;	*go, help, look, see, …*
	2. Prädikat	*Reading* ***can be*** *fun.*
***will*-future** ['fjuːtʃə]	Futur mit *will*	*I'm sure you'****ll like*** *the new maths teacher.*
yes/no question	Entscheidungsfrage	*Are you 14? Do you like oranges?*

Lösungen der Grammar-File-Aufgaben

p. 171
1 Katie: *Hannah and I* ***have decided*** *to go to that rock concert in Bath. Do you want to come with us?*
Daniel: *No, thanks. I* ***saw*** *both bands on TV last month, and I* ***didn't like*** *them.*
2 Thomas: *Hi Jessica.* ***Have*** *you* ***just arrived****?*
Jessica: *Yes, I'm a bit late.* ***Has*** *the meeting* ***started yet****?*
Thomas: *I think so. Mr Carter* ***went in*** *a few minutes ago.*

p. 172
1 *They'****ve been waiting for*** *a long time.*
2 *She'****s been reading since*** *lunchtime.*
3 *He'****s been playing for*** *an hour.*

p. 173
1 *Hannah* ***has been drawing*** *all afternoon, but she still* ***hasn't finished*** *her art homework.*
2 *Jonathan still* ***hasn't found*** *a present for his father although he'****s been looking*** *around the mall for hours.*
3 *Oh no, we'****ve been going*** *around in circles! This is the second time we'****ve seen*** *this sign.*
4 *Oliver* ***has been trying on*** *boots all morning. He'****s tried on*** *six pairs but can't decide which ones he likes.*

p. 174
1 *Holly didn't go to the cinema because she* ***had left*** *her money at home.*
2 *Holly didn't go to the cinema because the queue* ***was*** *too long.*
3 *Matthew bought lots of apples because they* ***were*** *very cheap.*
4 *Matthew bought lots of apples because his mother* ***had asked*** *him to get some fruit.*

p. 175
1 *Do you think it* ***will rain*** *tomorrow?*
2 *… – Yes, we'****re going to fly*** *to Spain.*
3 *… – Well, it's too small really. We'****re going to move*** *out again. We've already started looking.*
4 *… – No, I'****m meeting*** *Julian.*

p. 177
1 *If the weather* ***is*** *nice, we'****ll have*** *a picnic in the park.*
2 ***Would*** *you* ***change*** *anything if you* ***were*** *the headteacher at your school?*
3 *What* ***would*** *you* ***do*** *if your classmates* ***made*** *fun of you?*
4 *If we really* ***go*** *to Wales this summer, I'****ll try*** *to climb Mount Snowdon.*
5 *If I* ***had*** *more money, I* ***would travel*** *(I'****d travel****) all over Europe in the summer.*
6 *If you* ***don't hurry up*** *now, you'****ll be*** *late for school.*

p. 180
1 *We sailed* ***slowly*** *down the river.*
2 *The match got more* ***interesting*** *after a very* ***slow*** *start.*
3 *Suddenly there was a* ***loud*** *BANG and the lights went out.*
4 *Suddenly somebody sneezed very* ***loudly****.*
5 *She looked* ***nervously*** *at her watch. It was almost too late now.*
6 *She always plays with her hair when she's* ***nervous****.*
7 *I slept very* ***badly*** *last night.*
8 *I always take an umbrella in* ***bad*** *weather.*
9 *She smelled* ***happily*** *at the flowers and smiled.*
10 *The flowers smelled* ***wonderful****.*
11 *The man on the phone sounded very* ***excited****.*
12 *My new loudspeakers sound really* ***brilliant****.*

p. 182
1 *They're laughing at* ***each other****.*
2 *They might hurt* ***themselves****.*
3 *They're teaching* ***themselves*** *German.*
4 *They're talking to* ***each other*** *on the phone.*

p. 184, a)
1 **A** *it's raining*
2 **B** *he might arrive late*
3 **B** *it might rain*
4 **A** *the lights aren't on*
5 **A** *he doesn't have a dog*
6 **B** *Mum might text you*

p. 184, b)
1 ***If the shops hadn't been closed, we could have gone shopping.***
2 ***If Claire had turned off her computer, it wouldn't have been on all night***
3 ***If the weather had been good enough/better, we could have gone swimming.***
4 ***If I hadn't turned on the radio, I wouldn't have found out about the fire.***

Das **Vocabulary** (S.188 – 223) enthält alle Wörter und Wendungen deines Englischbuches, die du lernen musst.
Sie stehen in der Reihenfolge, in der sie im Buch zum ersten Mal vorkommen.

Hier siehst du, wie das **Vocabulary** aufgebaut ist:

Diese Zahl gibt die **Seite** an, auf der die Wörter zum ersten Mal vorkommen.
p. 11 = Seite 11

Die **Lautschrift** zeigt dir, wie ein Wort ausgesprochen wird.
Eine Übersicht über alle **Lautschriftzeichen** findest du auf S. 276.
Die Lautschriftzeichen stehen auch unten auf den **Vocabulary**-Seiten.

Eingerückte Wörter lernst du am besten zusammen mit dem vorausgehenden Wort, weil die beiden zusammengehören.

p. 11	**south** [saʊθ]	Süden; nach Süden; südlich	
	darkness ['dɑːknəs]	Dunkelheit, Finsternis	
	false [fɔːls]	falsch	**true** ◄► **false** (L) falsus, -a, -um
p. 14	**in fact** [ɪn 'fækt]	eigentlich, in Wirklichkeit	I thought he … Wales.
	fact [fækt]	Tatsache, Fakt	Here are some interesting **facts** about London. (L) factum, -i n
			The **figures** aren't correct. Please check them again. ! stress: **figure** ['fɪɡə]
			! Schreibung: **parliament** (F) le parlement
	(to) guard [gɑːd]	bewachen	

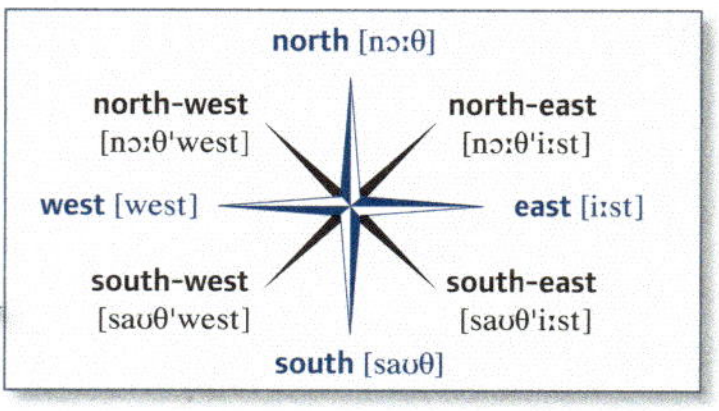

Dies ist das „Gegenteil"-Zeichen: **true** ist das Gegenteil von **false**.

Diese **Kästen** solltest du dir immer besonders gut ansehen: Hier sind Vokabeln zu einem bestimmten Thema zusammengestellt. Oder du erfährst mehr über ein Wort und wie es verwendet wird.

Das **rote Ausrufezeichen** bedeutet: Vorsicht, hier macht man leicht Fehler!

German "während"

• vor einem Nomen:	**during**	Jack phoned **during** the football match. Jack rief **während** des Fußballspiels an.
• vor einem Nebensatz:	**while**	Jack phoned **while** we were watching the football match. Jack rief an, **während** wir das Fußballspiel schauten.

Im **Vocabulary** werden folgende **Abkürzungen** verwendet:

p. = page (Seite) pp. = pages (Seiten)
sth. = something (etwas) sb. = somebody (jemand)
jn. = jemanden jm. = jemandem
pl = *plural* (Mehrzahl)
infml = *informal* (umgangssprachlich)
(F) = *verwandtes Wort im Französischen*
(L) = *verwandtes Wort im Lateinischen*

Wenn du **nachschlagen** möchtest, was ein englisches Wort bedeutet oder wie man es ausspricht, dann verwende das **English – German Dictionary** auf den Seiten 224 – 252. Und wenn du vergessen hast, wie etwas auf Englisch heißt, dann kann dir das **German – English Dictionary** auf den Seiten 253 – 276 eine erste Hilfe sein.

[iː] green · [i] happy · [ɪ] big · [e] red · [æ] cat · [ɑː] class · [ɒ] song · [ɔː] door · [uː] blue · [ʊ] book · [ʌ] mum · [ɜː] girl · [ə] a partner

Unit 1 This is London

pp. 8/9	**the best thing about …**	das Beste an …	**The best thing about** the film was the music.
	expert ['ekspɜːt]	Experte/Expertin	! stress: **ex**pert ['ekspɜːt] (F) l'expert *(m)*, l'experte *(f)*

Part A

p. 10	**huge** [hjuːdʒ]	riesig, sehr groß	Little Andrew got a **huge** teddy bear for his birthday.
	as soon as [əz 'suːn‿əz]	sobald, sowie	I'll call you **as soon as** I'm home.
	cathedral [kə'θiːdrəl]	Kathedrale, Dom	! Betonung: **ca<u>the</u>dral** [kə'θiːdrəl] (F) la cathédrale
	palace ['pæləs]	Palast, Schloss	! Betonung: **<u>pal</u>ace** ['pæləs] (F) le palais
	(to) **reply (to)** [rɪ'plaɪ]	antworten (auf); erwidern, entgegnen	Why didn't you **reply to** my email? "That isn't London Bridge," he **replied**. "It's Tower Bridge."
	Europe ['jʊərəp]	Europa	
	western ['westən]	westlich, West-	Spain is one of the biggest countries in **western** Europe.
	amazing [ə'meɪzɪŋ]	erstaunlich, unglaublich	
	How do you know …?	Woher weißt/kennst du …?	**How do you know** so much about cows? – My grandparents have a farm.
	post [pəʊst]	Posting *(auf Blog)*, Blog-Eintrag	
	carnival ['kɑːnɪvl]	Karneval, Fasching	**Carnival** is a big event in German cities like Cologne and Mainz, but people in Britain don't celebrate it. ! In Großbritannien wird mit **carnival** jegliche Art von Straßenumzügen mit Musik- und Tanzgruppen, Festwagen u.Ä. bezeichnet.
	(to) **be into** sth. *(infml)*	etwas mögen, auf etwas stehen	My sister **is into** reggae at the moment.
	(to) **enjoy** [ɪn'dʒɔɪ]	genießen	The film was fantastic. I really **enjoyed** it.
	by the way [ˌbaɪ ðə 'weɪ]	übrigens	Oh, **by the way,** Grandma called this morning.
p. 11	**south** [saʊθ]	Süden; nach Süden; südlich	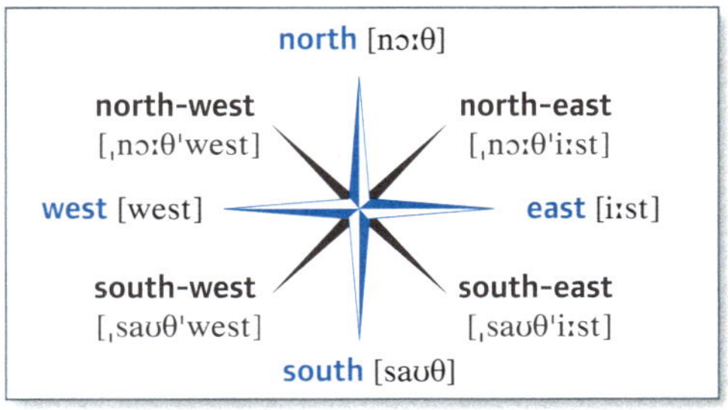
	darkness ['dɑːknəs]	Dunkelheit, Finsternis	
	clue [kluː]	(Lösungs-)Hinweis; Anhaltspunkt	Nobody knows who killed the man. The police are still looking for **clues** in his house.
	skyline ['skaɪlaɪn]	Skyline; Horizont	 a **skyline**
	false [fɔːls]	falsch	**true** ◄► **false** (L) falsus, -a, -um

[eɪ] name · [aɪ] time · [ɔɪ] boy · [əʊ] old ·
[aʊ] town · [ɪə] here · [eə] where · [ʊə] tour

p. 12	(to) **go together**	zusammenpassen, zueinander passen	I don't think pink and orange **go together**.
	the Tube [tju:b] *(no pl)*	die U-Bahn *(in London)*	In London, the underground is called "**the Tube**". *English:* **on the Tube** – *German:* **in der U-Bahn**
	timetable ['taɪmteɪbl]	Fahrplan	! **timetable** = **1.** Stundenplan; **2.** Fahrplan
	gallery ['gæləri]	Galerie	! Betonung: **gallery** ['gæləri] (F) la galerie
p. 13	**small talk**	Smalltalk *(spontan geführtes Gespräch)*	
	(to) **expect** sth. [ɪk'spekt]	etwas erwarten	(L) exspectare

Part B

p. 14	**attraction** [ə'trækʃn]	Attraktion; Anziehungspunkt	The British Museum is one of London's biggest tourist **attractions**. (F) l'attraction *(f)* (L) trahere *(ziehen)*
	entry ['entri]	Eintritt, Zutritt	**Entry** into museums is usually free in Britain. (F) l'entrée *(f)*
	in fact [ɪn 'fækt]	eigentlich, in Wirklichkeit	I thought he was English, but **in fact** he was Welsh.
	fact [fækt]	Tatsache, Fakt	Here are some interesting **facts** about London. (L) factum, -i *n*
	(to) **reserve** [rɪ'zɜ:v]	reservieren, buchen	We'll have to **reserve** a table if we want to eat there. (F) réserver
	step [step]	Stufe	! **step** = **1.** Stufe; **2.** Schritt
	chance [tʃɑ:ns]	Gelegenheit, Möglichkeit, Chance	If you have the **chance**, you should go to the British Museum. (F) la chance
p. 15	**figure** ['fɪgə]	Zahl, Ziffer	The **figures** aren't correct. Please check them again. ! stress: **figure** ['fɪgə]
	less (than) [les]	weniger (als)	I have **less** money than you. = You have more money than me.
	tortoise ['tɔ:təs]	(Land-)Schildkröte	
	on top of each other	übereinander, aufeinander	Please put those plates **on top of each other**.
	at one time	zur selben Zeit, gleichzeitig	It's hard to understand if everyone talks **at one time**.
	ticket office ['tɪkɪt‿ˌɒfɪs]	Fahrkartenschalter; Kasse *(für den Verkauf von Eintrittskarten)*	
	detail ['di:teɪl]	Detail, Einzelheit	! stress: **detail** ['di:teɪl] (F) le détail
	a family of four	eine vierköpfige Familie	
	during ['djʊərɪŋ]	während	

German "während"

- vor einem <u>Nomen</u>: **during** — Jack phoned **during** <u>the football match</u>. Jack rief **während** <u>des Fußballspiels</u> an.
- vor einem <u>Nebensatz</u>: **while** — Jack phoned **while** <u>we were watching the football match</u>. Jack rief an, **während** <u>wir das Fußballspiel schauten</u>.

	(to) **guard** [gɑ:d]	bewachen	It's the Beefeaters' job to **guard** the Tower.

[b] **boat** · [p] **pool** · [d] **dad** · [t] **ten** · [g] **good** · [k] **cat** · [m] **mum** · [n] **no** · [ŋ] **song** · [l] **hello** · [r] **red** · [w] **we** · [j] **you**

	raven ['reɪvn]	Rabe	a **raven** 
	blood [blʌd]	Blut	
	(to) **be home to** sth.	Heimat sein für etwas; etwas beheimaten	The Amazon area **is home to** the world's largest rainforest.
	jewels *(pl)* ['dʒuːəlz]	Juwelen	! stress: **jewels** ['dʒuːəlz]
	education [ˌedʒu'keɪʃn]	(Schul-, Aus-)Bildung; Erziehung	You need a good **education** if you want to get a good job. (F) l'éducation *(f)* (L) educere *(großziehen)*
p. 16	**instead of** [ɪn'sted‿əv]	anstelle von, statt	! • **instead of** = anstelle von – I'd like chips **instead of** rice, please. • **instead** = stattdessen – I don't like rice. Can I have chips **instead**?
	exact [ɪg'zækt]	genau	What's the **exact** size of London? Do you know?
	linking word ['lɪŋkɪŋ wɜːd]	Bindewort	
	worth [wɜːθ]	wert	The correct answer is **worth** five points.
	(to) **roar** [rɔː]	brüllen	I could hear the lion **roar** when we entered the zoo.
	crowded ['kraʊdɪd]	voller Menschen; überfüllt	The old city centre is often **crowded** with tourists.
p. 17	**feedback** ['fiːdbæk]	Rückmeldung, Feedback	The hotel wants to get some **feedback** from the people who have stayed there.
	(to) **improve** [ɪm'pruːv]	verbessern; sich verbessern	This book helps you to **improve** your English. Your English will **improve** if you watch English films.
	(to) **react (to)** [ri'ækt]	reagieren (auf)	I called him but he didn't **react**. (F) réagir
	content ['kɒntent]	Inhalt	(F) le contenu
	(to) **cover** ['kʌvə]	behandeln, abdecken, ansprechen *(Thema; Fragen)*	Any more questions? – No, you've **covered** everything.
	opinion [ə'pɪnjən]	Meinung	*English:* **In my opinion …** *German:* **Meiner Meinung nach …** (F) l'opinion *(f)* (L) opinio, -onis *f*
	argument ['ɑːgjumənt]	Argument	Try to present **arguments** for your opinion. ! stress: **argument** ['ɑːgjumənt]
	structure ['strʌktʃə]	Struktur, Gliederung	! stress: **structure** ['strʌktʃə]
	introduction [ˌɪntrə'dʌkʃn]	Einleitung, Einführung	(F) l'introduction *(f)*
	conclusion [kən'kluːʒn]	Schluss(folgerung)	(F) la conclusion
	(to) **join** sth. [dʒɔɪn]	etwas verbinden	You can **join** sentences with the words *and* and *or*. ! (to) **join** = **1.** *(in einen Klub/Verein)* eintreten **2.** verbinden
	(to) **sum** sth. **up** [ˌsʌm‿'ʌp]	etwas zusammenfassen	Can you **sum up** your life in five sentences? (L) sumere *(nehmen)*
	communication [kəˌmjuːnɪ'keɪʃn]	Kommunikation, Verständigung	(F) la communication (L) communis *(gemeinsam)*
	(to) **seem (to be/do)** [siːm]	(zu sein/zu tun) scheinen	He **seems (to be)** very sad. What's wrong?
	relaxed [rɪ'lækst]	entspannt	
	(to) **make eye contact** ['kɒntækt]	Blickkontakt herstellen	! stress: **contact** ['kɒntækt]

[f] father • [v] river • [s] sister • [z] please • [ʃ] shop • [ʒ] television •
[tʃ] teacher • [dʒ] Germany • [θ] thanks • [ð] this • [h] here

	(to) **point** sth. **out (to** sb.**)** [ˌpɔɪnt‿ˈaʊt]	(jn.) auf etwas hinweisen	"Be careful!" he said, and **pointed out** a snake in the grass.
p. 18	**northbound** [ˈnɔːθbaʊnd]	Richtung Norden	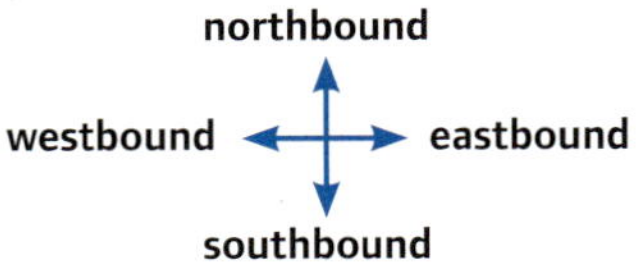
p. 19	(to) **be slow**	nachgehen *(Uhr)*	It's twenty past eight. – No, it isn't. It's half past eight. Your watch **is slow**. (to) **be slow** ◄► (to) **be fast**
	(to) **work**	funktionieren	I need your help. My computer doesn't **work**.
	(to) **head for** sth. [hed]	auf etwas zusteuern/zugehen/zufahren	As soon as we arrived at the coast, we **headed for** the beach.
	announcement [əˈnaʊnsmənt]	Durchsage, Ansage	We'll have to wait for the **announcement** to find out where our train leaves. Ⓕ l'annonce *(f)*
	message [ˈmesɪdʒ]	Botschaft, Aussage	! **message** = **1.** Nachricht – John left a **message** for you. **2.** Botschaft – I think the poem has an interesting **message**. Ⓕ le message

Part C

p. 20	(to) **be on**	eingeschaltet sein, an sein *(Radio, Licht usw.)*; laufen, übertragen werden *(Programm, Sendung)*	The lights **are on**, so they must be at home. (to) **be on** ◄► (to) **be off** Can we watch TV, Mum? The football **is on**.
	No way! [ˌnəʊ ˈweɪ]	Auf keinen Fall! / Kommt nicht in Frage!	Dad, can you give me £120 for a new pair of jeans? – £120? **No way!** You can have £70.
	for hours/weeks/...	seit Stunden/Wochen/...	"You've been watching TV **for hours**." –
	since 10 o'clock/last week/... [sɪns]	seit 10 Uhr/letzter Woche/...	"No, I haven't. I've been watching TV **since 10**."
	And anyway, ... [ˈeniweɪ]	Und überhaupt, ...	I don't have time to go. **And anyway**, it's too expensive.
	try [traɪ]	Versuch	verb: (to) **try** – noun: **try**
	remote control [rɪˌməʊt kənˈtrəʊl] (*kurz auch:* **remote**)	Fernbedienung	 some **remote controls**
	(to) **turn** sth. **up/down** [tɜːn]	etwas lauter/leiser stellen	Can you **turn up** the radio? I want to hear the news.

(to) turn

1. The London Eye **turns** very slowly.	**sich drehen**
2. The woman **turned** (*auch:* **turned round / turned around**) and looked at me.	**sich umdrehen**
3. The boy **turned to** his father and smiled.	**sich jm. zuwenden**
4. Please **turn on** the TV. And **turn up** the sound.	**einschalten ... lauter stellen**
5. First you **turn left**. Then you **turn right**.	**(nach) links/rechts abbiegen**

each other [iːtʃ‿ˈʌðə]	sich (gegenseitig), einander	Luke looked at Mo and Mo looked at Luke. = Luke and Mo looked at **each other**.

[iː] green · [i] happy · [ɪ] big · [e] red · [æ] cat · [ɑː] class · [ɒ] song · [ɔː] door · [uː] blue · [ʊ] book · [ʌ] mum · [ɜː] girl · [ə] a partner

	pub [pʌb]	Kneipe, Lokal	
	a while [waɪl]	eine Weile, einige Zeit	First we watched the monkeys **for a while**. (… eine Weile, eine Zeit lang)
	tap [tæp]	*(leichtes)* Klopfen	In the middle of night, we heard a **tap** on the door.
	Off you go now. [ɒf]	Ab mit euch jetzt! / Los mit euch jetzt!	

off

1. **weg, los** The thieves took our bag and ran **off**. She turned around and walked **off**.
2. **von … herunter** He fell **off** his bike and broke his leg. She jumped **off** the wall and ran away.

- (to) **get off the bus/boat/plane** aus dem Bus/Boot/Flugzeug aussteigen
- (to) **take sth. off** etwas ausziehen *(Kleidung)*; etwas absetzen *(Hut, Helm)*
- (to) **turn sth. off** etwas ausschalten *(Radio, Fernsehen, Licht)*

	towards the station/Mr Bell [tə'wɔːdz]	auf den Bahnhof/Mr Bell zu, in Richtung Bahnhof/Mr Bell	When the fire started, everyone ran **towards** the door.
p. 21	**tense** [tens]	(grammatische) Zeit, Tempus	the **past tense**, the **present tense**, the **future tense** (L) tempus, -oris *n*
	(to) **go on**	im Gang sein; andauern	The film was so boring, and it **went on** for hours.
	situation [ˌsɪtʃu'eɪʃn]	Situation	! stress: **situation** [ˌsɪtʃu'eɪʃn] (F) la situation
p. 22	**length** [leŋθ]	Länge; Dauer	The swimming pool has a **length** of 25 metres. adjective: **long** – noun: **length**
	for free	kostenlos, umsonst	There are a lot of things you can do **for free** in London.
p. 23	**route** [ruːt]	Strecke, Route	(F) la route
	speed [spiːd]	Geschwindigkeit	
	It was a pity that … ['pɪti]	Es war schade, dass …	**It's a pity that** Jake can't come to our party.

Text: The Notting Hill Carnival Parade

p. 24	(to) **hold onto** sth. [həʊld], **held, held** [held]	sich an etwas festhalten	She **held onto** the table and tried to stand up.
	(to) **scan** sth. **(for** sth.**)** [skæn]	etwas (nach etwas) absuchen	I **scanned** the crowd/the garden for my sister but couldn't see her.
	(to) **fill** [fɪl]	füllen	Can you **fill** the bucket with water, please?
	pavement ['peɪvmənt]	Gehweg, Bürgersteig	People were queuing on the **pavement**. 
	available [ə'veɪləbl]	erhältlich, verfügbar; erreichbar *(am Telefon)*	Tickets are **available** at the door.
	all around her	überall um sie herum	Suddenly there was darkness **all around** her.
	whistle ['wɪsl]	(Triller-)Pfeife	a **whistle** 
	(to) **blow the whistle** [bləʊ], **blew** [bluː], **blown** [bləʊn]	pfeifen *(auf der Trillerpfeife)*	

[eɪ] name · [aɪ] time · [ɔɪ] boy · [əʊ] old ·
[aʊ] town · [ɪə] here · [eə] where · [ʊə] tour

	(to) **panic** ['pænɪk]	in Panik geraten	❗ spelling: -ing form: **panicking**; simple past: **panicked** Ⓕ paniquer
	exactly [ɪg'zæktli]	genau	Sue and Jack are **exactly** the same size. Ⓕ exactement
	(to) **bend down** [bend], **bent**, **bent** [bent]	sich hinunterbeugen, sich bücken	She saw a coin on the ground and **bent down** to pick it up.
	rope [rəʊp]	Seil	
	wing [wɪŋ]	Flügel	
	rainbow ['reɪnbəʊ]	Regenbogen	
	dizzy ['dɪzi]	schwindlig	All the noise and the lights made her feel **dizzy**.
	hip [hɪp]	Hüfte	
	you	man	How do **you** say that in English? (Wie sagt man …?) That's not how **you** do it! (So macht man das nicht!)
	rhythm ['rɪðəm]	Rhythmus	Ⓕ le rythme
p. 25	(to) **scare** sb. [skeə]	jn. erschrecken; jm. Angst machen	verb: (to) **scare** – adjectives: **scared** (verängstigt) **scary** (unheimlich)
	loudspeaker [ˌlaʊd'spiːkə]	Lautsprecher; Megaphon	
	(to) **mind** [maɪnd]	etwas dagegen haben	

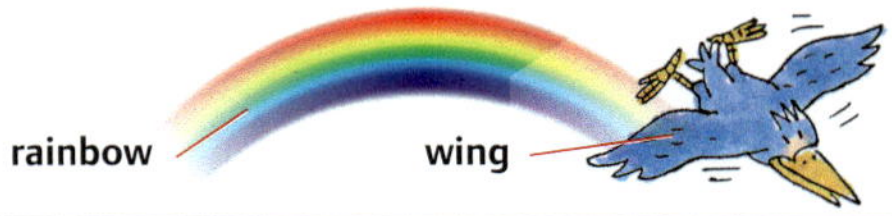

(to) mind

He **won't mind** if we sit down here for a while.	Es wird ihm nichts ausmachen. … / Er wird nichts dagegen haben, …
I'd like to ask you a question, **if you don't mind**.	…, wenn Sie nichts dagegen haben.
Do you mind if I open the window?	Stört es Sie, …? / Haben Sie etwas dagegen, …?

(to) **rest** [rest]	ruhen, sich ausruhen	They sat down in the park to **rest** for a moment.
no sign of … [saɪn]	keine Spur von …	I scanned the crowd, but there was **no sign of** my sister.
…, he said **under his breath.** [breθ]	…, sagte er flüsternd / murmelte er.	

Access to cultures: The Tower and the monarchs

p. 30	**monarch** ['mɒnək]	Monarch/in	❗ stress: **monarch** ['mɒnək]
	colourful ['kʌləfl]	farbenfroh, farbenprächtig, bunt	
	empire ['empaɪə]	Reich, Imperium	Ⓕ l'empire
	Celtic ['keltɪk], ['seltɪk]	keltisch	
	(to) **rule** sth. [ruːl]	etwas beherrschen, über etwas herrschen	Who **ruled** England after 1066?
	(to) **beat** [biːt], **beat** [biːt], **beaten** ['biːtn]	schlagen; besiegen	I **beat** my father at tennis last Sunday.
	(to) **belong to** sb. [bɪ'lɒŋ]	jm. gehören; zu jm. gehören	This bag **belongs to** Jill. (= This is Jill's bag.)
	(to) **remind** sb. [rɪ'maɪnd]	jn. erinnern	Please **remind** me that it's Grandma's birthday on Friday. I want to call her. Grandpa always says I **remind** him of his sister. ❗ • **remember sth.** = sich an etwas erinnern — Do you **remember** her name? • **remind sb.** = jn. erinnern — I mustn't forget. Please **remind** me.

[b] **boat** · [p] **pool** · [d] **dad** · [t] **ten** · [g] **good** · [k] **cat** · [m] **mum** · [n] **no** · [ŋ] **song** · [l] **hello** · [r] **red** · [w] **we** · [j] **you**

	(to) **spend time/money (on)** [spend], **spent, spent** [spent]	Zeit verbringen (mit); Geld ausgeben (für)	Mum says I **spend** too much time in front of my computer. My brother **spends** a lot of money **on** DVDs.
	rather than ['rɑːðə ðən]	statt, anstatt	I'd like tea **rather than** cocoa.
p. 31	(to) **remain** [rɪ'meɪn]	bleiben, verbleiben	My parents are divorced but the have **remained** good friends.
	as [æz]	da, weil	= because
	law [lɔː]	Gesetz	It's against the **law** to drive a car in a pedestrian zone.
	common ['kɒmən]	häufig; weit verbreitet	One of the most **common** names for girls in Britain today is Olivia. (L) communis, -e *(allgemein)*
	influence ['ɪnfluəns]	Einfluss	French words had a big **influence** on the English language.
	beginning [bɪ'gɪnɪŋ]	Anfang, Beginn	verb: (to) **begin** – nouns: **beginner / beginning**
	modern ['mɒdən]	modern	! stress: **modern** ['mɒdən] (F) moderne
p. 32	(to) **defeat** [dɪ'fiːt]	besiegen, schlagen	= (to) beat
	including [ɪn'kluːdɪŋ]	einschließlich; darunter (auch)	A lot of famous bands have played here, **including** *Deep Purple* and *Coldplay*. (L) includere *(einschließen)* ! • The price is £48, **including** breakfast. (… **einschließlich** Frühstück.) • Breakfast is **included**. (Frühstück ist **inbegriffen**.)
	population [ˌpɒpju'leɪʃn]	Bevölkerung, Einwohner(zahl)	(F) la population (L) populus, -i *m*
	trade [treɪd]	Handel	the activity of buying and selling
	wife [waɪf], *pl* **wives** [waɪvz]	Ehefrau	! seine (Ehe-)Frau = his **wife** (*not:* his ~~woman~~)
	husband ['hʌzbənd]	Ehemann	! ihr (Ehe-)Mann = her **husband** (*not:* her ~~man~~)
	divorce [dɪ'vɔːs]	Scheidung	adjective: **divorced** – noun: **divorce**
	pope [pəʊp]	Papst	
	head [hed]	Oberhaupt, Leiter/in	The prime minister is the **head** of the government in the UK.
	wedding ['wedɪŋ]	Hochzeit, Trauung	They lived together for ten years before their **wedding**.
	luxurious [lʌg'ʒʊəriəs]	luxuriös	
	prisoner ['prɪznə]	Gefangene(r)	
	Catholic ['kæθlɪk]	Katholik/in; katholisch	The pope is the head of the Roman **Catholic** church.
	Protestant ['prɒtɪstənt]	Protestant/in; protestantisch	! stress: **Protestant** ['prɒtɪstənt] / **Catholic** ['kæθlɪk]
	powerful ['paʊəfl]	mächtig, kräftig, stark	a **powerful** country/computer/car/storm
	power ['paʊə]	Macht; Kraft, Stärke; Energie, Strom	In the old days, kings had more **power** than today. Eating good food helps you to build up your **power**. How much **power** does a TV use?
p. 33	**age** [eɪdʒ]	Zeitalter	
	pirate ['paɪrət]	Pirat/in	! pronunciation and stress: **pirate** ['paɪrət]
	hero ['hɪərəʊ], *pl* **heroes**	Held/in	(F) le héros, la héroïne

[f] **f**ather · [v] ri**v**er · [s] **s**ister · [z] plea**s**e · [ʃ] **sh**op · [ʒ] televi**s**ion · [tʃ] **t**ea**ch**er · [dʒ] **G**ermany · [θ] **th**anks · [ð] **th**is · [h] **h**ere

return [rɪ'tɜːn]	Rückkehr	
(to) **overthrow** [ˌəʊvə'θrəʊ], **overthrew, overthrown**	stürzen *(Regierung, Staatsoberhaupt usw.)*	Do you remember Guy Fawkes? He wanted to **overthrow** the British government.
factor ['fæktə]	Faktor	
literature ['lɪtrətʃə]	Literatur	! stress: **li**terature ['lɪtrətʃə] (F) la littérature (L) litterae *f*
(to) **marry** ['mæri]	heiraten	verb: (to) **marry** – adjective: **married**
colony ['kɒləni]	Kolonie	! stress: **co**lony ['kɒləni] (F) la colonie (L) colonia *f (Siedlung)*
colonist ['kɒlənɪst]	Kolonist/in, Siedler/in	

Unit 2 Welcome to Snowdonia

Part A

p. 36 **empty** ['empti]	leer	**full ◄► empty**
scientist ['saɪəntɪst]	Naturwissenschaftler/in	someone who has studied science (L) scientia, -ae *f (Wissen)*
(to) **study** ['stʌdi]	studieren; untersuchen, beobachten; lernen	She **studied** English in Dublin in 1996. His dream was to **study** seals on the Welsh coast. There's a test on Monday so I have to **study** at the weekend. (L) studere
workshop ['wɜːkʃɒp]	Werkstatt	! **workshop** = **1.** Werkstatt; **2.** Lehrgang, Workshop
carpenter ['kɑːpəntə]	Tischler/in, Zimmerer/Zimmerin	someone who works with wood to make things like tables, chairs, etc.
furniture ['fɜːnɪtʃə] *(no pl)*	Möbel	! **furniture** hat keinen Plural: The **furniture is** new. Die **Möbel sind** neu. **ein Möbel(stück)** = **a piece of furniture**
oil [ɔɪl]	Öl	
a piece of … [piːs]	ein Stück …	 **a piece of wood**  **a piece of paper**
hammer ['hæmə]	Hammer	
(to) **come over (to)**	herüberkommen (zu/nach), vorbeikommen (bei)	Why don't you **come over to** our place on Friday evening?
probably ['prɒbəbli]	wahrscheinlich	! • adverb: **probably** („wahrscheinlich") – Jake is late. He's **probably** missed the bus again. • adjective: **probable** („wahrscheinlich") – How **probable** is a white Christmas this year?
(to) **make fun of** sb./sth.	sich über jn./etwas lustig machen	Don't **make fun of** me or I'll tell Mum!
(to) **give up**	aufgeben	
tonight [tə'naɪt]	heute Nacht, heute Abend	
p. 37 **architect** ['ɑːkɪtekt]	Architekt/in	! stress: **ar**chitect ['ɑːkɪtekt] (F) l'architecte *(m/f)* (L) architectus, -i *m*
astronaut ['æstrənɔːt]	Astronaut/in	! stress: **as**tronaut ['æstrənɔːt] (F) l'astronaute *(m/f)* (L) nauta, -ae *m (Seemann)*

[iː] green · [i] happy · [ɪ] big · [e] red · [æ] cat · [ɑː] class · [ɒ] song · [ɔː] door · [uː] blue · [ʊ] book · [ʌ] mum · [ɜː] girl · [ə] a partner

hairdresser ['heədresə]	Friseur/in	**at the hairdresser's** 
musician [mju'zɪʃn]	Musiker/in	someone who plays an instrument (F) le musicien, la musicienne
painter ['peɪntə]	Maler/in	(F) le/la peintre
natural ['nætʃrəl]	natürlich	the **natural** world = die Welt der Natur, die Natur (L) natura, ae *f* *(Geburt; Wesen)*
p. 38 **headword** ['hedwɜːd]	Stichwort *(im Wörterbuch)*	
part of speech [ˌpɑːt‿əv 'spiːtʃ]	Wortart	Nouns, verbs, adjectives, etc. are all **parts of speech**.
translation [træns'leɪʃn]	Übersetzung	verb: (to) **translate** – noun: **translation** (L) transferre *(hinübertragen)*
coal [kəʊl]	Kohle	**coal** 
underground [ˌʌndə'graʊnd]	unterirdisch, unter der Erde	Some animals – like rabbits – live **underground**.
(to) **ground** sb. [graʊnd]	jm. Hausarrest/Ausgehverbot erteilen	If you come home so late again, I'll **ground** you for two weeks.
official *(n)* [ə'fɪʃl]	Beamte(r), Beamtin	! **official** = **1.** *(adj)* amtlich, Amts- **2.** *(n)* Beamte(r), Beamtin (L) officium, -i *n* *(Dienst)*

(to) look after/around/for/…

• (to) **look after** sb.	I often have to **look after** my little brother.	**aufpassen auf; sich kümmern um**
• (to) **look around**	I like your new flat. Can I **look around**?	**sich umsehen**
• (to) **look for** sb./sth.	I'm **looking for** my keys. Have you seen them?	**suchen**
• (to) **look forward to** sth.	We're all **looking forward to** the summer holidays.	**sich freuen auf**
• (to) **look into** sth.	The officials are going to **look into** the problem.	**untersuchen, prüfen**
• (to) **look up**	She heard a noise and **looked up** from her book.	**hochsehen, aufschauen**
• (to) **look** sth. **up**	I don't understand this word. I'll have to **look** it **up**.	**nachschlagen** *(Wörter, Informationen)*

(to) come across/down/over/…

• (to) **come across** sb./sth.	Later we **came across** a beautiful village.	**stoßen auf,** *(zufällig)* **treffen**
• (to) **come down with** sth.	Jack can't take part. He's **come down with** a cold.	**bekommen** *(Krankheit)*, **erkranken an**
• (to) **come over**	John **came over** to watch the football with us.	**herüberkommen, vorbeikommen**
• (to) **come up with** sth.	Then my sister **came up with** a brilliant idea.	**haben, kommen auf** *(Idee, Vorschlag)*

p. 39 **difficult** ['dɪfɪkəlt]	schwierig, schwer	**easy ◄► difficult**
(to) **change** [tʃeɪndʒ]	wechseln	For some people, **changing** from one language to the other is easy. (F) changer
carrot ['kærət]	Möhre, Karotte	! stress: **carrot** ['kærət]
majority [mə'dʒɒrəti]	Mehrheit	There are 16 girls and 13 boys in my class. The girls are in the **majority**. (F) la majorité
minority [maɪ'nɒrəti]	Minderheit	The boys are in the **minority**. (F) la minorité **majority ◄► minority**
equally ['iːkwəli]	gleichermaßen, genauso	Do you think maths is **equally** important as English?

[eɪ] name · [aɪ] time · [ɔɪ] boy · [əʊ] old ·
[aʊ] town · [ɪə] here · [eə] where · [ʊə] tour

Part B

p. 40	**altogether** [ˌɔːltəˈgeðə]	insgesamt, alles in allem	We've raised a lot of money for charity – £400 **altogether**.
	hostel [ˈhɒstl]	Herberge, Wohnheim	
	(to) **wonder** [ˈwʌndə]	sich fragen, gern wissen wollen	Have you ever **wondered** why we have Christmas trees?
	(to) **pretend** [prɪˈtend]	so tun, als ob	He **pretended** to be ill so that he could miss school. The boys shouted after her, but she **pretended** not to hear them.
	Me neither. [ˈnaɪðə], [ˈniːðə]	Ich auch nicht.	"I don't know the answer." – "**Me neither.**" **Me too.** ◄► **Me neither.**
	(to) **go by**	vergehen, vorübergehen *(Zeit)*	Time always **goes by** too quickly in the holidays.
	stupid [ˈstjuːpɪd]	dumm, blöd	**stupid** ◄► **clever** (F) stupide
	downstream [ˌdaʊnˈstriːm]	flussabwärts	
	edge [edʒ]	Rand, Kante	 The ball rolled down the hill and dropped off the **edge** of the cliff.
	(to) **reach** [riːtʃ]	erreichen	If we leave now, we'll **reach** Wales before dinner.
	stick [stɪk]	Stock	
	(to) **grab** [græb]	schnappen, packen	I was late, so I **grabbed** my school bag and ran to the bus stop. 
p. 41	**steep** [stiːp]	steil	You can't ride your bike up that hill. It's too **steep**.
	(to) **join in**	mitmachen	We want to play football. Would you like to **join in**?
	before long	schon bald	The afternoon passed quickly and **before long** it was time to say goodbye.
	(to) **tell** sb. **(not) to do** sth.	jn. auffordern, etwas (nicht) zu tun; jm. sagen, dass er/sie etwas (nicht) tun soll	The teacher **told** the students **to** be quiet. How often do I have to **tell** you **not to** hit your brother?
p. 42	**warning** [ˈwɔːnɪŋ]	Warnung	
p. 43	**head teacher** [ˌhed ˈtiːtʃə]	Schulleiter/in	
	laptop [ˈlæptɒp]	Laptop *(tragbarer PC)*	
	(to) **allow** [əˈlaʊ]	erlauben, zulassen	**!** • (to) **allow** = erlauben, zulassen – **Does** your school **allow** you to use mobiles? • (to) **be allowed to do** sth. = etwas tun dürfen – **Are** you **allowed to use** mobiles at school?
p. 44	**No worries.** [ˈwʌriz] *(infml)*	Kein Problem! / Gern geschehen!	Thanks very much for helping me – **No worries.**
	a couple [ˈkʌpl]	ein Paar; ein paar	 **a young couple**  **a couple of sandwiches**

[b] **b**oat · [p] **p**ool · [d] **d**ad · [t] **t**en · [g] **g**ood · [k] **c**at · [m] **m**u**m** · [n] **n**o · [ŋ] so**ng** · [l] he**ll**o · [r] **r**ed · [w] **w**e · [j] **y**ou

p. 45	**topic sentence** [ˌtɒpɪk 'sentəns]	*Satz, der in das Thema eines Absatzes einführt*	
	(to) **be connected** [kə'nektɪd]	verbunden sein	

Numbers

- *English:* **3.5** = three **point** five
  German: **3,5** = drei **Komma** fünf
  Im Englischen steht ein **Punkt**, im Deutschen ein **Komma**.
- *English:* **1,500** = one thousand five hundred
  German: **1.500** = eintausendfünfhundert
  Im Englischen steht oft ein **Komma** in Zahlen, die größer als 1 000 sind. Im Deutschen steht dort manchmal ein **Punkt**.

climb [klaɪm]	Aufstieg, Anstieg	verb: (to) **climb** – noun: **climb**
summit ['sʌmɪt]	Gipfel	**summit**  Ⓕ le sommet Ⓛ summus, -a, -um *(höchster)*
(to) **manage** sth. ['mænɪdʒ]	etwas schaffen; etwas zustande bringen	We wanted to be back home at 6, but we didn't **manage** it. I didn't **manage** to visit the Tower while I was in London.
(to) **continue** sth. [kən'tɪnjuː]	etwas fortsetzen	We went inside and **continued** our conversation.
downhill [ˌdaʊn'hɪl]	bergab	**downhill** ◄► **uphill** (bergauf) **downstream** ◄► **upstream** (flussaufwärts)
energy ['enədʒi]	Energie, Kraft	! stress: **e**nergy ['enədʒi] Ⓕ l'énergie *(f)*
a total of … ['təʊtl]	eine Gesamtsumme von …; insgesamt	We raised **a total of** £ 400 for charity.
bar [bɑː]	Riegel *(Schokolade, Müsli)*, Tafel *(Schokolade)*	 **a bar of chocolate**  **a chocolate bar**
(to) **revise** [rɪ'vaɪz]	überarbeiten; *(Lernstoff)* wiederholen	He had to **revise** his work because there were too many mistakes. I have a test tomorrow, so I must **revise** tonight. Ⓕ réviser

Text: Snowdonia at night

p. 46	(to) **press** [pres]	drücken	
	finally ['faɪnəli]	endlich, schließlich	He tried again and again to open the door, and **finally** he managed it. Ⓕ finalement Ⓛ finis, -is *m* *(Ende, Ziel)*
	meal [miːl]	Mahlzeit, Essen	Me and my sister always prepare the evening **meal** on Fridays.
	(to) **keep doing** sth. [kiːp], **kept, kept** [kept]	etwas immer wieder / immer weiter tun; etwas ständig tun	I tried to speak, but he **kept interrupting** me. **Keep smiling** – and never give up.

corridor ['kɒrɪdɔː]	Gang, Korridor	a **corridor** 
star [stɑː]	Stern	
magical ['mædʒɪkl]	zauberhaft, wundervoll; magisch	The first time I was on stage with my band was one of the most **magical** moments in my life.
(to) **lie down** [ˌlaɪ 'daʊn], **lay** [leɪ], **lain** [laɪn]	sich hinlegen	I'm so tired. I think I'll **lie down** for half an hour. (to) **lie down** ◄► (to) **get up**
busy ['bɪzi]	belebt, geschäftig, hektisch	It was too **busy** in the dining room, so we went upstairs. (*etwa:* Im Esszimmer war zu viel los, …) The week before Christmas is a **busy** time for most shops.
(to) **clear** [klɪə]	räumen; abräumen	(to) **clear** the table / the dishes / your desk / the road
breeze [briːz]	Brise	
p. 47 (to) **have a look (at** sth.**)**	nachschauen; einen Blick auf etwas werfen	What was that noise in the garden? – I don't know. Let's go and **have a look**.
(to) **sit up**	sich aufsetzen	The sound of a bell woke her. She **sat up** and opened her eyes.
wooden ['wʊdn]	hölzern; Holz-	a **wooden** puppet 
figure ['fɪɡə]	Figur, Gestalt	! **figure** = **1.** Figur, Gestalt; **2.** Zahl, Ziffer stress: **figure** ['fɪɡə] Ⓛ figura, -ae *f*
note [nəʊt]	Note *(Musik)*	! **note** = **1.** Notiz, Mitteilung; **2.** Note
such a … [sʌtʃ]	so ein/e …; solch ein/e …	**such a** thing/person = a thing/person like that

such a + noun
Olivia is **such a** nice **person**.
… **so** ein netter Mensch
It was **such a** good **film** that I watched it twice.
… **so** ein guter Film

so + adjective
Olivia is **so nice**.
… **so** nett
The film was **so good** that I watched it twice.
… **so** gut

p. 48 (to) **make** sth. **up**	sich etwas ausdenken	Today we had to **make up** a story and tell it to our classmates.
(to) **argue** ['ɑːɡjuː]	streiten; sich streiten	My brother and sister **argue** from morning till night. "But, Mum …," he said. "**Don't argue**," she replied. („Widersprich mir nicht" …)
bite [baɪt]	Biss, Bissen	
director [də'rektə]	Leiter/in	Ⓕ le directeur, la directrice
office ['ɒfɪs]	Büro	Ⓛ officium, -i *n* *(Dienst)*

Question word + to-infinitive: how to … / what to … / who to … / where to …

Can you tell me **how to get** to the station?	Können Sie mir sagen, wie ich zum Bahnhof komme/kommen kann?
I don't know **what to do**.	Ich weiß nicht, was ich tun soll.
I need help, but I don't know **who to ask**.	Ich brauche Hilfe, aber ich weiß nicht, wen ich fragen kann/soll.
We had no idea **where to go**.	Wir hatten keine Ahnung, wohin wir gehen sollten.

[iː] green · [i] happy · [ɪ] big · [e] red · [æ] cat · [ɑː] class · [ɒ] song · [ɔː] door · [uː] blue · [ʊ] book · [ʌ] mum · [ɜː] girl · [ə] a partner

(to) **behave** [bɪˈheɪv]	sich verhalten, sich benehmen	If you **behave** like that again, I'll ground you for a month.
mop [mɒp]	Wischmopp	noun: **mop** – verb: (to) **mop** (wischen *(Fußboden)*)  He's **mopping** the floor.
(to) **splash** sb. [splæʃ]	jn. nass spritzen	
p. 49 **punishment** [ˈpʌnɪʃmənt]	Bestrafung, Strafe	
point of view [ˌpɔɪnt‿əv ˈvjuː]	Standpunkt	*English:* from my **point of view** *German:* von meinem **Standpunkt** aus gesehen; aus meiner **Sicht** (F) le point de vue

Checkpoint

p. 52 **a little**	ein bisschen, ein wenig, etwas	She speaks **a little** Welsh.

a little – a few

- You use **a little** with <u>nouns that have no plural</u>: **a little time, money, milk, music, bread, …**
  ein bisschen/ein wenig/etwas Zeit, Geld, Milch, Musik, Brot, …
- You use **a few** with the <u>plural of nouns</u>: **a few minutes, dollars, bottles, songs, sandwiches, …**
  einige/ein paar Minuten, Dollar, Flaschen, Lieder, belegte Brote, …

Access to cultures: Welcome to Wales

p. 54 **experience** [ɪkˈspɪəriəns] *(no pl)*	Erfahrung(en)	We'd love to hear about your **experience** during your trip to Liverpool. (F) l'expérience *(f)* (L) peritus, -a, -um *(erfahren)*
steel [stiːl]	Stahl	
industry [ˈɪndəstri]	Industrie	! stress: **industry** [ˈɪndəstri] (F) l'industrie *(f)* (L) industria
manufacturing (industry) [ˌmænjuˈfæktʃərɪŋ]	Fertigungsindustrie, verarbeitende Industrie	
health service [ˈhelθ ˌsɜːvɪs]	Gesundheitswesen	
social services *(pl)* [ˌsəʊʃl ˈsɜːvɪsɪz]	Sozialwesen, soziale Dienste	If teachers think that a student has problems, they can call **social services**.
rugby ground [ˈrʌgbi graʊnd]	Rugby-Platz, Rugby-Spielfeld	
below [bɪˈləʊ]	unter, unterhalb (von); unten, darunter	Your mouth is **below** your nose. From the plane, the buildings **below** were so small. **above** ◄► **below**
(to) **gaze** [geɪz]	blicken, starren	
reserve [rɪˈzɜːv]	Schutzgebiet	*English:* **dark sky reserve** *German:* **Lichtschutzgebiet**

p. 55	**whitewater rafting** [ˌwaɪtwɔːtə 'rɑːftɪŋ]	Wildwasserfahren *(im Schlauchboot)*	

whitewater rafting

	steam train ['stiːm treɪn]	*Zug mit Dampflok*	

	style [staɪl]	Stil	
	(to) **relax** [rɪ'læks]	sich entspannen, sich ausruhen	
	kayaking ['kaɪækɪŋ]	Kajakfahren	

kayaking

	bilingual [baɪ'lɪŋgwəl]	zweisprachig	(F) bilingue (L) bis *(zweimal)*, lingua *f (Sprache)*
	original [ə'rɪdʒənl]	Original-; ursprüngliche(r, s)	Who wrote the **original** version of this song? ! stress: **or<u>i</u>ginal** [ə'rɪdʒənl] (L) origo
	(to) **take place** [teɪk 'pleɪs]	stattfinden	Our next school trip will **take place** in October. ! „Falsche Freunde": *English:* (to) **take place** = *German:* **stattfinden** *English:* (to) **take a seat** = *German:* **Platz nehmen**
	mix [mɪks]	Mischung	
	(to) **promote** sth. [prə'məʊt]	etwas fördern; für etwas werben	The new rule will **promote** the rights of animals. Bands often give concerts to **promote** their new CDs.

Unit 3 My trip to the Southwest

pp. 58/59	**impression** [ɪm'preʃn]	Eindruck	(F) l'impression *(f)*
	skyscraper ['skaɪskreɪpə]	Wolkenkratzer	
	in downtown Albuquerque ['daʊntaʊn] *(AE)*	im Zentrum von Albuquerque	= *BE* in the centre of Albuquerque
	brochure ['brəʊʃə]	Broschüre, Prospekt	! stress: **<u>bro</u>chure** ['brəʊʃə] (F) la brochure
	practical ['præktɪkl]	praktisch	Your ideas are good, but can you give me some **practical** help, too? (F) pratique

Part A

p. 60	**coffee** ['kɒfi]	Kaffee	(F) le café
	an hour and a half	eineinhalb Stunden, anderthalb Stunden	*English:* **an hour and a half** *German:* **eineinhalb/anderthalb Stunden** *English:* **half an hour** *German:* **eine halbe Stunde**

[b] **b**oat · [p] **p**ool · [d] **d**ad · [t] **t**en · [g] **g**ood · [k] **c**at · [m] **m**um · [n] **n**o · [ŋ] so**ng** · [l] **h**ello · [r] **r**ed · [w] **w**e · [j] **y**ou

as well [əz 'wel]	auch, ebenso	We don't only sell books, we sell magazines **as well**. You might **as well** stay here tonight. (Du könntest heute Nacht ebenso gut hier bleiben.)
backpack ['bækpæk] (*BE auch:* **rucksack** ['rʌksæk])	Rucksack	 **backpacks** (*BE auch:* **rucksacks**)
(to) **form** [fɔːm]	bilden, formen	(L) forma, -ae *f* *(Form, Gestalt)*
column ['kɒləm]	Säule	(F) la colonne
(to) **rise up** [ˌraɪz_'ʌp], **rose** [rəʊz], **risen** ['rɪzn]	aufragen, emporragen *(Berge, Säulen, Türme, …)*	
gravestone ['ɡreɪvstəʊn]	Grabstein	a **gravestone** 
(to) **bury** ['beri]	begraben, beerdigen	He died on holiday in Spain, and they **buried** him there.
Native American [ˌneɪtɪv_ə'merɪkən]	amerikanischer Ureinwohner/ amerikanische Ureinwohnerin	
native ['neɪtɪv]	Mutter-	**native language** Muttersprache **native speaker** Muttersprachler/in (L) nasci *(geboren werden)*
god, God [ɡɒd]	Gott	
giant ['dʒaɪənt]	Riese	(F) le géant
challenge ['tʃælɪndʒ]	Herausforderung	My first day at *Gymnasium* was a **challenge** for me.
(to) **challenge** sb. (**to** sth.) ['tʃælɪndʒ]	jn. herausfordern (zu etwas)	We **challenged** them **to** a game of basketball. Maths doesn't really **challenge** me at the moment.
fierce [fɪəs]	heftig, wild	adjective: **fierce** – a **fierce** attack/fight/storm; **fierce** enemies adverb: **fiercely** – (to) fight **fiercely**; (to) defend/attack sth. **fiercely**
heaven ['hevn]	Himmel *(im religiösen Sinn)*	! clouds in the **sky** – God in **heaven**
(to) **be left** [left]	übrig sein	There **aren't** any biscuits **left**. I've eaten them all.
glad [ɡlæd]	froh, dankbar	
actually ['æktʃuəli]	eigentlich; übrigens; tatsächlich	

actually

Das Wort **actually** kann im Deutschen – je nach Situation – mit **eigentlich, übrigens, tatsächlich** wiedergegeben werden. Manchmal hat es auch überhaupt keine Entsprechung.

Man verwendet **actually**,

- wenn man jemanden höflich darauf hinweisen möchte, dass er/sie etwas Falsches gesagt hat
  I'm not English, **actually**: I'm Welsh.
  Actually, London is bigger than Paris.
- wenn man ausdrücken möchte, dass etwas in Wirklichkeit anders ist oder war, als man erwartet hat
  I didn't think I would enjoy the party, but it was **actually** fun.
- als entschuldigende Einleitung, wenn man etwas Unangenehmes mitzuteilen hat.
  When are you going to give me my MP3 player back?
  – **Actually**, I can't. I've lost it.

Shall I …? [ʃæl]	Soll ich …?	It's hot in here. **Shall I** open the window?
proud (of) [praʊd]	stolz (auf)	She's a very good student. We're **proud of** her.

[f] **f**ather · [v] **r**iver · [s] **s**ister · [z] plea**s**e · [ʃ] **sh**op · [ʒ] televi**s**ion · [tʃ] **t**ea**ch**er · [dʒ] **G**ermany · [θ] **th**anks · [ð] **th**is · [h] **h**ere

	none (of …) [nʌn]	keine(r, s) (von …)	He had 11 cousins but **none of** them lived near him.
	(to) **explore** [ɪk'splɔː]	erkunden, erforschen	It's exciting to **explore** new places. (F) explorer (L) explorare
	curious ['kjʊəriəs]	wissbegierig, neugierig	My brother is very **curious** and always wants to learn everything about everything. (F) curieux, se (L) cura, -ae *f* *(Sorge, Neugier)*
	impolite [ˌɪmpə'laɪt]	unhöflich	**polite** ◄► **impolite** (F) impoli, e
p. 61	**reservation** [ˌrezə'veɪʃn]	Reservat, Reservation	(L) servare *(retten, bewahren)*
	documentary [ˌdɒkju'mentri]	Dokumentarfilm	! stress: docu<u>men</u>tary [ˌdɒkju'mentri]
	narration [nə'reɪʃn]	Erzählung, Schilderung	
	narrator [nə'reɪtə]	Erzähler/in; Sprecher/in	
	host [həʊst]	Gastgeber/in; Moderator/in	
	(to) **guide** [gaɪd]	führen, begleiten	verb: (to) **guide** – noun: **guide**
	view [vjuː]	Ansicht, Meinung	**in my view** = in my opinion
p. 62	**border** ['bɔːdə]	Grenze	Spain only has a **border** with Portugal and France.
	(to) **change** [tʃeɪndʒ]	wechseln, umtauschen *(Geld)*	Don't forget to **change** money if you want to travel to Britain. (F) changer
	currency ['kʌrənsi]	Währung	Until 2001, Germany's **currency** was the *Deutsche Mark*.
	(to) **emigrate** ['emɪgreɪt]	auswandern, emigrieren	(F) émigrer
	the EU [ˌiː 'juː] **(the European Union** [ˌjʊərəpiːən 'juːniən]**)**	die Europäische Union	
	euro (€) ['jʊərəʊ]	Euro	

Pounds and euros

In **Britain**, you pay with **pounds** and **pence**.

You say:	*You write:*
fifty p [piː] / **fifty pence** [pens]	**50 p**
one pound / a pound	**£ 1**
two pounds fifty	**£ 2.50**

In **Germany**, you pay with **euros** and **cents**.

You say:	*You write:*
fifty cents [sents]	**€ 0.50**
one euro / a euro	**€ 1**
two euros fifty	**€ 2.50**

export ['ekspɔːt]	Export, Ausfuhr	(F) l'export *(m)*
governor ['gʌvənə]	Gouverneur/in	
ID card [ˌaɪ 'diː kɑːd]	Personalausweis	
independent [ˌɪndɪ'pendənt]	unabhängig	adjective: **independent** – noun: **independence**
nation ['neɪʃn]	Nation, Volk	(F) la nation (L) natio, -onis *f*
peace [piːs]	Friede, Frieden	**peace** ◄► **war** (F) la paix (L) pax, pacis *f*
police station [pə'liːs steɪʃn]	Polizeiwache, -revier	
republic [rɪ'pʌblɪk]	Republik	! stress: **re<u>pub</u>lic** [rɪ'pʌblɪk] (L) res publica *f*
the US [ˌjuː‿'es] **(the United States)**	die Vereinigten Staaten *(von Amerika)*	! Trotz des Plural-s („**states**") folgt ein <u>Verb im Singular</u>: The **United States has** a much bigger population than the United Kingdom.
visa ['viːzə]	Visum	Germans need a **visa** if they travel to India.

[iː] green · [i] happy · [ɪ] big · [e] red · [æ] cat · [ɑː] class · [ɒ] song · [ɔː] door · [uː] blue · [ʊ] book · [ʌ] mum · [ɜː] girl · [ə] a partner

north – northern / south – southern / …

north [nɔːθ]	Norden; nach Norden; nördlich	**northern** ['nɔːðən]	nördlich, Nord-
south [saʊθ]	Süden; nach Süden; südlich	**southern** ! ['sʌðən]	südlich, Süd-
east [iːst]	Osten; nach Osten; östlich	**eastern** ['iːstən]	östlich, Ost-
west [west]	Westen; nach Westen; westlich	**western** ['westən]	westlich, West-

the **southern** end of the island — *das südliche Ende der Insel*
They come from **eastern** Turkey. — *aus der östlichen Türkei*

	public ['pʌblɪk]	öffentliche(r, s)	This is a **public** library. Everyone can read books here. (F) public, publique (L) publicus, -a, -um
p. 63	**argument** ['ɑːgjumənt]	Streit, Auseinandersetzung	! **argument** = **1.** Argument; **2.** Streit, Auseinandersetzung stress: **argument** ['ɑːgjumənt]

Part B

p. 66	**petrol** ['petrəl] *(BE)*, **gas** [gæs] *(AE)*	Benzin	a **petrol station** *(BE)* / **gas station** *(AE)*
	like *(infml)*	als ob	What's he doing? – He looks **like** he's crying. ! Diese umgangssprachliche Verwendung von **like** wird von manchen als falsches Englisch empfunden. Besonders im Schriftlichen solltest du **as if** für das deutsche „als ob" benutzen: He looks **as if** he's crying.
	incredible [ɪn'kredəbl]	unglaublich	an **incredible** story/feeling/journey/… (L) incredibilis, e
	nephew ['nefjuː], ['nevjuː]	Neffe	your sister's or brother's son
	niece [niːs]	Nichte	your sister's or brother's daughter
	typical (of) ['tɪpɪkl]	typisch (für)	That's so **typical of** him – he's always like that. What food is **typical of** your area? (F) typique
	service ['sɜːvɪs]	Gottesdienst	(L) servire *(dienen)*
	(to) **suggest** sth. **(to** sb.**)** [sə'dʒest]	(jm.) etwas vorschlagen	*English:* Dad **suggested that we go** to the cinema. *German:* Dad **schlug vor**, ins Kino **zu gehen**. ! (*not:* Dad suggested ~~to go~~ …)
	(to) **check** sth. **out** [ˌtʃek‿'aʊt] *(infml)*	sich etwas anschauen, anhören; etwas ausprobieren	Our new CD is called "No sky above". **Check it out!**
	section ['sekʃn]	Abschnitt, Teilstück	My favourite **section** of this book is *Access to cultures*.
	painting ['peɪntɪŋ]	Gemälde, Bild	verb: (to) **paint** – noun: **painting**
	local ['ləʊkl]	örtlich, Lokal-; am/vom Ort	We like to buy food from **local** farmers. (F) local, e (L) locus, -i *m* *(Ort)*
p. 67	**skull** [skʌl]	Schädel	
	crazy ['kreɪzi]	verrückt	You want to go out in this rain? You must be **crazy**.
	She was like: "Stop …" *(infml)*	Und sie so: „Stopp …"	
	bank [bæŋk]	Bank; Flussufer	

[eɪ] name · [aɪ] time · [ɔɪ] boy · [əʊ] old ·
[aʊ] town · [ɪə] here · [eə] where · [ʊə] tour

kind of … *(infml)*	irgendwie; ganz schön	This place looks **kind of** scary to me. ! **kind of** + <u>**noun**</u>: What **kind of <u>music</u>** …? Welche **Art von Musik** …? **kind of** + <u>**adjective**</u>: He looked **kind of <u>excited</u>**. … **irgendwie aufgeregt** …
strict [strɪkt]	streng	Emily isn't allowed to watch TV after 9 o'clock. Her parents are very **strict** about that.
angel ['eɪndʒl]	Engel	(F) l'ange *(m)*
way [weɪ]	Art und Weise	

way ("Art und Weise")

Try to present your topic **in an interesting way**.	auf eine interessante Art und Weise
In this way, you will make sure that everyone enjoys your talk.	auf diese Weise
I like **the way** Oliver ended his talk.	die Art und Weise, wie …
John is like his father **in some/many ways**.	in mancher/vielerlei Hinsicht

(to) **miss** [mɪs]	vermissen	I enjoyed my trip to France, but I **missed** my friends. ! (to) **miss** = **1.** verpassen; **2.** vermissen
either … or … ['aɪðə], ['iːðə]	entweder … oder …	We can **either** walk **or** take the bus.
pot [pɒt]	Gefäß; Topf	**several pots** 
design [dɪ'zaɪn]	Design; Gestaltung	
jewellery *(BE)* **/ jewelry** *(AE)* *(no pl)* ['dʒuːəlri]	Schmuck	rings, earrings, etc.
pipe [paɪp]	(Tabaks-)Pfeife	 a **pipe**  a **whistle**
line [laɪn]	Reihe	! **line** = **1.** Linie; **2.** Zeile; **3.** Reihe
certainly ['sɜːtnli]	sicher(lich), auf jeden Fall, freilich	That is **certainly** true for Germany, but I'm not so sure about Britain. Ask Jonathan. He'll **certainly** help you.
awesome ['ɔːsəm] *(bes. AE, infml)*	klasse, großartig	= *BE* great, super, fantastic, cool
p. 68 **boyfriend** ['bɔɪfrend]	Freund	
girlfriend ['gɜːlfrend]	Freundin	
on foot	zu Fuß	(to) go **on foot** = (to) walk
p. 69 **coordinator** [kəʊ'ɔːdɪneɪtə]	Koordinator/in	
layout ['leɪaʊt]	Layout, Gestaltung	
editor ['edɪtə]	Redakteur/in; Herausgeber/in	(F) l'éditeur *(m)*, l'éditrice *(f)* (L) edere *(bekanntmachen)*
research *(no pl)* ['riːsɜːtʃ]	Recherche, Forschung(en)	I have to do some **research** on Ireland for homework.
discussion [dɪ'skʌʃn]	Diskussion	(F) la discussion
decision [dɪ'sɪʒn]	Entscheidung	verb: (to) **decide** – noun: **decision** (F) la décision

[b] **boat** · [p] **pool** · [d] **dad** · [t] **ten** · [g] **good** · [k] **cat** ·
[m] **mum** · [n] **no** · [ŋ] **song** · [l] **hello** · [r] **red** · [w] **we** · [j] **you**

Part C

p. 70	**owner** ['əʊnə]	Besitzer/in	verb: (to) **own** – noun: **owner**
	weird [wɪəd]	seltsam, komisch	I have a **weird** feeling that something is wrong.
	(to) **try hard**	sich anstrengen; sich (große) Mühe geben	They were from Scotland. I had to **try** very **hard** to understand them.
	(to) **stare (at** sb./sth.**)** [steə]	(jn./etwas an)starren	You shouldn't **stare at** people. It's impolite.
	guest [gest]	Gast	
	last [lɑːst]	zuletzt, das letzte Mal	When did you see them **last**?
	sense of humour [ˌsens‿əv 'hjuːmə]	(Sinn für) Humor	*English:* He has **a good sense of humour** / **no sense of humour.** *German:* Er hat **Humor** / **keinen Humor**.
	(to) **survive** [sə'vaɪv]	überleben	(F) survivre (L) vivere *(leben)*
	(to) **be alive** [ə'laɪv]	leben, am Leben sein	(to) **be alive** ◄► (to) **be dead**
p. 71	**ride** [raɪd]	Ritt, Ausritt	
	folk *(pl)* [fəʊk] *(infml)*	Leute	The **folk** round here are very friendly to tourists.
	round here [ˌraʊnd 'hɪə]	hier in der Gegend	**Round here**, we're all United fans.
	(to) **dislike** [dɪs'laɪk]	nicht mögen, nicht leiden können	(to) **like** ◄► (to) **dislike**
	(to) **unpack** [ˌʌn'pæk]	auspacken	(to) **pack** (packen, einpacken) ◄► (to) **unpack**
	rude [ruːd]	unhöflich; unverschämt	Staring at people is **rude**. **rude** ◄► **polite** (L) rudis
	(to) **care about** sth. [keə]	etwas wichtig nehmen	(L) curare *(sorgen für)*

(to) care

1. I **don't care** about money.	Geld ist mir egal.
2. In the city, people **wouldn't care** what I looked like.	In der Großstadt wäre es den Leuten egal, wie ich aussehe / würde sich niemand darum kümmern, wie ich aussehe.
3. I really **care** about animals.	Tiere liegen mir sehr am Herzen. / Tiere sind mir sehr wichtig.
4. Her parents are really rich. – Who **cares**?	Ihre Eltern sind richtig reich. – Na und? / Wen interessiert das?

accident ['æksɪdənt]	Unfall; Zufall	There's been an **accident**. We should call the police. Yesterday, Dad met an old friend **by accident**. (= zufällig)

möglich – wahrscheinlich – sicherlich

My parents	**may** **might** **could** **should** **must**	be at home now.	Meine Eltern	sind jetzt **vielleicht** daheim. **könnten** jetzt (**vielleicht**) daheim sein. **könnten** jetzt daheim sein. **sollten/müssten eigentlich** jetzt daheim sein. **müssen** jetzt daheim sein.

trail [treɪl]	Weg, Pfad	There are lots of good riding **trails** in the hills behind our house.
the trail I **used to take** with Oreo ['juːst tə]	der Weg, den ich (früher immer) mit Oreo genommen habe	

… used to be/do …

With **used to** you can talk about something that was true in the past but is usually not true any more:

I **used to do** a lot of sport, but I don't have the time now.	Ich habe früher (immer) viel Sport getrieben, …
There **used to be** trees in front of our house.	Früher standen Bäume vor unserem Haus.
My brother **used to cry** a lot when he was little.	Mein Bruder hat (immer) viel geweint, …

[f] **f**ather · [v] ri**v**er · [s] **s**ister · [z] plea**s**e · [ʃ] **sh**op · [ʒ] televi**s**ion · [tʃ] tea**ch**er · [dʒ] **G**ermany · [θ] **th**anks · [ð] **th**is · [h] **h**ere

	stream [striːm]	Bach	She stopped at the **stream** and drank some water.
	ashes *(pl)* ['æʃɪz]	Asche *(sterbliche Überreste)*	**!** • **ash** („Asche") wird verwendet für das, was übrig bleibt, wenn Holz, Papier, Kohle, Tabak verbrennt. • **ashes** *(pl)* („Asche") wird verwendet – für die sterblichen Überreste nach der Einäscherung eines Verstorbenen; – für die Überreste nach einem Brand (z.B. eines Hauses).
	(to) **complain** [kəm'pleɪn]	sich beschweren, sich beklagen	There was a disco right next to the hotel, and a lot of guests **complained** about the noise.
	(to) **get paid**	bezahlt werden	My sister is good at making videos. She even **gets paid** for them.
	I guess ...	Ich nehme an, ... / Ich denke, ...	That was the last question. **I guess** we're finished.
p. 73	**bang** [bæŋ]	Knall	
	dock [dɒk]	Hafen, Dock	
	(to) **end** [end]	enden; beenden	Most adverbs of manner **end** in *-ly*. (to) **start** ◄► (to) **end**
	quarter ['kwɔːtə]	(Stadt-)Viertel	(F) le quartier (L) quartus *(der Vierte)*
p. 74	**prediction** [prɪ'dɪkʃn]	Vorhersage, Voraussage	What is your **prediction** for the *Bundesliga* this year? Who will win? (L) praedicere *(vorhersagen)*
	date [deɪt]	Datum; Verabredung, Date	**!** **date** = **1.** Datum – What's the **date** today? **2.** Verabredung, Date – Guess what! I've got a **date** with Jeremy tomorrow.
	calendar ['kælɪndə]	Kalender	
	(to) **experience** [ɪk'spɪəriəns]	erfahren, erleben	verb: (to) **experience** - noun: **experience**
p. 75	(to) **pass** [pɑːs]	vergehen, vorübergehen *(Zeit)*	The lesson was so interesting that the time **passed** really quickly. (F) passer
	next [nekst]	als Nächstes	That was nice. What are we going to do **next**?
	junction ['dʒʌŋkʃn]	(Straßen-)Kreuzung	
	pedestrian [pə'destriən]	Fußgänger/in	
	(to) **walk the dog**	mit dem Hund rausgehen, den Hund ausführen	
	traffic light ['træfɪk laɪt] (*oft auch:* **traffic lights** *(pl)*)	(Verkehrs-)Ampel	

He's **walking the dog.**

traffic ['træfɪk]	Verkehr	There's not much **traffic** in our street – it's usually very quiet.
(to) **carry** ['kæri]	tragen	**!** He's **carrying** a heavy box. (Er **trägt** eine schwere Kiste.) He's **wearing** jeans and a red T-shirt. (Er **trägt** Jeans und ein rotes T-Shirt.)

[iː] green · [i] happy · [ɪ] big · [e] red · [æ] cat · [ɑː] class · [ɒ] song · [ɔː] door · [uː] blue · [ʊ] book · [ʌ] mum · [ɜː] girl · [ə] **a** partner

(to) **kick** [kɪk]	treten	
(to) **race** [reɪs]	rasen	A red car was **racing** across the junction.
(to) **turn** red/brown/cold/… [tɜːn]	rot/braun/kalt/… werden	! **turn** = „werden" wird hauptsächlich für Farbveränderungen und Wetterwechsel verwendet.
van [væn]	Transporter, Lieferwagen	
(to) **spin around** [ˌspɪn‿əˈraʊnd], **spun, spun** [spʌn]	sich (im Kreis) drehen; herumwirbeln	The girl **spun around** until she fell to the ground.
(to) **park** [pɑːk]	parken	
immediately [ɪˈmiːdiətli]	sofort	My dog comes **immediately** when I call her. (F) immédiatement
siren [ˈsaɪrən]	Sirene	! stress: **siren** [ˈsaɪrən]

Text: The horse ride

p. 76 **accent** [ˈæksənt]	Akzent	! stress: **accent** [ˈæksənt] (F) l'accent *(m)*
(to) **sigh** [saɪ]	seufzen	
reins *(pl)* [reɪnz]	Zügel	
ditch [dɪtʃ]	Graben	
famine [ˈfæmɪn]	Hungersnot	(L) fames, -is *f* *(Hunger)*
(to) **starve** [stɑːv]	hungern	*English:* (to) **be starving** *German:* **einen Riesenhunger haben**
disease [dɪˈziːz]	*(ansteckende)* Krankheit	! • **disease** wird für ansteckende oder sehr ernsthafte Erkrankungen verwendet: She has a blood **disease**. Thousands of trees died from **disease**. • Das allgemeinere Wort für „Krankheit" ist **illness**: After a week of **illness**, she went back to school.
silent [ˈsaɪlənt]	lautlos, leise; schweigend	(L) silentium, -i *n* *(Schweigen)*
straight [streɪt]	direkt, geradewegs	They entered the pub and went **straight** to the bar.
not until 1912	erst im Jahr 1912; nicht vor 1912	We wo**n't** arrive **until** 10 pm.
now that …	jetzt, wo … / nun, da …	**Now that** the school year is almost over, we can make plans for the holidays.
slippery [ˈslɪpəri]	rutschig, glatt	
dry [draɪ]	trocken	**dry** ◄► **wet**
(to) **protest** [prəˈtest]	protestieren	(F) protester (L) protestari *(öffentlich aussagen)*
protest [ˈprəʊtest]	Protest	! verb: (to) **protest** [prəˈtest] – noun: **protest** [ˈprəʊtest]
What's up?	Was gibt's? / Was ist los?	Can you come and help me? – Why, **what's up?**
just as rude/boring/exciting/…	genauso unhöflich/langweilig/aufregend/…	
shrub [ʃrʌb]	Strauch, Busch	
(to) **realize** sth. [ˈriːəlaɪz]	etwas erkennen; sich einer Sache bewusst werden	When I got home, I **realized** that I had left my bag on the train. (F) réaliser qc
(to) **tighten** [ˈtaɪtn]	spannen, festziehen, anziehen	You need to **tighten** the wheel of your bike before you go on your trip.

[eɪ] name · [aɪ] time · [ɔɪ] boy · [əʊ] old · [aʊ] town · [ɪə] here · [eə] where · [ʊə] tour

	(to) **lift** [lɪft]	heben, hochheben, anheben	This table is very heavy. Can you help me to **lift** it?
	calm [kɑːm]	ruhig	There was no wind and the sea was very **calm**. (F) calme
	still [stɪl]	still, ruhig	Stand **still**! Don't move!
	rattlesnake ['rætlsneɪk]	Klapperschlange	
p. 77	**battery** ['bætəri]	Batterie, Akku	! stress: **battery** ['bætəri] (F) la batterie
	(to) **charge** ['tʃɑːdʒ]	(auf)laden	I can't make any phone calls right now – I have to **charge** my mobile first. (F) charger
	vet [vet]	Tierarzt/Tierärztin	
	(to) **get lost** [lɒst]	sich verlaufen, sich verirren	Be careful. It's easy to **get lost** in the forest.
	death [deθ]	Tod	verb: (to) **die** – noun: **death**
	thought [θɔːt]	Gedanke	verb: (to) **think, thought, thought** – noun: **thought**
	motor ['məʊtə]	Motor	
	truck [trʌk] (*BE auch:* **lorry** ['lɒri])	Lastwagen, LKW	
	(to) **lead** [liːd], **led, led** [led]	führen, leiten	This road **leads** to the next village.

Checkpoint

p. 80	**semi-** ['semi]	halb-; Halb-	a **semi**-circle; the **semi**-finals
	luckily ['lʌkɪli]	glücklicherweise	There's been an accident. **Luckily**, nobody got hurt.
p. 81	(to) **grow up** [ˌɡrəʊ‿'ʌp], **grew up, grown up**	aufwachsen; erwachsen werden	My grandma **grew up** in a small village in Spain. When I **grow up**, I want to be an artist.

Access to cultures: Celebrating in America

p. 82	**holiday** ['hɒlədeɪ]	Feiertag	! **holiday** = **1.** Urlaub; **2.** Ferien

Unit 4 Inside New York

p. 84	**borough** [*AE:* 'bɜːrəʊ, *BE:* 'bʌrə]	(Stadt-)Bezirk	Manhattan is one of New York City's five **boroughs**.
	central ['sentrəl]	zentral, Zentral-, Mittel-	! stress: **central** ['sentrəl]
	statue ['stætʃuː]	Statue	! pronunciation: **statue** ['stætʃuː] (L) statua, -ae *f*
	liberty ['lɪbəti]	Freiheit	(F) la liberté (L) libertas *f*
p. 85	**exchange** [ɪks'tʃeɪndʒ]	Austausch; Austausch-	There are some **exchange** students from France at our school. (F) *l'échange (m)*

Part A

p. 86	**metal** ['metl]	Metall; Metall-	! stress: **metal** ['metl] (F) le métal
p. 87	(to) **hang out** [ˌhæŋ‿'aʊt], **hung, hung** [hʌŋ] *(infml)*	abhängen, rumhängen	What did you do last night? – I just **hung out** with some friends.

p. 88	**locker** ['lɒkə]	Schließfach, Spind	lockers 
	high school ['haɪ sku:l]	*(USA) Schule für 14- bis 18-Jährige*	
	railing ['reɪlɪŋ]	Geländer	a **railing**
	yacht [jɒt]	Jacht	! pronunciation: **yacht** [jɒt] (F) le métal
	shot [ʃɒt]	Aufnahme, Foto; *(Film)* Einstellung, Szene	
	he's **way too** good/clever/…	er ist viel zu gut/clever/…	He's **way too clever** to do something silly like that.
	pressure ['preʃə]	Druck	We're always under a lot of **pressure** before a test. (F) la pression (L) premere *(drücken)*
	memorial [mə'mɔ:riəl]	Denkmal; Gedenk-	There's a war **memorial** by the church in our village. (L) memoria, -ae *f (Erinnerung)*
	newspaper ['nju:speɪpə] (*kurz auch:* **paper**)	Zeitung	(L) novus, -a, -um *(neu)*
	block [blɒk]	(Häuser-, Wohn-)Block	
	(to) **roar** [rɔ:]	tosen, dröhnen	The waves **roared** as the hurricane got stronger.
	man-made [ˌmæn'meɪd]	künstlich, Kunst-	This isn't a natural lake. It's **man-made**. **natural; real ◄► man-made**
	(to) **cover** ['kʌvə]	bedecken, zudecken	It was cold so she **covered** her baby with her jacket. His desk is always **covered** with books and articles.
	surface ['sɜ:fɪs]	Oberfläche	(F) la surface
	rose [rəʊz]	Rose	(F) la rose
	if	ob	! **if** = **1.** ob – I don't know **if** I can come to your party. **2.** wenn, falls – I'll come to your party **if** I can.
p. 89	(to) **arrest** [ə'rest]	verhaften, festnehmen	After the body was found, the police quickly **arrested** a 32-year-old man. (F) arrêter qn.
	(to) **lean** [li:n]	sich lehnen; sich beugen	 He's **leaning** forward to talk to the driver.
	inch [ɪntʃ]	Zoll *(Längenmaß; 2,54 cm)*	12 **inches** = 1 foot (about 30 centimetres)
	one another	sich (gegenseitig), einander	The looked at **one another**. = … at **each other**.
	in fright [fraɪt]	ängstlich, erschrocken	When he saw the knife, he cried out **in fright**.
	(to) **be born** [bɔ:n]	geboren sein/werden	*English:* I **was born** in 2008. *(not:* I ~~am born~~ in …) *German:* Ich **bin** 2008 **geboren**.
	cemetery [*BE:* 'semətri, *AE:* 'seməteri]	Friedhof	an area of land where we bury the dead (F) le cimetière
	I'd better … (= **I had better …**)	Ich sollte lieber …	It's getting late. **I'd better** call Mum. (= I should call …) It's cold. **You'd better** put on a pullover. (= You should put on …)

[f] **f**ather · [v] **r**iver · [s] **s**ister · [z] plea**s**e · [ʃ] **sh**op · [ʒ] televi**s**ion · [tʃ] **t**ea**ch**er · [dʒ] **G**ermany · [θ] **th**anks · [ð] **th**is · [h] **h**ere

storey, *pl* **storeys** *(BE)*, **story**, *pl* **stories** *(AE)* ['stɔːri] — Stock, Stockwerk, Etage

> **German "Stock(werk)"**
> - You usually use **floor** when you want to say where somebody lives or works: We live on the third **floor**. / Our offices are on the sixth **floor**.
> - You usually use **storey** *(BE)*/**story** *(AE)* when you want to say how high a building is: a six-**storey** house *(ein sechsstöckiges Haus)* / The building is 14 **storeys** high.

indoor ['ɪndɔː] — Innen-; Hallen- — an **indoor** swimming pool; **indoor** games and activities
indoor ◄► **outdoor**

observation deck [ˌɒbzə'veɪʃn dek] — Aussichtsplattform — an **observation deck**

terrorist ['terərɪst] — terroristische(r, s); Terrorist/in — ! stress: **terrorist** ['terərɪst] — (F) le/la terroriste — (L) terrere *(erschrecken)*

(to) **crash** [kræʃ] — abstürzen *(Flugzeug; Computer)*

> **(to) crash**
> - My computer **crashed** and I lost lots of work.
> - The plane **crashed into** an office block. (… stürzte/krachte in ein Bürogebäude.)
> - The car went off the road and **crashed into** a tree. (… fuhr/krachte/knallte gegen …)

(to) **collapse** [kə'læps] — einstürzen; zusammenbrechen

p. 90

American English (I)

DIFFERENT WORDS

American English	British English
apartment	flat
cell phone	mobile phone
cookie	biscuit
elevator	lift
French fries	chips
garbage	rubbish
line	queue
pants	trousers
sidewalk	pavement
store	shop
subway	underground
vacation	holiday

DIFFERENT SPELLING

AE: -ter	BE: -tre
center	centre
meter	metre
theater	theatre
AE: -or	**BE: -our**
color	colour
favorite	favourite
neighbor	neighbour
AE:	**BE:**
traveled, traveling	travelled, travelling

American English (II)

DIFFERENT PRONUNCIATION

	AE	BE
ask, can't	AE: [æ] [æsk], [kænt]	BE: [ɑː] [ɑːsk], [kɑːnt]
new, Tuesday	AE: [uː] [nuː], ['tuːzdeɪ]	BE: [juː] [njuː], ['tjuːzdeɪ]
clock, hot	AE: [ɑː] [klɑːk], [hɑːt]	BE: [ɒ] [klɒk], [hɒt]

In American English, you can usually hear the **r** in words like **here, more, sure, shirt, farm, hard**.

In American English, the **t** between two vowels often sounds more like a **d**:
city ['sɪdi], **better** ['bedər], **writer** ['raɪdər]

[iː] green · [i] happy · [ɪ] big · [e] red · [æ] cat · [ɑː] class · [ɒ] song · [ɔː] door · [uː] blue · [ʊ] book · [ʌ] mum · [ɜː] girl · [ə] a partner

	(to) **be afraid (of** sth./sb.**)** [ə'freɪd]	Angst haben (vor etwas/jm.)	My mother **is afraid of** snakes.
p. 91	**emphasis** ['emfəsɪs]	Betonung, Hervorhebung	

Part B

p. 92	**weirdo** ['wɪədəʊ] *(infml)*	Spinner/in	Don't walk through the park. It's full of **weirdos** at night.
	(to) **be keen on** sth. [kiːn]	wild auf etwas sein	I'**m** really **keen on** sports. I go running every day.
	(to) **be keen on doing** sth.	wild darauf sein, etwas zu tun	I'**m not** very **keen on** going to that party on Friday. Do we have to go?
	pigeon ['pɪdʒɪn]	(Stadt-)Taube	 a **pigeon** (F) le pigeon
	insulted [ɪn'sʌltɪd]	beleidigt	When he said I was fat, I felt really **insulted**.
p. 93	**suggestion** [sə'dʒestʃən]	Vorschlag	My **suggestion** is that we stop work and go home. verb: (to) **suggest** – noun: **suggestion** (F) la suggestion
	move [muːv]	Zug *(bei Brettspielen)*	(L) movere *(bewegen, sich bewegen)*
	legendary ['ledʒəndri]	legendär, berühmt	! stress: **legendary** ['ledʒəndri] (F) légendaire
	Ladies and gentlemen [ˌleɪdiz‿ən 'dʒentlmən]	Meine Damen und Herren / Sehr geehrte Damen und Herren	
	timer ['taɪmə]	Zeitmesser	
	(to) **click** [klɪk]	klicken	Open the page and **click** on the link.
	(to) **concentrate (on** sth.**)** ['kɒnsntreɪt]	sich konzentrieren (auf etwas)	Please be quiet. I can't **concentrate** on my work. ! stress: **concentrate** ['kɒnsntreɪt] (F) se concentrer
p. 94	**takeout** ['teɪkaʊt] *(AE)*	Essen zum Mitnehmen	= *BE* takeaway
	onion ['ʌnjən]	Zwiebel	**preparing to cut onions**  ! pronunciation: **onion** ['ʌnjən]
p. 95	**body** ['bɒdi]	Hauptteil *(eines Textes)*	
	human ['hjuːmən]	menschlich; Mensch	! **human** = **1.** Mensch – animals and **humans** **2.** menschlich – It's only **human**. Für das deutsche „Mensch" wird oft auch **human being** verwendet: The earth is much older than **human beings**. (F) humain, e (L) humanus
	(to) **escape** [ɪ'skeɪp]	fliehen	His grandfather **escaped** from Germany in 1940. verb: (to) **escape** – noun: **escape**
	draw *(n)* [drɔː] *(bes. BE)*	Unentschieden	Nobody was able to win the match. It ended in a **draw**.
	standard ['stændəd]	Standard; Standard-	(F) le standard
	(to) **date from**	stammen aus *(zeitlich)*	Today's rules of chess **date from** the 19th century.
	board game ['bɔːd geɪm]	Brettspiel	*Chess* and *Monopoly* are **board games**.

[eɪ] name · [aɪ] time · [ɔɪ] boy · [əʊ] old · [aʊ] town · [ɪə] here · [eə] where · [ʊə] tour

	square [skweə]	Quadrat; *(in Städten)* Platz; *(auf Brettspiel)* Feld; *(auf Papier)* Kästchen	
	grid [ɡrɪd]	Gitter; Raster; Rechteckschema	

Part C

p. 98	(to) **take a walk** *(bes. AE)*	spazieren gehen, einen Spaziergang machen	(to) go for a walk
	track [træk]	(Bahn-)Gleis	
	railroad ['reɪlrəʊd] *(AE)*, **railway** ['reɪlweɪ] *(BE)*	Eisenbahn	**railway tracks** *(BE)*, **railroad tracks** *(AE)*
	unusual [ʌn'ju:ʒuəl]	ungewöhnlich	Snow is very **unusual** in June.
	usual ['ju:ʒuəl]	gewöhnlich, üblich	**usual** ◄► **unusual** adjective: **usual** – Dad came home earlier than **usual**. adverb: **usually** – He **usually** comes home later.
	frozen ['frəʊzn]	tiefgekühlt; gefroren	a **frozen** turkey 
	leader ['li:də]	Leiter/in	Our maths teacher is also **leader** of our school choir.
	(to) **tear** sth. **down** [ˌteə 'daʊn], **tore** [tɔ:], **torn** [tɔ:n]	etwas abreißen	They started **tearing** the Berlin Wall **down** in 1989.
	roller coaster ['rəʊlə kəʊstə]	Achterbahn	a **roller coaster** 
	shrub [ʃrʌb]	Strauch, Busch	
	(to) **bloom** [blu:m]	blühen	
	seed [si:d]	Samen	
	lawn [lɔ:n]	Rasen	**shrubs** **lawn** **seeds**
	(to) **spread, spread, spread** [spred]	(sich) ausbreiten, verbreiten	The fire quickly **spread** to other parts of the building.
	avenue ['ævənju:]	Allee, Boulevard	(F) l'avenue *(f)*
	work of art [ˌwɜ:k‿əv‿'ɑ:t]	Kunstwerk	(L) ars *f (Kunst)*
	performance [pə'fɔ:məns]	Aufführung, Vorstellung, Auftritt	
	(to) **perform** [pə'fɔ:m]	auftreten *(Künstler/in)*	The Beatles first **performed** in the USA in 1964.
	council ['kaʊnsl]	Ausschuss; Rat *(Stadtrat, Gemeinderat u.Ä.)*	
p. 99	**handout** ['hændaʊt]	Handout, Handzettel	
	transparency [træns'pærənsi]	Folie	
	bouldering ['bəʊldərɪŋ]	Bouldern *(Klettern in Absprunghöhe, ohne Seil)*	
	altitude ['æltɪtju:d]	Höhe	
	hold [həʊld]	Griff	verb: (to) **hold, held, held** – noun: **hold**
	improvement [ɪm'pru:vmənt]	Verbesserung	verb: (to) **improve** – noun: **improvement**

[b] **b**oat · [p] **p**ool · [d] **d**ad · [t] **t**en · [ɡ] **g**ood · [k] **c**at · [m] **m**um · [n] **n**o · [ŋ] so**ng** · [l] **h**e**ll**o · [r] **r**ed · [w] **w**e · [j] **y**ou

Text: Underground New York

p. 100	**novel** ['nɒvl]	Roman	(L) novus
	sight [saɪt]	Anblick	Look at those mountains! What a **sight**!
	risk [rɪsk]	Risiko	I'm much too nervous to take any **risks**. (F) le risque *English:* (to) **take a risk** *German:* **ein Risiko eingehen**
	(to) **yell** [jel]	schreien	
	chubby ['tʃʌbi]	pummelig, mollig	
	forearm ['fɔːrɑːm]	Unterarm	**forearm** 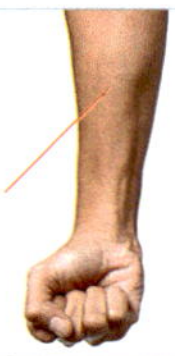
	hook [hʊk]	Haken	 some **hooks**
	skinny ['skɪni]	mager, dünn, dürr	
	entrance ['entrəns]	Eingang	verb: (to) **enter** – noun: **entrance**
	gravel ['grævl]	Kies, Schotter	**gravel** 
p. 101	**bit** [bɪt]	Stück(chen), Teil	! **a bit** = **1.** ein Stück(chen), Teil  **bits of glass**  **bits of wood** **2.** ein bisschen, etwas – We felt **a bit** tired after the walk.
	besides [bɪ'saɪdz]	außerdem	It's too late to go to the cinema. And **besides**, I've already seen the film.
	fault [fɔːlt]	Schuld, Fehler	Why didn't you wake me up this morning? It's your **fault** that I'll be late for school.
	pebble ['pebl]	Kieselstein	**pebbles on the beach** 
	whatever [ˌwɒt'evə]	was (auch) immer	We will help you, **whatever** happens.
	(to) **approach** [ə'prəʊtʃ]	sich nähern, herannahen	We are now **approaching** Augsburg main station.
	dust [dʌst]	Staub	
	(to) **blow the horn** [hɔːn], **blew, blown**	hupen	You should only **blow your horn** if the situation is dangerous.
	impatient [ɪm'peɪʃnt]	ungeduldig	**patient** (geduldig) ◄► **impatient**

patient(ly) – impatient(ly)

adjectives:	Be **patient**. It'll be your turn soon.	Please don't be **impatient**. I'm working as fast as I can.
adverbs:	She waited **patiently** for three hours.	He played **impatiently** with his pen.

[f] father · [v] river · [s] sister · [z] please · [ʃ] shop · [ʒ] television · [tʃ] teacher · [dʒ] Germany · [θ] thanks · [ð] this · [h] here

	thick [θɪk]	dick	❗ *German* **dick** = **1. fat** *(person, animal)* **2. thick** *(book, pullover, wall, …)*
	dirt [dɜːt]	Dreck	noun: **dirt** – adjective: **dirty**
	can [kæn]	Dose	❗ • In *BE*, people use the word **can** for drinks. To talk about food, the British usually use **tin**. • Americans use **can** for food and drinks.
	blanket ['blæŋkɪt]	Decke *(zum Zudecken)*	Are you cold? Shall I get you a **blanket**?
	doll [dɒl]	Puppe	a **doll** 
	rusty ['rʌsti]	rostig; verrostet	
	machine [mə'ʃiːn]	Maschine, Gerät	(L) machina
	(to) **be gone** [gɒn]	weg sein, nicht (mehr) da sein	I don't know where Steve is. He was here two minutes ago and now he**'s gone**.
	stuff [stʌf] *(infml)*	Zeug, Kram	What's the red **stuff** on your shirt? Blood?
	artwork ['ɑːtwɜːk]	Kunstwerk	
p. 102	**vigorous** ['vɪgərəs]	energisch, kräftig	adjective: **vigorous** – adverb: **vigorously** He had to run **vigorously** to get the bus.
	by mistake	aus Versehen	Sorry, I opened this letter **by mistake**, but it's for you.
	(to) **hop** [hɒp]	hüpfen	
	flashlight ['flæʃlaɪt] *(AE)*	Taschenlampe	= *BE* torch
	(to) **reach (for)** [riːtʃ]	greifen (nach)	Little Johnny tried to **reach for** the toy and fell over. ❗ (to) **reach** = **1.** erreichen; **2.** greifen
	switch [swɪtʃ]	Schalter	 **switches** 
	movement ['muːvmənt]	Bewegung	verb: (to) **move** – noun: **movement** (F) le mouvement (L) movere *(bewegen)*
	(to) **illuminate** [ɪ'luːmɪneɪt]	erleuchten, beleuchten	I love it at night when they **illuminate** all the old buildings in town.
p.103	**handshake** ['hændʃeɪk]	Handschlag, Händedruck	
	whether ['weðə]	ob	**Whether** you go or not, that is your decision. ❗ **whether** ist etwas förmlicher als **if**.
	(to) **grow** darker/old/…, **grew, grown**	(allmählich) dunkler/alt/… werden	My hair **grew** darker when I was about 14. ❗ (to) **grow** = **1.** wachsen; **2.** anbauen, anpflanzen; **3.** werden
	body ['bɒdi]	Leiche	❗ **body** = **1.** Körper; **2.** Leiche

Checkpoint

p.105	**transport** ['trænspɔːt]	Verkehrsmittel; Transport(wesen)	different forms of **transport** ❗ stress: **transport** ['trænspɔːt] (F) le transport (L) trans + portare 

[iː] green · [i] happy · [ɪ] big · [e] red · [æ] cat · [ɑː] class · [ɒ] song · [ɔː] door · [uː] blue · [ʊ] book · [ʌ] mum · [ɜː] girl · [ə] a partner

p.106	(to) **teach** [tiːtʃ], **taught, taught** [tɔːt]	unterrichten, lehren	*English:* (to) **teach sb. to do sth.** *German:* **jm. beibringen/jn. lehren, etwa zu tun** verb: (to) **teach** – noun: **teacher**
p.107	**nearly** [ˈnɪəli]	fast, beinahe	= almost

Access to cultures: In the New World

p.108	**apart** [əˈpɑːt]	auseinander; getrennt	My sister and I are three years **apart**. Josie's parents are living **apart** now.
	corn [kɔːn] *(AE, no pl)*	Mais	
	squash [skwɒʃ]	Kürbis	
	bean [biːn]	Bohne	

corn

squash

beans

p.109	**timeline** [ˈtaɪmlaɪn]	Zeitstrahl, Zeitleiste	
	pilgrim [ˈpɪlgrɪm]	Pilger/in	The **Pilgrims** (with a capital 'p') were the English colonists who arrived in America in 1620.
	harvest [ˈhɑːvɪst]	Ernte	
	(to) **found** [faʊnd]	gründen	! (to) **found** – **founded** – **founded** (gründen) (to) **find** – **found** – **found** (finden)
	(to) **govern** [ˈgʌvən]	regieren	verb: (to) **govern** – noun: **government** (F) gouverner
	according to … [əˈkɔːdɪŋ]	… zufolge; laut …	**According to** my dad, it's a great film. (= My dad says it's a great film.)
	Indian [ˈɪndiən]	Indianer/in	! • Der Begriff **Native American** wird heute dem älteren Begriff **Indian** vorgezogen. • **Indian** bedeutet auch „Inder/in".
	deer [dɪə], *pl* **deer**	Reh, Hirsch	
	shelter [ˈʃeltə]	Unterkunft	
	politics [ˈpɒlətɪks]	Politik	! • Das Wort **politics** ist Singular, trotz des **-s**: **Politics <u>is</u>** interesting for some people, and **<u>it is</u>** boring for others. • stress: **<u>po</u>litics** [ˈpɒlətɪks] (F) la politique
	generally [ˈdʒenrəli]	generell, allgemein	Mum doesn't eat much meat **generally**, but sometimes she has a steak.

Unit 5 New Orleans

p.110	**hurricane** [ˈhʌrɪkən, ˈhʌrɪkeɪn]	Hurrikan, Orkan	
	brass band [ˌbrɑːs ˈbænd]	Blaskapelle	a **brass band**

	swamp [swɒmp]	Sumpf, Marschland	
	alligator [ˈælɪgeɪtə]	Alligator	! stress: **<u>al</u>**ligator [ˈælɪgeɪtə]
	palm tree [ˈpɑːm triː]	Palme	! silent "**l**": **palm tree** [ˈpɑːm triː]
p.111	**object** [ˈɒbdʒɪkt]	Objekt, Gegenstand	

[eɪ] name · [aɪ] time · [ɔɪ] **boy** · [əʊ] **old** ·
[aʊ] **town** · [ɪə] **here** · [eə] **where** · [ʊə] **tour**

Part A

p. 112	**tropical** ['trɒpɪkl]	tropisch, Tropen-	a **tropical** island/rainforest/disease
	embarrassing [ɪm'bærəsɪŋ]	peinlich	My father saw us in the park. – How **embarrassing**.
	disgusting [dɪs'gʌstɪŋ]	ekelhaft, widerlich	I find the way some people eat **disgusting**. It makes me feel sick.
	buck [bʌk] *(infml)* (= **dollar ($)** ['dɒlə])	Dollar	
	chicken ['tʃɪkɪn]	Huhn; (Brat-)Hähnchen	**chickens** 
	barbecue ['bɑːbɪkjuː]	Grill; Grillfest, Grillparty	Shall I put some more meat on the **barbecue**? We're having a **barbecue** today. Do you want to come? 
p. 113	**dude** [djuːd] *(bes. AE, Slang)*	Typ, Kerl	You know Mick? Man, he's the coolest **dude** I know.
	That **sucks**! [sʌks] *(infml)*	Das ist echt übel!	I can't come to your party. I have to go to my grandma's birthday. – Man, **that sucks!**
	(to) **keep** [kiːp], **kept, kept** [kept]	halten; behalten	

(to) keep, kept, kept

1) (to) **keep**	behalten; aufbewahren	Can I **keep** the book or do you want it back? I **keep** all my books in my bedroom.
2) (to) **keep** sth. **warm/fresh**/… (to) **keep** sth. **out of/away from** …	halten	She put on some boots to **keep** her feet **warm**. Careful. **Keep** the fireworks **out of** the rain. And **keep** them **away from** the children. Dangerous area! **Keep out**!
3) (to) **keep (on) doing** sth.	etwas immer wieder/ immer weiter/ständig tun	She **kept (on) walking** till she got to a village. I tried to speak, but he **kept interrupting** me.

habit ['hæbɪt]	(An-)Gewohnheit	something people do regularly: Doing sport is a good **habit**. (L) habere *(eine Gewohnheit haben)*
(to) **block** [blɒk]	blockieren, sperren	(to) **block** emails; (to) **block** a phone number; (to) **block** sb.
jerk [dʒɜːk] *(infml)*	Trottel, Depp	
social media *(pl)* [ˌsəʊʃl 'miːdiə]	soziale Medien	
generation [ˌdʒenə'reɪʃn]	Generation	! stress: gene**ra**tion [ˌdʒenə'reɪʃn] (F) la génération
serious ['sɪəriəs]	ernst; ernsthaft	adj: **serious** – a **serious** illness/problem/… (F) sérieux, se (L) serius adv: **seriously** – **seriously** ill/injured/… (F) sérieusement
assignment [ə'saɪnmənt] *(AE)*	Aufgabe, Arbeitsauftrag *(in der Schule oder daheim zu erledigen)*	
(to) **compare** [kəm'peə]	vergleichen	**Compared to** Australia, Germany is very small. (Verglichen mit Australien …)

[b] **boat** · [p] **pool** · [d] **dad** · [t] **ten** · [g] **good** · [k] **cat** · [m] **mum** · [n] **no** · [ŋ] **song** · [l] **hello** · [r] **red** · [w] **we** · [j] **you**

advertisement [əd'vɜːtɪsmənt] (*kurz auch:* **ad** [æd], **advert** ['ædvɜːt])	Werbespot, Werbung; Anzeige, Inserat	We bought our dog after we saw an **advert** in the local paper.
(to) **advertise** ['ædvətaɪz]	Werbung machen (für); inserieren	*English:* (to) **advertise** clothes/cars/... *German:* **für** Kleidung/Autos/... **werben**
totally ['təʊtəli]	völlig, total	• adv: **totally** (völlig, total) – I **totally** disagree. (F) totalement • adj: **total** (Gesamt-) – the **total** number of pupils at this school (F) total, e
company ['kʌmpəni]	Firma, Gesellschaft	My uncle works for an oil **company** in Scotland.
(to) **match** sth. [mætʃ]	zu etwas passen	*English:* (to) **match** sth. *German:* **zu** etwas **passen** Her red shoes **matched** her dress very well.
image ['ɪmɪdʒ]	Bild, Abbild; Vorstellung	When I hear the word 'California', I have an **image** of beaches and surfers in my head. (F) l'image *(f)* (L) imago *f*
(to) **create** [kri'eɪt]	schaffen, erschaffen, kreieren	(F) créer (L) creare
p. 114 **account** [ə'kaʊnt]	Account, Konto	How do I change the password of my email **account**? You're too young to open a bank **account**.
cyberbullying ['saɪbəˌbʊliɪŋ]	Cyber-Mobbing *(Verleumdung/ Diffamierung in sozialen Medien)*	
(to) **download** sth. [ˌdaʊn'ləʊd]	etwas herunterladen	(to) **download** sth. ◄► (to) **upload** sth. etwas herunterladen ◄► etwas hochladen
(to) **enter** a **password** ['entə], ['pɑːswɜːd]	ein Passwort eingeben	! (to) **enter** = **1.** betreten; eintreten **2.** eingeben, eintragen *(Name, Passwort, ...)*
(to) **log in/out** [lɒg]	sich ein-/ausloggen	
on demand [dɪ'mɑːnd]	auf Abruf, nach Bedarf	Watching movies **on demand** is cheaper than buying the DVD.
(to) **stream** [striːm]	strömen; streamen	
(to) **update** sth. [ˌʌp'deɪt]	etwas aktualisieren, auf den neuesten Stand bringen	Do your apps **update** themselves automatically?
survey ['sɜːveɪ]	Umfrage, Studie	Here are the results of a 2017 **survey** of US teenagers.
daily ['deɪli]	täglich	nouns: **day** **week** **month** **year** adjectives: **daily** **weekly** **monthly** **yearly**
per day/hour/... [pə, pɜː]	pro Tag/Stunde/...	People say you should walk 10,000 steps **per** day.
type (of) [taɪp]	Typ, Art, Sorte (von)	
questionnaire [ˌkwestʃə'neə]	Fragebogen	Please anwer the questions in this **questionaire** now.
average ['ævərɪdʒ]	durchschnittlich; Durchschnitt	What's the **average** age of students in your year? I study two hours per day **on average**. (im Durchschnitt, durchschnittlich)
(to) **delete** [dɪ'liːt]	löschen; streichen	(to) **delete** a paragraph / a program / a link
comment ['kɒment]	Bemerkung, Kommentar	(F) le commentaire (L) commentari

[f] **f**ather · [v] ri**v**er · [s] **s**ister · [z] plea**s**e · [ʃ] **sh**op · [ʒ] televi**s**ion · [tʃ] tea**ch**er · [dʒ] **G**ermany · [θ] **th**anks · [ð] **th**is · [h] **h**ere

	(to) **comment (on** sth.**)** ['kɒment]	sich äußern (zu etwas), (etwas) kommentieren	When he saw her new car, he **commented** "Nice!". The President didn't want to **comment on** the news. (F) commenter
	harmless ['hɑːmləs]	harmlos	This animal looks **harmless** but is very dangerous.
p. 115	**salt** [sɔːlt]	Salz	**salt** and **pepper**  (L) sal *m*
p. 117	**element** ['elɪmənt]	Element	(L) elementum
	necessary ['nesəsəri]	notwendig, nötig	You can phone me on my mobile if **necessary**. (F) nécessaire (L) necesse est *(es ist notwendig)*

Part B

p. 118	(to) **tune** [tjuːn]	stimmen *(Instrument)*	That guitar sounds awful. He should **tune** it.
	(to) **reach over** [ˌriːtʃ‿'əʊvə]	die Hand ausstrecken	**Bob reached over**, took the guitar and started to play.
	string [strɪŋ]	Saite	 **strings**
	closet ['klɒzɪt] *(bes. AE)*	Wandschrank *(oft begehbar)*	 a **closet**
	ancestor ['ænsestə]	Vorfahr/in	Our **ancestors** lived shorter lives than we do. (F) l'ancêtre *(m)*
	porch [pɔːtʃ]	Veranda *(AE)*; Vorbau, Vordach *(BE)*	 **porch** *(AE)*  **porch** *(BE)*
	(to) **hum** [hʌm]	summen; brummen	
	tune [tjuːn]	Melodie	Dad always hums some old **tunes** when he's driving.

(to) wish

I **wish** I knew the answer to your questions.	Ich wünschte, ich wüsste die Antwort auf deine Fragen.
I **wish** it wasn't raining.	Ich wünschte, es regnete nicht/würde nicht regnen.
I **wish** I had known my grandparents.	Ich wünschte, ich hätte meine Großeltern gekannt.

In Wunschsätzen mit **I wish …** *(Ich wünschte, …)* steht das folgende Verb in einer Vergangenheitsform, obwohl sich die Sätze nicht auf die Vergangenheit beziehen, sondern auf die Gegenwart oder Zukunft. Im Deutschen steht der Konjunktiv.

You **would have liked** him.	Du hättest ihn gemocht.	• I **would have been** afraid. (Ich hätte Angst gehabt.) • You **could have asked** me. (Du hättest mich fragen können.) • She **must have liked** him. (Sie muss ihn gemocht haben.)
honey ['hʌni]	Honig; *(infml, als Anrede:)* Schatz, Schätzchen	

[iː] green · [i] happy · [ɪ] big · [e] red · [æ] cat · [ɑː] class · [ɒ] song · [ɔː] door · [uː] blue · [ʊ] book · [ʌ] mum · [ɜː] girl · [ə] a partner

	pile [paɪl]	Stapel, Haufen	I can't come, I have a **pile** of work to do.
	great-grandfather/ great-grandmother	Urgroßvater/ Urgroßmutter	
	handsome ['hænsəm]	attraktiv, gut aussehend	Her father was a very **handsome** man.
	(to) **pat** [pæt]	tätscheln	verb: (to) **pat** – noun: **pat** (Klaps; Tätscheln)
	carefully ['keəfəli]	sorgfältig, aufmerksam	! **carefully** = **1.** vorsichtig – Drive **carefully**. **2.** sorgfältig, aufmerksam – Listen **carefully**. / Read the report **carefully**.
	(to) **fold** [fəʊld]	falten	Take a sheet of paper and **fold** it in two. (… und falte es in der Mitte zusammen)
	jersey ['dʒɜːzi]	Trikot	Football **jerseys** are terribly expensive, aren't they?
p. 119	(to) **hunt** [hʌnt]	jagen	verb: (to) **hunt** – noun: **hunt**
p. 120	**pattern** ['pætn]	Muster	I like the **pattern** on your shirt. It looks African.
p. 121	(to) **bet, bet, bet** [bet]	wetten	I **bet** you can't sing as high as my sister.
	(to) **be in time for** the bus	den Bus erreichen; rechtzeitig zum Bus kommen	We were late, but were still **in time for the bus**, because it was late too.
	(to) **go wrong**	schiefgehen	Anything that can **go wrong** will **go wrong**.
	(to) **report** [rɪ'pɔːt]	berichten	verb: (to) **report** – noun: **report**

Part C

p. 122	(to) **try** sth. **on**	etwas anprobieren	I'm not sure if this T-shirt is the right size. Can I **try** it **on**?
	anthem ['ænθəm]	Hymne	
	doorway ['dɔːweɪ]	Eingang	They stood in the **doorway** and chatted for hours.
	round [raʊnd]	rund	
	coloured ['kʌləd]	farbig, bunt	I love the **coloured** windows in our church.
	(to) **speculate** ['spekjuleɪt]	spekulieren, Vermutungen anstellen	
	relationship [rɪ'leɪʃnʃɪp]	Beziehung, Verhältnis	(F) la relation
p. 123	**material** [mə'tɪəriəl]	Material, Stoff	(F) le matériel (L) materia
	shape [ʃeɪp]	Form, Gestalt	*English:* Those glasses **are** an interesting **shape**. *German:* Die Brille **hat** eine interessante **Form**.
	oval ['əʊvl]	oval	! stress: <u>o</u>val ['əʊvl] (L) ovum *(Ei)*
	cotton ['kɒtn]	Baumwolle	(F) le coton
	leather ['leðə]	Leder	
	light brown/blue/…	hellbraun/-blau/…	**light brown/blue/…** ◄► **dark brown/blue/…**
	medium ['miːdiəm]	mittelgroß; mittel-	(L) medius, -a, -um
	tiny ['taɪni]	winzig	**tiny** ◄► **huge**
	triangular [traɪ'æŋgjələ]	dreieckig	These **triangular** plates aren't very practical. Round ones or square ones are much better. (F) triangulaire (L) tres, tria *(drei)*; angulus *(Ecke, Winkel)*
	centimetre (cm) ['sentɪmiːtə]	Zentimeter	1 metre = 100 **centimetres** (F) le centimètre (L) centum *(hundert)*

	(to) **vary** ['veəri]	unterschiedlich sein, verschieden sein	The pronunciation of "butter" **varies** in different parts of the UK. (L) variare
	(to) **depend on** sth. [dɪ'pend]	von etwas abhängen; auf etwas angewiesen sein	I sometimes ride my bike to school – it **depends on** the weather. We live in a small village, so we **depend on** our car.
	actual ['æktʃuəl]	tatsächliche(r, s), wirkliche (r, s)	They call him Fred, but his **actual** name is Nathan.
	consequence ['kɒnsɪkwəns]	Folge, Konsequenz	Think of the **consequences** before you do that!
p. 124	(to) **skim a text** [skɪm]	einen Text überfliegen *(um den Inhalt grob zu erfassen)*	
	heading ['hedɪŋ]	Überschrift	
	sub-heading ['sʌbˌhedɪŋ]	Zwischenüberschrift; Kapitelüberschrift	Long articles in newspapers are often broken up with **sub-headings**.
	graphics *(pl)* ['græfɪks]	Grafiken	
p. 125	**youth** [juːθ]	Jugend; Jugend-	It's cheaper to stay at a **youth** hostel than at a hotel.
	(to) **rebuild** [ˌriː'bɪld], **rebuilt, rebuilt** [ˌriː'bɪlt]	wiederaufbauen	

Text: A true Fourth of July

p. 126	(to) **be attached to** sth. [ə'tætʃt]	an etwas hängen *(befestigt sein)*; an etwas angehängt/beigeheftet sein	A boat **was attached to** the back of the car. The **attached** translation can help you if you have problems with the French original.
	(to) **wave (at** sb.**)** [weɪv]	(jm. zu)winken	She **waved at** her fans before she got on the plane.
	balcony ['bælkəni]	Balkon	
	(to) **run, ran, run**	verlaufen *(Straße; Grenze)*	The path **runs** along both sides of the river.
	smoke [sməʊk]	Rauch	verb: (to) **smoke** – noun: **smoke**
	(to) **growl** [graʊl]	knurren	After a couple of hours, my stomach began to **growl**.
	(to) **set** sth. **up, set, set** [set]	etwas aufstellen, aufbauen, errichten, einrichten	It took half an hour to **set up** the tent.
	(to) **lay** [leɪ], **laid, laid** [leɪd]	legen	! • (to) **lie, lay, lain** = **liegen** – Our dog is not allowed to **lie** on the sofa. • (to) **lay, laid, laid** = **legen** – You can **lay** your jacket on the sofa. • (to) **lay sth. out, laid, laid** = **etwas ausbreiten** – We **laid out** the brochures on the table.
	(to) **sizzle** ['sɪzl]	brutzeln, zischen	The meat **sizzled** on the barbecue.
	stilts *(pl)* [stɪlts]	Stelzen	Can you walk on **stilts**?
	It's been **ages** ...	Es ist ewig her ...	It's been **ages** since we last met. I met him once or twice, but that was **ages** ago.
	landing ['lændɪŋ]	Landungssteg	
	(to) **grin** [grɪn]	grinsen	
	(to) **slither** ['slɪðə]	gleiten; schlittern	Snakes **were slithering** through the grass.
	(to) **shine** [ʃaɪn], **shone, shone** [ʃɒn]	leuchten; scheinen *(Sonne)*	Her earrings **shone** in the light of the candles.
	line [laɪn]	Leine, (Angel-)Schnur	(L) linea

[b] boat · [p] pool · [d] dad · [t] ten · [g] good · [k] cat · [m] mum · [n] no · [ŋ] song · [l] hello · [r] red · [w] we · [j] you

	sharp [ʃɑːp]	scharf	Be careful. That knife is very **sharp**.
	(to) **shoot** [ʃuːt], **shot, shot** [ʃɒt]	schießen; erschießen	She **shot** the man in the leg. John Lennon was **shot** in 1980.
p. 127	(to) **rock**	schaukeln, schwanken	The boat **rocked** and we nearly fell out.
	simple [ˈsɪmpl]	einfach, unkompliziert	Anyone can make this cake. It's a very **simple** recipe.
	harmonica [hɑːˈmɒnɪkə]	Mundharmonika	
	buoy [bɔɪ, *AE auch:* ˈbuːi]	Boje	
	(to) **get the hang of** sth. [hæŋ] *(infml)*	den Dreh raushaben/rausbekommen (bei etwas); etwas kapieren	Well done! I think you're **getting the hang of** it. It took me a while to **get the hang of** my new job.
	both ... and ... [bəʊθ]	sowohl ... als auch ...	People speak English **both** in Britain **and** in the USA.
	(to) **set, set, set** [set]	untergehen *(Sonne)*	
	vibration [vaɪˈbreɪʃn]	Vibration	
	(to) **explode** [ɪkˈspləʊd]	explodieren	Suddenly hundreds of fireworks **exploded** in the sky.
	mesmerizing [ˈmezməraɪzɪŋ]	fesselnd, hypnotisierend	It was a **mesmerizing** view.
	(to) **notice** [ˈnəʊtɪs]	merken, bemerken	I didn't **notice** Jeremy because he was so quiet. When I arrived, I **noticed** that I had lost my keys.
	(to) **rush** [rʌʃ]	eilen, stürzen	(to) hurry
	rough [rʌf]	rau; grob; hart	**rough** hands; a **rough** idea/plan; a **rough** first draft a **rough** time
	passenger [ˈpæsɪndʒə]	Passagier/in; Fahrgast	(F) le passager
	(to) **burst, burst, burst** [bɜːst]	platzen	The balloon **burst** with a loud bang.

Checkpoint

p. 129	**paraphrase** [ˈpærəfreɪz]	Umschreibung	Can you give me a **paraphrase** for this word? I don't know what it means. (L) paraphrasis *f* noun: **paraphrase** – verb: (to) **paraphrase** (umschreiben, mit anderen Worten sagen)
	civil rights *(pl)* [ˌsɪvl ˈraɪts]	Bürgerrechte	(L) civis *m, f (Bürger/in)*
p. 131	(to) **cook** [kʊk]	kochen; zubereiten	
	review [rɪˈvjuː]	Rezension, Besprechung, Kritik	Before I buy a book, I try to read a few **reviews** of it.

[f] **f**ather · [v] ri**v**er · [s] **s**i**s**ter · [z] plea**s**e · [ʃ] **sh**op · [ʒ] televi**s**ion · [tʃ] tea**ch**er · [dʒ] **G**ermany · [θ] **th**anks · [ð] **th**is · [h] **h**ere

Das **Dictionary** besteht aus **zwei alphabetischen Wörterlisten**:
English – German (S. 224–252) und **German – English** (S. 253–276)

Im **English – German Dictionary** kannst du nachschlagen, wenn du wissen möchtest, was ein englisches Wort bedeutet, wie man es ausspricht oder wie es geschrieben wird.

Im **Dictionary** werden folgende **Abkürzungen und Symbole** verwendet:

sth. = something (etwas)	sb. = somebody (jemand)	jn. = jemanden	jm. = jemandem
pl = plural (Mehrzahl)	*infml = informal* (umgangssprachlich)	*AE = American English*	*BE = British English*

° Mit diesem Kringel sind Wörter markiert, die nicht zum Lernwortschatz gehören.

Die **Fundstellenangaben** zeigen, wo ein Wort zum ersten Mal vorkommt:
I = erster Band (Jahrgangsstufe 5) • II = zweiter Band (Jahrgangsstufe 6) •
III 1 (33) = dritter Band (Jahrgangsstufe 7), Unit 1, Seite 33

Tipps zur Arbeit mit einem Wörterbuch findest du im Skills File auf den Seiten 166–167.

A

a [ə] ein, eine I **a 1960s band** eine Band aus den 60er Jahren *(des 20. Jahrhunderts)* II **... a day/week/year** ... pro Tag/Woche/Jahr I **a bit** ein bisschen, etwas I **a few** ein paar, einige II

°**abbey** ['æbi] Abtei, Kloster

abbreviation [əˌbriːvi'eɪʃn] Abkürzung II

able ['eɪbl]: **be able to do sth.** etwas tun können; fähig sein / in der Lage sein, etwas zu tun II

about [ə'baʊt]:
1. **about me/you/yourself/Miss Bell** über mich/dich/dich selbst/Frau Bell I **It's about a seagull.** Es geht um eine Möwe. / Es handelt von einer Möwe. I
the best thing about ... das Beste an III 1 (8/9) **What about you?** Und du? / Und was ist mit dir?; Und ihr? / Und was ist mit euch? I **What about ...?** Wie wäre es mit ...? II **What is the story about?** Wovon handelt die Geschichte? / Worum geht es in der Geschichte? I
2. **about 300 people** ungefähr 300 Leute I

above [ə'bʌv] über, oberhalb (von); oben, darüber II

accent ['æksənt] Akzent III 3 (76)

°**accept** [ək'sept] akzeptieren, annehmen

°**acceptable** [ək'septəbl] akzeptabel, zulässig

access ['ækses] Zugang, Zutritt I

accident ['æksɪdənt] Unfall; Zufall III 3 (71) **by accident** zufällig III 3 (71)

°**accompany** [ə'kʌmpəni] begleiten

according to ... [ə'kɔːdɪŋ] ... zufolge; laut ... III 4 (109)

account [ə'kaʊnt] Account, Konto III 5 (114)

across the moor/the street [ə'krɒs] (quer) über das Moor/die Straße II °**across the nation** überall im Land

°**acrostic** [ə'krɒstɪk] Akrostichon *(Gedicht, in dem die Anfangsbuchstaben ein Wort oder einen Spruch ergeben)*

act [ækt] schauspielern II **act sth. out** etwas vorspielen I

°**act** [ækt] Gesetz **Act of Union** Vereinigungsgesetz

action ['ækʃn] Action; Handlung, Tat I

°**active** ['æktɪv] aktiv

activity [æk'tɪvəti] Aktivität I **free-time activities** Freizeitaktivitäten I

actor ['æktə] Schauspieler/in I

actual ['æktʃuəl] tatsächliche(r, s), wirkliche (r, s) III 5 (123)

actually ['æktʃuəli] eigentlich; übrigens; tatsächlich III 3 (60)

ad [æd] (*kurz für:* **advert, advertisement**) Werbespot, Werbung; Anzeige, Inserat III 5 (113)

°**AD (anno Domini)** [ˌeɪ 'diː] n. Chr. (nach Christus)

add (to) [æd] hinzufügen, ergänzen, addieren (zu) I

adder ['ædə] Kreuzotter II

address [ə'dres] Adresse, Anschrift I

adjective ['ædʒɪktɪv] Adjektiv II

°**adobe** [ə'dəʊbi] Lehmziegel

adopted [ə'dɒptɪd] adoptiert, Adoptiv- II

adult ['ædʌlt] Erwachsene(r) II

adventure [əd'ventʃə] Abenteuer II

°**adventurer** [əd'ventʃərə] Abenteurer/in

adverb ['ædvɜːb] Adverb III 3 (63)

advert ['ædvɜːt] Werbespot, Werbung; Anzeige, Inserat III 5 (113)

advertise ['ædvətaɪz] Werbung machen (für); inserieren III 5 (113)

advertisement [əd'vɜːtɪsmənt] (*kurz auch:* **ad, advert**) Werbespot, Werbung; Anzeige, Inserat III 5 (113)

advertising ['ædvətaɪzɪŋ] Werbung, Reklame III 5 (113)

°**advice** *(no pl)* [əd'vaɪs] Rat, Ratschlag, Ratschläge

°**affect** [ə'fekt] betreffen, sich auswirken auf; beeinflussen

afraid [ə'freɪd]: **be afraid (of sth./sb.)** Angst haben (vor etwas/jm.) III 4 (90)

°**African American** [ˌæfrɪkən‿ə'merɪkən] Afroamerikaner/in; afroamerikanisch

after ['ɑːftə]:
1. nach I **after that** danach I
2. nachdem II
3. **run after sb.** hinter jm. herrennen I

afternoon [ˌɑːftə'nuːn] Nachmittag I **in the afternoon** nachmittags, am Nachmittag I **on Saturday afternoon** am Samstagnachmittag I

again [ə'gen] wieder; noch einmal I **again and again** immer wieder II

against [ə'genst] gegen I

age [eɪdʒ]:
1. Alter I **... is your age** ... ist in deinem Alter; ... ist so alt wie du II **It's been ages ...** Es ist ewig her ... III 5 (126) **That was ages ago.** Das ist ewig her. III 5 (126)
2. Zeitalter III 1 (33)

ago [ə'gəʊ]: **two days ago** vor zwei Tagen II

agree [ə'griː]: **agree with sb.** jm. zustimmen I **agree on sth.** sich auf etwas einigen I

air [eə] Luft II

airport ['eəpɔːt] Flughafen II

aisle [aɪl] Gang II

album ['ælbəm] Album II

°**alibi** ['æləbaɪ] Alibi

alive [ə'laɪv]: **be alive** leben, am Leben sein III 3 (70)

all [ɔːl] alles; alle I **all alone** ganz allein II **all around her** überall um sie herum III 1 (24) **all day** den ganzen Tag (lang) I **all in all** alles in allem III 1 (17) **all of Plymouth** ganz Plymouth, das ganze Plymouth I **all over the country / the city / the world** im ganzen Land / in der ganzen Stadt / auf der ganzen Welt II **all the time** die ganze Zeit II °**all year round** das ganze Jahr

alligator ['ælɪgeɪtə] Alligator III 5 (110)

allow [əˈlaʊ] erlauben, zulassen III 2 (43) **be allowed to do sth.** etwas tun dürfen II
all right [ɔːl ˈraɪt] okay; in Ordnung I
almost [ˈɔːlməʊst] fast, beinahe I
alone [əˈləʊn] allein II **all alone** ganz allein II
along [əˈlɒŋ]
1. along the street / the river / ... die Straße / den Fluss / ... entlang I
2. come along mitkommen, herkommen I °**sing along** mitsingen
aloud [əˈlaʊd]: **read aloud** laut (vor-)lesen II
°**alphabet** [ˈælfəbet] Alphabet
already [ɔːlˈredi] schon, bereits II
also [ˈɔːlsəʊ] auch I
°**alternative** [ɔːlˈtɜːnətɪv] alternative(r, s)
although [ɔːlˈðəʊ] obwohl II
altitude [ˈæltɪtjuːd] Höhe III 4 (99)
altogether [ˌɔːltəˈgeðə] insgesamt, alles in allem III 2 (40)
always [ˈɔːlweɪz] immer I
am: 4 am [ˌeɪ‿ˈem] 4 Uhr morgens I
amazing [əˈmeɪzɪŋ] erstaunlich, unglaublich III 1 (10)
°**America** [əˈmerɪkə]: **the Americas** *Nordamerika, Mittelamerika und Südamerika*
°**American football** [əˌmerɪkən ˈfʊtbɔːl] Football
°**among** [əˈmʌŋ] unter, zwischen *(mehreren Personen, Tieren, Dingen)*
an [æn, ən] ein, eine I **... an hour** ... pro Stunde III 1 (15)
ancestor [ˈænsestə] Vorfahr/in III 5 (118)
°**ancient** [ˈeɪnʃənt] (ur)alt; antik
and [ænd, ənd] und I **both ... and ...** sowohl ... als auch ... III 5 (127)
angel [ˈeɪndʒl] Engel III 3 (67)
angry [ˈæŋgri] wütend I **angry with sb.** wütend, böse auf jn. II
animal [ˈænɪml] Tier I
announcement [əˈnaʊnsmənt] Durchsage, Ansage III 1 (19)
another [əˈnʌðə]:
1. ein(e) andere(r, s) I
2. noch ein(e) I
answer [ˈɑːnsə]:
1. antworten; beantworten I **answer the phone** ans Telefon gehen II
2. Antwort I
ant [ænt] Ameise I
anthem [ˈænθəm] Hymne III 5 (122)
any [ˈeni]: **Are there any ...?** Gibt es (irgendwelche) ...? I **There aren't any ...** Es gibt keine / Es sind keine ... I **not ... any more** nicht mehr II
anybody [ˈenibɒdi]: **anybody?** (irgend) jemand? I **not ... anybody** niemand I
anyone [ˈeniwʌn]: **anyone?** (irgend)jemand? I **not ... anyone** niemand I
anything [ˈeniθɪŋ]: **anything?** (irgend) etwas? I **not ... anything** nichts I
Anyway, ... [ˈeniweɪ] Jedenfalls, .../ Wie dem auch sei, ... / Aber egal, ... II **And anyway, ...** Und überhaupt, ... III 1 (20)
apart [əˈpɑːt] auseinander; getrennt III 4 (108)
apartment [əˈpɑːtmənt] Wohnung II
apostrophe [əˈpɒstrəfi] Apostroph, Auslassungszeichen I
appear [əˈpɪə] erscheinen, auftauchen II
appointment [əˈpɔɪntmənt] Verabredung, Termin II
approach [əˈprəʊtʃ] sich nähern, herannahen III 4 (101)
April [ˈeɪprəl] April I
aquarium [əˈkweəriəm] Aquarium; Aquarienhaus I
architect [ˈɑːkɪtekt] Architekt/in III 2 (37)
°**archive** [ˈɑːkaɪv] Archiv
are [ˈɑː] bist; sind; seid I **The DVDs are ...** Die DVDs kosten ... I
area [ˈeəriə] Bereich; Gebiet, Gegend I
aren't [ɑːnt]: **you aren't** du bist nicht ...; du bist kein/e ...; ihr seid nicht ...; ihr seid kein/e ... I
argue [ˈɑːgjuː] streiten; sich streiten III 2 (48)
argument [ˈɑːgjumənt]:
1. Argument III 1 (17)
2. Streit, Auseinandersetzung III 3 (63)
arm [ɑːm] Arm II
°**armada** [ɑːˈmɑːdə] Armada, Kriegsflotte
armchair [ˈɑːmtʃeə] Sessel I
around [əˈraʊnd]:
1. around the library in der Bücherei umher, durch die Bücherei I **all around her** überall um sie herum III 1 (24)
2. around the lake um den See (herum) II
3. run/walk around herum-, umherrennen/-gehen II
arrange [əˈreɪndʒ] anordnen I
arrest [əˈrest] verhaften, festnehmen III 4 (89)
arrival [əˈraɪvl] Ankunft II
arrive [əˈraɪv] ankommen, eintreffen I
art [ɑːt] Kunst I **work of art** Kunstwerk III 4 (98)
article [ˈɑːtɪkl] Artikel II
artist [ˈɑːtɪst] Künstler/in II
artwork [ˈɑːtwɜːk] Kunstwerk III 4 (101)
as [æz, əz]:
1. als, während II
2. da, weil III 1 (31)
3. (not) as big as (nicht) so groß wie II
4. as a child als Kind II °**as one word** als ein Wort
5. as if als ob III 3 (66)
6. as soon as sobald, sowie III 1 (10)
7. as well auch, ebenso III 3 (60)
ash [æʃ] Asche III 3 (71) **ashes** *(pl)* Asche *(sterbliche Überreste)* III 3 (71)
°**Ash** [æʃ]: **Ash Wednesday** Aschermittwoch
°**Asian** [ˈeɪʃn], [ˈeɪʒn] asiatisch
ask [ɑːsk] fragen I **ask a question** eine Frage stellen I **ask for sth.** um etwas bitten II **ask sb. to do sth.** jemanden bitten, etwas zu tun I **ask sb. the way** jn. nach dem Weg fragen II
asleep [əˈsliːp]: **be asleep** schlafen II
assignment [əˈsaɪnmənt] *(AE)* Aufgabe, Arbeitsauftrag *(in der Schule oder daheim zu erledigen)* III 5 (113)
assistant [əˈsɪstənt] *(kurz für:* **shop assistant***)* Verkäufer/in II
astronaut [ˈæstrənɔːt] Astronaut/in III 2 (37)
at [æt, ət] *(in Ortsangaben)* an, bei, in; *(in Zeitangaben)* um, an I **at 14 Dean Street** in der Deanstraße 14 I **at first** zuerst, anfangs, am Anfang II **at Grandma's (house/flat)** bei Oma II **at home** daheim, zu Hause I **at last** endlich, schließlich I **at least** zumindest, wenigstens II **at lunchtime** mittags I °**at once** auf einmal; gleichzeitig **at one time** zur selben Zeit, gleichzeitig III 1 (15) **at the bottom (of)** unten, am unteren Ende (von) II **at the moment** gerade, im Moment I **at night** nachts, in der Nacht I **at school** in der Schule I **at the top (of)** oben, am oberen Ende, an der Spitze (von) II **at the weekend** am Wochenende I
ate [et, eɪt] *siehe* **eat**
Atlantic: the Atlantic (Ocean) [ətˈlæntɪk] der Atlantik, der Atlantische Ozean II
atmosphere [ˈætməsfɪə] Atmosphäre; Stimmung II
attached [əˈtætʃt]: **be attached to sth.** an etwas hängen *(befestigt sein)*; an etwas angehängt/beigeheftet sein III 5 (126)
attack [əˈtæk]:
1. angreifen II
2. Angriff II
°**attend school/a course** [əˈtend] die Schule/einen Kurs besuchen
°**attendance** [əˈtendəns] Teilnehmerzahl, Besucherzahl **take attendance** *(AE)* die Anwesenheit kontrollieren *(Schule)*
attic [ˈætɪk] Dachboden I **in the attic** auf dem Dachboden I
attraction [əˈtrækʃn] Attraktion; Anziehungspunkt III 1 (14)
audience [ˈɔːdiəns] Publikum, Zuschauer/innen, Zuhörer/innen II
audition [ɔːˈdɪʃn] Vorsprechen, Vorsingen, Vorspielen II
August [ˈɔːgəst] August I
aunt [ɑːnt] Tante I
author [ˈɔːθə] Autor/in I
autumn [ˈɔːtəm] Herbst I
available [əˈveɪləbl] erhältlich, verfügbar; erreichbar *(am Telefon)* III 1 (24)
avenue [ˈævənjuː] Allee, Boulevard III 4 (98)

average [ˈævərɪdʒ] durchschnittlich; Durchschnitt III 5 (114) **on average** im Durchschnitt; durchschnittlich III 5 (114)
away [əˈweɪ] weg, fort I
awesome [ˈɔːsəm] *(bes. AE, infml)* klasse, großartig III 3 (67)
awful [ˈɔːfl] schrecklich, fürchterlich II

B

baby seal [ˈbeɪbi siːl] Robbenjunges; Heuler I
back [bæk]
1. zurück I
2. Rücken II
from the back of the bus aus dem hinteren Teil des Busses II °**back then** damals
background [ˈbækgraʊnd] Hintergrund I **background file** Hintergrundinformation(en) I
°**back door** [ˌbæk ˈdɔː] Hintertür
backpack [ˈbækpæk] Rucksack III 3 (60)
bacon [ˈbeɪkən] Schinkenspeck II
bad [bæd] schlecht, schlimm I
bag [bæg] Tasche, Beutel, Tüte I **school bag** Schultasche I
°**baggy** [ˈbægi] weit (geschnitten) *(Hose)*
°**bake** [beɪk] backen
balcony [ˈbælkəni] Balkon III 5 (126)
ball [bɔːl] Ball I
balloon [bəˈluːn] (Luft-)Ballon II
band [bænd] Band, (Musik-)Gruppe I
bang [bæŋ] Knall III 3 (73)
°**banjo** [ˈbændʒəʊ] Banjo
bank [bæŋk]:
1. Bank III 3 (67)
2. Flussufer III 3 (67)
°**banner** [ˈbænə] Banner, Fahne
bar [bɑː] Riegel *(Schokolade, Müsli)*; Tafel *(Schokolade)* III 2 (45)
barbecue [ˈbɑːbɪkjuː] Grill; Grillfest, Grillparty III 5 (112)
bark [bɑːk] bellen I
barman [ˈbɑːmən], *pl* **barmen** [ˈbɑːmən] Barkeeper III 1 (20)
barn [bɑːn] Scheune, Stadel II
baseball [ˈbeɪsbɔːl] Baseball II
basket [ˈbɑːskɪt] Korb I
basketball [ˈbɑːskɪtbɔːl] Basketball I
bath [bɑːθ] Bad II
bathroom [ˈbɑːθruːm] Badezimmer I
battery [ˈbætəri] Batterie, Akku III 3 (77)
battle [ˈbætl] Schlacht; Kampf II
Bavaria [bəˈveəriə] Bayern I
°**bayou** [ˈbaɪuː] sumpfiger Flussarm
°**BBC** [ˌbiː biː ˈsiː] BBC *(öffentlich-rechtliche Rundfunkanstalt des Vereinigten Königreichs)*
be [bi], **was/were, been**:
1. sein I **Have you ever been to …?** Bist du jemals in … gewesen? II
°2. werden
beach [biːtʃ] Strand I
bear [beə] Bär I
bean [biːn] Bohne III 4 (108)
beard [bɪəd] Bart II
beat [biːt], **beat, beaten** schlagen; besiegen III 1 (30)
beaten [ˈbiːtn] *siehe* **beat**
beautiful [ˈbjuːtɪfl] schön I
became [bɪˈkeɪm] *siehe* **become**
because [bɪˈkɒz] weil I
become [bɪˈkʌm], **became, become** werden I
bed [bed] Bett I **bed & breakfast (B&B)** Frühstückspension; Zimmer mit Frühstück III 1 (12)
bedroom [ˈbedruːm] Schlafzimmer I
°**bee** [biː] Biene
beef [biːf] Rindfleisch II **roast beef** Rinderbraten I
°**Beefeater** [ˈbiːfiːtə] *Torwächter des Towers von London*
been [biːn]:
1. *siehe* **be**
2. **Have you ever been to …?** … Bist du jemals in … gewesen? II
beep [biːp] piepen II
before [bɪˈfɔː]:
1. bevor I
2. vor I **before school/lessons** vor der Schule *(vor Schulbeginn)* / vorm Unter-richt I **before long** schon bald III 2 (41)
°**before that** davor
3. (vorher) schon mal II **not/never before** (vorher) noch nie II
began [bɪˈgæn] *siehe* **begin**
begin [bɪˈgɪn], **began, begun** beginnen, anfangen II
beginner [bɪˈgɪnə] Anfänger/in III 3 (76)
beginning [bɪˈgɪnɪŋ] Anfang, Beginn III 1 (31)
begun [bɪˈgʌn] *siehe* **begin**
behave [bɪˈheɪv] sich verhalten, sich benehmen III 2 (48)
behind [bɪˈhaɪnd] hinter I **from behind** von hinten II
believe [bɪˈliːv] glauben II
°**believer** [bɪˈliːvə] Gläubige(r)
bell [bel] Klingel, Glocke I
belong to sb. [bɪˈlɒŋ] jm. gehören; zu jm. gehören III 1 (30)
below [bɪˈləʊ] unter, unterhalb (von); unten, darunter III 2 (54)
bend down [bend], **bent, bent** sich hinunterbeugen, sich bücken III 1 (24)
bent [bent] *siehe* **bend**
besides [bɪˈsaɪdz] außerdem III 4 (101)
best [best]: **the best …** der/die/das beste …; die besten … I **the best thing about …** das Beste an III 1 (8/9)
bet [bet], **bet, bet** wetten III 5 (121)
better [ˈbetə] besser I **better than ever** besser als je zuvor II **I'd better … (= I had better …)** Ich sollte lieber … III 4 (89)
between [bɪˈtwiːn] zwischen I
big [bɪg] groß I °**big cat** Großkatze **big wheel** Riesenrad I **the biggest …** [ˈbɪgɪst] der/die/das größte … I
bike [baɪk] Fahrrad I **ride a bike** Fahrrad fahren I
bilingual [baɪˈlɪŋgwəl] zweisprachig III 2 (55)
°**billion** [ˈbɪljən] Milliarde
°**binoculars** *(pl)* [bɪˈnɒkjələz] Fernglas
°**biography** [baɪˈɒgrəfi] Biografie
bird [bɜːd] Vogel I
birth [bɜːθ] Geburt I
birthday [ˈbɜːθdeɪ] Geburtstag I **My birthday is in May.** Ich habe im Mai Geburtstag. I **My birthday is on 5th August.** Ich habe am 5. August Geburtstag. I **When's your birthday?** Wann hast du Geburtstag? I
birthplace [ˈbɜːθpleɪs] Geburtsort II
biscuit [ˈbɪskɪt] Plätzchen, Keks I
°**bishop** [ˈbɪʃəp] *(Schach)* Läufer
bit [bɪt]:
1. *siehe* **bite**
2. Stück(chen), Teil III 4 (101) **a bit** ein bisschen, etwas I
bite [baɪt]:
1. (**bit, bitten**) beißen I
2. **bite** Biss, Bissen III 2 (48)
bitten [ˈbɪtn] *siehe* **bite**
black [blæk] schwarz I
blanket [ˈblæŋkɪt] Decke *(zum Zudecken)* III 4 (101)
blew [bluː] *siehe* **blow**
block [blɒk]:
1. (Häuser-, Wohn-)Block III 4 (88)
2. blockieren, sperren III 5 (113)
blog [blɒg] Blog *(Weblog, digitales Tagebuch)* II
blond *(bei Frauen oft:* **blonde***)* [blɒnd] blond I
blood [blʌd] Blut III 1 (15)
bloom [bluːm] blühen III 4 (98)
blow [bləʊ], **blew, blown**:
blow sth. out etwas auspusten, ausblasen II **blow the horn** hupen III 4 (101)
blow the whistle pfeifen *(auf der Trillerpfeife)* III 1 (24)
blown [bləʊn] *siehe* **blow**
blue [bluː] blau I
blueberry [ˈbluːbəri] Blaubeere, Heidelbeere II
°**bluebird** [ˈbɒnfaɪə] *dem Rotkehlchen verwandte Drossel*
board [bɔːd] (Wand-)Tafel I
board game [ˈbɔːd geɪm] Brettspiel III 4 (95)
boarding pass [ˈbɔːdɪŋ pɑːs] Bordkarte II
boarding school [ˈbɔːdɪŋ skuːl] Internat II
boat [bəʊt] Boot, Schiff I
body [ˈbɒdi]:
1. Körper I **part of the body** Körperteil II

2. Leiche III 4 (103)
3. Hauptteil *(eines Textes)* I I 4 (95)
°**bodysurfing** ['bɒdiˌsɜːfɪŋ] Bodysurfing *(Wellenreiten ohne Brett)*
°**bonfire** ['bɒnfaɪə] Lagerfeuer
book [bʊk] Buch I
bookshop ['bʊkʃɒp] Buchladen, Buchhandlung I
boot [buːt] Stiefel II
border ['bɔːdə] Grenze III 3 (62)
bored [bɔːd]: **be/feel bored** gelangweilt sein, sich langweilen II
boring ['bɔːrɪŋ] langweilig I
born [bɔːn]: **be born** geboren sein/werden III 4 (89)
borough [*AE:* 'bɜːrəʊ, *BE:* 'bʌrə] (Stadt-)Bezirk III 4 (84)
both [bəʊθ] beide II **both … and …** sowohl … als auch … III 5 (127)
bottle ['bɒtl] Flasche I
bottom ['bɒtəm]: **at the bottom (of)** unten, am unteren Ende (von) II
bought [bɔːt] *siehe* **buy**
bouldering ['bəʊldərɪŋ] Bouldern *(Klettern in Absprunghöhe, ohne Seil)* III 4 (99)
bow [baʊ] sich verbeugen, sich verneigen II
bowl [bəʊl] Schüssel II
°**bowls** *(pl)* [bəʊlz] Bowls *(Kugelspiel)*
box [bɒks] Kasten, Kiste, Kästchen I
Boxing Day ['bɒksɪŋ deɪ] 2. Weihnachtstag (26. Dezember) I
boy [bɔɪ] Junge, Bub I
boyfriend ['bɔɪfrend] Freund III 3 (68)
°**bracket** ['brækɪt] Klammer *(in Texten)*
brass band [ˌbrɑːs 'bænd] Blaskapelle III 5 (110)
bread [bred] Brot I
break [breɪk] Pause I
break [breɪk], **broke, broken**:
1. zerbrechen, kaputt machen I
2. brechen, kaputt gehen I
breakfast ['brekfəst] Frühstück I
have breakfast frühstücken I
°**breakthrough** ['breɪkθruː] Durchbruch
breath [breθ] Atem, Atemzug II **…, he said under his breath.** …, sagte er flüsternd / murmelte er. III 1 (25)
breeze [briːz] Brise III 2 (46)
bridge [brɪdʒ] Brücke II
bright [braɪt] strahlend, leuchtend, hell I
brilliant ['brɪliənt] großartig, genial, glänzend II
bring [brɪŋ], **brought, brought** (mit-, her)bringen I **bring in** *(hay)* einbringen *(Heu)* II
°**Brit** [brɪt] *(infml)* Brite/Britin
°**Brit award** ['brɪt‿əˌwɔːd] *Musikpreis der britischen Plattenindustrie*
British ['brɪtɪʃ] britisch I
brochure ['brəʊʃə] Broschüre, Prospekt III 3 (58/59)
broke [brəʊk] *siehe* **break**
broken ['brəʊkən]:
1. *siehe* **break**
2. zerbrochen, kaputt; gebrochen II
brother ['brʌðə] Bruder I
brought [brɔːt] *siehe* **bring**
brown [braʊn] braun I
°**brownstone** ['braʊnstəʊn]: **brownstone house** Sandsteinhaus
°**bubble** ['bʌbl]: **speech bubble** Sprechblase
buck [bʌk] *(infml)* (= **dollar**) Dollar III 5 (112)
bucket ['bʌkɪt] Eimer II
°**bug** [bʌg] Käfer
build [bɪld], **built, built** bauen II
building ['bɪldɪŋ] Gebäude II
built [bɪlt] *siehe* **build**
°**bullet point** ['bʊlɪt pɔɪnt] Aufzählungspunkt, Spiegelstrich
°**bump** [bʌmp] Stoß
buoy [bɔɪ], *AE auch:* ['buːi] Boje III 5 (127)
burger ['bɜːgə] Hamburger II
burst [bɜːst], **burst, burst** platzen III 5 (127) °**burst out** hervorbrechen
bury ['beri] begraben, beerdigen III 3 (60)
bus [bʌs] Bus I **go by bus** mit dem Bus fahren I
°**business** ['bɪznəs] Geschäft
busy ['bɪzi] belebt, geschäftig, hektisch III 2 (46) **be busy** beschäftigt sein; viel zu tun haben I
but [bʌt, bət] aber I
°**butter** ['bʌtə] Butter
butterfly ['bʌtəflaɪ] Schmetterling I
buy [baɪ], **bought, bought** kaufen I
°**buzz** [bʌz] vibrieren
by [baɪ]:
1. **by …** von … II
2. **by the sea** am Meer I
3. **go by car/minibus/…** mit dem Auto/Kleinbus/… fahren I
by accident zufällig III 3 (71) **by the way** übrigens III 1 (10) **by mistake** aus Versehen III 4 (102)
Bye. [baɪ] (*auch:* **Bye-bye.**) Servus. / Auf Wiedersehen. I

C

°**cabin** ['kæbɪn] Hütte
café ['kæfeɪ] Café I
cage [keɪdʒ] Käfig I
°**Cajun** ['keɪdʒən] Cajun
cake [keɪk] Kuchen I
calendar ['kælɪndə] Kalender III 3 (74)
call [kɔːl]:
1. rufen; anrufen; nennen I **call out the names** die Namen aufrufen II
2. Anruf; Telefongespräch I
called [kɔːld]: **be called** heißen, genannt werden I
caller ['kɔːlə] Anrufer/in II
calm [kɑːm] ruhig III 3 (76)
came [keɪm] *siehe* **come**
camera ['kæmərə] Kamera, Fotoapparat I
cameraman ['kæmrəmæn], *pl* **cameramen** ['kæmrəmer] Kameramann I
camping ['kæmpɪŋ] Camping, Zelten II
campsite ['kæmpsaɪt] Zeltplatz II
°**campus** ['kæmpəs] Campus, Universitätsgelände
can [kæn] Dose III 4 (101)
can [kæn, kən] können I **we cannot** ['kænɒt], **we can't** [kɑːnt] … wir können nicht … I
candle ['kændl] Kerze I
canteen [kæn'tiːn] Kantine, (Schul-) Mensa I
°**cap** [kæp] Mütze, Kappe
capital ['kæpɪtl] Hauptstadt I
capital letter [ˌkæpɪtl 'letə] Großbuchstabe I
captain ['kæptɪn] Kapitän/in I
caption ['kæpʃn] Bildunterschrift I
°**capture** ['kæptʃə] Gefangennahme; Schlagen *(Schach)*
car [kɑː] Auto I **go by car** mit dem Auto fahren I °**subway car** *(AE)* U-Bahn-Wagen
caravan ['kærəvæn] Wohnwagen II
card (to) [kɑːd] Karte (an) I
care [keə]: **care about sth.** etwas wichtig nehmen III 3 (71) **I don't care about money.** Geld ist mir egal. III 3 (71)
I really care about animals. Tiere liegen mir sehr am Herzen. / Tiere sind mir sehr wichtig. III 3 (71) **Who cares?** Na und? / Wen interessiert das? III 3 (71)
°**career** [kə'rɪə] Karriere
careful ['keəfl] vorsichtig I
carefully ['keəfəli]:
1. vorsichtig III 5 (118)
2. sorgfältig, aufmerksam III 5 (118)
°**Caribbean** [ˌkærɪ'biːən] karibisch
carnival ['kɑːnɪvl] Karneval, Fasching III 1 (10)
carpenter ['kɑːpəntə] Tischler/in, Zimmerer/Zimmerin III 2 (36)
carrot ['kærət] Möhre, Karotte III 2 (39)
carry ['kæri] tragen III 3 (75)
carry-on bag ['kæri‿ɒn] Handgepäckstück, (kleine) Reisetasche II
cart [kɑːt] Karren I
°**cartoon** [kɑː'tuːn] Cartoon, Witzzeichnung
cash desk ['kæʃ desk] Kasse *(in Geschäften)* II
cast [kɑːst] Besetzung; Mitwirkende *(Theaterstück, Film)* II
castle ['kɑːsl] Burg, Schloss I
cat [kæt] Katze I °**big cat** Großkatze
catch [kætʃ], **caught, caught**:
1. fangen I
°2. **We have to catch up on everything.** Wir haben uns viel zu erzählen. *(weil wir uns lange nicht gesehen haben)*
cathedral [kə'θiːdrəl] Kathedrale, Dom III 1 (10)
Catholic ['kæθlɪk] Katholik/in; katholisch III 1 (32)
caught [kɔːt] *siehe* **catch**
°**causeway** ['kɔːzweɪ] Damm
cave [keɪv] Höhle II

°**CE (Common Era)** [ˌkɒmən‿ˈɪərə] nach unserer Zeitrechnung
celebrate [ˈselɪbreɪt] feiern II
celebration [ˌselɪˈbreɪʃn] Feier II
°**celebrity** [səˈlebrəti] berühmte Persönlichkeit
cell phone [ˈsel fəʊn] *(AE)* Mobiltelefon, Handy II
°**Celt** [kelt] Kelte/Keltin
Celtic [ˈkeltɪk, ˈseltɪk] keltisch III 1 (30)
cemetery [*BE:* ˈsemətri, *AE:* ˈseməteri] Friedhof III 4 (89)
cent [sent] Cent III 3 (61)
centimetre (cm) [ˈsentɪmiːtə] Zentimeter III 5 (123)
central [ˈsentrəl] zentral, Zentral-, Mittel-
III 4 (84)
centre [ˈsentə] Zentrum; Mitte I
century [ˈsentʃəri] Jahrhundert I
°**ceremony** [ˈserəməni] Zeremonie
°**certain** [ˈsɜːtn] gewisse(r, s)
certainly [ˈsɜːtnli] sicher(lich), auf jeden Fall, freilich III 3 (67)
chain [tʃeɪn] Kette I
chair [tʃeə] Stuhl I
challenge [ˈtʃælɪndʒ]:
1. Herausforderung III 3 (60)
2. **challenge sb. (to sth.)** jn. herausfordern (zu etwas) III 3 (60)
champion [ˈtʃæmpiən] Meister/in, Champion II
°**championship** [ˈtʃæmpiənʃɪp] Meisterschaft
chance [tʃɑːns] Gelegenheit, Möglichkeit, Chance III 1 (14) °**take the chance to do sth.** die Gelegenheit nutzen, etwas zu tun
change [tʃeɪndʒ]:
1. (ver)ändern; sich (ver)ändern II
2. umsteigen II
3. wechseln III 2 (39); *(Geld)* umtauschen III 3 (62)
4. Veränderung III 3 (82)
5. Wechselgeld II
°**change one's mind** seine Meinung ändern
°**changing room** [ˈtʃeɪndʒɪŋ ruːm] Umkleideraum
chaos [ˈkeɪɒs] Chaos I
character [ˈkærəktə] Figur, Person *(in Roman, Film, Theaterstück)* I
charge [tʃɑːdʒ] (auf)laden III 3 (77)
charity [ˈtʃærəti] Wohlfahrtsorganisation; Wohltätigkeit, wohltätige Zwecke II
°**chart** [tʃɑːt] Tabelle, Schaubild
chat [tʃæt] chatten; plaudern III 3 (70)
cheap [tʃiːp] billig, preiswert I
check [tʃek]:
1. Überprüfung, Kontrolle I
2. (über)prüfen, kontrollieren I
3. **check sth. out** *(infml)* sich etwas anschauen, anhören; etwas ausprobieren III 3 (66)
4. **check sth. in** etwas einchecken, aufgeben *(Gepäck)* II

check-in desk [ˈtʃek‿ɪn ˌdesk] Abflugschalter, Abfertigungsschalter II
checklist [ˈtʃeklɪst] Checkliste III 1 (17)
°**checkmate** [ˌtʃekˈmeɪt]:
1. Schachmatt
2. **checkmate sb.** jn. matt setzen *(Schach)*
cheer [tʃɪə] jubeln II
°**cheerleader** [ˈtʃɪəliːdə] Cheerleader *(Stimmungsanheizer/in bei Sportereignissen)*
cheese [tʃiːz] Käse I
chemist [ˈkemɪst] *(BE)* Apotheker/in II
chess [tʃes] Schach I
chest [tʃest] Brust, Brustkorb II
°**Chevy** [ˈʃevi] *infml für „Chevrolet" (amerik. Automarke)*
°**chick** [tʃɪk] Küken
chicken [ˈtʃɪkɪn] Huhn; (Brat-)Hähnchen III 5 (112)
child [tʃaɪld], *pl* **children** [ˈtʃɪldrən] Kind I
chips *(pl)* [tʃɪps] *(BE)* Pommes frites II
chocolate [ˈtʃɒklət]:
1. Schokolade I
2. Praline II
°**choice** [tʃɔɪs] Wahl; Auswahl
choir [ˈkwaɪə] Chor II
choose [tʃuːz], **chose, chosen** aussuchen, (aus)wählen; sich aussuchen I
chorus [ˈkɔːrəs] Refrain II
chose [tʃəʊz] *siehe* **choose**
chosen [ˈtʃəʊzn] *siehe* **choose**
°**Christian** [ˈkrɪstʃən] Christ/in
Christmas [ˈkrɪsməs] Weihnachten I
Christmas Day 1. Weihnachtstag (25. Dezember) I **Christmas Eve** Heiligabend I **Christmas pudding** *kein Pudding, sondern ein Nachtisch aus Butter, Zucker, Mehl, Rosinen, Nüssen, Eiern, Gewürzen, der traditionell zu Weihnachten gegessen wird* I **Merry Christmas!** Frohe Weihnachten! I
chubby [ˈtʃʌbi] pummelig, mollig III 4 (100)
church [tʃɜːtʃ] Kirche I
°**chutzpah** [ˈ:ʊtspə], [ˈhʊtspə] Chuzpe, bewunderns.ierte Frechheit
cinema [ˈsɪnə ɪə] Kino I
circle [ˈsɜːkl] Kreis II
°**cite** [saɪt] zitieren
city [ˈsɪti] Stadt, Großstadt I
civil [ˈsɪvl]: **civil rights** *(pl)* Bürgerrechte III 5 (129) °**civil war** Bürgerkrieg
clap [klæp] (Beifall) klatschen I **Clap your hands.** Klatscht in die Hände. I
class [klɑːs] (Schul-)Klasse I
°**classical music** [ˈklæsɪkl] klassische Musik
classmate [ˈklɑːsmeɪt] Mitschüler/in, Klassenkamerad/in I
classroom [ˈklɑːsruːm] Klassenzimmer I
clean [kliːn]:
1. sauber machen, putzen I °**clean up** aufräumen, säubern
2. sauber II

clear [klɪə]:
1. klar, deutlich II
2. räumen; abräumen III 2 (46)
clever [ˈklevə] klug, schlau I
click [klɪk] klicken III 4 (93)
cliff [klɪf] Klippe II
°**climate** [ˈklaɪmət] Klima **climate change** Klimawandel
climb [klaɪm]:
1. klettern; hinaufklettern (auf) I
2. Aufstieg, Anstieg III 2 (45)
climb a tree/a tower auf einen Baum/einen Turm klettern I
clock [klɒk] (Wand-, Stand-, Turm-)Uhr I
°**clock face** Zifferblatt
close [kləʊz] schließen, zumachen II
close (to) [kləʊs] nah, dicht (bei, an) I
closed [kləʊzd] geschlossen I
closet [ˈklɒzɪt] *(bes. AE)* Wandschrank *(oft begehbar)* III 5 (118)
°**cloth** [klɒθ] Tuch
clothes *(pl)* [kləʊðz] Kleidung, Kleidungsstücke I
cloud [klaʊd] Wolke II
cloudy [ˈklaʊdi] bewölkt II
clown [klaʊn] Clown II
club [klʌb] Klub I **join a club** [dʒɔɪn] in einen Klub eintreten; sich einem Klub anschließen I
clue [kluː] (Lösungs-)Hinweis; Anhaltspunkt III 1 (11)
°**coach** [kəʊtʃ] Trainer/in
coal [kəʊl] Kohle III 2 (38) **coal mine** Kohlebergwerk III 2 (38)
coast [kəʊst] Küste I
coat [kəʊt] Mantel II
cocoa [ˈkəʊkəʊ] Kakao II
coffee [ˈkɒfi] Kaffee III 3 (60)
coin [kɔɪn] Münze I
cola [ˈkəʊlə] Cola II
cold [kəʊld]:
1. kalt I **be cold** frieren I
2. **have a cold** eine Erkältung haben, erkältet sein II
collapse [kəˈlæps] einstürzen; zusammenbrechen III 4 (89)
collect [kəˈlekt] sammeln I
°**college** [ˈkɒlɪdʒ] Hochschule
°**collocation** [ˌkɒləˈkeɪʃn] Kollokation *(Wörter, die oft zusammen vorkommen)*
colon [ˈkəʊlən] Doppelpunkt II
colonist [ˈkɒlənɪst] Kolonist/in, Siedler/in III 1 (33)
colony [ˈkɒləni] Kolonie III 1 (33)
colour [ˈkʌlə] Farbe I
coloured [ˈkʌləd] farbig, bunt III 5 (122)
colourful [ˈkʌləfl] farbenfroh, farbenprächtig, bunt III 1 (30)
column [ˈkɒləm]:
1. Säule III 3 (60)
°2. (Tabellen-)Spalte
°**combination** [ˌkɒmbɪˈneɪʃn] Kombination
°**combine** [kəmˈbaɪn] kombinieren, verbinden

come [kʌm], **came, come** kommen I **come across sb./sth.** auf jn./etwas stoßen, jn./etwas (zufällig) treffen III 2 (38) **come along** mitkommen, herkommen I **come down with sth.** etwas bekommen *(Krankheit)*, an etwas erkranken III 2 (38) **come home** nach Hause kommen I **come in** hereinkommen I **Come on, Dad.** Na los, Dad! / Komm, Dad! I **come over (to)** herüberkommen (zu/nach), vorbeikommen (bei) III 2 (36) **come up with sth.** etwas haben, auf etwas kommen (Idee, Vorschlag) III 2 (38) °**come to life** lebendig werden

°**comedian** [kə'miːdiən] Komiker/in, Komödiant/in

comedy ['kɒmədi] Comedyshow, Komödie II

comfortable ['kɒmftəbl] bequem II °**be more comfortable with** sich besser/wohler fühlen mit

°**comic strip** ['kɒmɪk ˌstrɪp] Comicstrip

comma ['kɒmə] Komma II

comment ['kɒment]:

1. Bemerkung, Kommentar III 5 (114)
2. **comment (on sth.)** sich äußern (zu etwas), (etwas) kommentieren III 5 (114)

°**commentary** ['kɒməntri] Kommentar

°**commentator** ['kɒmənteɪtə] (Radio-, Fernseh-)Kommentator/in

common ['kɒmən] häufig; weit verbreitet III 1 (31)

communication [kəˌmjuːnɪ'keɪʃn] Kommunikation, Verständigung III 1 (17)

°**community** [kə'mjuːnəti] Gemeinde; Gemeinschaft

company ['kʌmpəni] Firma, Gesellschaft III 5 (113)

compare [kəm'peə] vergleichen III 5 (113) **compared to …** verglichen mit … III 5 (113)

°**comparison** [kəm'pærɪsn] Vergleich

°**compete with** [kəm'piːt] im Wettstreit stehen mit; sich messen mit

competition [ˌkɒmpə'tɪʃn] Wettbewerb II

complain [kəm'pleɪn] sich beschweren, sich beklagen III 3 (71)

°**complete** [kəm'pliːt] vervollständigen

°**compose** [kəm'pəʊz] bilden, komponieren, verfassen

computer [kəm'pjuːtə] Computer I

°**con** [kɒn]: **the pros and cons** das Für und Wider; die Vor- und Nachteile

concentrate (on sth.) ['kɒnsntreɪt] sich konzentrieren (auf etwas) III 4 (93)

concert ['kɒnsət] Konzert I

conclusion [kən'kluːʒn] Schluss(folgerung) III 1 (17)

°**congress** ['kɒŋgres] Kongress

°**connect** [kə'nekt] verbinden, verknüpfen

connected [kə'nektɪd]: **be connected** verbunden sein III 2 (45)

°**connection** [kə'nekʃn] Verbindung

°**conqueror** ['kɒŋkərə] Eroberer/Eroberin

consequence ['kɒnsɪkwəns] Folge, Konsequenz III 5 (123)

°**conservation** [ˌkɒnsə'veɪʃn] (Umwelt-)Schutz, Erhaltung

consonant ['kɒnsənənt] Konsonant, Mitlaut I

content ['kɒntent] Inhalt III 1 (17)

context ['kɒntekst] (Text-, Satz-)Zusammenhang, Kontext II

continue [kən'tɪnjuː] sich fortsetzen, weitergehen III 3 (75) **continue sth.** etwas fortsetzen III 2 (45) °**to be continued** Fortsetzung folgt.

°**contradict** [ˌkɒntrə'dɪkt] widersprechen; im Widerspruch stehen zu

°**contradiction** [ˌkɒntrə'dɪkʃn] Widerspruch

°**contrast** [kən'trɑːst] kontrastieren

conversation [ˌkɒnvə'seɪʃn] Gespräch, Unterhaltung II

cook [kʊk] kochen; zubereiten III 5 (131)

cookie ['kʊki] *(AE)* Keks, Plätzchen I

cool [kuːl]:

1. cool I
2. kühl II

coordinator [kəʊ'ɔːdɪneɪtə] Koordinator/in III 3 (69)

copy ['kɒpi]:

1. kopieren, abschreiben I
2. Kopie; Exemplar II

corn [kɔːn] *(AE, no pl)* Mais III 4 (108)

corner ['kɔːnə] Ecke I **on the corner of Church Road and London Road** Church Road, Ecke London Road II **corner shop** Laden an der Ecke; Tante-Emma-Laden I

cornflakes ['kɔːnfleɪks] Cornflakes I

correct [kə'rekt]:

1. richtig, korrekt II
2. korrigieren, verbessern II

°**correction** [kə'rekʃn] Korrektur, Berichtigung

corridor ['kɒrɪdɔː] Gang, Korridor III 2 (46)

cost, cost, cost [kɒst] kosten II

costume ['kɒstjuːm] Kostüm, Verkleidung II

cottage ['kɒtɪdʒ] Häuschen, Cottage II

cotton ['kɒtn] Baumwolle III 5 (123)

cough [kɒf]: **have a cough** Husten haben II

could [kʊd]:

1. **he could …** er konnte … I **we couldn't …** ['kʊdnt] wir konnten nicht … I
2. **What could be better?** Was könnte besser sein? II

council ['kaʊnsl] Ausschuss; Rat *(Stadtrat, Gemeinderat u.Ä.)* III 4 (98)

count [kaʊnt] zählen I

°**countess** ['kaʊntəs], ['kaʊntes] Gräfin

country ['kʌntri] Land I

countryside ['kʌntrisaɪd] Landschaft, ländliche Gegend II

county ['kaʊnti] Grafschaft *(in Großbritannien)* I

couple ['kʌpl]: **a couple** ein Paar; ein paar III 2 (44)

course [kɔːs] Kurs, Lehrgang I

courtyard ['kɔːtjɑːd] Hof, Innenhof; Vorplatz II

cousin ['kʌzn] Cousin, Cousine I

cover ['kʌvə]:

1. bedecken, zudecken III 4 (88)
2. behandeln, abdecken, ansprechen *(Thema; Fragen)* III 1 (17)

°3. Umschlag

cow [kaʊ] Kuh II

crab [kræb] Krebs I

cracker ['krækə] Knallbonbon I

crash [kræʃ] crashen; abstürzen *(Flugzeug; Computer)* III 4 (89)

crazy ['kreɪzi] verrückt III 3 (67)

cream [kriːm] Sahne I °**cream tea** [ˌkriːm 'tiː] *Mahlzeit mit Tee, Scones, Marmelade und Sahne*

create [kri'eɪt] (er)schaffen, kreieren III 5 (113)

°**creative** [kri'eɪtɪv] kreativ

crib sheet ['krɪb ʃiːt] *(infml)* Spickzettel, Merkzettel II

cricket ['krɪkɪt] Cricket I

°**critic** ['krɪtɪk] Kritiker/in

°**critical** ['krɪtɪkl] kritisch

cross [krɒs] überqueren, kreuzen; sich kreuzen II °**cross sth.out** etwas durchstreichen

crowd [kraʊd] (Menschen-)Menge II

crowded ['kraʊdɪd] voller Menschen; überfüllt III 1 (16)

crown [kraʊn]:

1. Krone II

°2. krönen

°**cruel** ['kruːl] grausam

cry [kraɪ] schreien; weinen II

°**cult** [kʌlt] Kult; Kult-

°**cultural** ['kʌltʃərəl] kulturell

culture ['kʌltʃə] Kultur I

cup [kʌp]: **a cup of tea** eine Tasse Tee I

cupboard ['kʌbəd] Schrank I

curious ['kjʊəriəs] wissbegierig, neugierig III 3 (60)

currency ['kʌrənsi] Währung III 3 (62)

curry ['kʌri] Curry(gericht) I

cut [kʌt]:

1. **(cut, cut)** schneiden II
2. **Cut!** Schnitt! *(beim Filmen)* II

cyberbullying ['saɪbəˌbʊliɪŋ] Cyber-Mobbing *(Verleumdung/Diffamierung in sozialen Medien)* III 5 (114)

D

dad [dæd] Papa, Vati I

daily ['deɪli] täglich III 5 (114)

°**dam** [dæm] Damm, Staudamm

dance [dɑːns]:

1. tanzen I
2. Tanz II

dancer ['dɑːnsə] Tänzer/in II

danger ['deɪndʒə] Gefahr II

dangerous ['deɪndʒərəs] gefährlich I
dark [dɑːk]:
1. dunkel I
2. Dunkelheit III 2 (47)
darkness ['dɑːknəs] Dunkelheit, Finsternis III 1 (11)
date [deɪt]:
1. Datum III 3 (74)
2. Verabredung, Date III 3 (74)
3. date from stammen aus *(zeitlich)* III 4 (95)
daughter ['dɔːtə] Tochter II
day [deɪ] Tag I **all day** den ganzen Tag (lang) I **day of the week** Wochentag I °**one day** eines Tages
dead [ded] tot I
°**deadline** ['dedlaɪn] (Abgabe-)Termin, Frist
dear [dɪə] liebe(r, s) II **Oh dear!** Oje! II
death [deθ] Tod III 3 (77)
°**decade** ['dekeɪd] Jahrzehnt
December [dɪ'sembə] Dezember I
decide [dɪ'saɪd] beschließen, sich entscheiden I
decision [dɪ'sɪʒn] Entscheidung III 3 (69)
deck [dek]:
1. Deck *(eines Schiffes)* I
°**2.** Terrasse
declaration [ˌdeklə'reɪʃn] Erklärung, Verkündung II **the Declaration of Independence** die Unabhängigkeitserklärung *(der Vereinigten Staaten im Jahr 1776)* II
°**declare sth.** [dɪ'kleə] etwas erklären, verkünden
°**decorate** ['dekəreɪt] verzieren
°**decoration** [ˌdekə'reɪʃn] Dekoration, Schmuck
deep [diːp] tief II
deer, *pl* **deer** [dɪə] Reh, Hirsch III 4 (109)
defeat [dɪ'fiːt] besiegen, schlagen III 1 (32)
defend sb./sth. (against sb./sth.) [dɪ'fend] jn./etwas verteidigen (gegen jn./etwas) II
°**definition** [ˌdefɪ'nɪʃn] Definition
delete [dɪ'liːt] löschen; streichen III 5 (114)
delicious [dɪ'lɪʃəs] köstlich, lecker II
°**delivery** [dɪ'lɪvəri] Vortragsweise
°**demand** [dɪ'mɑːnd] fordern, verlangen
demand [dɪ'mɑːnd]: **on demand** auf Abruf, nach Bedarf III 5 (114)
demonstration [ˌdemən'streɪʃn] Demonstration, Vorführung II
dentist ['dentɪst] Zahnarzt/-ärztin II
depend on sth. [dɪ'pend] von etwas abhängen; auf etwas angewiesen sein III 5 (123)
describe sth. (to sb.) [dɪ'skraɪb] (jm.) etwas beschreiben II
°**description** [dɪ'skrɪpʃn] Beschreibung
°**desert** ['dezət] Wüste
°**deserted** [dɪ'zɜːtɪd] verlassen
design [dɪ'zaɪn] Design; Gestaltung III 3 (67) **design and technology** Design und Technik I

desk [desk] Schreibtisch I
dessert [dɪ'zɜːt] Nachtisch, Nachspeise I
destroy [dɪ'strɔɪ] zerstören II
detail ['diːteɪl] Detail, Einzelheit III 1 (15)
°**detective** [dɪ'tektɪv] Detektiv/in
°**Devil, devil** ['devl] Teufel
°**diagram** ['daɪəgræm] Diagramm
°**dialect** ['daɪəlekt] Dialekt, Mundart
dialogue ['daɪəlɒg] Dialog II
diary ['daɪəri] Tagebuch; Kalender I °**keep a diary** ein Tagebuch führen
dictionary ['dɪkʃənri] alphabetisches Wörterverzeichnis, Wörterbuch I
did [dɪd] *siehe* **do** **he didn't run** ['dɪdnt] Er rannte nicht. I
die [daɪ] sterben I **die out** aussterben III 3 (60)
°**diet** ['daɪət] Ernährung(sweise), Speiseplan
difference ['dɪfrəns] Unterschied II
different ['dɪfrənt] verschieden; anders I °**different from** anders als
difficult ['dɪfɪkəlt] schwierig, schwer III 2 (39)
digital ['dɪdʒɪtl] digital III 4 (106)
dining room ['daɪnɪŋ ruːm] Esszimmer I
dinner ['dɪnə] Abendessen, Abendbrot I **have dinner** zu Abend essen I
dinosaur ['daɪnəsɔː] Dinosaurier I
direct [də'rekt], [daɪ'rekt] direkt II
°**directions** *(pl)* [də'rekʃnz] Wegbeschreibung(en)
director [də'rektə]:
1. Leiter/in III 2 (48)
2. Regisseur/in II
dirt [dɜːt] Dreck III 4 (101)
dirty ['dɜːti] schmutzig II
°**disagree (with)** [ˌdɪsə'griː] anderer Meinung sein (als); nicht übereinstimmen (mit); nicht zustimmen
disappear [ˌdɪsə'pɪə] verschwinden II
°**disaster** [dɪ'zɑːstə] Desaster, Katastrophe
disco ['dɪskəʊ] Disko I
°**discovery** [dɪ'skʌvəri] Entdeckung
°**discuss sth.** [dɪ'skʌs] über etwas diskutieren, etwas besprechen
discussion [dɪ'skʌʃn] Diskussion III 3 (69)
disease [dɪ'ziːz] *(ansteckende)* Krankheit III 3 (76)
disgusting [dɪs'gʌstɪŋ] ekelhaft, widerlich III 5 (112)
°**dish** [dɪʃ] Gericht
dishes: wash the dishes *(pl)* [ˌwɒʃ ðə 'dɪʃɪz] das Geschirr abwaschen, spülen II
dislike [dɪs'laɪk] nicht mögen, nicht leiden können III 3 (71)
dislikes [dɪs'laɪks]: **likes and dislikes** *(pl)* Vorlieben und Abneigungen I
°**display** [dɪ'spleɪ]: **fireworks display** Feuerwerk
°**distance** ['dɪstəns] Distanz, Entfernung
ditch [dɪtʃ] Graben III 3 (76)
°**diver** ['daɪvə] Taucher/in
°**diverse** [daɪ'vɜːs] unterschiedlich, vielfältig

°**diversity** [daɪ'vɜːsəti] Vielfalt
divorce [dɪ'vɔːs] Scheidung III 1 (32)
divorced [dɪ'vɔːst] geschieden I
°**Diwali** [diː'wɑːli] *hinduistisches Fest („Lichterfest")*
dizzy ['dɪzi] schwindlig III 1 (24)
do [duː], **did, done** machen, tun I **do sport** Sport treiben I **Don't go.** Geh nicht. I **he doesn't have time** er hat keine Zeit I °**Does it now?** Tatsächlich? / Ist das so?
dock [dɒk] Hafen, Dock III 3 (73)
doctor ['dɒktə] Arzt/Ärztin, Doktor II
documentary [ˌdɒkju'mentri] Dokumentarfilm III 3 (61)
dog [dɒg] Hund I
doll [dɒl] Puppe III 4 (101)
dollar ['dɒlə] Dollar III 3 (112)
dome [dəʊm] Kuppel II
done [dʌn] *siehe* **do**
°**donkey** ['dɒŋki] Esel
door [dɔː] Tür I
doorbell ['dɔːbel] Türklingel, Türglocke II
doorway ['dɔːweɪ] Eingang III 5 (122)
°**dot** [dɒt] Punkt, Pünktchen
double ['dʌbl] Doppel- I
down [daʊn] hinunter, herunter; nach unten I **down there** dort unten II **up and down** auf und ab; rauf und runter I
downhill [ˌdaʊn'hɪl] bergab III 2 (45)
download sth. [ˌdaʊn'ləʊd] etwas herunterladen III 5 (114)
downstairs [ˌdaʊn'steəz] unten; nach unten *(im Haus)* I
downstream [ˌdaʊn'striːm] flussabwärts III 2 (40)
downtown ['daʊntaʊn]: **in downtown Albuquerque** *(AE)* im Zentrum von Albuquerque III 3 (58/59)
draft [drɑːft] Entwurf II
°**dragon** ['drægən] Drache
drama ['drɑːmə] Schauspiel; darstellende Kunst II
drank [dræŋk] *siehe* **drink**
draw [drɔː] *(bes. BE)* Unentschieden III 4 (95)
draw [drɔː], **drew, drawn** zeichnen I
drawing ['drɔːɪŋ] Zeichnung I
drawn [drɔːn] *siehe* **draw**
dream [driːm]:
1. Traum I
°**2.** träumen
dress [dres] Kleid I
dress up [ˌdres_'ʌp] sich verkleiden; sich schick anziehen II
drew [druː] *siehe* **draw**
drink [drɪŋk]:
1. (drank, drunk) trinken I
2. Getränk I
drive [draɪv], **drove, driven** *(ein Auto/ mit dem Auto)* fahren I
driven ['drɪvn] *siehe* **drive**
°**driver's license** *(AE)* **/ driving licence** *(BE)* ['laɪsns] Führerschein, Fahrerlaubnis

drop [drɒp]:
1. fallen III 2 (40)
2. drop sth. etwas fallen lassen II
°**drought** [draʊt] Dürre, Trockenheit
drove [drəʊv] *siehe* **drive**
drum [drʌm] Trommel I **drums** *(pl)* Schlagzeug I **play the drums** Schlagzeug spielen I
drummer ['drʌmə] Trommler/in; Schlagzeuger/in III 1 (24)
drunk [dræŋk] *siehe* **drink**
dry [draɪ] trocken III 3 (76)
dude [dju:d] *(bes. AE, Slang)* Typ, Kerl III 5 (113)
°**dues** [dju:z]: **I've paid my dues** *etwa:* Ich habe für meine Missetaten gebüßt.
during ['djʊərɪŋ] während III 1 (15)
dust [dʌst] Staub III 4 (101)
DVD [ˌdi:vi:'di:] DVD I

E

each [i:tʃ] jeder, jede, jedes (einzelne) II **They're £ 2.75 each.** Sie kosten je 2 Pfund 75. *(2,75 pro Stück)* I **each other** sich (gegenseitig), einander III 1 (20)
ear [ɪə] Ohr I
early ['ɜ:li] früh I
°**earn** [ɜ:n] verdienen
earphones *(pl)* ['ɪəfəʊnz] Ohrhörer, Kopfhörer II
earring ['ɪərɪŋ] Ohrring III 5 (118)
earth [ɜ:θ]: **(the) earth** *(oft auch:* **Earth***)* (die) Erde *(der Planet)* II
east [i:st] Osten; nach Osten; östlich III 1 (11)
Easter ['i:stə] Ostern I
eastern ['i:stən] östlich, Ost- III 3 (62)
easy ['i:zi] leicht, einfach I
eat [i:t], **ate, eaten** essen I
eaten ['i:tn] *siehe* **eat**
°**echo** ['ekəʊ] widerhallen
°**economy** [ɪ'kɒnəmi] Wirtschaft
edge [edʒ] Rand, Kante III 2 (40)
edit ['edɪt] bearbeiten; schneiden *(Film, Video)* I
editor ['edɪtə] Redakteur/in; Herausgeber/in III 3 (69)
education [ˌedʒu'keɪʃn] (Schul-, Aus-) Bildung; Erziehung III 1 (15)
e.g. [ˌi: 'dʒi:] *(from Latin:* exempli gratia*)* z.B. (zum Beispiel) II
egg [eg] Ei I
eight [eɪt] acht I
either ['aɪðə, 'i:ðə]: **either … or …** entweder … oder … III 3 (67) **not … either** auch nicht I
°**electricity** [ɪˌlek'trɪsəti] Elektrizität, Strom
element ['elɪmənt] Element III 5 (117)
elephant ['elɪfənt] Elefant I
elevator ['elɪveɪtə] *(bes. AE)* Fahrstuhl, Aufzug, Lift II
eleven [ɪ'levn] elf I
°**else** [els]: **what else?** was (sonst) noch?
email ['i:meɪl] E-Mail I
embarrassing [ɪm'bærəsɪŋ] peinlich III 5 (112)
emigrate ['emɪgreɪt] auswandern, emigrieren III 3 (62)
emphasis ['emfəsɪs] Betonung, Hervorhebung III 4 (91)
empire ['empaɪə] Reich, Imperium III 1 (30)
empty ['empti] leer III 2 (36)
encore ['ɒŋkɔ:] Zugabe II
end [end]:
1. Ende, Schluss I °**in the end** schließlich, am Ende, zum Schluss
2. enden; beenden III 3 (73)
ending ['endɪŋ]:
1. Ende, (Ab-)Schluss II
2. Endung I
enemy ['enəmi] Feind/in II
energy ['enədʒi] Energie, Kraft III 2 (45)
English ['ɪŋglɪʃ] Englisch; englisch I **in English** auf Englisch I
enjoy [ɪn'dʒɔɪ] genießen III 1 (10) **Enjoy yourself!** Viel Spaß! / Amüsiere dich gut! III 3 (71/72)
enough [ɪ'nʌf] genug I
enter ['entə]:
1. betreten, hineingehen in; eintreten II
2. enter a password ein Passwort eingeben III 5 (114)
°**entertainment** [ˌentə'teɪnmənt] Unterhaltung
entrance ['entrəns] Eingang III 4 (100)
entry ['entri]:
1. Eintritt, Zutritt III 1 (14)
2. Eintrag, Eintragung *(im Tagebuch, Wörterbuch)* II
°**equal to** ['i:kwəl] größengleich mit, entsprechend
equally ['i:kwəli] gleichermaßen, genauso III 2 (39)
equipment *(no pl)* [ɪ'kwɪpmənt] Ausrüstung II
escape [ɪ'skeɪp]:
1. fliehen III 4 (95)
2. Flucht III 4 (95)
especially [ɪ'speʃli] besonders, vor allem II
etc. (et cetera) [et'setərə] usw. (und so weiter) I
EU: the EU [ˌi: 'ju:] die Europäische Union III 3 (62)
euro (€) ['jʊərəʊ] Euro III 3 (62)
Europe ['jʊərəp] Europa III 1 (10)
European: the European Union (EU) [ˌjʊərəpi:ən 'ju:niən] die Europäische Union III 3 (62)
even ['i:vn] sogar II **even if** selbst wenn II **not even** (noch) nicht einmal II
evening ['i:vnɪŋ] Abend I **in the evening** abends, am Abend I
event [ɪ'vent] Ereignis II
ever ['evə] jemals II **better than ever** besser als je zuvor II
every day/colour/boat ['evri] jeder Tag / jede Farbe / jedes Boot I
everybody ['evribɒdi] jeder; alle I
everyday ['evrideɪ] Alltags- I
everyone ['evriwʌn] jeder; alle I
everything ['evriθɪŋ] alles I
everywhere ['evriweə] überall II
exact [ɪg'zækt] genau III 1 (16)
exactly [ɪg'zæktli] genau III 1 (24)
example [ɪg'zɑ:mpl] Beispiel II **for example** zum Beispiel II
excellent ['eksələnt] ausgezeichnet, hervorragend I
except [ɪk'sept] außer, bis auf II
exchange [ɪks'tʃeɪndʒ]:
1. Austausch; Austausch- III 4 (85)
°**2.** austauschen
excited [ɪk'saɪtɪd] aufgeregt, gespannt I
exciting [ɪk'saɪtɪŋ] aufregend, spannend I
exclamation mark [ˌekskla'meɪʃn mɑ:k] Ausrufezeichen II
Excuse me, … [ɪk'skju:z mi:] Entschuldigung, … / Entschuldigen Sie, … II
exercise ['eksəsaɪz] Aufgabe, Übung I
exercise book ['eksəsaɪz bʊk] Schulheft, Übungsheft I
°**exhibit** [ɪg'zɪbɪt] Ausstellungsstück
°**exhibition** [ˌeksɪ'bɪʃn] Ausstellung
°**exit** ['eksɪt, 'egzɪt] *(von der Bühne)* abgehen *(Theater)*
expect sth. [ɪk'spekt] etwas erwarten III 1 (13)
°**expenses** *(pl)* [ɪk'spensɪz]: **travel expenses** Reisekosten
expensive [ɪk'spensɪv] teuer I
experience [ɪk'spɪəriəns]:
1. *(no pl)* Erfahrung(en) III 2 (54)
2. erfahren, erleben III 3 (74)
expert ['ekspɜ:t] Experte/Expertin III 1 (8/9)
explain sth. to sb. [ɪk'spleɪn] jm. etwas erklären, erläutern I
°**explanation** [ˌekspla'neɪʃn] Erklärung
explode [ɪk'spləʊd] explodieren III 5 (127)
explore [ɪk'splɔ:] erkunden, erforschen III 3 (60)
°**explosion** [ɪk'spləʊʒn] Explosion
export ['ekspɔ:t] Export, Ausfuhr III 3 (62)
°**express** [ɪk'spres] ausdrücken, zum Ausdruck bringen
°**expression** [ɪk'spreʃn] Ausdruck
eye [aɪ] Auge I

F

face [feɪs] Gesicht I °**face down** mit der Vorderseite nach unten *(Karten)*
°**facilities** *(pl)* [fə'sɪlətiz] Einrichtungen, Anlagen
fact [fækt] Tatsache, Fakt III 1 (14) **in fact** eigentlich, in Wirklichkeit III 1 (14)
factor ['fæktə] Faktor III 1 (33)
factory ['fæktri] Fabrik II

°**fail** [feɪl] nicht bestehen *(Test, Prüfung)*; durchfallen
fair [feə] fair, gerecht I
°**fairy** ['feəri] Fee
fall [fɔːl], **fell, fallen** fallen, stürzen; hinfallen I **fall asleep** einschlafen I **fall off a bike** vom Fahrrad (herunter)fallen III 1 (20) °**fall in love (with sb.)** sich (in jn.) verlieben
fall [fɔːl] *(AE)* Herbst II
fallen ['fɔːlən] *siehe* **fall**
°**falls** *(pl)* [fɔːlz] Wasserfälle
false [fɔːls] falsch III 1 (11)
family ['fæməli] Familie I **the Blackwell family** (die) Familie Blackwell I **a family of four** eine vierköpfige Familie III 1 (15) °**family name** Familienname, Nachname **family tree** (Familien-) Stammbaum I
famine ['fæmɪn] Hungersnot III 3 (76)
famous (for) ['feɪməs] berühmt (für, wegen) I
fan [fæn] Fan, Anhänger/in I
fantastic [fæn'tæstɪk] fantastisch I
far [fɑː] weit (entfernt) I **so far** bis jetzt; bis hierher II °**far and wide** weit und breit
farm [fɑːm] Bauernhof, Farm I °**farm worker** Landarbeiter/in
farmer ['fɑːmə] Bauer/Bäuerin, Landwirt/in I
fashion ['fæʃn] Mode II
fast [fɑːst] schnell I **be fast** vorgehen *(Uhr)* III 1 (19)
°**fast** [fɑːst] fasten
fat [fæt] dick, fett I
father ['fɑːðə] Vater I
fault [fɔːlt] Schuld, Fehler III 4 (101)
favourite ['feɪvərɪt]: **my favourite day** mein Lieblingstag I
°**fear** [fɪə] fürchten
February ['februəri] Februar I
fed [fed] *siehe* **feed**
°**federal** ['fedərəl] Bundes-; bundesweit
feed [fiːd], **fed, fed** füttern I **feeding time** Fütterungszeit I
feedback *(no pl)* ['fiːdbæk] Rückmeldung, Feedback III 1 (17)
feel [fiːl], **felt, felt** fühlen; sich fühlen I; sich anfühlen III 2 (36) **I don't feel well.** Ich fühle mich nicht gut. / Mir geht's nicht gut. II **I feel sick.** Mir ist schlecht. II
feeling ['fiːlɪŋ] Gefühl I
feet [fiːt] *plural of* **foot** II
fell [fel] *siehe* **fall**
felt [felt] *siehe* **feel**
felt pen [ˌfelt 'pen] Filzstift I
fence [fens] Zaun II
ferry ['feri] Fähre I
festival ['festɪvl] Fest, Festival II
few: a few [ə 'fjuː] ein paar, einige II
field [fiːld] Feld, Acker, Weide II
fierce [fɪəs] heftig, wild III 3 (60)
fight [faɪt]:
1. (fought, fought) kämpfen I **fight sb.** jn. bekämpfen; gegen jn. kämpfen II °**fight for sth.** um etwas kämpfen
°**2.** Kampf, Schlägerei
fighter ['faɪtə] Kämpfer/in II
figure ['fɪgə]:
1. Zahl, Ziffer III 1 (15)
2. Figur, Gestalt III 2 (47)
file [faɪl]: **background file** Hintergrundinformation(en) I **grammar file** Zusammenfassung der Grammatik jeder Unit I
skills file Übersicht über Lern- und Arbeitstechniken I
fill [fɪl] füllen III 1 (24) °**fill sth. in**
1. etwas einsetzen; **2.** etwas ausfüllen
film [fɪlm]:
1. filmen I
2. Film I
final ['faɪnl]:
1. Finale, Endspiel I
°**2.** letzte(r, s), End-; endgültige(r, s)
finally ['faɪnəli] endlich, schließlich III 2 (46)
find [faɪnd], **found, found** finden I **Find someone who ...** Finde jemanden, der ... I **find sth. out** etwas herausfinden II
fine [faɪn] gut, in Ordnung, prima II **Fine, thanks.** Gut, danke. I
finger ['fɪŋgə] Finger II
finish ['fɪnɪʃ]:
1. enden I
2. finish sth. etwas beenden; mit etwas fertig werden/sein I **We're finished.** Wir sind fertig. I
°**3.** vervollständigen; abschließen
fire ['faɪə] Feuer II
fireplace ['faɪəpleɪs] Kamin II
firework ['faɪəwɜːk] Feuerwerkskörper II **fireworks** *(pl)* Feuerwerk II
first [fɜːst] zuerst, als Erstes I **at first** zuerst, anfangs, am Anfang II **the first day** der erste Tag I **First, ...** Erstens, ... I
°**first-aid kit** [fɜːst‿'eɪd ˌkɪt] Erste-Hilfe-Kasten
fish [fɪʃ]:
1. *pl* **fish** Fisch I
2. fish sth. out etwas herausfischen III 2 (40)
°**fishing** ['fɪʃɪŋ] Angeln, Fischen
fishing village ['fɪʃɪŋ ˌvɪlɪdʒ] Fischerdorf II
fit [fɪt] fit II
five [faɪv] fünf I
fixed [fɪkst] fest, festgelegt II
flag [flæg] Fahne, Flagge II
flash [flæʃ]:
1. Lichtblitz II **a flash of lightning** ein Blitz II
°**2. he flashed his smile** er ließ sein Lächeln aufblitzen
flashlight ['flæʃlaɪt] *(AE)* Taschenlampe III 4 (102)
flat [flæt] Wohnung I
flavour *(BE)*, **flavor** *(AE)* ['fleɪvə] Geschmack, Geschmacksrichtung II
flew [fluː] *siehe* **fly**
°**flight** [flaɪt] Flug
floor [flɔː]:
1. Fußboden I
2. Stock(werk) I
flower ['flaʊə] Blume; Blüte II
flown [fləʊn] *siehe* **fly**
fly [flaɪ], **flew, flown** fliegen II
°**flyer** ['flaɪə] Flyer, Flugblatt
°**foal** [fəʊl] Fohlen
°**focus** ['fəʊkəs] Mittelpunkt, Schwerpunkt
°**foil** [fɔɪl] Folie *(Alufolie)*
fold [fəʊld] falten III 5 (118)
°**folder** ['fəʊldə] Mappe
folk *(pl)* [fəʊk] *(infml)* Leute III 3 (71)
follow ['fɒləʊ] folgen I **Follow me.** Folg(t) mir. I
food [fuːd] Essen; Lebensmittel; Futter I
foot [fʊt], *pl* **feet** [fiːt] Fuß *(auch Längenmaß: 30,5 cm)* II **on foot** zu Fuß III 3 (68)
football ['fʊtbɔːl] Fußball I °**American football** Football
°**footbridge** ['fʊtbrɪdʒ] Fußgängerbrücke
°**footpath** ['fʊtpɑːθ] Fußweg, Pfad
footprint ['fʊtprɪnt] Fußabdruck II
for [fɔː, fə] für I **for a while** eine Weile, eine Zeit lang III 1 (20) **for ever** (für) immer; ewig II **for example** zum Beispiel II **for free** kostenlos, umsonst III 1 (22) **for hours/weeks/...** seit Stunden/Wochen/... III 1 (20) **for miles** meilenweit I **for the first time** zum ersten Mal III 1 (14) **What's for lunch?** Was gibt es zum Mittagessen? I **What's for homework?** Was haben wir als Hausaufgabe auf? I
forearm ['fɔːrɑːm] Unterarm III 4 (100)
forever [fər'evə] (für) immer; ewig III 5 (114)
foreground ['fɔːgraʊnd] Vordergrund I
forest ['fɒrɪst] Wald II
forget [fə'get], **forgot, forgotten** vergessen I
forgot [fə'gɒt] *siehe* **forget**
forgotten [fə'gɒtn] *siehe* **forget**
fork [fɔːk] Gabel II
form [fɔːm]:
1. bilden, formen III 3 (60)
2. Form I
former ['fɔːmə] ehemalige(r, s), frühere(r, s) I
°**Forty-Niner** [ˌfɔːti 'naɪnə] *Teilnehmer/in am Kalifornischen Goldrausch (1848–1854)* **the 49ers** die San Francisco 49ers *(American football team)*
°**forum** ['fɔːrəm] Forum *(Platz im alten Rom)*
forward ['fɔːwəd]: **look forward to sth.** sich auf etwas freuen II
fought [fɔːt] *siehe* **fight**

found [faʊnd]:
1. *siehe* **find**
2. gründen III 4 (109)
°**fountain** ['faʊntɪn] Fontäne
four [fɔː] vier I
°**frame** [freɪm] Rahmen
free [friː]:
1. frei I **free time** Freizeit, freie Zeit I **free-time activities** Freizeitaktivitäten I
2. kostenlos II **for free** kostenlos, umsonst III 1 (22)
°**freedom** ['friːdəm] Freiheit
French [frentʃ] Französisch I
French fries *(pl)* [ˌfrentʃ 'fraɪz] *(AE)* Pommes Frites III 4 (90)
fresh [freʃ] frisch II
Friday ['fraɪdeɪ, 'fraɪdi] Freitag I
friend ['frend] Freund/in I
friendly ['frendli] freundlich I
fries *(pl)* [fraɪz] *(kurz für:* **French fries***)* *(AE)* Pommes frites II
fright [fraɪt]: **in fright** ängstlich, erschrocken III 4 (89)
frisbee ['frɪzbi] Frisbee II
frog [frɒg] Frosch I
from [frɒm, frəm] aus, von I **from behind** von hinten II **from the back of the bus** aus dem hinteren Teil des Busses II **from … to …** von … bis … I
front [frʌnt] Vorderseite I **in front of** vor *(räumlich)* I **to the front** nach vorn II
frown [fraʊn] die Stirn runzeln II
frozen ['frəʊzn] tiefgekühlt; gefroren III 4 (98)
fruit [fruːt] Obst, Früchte; Frucht I **fruit salad** Obstsalat I
°**frying pan** ['fraɪɪŋ pæn] Bratpfanne
full (of) [fʊl] voll (von/mit) I **full moon** Vollmond II **full sentence** ganzer Satz II **full stop** Punkt II
fun [fʌn] Spaß I **have fun** Spaß haben, sich amüsieren I **make fun of sb./sth.**
sich über jn./etwas lustig machen III 2 (36)
That sounds fun. Das klingt nach Spaß. I **That's fun.** Das macht Spaß. I **Was it fun?** Hat es Spaß gemacht? I
funny ['fʌni] witzig, komisch I
fun park ['fʌn pɑːk] Vergnügungspark I
furniture *(no pl)* ['fɜːnɪtʃə] Möbel III 2 (36)
further ['fɜːðə] weiter II
furthest ['fɜːðɪst] am weitesten II
future ['fjuːtʃə] Zukunft; zukünftige(r, s) II

G

°**Gaelic** ['geɪlɪk] Gälisch *(die irische Sprache)*
gallery ['gæləri] Galerie III 1 (12)
°**galley** ['gæli] Kombüse, Bordküche
game [geɪm] Spiel I
°**game plan** ['geɪm plæn] Strategie, Schlachtplan
°**gang** [gæŋ] Gruppe
°**gap** [gæp] Lücke
garage ['gærɑːʒ, 'gærɪdʒ] Garage I
garbage ['gɑːbɪdʒ] *(AE)* Müll, Abfall III 4 (90)
garden ['gɑːdn] Garten I
gardener ['gɑːdnə] Gärtner/in III 4 (96)
gardening ['gɑːdnɪŋ] Gärtnern, Gartenarbeit I
gas [gæs] *(AE)* Benzin III 3 (66) **gas station** *(AE)* Tankstelle III 3 (66)
gate [geɪt] Tor, Pforte, Gatter II
°**gatehouse** ['geɪthaʊs] Pförtnerhaus
gave [geɪv] *siehe* **give**
gaze [geɪz] blicken, starren III 2 (54)
gel [dʒel] Gel II
°**general** ['dʒenrəl] allgemeine(r, s)
generally ['dʒenrəli] generell, allgemein III 4 (109)
generation [ˌdʒenə'reɪʃn] Generation III 5 (113)
geography [dʒi'ɒgrəfi] Geografie I
German ['dʒɜːmən] Deutsch; deutsch I **in German** auf Deutsch I
get [get], **got, got**:
1. bekommen, erhalten I **Did you get it?** *(infml)* Hast du es verstanden? / Hast du es mitbekommen? I **get the hang of sth.** *(infml)* den Dreh raushaben/ rausbekommen (bei etwas); etwas kapieren
III 5 (127)
2. **get sth.** (sich) etwas besorgen, (sich) etwas holen II
3. gelangen, (hin)kommen I **get in touch (with sb.)** [tʌtʃ] (mit jm.) Kontakt aufnehmen; sich (mit jm.) in Verbindung setzen II **get into trouble** in Schwierigkeiten geraten, Ärger kriegen III 2 (46) **get lost** sich verlaufen, sich verirren III 3 (77) **get on** vorankommen, zurechtkommen II
4. **get in(to) a car/taxi** in ein Auto/ Taxi einsteigen II **get off (the bus/ boat)**
(aus dem Bus/Boot) aussteigen I **get on (the bus/boat** (in den Bus/das Boot) einsteigen II **get out of a car/ taxi** aus einem Auto/Taxi aussteigen II
5. **get angry/cold/…** wütend/kalt/… werden I **get paid** bezahlt werden III 3 (71) **get ready (for)** sich fertig machen (für); sich vorbereiten (auf) II
6. **get up** aufstehen I
ghost [gəʊst] Geist, Gespenst I
giant ['dʒaɪənt] Riese III 3 (60)
giraffe [dʒə'rɑːf] Giraffe I
girl [gɜːl] Mädchen I
girlfriend ['gɜːlfrend] Freundin III 3 (68)
give [gɪv], **gave, given** geben I **give a talk (about)** einen Vortrag / eine Rede halten (über) I **give sb. a hug** jn. umarmen II **give sb. a lift** jn. mitnehmen II
give up aufgeben III 2 (36)
given ['gɪvn] *siehe* **give**
glad [glæd] froh, dankbar III 3 (60)
glass [glɑːs] Glas II **a glass of …** ein Glas … II
glasses *(pl)* ['glɑːsɪz] (eine) Brille II
glove [glʌv] Handschuh II
glue [gluː] Klebstoff I
glue stick ['gluː stɪk] Klebestift I
go [gəʊ], **went, gone**:
1. gehen; fahren I **go by** vergehen, vorübergehen *(Zeit)* III 2 (40) **go by car/ bus/…** mit dem Auto/Bus/… fahren I **go camping** zelten gehen II **go down** untergehen *(Sonne)* I **go for a walk** spazieren gehen, einen Spaziergang machen I **go hard/bad/mad** hart/ schlecht/verrückt werden II **go home** nach Hause gehen I **go in** hineingehen II °**go marching** marschieren **go on**
1. im Gang sein; andauern III 1 (21);
2. weiterreden, fortfahren; weitermachen I **go on a boat trip** einen Bootsausflug machen I **go red** rot werden, erröten II **go sailing** segeln; segeln gehen I **go shopping** einkaufen gehen I **go together** zusammenpassen, zueinander passen III 1 (12) **go well** gut laufen, gut gehen II **go with sth.** zu etwas gehören, zu etwas passen I **go wrong** schiefgehen III 5 (121) **Here we go.** Los geht's. / Jetzt geht's los. I
2. **Have a go.** Versuch's mal. I
goal [gəʊl] Tor *(Sport)* II
goat [gəʊt] Ziege II
God, god [gɒd] Gott III 3 (60)
°**goddess** ['gɒdes] Göttin
going to ['gəʊɪŋ tʊ]: **He is going to visit his dad.** Er hat vor, seinen Vater zu besuchen. / Er wird seinen Vater besuchen. I
go-kart ['gəʊ kɑːt] Gokart II
gold [gəʊld]:
1. Gold I
2. golden, Gold- II
°**golden** ['gəʊldən] golden
°**golf course** ['gɒlf kɔːs] Golfplatz
gone [gɒn] *siehe* **go**
be gone weg sein, nicht (mehr) da sein III 4 (101)
good [gʊd]:
1. gut I **be good at kung fu** gut sein in Kung-Fu; gut Kung-Fu können I **Good luck!** Viel Glück! I **Good morning.** Guten Morgen. I
2. brav II
Goodbye. [ˌgʊd'baɪ] Auf Wiedersehen. I
good-looking [ˌgʊd'lʊkɪŋ] gutaussehend II
goods *(pl)* [gʊdz] Waren, Güter I
got [gɒt]:
1. **get**
2. **Have you got …?** Haben Sie …? / Hast du …? / Habt ihr …? I
°**gourd** [gʊəd, gɔːd] Kalebasse, Kürbis

govern ['gʌvən] regieren III 4 (109)
government ['gʌvənmənt] Regierung II
governor ['gʌvənə] Gouverneur/in III 3 (62)
grab [græb] schnappen, packen III 2 (40)
°**grade** [greɪd]:
1. *(AE)* Jahrgangsstufe, Klasse
2. *(bes. AE)* (Schul-)Note, Zensur
°**graffiti** [grə'fi:ti] Graffiti
gram [græm] Gramm II
grammar file ['græmə ˌfaɪl] Zusammenfassung der Grammatik I
grandfather ['grænfɑ:ðə] Großvater I
grandma ['grænmɑ:] Oma I
grandmother ['grænmʌðə] Großmutter I
grandpa ['grænpɑ:] Opa I
grandparents *(pl)* ['grænpeərənts] Großeltern I
graphics *(pl)* ['græfɪks] Grafiken III 5 (124)
grass [grɑ:s] Gras; Rasen I
grave [greɪv] Grab II
gravel ['grævl] Kies, Schotter III 4 (100)
gravestone ['greɪvstəʊn] Grabstein III 3 (60)
great [greɪt] großartig I **great-grandfather/great-grandmother** Urgroßvater/Urgroßmutter III 5 (118)
Great Britain (GB) [ˌgreɪt 'brɪtn] Großbritannien I
green [gri:n] grün I
°**greetings** *(pl)* ['gri:tɪŋz] Grüße
grew [gru:] *siehe* **grow**
grey [greɪ] grau I
°**grey seal** [ˌgreɪ 'si:l] Kegelrobbe
grid [grɪd] Gitter; Raster; Rechteckschema III 4 (95)
grin [grɪn] grinsen III 5 (126)
groan [grəʊn]:
1. stöhnen II
2. Stöhnen II
ground [graʊnd]:
1. (Erd-)Boden II
2. **ground sb.** jm. Hausarrest/Ausgehverbot erteilen III 2 (38)
group (of) [gru:p] Gruppe I °**group word** Oberbegriff
grow [grəʊ], **grew, grown:**
1. anbauen, anpflanzen I
2. wachsen I
3. **grow darker/old/...** (allmählich) dunkler/alt/... werden III 4 (103)
4. **grow up** aufwachsen; erwachsen werden III 3 (81)
growl [graʊl] knurren III 5 (126)
grown [grəʊn] *siehe* **grow**
°**gruff** [grʌf]: **in a gruff voice** barsch, schroff
guard [gɑ:d]:
1. Wachposten, Wache II
2. bewachen III 1 (15)
guess [ges] raten, erraten I **Guess what, Dad ...** Stell dir vor, Papa .../ Weißt du was, Papa ... I **I guess ...** Ich nehme an, ... / Ich denke, ... III 3 (71)
guest [gest] Gast III 3 (70)
guide [gaɪd]:
1. Fremdenführer/in; Reiseleiter/in II
2. führen, begleiten III 3 (61)
guinea pig ['gɪni pɪg] Meerschweinchen I
guitar [gɪ'tɑ:] Gitarre I **play the guitar** Gitarre spielen I
°**gumbo** ['gʌmbəʊ] Eintopfgericht
°**gun** [gʌn] Waffe
guy [gaɪ] Typ, Kerl II **guys** *(pl)* Leute II
gym [dʒɪm] Turnhalle I
gymnastics [dʒɪm'næstɪks] Gymnastik, Turnen I

H

habit ['hæbɪt] (An-)Gewohnheit III 5 (113)
had [hæd] *siehe* **have** *und* **have got**
hair [heə] Haar, Haare I
hairdresser ['heədresə] Friseur/in III 2 (37)
half [hɑ:f], *pl* **halves** [hɑ:vz] Hälfte; Halbzeit I **half past ten** halb elf (10.30 / 22.30) I **an hour and a half** eineinhalb Stunden, anderthalb Stunden III 3 (60) **half an hour** eine halbe Stunde III 3 (60) °**half the population** die Hälfte der Bevölkerung
hamburger ['hæmbɜ:gə] Hamburger II
hammer ['hæmə]:
1. Hammer III 2 (36)
2. hämmern III 2 (41)
hamster ['hæmstə] Hamster II
hand [hænd]:
1. Hand I
2. **hand sb. sth.** jm. etwas geben, reichen III 5 (118) **hand sth. in** etwas abgeben; etwas einreichen II °**hand sth. out** etwas austeilen
°**handle** ['hændl] Griff; Klinke III 5 (127)
°**handmade** [ˌhænd'meɪd] von Hand gefertigt
handout ['hændaʊt] Handout, Handzettel III 4 (99)
handshake ['hændʃeɪk] Handschlag, Händedruck III 4 (103)
handsome ['hænsəm] attraktiv, gut aussehend III 5 (118)
hang [hæŋ], **hung, hung** hängen II **hang out** *(infml)* abhängen, rumhängen III 4 (87) °**hang sth. up** etwas aufhängen
hang [hæŋ]: **get the hang of sth.** *(infml)* den Dreh raushaben/rausbekommen (bei etwas); etwas kapieren III 5 (127)
happen (to) ['hæpən] passieren, geschehen (mit) I °**make sth. happen** etwas möglich machen
happy ['hæpi] glücklich, froh I
harbour ['hɑ:bə] Hafen I
hard [hɑ:d] schwer, schwierig; hart I **try hard** sich anstrengen; sich (große) Mühe geben III 3 (70)
harmless ['hɑ:mləs] harmlos III 5 (114)
harmonica [hɑ:'mɒnɪkə] Mundharmonika III 5 (127)
harvest ['hɑ:vɪst] Ernte III 4 (109)
has [hæz]: **he/she has** er/sie hat I
hat [hæt] Hut I
have [hæv, həv], **had, had** haben I **Have a go.** Versuch's mal. I **have a cold** eine Erkältung haben, erkältet sein II **have a cough/a temperature** Husten/Fieber haben II **have a look (at sth.)** nachschauen; einen Blick auf etwas werfen III 2 (47) **have a shower** (sich) duschen II **have a toothache/a headache** Zahnschmerzen/Kopfschmerzen haben II **have breakfast** frühstücken I **have dinner** zu Abend essen I **have fun** Spaß haben, sich amüsieren I **have lunch** zu Mittag essen I **have to do** tun müssen I **Have you ever been to ...?** Bist du jemals in ... gewesen? II **Have you got ...?** Haben Sie ...? / Hast du ...? / Habt ihr ...? II **I'll have a tea/a burger/...** Ich nehme einen Tee/ einen Hamburger/... *(beim Essen, im Restaurant)* II °**Just have a look.** Schau einfach mal.
have got [hæv 'gɒt, həv 'gɒt], **had, had** haben I **Have you got ...?** Haben Sie ...? / Hast du ...? / Habt ihr ...? I
hay [heɪ] Heu II
he [hi:] er I
head [hed]:
1. Kopf I
2. Oberhaupt, Leiter/in III 1 (32)
3. **head for sth.** auf etwas zusteuern/ zugehen/zufahren III 1 (19)
headache ['hedeɪk]: **have a headache** Kopfschmerzen haben II
heading ['hedɪŋ] Überschrift III 5 (124)
°**headline** ['hedlaɪn] Schlagzeile, Überschrift
head teacher [ˌhed 'ti:tʃə] Schulleiter/ in III 2 (43)
headword ['hedwɜ:d] Stichwort *(im Wörterbuch)* III 2 (38)
health service ['helθ ˌsɜ:vɪs] Gesundheitswesen III 2 (54)
hear [hɪə], **heard, heard** hören I
heard [hɜ:d] *siehe* **hear**
heart [hɑ:t] Herz II
°**heath** [hi:θ] Heide
heaven ['hevn] Himmel *(im religiösen Sinn)* III 3 (60)
heavy ['hevi] schwer *(von Gewicht)* II **heavy rain** starker/heftiger Regen II
held [held] *siehe* **hold**
helicopter ['helɪkɒptə] Helikopter, Hubschrauber III 2 (53)
Hello. [hə'ləʊ] Hallo. / Grüß Gott. I **Say hello to ... for me.** Grüß ... von mir. II
°**helmet** ['helmɪt] Helm
help [help]:
1. Hilfe I
2. helfen I

Help yourself! Greif zu! / Bedien dich! III 3 (71/72)
helper ['helpə] Helfer/in II
her [hɜː, hə]:
1. ihr, ihre I **her best friend** ihr bester Freund / ihre beste Freundin I
2. sie; ihr I
here [hɪə] hier; hierher I **Here we go.** Los geht's. / Jetzt geht's los. I **Here you are.** Bitte sehr. / Hier bitte. II **near here** (hier) in der Nähe I **over here** hier herüber; hier drüben II **up here** hier oben; nach hier oben II
°**heritage** ['herɪtɪdʒ] (Kultur-, Natur-)Erbe
hero ['hɪərəʊ], *pl* **heroes** Held/in III 1 (33)
hers [hɜːz] ihrer, ihre, ihrs II
herself [hɜː'self] sich III 3 (71/72); selbst, selber III 4 (91)
hid [hɪd] *siehe* **hide**
hidden ['hɪdn] *siehe* **hide**
hide [haɪd], **hid, hidden** verstecken; sich verstecken I
high [haɪ] hoch I **high school** ['haɪ skuːl] *(USA) Schule für 14- bis 18-Jährige* III 4 (88)
highlight ['haɪlaɪt]:
1. hervorheben, markieren *(mit Textmarker)* II
°**2.** Höhepunkt
high school ['haɪ skuːl] *(USA) Schule für 14- bis 18-Jährige* III 4 (88)
°**high-tech** [ˌhaɪ'tek] Hightech-
hill [hɪl] Hügel I
°**hillwalking** ['hɪlwɔːkɪŋ] Bergwandern
him [hɪm] ihn; ihm I
himself [hɪm'self] sich III 3 (71/72); selbst, selber III 4 (91)
hip [hɪp] Hüfte III 1 (24)
°**hire** ['haɪə] Leihgebühr
his [hɪz]:
1. his friend sein Freund / seine Freundin I
2. seiner, seine, seins II
°**Hispanic** [hɪ'spænɪk] lateinamerikanisch, hispanisch
hiss [hɪs] zischen II
historic [hɪ'stɒrɪk] historisch *(geschichtlich bedeutsam)* II
°**historical** [hɪ'stɒrɪkl] historisch
history ['hɪstri] Geschichte I **natural history** [ˌnætʃrəl 'hɪstri] Naturkunde I
hit [hɪt], **hit, hit**:
1. schlagen II
2. prallen, stoßen gegen I
3. treffen II
hobby ['hɒbi] Hobby I
hockey ['hɒki] Hockey II
°**hogan** ['həʊgn] *Wohnhaus der Navajos*
hold [həʊld]:
1. (held, held) halten I
°**2. (held, held)** abhalten, durchführen *(Veranstaltung)*
3. Griff III 4 (99)
Hold on a minute. *(oft auch kurz:* **Hold on.***)* Bleib / Bleiben Sie am Apparat. *(am Telefon)* II **hold onto sth.** sich an etwas festhalten III 1 (24)
hole [həʊl] Loch II
holiday ['hɒlədeɪ]:
1. Urlaub I **be/go on holiday** in Urlaub sein/fahren I **holidays** *(pl)* Ferien I
2. Feiertag III 3 (82)
°**holidaymaker** ['hɒlədeɪˌmeɪkə] Urlauber/in
home [həʊm] Heim, Zuhause I **at home** daheim, zu Hause I **come/go home** nach Hause kommen/gehen I **be home to sth.** Heimat sein für etwas; etwas beheimaten III 1 (15)
°**homely** ['həʊmli] behaglich, wohnlich
hometown [ˌhəʊm'taʊn] Heimatstadt I
homework ['həʊmwɜːk] Hausaufgabe(n) I **Do your homework.** Mach deine Hausaufgaben. I **What's for homework?** Was haben wir als Hausaufgabe auf? I
honey ['hʌni] Honig; *(infml, als Anrede:)* Schatz, Schätzchen III 5 (118)
honour ['ɒnə] Ehre II
hook [hʊk]
1. Haken III 4 (100)
°**2.** an den (Angel-)Haken bekommen
hop [hɒp] hüpfen III 4 (102)
hope [həʊp] hoffen I
horn [hɔːn] Hupe III 4 (101) **blow the horn** hupen III 4 (101)
horse [hɔːs] Pferd I
°**horseback** ['hɔːsbæk]: **on horseback** zu Pferd
hospital ['hɒspɪtl] Krankenhaus II
host [həʊst]:
1. Gastgeber/in; Moderatorin III 3 (61)
°**2. a host of …** eine Fülle von …
hostel ['hɒstl] Herberge, Wohnheim III 2 (40)
host family ['həʊst fæməli] Gastfamilie II
hot [hɒt] heiß I
hotel [həʊ'tel] Hotel II
hour ['aʊə] Stunde I **an hour and a half** eineinhalb Stunden, anderthalb Stunden III 3 (60) **half an hour** eine halbe Stunde III 3 (60)
house [haʊs] Haus I
how [haʊ] wie I **How are you?** Wie geht's? / Wie geht es dir/euch? I **How do you know …?** Woher weißt/kennst du …? III 1 (10) **How do you like it?** Wie findest du es (sie/ihn)? / Wie gefällt es (sie/er) dir? I **How many?** Wie viele? I **How much?** Wie viel? I **How much are …?** Was kosten …? I **How much is …?** Was kostet …? I **How old are you?** Wie alt bist du? I **how to do sth.** wie man etwas macht / machen kann / machen soll I
°**however** [haʊ'evə] aber; allerdings; jedoch
hug [hʌg]:
1. umarmen II
2. give sb. a hug jn. umarmen II
huge [hjuːdʒ] riesig, sehr groß III 1 (10)
hum [hʌm] summen; brummen III 5 (118)
human ['hjuːmən]:
1. Mensch III 4 (95)
2. menschlich III 4 (95)
humour: sense of humour [ˌsens‿əv 'hjuːmə] (Sinn für) Humor III 3 (70)
hundred: a/one hundred [ə'hʌndrəd, ˌwʌn'hʌndrəd] einhundert I
hung [hʌŋ] *siehe* **hang**
hungry ['hʌŋgri]: **be hungry** hungrig sein, Hunger haben I
hunt [hʌnt]:
1. jagen III 5 (119)
2. Jagd 5 (119)
°**hurrah** [hə'rɑː] hurra
hurricane ['hʌrɪkən, 'hʌrɪkeɪn] Hurrikan, Orkan III 5 (110)
hurry ['hʌri] eilen; sich beeilen II **hurry up** sich beeilen I
hurt, hurt, hurt [hɜːt] schmerzen, wehtun; verletzen I
husband ['hʌzbənd] Ehemann III 1 (32)
hyphen ['haɪfən] Bindestrich II

I

I [aɪ] ich I **I'm (= I am)** Ich bin I **I'm two years old.** Ich bin zwei Jahre alt. I **I see.** Aha! / Verstehe. II °**I spy with my little eye** *entspricht dem Spiel „Ich sehe was, was du nicht siehst"*
ice [aɪs] Eis II **iced tea** Eistee II
ice cream [ˌaɪs 'kriːm] (Speise-)Eis I
°**ice hockey** ['aɪs hɒki] Eishockey
°**ice rink** ['aɪs rɪŋk] Eislaufbahn
ice skating ['aɪs skeɪtɪŋ] Schlittschuhlaufen II
ICT [ˌaɪ siː 'tiː] Informations- und Kommunikationstechnologie I
ID card [ˌaɪ 'diː kɑːd] Personalausweis III 3 (62)
idea [aɪ'dɪə] Idee; Vorstellung I
°**identify with** [aɪ'dentɪfaɪ] sich identifizieren mit
if [ɪf]:
1. ob III 4 (88) **as if** als ob III 3 (66)
2. wenn, falls I **if-clause** Nebensatz mit *if* III 2 (42)
ill [ɪl] krank II
°**illegal** [ɪ'liːgl] illegal, ungesetzlich
illness ['ɪlnəs] Krankheit III 3 (76)
illuminate [ɪ'luːmɪneɪt] erleuchten, beleuchten III 4 (102)
°**illustration** [ˌɪlə'streɪʃn] Illustration
image ['ɪmɪdʒ] Bild, Abbild; Vorstellung III 5 (113)
imagine sth. [ɪ'mædʒɪn] sich etwas vorstellen I
immediately [ɪ'miːdiətli] sofort III 3 (75)
°**immigrant** ['ɪmɪgrənt] Einwanderer/Einwanderin

°**immigration** [ˌɪmɪ'greɪʃn] Einwanderung
impatient [ɪm'peɪʃnt] ungeduldig III 4 (101)
impolite [ˌɪmpə'laɪt] unhöflich III 3 (60)
°**importance** [ɪm'pɔːtəns] Wichtigkeit, Bedeutung
important [ɪm'pɔːtnt] wichtig I
impossible [ɪm'pɒsəbl] unmöglich II
impression [ɪm'preʃn] Eindruck III 3 (58/59)
improve [ɪm'pruːv] verbessern; sich verbessern III 1 (17)
improvement [ɪm'pruːvmənt] Verbesserung III 4 (99)
in [ɪn] in I **be in** daheim sein II **come in** hereinkommen I **in 1580** im Jahr 1580 I **in fact** eigentlich, in Wirklichkeit III 1 (14) **in England** in England I **in fright** ängstlich, erschrocken III 4 (89) **in front of** vor *(räumlich)* I **in German/English** auf Deutsch/Englisch I **in my opinion** meiner Meinung nach III 1 (17) **in some/many ways** in mancher/vielerlei Hinsicht III 3 (67) **in this way** auf diese Weise III 3 (67) **in the afternoon** nachmittags, am Nachmittag I **in the attic** auf dem Dachboden I
°**in the end** schließlich, am Ende, zum Schluss **in the evening** abends, am Abend I **in the middle** in der Mitte I **in the morning** morgens, vormittags, am Morgen/Vormittag I **in the photo** auf dem Foto I **in the picture** auf dem Bild I **in the world** auf der Welt I
inch [ɪntʃ] Zoll *(Längenmaß; 2,54 cm)* III 4 (89)
°**include** [ɪn'kluːd] einbeziehen, berücksichtigen
included [ɪn'kluːdɪd] inbegriffen III 4 (89)
including [ɪn'kluːdɪŋ] einschließlich; darunter (auch) III 1 (32)
incredible [ɪn'kredəbl] unglaublich III 3 (66)
independence [ˌɪndɪ'pendəns] Unabhängigkeit II **the Declaration of Independence** die Unabhängigkeitserklärung *(der Vereinigten Staaten im Jahr 1776)* II
independent [ˌɪndɪ'pendənt] unabhängig III 3 (62)
°**index card** ['ɪndeks kɑːd] Karteikarte
Indian ['ɪndiən]:
1. Inder/in; indisch II
2. Indianer/in III 4 (109)
°**indigenous** [ɪn'dɪdʒənəs] indigen, einheimisch, Ur-
indoor ['ɪndɔː] Innen-; Hallen- III 4 (89)
industry ['ɪndəstri] Industrie III 2 (54)
infinitive [ɪn'fɪnətɪv] Infinitiv III 2 (42)
influence ['ɪnfluəns]:
1. Einfluss III 1 (31)
°2. beeinflussen
information (about/on) *(no pl)* [ˌɪnfə'meɪʃn] Information(en) (über) I **Information and Communications Technology** Informations- und Kommunikationstechnologie I
°**inn** [ɪn] Gasthof
°**insect** ['ɪnsekt] Insekt
inside [ˌɪn'saɪd]:
1. drinnen; nach drinnen I °**inside sth.** innerhalb von etwas
2. **the inside** die Innenseite; das Innere III 1 (14) °**inside cover** Umschlaginnenseite
instead [ɪn'sted] stattdessen II
instead of [ɪn'sted‿əv] anstelle von, statt III 1 (16)
°**instruction** [ɪn'strʌkʃn] Anweisung
instrument ['ɪnstrəmənt] Instrument I
insulted [ɪn'sʌltɪd] beleidigt III 4 (92)
°**insurance** [ɪn'ʃʊərəns] Versicherung
interested ['ɪntrəstɪd]: **be interested (in)** interessiert sein (an), sich interessieren (für) II
interesting ['ɪntrəstɪŋ] interessant I
international [ˌɪntə'næʃnəl] international I
internet ['ɪntənet] Internet I **on the internet** im Internet I
interrupt [ˌɪntə'rʌpt] unterbrechen II
interview ['ɪntəvjuː]:
1. Interview II
°2. interviewen, befragen
into ['ɪntʊ]: **into the kitchen** in die Küche (hinein) I **be into sth.** *(infml)* etwas mögen, auf etwas stehen III 1 (10)
intonation [ˌɪntə'neɪʃn] Intonation, Satzmelodie I
introduce sth./sb. (to sb.) [ˌɪntrə'djuːs] etwas/jn. (jm.) vorstellen II
introduction [ˌɪntrə'dʌkʃn] Einleitung, Einführung III 1 (17)
invade (a country) [ɪn'veɪd] (in ein Land) einmarschieren II
invitation (to) [ˌɪnvɪ'teɪʃn] Einladung (zu, nach) I
invite sb. [ɪn'vaɪt]:
1. jn. einladen II
2. jn. auffordern III 1 (17)
°**involve** [ɪn'vɒlv] umfassen, mit sich bringen °**be involved in** beteiligt sein (an); etwas zu tun haben (mit)
irregular [ɪ'regjələ] unregelmäßig II
is [ɪz]: **Is it Monday?** Ist es Montag? I **Is that you?** Bist du's? / Bist du das? I **The camera is ...** Die Kamera kostet ... I
island ['aɪlənd] Insel I
isn't ['ɪznt]: **he/she/it isn't (= is not)** er/sie/es ist nicht ... I
°**IT** [ˌaɪ 'tiː] Informationstechnologie
it [ɪt] er, sie, es I **it's ... (= it is)** er/sie/es ist ... I
°**item** ['aɪtəm] Punkt, Posten *(auf Liste)*
itself [ɪt'self] sich III 3 (71/72); selbst, selber III 4 (91)
its name [ɪts] sein Name / ihr Name I

J

jacket ['dʒækɪt] Jacke, Jackett II °**jacket potato** Backkartoffel
jam [dʒæm] Marmelade I
January ['dʒænjuəri] Januar I
jeans *(pl)* [dʒiːnz] Jeans I
jeep [dʒiːp] Jeep III 3 (73)
jerk [dʒɜːk] (infml) Trottel, Depp III 5 (113)
jersey ['dʒɜːzi] Trikot III 5 (118)
jewellery *(BE)*/**jewelry** *(AE)* *(no pl)* ['dʒuːəlri] Schmuck III 3 (67)
jewels *(pl)* ['dʒuːəlz] Juwelen III 1 (15)
jigsaw ['dʒɪgsɔː] Puzzle II
job [dʒɒb]:
1. Job, (Arbeits-)Stelle I
2. Aufgabe II
join [dʒɔɪn]:
1. **join sth.** etwas verbinden III 1 (17)
2. **join a club** in einen Klub eintreten; sich einem Klub anschließen I **join in** mitmachen III 2 (41)
joke [dʒəʊk]:
1. Witz I
°2. scherzen
journey ['dʒɜːni] Reise, Fahrt II
judo ['dʒuːdəʊ] Judo I
juggle sth. ['dʒʌgl] mit etwas jonglieren II
juggler ['dʒʌglə] Jongleur/in II
juice [dʒuːs] Saft II
July [dʒu'laɪ] Juli I
jump [dʒʌmp]:
1. springen I **jump up** aufspringen, hochspringen II
2. Sprung I
junction ['dʒʌŋkʃn] (Straßen-)Kreuzung III 3 (75)
June [dʒuːn] Juni I
°**jungle** ['dʒʌŋgl] Dschungel
junior team ['dʒuːniə tiːm] Jugendmannschaft, Juniorenmannschaft I
just [dʒʌst]:
1. (einfach) nur, bloß I °**Just have a look.** Schau einfach mal.
2. gerade (eben), soeben II **just after ...** gleich nachdem ...; kurz nachdem ... II **just then** genau in dem Moment; gerade dann II
3. **just like ...** genau wie ... II **just as boring/exciting/...** genauso langweilig/aufregend/... III 3 (76)

K

°**karate** [kə'rɑːti] Karate
kayak ['kaɪæk] Kajak III 2 (55)
kayaking Kajakfahren III 2 (55)
keen: be keen on sth. [kiːn] wild auf etwas sein III 4 (92) **be keen on doing sth.** wild darauf sein, etwas zu tun III 4 (92)

keep [ki:p], **kept, kept** [kept]:
1. halten III 5 (113)
2. behalten III 5 (113)
3. aufbewahren III 5 (113)
4. **keep doing sth.** etwas immer wieder/immer weiter tun; etwas ständig tun III 2 (46)
keep sth. away from etwas fernhalten von III 5 (113) **keep sth. out of** etwas heraushalten aus III 5 (113) **keep sth. warm/fresh** etwas warm/frisch halten III 5 (113) °**keep a diary** ein Tagebuch führen °**keep fit** gesund/fit bleiben
°**keeper** ['ki:pə]: **animal keeper** Tierwärter/in
kept [kept] *siehe* **keep**
key [ki:]:
1. Schlüssel II
°2. Legend *(auf Karten u.Ä.)*
key point ['ki: pɔɪnt] Kernpunkt, Hauptpunkt II
keyword ['ki:wɜ:d] Schlüsselwort I
kick [kɪk] treten III 3 (75)
kid [kɪd] Kind I
kill [kɪl] töten II
kilogram, kilo (kg) ['kɪləgræm, 'ki:ləʊ] Kilogramm, Kilo I
kilometre ['kɪləmi:tə], [kɪ'lɒmɪtə] Kilometer II
kind [kaɪnd]:
1. *(adj)* freundlich, nett II
2. *(n)* **a kind of ...** eine Art (von) ... I
3. *(adv)* **kind of scary/...** *(infml)* irgendwie unheimlich/...; ganz schön unheimlich/... III 3 (67)
king [kɪŋ] König II
kingdom ['kɪŋdəm] Königreich III 1 (14)
kiss [kɪs] küssen; sich küssen II
kit [kɪt] Ausrüstung I
kitchen ['kɪtʃɪn] Küche I
knee [ni:] Knie II
kneel [ni:l], **knelt, knelt** knien II
knelt [nelt] *siehe* **kneel**
knew [nju:] *siehe* **know**
knife [naɪf], *pl* **knives** [naɪvz] Messer II
knight [naɪt]:
1. Ritter II
°2. *(Schach)* Springer
°**knock sth. over** [ˌnɒk‿'əʊvə] etwas umstoßen
know [nəʊ], **knew, known** wissen; kennen I **know about sth.** sich mit etwas auskennen; über etwas Bescheid wissen I **How do you know ...?** Woher weißt/kennst du ...? III 1 (10) **I don't know.** Ich weiß (es) nicht. I **..., you know.** ..., weißt du. / ..., wissen Sie. I
known [nəʊn] *siehe* **know**
well known bekannt II
kung fu [ˌkʌŋ 'fu:] Kung Fu I

L

label ['leɪbl]:
1. Beschriftung; Schild, Etikett II
2. beschriften; etikettieren II
°**ladder** ['lædə] (die) Leiter
Ladies and gentlemen [ˌleɪdiz‿ən 'dʒentlmən] Meine Damen und Herren / Sehr geehrte Damen und Herren III 4 (93)
°**lady** ['leɪdi] Dame
laid [leɪd] *siehe* **lay**
lain [leɪn] *siehe* **lie**
lake [leɪk] (Binnen-)See I
lamb [læm] Lamm II
lamp [læmp] Lampe I
°**lamppost** ['læmpəʊst] Laternenpfahl
land [lænd]:
1. Land II
2. landen; an Land gehen II
landing ['lændɪŋ] Landungssteg III 5 (126)
language ['læŋgwɪdʒ] Sprache I
laptop ['læptɒp] Laptop *(tragbarer PC)* III 2 (43)
large [lɑ:dʒ] groß I
last [lɑ:st]:
1. **last weekend/Friday** letztes Wochenende / letzten Freitag I **last year's musical** das Musical vom letzten Jahr II
2. **When did you see them last?** Wann hast du sie zuletzt/das letzte Mal gesehen? III 3 (70)
3. **at last** endlich, schließlich I
late [leɪt] spät I **You're late.** Du bist spät dran. / Du bist zu spät. I
later ['leɪtə] später I **See you later.** Bis bald. / Bis nachher. I
°**Latin America** [ˌlætɪn‿ə'merɪkə] Lateinamerika
°**Latino** [læ'ti:nəʊ] Amerikaner lateinamerikanischer Herkunft *(weibliche Form:* **Latina** [læ'ti:nə])
laugh [lɑ:f] lachen I **laugh at sb./sth.** über jn./etwas lachen; jn. auslachen III 2 (36)
°**lava** ['lɑ:və] Lava(gestein)
°**lavender** ['lævəndə] Lavendel
law [lɔ:] Gesetz III 1 (31)
lawn [lɔ:n] Rasen III 4 (98)
lay [leɪ]:
1. *siehe* **lie**
2. **(laid, laid)** legen III 5 (126) **lay sth. out** etwas ausbreiten
layout ['leɪaʊt] Layout, Gestaltung III 3 (69)
lead [li:d], **led, led** führen, leiten III 3 (77)
leader ['li:də] Leiter/in III 4 (98)
°**league** [li:g] Liga
lean [li:n] sich lehnen; sich beugen III 4 (89)
learn [lɜ:n] lernen I °**learn sth. by heart** etwas auswendig lernen
least [li:st]: **at least** zumindest, wenigstens II
leather ['leðə] Leder III 5 (123)

leave [li:v], **left, left**:
1. (ab)fahren; (weg)gehen I
2. verlassen; zurücklassen I
3. lassen II **leave sth.** etwas übrig lassen II **leave sth. out** etwas weglassen, auslassen II **leave a message** eine Nachricht hinterlassen II °**leave room** Platz lassen
led [led] *siehe* **lead**
left [left]:
1. *siehe* **leave** **be left** übrig sein III 3 (60)
2. linke(r, s); (nach) links I **on the left** links/auf der linken Seite I **turn left** (nach) links abbiegen II
leg [leg] Bein I
°**legal** ['li:gl] legal
legend ['ledʒənd] Legende, Sage II
legendary ['ledʒəndri] legendär, berühmt III 4 (93)
leisure centre ['leʒə sentə] Freizeitpark, Freizeitzentrum II
°**lemon** ['lemən] Zitrone
length [leŋθ] Länge; Dauer III 1 (22)
°**Lent** [lent] Fastenzeit
°**leprechaun** ['leprəkɔ:n] Leprechaun, Kobold *(Wesen der irischen Mythologie)*
less (than) [les] weniger (als) III 1 (15)
lesson ['lesn] (Unterrichts-)Stunde I
before lessons vorm Unterricht I
let [let], **let, let**: lassen I **Let me show you ...** Lass mich dir ... zeigen. I **Let's ...** Lass(t) uns ... I
letter ['letə]:
1. Brief I
2. Buchstabe I
°**letterbox** ['letəbɒks] Briefkasten
°**letterboxing** ['letəbɒksɪŋ] *Spiel für draußen, bei dem mit Hilfe von Karte u. Kompass versteckte Behälter gefunden werden müssen*
°**level** ['levl] Niveau
°**LGBTQ+ people** lesbische, schwule, bisexuelle, transsexuelle, transgender, queere, intersexuelle u. asexuelle Menschen
liberty ['lɪbəti] Freiheit III 4 (84)
library ['laɪbrəri] Bibliothek, Bücherei I
lie [laɪ], **lay, lain** [leɪn] liegen II **lie down** sich hinlegen III 2 (46)
life [laɪf], *pl* **lives** [laɪvz] Leben I
life jacket ['laɪf dʒækɪt] Schwimmweste I
lift [lɪft]:
1. Fahrstuhl, Aufzug, Lift II
2. Mitfahrgelegenheit II **give sb. a lift** jn. mitnehmen II
3. **lift sth.** etwas heben, hochheben, anheben
light [laɪt]:
1. *(n)* Licht I
2. *(v)* **(lit, lit)** anzünden II **light up** aufleuchten III 5 (126) **light sth. up** etwas erhellen *(aufleuchten lassen)* II

3. *(adv)* **light brown/blue/...** hellbraun/-blau/... III 5 (123)
lightning *(no pl)* ['laɪtnɪŋ] Blitz(e) II
a flash of lightning ein Blitz II
like [laɪk]:
1. mögen, gernhaben I **I like ...** Ich mag ... I **I like swimming/sailing/...** Ich schwimme/segele/... gern. I **I don't like ...** Ich mag ... nicht. / Ich mag kein ... I **I'd like ...** Ich hätte gern .../ Ich möchte ... I **I'd like to go** Ich möchte gehen / Ich würde gern gehen I **I'd like you to go.** Ich möchte/hätte gerne, dass du gehst. II °**like sth. about sth.** etwas an etwas mögen
2. *(conjunction; infml)* als ob III 3 (66)
3. **like boys** wie Jungen, wie Buben I **like this** so *(auf diese Weise)* I **like that** so *(auf diese Weise)* I **What's she like?** Wie ist sie? / Wie ist sie so? I **What was it like?** Wie war es? II
4. **She was like: "Stop ..."** *(infml)* Und sie so: „Stopp ..." III 3 (67)
likes and dislikes *(pl)* [ˌlaɪks_ən 'dɪslaɪks] Vorlieben und Abneigungen I
°**lily** ['lɪli] Lilie
line [laɪn]:
1. Zeile I
2. Leine, (Angel-)Schnur III 5 (126)
3. (U-Bahn-)Linie II
4. Reihe III 3 (67); *(AE)* Schlange, Reihe *(wartender Menschen)* III 4 (90) **be/stand/wait in line** *(AE)* Schlange stehen, sich anstellen II
link [lɪŋk]:
1. verbinden, verknüpfen I
2. Link III 2 (44)
linking word ['lɪŋkɪŋ wɜːd] Bindewort III 1 (16)
lion ['laɪən] Löwe I
lip [lɪp] Lippe II
list [lɪst]:
1. Liste I
°2. auflisten
listen ['lɪsn] zuhören, horchen I **listen to sb.** jm. zuhören I **listen to sth.** sich etwas anhören I
listener ['lɪsənə] Zuhörer/in II
lit [lɪt] *siehe* **light**
literature ['lɪtrətʃə] Literatur III 1 (33)
°**litre** ['liːtə] Liter
litter ['lɪtə] Abfall II **litter bin** Abfalleimer II
little ['lɪtl] klein I **a little** ein bisschen, ein wenig, etwas III 1 (52) °**little by little** nach und nach
live [lɪv] leben; wohnen I
°**live** [laɪv] lebend, lebendig
living room ['lɪvɪŋ ruːm] Wohnzimmer I
lobster ['lɒbstə] Hummer II
local ['ləʊkl] örtlich, Lokal-; am/vom Ort III 3 (66)
°**location** [ləʊ'keɪʃn] Position, Standort
locker ['lɒkə] Schließfach, Spind III 4 (88)
log in/out [lɒg] sich ein-/ausloggen III 5 (114)
logbook ['lɒgbʊk] Fahrtenbuch II
lonely ['ləʊnli] einsam I
long [lɒŋ] lang I **(the) longest ...** ['lɒŋgɪst] der/die/das längste ...; am längsten II °**no longer** nicht mehr, nicht länger
look [lʊk]:
1. schauen I **look after sb.** auf jn. aufpassen; sich um jn. kümmern II **look around (the farm)** sich (auf der Farm) umsehen II **look at** anschauen, ansehen I **look happy/angry/...** glücklich/wütend/... aussehen I **look for sth.** etwas suchen I **look forward to sth.** sich auf etwas freuen II **look into sth.** etwas untersuchen, prüfen III 2 (38) **look up** hochsehen, aufschauen II **look sth. up** etwas nachschlagen III 2 (38)
2. **have a look (at sth.)** nachschauen; einen Blick auf etwas werfen III 2 (47)
°**lord** [lɔːd] Lord; Feudalherr
°**Lord Mayor** [ˌlɔːd 'meə] Oberbürgermeister/in
lorry ['lɒri] *(BE)* Lastwagen, LKW III 3 (77)
lose [luːz], **lost, lost** verlieren II
lost [lɒst] *siehe* **lose**
lot [lɒt]: **a lot** viel I **That helped us a lot.** Das hat uns sehr geholfen. I **lots of .../a lot of ...** viel ..., viele ... I
loud [laʊd] laut I °**read sth. out loud** etwas vorlesen
loudspeaker [ˌlaʊd'spiːkə] Lautsprecher; Megaphon III 1 (25)
love [lʌv] lieben, sehr mögen I **I'd love to ...** Ich würde sehr gern ... I
Love, ... [lʌv] Alles Liebe, ... / Liebe Grüße, ... *(Briefschluss)* II
lovely ['lʌvli] schön, hübsch, herrlich II
°**low** [ləʊ] niedrig **lower** untere(r, s)
luck [lʌk]: **Good luck!** Viel Glück! I
luckily ['lʌkɪli] glücklicherweise III 3 (80)
lucky ['lʌki]: **be lucky** Glück haben I **Lucky you.** Du Glückspilz. II
lunch [lʌntʃ] Mittagessen I **have lunch** zu Mittag essen I **What's for lunch?** Was gibt es zum Mittagessen? I
lunchtime ['lʌntʃtaɪm] Mittagszeit I **at lunchtime** mittags I
luxurious [lʌg'ʒʊəriəs] luxuriös III 1 (32)
°**lynch** [lɪntʃ] lynchen *(eigenmächtig und illegal hinrichten)*

M

machine [mə'ʃiːn] Maschine, Gerät III 4 (101)
mad [mæd] verrückt I
made [meɪd] *siehe* **make**
be made of sth. aus etwas (gemacht) sein II °**be made up of** bestehen aus
°**madhouse** ['mædhaʊs] Irrenhaus
°**madman** ['mædmən] Irrer, Verrückter
magazine [ˌmægə'ziːn] Zeitschrift I
magic ['mædʒɪk] magisch, Zauber- II
magical ['mædʒɪkl] zauberhaft, wundervoll; magisch III 2 (46)
mail [meɪl] E-Mail II
main [meɪn] Haupt- II **main clause** Hauptsatz II
°**mainland** ['meɪnlænd] Festland
°**maintain** [meɪn'teɪn] instandhalten
°**majesty** ['mædʒəsti]: **Your majesty** Eure Majestät
°**major** ['meɪdʒə] bedeutende(r, s); Haupt-
majority [mə'dʒɒrəti] Mehrheit III 2 (39)
make [meɪk], **made, made**:
1. machen; herstellen I **make a wish** sich etwas wünschen I °**make comparisons** Vergleiche anstellen; vergleichen
make eye contact Blickkontakt herstellen III 1 (17) **make friends** Freunde finden I **make fun of sb./sth.** sich über jn./etwas lustig machen III 2 (36) **make notes (on sth.)** (sich) Notizen machen (über/zu etwas) *(zur Vorbereitung)* II **make sb. sth.** jn. zu etwas machen II °**make sth. happen** etwas möglich machen **make sth. into sth.** etwas in etwas umwandeln III 4 (96) **make sth. up** sich etwas ausdenken III 2 (48) **make sure that ...** sich vergewissern, dass ...; darauf achten/dafür sorgen, dass ... II
°2. bilden °**be made up of** bestehen aus
make-up ['meɪk_ʌp] Make-up II
malaria [mə'leəriə] Malaria III 2 (38)
°**male** [meɪl] männlich
mall [mɔːl] (großes) Einkaufszentrum I
man [mæn], *pl* **men** [men] Mann I
manage sth. ['mænɪdʒ] etwas schaffen; etwas zustande bringen III 2 (45)
man-made [ˌmæn'meɪd] künstlich, Kunst- III 4 (88)
°**mansion** ['mænʃn] Herrenhaus
manufacturing (industry) [ˌmænju'fæktʃərɪŋ] Fertigungsindustrie, verarbeitende Industrie III 2 (54)
many ['meni] viele I **How many?** Wie viele? I
°**Maori** ['maʊri] Maori; maorisch
map [mæp] Landkarte; Stadtplan I **on the map** auf der Landkarte; auf dem Stadtplan I
°**maple syrup** [ˌmeɪpl 'sɪrəp] Ahornsirup
marathon ['mærəθən] Marathon II
March [mɑːtʃ] März I
°**marching** ['mɑːtʃɪŋ]: **go marching** marschieren
°**marching band** ['mɑːtʃɪŋ bænd] Blaskapelle, Marschkapelle
°**Mardi Gras** [ˌmɑːdi 'grɑː] Faschingsdienstag *(auch:* die Karnevalsfeiern in New Orleans)
mark [mɑːk]:
1. markieren II **mark sth. up** etwas

markieren, kennzeichnen II
°**2.** Zeichen
°**marker** ['mɑːkə] Kennzeichnung, Markierung
market ['mɑːkɪt] Markt I
marmalade ['mɑːməleɪd] Marmelade *(aus Zitrusfrüchten)* I
marry ['mæri] heiraten III 1 (33)
married (to) ['mærɪd] verheiratet (mit) I
°**marshmallows** *(pl)* [ˌmɑːʃ'mæləʊz] Marshmallows, Mäusespeck
°**mascot** ['mæskət] Maskottchen
°**mashed** [mæʃt]: **mashed potatoes** *(pl)* Kartoffelbrei
mask [mɑːsk] Maske II
°**massage** ['mæsɑːʒ] Massage
master ['mɑːstə] Meister/in I
match [mætʃ]:
1. Spiel, Wettkampf, Match I
2. match sth. zu etwas passen III 5 (113)
°**match sth. to sth.** etwas zu etwas zuordnen
material [mə'tɪəriəl] Material, Stoff III 5 (123)
maths [mæθs] Mathematik I
matter: What's the matter? ['mætə] Was ist denn? / Was ist los? I
°**maximum** ['mæksɪməm] Höchstbetrag
may [meɪ]:
1. dürfen II **May I have a word with you?** Kann ich Sie kurz sprechen? II
2. they may be at home sie sind vielleicht daheim III 3 (71)
May [meɪ] Mai I
maybe ['meɪbi] vielleicht I
mayor [meə] Bürgermeister/in II
me [miː] mich; mir I **It's me.** Ich bin's. I
Me too. Ich auch. I
meal [miːl] Mahlzeit, Essen III 2 (46)
mean [miːn], **meant, meant** [ment]:
1. bedeuten II
2. meinen, sagen wollen II
meaning ['miːnɪŋ] Bedeutung II
meant [ment] *siehe* **mean**
meat [miːt] Fleisch I
medal ['medl] Medaille I
media *(pl)* ['miːdiə] Medien III 5 (113)
°**mediate** ['miːdieɪt] vermitteln *(auch sprachlich)*
mediation [ˌmiːdi'eɪʃn] Sprachmittlung, Mediation I
medicine ['medsn, 'medɪsn] Medizin; Arznei II
°**medieval** [ˌmedi'iːvl] mittelalterlich
medium ['miːdiəm] mittelgroß; mittel- III 5 (123)
meet [miːt], **met, met**:
1. treffen; kennenlernen I **Meet your classmates.** Triff deine Mitschüler/innen. / Lerne deine Mitschüler/innen kennen. I **Nice to meet you.** Freut mich, dich/euch/Sie kennenzulernen. I
2. sich treffen I
°**meeting** ['miːtɪŋ] Begegnung; Treffen; Besprechung

melt [melt] schmelzen II
°**member** ['membə] Mitglied
meme [miːm] (Internet-)Mem III 5 (114)
memorial [mə'mɔːriəl] Denkmal; Gedenk- III 4 (88)
memory ['meməri] Erinnerung II
men [men] *plural of* **man** I
°**menu** ['menjuː] Speisekarte
°**merchandise** ['mɜːtʃəndaɪz] Werbeartikel
Merry Christmas! [ˌmeri 'krɪsməs] Frohe Weihnachten! I
mesmerizing ['mezməraɪzɪŋ] fesselnd, hypnotisierend III 5 (127)
message ['mesɪdʒ]:
1. Nachricht II **leave a message** eine Nachricht hinterlassen II
2. Botschaft, Aussage III 1 (19)
met [met] *siehe* **meet**
metal ['metl] Metall; Metall- III 4 (86)
°**methinks** *(altmodisch)* [mɪ'θɪŋks] mich dünkt; ich denke
metre ['miːtə] Meter I °**square metre** Quadratmeter
°**mice** [maɪs] *plural of* **mouse**
middle ['mɪdl] Mitte I
°**Middle Eastern** [ˌmɪdl‿'iːstən] aus dem Nahen Osten
midnight ['mɪdnaɪt] Mitternacht I
might [maɪt]: **that might be the reason** das könnte (vielleicht) der Grund sein II
mile [maɪl] Meile *(ca. 1,6 km)* I **for miles** meilenweit I
milk [mɪlk] Milch I
°**Milky Way** [ˌmɪlki 'weɪ] Milchstraße
million ['mɪljən] Million I
°**mime** [maɪm] vorspielen, pantomimisch darstellen
°**mince** [mɪns] Hackfleisch
mind [maɪnd] etwas dagegen haben III 1 (25) **Do you mind …?** Stört es Sie, …? / Haben Sie etwas dagegen, …? III 1 (25) **if you don't mind** wenn Sie nichts dagegen haben III 1 (25)
mind map ['maɪnd mæp] Mindmap I
mine [maɪn]:
1. meiner, meine, meins II
2. Bergwerk, Mine III 2 (38) **coal mine** Kohlebergwerk III 2 (38)
3. Mine *(Militär)* III 2 (38)
4. abbauen *(Bodenschätze)* III 2 (38)
minibus ['mɪnibʌs] Kleinbus I
minority [maɪ'nɒrəti] Minderheit III 2 (39)
minute ['mɪnɪt] Minute I **Hold on a minute.** *(oft auch kurz:* **Hold on.***)* Bleib / Bleiben Sie am Apparat. *(am Telefon)* II **wait a minute** Warte einen Moment. / Moment mal. I **a two-minute talk** ein zweiminütiger Vortrag II
mirror ['mɪrə] Spiegel II
miss [mɪs]:
1. verpassen I
2. vermissen III 3 (67)
Miss [mɪs]: **Miss Bell** Frau Bell *(übliche Anrede von Lehrerinnen)* I

missing ['mɪsɪŋ]: **be missing** fehlen II **the missing words** die fehlenden Wörter I
mist [mɪst] (leichter) Nebel, Dunst(schleier) II
mistake [mɪ'steɪk] Fehler II **by mistake** aus Versehen III 4 (102)
°**misunderstanding** [ˌmɪsʌndə'stændɪŋ] Missverständnis
mix [mɪks] Mischung III 2 (55)
mixed [mɪkst] gemischt I **mixed bag** *etwa:* bunte Mischung I
°**mob** [mɒb] Pöbel
mobile (phone) [ˌməʊbaɪl 'fəʊn] Mobiltelefon, Handy I
model ['mɒdl] Modell III 1 (16)
modern ['mɒdən] modern III 1 (31)
°**mom** [mɑːm] *(AE)* Mama, Mutti
moment ['məʊmənt] Moment I **at the moment** gerade, im Moment I
monarch ['mɒnək] Monarch/in III 1 (30)
Monday ['mʌndeɪ, 'mʌndi] Montag I **on Monday** am Montag I
money ['mʌni] Geld I
monkey ['mʌŋki] Affe I
monster ['mɒnstə] Monster I
month [mʌnθ] Monat I
monthly ['mʌnθli] monatlich III 5 (114)
°**monument (to)** ['mɒnjumənt] Denkmal, Monument (für / zum Gedenken an)
moon [muːn] Mond I
moonlight ['muːnlaɪt] Mondlicht III 2 (46)
moor [mɔː], [mʊə] Hochmoor II
°**moose** [muːs] Elch
mop [mɒp]:
1. wischen *(Fußboden)* III 2 (48)
2. Wischmopp III 2 (48)
more [mɔː] mehr I **one more photo** noch ein Foto; ein weiteres Foto II **more beautiful (than)** schöner (als) II **not … any more** nicht mehr II
morning ['mɔːnɪŋ] Morgen, Vormittag I **Good morning.** Guten Morgen. I **in the morning** morgens, vormittags, am Morgen/Vormittag I
most [məʊst]: **(the) most beautiful** der/die/das schönste …; am schönsten II **most people / most of them** die meisten Menschen / die meisten von ihnen II
°**mostly** ['məʊstli] größtenteils, hauptsächlich; meistens
mother ['mʌðə] Mutter I
°**mother tongue** [mʌðə 'tʌŋ] Muttersprache
motor ['məʊtə] Motor III 3 (77)
mountain ['maʊntən] Berg I
mountain-biking ['maʊntən ˌbaɪkɪŋ] Mountainbiken III 2 (55)
°**mouse** [maʊs], *pl* **mice** [maɪs] Maus
mouth [maʊθ] Mund; Maul I
move [muːv]:
1. bewegen; sich bewegen I °**move in on sth./sb.** gegen etwas/jn. vorgehen; etwas/jn. angreifen

2. move (to) umziehen (nach) II **move in** einziehen II **move into a house** einziehen in ein Haus… II **3.** Zug *(bei Brettspielen)* III 4 (93)
movement ['mu:vmənt] Bewegung III 4 (102)
movie ['mu:vi] *(bes. AE)* Film II
MP3 player [ˌem pi: 'θri: ˌpleɪə] MP3-Spieler I
Mr Schwarz ['mɪstə] Herr Schwarz I
Mrs Schwarz ['mɪsɪz] Frau Schwarz I
much [mʌtʃ] viel I **How much …?** Wie viel …? I **How much are …?** Was kosten …? I **How much is …?** Was kostet …? I
mud [mʌd] Schlamm, Matsch II
mug [mʌg]: **a mug (of)** ein Becher II
mum [mʌm] Mama, Mutti I
museum [mju'zi:əm] Museum I
music ['mju:zɪk] Musik I
musical ['mju:zɪkl] Musical II
musician [mju'zɪʃn] Musiker/in III 2 (37)
must [mʌst] müssen I **you mustn't do it** ['mʌsnt] du darfst es nicht tun I
my [maɪ] mein/e I **My birthday is in May.** Ich habe im Mai Geburtstag. I **My birthday is on 5th August.** Ich habe am 5. August Geburtstag. I **my favourite day** mein Lieblingstag I **My name is …** Ich heiße … I
myself [maɪ'self] mich, mir III 3 (71/72); selbst, selber III 4 (91)

N

name [neɪm]:
1. Name I **My name is …** Ich heiße … I **What's your name?** Wie heißt du? / Wie heißt ihr? I
°**2.** (be)nennen
narration [nə'reɪʃn] Erzählung, Schilderung III 3 (61)
narrator [nə'reɪtə] Erzähler/in; Sprecher/in III 3 (61)
narrow ['nærəʊ] schmal, eng II
nation ['neɪʃn] Nation, Volk III 3 (62)
national ['næʃnəl] national, National- I °**national holiday** Nationalfeiertag
native ['neɪtɪv] Mutter- III 3 (60) **Native American** amerikanischer Ureinwohner/amerikanische Ureinwohnerin III 3 (60) **native language** Muttersprache III 3 (60) **native speaker** Muttersprachler/in III 3 (60)
natural ['nætʃrəl] natürlich III 2 (37) **natural history** [ˌnætʃrəl 'hɪstri] Naturkunde I **natural world** (Welt der) Natur III 2 (37)
°**nature** ['neɪtʃə] Natur
°**Navajo** ['nɑ:vəhəʊ] Navajo, Navaho
°**naval** ['neɪvl] Marine-
navy ['neɪvi] Marine I
near [nɪə] in der Nähe von, nahe (bei) I **near here** (hier) in der Nähe I

nearby ['nɪəbaɪ]: **a nearby town** eine nahegelegene Stadt II
nearly ['nɪəli] fast, beinahe III 4 (107)
necessary ['nesəsəri] notwendig, nötig III 5 (117)
neck [nek] Hals II
need [ni:d] brauchen, benötigen I **need to do sth.** etwas tun müssen II **you needn't do it** ['ni:dnt] du musst es nicht tun I
°**negative** ['negətɪv] negativ
neighbour ['neɪbə] Nachbar/in II
°**neighbourhood** ['neɪbəhʊd] (*AE:* **neighborhood**) Viertel, Gegend, Umgebung; Nachbarschaft
neither ['naɪðə, 'ni:ðə]: **Me neither.** Ich auch nicht. III 2 (40)
nephew ['nefju:], ['nevju:] Neffe III 3 (66)
nervous ['nɜ:vəs] nervös, aufgeregt I
netball ['netbɔ:l] Korbball II
never ['nevə] nie, niemals I
new [nju:] neu I
New Year's Eve [ˌnju: jɪəz_'i:v] Silvester II
news *(no pl)* [nju:z]:
1. Nachrichten I
2. Neuigkeiten II
newspaper ['nju:speɪpə] *(kurz auch:* **paper***)* Zeitung III 4 (88)
next [nekst]:
1. als Nächstes III 3 (75)
2. next year's musical das Musical vom nächsten Jahr II **the next picture/question** das nächste Bild / die nächste Frage I
next to ['nekst tʊ] neben I
nice [naɪs] nett, schön I **Nice to meet you.** Freut mich, dich/euch/Sie kennenzulernen. I
°**niche** [ni:ʃ] Nische
niece [ni:s] Nichte III 3 (66)
night [naɪt] Nacht I **at night** nachts, in der Nacht I
nine [naɪn] neun I
no [nəʊ]:
1. nein I
2. kein, keine I
no one niemand I **No way!** Auf keinen Fall! / Kommt nicht in Frage! III 1 (20) **No worries.** *(infml)* Kein Problem! / Gern geschehen! III 2 (44) °**no more** nicht (mehr) wieder
nobody ['nəʊbədi] niemand I
nod [nɒd] nicken II
noise [nɔɪz] Geräusch, Lärm I
noisy ['nɔɪzi] laut, lärmend, voller Lärm I
°**non-** [nɒn] nicht- **non-native** nicht einheimisch; standortfremd
none (of …) [nʌn] keine(r, s) (von …) III 3 (60)
°**noodle** ['nu:dl] Nudel
no one ['nəʊ wʌn] niemand I
°**nope** [nəʊp] *(infml)* nein, nee

north [nɔ:θ] Norden; nach Norden; nördlich III 1 (11)
northbound ['nɔ:θbaʊnd] Richtung Norden III 1 (18)
north-east [ˌnɔ:θ'i:st] Nordosten; nach Nordosten; nordöstlich III 1 (11)
northern ['nɔ:ðən] nördliche(r, s), Nord- II
north-west [ˌnɔ:θ'west] Nordwesten; nach Nordwesten; nordwestlich III 1 (11)
nose [nəʊz] Nase I
not [nɒt] nicht I **not … any more** nicht mehr II **not even** (noch) nicht einmal II **not till three** erst um drei, nicht vor drei II **not until ten** erst um zehn, nicht vor zehn III 3 (76) **not … yet** noch nicht I
note [nəʊt]:
1. Note *(Musik)* III 2 (47)
2. Notiz, Mitteilung I **make notes (on sth.)** (sich) Notizen machen (über/zu etwas) *(zur Vorbereitung)* II **take notes** (sich) Notizen machen *(beim Lesen oder Zuhören)* II
°**3. note sth. down** (sich) etwas notieren; etwas aufschreiben
nothing ['nʌθɪŋ] (gar) nichts I
notice ['nəʊtɪs] merken, bemerken III 5 (127)
noun [naʊn] Nomen III 1 (12)
novel ['nɒvl] Roman III 4 (100)
November [nəʊ'vembə] November I
now [naʊ] nun, jetzt I **Now that …** Jetzt, wo … / Nun, da … III 3 (76)
nowhere ['nəʊweə] nirgendwo; nirgendwohin II
number ['nʌmbə] Zahl, Nummer, Ziffer I

O

o [əʊ] Null *(in Telefonnummern)* I
object ['ɒbdʒɪkt] Objekt, Gegenstand III 5 (111)
observation deck [ˌɒbzə'veɪʃn dek] Aussichtsplattform III 4 (89)
°**occupy** ['ɒkjəpaɪ] einnehmen, beanspruchen *(Platz)*
ocean ['əʊʃn] Ozean I
o'clock: ten o'clock [ə'klɒk] 10 / 22 Uhr I
October [ɒk'təʊbə] Oktober I
°**octopus** ['ɒktəpəs] Krake
of [ɒv, əv] von I **of all time** aller Zeiten II
of course [əv 'kɔ:s] natürlich, selbstverständlich I
off [ɒf] von … herunter III 1 (20) **Off you go now.** Ab mit euch jetzt! / Los mit euch jetzt! III 1 (20) **be off** aus(geschaltet) sein *(Radio, Licht usw.)* III 1 (20) **fall off a bike** vom Fahrrad (herunter)fallen III 1 (20) **run off** wegrennen III 1 (20)

offer sth. ['ɒfə] etwas anbieten II
office ['ɒfɪs] Büro III 2 (48)
°**officer** ['ɒfɪsə] Beamte/Beamtin, Angestellte
official [ə'fɪʃl]:
1. Beamte(r), Beamtin III 2 (38)
2. amtlich, Amts- I
often ['ɒfn, 'ɒftən] oft I
°**ogre** ['əʊgə] Ungeheuer
oh [əʊ]: **Oh dear!** Oje! II **Oh, it's you.** Ach, du bist es. I
oil [ɔɪl] Öl III 2 (36)
old [əʊld] alt I **How old are you?** Wie alt bist du? I
°**Olympic Games** *(pl)* [əˌlɪmpɪk 'geɪmz] Olympische Spiele
°**OMG** [ˌəʊ‿em 'dʒiː] (= **Oh my God**) Oh mein Gott!
on [ɒn] auf I **on earth** auf der Erde II **on Monday** am Montag I **on Monday afternoon** am Montagnachmittag I **on the corner of Church Road and London Road** Church Road, Ecke London Road II **on the map** auf der Landkarte; auf dem Stadtplan I **on the left** links/auf der linken Seite I **on the right** rechts/auf der rechten Seite I **on the phone** am Telefon II **on the plane** im Flugzeug II **on the radio** im Radio II **on top of each other** übereinander, aufeinander III 1 (15) **on TV** im Fernsehen III 1 (20) **on my/your/their/… own** allein II **straight on** geradeaus weiter II **be on** eingeschaltet sein, an sein *(Radio, Licht usw.)*; laufen, übertragen werden *(Programm, Sendung)* III 1 (20)
walk/run/sail/… on weitergehen/-laufen/-segeln/… II
once [wʌns]:
1. einmal I °**once again** nochmals
2. einst, (früher) einmal II
one [wʌn]:
1. eins I **one by one** einzeln; einer nach dem anderen II **one more photo** noch ein Foto; ein weiteres Foto II **one night/day** eines Nachts/Tages II
2. **one another** sich (gegenseitig), einander III 4 (89)
3. **a white one** ein weißer/eine weiße/ein weißes II **this one** diese(r,s) II **two black ones** zwei schwarze II **Which one?** Welche(r, s)? II
onion ['ʌnjən] Zwiebel III 4 (94)
online [ˌɒn'laɪn] online II
only ['əʊnli]:
1. nur, bloß I **the only …** der/die/das einzige …; die einzigen … II
2. erst I
onto ['ɒntʊ] auf (… hinauf) I
open ['əʊpən]:
1. öffnen, aufmachen I; sich öffnen I
2. geöffnet, offen I
opening ['əʊpənɪŋ] Öffnung III 4 (100)
opening times Öffnungszeiten III 1 (15)
opinion [ə'pɪnjən] Meinung III 1 (17)
in my opinion meiner Meinung nach III 1 (17)
opposite ['ɒpəzɪt]:
1. Gegenteil I
2. gegenüber (von) II
or [ɔː] oder I **either … or …** ['aɪðə], ['iːðə] entweder … oder … III 3 (67)
orange ['ɒrɪndʒ]:
1. Orange, Apfelsine II
2. orange(farben) I
°**orchestra** ['ɔːkɪstrə] Orchester
order ['ɔːdə]:
1. Reihenfolge I
2. bestellen II
°**3.** ordnen
°**ordinal number** [ˌɔːdɪnl 'nʌmbə] Ordinalzahl, Ordnungszahl
organize ['ɔːgənaɪz] organisieren; ordnen I
°**origin** ['ɒrɪdʒɪn] Ursprung
original [ə'rɪdʒənl] Original-; ursprüngliche(r, s) III 2 (55)
other ['ʌðə] andere(r, s) I
°**otter** ['ɒtə] Otter
our [aʊə] unser/e I
ours ['aʊəz] unserer, unsere, unseres II
ourselves [ɑː'selvz], [aʊə'selvz] uns III 3 (71/72); selbst, selber III 4 (91)
out [aʊt] heraus, hinaus, nach draußen II
out of … aus … (heraus/hinaus) I **out and about** unterwegs II **be out** nicht zu Hause sein, nicht daheim sein II
°**read sth. out loud** etwas vorlesen
outdoor ['aʊtdɔː] Außen-, im Freien II
outside [ˌaʊt'saɪd]:
1. draußen; nach draußen I **outside Rosie's Diner** vor Rosie's Diner; außerhalb von Rosie's Diner II
2. **the outside** die Außenseite; das Äußere III 1 (14)
°**outta** ['aʊtə] *(Slang:* **out of***)* aus (… heraus)
oval ['əʊvl] oval III 5 (123)
°**oven** ['ʌvn] Ofen, Backofen
over ['əʊvə]:
1. über I **over here** hier herüber; hier drüben II **over there** da drüben, dort drüben II **over to …** hinüber zu/nach … I **run over (to)** hinüberrennen (zu/nach) II
2. **over 20 people/years/…** über 20 Leute/Jahre/… I
3. **be over** vorbei sein, zu Ende sein I
overthrow [ˌəʊvə'θrəʊ], **overthrew, overthrown** stürzen *(Regierung, Staatsoberhaupt usw.)* III 1 (33)
own [əʊn]:
1. besitzen II
2. **my own film/room/…** mein eigener Film / mein eigenes Zimmer / … II
3. **on my/your/their/… own** allein II
owner ['əʊnə] Besitzer/in III 3 (70)

P

p [piː] *Abkürzung für „pence", „penny"* I
pack [pæk] packen; einpacken II
packet ['pækɪt] Packung, Päckchen II
°**paddle** ['pædl] paddeln
°**pads** *(pl)* ['pædz] (Schutz-)Polster
page [peɪdʒ] Seite I **What page are we on?** Auf welcher Seite sind wir? I
paid [peɪd] *siehe* **pay**
paint [peɪnt]:
1. (an)streichen; (an)malen II
°**2.** Farbe
painted ['peɪntɪd] bemalt, angemalt II
painter ['peɪntə] Maler/in III 2 (37)
painting ['peɪntɪŋ] Gemälde, Bild III 3 (66)
pair [peə] Paar I **a pair of …** ein Paar … I
°**pajamas** *(AE; pl)* / **pyjamas** *(BE; pl)* [pə'dʒɑːməz] Schlafanzug
palace ['pæləs] Palast, Schloss III 1 (10)
palm tree ['pɑːm triː] Palme III 5 (110)
pancake ['pænkeɪk] Pfannkuchen, Eierkuchen II
panic ['pænɪk] in Panik geraten III 1 (24)
pants *(pl)* [pænts] *(AE)* Hose III 4 (90)
paper ['peɪpə]:
1. Zeitung I
2. Papier I °**a piece of paper** ein Stück Papier
parade [pə'reɪd] Parade, Umzug II
paragraph ['pærəgrɑːf] Absatz *(in einem Text)* I
paraphrase ['pærəfreɪz]:
1. Umschreibung III 5 (129)
2. umschreiben, mit anderen Worten sagen III 5 (129)
parents *(pl)* ['peərənts] Eltern I
park [pɑːk]:
1. Park I
2. parken III 3 (75)
parliament ['pɑːləmənt] Parlament I
part [pɑːt] Teil I **part of the body** Körperteil II **part of speech** Wortart III 2 (38) **take part in sth.** an etwas teilnehmen II
partner ['pɑːtnə] Partner/in I
party ['pɑːti] Party I
pass [pɑːs]:
1. vergehen, vorübergehen *(Zeit)* III 3 (75)
°**2.** bestehen *(Test, Prüfung)*
3. **pass sth./sb.** an etwas/jm. vorbeigehen/vorbeifahren II
4. **pass sth. around** etwas herumgeben, herumreichen II
passenger ['pæsɪndʒə] Passagier/in; Fahrgast III 5 (127)
passport ['pɑːspɔːt] (Reise-)Pass II
password ['pɑːswɜːd] Passwort III 5 (114)
past [pɑːst]:
1. Vergangenheit I
2. **half past ten** halb elf (10.30 / 22.30) I **quarter past ten** Viertel nach zehn

(10.15 / 22.15) I
3. vorbei (an), vorüber (an) II

°**pasty** ['pæsti] Pastete *(Fleisch und Gemüse in Teig)*

pat [pæt]:
1. tätscheln III 5 (118)
2. Klaps; Tätscheln III 5 (118)

path [pɑːθ] Pfad, Weg II

patient ['peɪʃnt] geduldig III 4 (101)

pattern ['pætn] Muster III 5 (120)

pause [pɔːz] innehalten, pausieren; eine Pause einlegen II

pavement ['peɪvmənt] Gehweg, Bürgersteig III 1 (24)

°**paw prints** *(pl)* ['pɔː prɪnts] Pfotenabdrücke, Pfotenspuren

°**pawn** [pɔːn] *(Schach)* Bauer

pay (for sth.) [peɪ], **paid, paid** (etwas) bezahlen II **get paid** bezahlt werden III 3 (71) °**pay attention to sth.** etwas beachten; auf etwas achten

PE [ˌpiː‿'iː] Sportunterricht, Turnen I

peace [piːs] Friede, Frieden III 3 (62)

peaceful ['piːsfl] friedlich II

peak [piːk] Gipfel II

pebble ['pebl] Kieselstein III 4 (101)

pedestrian [pə'destriən] Fußgänger/in III 3 (75) **pedestrian zone** [pə'destrɪən zəʊn] Fußgängerzone II

pen [pen] Kugelschreiber, Stift, Füller I

pence [pens] Pence *(plural of* **penny***)* I

pencil ['pensl] Bleistift I

pencil case ['pensl keɪs] Federmäppchen I

people ['piːpl] Leute, Menschen I

pepper ['pepə] Pfeffer I

per day/hour/... [pə, pɜː] pro Tag/Stunde/... III 5 (114) **per cent (%)** [pə'sent] Prozent I

perfect ['pɜːfɪkt] perfekt, ideal I

perform [pə'fɔːm] auftreten *(Künstler/in)* III 4 (98)

performance [pə'fɔːməns] Aufführung, Vorstellung, Auftritt III 4 (98)

°**period** ['pɪəriəd] *(bes. AE)* Unterrichtsstunde, Schulstunde

person ['pɜːsn] Person I

°**personal assistant** [ˌpɜːsənl‿ə'sɪstənt] persönliche(r) Assistent/in

°**personality** [ˌpɜːsə'næləti] Persönlichkeit

pet [pet] Haustier I

petrol ['petrəl] Benzin III 3 (66) **petrol station** Tankstelle III 3 (66)

phone [fəʊn]:
1. Telefon I **answer the phone** ans Telefon gehen II
2. phone sb. jn. anrufen I

phone call ['fəʊn kɔːl] Anruf; Telefongespräch I

photo ['fəʊtəʊ] Foto I **in the photo** auf dem Foto I **take photos** fotografieren, Fotos machen I

phrase [freɪz] Ausdruck, (Rede-)Wendung I

Physical Education [ˌfɪzɪkl‿ˌedʒu'keɪʃn] Sportunterricht, Turnen I

piano [pi'ænəʊ] Klavier, Piano I **play the piano** Klavier spielen I

°**pick** [pɪk] wählen, auswählen, aussuchen

pick sb. up [ˌpɪk‿'ʌp] jn. abholen II

pick sth. up [ˌpɪk‿'ʌp] etwas aufheben *(vom Boden)*, etwas hochheben II

picnic ['pɪknɪk] Picknick I

picture ['pɪktʃə] Bild I **in the picture** auf dem Bild I

pie ['paɪ] Obstkuchen; Pastete II

piece [piːs]:
1. Stück III 2 (36) **a piece of ...** ein Stück ... III 2 (36)
°**2.** *(Schach)* Figur

°**pier** [pɪə] Seebrücke

pig [pɪg] Schwein I

pigeon ['pɪdʒɪn] (Stadt-)Taube III 4 (92)

pile [paɪl] Stapel, Haufen III 5 (118)

pilgrim ['pɪlgrɪm] Pilger/in III 4 (109)

pink [pɪŋk] pink, rosa I

°**pioneer** [ˌpaɪə'nɪə] Pionier/in

pipe [paɪp] (Tabaks-)Pfeife III 3 (67)

pirate ['paɪrət] Pirat/in III 1 (33)

°**pitch** [pɪtʃ] (Sport-)Platz, Spielfeld

pity ['pɪti]: **It was a pity that ...** Es war schade, dass ... III 1 (23)

°**pixie** ['pɪksi] *Wesen aus der englischen Mythologie, ähnlich wie Kobolde und Feen*

pizza ['piːtsə] Pizza I

place [pleɪs] Ort, Platz, Stelle I **take place** stattfinden; spielen, sich abspielen *(Geschichte, Handlung)* I

plan [plæn]:
1. Plan I
2. planen II

plane [pleɪn] Flugzeug II

planet ['plænɪt] Planet I

plant [plɑːnt]
1. Pflanze II
2. pflanzen II
°**3. power plant** Kraftwerk

plaster ['plɑːstə] (Heft-)Pflaster II

plastic ['plæstɪk] Plastik, Kunststoff II

plate [pleɪt]: **a plate of ...** ein Teller ... I

°**plateau** [*BE:* 'plætəʊ, *AE:* plæ'təʊ], *pl* **plateaux** *or* **plateaus** Hochebene

platform ['plætfɔːm] Bahnsteig, Gleis II

play [pleɪ]:
1. spielen I **play sb.** gegen jn. spielen III 4 (88) **play the drums** Schlagzeug spielen I **play the guitar** Gitarre spielen I **play the piano** Klavier spielen I
2. abspielen *(CD, DVD)* I
3. Theaterstück I

player ['pleɪə] Spieler/in I

°**playground** ['pleɪgraʊnd] Spielplatz

please [pliːz] bitte I

pm: 4 pm [ˌpiː‿'em] 4 Uhr nachmittags / 16 Uhr I

pocket ['pɒkɪt] Tasche *(Manteltasche, Hosentasche usw.)* II

poem ['pəʊɪm] Gedicht II

point [pɔɪnt]:
1. Punkt I **3.5 (three point five)** 3,5 (drei Komma fünf) III 2 (45) **point of view** Standpunkt III 2 (49) **from my point of view** aus meiner Sicht III 2 (49)
2. point to sth. auf etwas zeigen, deuten I **point sth. at sb.** etwas auf jn. richten I **point sth. out (to sb.)** (jn.) auf etwas hinweisen III 1 (17)

police *(pl)* [pə'liːs] Polizei I

police officer [pə'liːs‿ɒfɪsə] Polizist/in I

policeman [pə'liːsmən] Polizist I

police station [pə'liːs steɪʃn] Polizeiwache, -revier III 3 (62)

Polish ['pəʊlɪʃ] Polnisch; polnisch I

polite [pə'laɪt] höflich II

°**political** [pə'lɪtɪkl] politisch

politics ['pɒlətɪks] Politik III 4 (109)

pony ['pəʊni] Pony II

pool [puːl]:
1. Schwimmbad, -becken I
°**2.** Becken

poor [pɔː, pʊə] arm I

pop (music) [pɒp] Popmusik II

pope [pəʊp] Papst III 1 (32)

popular (with) ['pɒpjələ] populär, beliebt (bei) I

population [ˌpɒpju'leɪʃn] Bevölkerung, Einwohner(zahl) III 1 (32)

porch [pɔːtʃ] Veranda *(AE)*; Vorbau, Vordach *(BE)* III 5 (118)

°**pork** [pɔːk] Schweinefleisch

port [pɔːt] Hafenstadt I

°**positive** ['pɒzətɪv] positiv

possible ['pɒsəbl] möglich II

post [pəʊst]:
1. Posting *(auf Blog)*, Blog-Eintrag III 1 (10)
2. post sth. etwas posten III 5 (113)

postcard ['pəʊstkɑːd] Postkarte I

poster ['pəʊstə] Poster I

post office ['pəʊst‿ɒfɪs] Postamt II

pot [pɒt] Gefäß; Topf III 3 (67)

potato [pə'teɪtəʊ], *pl* **potatoes** Kartoffel I **roast potatoes** *(pl) im Backofen in Fett gebackene Kartoffeln* I

pound [paʊnd] Pfund *(britische Währung)*
I

pour [pɔː] gießen II

power ['paʊə]:
1. Macht; Kraft, Stärke III 1 (32)
2. Energie, Strom III 1 (32)

powerful ['paʊəfl] mächtig, kräftig, stark III 1 (32)

°**power plant** ['paʊə plɑːnt] Kraftwerk

practical ['præktɪkl] praktisch III 3 (58/59)

practice ['præktɪs]:
1. Übung I
°**2.** *(AE)* praktizieren; üben, trainieren

practise ['præktɪs] üben, trainieren I

prediction [prɪ'dɪkʃn] Vorhersage, Voraussage III 3 (74)

°**prefer sth.** [prɪ'fɜː] etwas vorziehen, etwas lieber mögen

prepare (for) [prɪ'peə] sich vorbereiten (auf) I **prepare sth.** etwas vorbereiten I
°**preposition** [ˌprepə'zɪʃn] Präposition
prescription [prɪ'skrɪpʃn] *(ärztliches)* Rezept II
present ['preznt]:
1. Geschenk I
2. Gegenwart II
°**3.** vorhanden, anwesend
present sth. (to sb.) [prɪ'zent] (jm.) etwas präsentieren, vorstellen II
presentation [ˌprezn'teɪʃn] Präsentation, Vorstellung II
president ['prezɪdənt] Präsident/in II
press [pres] drücken III 2 (46)
pressure ['preʃə] Druck III 4 (88)
pretend [prɪ'tend] so tun, als ob III 2 (40)
pretty ['prɪti] hübsch II
price [praɪs] (Kauf-)Preis I
prime minister [ˌpraɪm 'mɪnɪstə] Premierminister/in II
prince [prɪns] Prinz II
princess [ˌprɪn'ses], ['prɪnses] Prinzessin II
prison ['prɪzn] Gefängnis I
prisoner ['prɪznə] Gefangene(r) III 1 (32)
°**private** ['praɪvət] privat
prize [praɪz] Preis, Gewinn II °**prize fighter** Preisboxer/in
°**pro** [prəʊ]: **the pros and cons** das Für und Wider; die Vor- und Nachteile
probable ['prɒbəbl] wahrscheinlich III 2 (36)
probably ['prɒbəbli] wahrscheinlich II
problem ['prɒbləm] Problem I
°**problematic** [ˌprɒblə'mætɪk] problematisch
°**professional** [prə'feʃənl] professionell, Profi-
profile ['prəʊfaɪl] Profil; Beschreibung, Porträt I
°**program** ['prəʊgræm] programmieren
programme ['prəʊgræm] Programm *(auch im Theater usw.)*; (Radio-, Fernseh-)Sendung I **What programmes ...?** Welche Programme ...? / Welche Art von Programmen ...? I
project ['prɒdʒekt] Projekt II
°**projector** [prə'dʒektə] Projektor, Beamer
promise ['prɒmɪs]:
1. versprechen II
°**2.** Versprechen
promote sth. [prə'məʊt] etwas fördern; für etwas werben III 2 (55)
°**pronounce** [prə'naʊns] aussprechen
pronunciation [prəˌnʌnsi'eɪʃn] Aussprache I
°**propeller** [prə'pelə] Propeller
°**props** *(pl)* [prɒps] Requisiten
°**protect** [prə'tekt] (be)schützen
protest:
1. [prə'test] protestieren III 3 (76)
2. ['prəʊtest] Protest III 3 (76)
Protestant ['prɒtɪstənt] Protestant/in; protestantisch III 1 (32)
proud (of) [praʊd] stolz (auf) III 3 (60)
°**provide** [prə'vaɪd] bereitstellen
pub [pʌb] Kneipe, Lokal III 1 (20)
public ['pʌblɪk] öffentliche(r, s) III 3 (62)
°**Pueblo Indian** [ˌpwebləʊ‿'ɪndiən] pueblo-indianisch; Pueblo-Indianer/in
pull [pʊl] ziehen I **pull sth. out** etwas herausziehen II ° **pull into the station** *(Zug)* in den Bahnhof einfahren °**pull up** herausreißen
pullover ['pʊləʊvə] Pullover II
punctuation [ˌpʌŋktʃu'eɪʃn] Zeichensetzung II
punishment ['pʌnɪʃmənt] Bestrafung, Strafe III 2 (49)
puppet ['pʌpɪt] Marionette, Handpuppe II
purple ['pɜːpl] violett, lila I
push [pʊʃ] drücken, schieben, stoßen I
put [pʊt], **put, put** legen, stellen, *(etwas wohin)* tun I **put sth. down** etwas hinlegen III 2 (36) **put sth. on** etwas anziehen *(Kleidung)*; etwas aufsetzen *(Hut, Helm)* II °**put sth. in** etwas einsetzen °**Put up your hand.** Melde dich. / Heb deine Hand.
puzzle ['pʌzl] Rätsel II

Q

quarter ['kwɔːtə]:
1. (Stadt-)Viertel III 3 (73)
2. quarter past ten Viertel nach zehn (10.15 / 22.15) I **quarter to eleven** Viertel vor elf (10.45 / 22.45) I
°**quarterback** ['kwɔːtəbæk] Quarterback *(Angriffsspieler beim American Football)*
queen [kwiːn] Königin I
question ['kwestʃən] Frage I
question mark ['kwestʃən mɑːk] Fragezeichen II
questionnaire [ˌkwestʃə'neə] Fragebogen III 5 (114)
queue [kjuː]:
1. Schlange, Reihe *(wartender Menschen)* II
2. Schlange stehen, sich anstellen II
quick [kwɪk] schnell II
quiet ['kwaɪət] ruhig, still, leise I
quite [kwaɪt] ziemlich II
quiz [kwɪz] Quiz, Ratespiel I

R

rabbit ['ræbɪt] Kaninchen I
race [reɪs]:
1. Rennen, (Wett-)Lauf I
2. rasen III 3 (75)
radio ['reɪdiəʊ] Radio II **on the radio** im Radio II
raft [rɑːft] Schlauchboot *(wildwassertauglich)*; Floß III 2 (55)
railing ['reɪlɪŋ] Geländer III 4 (88)
railroad ['reɪlrəʊd] *(AE)* Eisenbahn III 4 (98)
railway ['reɪlweɪ] *(BE)* Eisenbahn III 4 (98)
rain [reɪn]:
1. regnen II
2. Regen II
rainbow ['reɪnbəʊ] Regenbogen III 1 (24)
raincoat ['reɪnkəʊt] Regenmantel II
°**raindrop** ['reɪndrɒp] Regentropfen
rainforest ['reɪnfɒrɪst] Regenwald II
rainy ['reɪni] regnerisch II
raise money (for) [reɪz] Geld sammeln (für) II
rally ['ræli] Rallye II
ran [ræn] *siehe* **run**
rang [ræŋ] *siehe* **ring**
°**ranger** ['reɪndʒə] Ranger/in, Aufseher/in, Fremdenführer/in *(in Nationalparks u.Ä.)*
rat [ræt] Ratte I
°**rate** [reɪt] Rate, Frequenz
rather than ['rɑːðə ðən] statt, anstatt III 1 (30)
°**rattle** ['rætl] klappern
rattlesnake ['rætlsneɪk] Klapperschlange III 3 (76)
raven ['reɪvn] Rabe III 1 (15)
reach [riːtʃ] erreichen III 2 (40) **reach (for)** greifen (nach) III 4 (102) **reach over** die Hand ausstrecken III 5 (118)
react (to) [ri'ækt] reagieren (auf) III 1 (17)
read [riːd], **read, read** [red] lesen I **read aloud** laut (vor)lesen II °**read sth. out loud** etwas vorlesen
reader ['riːdə] Leser/in II
ready ['redi] bereit, fertig I **get ready (for)** sich fertig machen (für); sich vorbereiten (auf) II
real ['riːəl] echt, wirklich II
°**reality** [ri'æləti] Realität, Wirklichkeit
realize sth. ['riːəlaɪz] etwas erkennen; sich einer Sache bewusst werden III 3 (76)
really ['rɪəli] echt, wirklich I
reason ['riːzn] Grund I
rebuild [ˌriː'bɪld], **rebuilt, rebuilt** [ˌriː'bɪlt] wiederaufbauen III 5 (125)
recipe ['resəpi] (Koch-)Rezept II
°**recognize** ['rekəgnaɪz] erkennen
°**record:**
1. ['rekɔːd] Schallplatte
2. [rɪ'kɔːd] aufzeichnen *(Musik, Daten)*
recorder [rɪ'kɔːdə] Blockflöte II
°**recruit** [rɪ'kruːt] anwerben, rekrutieren
red [red] rot I **go red** rot werden, erröten II
°**refer to sth.** [rɪ'fɜː] sich auf etwas beziehen
°**referee** [ˌrefə'riː] Schiedsrichter/in
region ['riːdʒən] Region II
°**registration** [ˌredʒɪ'streɪʃn] *Durchgang durch die Klassenliste, um die Anwesenheit zu überprüfen*

regular ['regjələ] regelmäßig II
°**rehearsal** [rɪ'hɜːsl] Probe
°**rehearse** [rɪ'hɜːs] proben
reins *(pl)* [reɪnz] Zügel III 3 (76)
relationship [rɪ'leɪʃnʃɪp] Beziehung, Verhältnis III 5 (122)
relax [rɪ'læks] sich entspannen, sich ausruhen III 2 (55)
relaxed [rɪ'lækst] entspannt III 1 (17)
religion [rɪ'lɪdʒən] Religion I
remain [rɪ'meɪn] bleiben, verbleiben III 1 (31)
remember sth. [rɪ'membə]:
1. sich an etwas erinnern I
2. an etwas denken *(etwas nicht vergessen)* II
3. sich etwas merken II
°4. gedenken
remind sb. [rɪ'maɪnd] jn. erinnern III 1 (30)
remote control [rɪˌməʊt kən'trəʊl] *(kurz auch:* **remote**) Fernbedienung III 1 (20)
°**remove** [rɪ'muːv] entfernen, beseitigen
°**repair** [rɪ'peə] reparieren, ausbessern
repeat [rɪ'piːt] wiederholen II
°**replace sth. (with)** [rɪ'pleɪs] etwas ersetzen (durch); austauschen
°**replica** ['replɪkə] Nachbildung, Modell
reply (to) [rɪ'plaɪ]:
1. antworten (auf); erwidern, entgegnen III 1 (10):
°2. Antwort (auf)
report [rɪ'pɔːt]:
1. berichten III 5 (121)
2. Bericht, Reportage II
°**reporter** [rɪ'pɔːtə] Reporter/in
republic [rɪ'pʌblɪk] Republik III 3 (62)
°**require** [rɪ'kwaɪə] erfordern, benötigen
rescue ['reskjuː]:
1. retten II
2. Rettung; Rettungs- I °**rescue centre** Rettungsstelle, -station
research *(no pl)*:
1. ['riːsɜːtʃ, rɪ'sɜːtʃ] Recherche, Forschung(en) III 3 (69)
°2. [rɪ'sɜːtʃ] recherchieren
reservation [ˌrezə'veɪʃn] Reservat, Reservation III 3 (61)
reserve [rɪ'zɜːv]:
1. reservieren, buchen III 1 (14)
2. Schutzgebiet III 2 (54)
°**resort: ski resort** ['skiː rɪˌzɔːt] Skiort, Wintersportort
°**respect** [rɪ'spekt] respektieren
responsible [rɪ'spɒnsəbl] verantwortlich II
rest [rest]:
1. ruhen, sich ausruhen III 1 (25)
2. Rest III 2 (48)
restaurant ['restrɒnt] Restaurant I
result [rɪ'zʌlt] Ergebnis, Resultat II
return [rɪ'tɜːn] Rückkehr III 1 (33)
return ticket (Hin- und) Rückfahrkarte II
review [rɪ'vjuː]:
1. Rezension, Besprechung, Kritik III 5 (131)
°2. besprechen
revise [rɪ'vaɪz] überarbeiten; *(Lernstoff)* wiederholen III 2 (45)
revision [rɪ'vɪʒn] Wiederholung *(des Lernstoffs)* II
°**rewrite** [ˌriː'raɪt] neu schreiben, umarbeiten
rhyme [raɪm] Reim; Vers I
rhythm ['rɪðəm] Rhythmus III 1 (24)
rich [rɪtʃ] reich I
ridden ['rɪdn] *siehe* **ride**
ride [raɪd]:
1. Fahrt I
2. Ritt, Ausritt III 3 (71)
3. **(rode, ridden)** reiten II **ride a bike** Fahrrad fahren I
riding ['raɪdɪŋ] Reiten I
right [raɪt]:
1. richtig I **sb. is right** jemand hat Recht I **..., right?** ..., nicht wahr? II
2. rechte(r, s); (nach) rechts I **on the right** rechts/auf der rechten Seite I **turn right** (nach) rechts abbiegen II
3. **right now** jetzt gerade, momentan II **right behind you** direkt hinter dir, genau hinter dir II **right after you** gleich nach dir II °**right away** sofort
rights *(pl)* [raɪts] Rechte III 5 (129)
ring [rɪŋ]:
1. **(rang, rung)** klingeln, läuten II
2. Ring II
°**ring out the hour** durch den Glockenschlag die Uhrzeit bekanntgeben
rise up [ˌraɪz‿'ʌp], **rose, risen** aufragen, emporragen *(Berge, Säulen, Türme, ...)* III 3 (60)
risen ['rɪzn] *siehe* **rise**
risk [rɪsk] Risiko III 4 (100) **take a risk** ein Risiko eingehen III 4 (100)
°**risk assessment** ['rɪsk‿əˌsesmənt] Risikoeinschätzung
river ['rɪvə] Fluss I
°**riverboat** ['rɪvəbəʊt] Flussschiff, Binnenschiff
road [rəʊd] Straße I **at 8 Beach Road** in der Beach Road (Nummer) 8 I **in Beach Road** in der Beach Road I
°**road trip** ['rəʊd trɪp] Autoreise
roar [rɔː] brüllen III 1 (16); tosen, dröhnen III 4 (88)
°**roast** [rəʊst] rösten, braten
roast beef [ˌrəʊst 'biːf] Rinderbraten I
roast potatoes *(pl)* [ˌrəʊst pə'teɪtəʊz] *im Backofen in Fett gebackene Kartoffeln* I
°**robot** ['rəʊbɒt] Roboter
rock [rɒk]:
1. Fels, Felsen I
2. schaukeln, schwanken III 5 (127)
rock (music) Rock(musik) II °**rock pool** Gezeitentümpel
rocky ['rɒki] felsig, steinig II
rode [rəʊd] *siehe* **ride**
role [rəʊl] Rolle *(in einem Theaterstück, Film)* II
roll [rəʊl] rollen II
roller coaster ['rəʊlə kəʊstə] Achterbahn III 4 (98)
Roman ['rəʊmən] Römer/in; römisch II
roof [ruːf] Dach II
°**rook** [rʊk] *(Schach)* Turm
room [ruːm] Zimmer, Raum I
rope [rəʊp] Seil III 1 (24)
rose [rəʊz] Rose III 4 (88)
rose [rəʊz] *siehe* **rise**
rough [rʌf] rau; grob; hart III 5 (127)
round [raʊnd]:
1. rund III 5 (122)
2. **round here** hier in der Gegend III 3 (71)
°3. **round up ponies** Ponys zusammentreiben
roundabout ['raʊndəbaʊt] Kreisverkehr II
route [ruːt] Strecke, Route III 1 (23)
routine [ruː'tiːn] Routine I
royal ['rɔɪəl] königlich II
rubber ['rʌbə] Radiergummi I
rubbish ['rʌbɪʃ] Müll, Abfall II
rucksack ['rʌksæk] *(BE)* Rucksack I
rude [ruːd] unhöflich; unverschämt III 3 (71)
rugby ['rʌgbi] Rugby III 2 (54)
rugby ground ['rʌgbi graʊnd] Rugby-Platz, Rugby-Spielfeld III 2 (54)
ruin ['ruːɪn] Ruine II
rule [ruːl]:
1. Regel, Vorschrift II
2. **rule sth.** etwas beherrschen, über etwas herrschen III 1 (30)
ruler ['ruːlə] Lineal I
run [rʌn], **ran, run**:
1. rennen, laufen I
2. verlaufen *(Straße; Grenze)* III 5 (126)
run after sb. hinter jm. herrennen I **run off** wegrennen III 1 (20) **run over (to)** hinüberrennen (zu/nach) II °**run around** herumrennen
rung [rʌŋ] *siehe* **ring**
runner ['rʌnə] Läufer/in II
running water [ˌrʌnɪŋ 'wɔːtə] fließend(es) Wasser II
°**rural** ['rʊərəl] ländlich, Land-
rush [rʌʃ] eilen, stürzen III 5 (127)
rusty ['rʌsti] rostig; verrostet III 4 (101)

S

sad [sæd] traurig I
°**sadness** ['sædnəs] Traurigkeit
safari [sə'fɑːri] Safari II
safe [seɪf] sicher, in Sicherheit II
said [sed] *siehe* **say**
sail [seɪl]:
1. segeln I **go sailing** segeln gehen I
°2. fahren *(Schiff)*, auslaufen, in See stechen

sailing boat ['seɪlɪŋ bəʊt] Segelboot I
°**sailor** ['seɪlə] Seemann, Matrose, Matrosin
salad ['sæləd] Salat *(als Gericht oder Beilage)* I **fruit salad** Obstsalat I
sales *(pl)* [seɪlz] Umsatz, Absatz; Verkäufe II
salt [sɔːlt] Salz III 5 (115)
samba ['sæmbə] Samba I
same [seɪm]: **the same** der-/die-/dasselbe; dieselben I
°**sanctuary** ['sæŋktʃuəri] (Natur-, Tier-, Vogel-)Schutzgebiet, Schutzgehege
sand [sænd] Sand I
sandwich ['sænwɪtʃ, 'sænwɪdʒ] Sandwich, (zusammengeklapptes) belegtes Brot I
°**sandy** ['sændi] sandig
sang [sæŋ] *siehe* **sing**
°**Santa (Claus)** ['sæntə klɔːz] der Weihnachtsmann
sat [sæt] *siehe* **sit**
°**satisfied** ['sætɪsfaɪd] zufrieden
Saturday ['sætədeɪ, 'sætədi] Samstag I **on Saturday afternoon** am Samstagnachmittag I
°**sauna** ['sɔːnə, 'saʊnə] Sauna
save [seɪv] retten I °**be saved** gerettet werden
saw [sɔː] *siehe* **see**
say [seɪ], **said, said** sagen I **It says here: …** [sez] Hier steht: … / Es heißt hier: … I **Say hello to … for me.** Grüß … von mir. II
scan sth. (for sth.) [skæn] etwas (nach etwas) absuchen III 1 (24) **scan a text** einen Text schnell nach bestimmten Wörtern/Informationen absuchen II
scare sb. [skeə] jn. erschrecken; jm. Angst machen III 1 (25)
scared [skeəd] verängstigt II
°**scarf** [skɑːf] Schal
scary ['skeəri] unheimlich, gruselig I
scene [siːn] Szene I
°**scholarship** ['skɒləʃɪp] Stipendium
school [skuːl] Schule I **at school** in der Schule I **before school** vor der Schule *(vor Schulbeginn)* I **in front of the school** vor der Schule *(vor dem Schulgebäude)* I **school bag** Schultasche I
science ['saɪəns] Naturwissenschaft I
scientist ['saɪəntɪst] Naturwissenschaftler/in III 2 (36)
scone [skɒn] *kleines rundes Milchbrötchen, leicht süß* I
°**scoop** [skuːp] schöpfen
score [skɔː] ein Tor schießen, einen Treffer erzielen I
°**scorpion** ['skɔːpiən] Skorpion
scream [skriːm] schreien II
screen [skriːn] Bildschirm II
°**sculpture** ['skʌlptʃə] Skulptur
sea [siː] Meer I **sea level** Meeresspiegel II

seafood ['siːfuːd] Meeresfrüchte II
seagull ['siːgʌl] Möwe I
seal [siːl] Robbe I
sea level ['siː levl] Meeresspiegel II
°**seaman** ['siːmən], *pl* **seamen** ['siːmən] Matrose, Seemann
°**seaside** ['siːsaɪd] Meeresküste, Strand; Meeres-; am Meer
°**season** ['siːzn] Jahreszeit
seat [siːt] Sitz, Platz II **take a seat** Platz nehmen III 2 (55)
second ['sekənd]:
1. zweite(r, s) I **Second, …** Zweitens, … I
2. Sekunde II
section ['sekʃn] Abschnitt, Teilstück III 3 (66)
see [siː], **saw, seen** sehen; besuchen I **I see.** Aha! / Verstehe. II **see a doctor** einen Arzt aufsuchen II **See you.** Bis gleich. / Bis bald. II **See you later.** Bis bald. / Bis nachher. I **…, you see.** …, weißt du. II
seed [siːd] Samen III 4 (98)
seem (to be/do) [siːm] (zu sein/zu tun) scheinen III 1 (17)
seen [siːn] *siehe* **see**
sell [sel], **sold, sold** verkaufen I
semi- ['semi] halb-; Halb- III 3 (80)
send [send], **sent, sent**:
send sth. to sb. jm. etwas schicken, senden I
sense of humour [ˌsens‿əv 'hjuːmə] (Sinn für) Humor III 3 (70)
sent [sent] *siehe* **send**
sentence ['sentəns] Satz I
°**separate** ['seprət] getrennt, separat
September [sep'tembə] September I
serious ['sɪəriəs] ernst; ernsthaft III 5 (113)
seriously ['sɪəriəsli] ernsthaft, ernstlich III 5 (113)
service ['sɜːvɪs]:
1. Gottesdienst III 3 (66)
°**2.** Dienst, Service
set [set] Satz, Set II
set [set], **set, set** untergehen *(Sonne)* III 5 (127) **set sth. up** etwas aufstellen, aufbauen, errichten, einrichten III 5 (126)
°**set a deadline** eine Frist setzen
°**set square** ['set skweə] Geodreieck®
°**setting** ['setɪŋ] Schauplatz
settle ['setl] sich niederlassen, sich ansiedeln II
settler ['setlə] Siedler/in II
seven ['sevn] sieben I
several ['sevrəl] mehrere, verschiedene II
°**shade** [ʃeɪd] Schatten *(vor der Sonne geschützter Platz)*
shadow ['ʃædəʊ] Schatten *(den jemand/etwas wirft)* II
shake [ʃeɪk], **shook, shaken** schütteln II
shaken ['ʃeɪkn] *siehe* **shake**
Shall I …? [ʃæl] Soll ich …? III 3 (60)
shape [ʃeɪp] Form, Gestalt III 5 (123)
°**shard** [ʃɑːd] Scherbe
°**share sth.** [ʃeə] (sich) etwas teilen

shark [ʃɑːk] Hai I
sharp [ʃɑːp] scharf III 5 (126)
sharpener ['ʃɑːpnə] (An-)Spitzer I
she [ʃiː] sie I
sheep, *pl* **sheep** [ʃiːp] Schaf II
°**sheet** [ʃiːt] Blatt, Bogen *(Papier)*
shelf [ʃelf], *pl* **shelves** [ʃelvz] Regal I
shelter ['ʃeltə] Unterkunft III 4 (109)
°**shepherd** ['ʃepəd] Schafhirte/-hirtin
°**shift** [ʃɪft] verschieben
°**shimmer** ['ʃɪmə] schimmern
shine [ʃaɪn], **shone, shone** leuchten; scheinen *(Sonne)* III 5 (126)
ship [ʃɪp] Schiff I
shirt [ʃɜːt] Hemd II
°**shock** [ʃɒk] schockieren
shocked [ʃɒkt] schockiert, entsetzt II
shoe [ʃuː] Schuh I
shone [ʃɒn] *siehe* **shine**
shook [ʃʊk] *siehe* **shake**
shoot [ʃuːt], **shot, shot** schießen; erschießen III 5 (126)
°**shooting star** [ˌʃuːtɪŋ 'stɑː] Sternschnuppe
shop [ʃɒp]:
1. Laden I **corner shop** Laden an der Ecke; Tante-Emma-Laden I
2. einkaufen II
shop assistant ['ʃɒp‿əˌsɪstənt] *(kurz auch:* **assistant***)* Verkäufer/in II
shopping ['ʃɒpɪŋ]: **do the/some shopping** einkaufen gehen; Einkäufe erledigen II **go shopping** einkaufen gehen I **shopping centre** Einkaufszentrum I **shopping mall** (großes) Einkaufszentrum I
shore [ʃɔː] Ufer *(eines Sees)*, Strand II
short [ʃɔːt] kurz I °**short form** Kurzform
shorts *(pl)* [ʃɔːts] Shorts, kurze Hose I
shot [ʃɒt]:
1. *siehe* **shoot**
2. Aufnahme, Foto; *(Film)* Einstellung, Szene III 4 (88)
should [ʃʊd], [ʃəd]: **You should …** Du solltest … / Ihr solltet … II
shoulder ['ʃəʊldə] Schulter II
shout [ʃaʊt]:
1. schreien, rufen I
°**2.** Ruf
show [ʃəʊ]:
1. (showed, shown) zeigen I
2. Show, Vorstellung II
shower ['ʃaʊə] Dusche II **have/take a shower** (sich) duschen II
shrub [ʃrʌb] Strauch, Busch III 3 (76)
shy [ʃaɪ] schüchtern, scheu II
sick [sɪk] krank I **I feel sick.** Mir ist schlecht. II **I'm going to be sick** Ich muss mich übergeben. II
sickness ['sɪknəs] Krankheit II
side [saɪd] Seite II °**side by side** nebeneinander, Seite an Seite
sidewalk ['saɪdwɔːk] *(AE)* Gehweg, Bürgersteig III 4 (90)
sigh [saɪ] seufzen III 3 (76)

sight [saɪt] Anblick III 4 (100) **sights** *(pl)* [saɪts] Sehenswürdigkeiten I
sign [saɪn]:
1. Schild; Zeichen I **no sign of …** keine Spur von … III 1 (25)
°2. unterschreiben, unterzeichnen
signal ['sɪgnəl] Signal, Zeichen II
silent ['saɪlənt] lautlos, leise; schweigend III 3 (76)
silky ['sɪlki] seidig I
silly ['sɪli]:
1. albern; blöd I
2. Dummerchen I
similar (to sth./sb.) ['sɪmələ] (etwas/jm.) ähnlich II
simple ['sɪmpl] einfach, unkompliziert III 5 (127)
since [sɪns]: **since 10 o'clock/last week/…** seit 10 Uhr/letzter Woche/… III 1 (20)
sing [sɪŋ], **sang, sung** singen I
singer ['sɪŋə] Sänger/in II
single ['sɪŋgl]:
1. ledig, alleinstehend I
2. *(kurz für:* **single ticket***)* Einzelfahrschein; einfache Fahrkarte II
°3. einzige(r, s)
°**sip** [sɪp] (kleiner) Schluck
°**sir** [sɜː] Sir *(höfliche Anrede, z. B. für Kunden, Vorgesetzte oder Lehrer)*
siren ['saɪrən] Sirene III 3 (75)
sister ['sɪstə] Schwester I
sit [sɪt], **sat, sat** sitzen; sich setzen I **sit down** sich hinsetzen I **sit up** sich aufsetzen III 2 (47)
°**site** [saɪt] Ort **work site** Arbeitsort, Einsatzort
°**sit-in** ['sɪt‿ɪn] Sit-in, Sitzstreik
situation [ˌsɪtʃu'eɪʃn] Situation III 1 (21)
six [sɪks] sechs I
size [saɪz] Größe I **What size tea would you like?** Wie groß soll der/dein Tee sein? II
sizzle ['sɪzl] brutzeln, zischen III 5 (126)
skates [skeɪts] Inlineskates I
skating ['skeɪtɪŋ]:
1. Inlineskaten, Rollschuhlaufen I
2. *(kurz für:* **ice skating***)* Schlittschuhlaufen II
skill [skɪl] Fertigkeit II **skills file** Übersicht über Lern- und Arbeitstechniken I **study skills** Lern- und Arbeitstechniken I
skim a text [skɪm] einen Text überfliegen *(um den Inhalt grob zu erfassen)* III 5 (124)
skinny ['skɪni] mager, dünn, dürr III 4 (100)
°**ski resort** ['skiː rɪˌzɔːt] Skiort, Wintersportort
skirt [skɜːt] Rock II
skull [skʌl] Schädel III 3 (67)
sky [skaɪ] Himmel II
skyline ['skaɪlaɪn] Skyline; Horizont III 1 (11)
°**skype** [skaɪp] per Skype telefonieren
skyscraper ['skaɪskreɪpə] Wolkenkratzer III 3 (58/59)
sleep [sliːp]:
1. **(slept, slept)** schlafen I
2. Schlaf III 2 (37)
sleepover ['sliːpəʊvə] Pyjama-Party, Schlafparty I
°**sleeping beauty** [ˌsliːpɪŋ 'bjuːti] Dornröschen *(„schlafende Schöne")*
sleepy ['sliːpi] schläfrig II
slept [slept] *siehe* **sleep**
°**slide** [slaɪd], **slid, slid** gleiten
slippery ['slɪpəri] rutschig, glatt III 3 (76)
slither ['slɪðə] gleiten; schlittern III 5 (126)
slow [sləʊ]:
1. langsam I **be slow** nachgehen *(Uhr)* III 1 (19)
°2. verlangsamen
small [smɔːl] klein I **small talk** Smalltalk *(spontan geführtes Gespräch)* III 1 (13)
smell [smel]:
1. riechen I **smell sth.** an etwas riechen I **smell good** gut riechen II
2. Geruch III 4 (101)
smile [smaɪl]:
1. lächeln I **smile at sb.** jn. anlächeln I
2. Lächeln I
smiley ['smaɪli] Smiley I
smoke [sməʊk]:
1. rauchen III 5 (126)
2. Rauch III 5 (126)
smuggle ['smʌgl] schmuggeln I
smuggler ['smʌglə] Schmuggler/in I
smuggling ['smʌglɪŋ] der Schmuggel, das Schmuggeln I
snack [snæk] Snack, Imbiss I
snake [sneɪk] Schlange I
sneeze [sniːz] niesen I
°**snort** [snɔːt] Schnauben, Prusten
snow [snəʊ] Schnee II
°**snow leopard** [ˌsnəʊ 'lepəd] Schneeleopard
so [səʊ]:
1. also; deshalb, daher I
2. **so cool/nice** so cool/nett I **so far** bis jetzt; bis hierher II
3. **So?** Und? / Na und? I
4. **so that …** *(oft auch kurz:* **so …***)* sodass …, damit … II
soccer ['sɒkə] Fußball II
social media *(pl)* [ˌsəʊʃl 'miːdiə] soziale Medien III 5 (113)
social services *(pl)* [ˌsəʊʃl 'sɜːvɪsɪz] Sozialwesen, soziale Dienste III 2 (54)
°**social studies** [ˌsəʊʃl 'stʌdiz] Gemeinschaftskunde, Sozialkunde, Politische Bildung
sock [sɒk] Socke II
sofa ['səʊfə] Sofa I
soft [sɒft] weich I **in a soft voice** sanft; mit leiser Stimme II
sold [səʊld] *siehe* **sell**
soldier ['səʊldʒə] Soldat/in II
solo ['səʊləʊ] Solo- II
some [sʌm] einige, ein paar; etwas I
somebody ['sʌmbədi] jemand I
someone ['sʌmwʌn] jemand I
something ['sʌmθɪŋ] etwas I
sometimes ['sʌmtaɪmz] manchmal I
somewhere ['sʌmweə] irgendwo, irgendwohin II
son [sʌn] Sohn II
song [sɒŋ] Lied, Song I
soon [suːn] bald I **as soon as** sobald, sowie III 1 (10)
sore [sɔː] wund II **have a sore throat** Halsschmerzen haben II
sorry ['sɒri]: **(I'm) sorry.** Tut mir leid. / Entschuldigung. I **I'm sorry about …** Es tut mir leid wegen … I
sound [saʊnd]:
1. klingen, sich anhören I
2. Geräusch; Klang I
3. Laut I °**sound group** Lautgruppe
°**sound** [saʊnd] Meerenge, Sund
°**sound system** ['saʊnd ˌsɪstm] Tonanlage
soup [suːp] Suppe I
°**source** [sɔːs] Quelle
south [saʊθ] Süden; nach Süden; südlich III 1 (11) **south-east** Südosten; nach Südosten; südöstlich III 1 (11) **southern** ['sʌðən] südlich, Süd- III 3 (62) **south-west** Südwesten; nach Südwesten; südwestlich III 1 (11)
souvenir [ˌsuːvə'nɪə] Andenken, Souvenir II
space [speɪs] Platz, Raum; Weltraum II
spaghetti [spə'geti] Spagetti I
Spanish ['spænɪʃ] Spanisch; spanisch I
speak [spiːk], **spoke, spoken** sprechen, reden I **speak to sb.** mit jm. sprechen II
speaker ['spiːkə] Sprecher/in I; Redner/in II
special ['speʃl] besondere(r, s) I
°**specific** [spə'sɪfɪk] bestimmte(r, s), spezifische(r, s)
speculate ['spekjuleɪt] spekulieren, Vermutungen anstellen III 5 (122)
speech [spiːtʃ] *(offizielle)* Rede II **part of speech** Wortart III 2 (38)
°**speech bubble** ['spiːtʃ bʌbl] Sprechblase
speed [spiːd] Geschwindigkeit III 1 (23)
°**speed sth. up** [ˌspiːd‿'ʌp] etwas beschleunigen
spell [spel] buchstabieren I
spelling ['spelɪŋ] Rechtschreibung; Schreibweise II
spend time/money (on) [spend], **spent, spent** Zeit verbringen (mit); Geld ausgeben (für) III 1 (30)
spent [spent] *siehe* **spend**
°**spider** ['spaɪdə] Spinne
spin around [ˌspɪn‿ə'raʊnd], **spun, spun** sich (im Kreis) drehen; herumwirbeln III 3 (75)
splash sb. [splæʃ] jn. nass spritzen III 2 (48)
°**split** [splɪt] aufteilen
spoke [spəʊk] *siehe* **speak**
spoken ['spəʊkn] *siehe* **speak**

spoon [spuːn] Löffel II
°**spoonful** ['spuːnfʊl]: **a spoonful of sth.** ein Esslöffel (voll) etwas
sport [spɔːt] Sport; Sportart I **do sport** Sport treiben I
spot [spɒt] Fleck, Punkt I
°**spray** [spreɪ] sprühen
spread [spred], **spread, spread** (sich) ausbreiten, verbreiten III 4 (98)
spring [sprɪŋ]:
1. Frühling I
°2. Quelle
spun [spʌn] *siehe* **spin**
°**spy** [spaɪ]: **I spy with my little eye** *entspricht dem Spiel „*Ich sehe was, was du nicht siehst"
square [skweə]:
1. Quadrat III 4 (95) **square kilometre (sq km)** Quadratkilometer (km²) II
2. Feld *(auf Brettspiel)* III 4 (95)
3. Platz *(in der Stadt)* II
4. Kästchen *(auf Papier)*
5. quadratisch III 4 (100)
squash [skwɒʃ] Kürbis III 4 (108)
°**squeeze** [skwiːz]: **give sb. a squeeze** jn. drücken
°**stadium** ['steɪdiəm] Stadion
stage [steɪdʒ] Bühne II
stairs *(pl)* [steəz] Treppe; Treppenstufen II
stall [stɔːl] (Markt-)Stand II
stamp [stæmp] Stempel II
stand [stænd], **stood, stood** stehen; sich (hin)stellen II **stand up** aufstehen I
standard ['stændəd] Standard; Standard- III 4 (95)
star [stɑː]:
1. (Film-, Pop-)Star I
2. Stern III 2 (46)
stare (at sb./sth.) [steə] (jn./etwas an) starren III 3 (70)
°**starfleet** ['stɑːfliːt] Sternenflotte
°**star-spangled** ['stɑː spæŋgld] mit Sternen übersät
start [stɑːt] anfangen, beginnen I
starve [stɑːv] hungern III 3 (76) **be starving** einen Riesenhunger haben III 3 (76)
state [steɪt] Staat I **state animal** Wappentier II
°**statement** ['steɪtmənt] Aussage
station ['steɪʃn] Bahnhof II
statue ['stætʃuː] Statue III 4 (84)
°**status** ['steɪtəs] Status
stay [steɪ]:
1. bleiben I **stay (at/with)** *(vorübergehend)* wohnen, übernachten (in/bei) II **stay in touch (with sb.)** (mit jm.) Kontakt halten; (mit jm.) in Verbindung bleiben II **stay up late** lang aufbleiben II
°2. Aufenthalt
°**steady** ['stedi] fest, ruhig, gleichmäßig, konstant
steam [stiːm] Dampf III 2 (55) **steam train** *Zug mit Dampflok* III 2 (55)
steel [stiːl] Stahl III 2 (54)
steep [stiːp] steil III 2 (41)
steer [stɪə] steuern, lenken I
steering wheel ['stɪərɪŋ wiːl] Lenkrad II
step [step]:
1. Schritt I
2. Stufe III 1 (14)
°3. **step in** eintreten; hineingehen **step on sth.** auf etwas treten **step up** vortreten
stick:
1. Stock III 2 (40)
2. **stick sth. into sth., stuck, stuck** etwas in etwas stechen, stecken II
sticky ['stɪki] klebrig II
still [stɪl]:
1. *(adv)* (immer) noch I
2. *(adv)* trotzdem, dennoch II
3. *(adj)* still, ruhig III 3 (76)
stilts *(pl)* [stɪlts] Stelzen III 5 (126)
°**still** [stɪl] Standfoto
stomach ['stʌmək] Magen II
stone [stəʊn] Stein II
stood [stʊd] *siehe* **stand**
°**stoop** [stuːp] *(AE)* offene Veranda; Aufgang zum Hauseingang
stop [stɒp]:
1. anhalten, stoppen I
2. aufhören II
3. Halt; Station, Haltestelle II
Stop it! *(infml)* Hör auf (damit)! / Lass das! II
store [stɔː] *(AE)* Laden, Geschäft II
storey ['stɔːri] *(BE)* Stock, Stockwerk, Etage III 4 (89)
storm [stɔːm] Sturm, Unwetter, Gewitter II
story ['stɔːri]:
1. Geschichte, Erzählung I
2. *(AE)* Stock, Stockwerk, Etage III 4 (89)
straight [streɪt]:
1. gerade II
2. direkt, geradewegs III 3 (76)
straight on geradeaus weiter II
strange [streɪndʒ] seltsam, komisch I
°**strangle** ['stræŋgl] erdrosseln
strawberry ['strɔːbəri] Erdbeere II
stream [striːm]:
1. Bach III 3 (71)
2. strömen; streamen III 5 (114)
street [striːt] Straße I **at 14 Dean Street** in der Deanstraße 14 I **in Dean Street** in der Dean Street I
street artist ['striːt‿ˌɑːtɪst] Straßenkünstler/in II
stress [stres] Betonung I
°**stressed syllable** [strest 'sɪləbl] betonte Silbe
strict [strɪkt] streng III 3 (67)
°**stride** [straɪd] Schritt
string [strɪŋ] Saite III 5 (118)
°**stripe** [straɪp] Streifen
strong [strɒŋ] stark, kräftig II
structure ['strʌktʃə]:
1. Struktur, Gliederung III 1 (17)
°2. strukturieren
stuck [stʌk] *siehe* **stick**
student ['stjuːdənt] Schüler/in; Student/in I
studio ['stjuːdiəʊ] Studio I
study ['stʌdi] studieren; untersuchen, beobachten; lernen III 2 (36)
study poster ['stʌdi ˌpəʊstə] Lernposter II
study skills ['stʌdi ˌskɪlz] Lern- und Arbeitstechniken I
stuff [stʌf] *(infml)* Zeug, Kram III 4 (101)
stupid ['stjuːpɪd] dumm, blöd III 2 (40)
style [staɪl] Stil III 2 (55)
sub-clause ['sʌbklɔːz] Nebensatz I
sub-heading ['sʌbˌhedɪŋ] Zwischenüberschrift; Kapitelüberschrift III 5 (124)
subject ['sʌbdʒɪkt] Schulfach I
subtitle ['sʌbtaɪtl] Untertitel I
°**suburb** ['sʌbɜːb] Vorort
°**suburban** [sə'bɜːbən] Vorort-, Vorstadt-; vorstädtisch
subway ['sʌbweɪ] *(AE)* U-Bahn II
°**subway car** *(AE)* U-Bahn-Wagen
successful [sək'sesfl] erfolgreich II
such a … [sʌtʃ] so ein/e …; solch ein/e … III 2 (47)
suck [sʌk]: **That sucks!** *(infml)* Das ist echt übel! III 5 (113) °**suck up** aufsaugen
°**sudden** ['sʌdn] plötzliche(r, s)
suddenly ['sʌdnli] plötzlich, auf einmal I
°**sugar** ['ʃʊgə] Zucker
suggest sth. (to sb.) [sə'dʒest] (jm.) etwas vorschlagen III 3 (66)
suggestion [sə'dʒestʃən] Vorschlag III 4 (93)
°**suitable** ['suːtəbl] passend, geeignet
sum sth. up [ˌsʌm‿'ʌp] etwas zusammenfassen III 1 (17)
summer ['sʌmə] Sommer I
summit ['sʌmɪt] Gipfel III 2 (45)
sun [sʌn] Sonne I
Sunday ['sʌndeɪ, 'sʌndi] Sonntag I
sung [sʌŋ] *siehe* **sing**
sunglasses *(pl)* ['sʌnglɑːsɪz] (eine) Sonnenbrille II
sunny ['sʌni] sonnig II
supermarket ['suːpəmɑːkɪt] Supermarkt I
°**supply (with)** [sə'plaɪ] versorgen (mit)
°**support** [sə'pɔːt]:
1. unterstützen
2. Unterstützung
°**supporter** [sə'pɔːtə] Befürworter/in; Unterstützer/in
°**Supreme Court** [suˌpriːm kɔːt] Oberster Gerichtshof
sure [ʃʊə, ʃɔː] sicher I **make sure that …** sich vergewissern, dass …; darauf achten, dass …; dafür sorgen, dass … II
surf [sɜːf] surfen II
surface ['sɜːfɪs] Oberfläche III 4 (88)
surfing ['sɜːfɪŋ] Wellenreiten, Surfen II
surprise [sə'praɪz]:
1. Überraschung I
°2. überraschen
surprised [sə'praɪzd] überrascht I

°**surprising** [sə'praɪzɪŋ] überraschend
survey ['sɜːveɪ] Umfrage, Studie III 5 (114)
survive [sə'vaɪv] überleben III 3 (70)
swam [swæm] *siehe* **swim**
swamp [swɒmp] Sumpf, Marschland III 5 (110)
°**swap** [swɒp] tauschen
sweet [swiːt] süß II
sweets *(pl)* [swiːts] Süßigkeiten II
swim [swɪm], **swam, swum** schwimmen I
swimmer ['swɪmə] Schwimmer/in I
swng pool ['swɪmɪŋ puːl] Schwimmbad, Schwimmbecken I
switch [swɪtʃ] Schalter III 4 (102)
sword [sɔːd] Schwert I
swum [swʌm] *siehe* **swim**
syllable ['sɪləbl] Silbe II °**stressed syllable** betonte Silbe
symbol ['sɪmbl] Symbol I

T

table ['teɪbl]:
1. Tisch I
2. Tabelle I
table tennis Tischtennis II
tablet ['tæblət] *(bes. BE)* Tablette II
°**tag** [tæg] Fangen *(Spiel)*
take [teɪk], **took, taken**:
1. nehmen, mitnehmen; (weg-, hin-) bringen I
2. *(Zeit)* brauchen; dauern II
take a risk ein Risiko eingehen III 4 (100)
take a seat Platz nehmen III 2 (55) **take a shower** (sich) duschen II **take a walk** *(bes. AE)* spazieren gehen, einen Spaziergang machen III 4 (98) **take place** stattfinden; spielen, sich abspielen *(Geschichte, Handlung)* I **take notes** (sich) Notizen machen *(beim Lesen oder Zuhören)* II
take part in sth. an etwas teilnehmen II
take photos fotografieren I **take sth. off** etwas ausziehen *(Kleidung)*; etwas absetzen *(Hut, Helm)* II **take sth. out** etwas herausnehmen II °**take the chance to do sth.** die Gelegenheit nutzen, etwas zu tun °**take turns** sich abwechseln
takeaway ['teɪkəweɪ]:
1. *Restaurant/Imbissgeschäft, das auch Essen zum Mitnehmen verkauft* II
2. *Essen zum Mitnehmen* II
taken ['teɪkn] *siehe* **take**
takeout ['teɪkaʊt] *(AE)* Essen zum Mitnehmen III 4 (94)
talent ['tælənt] Talent, Begabung II
talented ['tæləntɪd] begabt, talentiert II
talk [tɔːk]:
1. Vortrag, Referat, Rede I **give a talk (about)** einen Vortrag / eine Rede halten (über) I
2. talk (to) reden (mit), sich unterhalten (mit) I
tall [tɔːl] groß *(Person)*; hoch *(Gebäude, Baum)* II
tap [tæp]:
1. tippen, *(vorsichtig)* klopfen II °**she taps her foot** sie wippt mit dem Fuß
2. (leichtes) Klopfen III 1 (20)
task [tɑːsk] Aufgabe I
taste [teɪst] schmecken I **taste sth.** etwas kosten *(probieren)* II
tasty ['teɪsti] lecker II
°**tattoo** [tə'tuː] Tätowierung
taught [tɔːt] *siehe* **teach**
tea [tiː] Tee I; *(auch:) leichte Nachmittags- oder Abendmahlzeit* II
teach [tiːtʃ], **taught, taught** unterrichten, lehren III 4 (106) **teach sb. to do sth.** jm. beibringen/jn. lehren, etwas zu tun III 4 (106)
teacher ['tiːtʃə] Lehrer/in I
team [tiːm] Team, Mannschaft I
tear [tɪə] Träne II
tear sth. down [ˌteə 'daʊn], **tore, torn** etwas abreißen III 4 (98)
°**tease sb.** [tiːz] sich über jn. lustig machen
teaspoon ['tiːspuːn] Teelöffel II
°**technique** [tek'niːk] Technik, Methode
°**technology** [tek'nɒlədʒi] Technologie
teen [tiːn] Teenager/in II
teeth [tiːθ] *plural of* **tooth**
telephone ['telɪfəʊn] Telefon I **telephone box** Telefonzelle III 1 (15)
tell [tel], **told, told**:
tell sb. about sth. jm. von etwas erzählen; jm. über etwas berichten I **tell sb. the way (to …)** jm. den Weg (nach …) beschreiben II **tell sb. (not) to do sth.**
jn. auffordern, etwas (nicht) zu tun; jm. sagen, dass er/sie etwas (nicht) tun soll III 2 (41)
temperature ['temprətʃə] Temperatur, Fieber II **have a temperature** Fieber haben II
°**temple** ['templ] Tempel
ten [ten] zehn I
tennis ['tenɪs] Tennis I
tense [tens] (grammatische) Zeit, Tempus
III 1 (21)
tent [tent] Zelt II
term [tɜːm] Trimester II
terrible ['terəbl] schrecklich, furchtbar II
terrorist ['terərɪst] terroristische(r, s); Terrorist/in III 4 (89)
test [test]:
1. testen, prüfen III 2 (40)
2. Test I
text [tekst]:
1. Text I
2. SMS II
3. text sb. jm. eine SMS schicken I
text message ['tekst mesɪdʒ] *(kurz auch:* **text***)* SMS II
than [ðæn], [ðən]: **bigger than** größer als II
Thank you. [θæŋk] Danke. I **Thanks.** Danke. I **thanks to Maya** dank Maya II
°**Thanksgiving** [θæŋks'gɪvɪŋ] Erntedankfest *(amerikanischer Feiertag am 4. Donnerstag im November)*
that [ðæt, ðət]:
1. it shows that … es zeigt, dass … I **Now that …** Jetzt, wo … / Nun, da … III 3 (76)
2. that group die Gruppe (dort), jene Gruppe I **that way** dort entlang; in die Richtung II
3. that's das ist I **that's why** deshalb, darum I **after that** danach I
4. der/die/das; die *(Relativpronomen)* II
the [ðə] der, die, das; die I
theatre ['θɪətə] Theater I
their [ðeə] ihr I **their first day** ihr erster Tag I
theirs [ðeəz] ihrer, ihre, ihrs II
them [ðem, ðəm] sie; ihnen I
theme [θiːm] Thema II
themselves [ðəm'selvz] sich III 3 (71/72); selbst, selber III 4 (91)
then [ðen] dann I **just then** genau in dem Moment; gerade dann II
there [ðeə] da, dort; dahin, dorthin I **over there** da drüben, dort drüben II **There are …** Es sind … / Es gibt … I **There's …** Es ist/gibt … I
thermometer [θə'mɒmɪtə] Thermometer
II
these [ðiːz] diese (hier) I
they [ðeɪ] sie *(Plural)* I **they're (= they are)** sie sind … I
thick [θɪk] dick III 4 (101)
thief [θiːf], *pl* **thieves** [θiːvz] Dieb/in I
thing [θɪŋ] Sache, Ding, Gegenstand I
think [θɪŋk], **thought, thought** denken, glauben I **think (about)** nachdenken (über) I **think of sth.** sich etwas ausdenken; an etwas denken I
third [θɜːd] dritte(r, s) I **Third, …** Drittens, … I
thirsty ['θɜːsti]: **be thirsty** durstig sein, Durst haben I
this [ðɪs]:
1. This is … Dies ist … / Das ist … I
2. this place/break/subject dieser Ort / diese Pause / dieses Fach I **this afternoon/evening/…** heute Nachmittag/Abend/… II **this one** diese(r, s) II
this time dieses Mal II **this year's musical** das diesjährige Musical II
those [ðəʊz] die … dort; jene … I
thought [θɔːt]:
1. *siehe* **think**
2. Gedanke III 3 (77)

thousand ['θaʊznd] Tausend, tausend II
three [θriː] drei I
threw [θruː] *siehe* **throw**
throat [θrəʊt] Hals, Kehle II **have a sore throat** Halsschmerzen haben II
through [θruː]:
1. durch I
°2. *(AE)* bis
throw [θrəʊ], **threw, thrown** werfen I
thrown [θrəʊn] *siehe* **throw**
thunder ['θʌndə] Donner II
Thursday ['θɜːzdeɪ, 'θɜːzdi] Donnerstag I
°**tick** [tɪk] ankreuzen, abhaken
ticket ['tɪkɪt]:
1. Eintrittskarte I
2. Fahrkarte I
ticket office Fahrkartenschalter; Kasse *(für den Verkauf v. Eintrittskarten)* III 1 (15)
°**tickle** ['tɪkl] kitzeln
°**tiger** ['taɪgə] Tiger
tighten ['taɪtn] spannen, festziehen, nachziehen III 3 (76)
till [tɪl]: **till 1 o'clock** bis 1 Uhr I **not till three** erst um drei, nicht vor drei II
°**tiller** ['tɪlə] Ruder, Ruderpinne
time [taɪm]:
1. Zeit; Uhrzeit I **all the time** die ganze Zeit II **at one time** zur selben Zeit, gleichzeitig III 1 (15) **be in time for the bus** den Bus erreichen; rechtzeitig zum Bus kommen III 5 (121) **feeding time** Fütterungszeit I **free time** Freizeit, freie Zeit I **free-time activities** Freizeitaktivitäten I **of all time** aller Zeiten II **What time is it?** Wie spät ist es? I °**time traveller** Zeitreisende(r)
2. Mal I **for the first time** zum ersten Mal III 1 (14)
timeline ['taɪmlaɪn] Zeitstrahl, Zeitleiste III 4 (109)
timer ['taɪmə] Zeitmesser III 4 (93)
timetable ['taɪmteɪbl]:
1. Stundenplan I
2. Fahrplan III 1 (12)
tin [tɪn] Dose II
tiny ['taɪni] winzig III 5 (123)
tip [tɪp] Tipp I
tired ['taɪəd] müde I
title ['taɪtl] Titel, Überschrift I
to [tu, tə]:
1. zu, nach I **from ... to ...** von ... bis ... I **to the front** nach vorn II
2. **Nice to meet you.** Freut mich, dich/euch/Sie kennenzulernen. I
3. um zu II °**to be continued** Fortsetzung folgt.
4. **quarter to eleven** Viertel vor elf (10.45 / 22.45) I
toast [təʊst] Toast(brot) III 2 (47)
today [tə'deɪ] heute I
toe [təʊ] Zeh II
°**toffee apple** ['tɒfi‿æpl] kandierter Apfel

together [tə'geðə] zusammen I
toilet ['tɔɪlət] Toilette I
told [təʊld] *siehe* **tell**
tomato [tə'mɑːtəʊ], *pl* **tomatoes** Tomate I
tomorrow [tə'mɒrəʊ] morgen II
tomorrow morning morgen früh, morgen Vormittag II
tongue [tʌŋ] Zunge II
tongue-twister ['tʌŋˌtwɪstə] Zungenbrecher II
tonight [tə'naɪt] heute Nacht, heute Abend III 2 (36)
too [tuː]:
1. auch I
2. **too late/cold/big/...** zu spät/kalt/groß/... I
took [tʊk] *siehe* **take**
°**tool** [tuːl] Werkzeug
tooth [tuːθ], *pl* **teeth** [tiːθ] Zahn II
toothache ['tuːθeɪk]: **have a toothache**
Zahnschmerzen haben II
top [tɒp]:
1. Spitze, oberes Ende I
2. Spitzen- I
3. Top, Oberteil I
on top of each other übereinander, aufeinander III 1 (15)
topic ['tɒpɪk] Thema, Themengebiet II
topic sentence Satz, der in das Thema eines Absatzes einführt III 2 (45)
°**tor** [tɔː] *kahler Hügel in Südwestengland*
torch [tɔːtʃ]:
1. Taschenlampe II
2. Fackel II
tore [tɔː] *siehe* **tear**
torn [tɔːn] *siehe* **tear**
tortoise ['tɔːtəs] (Land-)Schildkröte III 1 (15)
°**toss** [tɒs]: **toss a pancake** einen Pfannkuchen hochwerfen und wenden
total ['təʊtl]: **a total of ...** eine Gesamtsumme von ...; insgesamt III 2 (45)
totally ['təʊtəli] völlig, total III 5 (113)
touch [tʌtʃ] berühren, anfassen I **get in touch (with sb.)** (mit jm.) Kontakt aufnehmen; sich (mit jm.) in Verbindung setzen II **stay in touch (with sb.)** (mit jm.) Kontakt halten; (mit jm.) in Verbindung bleiben II
tour (of) ['tʊər‿əv] Rundgang, Rundfahrt, Reise (durch) I
°**tourism** ['tʊərɪzəm] Tourismus
tourist ['tʊərɪst] Tourist/in I
°**tournament** ['tʊənəmənt] Turnier
towards the station/Mr Bell [tə'wɔːdz] auf den Bahnhof/auf Mr Bell zu, in Richtung Bahnhof/Mr Bell III 1 (20)
tower ['taʊə] Turm I
town [taʊn] Stadt I °**town crier** Stadtausrufer/in
toy [tɔɪ] Spielzeug I
track [træk]:
1. (Bahn-)Gleis III 4 (98)
°2. Piste, Laufbahn *(Sport)*
°**track and field** *(AE)* Leichtathletik
tractor ['træktə] Traktor II
trade [treɪd] Handel III 1 (32)
°**trader** ['treɪdə] Händler/in
tradition [trə'dɪʃn] Tradition I
traditional [trə'dɪʃənl] traditionell II
°**traditionally** traditionellerweise
traffic ['træfɪk] Verkehr III 3 (75)
traffic light ['træfɪk laɪt] *(oft auch:* **traffic lights** *(pl))* (Verkehrs-) Ampel III 3 (75)
°**tragic** ['trædʒɪk] tragisch
trail [treɪl]:
1. Weg, Pfad III 3 (71)
°2. ziehen
train [treɪn]:
1. Zug I
2. trainieren II
trainer ['treɪnə] Turnschuh I
training ['treɪnɪŋ] Training(sstunde) I
°**trampoline** ['træmpəliːn] Trampolin
trance [trɑːns] Trance III 4 (91)
translate [træns'leɪt] übersetzen II
translation [træns'leɪʃn] Übersetzung III 2 (38)
transparency [træns'pærənsi] Folie III 4 (99)
transport ['trænspɔːt] Verkehrsmittel; Transport(wesen) III 4 (105)
travel ['trævl] reisen I **travel sickness**
Reisekrankheit II
traveller ['trævələ] Reisende(r) I
°**time traveller** Zeitreisende(r)
°**treason** ['triːzn] (Hoch-)Verrat
tree [triː] Baum I
°**triangle** ['traɪæŋgl] Dreieck
triangular [traɪ'æŋgjələ] dreieckig III 5 (123)
tribe [traɪb] (Volks-)Stamm II
trick [trɪk] Kunststück, Trick II
°**trigger** ['trɪgə] auslösen
trip [trɪp] Ausflug; Reise I **go on a boat trip** einen Bootsausflug machen I
trophy ['trəʊfi] Pokal; Trophäe I
tropical ['trɒpɪkl] tropisch, Tropen- III 5 (112)
trouble ['trʌbl]: **be in trouble** in Schwierigkeiten sein; Ärger kriegen I **get into trouble** in Schwierigkeiten geraten, Ärger kriegen III 2 (46)
trousers *(pl)* ['traʊzəz] Hose II
truck [trʌk] Lastwagen, LKW III 3 (77)
true [truː] wahr I
trumpet ['trʌmpɪt] Trompete I
°**trunk** [trʌŋk] Rüssel
truth [truːθ] Wahrheit II
try [traɪ]:
1. (aus)probieren; versuchen I
2. Versuch III 1 (20)
try hard sich anstrengen; sich (große) Mühe geben III 3 (70) **try sth. on** etwas anprobieren III 5 (122)
T-shirt ['tiːʃɜːt] T-Shirt I

Tube [tjuːb]: **the Tube** *(no pl)* die U-Bahn *(in London)* III 1 (12)
Tuesday ['tjuːzdeɪ, 'tjuːzdi] Dienstag I **on Tuesday** am Dienstag I
tulip ['tjuːlɪp] Tulpe II
tune [tjuːn]:
1. Melodie III 5 (118)
2. stimmen *(Instrument)* III 5 (118)
tunnel ['tʌnl] Tunnel II
turkey ['tɜːki] Pute, Truthahn I
turn [tɜːn]:
1. (It's) my turn. Ich bin dran / an der Reihe. I °**take turns** sich abwechseln *(etwas zu tun)* °**Whose turn is it?** Wer ist dran / Wer ist an der Reihe?
2. turn red/brown/cold/… rot/braun/kalt/… werden III 3 (75)
3. turn to sb. sich jm. zuwenden; sich an jn. wenden II **turn (a)round** sich umdrehen I; wenden, umdrehen I **turn left/right** (nach) links/rechts abbiegen II
4. turn sth. up/down etwas lauter/leiser stellen III 1 (20) **turn sth. on** etwas einschalten I **turn sth. off** etwas ausschalten II
TV [,tiː'viː] Fernsehen, Fernsehgerät I **on TV** im Fernsehen III 1 (20)
twelve [twelv] zwölf I
twice [twaɪs] zweimal II
°**twin** [twɪn] Zwillings-
twins *(pl)* [twɪnz] Zwillinge I
two [tuː] zwei I °**two by two** zu zweit; in Zweiergruppen
type (of) [taɪp] Typ, Art, Sorte (von) III 5 (114)
typical (of) ['tɪpɪkl] typisch (für) III 3 (66)

U

°**ugly** ['ʌgli] hässlich
umbrella [ʌm'brelə] Schirm, Regenschirm I
°**unarmed** [,ʌn'ɑːmd] unbewaffnet
uncle ['ʌŋkl] Onkel I
uncomfortable [ʌn'kʌmftəbl] unbequem II
under ['ʌndə] unter I
underground:
1. [,ʌndə'graʊnd] unterirdisch, unter der Erde III 2 (38)
2. ['ʌndəgraʊnd] *(BE)* U-Bahn II
underline [,ʌndə'laɪn] unterstreichen II °**underlined** unterstrichen
understand [,ʌndə'stænd], **understood, understood** verstehen I
understood [,ʌndə'stʊd] *siehe* **understand**
°**underweight** [,ʌndə'weɪt] untergewichtig
unfair [ʌn'feə] unfair III 3 (71)
unfriendly [ʌn'frendli] unfreundlich I
unhappy [ʌn'hæpi] unglücklich I
uniform ['juːnɪfɔːm] Uniform I
°**unify** ['juːnɪfaɪ] (ver)einigen, (ver)einen
°**uninvited** [,ʌnɪn'vaɪtɪd] un(ein)geladen, ungebeten
°**union** ['juːniən] Vereinigung, Union
unit ['juːnɪt] Kapitel, Lektion I
°**unite** [ju'naɪt] vereinigen
united [ju'naɪtɪd] vereinigt I **the United Kingdom (UK)** [ju,naɪtɪd 'kɪŋdəm] das Vereinigte Königreich I **the United States (US)** die Vereinigten Staaten *(von Amerika)* III 3 (62)
university [,juːnɪ'vɜːsəti] Universität II
unpack [,ʌn'pæk] auspacken III 3 (71)
until [ən'tɪl] bis II **not until ten** erst um zehn, nicht vor zehn III 3 (76)
°**untouched** [ʌn'tʌtʃt] unberührt, unverändert
unusual [ʌn'juːʒuəl] ungewöhnlich III 4 (98)
up [ʌp] hinauf, herauf; (nach) oben I **up and down** auf und ab; rauf und runter I **up here** hier oben; nach hier oben II **up to** bis (zu) II **What's up?** Was gibt's? / Was ist los? III 3 (76)
update sth. [,ʌp'deɪt] etwas aktualisieren, auf den neuesten Stand bringen III 5 (114)
uphill [,ʌp'hɪl] bergauf III 2 (45)
upload sth. [,ʌp'ləʊd] etwas hochladen III 5 (114)
°**upper** ['ʌpə] obere(r, s)
°**upset** [,ʌp'set] aufgebracht, gekränkt
upstairs [,ʌp'steəz] oben; nach oben *(im Haus)* I
upstream [,ʌp'striːm] flussaufwärts III 2 (45)
°**urban** ['ɜːbən] städtisch, Stadt-
us [ʌs, əs] uns I
use [juːz] benutzen, verwenden I
used to ['juːst tə]: **the trail I used to take** der Weg, den ich (früher immer) genommen habe III 3 (71)
°**useful** ['juːsfl] nützlich
usual ['juːʒuəl] gewöhnlich, üblich III 4 (98)
usually ['juːʒuəli] meistens, normalerweise, gewöhnlich I

V

vacation [və'keɪʃn] *(AE)* Urlaub II
valley ['væli] Tal II
°**vampire** ['væmpaɪə] Vampir/in
van [væn] Transporter, Lieferwagen III 3 (75)
vary ['veəri] unterschiedlich sein, verschieden sein III 5 (123)
°**vase** [vɑːz] Vase
vegetables *(pl)* ['vedʒtəblz] Gemüse I
vegetarian [,vedʒə'teəriən] Vegetarier/in; vegetarisch II
verb [vɜːb] Verb III 1 (12)
verse [vɜːs] Vers, Strophe II
very ['veri] sehr I
vet [vet] Tierarzt/-ärztin III 3 (77)
°**veteran** ['vetərən] Veteran/in
vibration [vaɪ'breɪʃn] Vibration III 5 (127)
video ['vɪdiəʊ] Video I
video camera ['vɪdiəʊ ,kæmərə] Videokamera I
view [vjuː]:
1. Aussicht, Blick (auf) I
2. Ansicht, Meinung III 3 (61)
in my view meiner Meinung nach III 3 (61)
vigorous ['vɪgərəs] energisch, kräftig III 4 (102)
village ['vɪlɪdʒ] Dorf I
°**vinegar** ['vɪnɪgə] Essig
°**virgin** ['vɜːdʒɪn]: **the Virgin Queen** die jungfräuliche Königin
visa ['viːzə] Visum III 3 (62)
visit ['vɪzɪt]:
1. besuchen I
2. Besuch I
visitor ['vɪzɪtə] Besucher/in, Gast I
vocabulary [və'kæbjələri] Vokabelverzeichnis, Wörterverzeichnis I
voice [vɔɪs] Stimme I **in a soft voice** sanft; mit leiser Stimme II
°**volcano** [vɒl'keɪnəʊ] Vulkan
°**volunteer** [,vɒlən'tɪə]:
1. sich freiwillig melden; freiwillig/ehrenamtlich arbeiten *(unbezahlt)*:
2. Freiwillige(r), Ehrenamtliche(r)
vowel ['vaʊəl] Vokal, Selbstlaut I

W

°**wage a war** [weɪdʒ] Krieg führen
waist [weɪst] Taille II
wait (for) [weɪt] warten (auf) I **wait a minute** Warte einen Moment. / Moment mal. I **I can't wait to see …** Ich kann es kaum erwarten, … zu sehen. II
wake up [,weɪk‿'ʌp], **woke up, woken up**:
1. aufwachen I
2. wake sb. up jn. (auf)wecken II
walk [wɔːk]:
1. Spaziergang I **go for a walk** spazieren gehen, einen Spaziergang machen I
take a walk *(bes. AE)* spazieren gehen, einen Spaziergang machen III 4 (98)
2. (zu Fuß) gehen I **walk the dog** mit dem Hund rausgehen, den Hund ausführen III 3 (75) °**walk around** herumlaufen
wall [wɔːl] Mauer; Wand II
wander ['wɒndə] herumlaufen; herumirren II
want [wɒnt]: **want sth.** etwas (haben) wollen I **want to do sth.** etwas tun wollen I **I want you to …** Ich möchte, dass du … II
°**war** [wɔː] Krieg
warm [wɔːm] warm I
warning ['wɔːnɪŋ] Warnung III 2 (42)

was [wɒz, wəz] *siehe* **be**
wash [wɒʃ] waschen; wischen III 2 (48)
wash the dishes *(pl)* das Geschirr abwaschen, spülen II °**washed in light** hell erleuchtet
°**wasp** [wɒsp] Wespe
watch [wɒtʃ]:
1. Armbanduhr I
2. sich etwas anschauen; beobachten I **watch TV** fernsehen I **Watch out!** Pass auf! / Vorsicht! I
°**watchdog** ['wɒtʃdɒg] Wächter/in, Aufpasser/in
watcher ['wɒtʃə] Beobachter/in I
water ['wɔːtə] Wasser I
waterfall ['wɔːtəfɔːl] Wasserfall II
°**waterproofs** *(pl)* ['wɔːtəpruːfs] wasserdichte Kleidung
°**watery** ['wɔːtəri] wässrig
wave [weɪv]:
1. Welle II
2. **wave (at sb.)** (jm. zu)winken III 5 (126)
way [weɪ]:
1. Weg I **ask sb. the way** jn. nach dem Weg fragen II **on the way to ...** auf dem Weg zu/nach ... I **tell sb. the way (to ...)** jm. den Weg (nach ...) beschreiben II **that way** dort entlang; in die Richtung II
2. Art, Weise III 3 (67) **in some/many ways** in mancher/vielerlei Hinsicht III 3 (67) **in this way** auf diese Weise III 3 (67)
3. **by the way** übrigens III 1 (10) **No way!** Auf keinen Fall! / Kommt nicht in Frage! III 1 (20)
4. **he's way too good/clever/...** *(bes. AE)* er ist viel zu gut/clever/... III 4 (88)
we [wiː] wir I
wear [weə], **wore, worn** tragen *(Kleidung)* I
weather ['weðə] Wetter II
website ['websaɪt] Website I
wedding ['wedɪŋ] Hochzeit, Trauung III 1 (32)
Wednesday ['wenzdeɪ, 'wenzdi] Mittwoch I
week [wiːk] Woche I
weekend [ˌwiːk'end] Wochenende I **at the weekend** am Wochenende I
weekly ['wiːkli] wöchentlich III 5 (114)
weigh [weɪ] wiegen I
weird [wɪəd] seltsam, komisch III 3 (70)
weirdo ['wɪədəʊ] *(infml)* Spinner/in III 4 (92)
welcome ['welkəm]:
1. **Welcome to Plymouth.** Willkommen in Plymouth. I
2. **You're welcome.** Bitte, gern geschehen. / Nichts zu danken. II
°3. **welcome sb. (to)** jn. begrüßen (in), jn. willkommen heißen (in)
Welsh [welʃ] Walisisch; walisisch I
well [wel]:
1. gut II **go well** gut laufen, gut gehen II **well known** [ˌwel 'nəʊn], ['wel nəʊn] bekannt II
2. *(gesundheitlich)* gesund II **I don't feel well.** Ich fühle mich nicht gut. / Mir geht's nicht gut. II
3. **as well** auch, ebenso III 3 (60)
Well, ... [wel] Nun, ... / Also, ... / Na ja, ... I
°**wellies** *(pl)* ['weliz] *(infml)* Gummistiefel
went [went] *siehe* **go**
were [wɜː, wə] *siehe* **be**
west [west] Westen; nach Westen; westlich III 1 (11)
western ['westən] westlich, West- III 1 (10)
wet [wet] nass I
whale [weɪl] Wal I
what? [wɒt] was? I **What about you?** Und du/ihr? / Und was ist mit dir/euch? I
What about ...? Wie wäre es mit ...? II
What colour ...? Welche Farbe ...? I
What is the story about? Wovon handelt die Geschichte? Worum geht es in der Geschichte? I **What page are we on?** Auf welcher Seite sind wir? I **What programmes ...?** Welche Programme ...? / Welche Art von Programmen ...? I **What size tea would you like?** Wie groß soll der/dein Tee sein? II **What time is it?** Wie spät ist es? I **What was it like?** Wie war es? II **What would you like?** Was hättest du gern? / Was möchtest du? I **What would you like to eat?** Was möchtest du essen? I **What's your name?** Wie heißt du? / Wie heißt ihr? I
What's for lunch? Was gibt es zum Mittagessen? I **What's for homework?** Was haben wir als Hausaufgabe auf? I **What's she like?** Wie ist sie (so)? I **What's up?** Was gibt's? / Was ist los? III 3 (76)
wver [ˌwɒt'evə] was (auch) immer III 4 (101)
wheel [wiːl]:
1. Rad II **big wheel** Riesenrad I
2. *(kurz für:* **steering wheel***)* Lenkrad II
°**wheelchair** ['wiːltʃeə] Rollstuhl
when [wen]:
1. wenn I
2. als I
3. wann I **When's your birthday?** Wann hast du Geburtstag? I
where? [weə] wo? / wohin? I **Where are you from?** Woher kommst du? I
°**wherever** [ˌweər'evə] wo (auch) immer
whether ['weðə] ob III 4 (103)
which [wɪtʃ]:
1. *(Fragewort)* welche(r, s) I **Which one?** Welche(r, s)? II
2. *(Relativpronomen)* der/die/das; die II
while [waɪl]:
1. während II
2. **a while** eine Weile, einige Zeit III 1 (20)
for a while eine Weile, eine Zeit lang III 1 (20)
whisper ['wɪspə] flüstern II
whistle ['wɪsl]:
1. pfeifen II
2. (Triller-)Pfeife III 1 (24)
white [waɪt] weiß I
whitewater ['waɪtwɔːtə] Wildwasser III 2 (55) **whitewater rafting** Wildwasserfahren *(im Schlauchboot)* III 2 (55)
who [huː]:
1. **Who likes Abby?** Wer mag Abby? I **Who does Maya like?** Wen mag Maya? II **Who did Maya help?** Wem hat Maya geholfen? II
2. der/die/das; die *(Relativpronomen)* II
°**whoever** [huː'evə] wer (auch) immer
whole [həʊl] ganze(r, s), gesamte(r, s) II
whose [huːz]:
1. *(Fragewort)* wessen I
2. *(Relativpronomen)* **cities whose names ...** Städte, deren Namen ... II
why? [waɪ] warum? I **that's why** deshalb, darum I
°**wicked** ['wɪkɪd] böse, schlecht
wide [waɪd] breit II °**far and wide** weit und breit
wife [waɪf], *pl* **wives** [waɪvz] Ehefrau III 1 (32)
°**wildlife** ['waɪldlaɪf] Tier- und Pflanzenwelt
will [wɪl]: **we'll miss the girls (= we will miss the girls)** wir werden die Mädchen verpassen II
wild [waɪld] wild I
°**wildlife** ['waɪldlaɪf] Tierwelt, frei lebende Tiere
win [wɪn], **won, won** gewinnen I
wind [wɪnd] Wind II
window ['wɪndəʊ] Fenster I
windy ['wɪndi] windig II
wing [wɪŋ] Flügel III 1 (24)
winner ['wɪnə] Gewinner/in, Sieger/in I
winter ['wɪntə] Winter I
wise [waɪz] weise II
wish [wɪʃ]:
1. wünschen II **I wish it was warmer.** Ich wünschte, es wäre wärmer. II
2. Wunsch I **make a wish** sich etwas wünschen I
°**witch** [wɪtʃ] Hexe
with [wɪð]:
1. mit I
2. bei I
without [wɪ'ðaʊt] ohne I
wives [waɪvz] *plural of* **wife**
°**wizard** ['wɪzəd] Zauberer
woke [wəʊk] *siehe* **wake**

woken ['wəʊkn] *siehe* **wake**
woman ['wʊmən], *pl* **women** ['wɪmɪn] Frau I
won [wʌn] *siehe* **win**
wonder ['wʌndə] sich fragen, gern wissen wollen III 2 (40)
wonderful ['wʌndəfəl] wunderbar II
wood [wʊd] Holz II
wooden ['wʊdn] hölzern; Holz- III 2 (47)
°**woodland** ['wʊdlənd] Wald(gelände)
°**woollen hat** (*AE:* **woolen)** [ˌwʊlən 'hæt] Wollmütze, Strickmütze
word [wɜːd] Wort I °**group word** Obergriff **word order** Wortstellung I
wordbank ['wɜːdˌbæŋk] „Wortspeicher" I
wore [wɔː] *siehe* **wear**
work [wɜːk]
1. arbeiten I
2. funktionieren III 1 (19)
3. Arbeit I
work of art [ˌwɜːk‿əv‿'ɑːt] Kunstwerk III 4 (98)
workbook ['wɜːkbʊk] Arbeitsheft I
worker ['wɜːkə] Arbeiter/in II
°**workplace** ['wɜːkpleɪs] Arbeitsplatz
worksheet ['wɜːkʃiːt] Arbeitsblatt II
workshop ['wɜːkʃɒp]:
1. Werkstatt III 2 (36)
2. Workshop, Lehrgang II
°**work site** ['wɜːk saɪt] Arbeitsort, Einsatzort
world [wɜːld] Welt I **in the world** auf der Welt I
worn [wɔːn] *siehe* **wear**
worried ['wʌrid] besorgt, beunruhigt I
worry (about) ['wʌri] sich Sorgen machen (wegen, um) II **No worries.** *(infml)* Kein Problem! / Gern geschehen! III 2 (44)
worse [wɜːs] schlechter II
°**worship sb.** ['wɜːʃɪp] jn. anbeten
worst [wɜːst]: **the worst ...** der/die/das schlechteste ...; die schlechtesten ... II
worth [wɜːθ] wert III 1 (16)
would [wʊd]: **it would be ...** es wäre ... II **I'd (= I would) like ...** Ich möchte ... I **What would you like?** Was hättest du gern? / Was möchtest du? I **What would you like to eat?** Was möchtest du essen? I **You would have liked him.** Du hättest ihn gemocht. III 5 (118)
°**wrap** [ræp] wickeln
°**wrestling** ['reslɪŋ] Ringen
write [raɪt], **wrote, written** schreiben I **write sth. down** etwas aufschreiben II
writer ['raɪtə] Schreiber/in; Schriftsteller/in III 3 (69)
°**writing** ['raɪtɪŋ] Inschrift
written ['rɪtn] *siehe* **write**
wrong [rɒŋ]:
1. falsch, verkehrt I **What's wrong with Justin/you?** Was fehlt Justin/dir? / Was ist los mit Justin/dir? II **go wrong** schiefgehen III 5 (121)
2. **sb. is wrong** jemand irrt sich; jemand hat Unrecht I
wrote [rəʊt] *siehe* **write**

Y

yacht [jɒt] Jacht III 4 (88)
year [jɪə]:
1. Jahr I
2. Jahrgang(sstufe) I
this year's musical das diesjährige Musical II
yearly ['jɪəli] jährlich III 5 (114)
yell [jel] schreien III 4 (100)
yellow ['jeləʊ] gelb I
yes [jes] ja I
yesterday ['jestədeɪ, 'jestədi] gestern I
yet [jet]:
1. **Have you ... yet?** Hast du schon ...? II
2. **not ... yet** noch nicht I
yoga ['jəʊgə] Yoga I
yoghurt ['jɒgət] Joghurt I
you [juː]
1. du; Sie; ihr I
2. dir; dich; euch; Ihnen I
3. man III 1 (24)
young [jʌŋ] jung I
your [jɔː, jə] dein/e; euer/eure; Ihr/Ihre I
yours [jɔːz] deiner, deine, deins; eurer, eure, eures II
yourself [jɔː'self] dich, dir; sich *(bei „Sie")* III 3 (71/72); selbst, selber III 4 (91)
about yourself über dich selbst I
Enjoy yourself! Viel Spaß! / Amüsiere dich gut! III 3 (71/72) **Help yourself!** Greif zu! / Bedien dich! III 3 (71/72)
youth [juːθ] Jugend; Jugend- III 5 (125)
yourselves [jɔː'selvz] euch; sich *(bei „Sie")* III 3 (71/72); selbst, selber III 4 (91)
yummy *(infml)* ['jʌmi] lecker I

Z

zoo [zuː] Zoo I
°**zookeeper** ['zuːkiːpə] Zoowärter/in
°**Zulu** ['zuːluː] Zulu

Das **German – English Dictionary** enthält den **Lernwortschatz** von **Access Bayern**, Bände **5 – 7**.
Es kann dir eine erste Hilfe sein, wenn du vergessen hast, wie etwas auf Englisch heißt.

Wenn du wissen möchtest, wo das entsprechende englische Wort zum ersten Mal in **Access Bayern** vorkommt, dann kannst du im **English – German Dictionary** (224 – 252) nachschlagen.

Im **German – English Dictionary** werden folgende **Abkürzungen** verwendet:

sth. = something (etwas) sb. = somebody (jemand) jn. = jemanden jm. = jemandem
pl = *plural* (Mehrzahl) *infml* = *informal* (umgangssprachlich) *AE* = *American English* *BE* = *British English*

A

ab: auf und ab up and down [ˌʌp‿ən ˈdaʊn]
abbauen: etwas abbauen *(Bodenschätze)* mine sth. [maɪn]
abbiegen: (nach) links/rechts abbiegen turn left/right [tɜːn]
Abbild image [ˈɪmɪdʒ]
abdecken *(Thema; Fragen)* cover [ˈkʌvə]
Abend evening [ˈiːvnɪŋ] **am Abend** in the evening **heute Abend** tonight [təˈnaɪt] **zu Abend essen** have dinner [ˈdɪnə]
Abendbrot, Abendessen dinner [ˈdɪnə]
abends in the evening [ˈiːvnɪŋ]
Abenteuer adventure [ədˈventʃə]
aber but [bʌt], [bət]
abfahren leave [liːv]
Abfall rubbish [ˈrʌbɪʃ] *(bes. BE)*; garbage [ˈɡɑːbɪdʒ] *(AE)*
Abfalleimer litter bin [ˈlɪtə bɪn]
Abfertigungsschalter check-in desk [ˈtʃek‿ɪn ˌdesk]
Abflugschalter check-in desk [ˈtʃek‿ɪn ˌdesk]
abgeben: etwas abgeben *(einreichen)* hand sth. in
abhängen 1. *(rumhängen)* hang out [ˌhæŋ‿ˈaʊt] *(infml)*
2. **von etwas abhängen** depend on sth. [dɪˈpend]
abholen: jn. abholen pick sb. up [ˌpɪk‿ˈʌp]
Abkürzung abbreviation [əˌbriːviˈeɪʃn]
Abneigungen: Vorlieben und Abneigungen likes and dislikes *(pl)* [ˌlaɪks‿ən ˈdɪslaɪks]
abräumen clear [klɪə]
abreißen: etwas abreißen tear sth. down [ˌteə ˈdaʊn]
Abruf: auf Abruf *(nach Bedarf)* on demand [dɪˈmɑːnd]
Absatz 1. *(in einem Text)* paragraph [ˈpærəɡrɑːf]
2. *(Umsatz; Verkäufe)* sales *(pl)* [seɪlz]
Abschluss *(Ende)* ending
Abschnitt *(Teilstück)* section [ˈsekʃn]
abschreiben copy [ˈkɒpi]
absetzen: etwas absetzen *(Hut, Helm)* take sth. off [ˌteɪk‿ˈɒf]
abspielen *(CD usw.)* play [pleɪ] **sich abspielen** *(Geschichte, Handlung)* take place
abstürzen *(Flugzeug; Computer)* crash [kræʃ]
absuchen: etwas (nach etwas) absuchen scan sth. (for sth.) [skæn] **einen Text schnell nach bestimmten Wörtern/Informationen absuchen** scan a text
abwaschen: das Geschirr abwaschen wash the dishes *(pl)* [ˈdɪʃɪz]
Account *(Konto)* account [əˈkaʊnt]
acht eight [eɪt]
achten: darauf achten, dass … *(dafür sorgen, dass …)* make sure that …
Achterbahn roller coaster [ˈrəʊlə kəʊstə]
Acker field [fiːld]
addieren (zu) add (to) [æd]
adoptiert adopted [əˈdɒptɪd]
Adresse address [əˈdres]
Adverb adverb [ˈædvɜːb]
Affe monkey [ˈmʌŋki]
Aha! *(Verstehe.)* I see.
ähnlich: (etwas/jm.) ähnlich similar (to sth./sb.) [ˈsɪmələ]
Akku battery [ˈbætəri]
Aktivität activity [ækˈtɪvəti]
aktualisieren: etwas aktualisieren update sth. [ˌʌpˈdeɪt]
Akzent accent [ˈæksənt]
albern silly [ˈsɪli]
alle all [ɔːl]; *(jeder)* everyone [ˈevriwʌn], everybody [ˈevribɒdi] **aller Zeiten** of all time
Allee avenue [ˈævənjuː]
allein alone [əˈləʊn]; on my/your/their/… own [əʊn]
alleinstehend *(ledig)* single [ˈsɪŋɡl]
alles all [ɔːl]; everything [ˈevriθɪŋ] **alles in allem** all in all; altogether [ˌɔːltəˈɡeðə] **Alles Liebe, …** *(Briefschluss)* Love, … **vor allem** especially [ɪˈspeʃli]
allgemein *(generell)* generally [ˈdʒenrəli]
Alligator alligator [ˈælɪɡeɪtə]
Alltags- everyday [ˈevrideɪ]
als 1. *(zeitlich)* when [wen]; *(während)* as [æz], [əz] **als Erstes** first [fɜːst] **als Nächstes** next [nekst]
2. **als Kind** as a child [æz, əz]
3. **größer als** bigger than [ðæn], [ðən] **schöner als** more beautiful than
4. **als ob** as if; *(infml)* like **so tun, als ob** pretend [prɪˈtend]
5. **sowohl … als auch …** both … and … [bəʊθ]
also 1. *(deshalb, daher)* so [səʊ]
2. **Also, …** Well, … [wel]
alt old [əʊld] **Ich bin zwei Jahre alt.** I'm two years old. **Wie alt bist du?** How old are you?
Alter age [eɪdʒ]
am 1. *(in Ortsangaben)* at [æ], [ət] **am Meer** by the sea [baɪ]
2. *(in Zeitangaben)* **am Abend** in the evening **am Montag/Dienstag/…** on Monday/Tuesday/… **am Morgen** in the morning **am Nachmittag** in the afternoon **am Samstagmorgen** on Saturday afternoon **am Wochenende** at the weekend
Ameise ant [ænt]
amerikanischer Ureinwohner/amerikanische Ureinwohnerin Native American [ˌneɪtɪv‿əˈmerɪkən]
Ampel traffic light [ˈtræfɪk laɪt] *(oft auch: traffic lights (pl))*
amtlich, Amts- official [əˈfɪʃl]
amüsieren: sich amüsieren have fun [fʌn] **Amüsiere dich gut!** Enjoy yourself!
an 1. *(in Ortsangaben)* at [æ], [ət] **an britischen Schulen** at British schools
2. **an sein** *(Radio, Licht usw.: eingeschaltet sein)* be on
anbauen *(anpflanzen)* grow [ɡrəʊ]
anbieten offer [ˈɒfə]
Anblick sight [saɪt]
andauern *(im Gang sein)* go on
Andenken souvenir [ˌsuːvəˈnɪə]
andere(r, s) other [ˈʌðə] **ein anderer …/eine andere …/ein anderes …** another … [əˈnʌðə] **einer nach dem anderen** one by one
ändern; sich ändern change [tʃeɪndʒ]
anders *(verschieden)* different [ˈdɪfrənt]
anderthalb Stunden an hour and a half
Anfang beginning [bɪˈɡɪnɪŋ] **am Anfang** at first [ət ˈfɜːst]
anfangen start [stɑːt]; begin [bɪˈɡɪn]

Anfänger/in beginner [bɪ'gɪnə]
anfangs at first [ət 'fɜːst]
anfassen touch [tʌtʃ]
anfühlen: sich anfühlen feel
angemalt *(bemalt)* painted ['peɪntɪd]
angewiesen: auf etwas angewiesen sein *(von etwas abhängen)* depend on sth. [dɪ'pend]
Angewohnheit habit ['hæbɪt]
angreifen attack [ə'tæk]
Angriff attack [ə'tæk]
Angst: Angst haben (vor etwas/jm.) be afraid (of sth./sb.) [ə'freɪd] **jm. Angst machen** scare sb. [skeə]
ängstlich *(erschrocken)* in fright [fraɪt]
anhalten stop [stɒp]
Anhaltspunkt *(Lösungshinweis)* clue [kluː]
anhören 1. sich etwas anhören listen to sth. ['lɪsn] **Hör dir/Hört euch den Song an.** Listen to the song. **2. sich gut anhören** *(gut klingen)* sound good [saʊnd]
ankommen arrive [ə'raɪv]
Ankunft arrival [ə'raɪvl]
anlächeln: jn. anlächeln smile at sb. [smaɪl]
anmalen paint [peɪnt]
annehmen: Ich nehme an, ... I guess ...
anordnen *(in eine bestimmte Ordnung bringen)* arrange [ə'reɪndʒ]
anpflanzen grow [grəʊ]
anprobieren: etwas anprobieren try sth. on
Anruf phone call ['fəʊn kɔːl], *(kurz auch:)* call
anrufen call [kɔːl]; phone [fəʊn]
Ansage announcement [ə'naʊnsmənt]
anschauen: sich etwas anschauen watch sth. [wɒtʃ]; look at sth. [lʊk]
anschließen: sich einem Klub anschließen join a club [dʒɔɪn]
Anschrift address [ə'dres]
ansehen: sich etwas ansehen watch sth. [wɒtʃ]; look at sth. [lʊk]
Ansicht *(Meinung)* view [vjuː]
ansiedeln: sich ansiedeln settle ['setl]
Anspitzer sharpener ['ʃɑːpnə]
ansprechen *(Thema; Fragen)* cover ['kʌvə]
anstarren: jn./etwas anstarren stare at sb./sth. [steə]
anstatt rather than ['rɑːðə ðən]
anstelle von instead of [ɪn'sted_əv]
anstellen: sich anstellen *(Schlange stehen)* queue [kjuː] *(BE)*; be/stand/wait in line *(AE)*
Anstieg *(am Berg)* climb [klaɪm]
anstreichen paint [peɪnt]
anstrengen: sich anstrengen try hard
Antwort answer ['ɑːnsə]
antworten answer ['ɑːnsə] **antworten (auf)** reply (to) [rɪ'plaɪ]
Anzeige *(Inserat)* advertisement [əd'vɜːtɪsmənt] *(kurz auch:* advert ['ædvɜːt], ad [æd])
anziehen: etwas anziehen *(Kleidung)* put sth. on [ˌpʊt_'ɒn] **sich schick anziehen** dress up [ˌdres_'ʌp]
anzünden light [laɪt]
Apfelsine orange ['ɒrɪndʒ]
Apostroph apostrophe [ə'pɒstrəfi]
Apotheker/in chemist ['kemɪst] *(BE)*
Apparat: Bleib/Bleiben Sie am Apparat. *(am Telefon)* Hold on (a minute). [ˌhəʊld_'ɒn]
April April ['eɪprəl]
Aquarienhaus aquarium [ə'kweəriəm]
Aquarium aquarium [ə'kweəriəm]
Arbeit work [wɜːk]; *(Job, Stelle)* job [dʒɒb]
arbeiten work [wɜːk]
Arbeitsauftrag assignment [ə'saɪnmənt] *(AE)*
Arbeitsblatt worksheet ['wɜːkʃiːt]
Arbeitsheft workbook ['wɜːkbʊk]
Architekt/in architect ['ɑːkɪtekt]
Ärger haben be in trouble ['trʌbl] **Ärger kriegen** get into trouble
Argument argument ['ɑːgjumənt]
arm poor [pɔː], [pʊə]
Arm arm [ɑːm]
Armbanduhr watch [wɒtʃ]
Art: eine Art (von) ... a kind of ... [kaɪnd]; a type of ... [kaɪnd] **Art und Weise** way [weɪ] **auf eine interessante Art und Weise** in an interesting way
Artikel article ['ɑːtɪkl]
Arznei medicine ['medsn, 'medɪsn]
Asche ash [æʃ]; *(sterbliche Überreste)* ashes *(pl)* ['æʃɪz]
Astronaut/in astronaut ['æstrənɔːt]
Atem breath [breθ]
Atemzug breath [breθ]
Atlantik: der Atlantik, der Atlantische Ozean the Atlantic (Ocean) [ət'læntɪk]
Atmosphäre atmosphere ['ætməsfɪə]
Attraktion attraction [ə'trækʃn]
attraktiv handsome ['hænsəm]
auch too [tuː]; also ['ɔːlsəʊ]; as well [əz 'wel] **Ich auch.** Me too. **auch nicht** not ... either ['aɪðə, 'iːðə] **Ich auch nicht.** Me neither. ['naɪðə, 'niːðə] **sowohl ... als auch ...** both ... and ... [bəʊθ]
auf on [ɒn] **auf das Boot (hinauf)** onto the boat ['ɒntʊ] **auf dem Bild/Foto** in the picture/photo **auf dem Dachboden** in the attic **auf dem Weg zu/nach ...** on the way to ... **auf den Bahnhof/Mr Bell zu** towards the station/Mr Bell [tə'wɔːdz] **auf der Welt** in the world **auf der Landkarte/auf dem Stadtplan** on the map **auf Deutsch/Englisch** in German/English **auf einmal** suddenly ['sʌdnli] **auf etwas zusteuern/zugehen/zufahren** head for sth. **Auf keinen Fall!** No way! **auf und ab** up and down **Auf welcher Seite sind wir?** What page are we on? **Auf Wiedersehen.** Goodbye.; Bye-bye.; Bye.
aufbauen: etwas aufbauen set sth. up [set]
aufbewahren keep
aufbleiben: lang aufbleiben stay up late
aufeinander on top of each other
auffordern: jn. auffordern, etwas (nicht) zu tun tell sb. (not) to do sth.
Aufführung *(Vorstellung)* performance [pə'fɔːməns]
Aufgabe task; exercise ['eksəsaɪz]; assignment [ə'saɪnmənt] *(AE)*
aufgeben give up **etwas aufgeben** *(Gepäck)* check sth. in [ˌtʃek_'ɪn]
aufgeregt *(gespannt)* excited [ɪk'saɪtɪd]; *(nervös)* nervous ['nɜːvəs]
aufheben: etwas aufheben *(vom Boden)* pick sth. up [ˌpɪk_'ʌp]
aufhören: Hör auf (damit)! Stop it! *(infml)*
aufladen *(Handy, Batterien)* charge ['tʃɑːdʒ]
aufleuchten light up
aufmachen open ['əʊpən]
aufmerksam *(sorgfältig)* carefully ['keəfəli]
Aufnahme *(Film)* shot [ʃɒt]
aufpassen: auf jn. aufpassen look after sb.
aufragen *(Berge, Säulen, Türme, ...)* rise up [ˌraɪz_'ʌp]
aufregend exciting [ɪk'saɪtɪŋ]
aufrufen: die Namen aufrufen call out the names
aufschauen *(hochsehen)* look up [ˌlʊk_'ʌp]
aufschreiben: etwas aufschreiben write sth. down
aufsetzen: sich aufsetzen sit up **etwas aufsetzen** *(Hut, Helm)* put sth. on [ˌpʊt_'ɒn]
aufstehen stand up [ˌstænd_'ʌp]; get up [ˌget_'ʌp]; *(aus dem Bett)* get up
aufstellen: etwas aufstellen set sth. up [set]
Aufstieg *(am Berg)* climb [klaɪm]
aufsuchen: einen Arzt aufsuchen see a doctor
auftauchen *(erscheinen)* appear [ə'pɪə]
auftreten *(Künstler/in)* perform [pə'fɔːm]
Auftritt *(Künstler/in)* performance [pə'fɔːməns]
aufwachen wake up [ˌweɪk_'ʌp]
aufwachsen grow up [ˌgrəʊ_'ʌp]
aufwecken: jn. aufwecken wake sb. up [ˌweɪk_'ʌp]
Aufzug *(Lift)* elevator ['elɪveɪtə] *(bes. AE; BE auch:* lift*)*
Auge eye [aɪ]
Augenblick moment ['məʊmənt]
August August ['ɔːgəst]
aus 1. from [frɒm], [frəm] **aus etwas (gemacht) sein** be made of sth. **eine Band aus den 60er Jahren** a 1960s band **aus ... heraus/hinaus** out of ...

['aʊt‿əv] **Ich bin aus/komme aus Plymouth.** I'm from Plymouth.
2. aus sein *(ausgeschaltet sein)* be off
ausblasen: etwas ausblasen blow sth. out [ˌbləʊ‿'aʊt]
ausbreiten: (sich) ausbreiten spread [spred]
ausdenken: sich etwas ausdenken *(erfinden)* make sth. up; *(sich vorstellen)* think of sth.
Ausdruck expression [ɪk'spreʃn]; phrase [freɪz]
auseinander apart [ə'pɑːt]
Auseinandersetzung *(Streit)* argument ['ɑːgjumənt]
Ausflug trip [trɪp]
Ausfuhr export ['ekspɔːt]
ausführen: den Hund ausführen walk the dog
ausgeben: Geld ausgeben (für) spend money (on) [spend]
Ausgehverbot: jm. Ausgehverbot erteilen ground sb. [graʊnd]
ausgezeichnet excellent ['eksələnt]
auskennen: sich mit etwas auskennen know about sth.
auslachen: jn. auslachen laugh at sb./sth.
auslassen: etwas auslassen *(weglassen)* leave sth. out [ˌliːv‿'aʊt]
Auslassungszeichen *(Apostroph)* apostrophe [ə'pɒstrəfi]
ausloggen: sich ausloggen log out [lɒg]
auspacken unpack [ˌʌn'pæk]
ausprobieren try [traɪ]; *(probeweise anschauen, anhören)* check out [ˌtʃek‿'aʊt] *(infml)*
auspusten: etwas auspusten blow sth. out [ˌbləʊ‿'aʊt]
ausruhen: sich ausruhen relax [rɪ'læks]; rest [rest]
Ausrüstung equipment *(no pl)* [ɪ'kwɪpmənt]; kit [kɪt]
Aussage *(Botschaft)* message ['mesɪdʒ]
ausschalten: etwas ausschalten turn sth. off [ˌtɜːn‿'ɒf]
Ausschuss *(Politik)* council ['kaʊnsl]
aussehen: glücklich/wütend/... aussehen look happy/angry/... **gut aussehend** handsome ['hænsəm]
Außen- *(im Freien)* outdoor ['aʊtdɔː]
außer *(bis auf)* except [ɪk'sept]
außerdem besides [bɪ'saɪdz]
außerhalb von Rosie's Diner outside Rosie's Diner [ˌaʊt'saɪd]
äußern: sich äußern (zu etwas) *(etwas kommentieren)* comment (on sth.) ['kɒment]
Außenseite *(das Äußere)* outside
Aussicht (auf) view (of) [vjuː]
Aussichtsplattform observation deck [ˌɒbzə'veɪʃn dek]
Aussprache pronunciation [prəˌnʌnsi'eɪʃn]
aussteigen: aus einem Bus/Flugzeug/Zug aussteigen get off a bus/plane/train **aus einem Auto/Taxi aussteigen** get out of a car/taxi
aussterben die out [ˌdaɪ‿'aʊt]
ausstrecken: die Hand ausstrecken reach over [ˌriːtʃ‿'əʊvə]
aussuchen: (sich) etwas aussuchen choose sth. [tʃuːz]
Austausch exchange [ɪks'tʃeɪndʒ]
auswählen: etwas auswählen choose sth. [tʃuːz]
auswandern emigrate ['emɪgreɪt]
ausziehen: etwas ausziehen *(Kleidung)* take sth. off [ˌteɪk‿ɒf]
Auto car [kɑː] **mit dem Auto fahren** go by car
Autor/in author ['ɔːθə]

B

Bach stream [striːm]
Bad bath [bɑːθ]
Badezimmer bathroom ['bɑːθruːm]
Bahnhof station ['steɪʃn]
Bahnsteig platform ['plætfɔːm]
bald soon [suːn] **Bis bald.** See you (later). **schon bald** before long
Balkon balcony ['bælkəni]
Ball ball [bɔːl]
Ballon balloon [bə'luːn]
Band *(Musikgruppe)* band [bænd]
Bank *(Geldinstitut)* bank [bæŋk]
Bär bear [beə]
Barkeeper barman ['bɑːmən], *pl* barmen ['bɑːmən]
Bart beard [bɪəd]
Basketball basketball ['bɑːskɪtbɔːl]
Batterie battery ['bætəri]
bauen build [bɪld]
Bauer/Bäuerin farmer ['fɑːmə]
Bauernhof farm [fɑːm]
Baum tree [triː]
Baumwolle cotton ['kɒtn]
Bayern Bavaria [bə'veəriə]
Beamte(r), Beamtin official [ə'fɪʃl]
beantworten answer ['ɑːnsə]
bearbeiten *(Texte, Videos)* edit ['edɪt]
Becher mug [mʌg]
Bedarf: nach Bedarf on demand [dɪ'mɑːnd]
bedecken cover ['kʌvə]
bedeuten mean [miːn]
Bedeutung meaning ['miːnɪŋ]
Bedien dich! Help yourself!
beeilen: sich beeilen hurry ['hʌri], hurry up [ˌhʌri‿'ʌp]
beenden: etwas beenden finish sth. ['fɪnɪʃ]; end sth.
beerdigen bury ['beri]
Begabung talent ['tælənt]
begabt talented ['tæləntɪd]
Beginn beginning [bɪ'gɪnɪŋ]
beginnen start [stɑːt], begin [bɪ'gɪn]
begleiten *(führen)* guide [gaɪd]
behalten keep [kiːp]
behandeln *(Thema; Fragen)* cover ['kɒvə]
beherrschen: etwas beherrschen *(über etwas herrschen)* rule sth. [ruːl]
bei *(in Ortsangaben)* at [æt], [ət] **bei Oma** at Grandma's **bei den Blackwells daheim** at the Blackwells' house **bei jm. sein** be with sb.
beibringen: jm. beibringen, etwas zu tun teach sb. to do sth.
beide both [bəʊθ]
Beifall klatschen clap [klæp]
beigeheftet sein (an etwas) be attached (to sth.) [ə'tætʃt]
Bein leg [leg]
beinahe almost ['ɔːlməʊst]; nearly ['nɪəli]
Beispiel: zum Beispiel for example [fər‿ɪg'zɑːmpl]
beißen bite [baɪt]
bekämpfen: jn. bekämpfen fight sb. [faɪt]
bekannt well known [ˌwel 'nəʊn], ['wel nəʊn]
beklagen: sich beklagen complain [kəm'pleɪn]
bekommen get [get] **etwas bekommen** *(Grippe u.Ä.)* come down with sth.
belebt busy ['bɪzi]
beleidigt insulted [ɪn'sʌltɪd]
beleuchten illuminate [ɪ'luːmɪneɪt]
beliebt (bei) popular (with) ['pɒpjələ]
bellen bark [bɑːk]
bemalt painted ['peɪntɪd]
bemerken *(wahrnehmen)* notice ['nəʊtɪs]
Bemerkung *(Kommentar)* comment ['kɒment]
benehmen: sich benehmen behave [bɪ'heɪv]
benötigen need [niːd]
benutzen use [juːz]
Benzin petrol ['petrəl] *(BE)*; gas [gæs] *(AE)*
beobachten watch [wɒtʃ]; *(untersuchen)* study ['stʌdi]
Beobachter/in watcher ['wɒtʃə]
bequem comfortable ['kʌmftəbl]
Bereich area ['eəriə]
bereit ready ['redi]
bereits already [ɔːl'redi]
Berg mountain ['maʊntən]
bergab downhill [ˌdaʊn'hɪl]
bergauf uphill [ˌʌp'hɪl]
Bergwerk *(Mine)* mine [maɪn]
Bericht report [rɪ'pɔːt]
berichten report [rɪ'pɔːt] **jm. etwas berichten** tell sb. about sth. [tel]
berühmt (für, wegen) famous (for) ['feɪməs]; *(legendär)* legendary ['ledʒəndri]
berühren touch [tʌtʃ]
beschäftigt sein *(viel zu tun haben)* be busy ['bɪzi]
Bescheid: über etwas Bescheid wissen know about sth.
beschließen decide [dɪ'saɪd]
beschreiben: (jm.) etwas beschreiben describe sth. (to sb.) [dɪ'skraɪb] **jm. den**

Weg (nach …) beschreiben tell sb. the way (to …)
beschriften *(etikettieren)* label ['leɪbl]
Beschriftung *(Etikett)* label ['leɪbl]
beschweren: sich beschweren complain [kəm'pleɪn]
Besetzung *(Theaterstück, Film)* cast [kɑːst]
besiegen beat [biːt]; defeat [dɪ'fiːt]
besitzen own [əʊn]
Besitzer/in owner ['əʊnə]
besondere(r, s) special ['speʃl]
besonders especially [ɪ'speʃli]
besorgen: (sich) etwas besorgen get sth.
besorgt worried ['wʌrid]
Besprechung *(von Film, Buch u.Ä.)* review [rɪ'vjuː]
besser better ['betə] **besser als je zuvor** better than ever
beste(r, s) best [best] **ihr bester Freund / ihre beste Freundin** her best friend **das Beste an …** the best thing about …
bestellen order ['ɔːdə]
Bestrafung punishment ['pʌnɪʃmənt]
Besuch visit ['vɪzɪt]
besuchen: jn. besuchen visit sb. ['vɪzɪt]; see sb. [siː]
Besucher/in visitor ['vɪzɪtə]
Betonung stress [stres]; *(Hervorhebung)* emphasis ['emfəsɪs]
betreten *(hineingehen)* enter ['entə]
Bett bed [bed]
beugen: sich beugen *(lehnen)* lean [liːn]
beunruhigt worried ['wʌrid]
Beutel bag [bæg]
Bevölkerung population [ˌpɒpju'leɪʃn]
bevor before [bɪ'fɔː]
bewachen guard [gɑːd]
bewegen; sich bewegen move [muːv]
Bewegung movement ['muːvmənt]
bewölkt cloudy ['klaʊdi]
bewusst: sich einer Sache bewusst werden realize sth. ['riːəlaɪz]
bezahlen: etwas bezahlen pay for sth. [peɪ] **bezahlt werden** get paid
Beziehung relationship [rɪ'leɪʃnʃɪp]
Bezirk: (Stadt-)Bezirk borough [*AE:* 'bɜːrəʊ, *BE:* 'bʌrə]
Bibliothek library ['laɪbrəri]
Bild picture ['pɪktʃə]; *(Gemälde)* painting ['peɪntɪŋ]; *(Abbild)* image ['ɪmɪdʒ] **auf dem Bild** in the picture
bilden *(formen)* form [fɔːm]
Bildschirm screen [skriːn]
Bildung *(Ausbildung; Erziehung)* education [ˌedʒu'keɪʃn]
Bildunterschrift caption ['kæpʃn]
billig cheap [tʃiːp]
Bindewort linking word ['lɪŋkɪŋ wɜːd]
bis **1.** till [tɪl]; until [ən'tɪl] **bis zwölf Uhr** till/until twelve o'clock **bis jetzt** so far **Bis bald. / Bis nachher.** See you later. **bis (zu)** up to **von … bis …** from … to …
2. bis auf *(außer)* except [ɪk'sept]
Biss, Bissen bite [baɪt]
bisschen: ein bisschen a little **ein bisschen traurig** a bit sad [bɪt]
Bissen bite [baɪt]
bitte **1.** *(in Fragen und Aufforderungen)* please [pliːz]
2. Bitte sehr. / Hier bitte. Here you are.
3. Bitte, gern geschehen. *(Nichts zu danken.)* You're welcome. ['welkəm]
bitten: jemanden bitten, etwas zu tun ask sb. to do sth. [ɑːsk] **um etwas bitten** ask for sth.
Blaskapelle brass band [ˌbrɑːs 'bænd]
blau blue [bluː]
Blaubeere blueberry ['bluːbəri]
bleiben stay [steɪ]; remain [rɪ'meɪn]
Bleib/Bleiben Sie am Apparat. *(am Telefon)* Hold on (a minute). [ˌhəʊld‿'ɒn]
Bleistift pencil ['pensl]
Blick (auf) *(Aussicht)* view (of) [vjuː]
einen Blick auf etwas werfen have a look at sth.
blicken gaze [geɪz]
Blickkontakt herstellen make eye contact ['kɒntækt]
Blitz(e) lightning *(no pl)* ['laɪtnɪŋ] **ein Blitz** a flash of lightning
Block: (Häuser-, Wohn-)Block block [blɒk]
Blockflöte recorder [rɪ'kɔːdə]
blockieren block [blɒk]
blöd *(albern)* silly ['sɪli]
Blog-Eintrag post [pəʊst]
blond blond *(bei Frauen oft:* blonde)
[blɒnd]
bloß only ['əʊnli]; *(einfach nur)* just [dʒʌst]
blühen bloom [bluːm]
Blume flower ['flaʊə]
Blut blood [blʌd]
Blüte flower ['flaʊə]
Boden *(Erdboden)* ground [graʊnd]
Bohne bean [biːn]
Boje buoy [bɔɪ], *AE auch:* ['buːi]
Boot boat [bəʊt] **einen Bootsausflug machen** go on a boat trip
Bordkarte boarding pass ['bɔːdɪŋ pɑːs]
Botschaft *(Aussage)* message ['mesɪdʒ]
Boulevard avenue ['ævənjuː]
brauchen need [niːd]; *(Zeit)* take [teɪk]
braun brown [braʊn]
brav good
brechen *(kaputt gehen)* break [breɪk]
breit wide [waɪd]
Brettspiel board game ['bɔːd geɪm]
Brief letter ['letə]
Brille glasses *(pl)* ['glɑːsɪz]
bringen *(weg-, hinbringen)* take [teɪk]; *(mitbringen, herbringen)* bring [brɪŋ]
etwas zustande bringen manage sth. ['mænɪdʒ]
Brise breeze [briːz]
britisch British ['brɪtɪʃ]
Broschüre brochure ['brəʊʃə]
Brot bread [bred]
Brücke bridge [brɪdʒ]
Bruder brother ['brʌðə]
brüllen roar [rɔː]
brummen hum [hʌm]
Brust(korb) chest [tʃest]
brutzeln sizzle ['sɪzl]
Bub boy [bɔɪ]
Buch book [bʊk]
buchen *(reservieren)* reserve [rɪ'zɜːv]
Bücherei library ['laɪbrəri]
Buchhandlung bookshop ['bʊkʃɒp]
Buchstabe letter ['letə]
buchstabieren spell [spel]
bücken: sich bücken bend down [bend]
Bühne stage [steɪdʒ]
bunt colourful ['kʌləfl]; coloured ['kʌləd]
Burg castle ['kɑːsl]
Bürgermeister/in mayor [meə]
Bürgerrechte civil rights *(pl)* [ˌsɪvl 'raɪts]
Bürgersteig pavement ['peɪvmənt] *(BE)*; sidewalk ['saɪdwɔːk] *(AE)*
Büro office ['ɒfɪs]
Bus bus **mit dem Bus fahren** go by bus
Busch shrub [ʃrʌb]

C

Café café ['kæfeɪ]
Camping camping ['kæmpɪŋ]
Cent cent [sent]
Chance chance [tʃɑːns]
Chaos chaos ['keɪɒs]
chatten chat
Checkliste checklist
Chor choir ['kwaɪə]
Clown clown [klaʊn]
Computer computer [kəm'pjuːtə]
cool cool [kuːl]
Cornflakes cornflakes ['kɔːnfleɪks]
Cousin, Cousine cousin ['kʌzn]
Cyber-Mobbing *(Verleumdung/Diffamierung in sozialen Medien)* cyberbullying ['saɪbəˌbʊliɪŋ]

D

da *(weil)* as [æz, əz]
da, dahin *(dort, dorthin)* there [ðeə] **da drüben** over there **nicht da sein** be out **nicht mehr da sein** be gone [gɒn]
Dach roof [ruːf]
Dachboden attic ['ætɪk] **auf dem Dachboden** in the attic
dagegen: etwas dagegen haben mind [maɪnd] **Haben Sie etwas dagegen, …?** Do you mind …? **wenn Sie nichts dagegen haben** if you don't mind
daheim at home [ət 'həʊm]
daher *(deshalb)* so [səʊ]
Dame: Meine Damen und Herren / Sehr geehrte Damen und Herren

Ladies and gentlemen [ˌleɪdiz‿ən ˈdʒentlmən]
damit *(sodass)* so (that)
Dampf steam [stiːm]
danach after that
dank Maya thanks to Maya
dankbar *(froh)* glad [glæd]
Danke. Thank you. [ˈθæŋk juː]; Thanks. **Danke, gut.** Fine, thanks.
dann then [ðen] **gerade dann/genau dann** just then
darstellende Kunst drama [ˈdrɑːmə]
darüber *(oberhalb von etwas)* above [əˈbʌv]
darum that's why
darunter **1.** *(unter etwas)* below [bɪˈləʊ] **2. darunter auch** *(einschließlich)* including [ɪnˈkluːdɪŋ]
das *(Artikel)* the [ðə]
das (dort) that [ðæt] **das (dort) ist …** that's … **das (dort) sind …** those are …
dass that [ðæt], [ðət] **es zeigt, dass …** it shows that …
dasselbe the same [seɪm]
Datum date [deɪt]
Dauer *(Länge)* length [leŋθ]
dauern *(Zeit brauchen)* take [teɪk]
Deck deck [dek]
Decke *(zum Zudecken)* blanket [ˈblæŋkɪt]
dein(e) … your … [jɔː], [jə]
deiner, deine, deins yours [jɔːz]
Demonstration demonstration [ˌdemənˈstreɪʃn]
denken think [θɪŋk] **an etwas denken** think of sth.; *(sich etwas merken)* remember sth.
Denkmal memorial [məˈmɔːriəl]
denn: Was ist denn? What's the matter? [ˈmætə]
dennoch still [stɪl]
Depp jerk [dʒɜːk] *(infml)*
der *(Artikel)* the [ðə]
der … (dort) that … [ðæt] **der … (hier)** this … [ðɪs]
der *(Relativpronomen)*: **Finde jemanden, der …** Find someone who …
deren *(Relativpronomen)*: **Städte, deren Namen …** cities whose names … [huːz]
derselbe the same [seɪm]
deshalb so [səʊ]; that's why
dessen *(Relativpronomen)*: **ein Junge/ Mädchen, dessen Namen …** a boy/girl whose name … [huːz]
Design design [dɪˈzaɪn]
Detail detail [ˈdiːteɪl]
deuten: auf etwas deuten *(zeigen)* point to sth. [pɔɪnt]
deutlich clear [klɪə]
Deutsch; deutsch German [ˈdʒɜːmən]
Dezember December [dɪˈsembə]
Dialog dialogue [ˈdaɪəlɒg]
dich you [juː]; yourself [jɔːˈself]
dicht (bei, an) close (to) [kləʊs]
dick *(Person, Tier)* fat [fæt]; *(Dinge)* thick [θɪk]
die *(Artikel)* the [ðə]
die … (dort) *(Singular)* that … [ðæt]; *(Plural)* those … [ðəʊz] **die … (hier)** *(Singular)* this … [ðɪs]; *(Plural)* these … [ðiːz]
Dieb/in thief [θiːf], *pl* thieves [θiːvz]
Dienstag Tuesday [ˈtjuːzdeɪ, ˈtjuːzdi]
dies (hier) this [ðɪs] **dies (hier) ist …** this is … **dies (hier) sind …** these are …
diese(r, s): dieser Ort / diese Pause / dieses Fach this place/break/subject **diese Orte/Pausen/Fächer** these places/breaks/subjects **Diese(r, s) (hier).** This one.
dieselbe(n) wie the same [seɪm]
diesjährig: das diesjährige Musical this year's musical
digital digital [ˈdɪdʒɪtl]
Ding thing [θɪŋ]
Dinosaurier dinosaur [ˈdaɪnəsɔː]
dir you [juː]; yourself [jɔːˈself]
direkt direct [dəˈrekt], [daɪˈrekt]; *(geradewegs)* straight [streɪt]
Disko disco [ˈdɪskəʊ]
Diskussion discussion [dɪˈskʌʃn]
Dokumentarfilm documentary [ˌdɒkjuˈmentri]
Dollar dollar [ˈdɒlə]; *(infml)* buck [bʌk]
Dom cathedral [kəˈθiːdrəl]
Donner thunder [ˈθʌndə]
Donnerstag Thursday [ˈθɜːzdeɪ, ˈθɜːzdi]
Doppel- double [ˈdʌbl]
Dorf village [ˈvɪlɪdʒ]
dort, dorthin there [ðeə] **dort drüben** over there **dort entlang** that way [weɪ]
Dose *(Lebensmittel)* tin [tɪn]; *(Getränk)* can [kæn]
dran: Ich bin dran. (It's) my turn. [tɜːn]
draußen outside [ˌaʊtˈsaɪd] **nach draußen** out; outside
Dreck dirt [dɜːt]
Dreh: den Dreh raushaben/rausbekommen (bei etwas) get the hang of sth. *(infml)*
drehen: sich (im Kreis) drehen spin around [ˌspɪn‿əˈraʊnd]
drei three [θriː]
dreieckig triangular [traɪˈæŋgjələ]
drinnen inside [ˌɪnˈsaɪd] **nach drinnen** inside
dritte(r, s) third [θɜːd] **Drittens, …** Third, …
dröhnen roar [rɔː]
drüben: da/dort drüben over there **hier drüben** over here
Druck pressure [ˈpreʃə]
drücken press [pres]; *(schieben, stoßen)* push [pʊʃ]
du you [juː]
dumm stupid [ˈstjuːpɪd]
Dummerchen silly [ˈsɪli]
dunkel dark [dɑːk]
Dunkelheit dark; darkness [ˈdɑːknəs]
dünn *(mager, dürr)* skinny [ˈskɪni]
durch through [θruː]
Durchsage announcement [əˈnaʊnsmənt]
Durchschnitt average [ˈævərɪdʒ] **im Durchschnitt** on average
durchschnittlich **1.** *(adj)* average 2. *(adv)* on average
dürfen can; may; be allowed to [əˈlaʊd] **du darfst es nicht tun** you mustn't do it [ˈmʌsnt]
dürr *(mager)* skinny [ˈskɪni]
Durst haben be thirsty [ˈθɜːsti]
durstig sein be thirsty [ˈθɜːsti]
Dusche shower [ˈʃaʊə]
duschen; sich duschen have/take a shower [ˈʃaʊə]
DVD DVD [ˌdiːviːˈdiː]

E

eben: gerade eben just [dʒʌst]
ebenso as well [əz ˈwel]
echt *(wirklich)* real [ˈriːəl] **Das ist echt übel!** That sucks! [sʌks] *(infml)*
Ecke corner [ˈkɔːnə] **Laden an der Ecke** *(„Tante-Emma-Laden")* corner shop [ˈkɔːnə ʃɒp] **Church Road, Ecke London Road** on the corner of Church Road and London Road
egal: Geld ist mir egal. I don't care about money.
Ehefrau wife [waɪf], *pl* wives [waɪvz]
ehemalige(r, s) former [ˈfɔːmə]
Ehemann husband [ˈhʌzbənd]
Ehre honour [ˈɒnə]
Ei egg [eg]
Eierkuchen pancake [ˈpænkeɪk]
eigen: mein eigener Film/mein eigenes Zimmer/… my own film/room/… [əʊn]
eigentlich actually [ˈæktʃuəli]; in fact [ɪn ˈfækt]
eilen rush [rʌʃ] **sich beeilen** hurry (up) [ˈhʌri]
Eimer bucket [ˈbʌkɪt]
ein(e) *(Artikel)* a, an [ə], [ən] **ein anderer …/eine andere …/ein anderes …** another … [əˈnʌðə] **einer nach dem anderen** one by one **ein paar** *(einige)* some [sʌm], [səm] **eines Nachts/Tages** one night/day
einander *(sich gegenseitig)* each other [iːtʃ‿ˈʌðə]; one another
einchecken: etwas einchecken *(Gepäck)* check sth. in [ˌtʃek‿ˈɪn]
Eindruck impression [ɪmˈpreʃn]
eineinhalb Stunden an hour and a half
einfach **1.** *(nicht schwierig)* easy [ˈiːzi]; *(unkompliziert)* simple [ˈsɪmpl] **2. einfach nur** just [dʒʌst] **3. einfache Fahrkarte** single (ticket) [ˈsɪŋgl]
Einfluss influence [ˈɪnfluəns]
Einführung introduction [ˌɪntrəˈdʌkʃn]
Eingang entrance [ˈentrəns]; *(Türeingang)* doorway
eingeben: ein Passwort eingeben enter a password [ˈentə], [ˈpɑːswɜːd]

eingeschaltet sein *(Radio, Licht usw.)* be on
einhundert a hundred, one hundred ['hʌndrəd]
einige some [sʌm], [səm]; *(ein paar)* a few [ə 'fjuː]
einigen: sich auf etwas einigen agree on sth. [ə'griː]
einkaufen gehen go shopping ['ʃɒpɪŋ]
Einkaufszentrum shopping centre; (shopping) mall [mɔːl]
einladen: jn. einladen (zu) invite sb. (to) [ɪn'vaɪt]
Einladung (zu, nach) invitation (to) [ˌɪnvɪ'teɪʃn]
Einleitung introduction [ˌɪntrə'dʌkʃn]
einloggen: sich einloggen log in [lɒg]
einmal **1.** once [wʌns] **noch einmal** again [ə'gen]
2. früher einmal *(einst)* once [wʌns]
3. auf einmal *(plötzlich)* suddenly ['sʌdnli]
4. (noch) nicht einmal not even
einmarschieren (in ein Land) invade (a country) [ɪn'veɪd]
einpacken pack [pæk]
einreichen: etwas einreichen hand sth. in
einrichten: etwas einrichten set sth. up [set]
eins one [wʌn]
einsam lonely ['ləʊnli]
einschalten: etwas einschalten turn sth. on [ˌtɜːn_'ɒn]
einschlafen fall asleep [ˌfɔːl_ə'sliːp]
einschließlich including [ɪn'kluːdɪŋ]
einst *(früher einmal)* once [wʌns]
einsteigen: in ein Auto/Taxi einsteigen get in(to) a car/taxi **in einen Bus/ein Flugzeug/einen Zug einsteigen** get on a bus/plane/train
Einstellung *(Film)* shot [ʃɒt]
einstürzen collapse [kə'læps]
Eintrag(ung) *(im Tagebuch, Wörterbuch)* entry ['entri]
eintreffen arrive [ə'raɪv]
eintreten *(hineingehen)* enter ['entə] **in einen Klub eintreten** join a club [dʒɔɪn]
Eintritt *(Zutritt)* entry ['entri]
Eintrittskarte ticket ['tɪkɪt]
Einwohner(zahl) population [ˌpɒpju'leɪʃn]
Einzelfahrschein single (ticket) ['sɪŋgl]
Einzelheit detail ['diːteɪl]
einzig: der/die/das einzige ...; die einzigen... the only ... ['əʊnli]
Eis ice [aɪs]; *(Speiseeis)* ice cream [ˌaɪs 'kriːm]
Eisenbahn railroad ['reɪlrəʊd] *(AE)*, railway ['reɪlweɪ] *(BE)*
Eistee iced tea [ˌaɪst 'tiː]
ekelhaft disgusting [dɪs'gʌstɪŋ]
Elefant elephant ['elɪfənt]
elf eleven [ɪ'levn]
Element element ['elɪmənt]
Eltern parents ['peərənts]

E-Mail email ['iːmeɪl]; mail [meɪl]
emigrieren emigrate ['emɪgreɪt]
emporragen *(Berge, Säulen, Türme, ...)* rise up [ˌraɪz_'ʌp]
Ende end [end]; *(Abschluss)* ending ['endɪŋ] **am unteren Ende (von)** at the bottom (of) ['bɒtəm] **zu Ende sein** be over ['əʊvə]
enden finish ['fɪnɪʃ]; end
endlich *(schließlich)* at last [ət 'lɑːst]; finally ['faɪnəli]
Endspiel final ['faɪnl]
Endung ending ['endɪŋ]
Energie energy ['enədʒi]
energisch *(kräftig)* vigorous ['vɪgərəs]
eng *(schmal)* narrow ['nærəʊ]
Engel angel ['eɪndʒl]
Englisch; englisch English ['ɪŋglɪʃ]
entgegnen reply (to) [rɪ'plaɪ]
entlang: die Straße/den Fluss/... entlang along the street/the river/... [ə'lɒŋ] **dort entlang** that way [weɪ]
entscheiden: sich entscheiden decide [dɪ'saɪd]
Entscheidung decision [dɪ'sɪʒn]
Entschuldigung. **1.** *(Tut mir leid.)* (I'm) sorry. ['sɒri]
2. Entschuldigung, ... / Entschuldigen Sie, ... *(Darf ich mal stören?)* Excuse me, ... [ɪk'skjuːz miː]
entsetzt shocked [ʃɒkt]
entspannen: sich entspannen relax [rɪ'læks]
entspannt relaxed [rɪ'lækst]
entweder ... oder ... either ... or ... ['aɪðə], ['iːðə]
Entwurf draft [drɑːft]
er **1.** *(männliche Person)* he [hiː]
2. *(Ding; Tier)* it [ɪt]
Erdbeere strawberry ['strɔːbəri]
Erdboden ground [graʊnd]
Erde *(der Planet)* (the) earth [ɜːθ] *(oft auch:* Earth)
Ereignis event [ɪ'vent]
erfahren experience [ɪk'spɪəriəns]
Erfahrung(en) experience *(no pl)* [ɪk'spɪəriəns]
erfolgreich successful [sək'sesfl]
erforschen explore [ɪk'splɔː]
ergänzen (zu) add (to) [æd]
Ergebnis result [rɪ'zʌlt]
erhalten get
erhältlich available [ə'veɪləbl]
erhellen: etwas erhellen *(aufleuchten lassen)* light sth. up [ˌlaɪt_'ʌp]
erinnern **1. sich an etwas erinnern** remember sth. [rɪ'membə]
2. jn. erinnern remind sb. [rɪ'maɪnd]
Erinnerung memory ['meməri]
erkältet sein have a cold [kəʊld]
Erkältung: eine Erkältung haben have a cold [kəʊld]
erkennen: etwas erkennen *(sich einer Sache bewusst werden)* realize sth. ['riːəlaɪz]

erklären: jm. etwas erklären explain sth. to sb. [ɪk'spleɪn]
Erklärung *(Verkündung)* declaration [ˌdeklə'reɪʃn]
erkranken: an etwas erkranken come down with sth.
erkunden *(erforschen)* explore [ɪk'splɔː]
erlauben allow [ə'laʊ]
erläutern: jm. etwas erläutern explain sth. to sb. [ɪk'spleɪn]
erleben experience [ɪk'spɪəriəns]
erleuchten illuminate [ɪ'luːmɪneɪt]
ernst(haft) *(adj)* serious ['sɪəriəs]
ernstlich *(adv)* seriously ['sɪəriəsli]
Ernte harvest ['hɑːvɪst]
erraten guess [ges]
erreichbar *(am Telefon)* available [ə'veɪləbl]
erreichen reach [riːtʃ] **den Bus erreichen** *(rechtzeitig)* be in time for the bus
errichten: etwas errichten set sth. up [set]
erröten go red
erschaffen create [kri'eɪt]
erscheinen appear [ə'pɪə]
erschießen shoot [ʃuːt]
erschrecken: jn. erschrecken scare sb. [skeə]
erschrocken in fright [fraɪt]
erst only ['əʊnli] **erst um drei** *(nicht vor drei)* not till three, not until three
erstaunlich amazing [ə'meɪzɪŋ]
erste(r, s) first [fɜːst] **als Erstes** first **der erste Tag** the first day **Erstens, ...** First, ...
erteilen: jm. Hausarrest/Ausgehverbot erteilen ground sb. [graʊnd]
erwachsen werden grow up [ˌgrəʊ_'ʌp]
Erwachsene(r) adult ['ædʌlt]
erwarten: etwas erwarten expect sth. [ɪk'spekt] **Ich kann es kaum erwarten, ... zu ...** I can't wait to ...
erwidern reply (to) [rɪ'plaɪ]
erzählen (von) tell (about) [tel]
Erzähler/in narrator [nə'reɪtə]
Erzählung story ['stɔːri]; *(Schilderung)* narration [nə'reɪʃn]
Erziehung education [ˌedʒu'keɪʃn]
erzielen: einen Treffer erzielen score [skɔː]
es it [ɪt] **es ist ... / es gibt ...** there's ... **es sind ... / es gibt ...** there are ... **Ach, du bist es.** Oh, it's you. **Bist du es?** Is that you? **es wäre ...** it would be ... [wʊd]
essen eat [iːt] **zu Abend / zu Mittag essen** have dinner / have lunch
Essen *(Lebensmittel)* food [fuːd]; *(Mahlzeit)* meal [miːl]; *(zum Mitnehmen)* takeout ['teɪkaʊt] *(AE)*
Esszimmer dining room ['daɪnɪŋ ruːm]
Etage *(Stockwerk)* floor [flɔː]; storey, *pl* storeys *(BE)*, story, *pl* stories *(AE)* ['stɔːri]
Etikett label
etikettieren label ['leɪbl]

etwas **1.** something ['sʌmθɪŋ]; *(in Fragen)* anything ['eniθɪŋ]
2. *(ein wenig)* some [sʌm], [səm]; a little **etwas traurig** a bit sad
euch you [juː]; yourselves [jɔː'selvz]
euer .../eure ... your ... [jɔː], [jə]
eurer, eure, eures yours [jɔːz]
Euro euro (€) ['jʊərəʊ]
Europa Europe ['jʊərəp]
europäisch: die Europäische Union the European Union [ˌjʊərəpiːən 'juːniən] (the EU [ˌiː 'juː])
ewig *(für immer)* for ever [fər‿'evə], forever **Es ist ewig her.** It's been ages. / That was ages ago.
Exemplar copy ['kɒpi]
Experte/Expertin expert ['ekspɜːt]
explodieren explode [ɪk'spləʊd]
Export export ['ekspɔːt]

F

Fabrik factory ['fæktri]
Fackel torch [tɔːtʃ]
Fahne *(Flagge)* flag [flæg]
fähig sein, etwas zu tun be able to do sth. ['eɪbl]
Fähre ferry ['feri]
fahren go [gəʊ]; *(ein Auto)* drive [draɪv]; *(abfahren)* leave [liːv] **mit dem Bus/Auto fahren** go by bus/car **Rad fahren** ride a bike [ˌraɪd‿ə 'baɪk]
Fahrgast passenger ['pæsɪndʒə]
Fahrkarte ticket ['tɪkɪt]
Fahrkartenschalter ticket office ['tɪkɪt‿ˌɒfɪs]
Fahrplan timetable ['taɪmteɪbl]
Fahrrad bike [baɪk]
Fahrstuhl elevator ['elɪveɪtə] *(bes. AE; BE auch:* lift)
Fahrt ride [raɪd]; *(Reise)* journey ['dʒɜːni]
Fahrtenbuch logbook ['lɒgbʊk]
fair fair [feə]
Fakt fact [fækt]
Faktor factor ['fæktə]
Fall: auf jeden Fall certainly ['sɜːtnli] **Auf keinen Fall!** No way! [ˌnəʊ 'weɪ]
fallen drop [drɒp]; fall [fɔːl] **etwas fallen lassen** drop sth. **vom Fahrrad fallen** fall off a bike
falls if [ɪf]
falsch false [fɔːls]; wrong [rɒŋ] **Nein, das ist falsch.** No, that's wrong.
falten fold [fəʊld]
Familie family ['fæməli] **Familie Blackwell** the Blackwell family **eine vierköpfige Familie** a family of four
Fan fan [fæn]
fangen catch [kætʃ]
fantastisch fantastic [fæn'tæstɪk]
Farbe colour ['kʌlə]
farbenfroh, farbenprächtig colourful ['kʌləfl]
farbig coloured ['kʌləd]
Farm farm [fɑːm]
Fasching carnival ['kɑːnɪvl]
fast almost ['ɔːlməʊst]; nearly ['nɪəli]
Februar February ['februəri]
Federmäppchen pencil case ['pensl keɪs]
fehlen be missing ['mɪsɪŋ] **die fehlenden Wörter** the missing words **Was fehlt Justin/dir?** What's wrong with Justin/you?
Fehler mistake [mɪ'steɪk]; *(Schuld)* fault [fɔːlt]
Feier celebration [ˌselɪ'breɪʃn]
feiern celebrate ['selɪbreɪt]
Feiertag holiday ['hɒlədeɪ]
Feind/in enemy ['enəmi]
Feld field [fiːld]; *(auf Brettspiel)* square [skweə]
Fels, Felsen rock [rɒk]
felsig rocky ['rɒki]
Fenster window ['wɪndəʊ]
Ferien holidays *(pl)* ['hɒlədeɪz]
Fernbedienung remote control [rɪˌməʊt kən'trəʊl] *(kurz auch:* remote)
fernhalten: etwas fernhalten von keep sth. away from
fernsehen watch TV [ˌwɒtʃ tiː'viː]
Fernsehen, Fernsehgerät TV [ˌtiː'viː] **im Fernsehen** on TV
fertig **1. mit etwas fertig werden/sein** finish sth. ['fɪnɪʃ] **Wir sind fertig.** *(Wir haben es erledigt.)* We're finished. ['fɪnɪʃt]
2. *(bereit)* ready ['redi] **sich fertig machen (für)** get ready (for) **Wir sind fertig.** *(Wir sind bereit.)* We're ready.
Fertigkeit skill [skɪl]
Fertigungsindustrie manufacturing industry [ˌmænju'fæktʃərɪŋ]
fesselnd *(hypnotisierend)* mesmerizing ['mezməraɪzɪŋ]
Fest, Festival festival ['festɪvl]
fest(gelegt) fixed [fɪkst]
festhalten: sich an etwas festhalten hold onto sth. [həʊld]
festnehmen arrest [ə'rest]
festziehen *(spannen)* tighten ['taɪtn]
fett fat [fæt]
Feuer fire ['faɪə]
Feuerwerk fireworks *(pl)* ['faɪəwɜːks]
Feuerwerkskörper firework ['faɪəwɜːk]
Fieber temperature ['temprətʃə] **Fieber haben** have a temperature
Figur *(Gestalt)* figure ['fɪgə]; *(in Roman, Film, Theaterstück usw.)* character ['kærəktə]
Film film [fɪlm]; movie ['muːvi]
filmen film [fɪlm]
Filzstift felt pen [ˌfelt 'pen]
Finale final ['faɪnl]
finden find [faɪnd] **Freunde finden** make friends **Wie findest du ...?** How do you like ...?
Finger finger ['fɪŋgə]
Finsternis darkness ['dɑːknəs]
Firma company ['kʌmpəni]
Fisch fish [fɪʃ], *pl* fish
Fischerdorf fishing village ['fɪʃɪŋ ˌvɪlɪdʒ]
fit fit [fɪt]
Flagge flag [flæg]
Flasche bottle ['bɒtl]
Fleck spot [spɒt]
Fleisch meat [miːt]
fliegen fly [flaɪ]
fliehen escape [ɪ'skeɪp]
fließend(es) Wasser running water [ˌrʌnɪŋ 'wɔːtə]
Floß raft [rɑːft]
Flucht escape [ɪ'skeɪp]
Flügel wing [wɪŋ]
Flughafen airport ['eəpɔːt]
Flugzeug plane [pleɪn]
Fluss river ['rɪvə]
flussabwärts downstream [ˌdaʊn'striːm]
flussaufwärts upstream [ˌʌp'striːm]
flüstern whisper ['wɪspə] **..., sagte er flüsternd.** ..., he said under his breath. [breθ]
Flussufer bank [bæŋk]
Folge *(Konsequenz)* consequence ['kɒnsɪkwəns]
folgen follow ['fɒləʊ]
Folie *(für Präsentationen)* transparency [træns'pærənsi]
fördern: etwas fördern *(für etwas werben)* promote sth. [prə'məʊt]
Form form [fɔːm]; *(Gestalt)* shape [ʃeɪp]
formen form [fɔːm]
Forschung(en) research *(no pl)* ['riːsɜːtʃ]
fort away [ə'weɪ]
fortfahren *(weiterreden)* go on [ˌgəʊ‿'ɒn]
fortsetzen: etwas fortsetzen continue sth. [kən'tɪnjuː] **sich fortsetzen** *(weitergehen)* continue
Foto photo ['fəʊtəʊ] **auf dem Foto** in the photo **Fotos machen** take photos
Fotoapparat camera ['kæmərə]
fotografieren take photos [ˌteɪk 'fəʊtəʊz]
Frage question ['kwestʃn] **eine Frage stellen** ask a question **Kommt nicht in Frage!** No way!
Fragebogen questionnaire [ˌkwestʃə'neə]
fragen ask [ɑːsk] **jn. nach dem Weg fragen** ask sb. the way **sich fragen** wonder ['wʌndə]
Französisch; französisch French [frentʃ]
Frau **1.** woman ['wʊmən], *pl* women ['wɪmɪn]
2. Frau Schwarz Mrs Schwarz ['mɪsɪz]
3. *(übliche Anrede von Lehrerinnen)* **Frau Bell** Miss Bell [mɪs]
frei free [friː]
Freiheit liberty ['lɪbəti]
freilich certainly ['sɜːtnli]
Freitag Friday ['fraɪdeɪ], ['fraɪdi]
Freizeit free time [ˌfriː 'taɪm]
Freizeitaktivitäten free-time activities [ˌfriːtaɪm‿æk'tɪvətiz]
Freizeitpark, -zentrum leisure centre ['leʒə sentə]
Fremdenführer/in guide [gaɪd]

freuen: Freut mich, dich/euch/Sie kennenzulernen. Nice to meet you. **sich auf etwas freuen** look forward to sth. ['fɔːwəd]
Freund friend [frend]; *(Partner)* boyfriend ['bɔɪfrend]
Freundin friend [frend]; *(Partnerin)* girlfriend ['gɜːlfrend]
freundlich friendly ['frendli]; kind [kaɪnd]
Freut mich, dich/euch/Sie kennenzulernen. Nice to meet you.
Friede, Frieden peace [piːs]
Friedhof cemetery [*BE:* 'semətri, *AE:* 'seməteri]
friedlich peaceful ['piːsfl]
frieren be cold [kəʊld]
Frisbee frisbee ['frɪzbi]
frisch fresh [freʃ]
Friseur/in hairdresser ['heədresə]
froh *(glücklich)* happy ['hæpi]; *(dankbar)* glad [glæd] **Frohe Weinachten!** Merry Christmas!
Frosch frog [frɒg]
Frucht fruit [fruːt]
früh early ['ɜːli]
früher: der Weg, den ich früher (immer) genommen habe the trail I used to take ['juːst tə]
frühere(r, s) former ['fɔːmə]
Frühling spring [sprɪŋ]
Frühstück breakfast ['brekfəst]
frühstücken have breakfast
Frühstückspension bed & breakfast
fühlen; sich fühlen feel [fiːl]
führen *(leiten)* lead [liːd]; *(begleiten)* guide [gaɪd]
füllen fill [fɪl]
Füller pen [pen]
fünf five [faɪv]
funktionieren work
für for [fɔː], [fə] **für immer** for ever [fər‿'evə], forever
furchtbar, fürchterlich terrible ['terəbl], awful ['ɔːfl]
Fuß *(auch Längenmaß: 30,5 cm)* foot [fʊt], *pl* feet [fiːt] **zu Fuß** on foot **zu Fuß gehen** walk [wɔːk]; go on foot
Fußabdruck footprint ['fʊtprɪnt]
Fußball football ['fʊtbɔːl]; soccer ['sɒkə]
Fußboden floor [flɔː]
Fußgänger/in pedestrian [pə'destriən]
Fußgängerzone pedestrian zone [pə'destriən zəʊn]
Futter food [fuːd]
füttern feed [fiːd]
Fütterungszeit feeding time ['fiːdɪŋ taɪm]

G

Gabel fork [fɔːk]
Galerie gallery ['gæləri]
Gang aisle [aɪl]; *(Korridor)* corridor ['kɒrɪdɔː] **im Gang sein** go on
ganze(r, s) whole [həʊl] **das ganze Plymouth, ganz Plymouth** all of Plymouth **den ganzen Tag (lang)** all day **ganzer Satz** full sentence **im ganzen Land / in der ganzen Stadt / auf der ganzen Welt** all over the country / the city / the world
gar nichts nothing ['nʌθɪŋ]
Garage garage ['gærɑːʒ], ['gærɪdʒ]
Garten garden ['gɑːdn]
Gartenarbeit gardening ['gɑːdnɪŋ]
Gärtner/in gardener ['gɑːdnə]
Gärtnern gardening ['gɑːdnɪŋ]
Gast guest [gest]; *(Besucher/in)* visitor ['vɪzɪtə]
Gastfamilie host family ['həʊst fæməli]
Gastgeber/in host [həʊst]
Gatter *(Tor, Pforte)* gate [geɪt]
gebackene Kartoffeln *(im Backofen in Fett gebacken)* roast potatoes [rəʊst pə'teɪtəʊz]
Gebäude building ['bɪldɪŋ]
geben give [gɪv] **jm. etwas geben** *(reichen)* hand sb. sth. **Es gibt …** *(Singular)* There's …; *(Plural)* There are … **Gibt es (irgendwelche) …?** Are there any …? ['eni] **Was gibt es zum Mittagessen?** What's for lunch?
Gebiet area ['eəriə]
geboren sein/werden be born [bɔːn]
gebrochen broken ['brəʊkən]
Geburt birth [bɜːθ]
Geburtsort birthplace ['bɜːθpleɪs]
Geburtstag birthday ['bɜːθdeɪ] **Ich habe am 5. Mai Geburtstag.** My birthday is on 5th May. **Ich habe im Mai Geburtstag.** My birthday is in May. **Wann hast du Geburtstag?** When's your birthday?
Gedanke thought [θɔːt]
Gedicht poem ['pəʊɪm]
geduldig patient ['peɪʃnt]
geehrte(r, s): Sehr geehrte Damen und Herren Ladies and gentlemen [ˌleɪdiz‿ən 'dʒentlmən]
Gefahr danger ['deɪndʒə]
gefährlich dangerous ['deɪndʒərəs]
gefallen: Wie gefällt dir …? How do you like …?
Gefangene(r) prisoner ['prɪznə]
Gefängnis prison ['prɪzn]
Gefäß *(Topf)* pot [pɒt]
gefroren frozen ['frəʊzn]
Gefühl feeling ['fiːlɪŋ]
gegen against [ə'genst]
Gegend area ['eəriə]; *(Landschaft)* countryside ['kʌntrisaɪd] **hier in der Gegend** round here [ˌraʊnd 'hɪə]
Gegenstand object ['ɒbdʒɪkt]
Gegenteil opposite ['ɒpəzɪt]
gegenüber (von) opposite ['ɒpəzɪt]
Gegenwart present ['preznt]
gehen 1. go [gəʊ]; *(zu Fuß gehen)* walk [wɔːk] **an Land gehen** land [lænd] **ans Telefon gehen** answer the phone **einkaufen gehen** go shopping ['ʃɒpɪŋ] **Los geht's. / Jetzt geht's los.** Here we go. **nach Hause gehen** go home **segeln gehen** go sailing ['seɪlɪŋ] **spazieren gehen** go for a walk [wɔːk]; take a walk *(bes. AE)*
2. Wie geht's? / Wie geht es dir/euch/Ihnen? How are you? **Mir geht's nicht gut.** I don't feel well.
3. Worum geht es in der Geschichte? What is the story about? **Es geht um eine Möwe.** It's about a seagull.
gehören: jm. gehören belong to sb. [bɪ'lɒŋ] **zu etwas gehören** *(zu etwas passen)* go with sth.
Gehweg pavement ['peɪvmənt] *(BE)*; sidewalk ['saɪdwɔːk] *(AE)*
Geist ghost [gəʊst]
Gel gel [dʒel]
Geländer railing ['reɪlɪŋ]
gelangen *(hinkommen)* get [get]
gelangweilt sein be/feel bored [bɔːd]
gelb yellow ['jeləʊ]
Geld money ['mʌni] **Geld sammeln (für)** raise money (for) [reɪz]
Gelegenheit *(Möglichkeit, Chance)* chance [tʃɑːns]
Gemälde painting ['peɪntɪŋ]
gemischt mixed [mɪkst]
Gemüse vegetables *(pl)* ['vedʒtəblz]
genannt werden *(heißen)* be called [kɔːld]
genau 1. *(Adjektiv)* exact [ɪg'zækt] **2.** *(Adverb)* exactly [ɪg'zæktli] **genau in dem Moment** just then **genau wie …** just like … ['dʒʌst laɪk]
genauso *(gleichermaßen)* equally ['iːkwəli] **genauso langweilig/aufregend/…** just as boring/exciting/…
Generation generation [ˌdʒenə'reɪʃn]
generell generally ['dʒenrəli]
genial brilliant ['brɪliənt]
genießen enjoy [ɪn'dʒɔɪ]
genug enough [ɪ'nʌf]
geöffnet open ['əʊpən]
Geografie geography [dʒi'ɒgrəfi]
gerade 1. *(im Moment)* at the moment ['məʊmənt] **gerade dann** just then **gerade eben** just [dʒʌst] **jetzt gerade** *(in diesem Moment)* right now [raɪt 'naʊ] **2.** *(nicht gekrümmt)* straight [streɪt]
geradeaus weiter straight on [streɪt‿'ɒn]
geradewegs *(direkt)* straight [streɪt]
Gerät *(Maschine)* machine [mə'ʃiːn]
geraten: in Panik geraten panic ['pænɪk] **in Schwierigkeiten geraten** get into trouble
Geräusch sound [saʊnd]; *(Lärm)* noise [nɔɪz]
gern: Ich tanze/singe/… gern. I like dancing/singing/… **Ich hätte gern …** I'd like … [ˌaɪd 'laɪk] (= I would like …) **Ich würde gern gehen.** I'd like to go. **Ich würde sehr gern …** I'd love to … **Was hättest du gern?** What would you like? [wʊd] **Bitte, gern geschehen.**

(Nichts zu danken.) You're welcome. ['welkəm]
gernhaben like [laɪk]
Geruch smell
gesamte(r, s) whole [həʊl]
Gesamtsumme: eine Gesamtsumme von … a total of … ['təʊtl]
Geschäft *(Laden)* shop [ʃɒp]
geschäftig *(belebt)* busy ['bɪzi]
geschehen (mit) happen (to) ['hæpən]
Geschenk present ['preznt]
Geschichte **1.** *(vergangene Zeiten)* history ['hɪstri] **2.** *(Erzählung)* story ['stɔːri]
geschieden divorced [dɪ'vɔːst]
Geschirr: das Geschirr abwaschen, spülen wash the dishes *(pl)* [ˌwɒʃ ðə 'dɪʃɪz]
geschlossen closed [kləʊzd]
Geschmack, Geschmacksrichtung flavour *(BE)*, flavor *(AE)* ['fleɪvə]
Geschwindigkeit speed [spiːd]
Gesellschaft *(Firma)* company ['kʌmpəni]
Gesetz law [lɔː]
Gesicht face [feɪs]
gespannt *(aufgeregt)* excited [ɪk'saɪtɪd]
Gespenst ghost [gəʊst]
Gespräch conversation [ˌkɒnvə'seɪʃn]
Gestalt *(Form)* shape [ʃeɪp]; *(Figur)* figure ['fɪgə]
Gestaltung *(Layout)* layout ['leɪaʊt]
gestern yesterday ['jestədeɪ], ['jestədi]
Gesundheitswesen health service ['helθ ˌsɜːvɪs]
Getränk drink [drɪŋk]
getrennt *(auseinander)* apart [ə'pɑːt]
Gewinn *(Preis)* prize [praɪz]
gewinnen win [wɪn]
Gewinner/in winner ['wɪnə]
Gewitter storm [stɔːm]
Gewohnheit *(Angewohnheit)* habit ['hæbɪt]
gewöhnlich usual ['juːʒuəl] *(adj)*; *(normalerweise)* usually ['juːʒuəli] *(adv)*
gießen pour [pɔː]
Gipfel peak [piːk]; summit ['sʌmɪt]
Giraffe giraffe [dʒə'rɑːf]
Gitarre guitar [gɪ'tɑː] **Gitarre spielen** play the guitar
Gitter grid [grɪd]
glänzend brilliant ['brɪliənt]
Glas glass [glɑːs]
glatt *(rutschig)* slippery ['slɪpəri]
glauben believe [bɪ'liːv]; *(denken)* think [θɪŋk]
gleich nachdem … just after …
gleichermaßen equally ['iːkwəli]
gleichzeitig *(zur selben Zeit)* at one time
Gleis track [træk]; *(Bahnsteig)* platform ['plætfɔːm]
gleiten slither ['slɪðə]
Gliederung *(Struktur)* structure ['strʌktʃə]
Glocke bell [bel]
Glück: Viel Glück! Good luck! [lʌk] **Glück haben** be lucky ['lʌki] **Du Glückspilz.** Lucky you. ['lʌki]
glücklich happy ['hæpi]
glücklicherweise luckily ['lʌkɪli]
Gold gold [gəʊld]
golden, Gold- gold [gəʊld]
Gott God [gɒd]
Gottesdienst service ['sɜːvɪs]
Gouverneur/in governor ['gʌvənə]
Grab grave [greɪv]
Graben ditch [dɪtʃ]
Grabstein gravestone ['greɪvstəʊn]
Grafiken graphics *(pl)* ['græfɪks]
Grafschaft *(in Großbritannien)* county ['kaʊnti]
Gramm gram [græm]
Gras grass [grɑːs]
grau grey [greɪ]
greifen (nach) reach (for) [riːtʃ] **Greif zu!** *(Bedien dich!)* Help yourself!
Grenze border ['bɔːdə]
Griff hold [həʊld]; *(Klinke)* handle ['hændl]
Grill barbecue ['bɑːbɪkjuː]
Grillfest, -party barbecue ['bɑːbɪkjuː]
grinsen grin [grɪn]
grob rough [rʌf]
groß big [bɪg]; large [lɑːdʒ]; *(Person)* tall [tɔːl] **Wie groß soll der/dein Tee sein?** What size tea would you like? [saɪz] **der/die/das größte …; die größten …** the biggest … ['bɪgɪst]
großartig great [greɪt]; brilliant ['brɪliənt]; awesome ['ɔːsəm] *(bes. AE, infml)*
Großbuchstabe capital letter [ˌkæpɪtl 'letə]
Größe size [saɪz]
Großeltern grandparents ['grænpeərənts]
Großmutter grandmother ['grænmʌðə]
Großstadt city ['sɪti]
Großvater grandfather ['grænfɑːðə]
grün green [griːn]
Grund *(Begründung)* reason ['riːzn]
gründen found [faʊnd]
Gruppe group (of) [gruːp]
gruselig scary ['skeəri]
Grüß Gott. Hello. [hə'ləʊ] **Grüß … von mir.** Say hello to … for me.
Grüße: Liebe Grüße, … *(Briefschluss)* Love, …
gucken look [lʊk]
gut good [gʊd]; *(in Ordnung, prima)* fine [faɪn]; *(gesundheitlich)* well **gut sein in Kung-Fu / gut Kung-Fu können** be good at kung fu **gut laufen, gut gehen** go well [wel] **Danke, gut.** Fine, thanks. **Guten Morgen.** Good morning. [gʊd 'mɔːnɪŋ] **Ich fühle mich nicht gut. / Mir geht's nicht gut.** I don't feel well.
gutaussehend good-looking [ˌgʊd'lʊkɪŋ]
Güter goods *(pl)* [gʊdz]
Gymnastik gymnastics [dʒɪm'næstɪks]

H

Haar, Haare hair [heə]
haben have [hæv], [həv]; have got **Durst haben** be thirsty ['θɜːsti] **Glück haben** be lucky **Hunger haben** be hungry ['hʌŋgri] **Ich habe im Mai Geburtstag.** My birthday is in May. **jemand hat Recht** someone is right **jemand hat Unrecht** someone is wrong **viel zu tun haben** *(beschäftigt sein)* be busy ['bɪzi] **Wann hast du Geburtstag?** When's your birthday?
Hafen harbour ['hɑːbə]
Hafenstadt port [pɔːt]
Hähnchen chicken ['tʃɪkɪn]
Hai shark [ʃɑːk]
Haken hook [hʊk]
halb-; Halb- semi- ['semi]
halb: eine halbe Stunde half an hour **halb elf (10.30 / 22.30)** half past ten ['hɑːf pɑːst]
Halbzeit half [hɑːf], *pl* halves [hɑːvz]
Hälfte half [hɑːf], *pl* halves [hɑːvz]
Hallo. Hello. [hə'ləʊ]
Hals neck [nek]; *(Kehle)* throat [θrəʊt]
Halsschmerzen haben have a sore throat [sɔː 'θrəʊt]
Halt stop [stɒp]
halten hold [həʊld]; keep [kiːp] **einen Vortrag/eine Rede halten (über)** give a talk (about) **etwas warm/frisch halten** keep sth. warm/fresh
Haltestelle stop [stɒp]
Hammer hammer ['hæmə]
hämmern hammer ['hæmə]
Hand hand [hænd]
Händedruck handshake ['hændʃeɪk]
Handel trade [treɪd]
handeln: Es handelt von einer Möwe. It's about a seagull. **Wovon handelt die Geschichte?** What is the story about?
Handgepäckstück carry-on bag ['kæri‿ɒn]
Handout handout ['hændaʊt]
Handschlag handshake ['hændʃeɪk]
Handschuh glove [glʌv]
Handy mobile phone [ˌməʊbaɪl 'fəʊn], *(kurz auch:)* mobile
Handzettel handout ['hændaʊt]
hängen hang [hæŋ] **an etwas hängen** *(befestigt sein)* be attached to sth. [ə'tætʃt]
harmlos harmless ['hɑːmləs]
hart hard [hɑːd]; rough [rʌf]
hätte: Du hättest ihn gemocht. You would have liked him. **Du hättest mich fragen können.** You could have asked me.
Haufen *(Stapel, Stoß)* pile [paɪl]
häufig *(Adjektiv: weit verbreitet)* common ['kɒmən]
Haupt- main [meɪn]
Hauptsatz main clause
Hauptstadt capital ['kæpɪtl]

Hauptteil *(eines Textes)* body ['bɒdi]
Haus house [haʊs] **nach Hause gehen** go home **nach Hause kommen** come home **zu Hause** at home **zu Hause sein** be in **nicht zu Hause sein** be out
Hausarrest: jm. Hausarrest erteilen ground sb. [graʊnd]
Hausaufgabe(n) homework ['həʊmwɜːk] **Hausaufgaben machen** do my / your / … homework **Was haben wir als Hausaufgabe auf?** What's for homework?
Häuschen cottage ['kɒtɪdʒ]
Haustier pet [pet]
heben lift [lɪft]
heftig *(wild)* fierce [fɪəs] **heftiger Regen** heavy rain ['hevi]
Heidelbeere blueberry ['bluːbəri]
Heiligabend Christmas Eve [ˌkrɪsməs‿'iːv]
Heim *(Zuhause)* home [həʊm]
Heimat sein für etwas be home to sth.
Heimatstadt hometown [ˌhəʊm'taʊn]
heiraten marry ['mæri]
heiß hot [hɒt]
heißen *(genannt werden)* be called [kɔːld] **Es heißt hier: …** It says here: … **Ich heiße …** My name is … **Wie heißt du?** What's your name?
hektisch *(belebt, geschäftig)* busy ['bɪzi]
Held/in hero ['hɪərəʊ], *pl* heroes
helfen help [help]
Helikopter helicopter ['helɪkɒptə]
hell bright [braɪt]
hellbraun/-blau/… light brown/ blue/…
Hemd shirt [ʃɜːt]
herannahen approach [ə'prəʊtʃ]
herauf up [ʌp]
heraus out [aʊt] **aus … heraus** out of … ['aʊt‿əv]
herausfordern: jn. herausfordern (zu etwas) challenge sb. (to sth.) ['tʃælɪndʒ]
Herausforderung challenge ['tʃælɪndʒ]
Herausgeber/in editor ['edɪtə]
heraushalten: etwas heraushalten aus keep sth. out of
Herberge hostel ['hɒstl]
herbringen bring [brɪŋ]
Herbst autumn *(BE)* ['ɔːtəm], fall *(AE)* [fɔːl]
hereinkommen come in [ˌkʌm‿'ɪn]
Herr Schwarz Mr Schwarz ['mɪstə] **Meine Damen und Herren / Sehr geehrte Damen und Herren** Ladies and gentlemen [ˌleɪdiz‿ən 'dʒentlmən]
herrennen: hinter jm. herrennen run after sb. [ˌrʌn‿'ɑːftə]
herrlich lovely ['lʌvli]
herrschen: über etwas herrschen rule sth. [ruːl]
herüber: hier herüber over here
herüberkommen (zu/nach) come over (to)
herum: um … herum around … [ə'raʊnd] **überall um sie herum** all around her
herum-: etwas herumgeben, herumreichen pass sth. around [ˌpɑːs‿ə'raʊnd] **herumirren, herumlaufen** wander ['wɒndə] **herumwirbeln** *(sich im Kreis drehen)* spin around [ˌspɪn‿ə'raʊnd]
herunter down [daʊn] **von … herunter** off … **etwas herunterladen** download sth. [ˌdaʊn'ləʊd] **vom Fahrrad herunterfallen** fall off a bike
hervorheben *(mit Textmarker markieren)* highlight ['haɪlaɪt]
Hervorhebung emphasis ['emfəsɪs]
hervorragend excellent ['eksələnt]
Herz heart [hɑːt] **Tiere liegen mir sehr am Herzen.** I really care about animals.
Heu hay [heɪ]
Heuler *(Robbenjunges)* baby seal ['beɪbi siːl]
heute today [tə'deɪ] **heute Nachmittag/Abend/…** this afternoon/evening/… **heute Nacht/heute Abend** tonight [tə'naɪt]
hier here [hɪə] **hier in der Gegend** round here [ˌraʊnd 'hɪə] **hier in der Nähe** near here **hier herüber; hier drüben** over here **(nach) hier oben** up here
hierher here [hɪə] **bis hierher** so far
Hilfe help [help]
Himmel sky [skaɪ]; *(im religiösen Sinn)* heaven ['hevn]
Hin- und Rückfahrkarte return (ticket) [rɪ'tɜːn]
hinauf up [ʌp] **auf das Boot hinauf** onto the boat ['ɒntʊ]
hinaufklettern (auf) climb [klaɪm]
hinaus out [aʊt] **aus … hinaus** out of … ['aʊt‿əv]
hinbringen take [teɪk]
hinein: in die Küche hinein into the kitchen ['ɪntʊ]
hineingehen in enter ['entə]
hinfallen fall [fɔːl]
hinkommen *(gelangen)* get [get]
hinlegen: etwas hinlegen put sth. down **sich hinlegen** lie down [ˌlaɪ 'daʊn]
hinsetzen: sich hinsetzen sit down [ˌsɪt 'daʊn]
Hinsicht: in mancher/vielerlei Hinsicht in some/many ways
hinstellen: sich hinstellen stand [stænd]
hinten: von hinten from behind [bɪ'haɪnd]
hinter behind [bɪ'haɪnd] **hinter jm. herrennen** run after sb. [ˌrʌn‿'ɑːftə] **aus dem hinteren Teil des Busses** from the back of the bus
Hintergrund background ['bækgraʊnd]
hinterlassen: eine Nachricht hinterlassen leave a message [ˌliːv‿ə 'mesɪdʒ]
hinüber zu/nach … over to … ['əʊvə]
hinüberrennen (zu/nach) run over (to)
hinunter down [daʊn]
hinunterbeugen: sich hinunterbeugen bend down [bend]
Hinweis *(Lösungshinweis; Anhaltspunkt)* clue [kluː]
hinweisen: (jn.) auf etwas hinweisen point sth. out (to sb.) [ˌpɔɪnt‿'aʊt]
hinzufügen (zu) add (to) [æd]
Hirsch deer [dɪə]
historisch *(geschichtlich bedeutsam)* historic [hɪ'stɒrɪk]
Hobby hobby ['hɒbi]
hoch high [haɪ]; *(Gebäude, Baum)* tall [tɔːl]
hochheben: etwas hochheben pick sth. up [ˌpɪk‿'ʌp]
hochladen upload
Hochmoor moor [mɔː], [mʊə]
hochsehen look up [lʊk‿'ʌp]
Hochzeit wedding ['wedɪŋ]
Hof *(Innenhof, Vorplatz)* courtyard ['kɔːtjɑːd]
hoffen hope [həʊp]
höflich polite [pə'laɪt]
Höhe altitude ['æltɪtjuːd]
Höhle cave [keɪv]
holen: (sich) etwas holen get sth.
Holz wood [wʊd]
hölzern wooden ['wʊdn]
Honig honey ['hʌni]
horchen listen ['lɪsn]
hören hear [hɪə]
Hose trousers *(pl)* ['traʊzəz]; pants *(pl)* [pænts] *(AE)*
hübsch pretty ['prɪti]; lovely ['lʌvli]
Hubschrauber helicopter ['helɪkɒptə]
Hüfte hip [hɪp]
Hügel hill [hɪl]
Huhn chicken ['tʃɪkɪn]
Hummer lobster ['lɒbstə]
Humor: Sinn für Humor sense of humour [ˌsens‿əv 'hjuːmə]
Hund dog [dɒg] **mit dem Hund rausgehen** *(den Hund ausführen)* walk the dog
Hunger haben be hungry ['hʌŋgri]
hungern starve [stɑːv]
Hungersnot famine ['fæmɪn]
hungrig sein be hungry ['hʌŋgri]
Hupe horn [hɔːn]
hupen blow the horn [hɔːn]
hüpfen hop [hɒp]
Hurrikan hurricane ['hʌrɪkən, hʌrɪkeɪn]
Husten haben have a cough [kɒf]
Hut hat [hæt]
Hymne anthem ['ænθəm]
hypnotisierend *(fesselnd)* mesmerizing ['mezməraɪzɪŋ]

I

ich I [aɪ] **Ich auch.** Me too. **Ich bin's.** It's me.
ideal *(perfekt)* perfect ['pɜːfɪkt]
Idee idea [aɪ'dɪə]
ihm him [hɪm]; *(bei Dingen, Tieren)* it

ihn him [hɪm]; *(bei Dingen, Tieren)* it
ihnen them [ðem], [ðəm]
Ihnen *(höfliche Anrede)* you [juː]
ihr *(Plural von „du")* you [juː]
ihr: Hilf ihr. Help her. [hɜː]
ihr(e) … *(vor Nomen; besitzanzeigend)*
1. *(zu „she")* her … [hɜː, hə]
2. *(zu „it")* its … [ɪts]
3. *(zu „they")* their … [ðeə]
Ihr(e) … *(vor Nomen; besitzanzeigend)* *(zur höflichen Anrede „you")* your … [jɔː, jə]
ihrer, ihre, ihrs hers [hɜːz]
im: im Jahr 1580 in 1580 **im Fernsehen** on TV **im Gang sein** go on
Imbiss snack [snæk]
immer always ['ɔːlweɪz] **immer noch** still [stɪl] **immer wieder** again and again **für immer** for ever [fər‿'evə], forever **etwas immer wieder / immer weiter tun** keep doing sth. [kiːp] **was (auch) immer** whatever [ˌwɒt'evə]
Imperium empire ['empaɪə]
in in [ɪn]; *(in Ortsangaben auch oft:)* at [æt], [ət] **in der Beach Road** in Beach Road **in der Beach Road 8** at 8 Beach Road **in der Dean Street** in Dean Street **in der Dean Street 14** at 14 Dean Street **in der Nacht** at night **in der Nähe von** near **in der Schule** at school **in die Küche (hinein)** into the kitchen **in England** in England **in Ordnung** all right **in Richtung Bahnhof/Mr Bell** towards the station/Mr Bell [tə'wɔːdz] **in Schwierigkeiten sein** be in trouble ['trʌbl]
inbegriffen included [ɪn'kluːdɪd]
Inder/in; indisch Indian ['ɪndiən]
Indianer/in Indian ['ɪndiən]
Industrie industry ['ɪndəstri] **verarbeitende Industrie** manufacturing industry [ˌmænju'fæktʃərɪŋ]
Infinitiv infinitive [ɪn'fɪnətɪv]
Information(en) (über) information (about) *(no pl)* [ˌɪnfə'meɪʃn]
Informations- und Kommunikationstechnologie ICT [ˌaɪ siː 'tiː] (Information and Communication Technology)
Inhalt content ['kɒntent]
Inlineskaten skating ['skeɪtɪŋ]
Inlineskates skates [skeɪts]
innehalten *(eine Pause einlegen)* pause [pɔːz]
Innere: das Innere *(die Innenseite)* the inside
Insel island ['aɪlənd]
Inserat advertisement [əd'vɜːtɪsmənt] (*kurz auch:* advert ['ædvɜːt], ad [æd])
insgesamt *(alles in allem)* altogether [ˌɔːltə'geðə]
Instrument instrument ['ɪnstrəmənt]
interessant interesting ['ɪntrəstɪŋ]
interessieren: sich interessieren (für) be interested (in) ['ɪntrəstɪd]
interessiert sein (an) be interested (in) ['ɪntrəstɪd] **Wen interessiert das?** Who cares?
Internat boarding school ['bɔːdɪŋ skuːl]
international international [ˌɪntə'næʃnəl]
Internet internet ['ɪntənet] **im Internet** on the internet
Interview interview ['ɪntəvjuː]
Intonation intonation [ˌɪntə'neɪʃn]
irgendetwas? anything? ['eniθɪŋ]
irgendjemand? anybody? / anyone? ['enibɒdi, 'eniwʌn]
irgendwelche: Gibt es irgendwelche …? Are there any …? ['eni]
irgendwie unheimlich/… kind of scary/… *(infml)*
irgendwo(hin) somewhere ['sʌmweə]
irren: jemand irrt sich *(jemand hat Unrecht)* someone is wrong [rɒŋ]

J

ja yes [jes] **Ja, das ist richtig. / Ja, das stimmt.** Yes, that's right.
Jacht yacht [jɒt]
Jacke, Jackett jacket ['dʒækɪt]
Jagd hunt [hʌnt]
jagen hunt [hʌnt]
Jahr year [jɪə] **eine Band aus den 60er Jahren** a 1960s band
Jahrgang, Jahrgangsstufe year [jɪə]
Jahrhundert century ['sentʃəri]
jährlich yearly ['jɪəli]
Januar January ['dʒænjuəri]
je **1. Sie kosten je 2 Pfund 75.** *(2,75 pro Stück)* They're £ 2.75 each. [iːtʃ]
2. besser als je zuvor better than ever
Jeans jeans *(pl)* [dʒiːnz]
jede(r, s): jeder Tag / jede Farbe / jedes Boot every day/colour/boat ['evri]
Jedenfalls, … *(Wie dem auch sei)* Anyway, … ['eniweɪ]
jeder *(alle)* everyone ['evriwʌn], everybody ['evribɒdi]; *(jeder einzelne)* each [iːtʃ]
Jeep jeep [dʒiːp]
jemals ever ['evə] **Bist du jemals in … gewesen?** Have you ever been to …?
jemand someone ['sʌmwʌn], somebody ['sʌmbədi]; *(in Fragen)* anybody? / anyone? ['enibɒdi, 'eniwʌn] **Finde jemanden, der …** Find someone who …
jene(r, s): jene Gruppe that group **jene Gruppen** those groups
jetzt now [naʊ] **jetzt gerade** right now [raɪt 'naʊ] **bis jetzt** so far **Jetzt, wo du …** Now that you …
Job job [dʒɒb]
Joghurt yoghurt ['jɒgət]
Jongleur/in juggler ['dʒʌglə]
jonglieren: mit etwas jonglieren juggle sth. ['dʒʌgl]
jubeln cheer [tʃɪə]
Judo judo ['dʒuːdəʊ]
Jugend; Jugend- youth [juːθ]
Jugendliche(r) kid [kɪd] *(infml)*
Jugendmannschaft junior team ['dʒuːniə tiːm]
Juli July [dʒu'laɪ]
jung young [jʌŋ]
Junge boy [bɔɪ]
Juni June [dʒuːn]
Juniorenmannschaft junior team ['dʒuːniə tiːm]
Juwelen jewels *(pl)* ['dʒuːəlz]

K

Kaffee coffee ['kɒfi]
Käfig cage [keɪdʒ]
Kajak kayak ['kaɪæk]
Kajakfahren kayaking ['kaɪækɪŋ]
Kakao cocoa ['kəʊkəʊ]
Kalender calendar ['kælɪndə]; diary ['daɪəri]
kalt cold [kəʊld]
Kamera camera ['kæmərə]
Kameramann cameraman, *pl* -men ['kæmrəmən]
Kamin fireplace ['faɪəpleɪs]
kämpfen fight [faɪt] **gegen jn. kämpfen** fight sb.
Kaninchen rabbit ['ræbɪt]
Kante *(Rand)* edge [edʒ]
Kantine canteen [kæn'tiːn]
Kapitän/in captain ['kæptɪn]
Kapitelüberschrift sub-heading ['sʌbˌhedɪŋ]
kaputt *(zerbrochen)* broken ['brəʊkən] **kaputt gehen** break [breɪk] **etwas kaputt machen** break sth.
Karneval carnival ['kɑːnɪvl]
Karotte carrot ['kærət]
Karren cart [kɑːt]
Karte (an) card (to) [kɑːd]
Kartoffel potato [pə'teɪtəʊ], *pl* potatoes
Käse cheese [tʃiːz]
Kästchen box [bɒks]; *(auf Papier)* square [skweə]
Kasse *(in Geschäften)* cash desk ['kæʃ desk]; *(für den Verkauf von Eintrittskarten)* ticket office ['tɪkɪt‿ˌɒfɪs]
Kasten box [bɒks]
Kathedrale cathedral [kə'θiːdrəl]
Katholik/in Catholic ['kæθlɪk]
katholisch Catholic ['kæθlɪk]
Katze cat [kæt]
kaufen buy [baɪ]
kaum: Ich kann es kaum erwarten, … zu sehen. I can't wait to see …
Kehle throat [θrəʊt]
kein(e) no [nəʊ] **keine(r, s) (von …)** none (of …) [nʌn] **Es gibt/sind keine …** There aren't any … ['eni] **Ich bin kein Junge.** I'm not a boy. **Ich mag kein Grün.** I don't like green.
Keks biscuit ['bɪskɪt]
keltisch Celtic ['keltɪk, 'seltɪk]

kennen know [nəʊ] **Woher kennst du ...?** How do you know ...?
kennenlernen meet [mi:t] **Freut mich, dich/euch/Sie kennenzulernen.** Nice to meet you.
kennzeichnen: etwas kennzeichnen *(markieren)* mark sth. up [ˌmɑ:k_'ʌp]
Kerl *(Typ)* guy [gaɪ]; dude [dju:d] *(bes. AE, Slang)*
Kernpunkt key point
Kerze candle ['kændl]
Kette chain [tʃeɪn]
Kies gravel ['grævl]
Kieselstein pebble ['pebl]
Kilogramm, Kilo (kg) kilogram ['kɪləgræm], kilo ['ki:ləʊ] (kg)
Kilometer kilometre ['kɪləmi:tə], [kɪ'lɒmɪtə] (km)
Kind child [tʃaɪld], *pl* children ['tʃɪldrən]; *(infml auch:)* kid [kɪd]
Kino cinema ['sɪnəmə]
Kirche church [tʃɜ:tʃ]
Kiste box [bɒks]
Klang sound [saʊnd]
Klapperschlange rattlesnake ['rætlsneɪk]
Klaps *(Tätscheln)* pat [pæt]
klar clear [klɪə]
Klasse class [klɑ:s]
Klassenkamerad/in classmate ['klɑ:smeɪt]
Klassenzimmer classroom ['klɑ:sru:m]
klatschen *(Beifall)* clap [klæp]
Klavier piano [pi'ænəʊ] **Klavier spielen** play the piano
Klebestift glue stick ['glu: stɪk]
klebrig sticky ['stɪki]
Klebstoff glue [glu:]
Kleid dress [dres]
Kleidung, Kleidungsstücke clothes *(pl)* [kləʊðz]
klein little ['lɪtl]; small [smɔ:l]
klettern climb [klaɪm] **auf einen Baum/einen Turm klettern** climb a tree/a tower
Klingel bell [bel]
klingeln ring [rɪŋ]
klingen sound [saʊnd]
Klinke handle ['hændl]
Klippe cliff [klɪf]
klopfen *(tippen)* tap [tæp]
Klub club [klʌb] **in einen Klub eintreten / sich einem Klub anschließen** join a club [dʒɔɪn]
klug clever ['klevə]
Knall bang [bæŋ]
Knallbonbon cracker ['krækə]
Kneipe pub [pʌb]
Knie knee [ni:]
knien kneel [ni:l]
knurren growl [graʊl]
kochen cook [kʊk]
Kochrezept recipe ['resəpi]
Kohle coal [kəʊl]
Kohlebergwerk coal mine
Kolonie colony ['kɒləni]
Kolonist/in colonist ['kɒlənɪst]
komisch 1. *(lustig)* funny ['fʌni] **2.** *(seltsam, merkwürdig)* funny; strange [streɪndʒ]; weird [wɪəd]
Komma comma ['kɒmə] **3,5 (drei Komma fünf)** 3.5 (three point five)
kommen come [kʌm]; *(gelangen, hinkommen)* get [get] **Ich komme aus Plymouth.** I'm from Plymouth. **Komm, Dad!** *(Na los, Dad!)* Come on, Dad. **nach Hause kommen** come home **auf etwas kommen** *(Idee)* come up with sth.
Kommentar comment ['kɒment]
kommentieren: etwas kommentieren comment on sth. ['kɒment]
Kommunikation communication [kəˌmju:nɪ'keɪʃn]
König king [kɪŋ]
Königin queen [kwi:n]
königlich royal ['rɔɪəl]
Königreich kingdom ['kɪŋdəm] **das Vereinigte Königreich** the United Kingdom (UK) [juˌnaɪtɪd 'kɪŋdəm]
können can [kæn], [kən]; be able to ['eɪbl] **ich kann nicht ... / du kannst nicht ...** *usw.* I can't ... / you can't ... *etc.* [kɑ:nt] **gut Kung-Fu können** be good at kung fu **Kann ich Sie kurz sprechen?** May I have a word with you?
konnte(n): ich konnte ... / du konntest ... *usw.* I could ... / you could ... *etc.* [kʊd] **ich konnte nicht ... / du konntest nicht ...** *usw.* I couldn't ... / you couldn't ... *etc.* [kʊdnt]
könnte(n): **Was könnte besser sein?** What could be better? [kʊd], [kəd] / What might be better? [maɪt]
Konsequenz consequence ['kɒnsɪkwəns]
Konsonant consonant ['kɒnsənənt]
Kontakt aufnehmen (mit jm.) get in touch (with sb.) [tʌtʃ] **Kontakt halten (mit jm.)** stay in touch (with sb.)
Kontext *(Text-, Satzzusammenhang)* context ['kɒntekst]
Konto account [ə'kaʊnt]
Kontrolle *(Überprüfung)* check [tʃek]
kontrollieren *(überprüfen)* check [tʃek]
konzentrieren: sich konzentrieren (auf etwas) concentrate (on sth.) ['kɒnsntreɪt]
Konzert concert ['kɒnsət]
Koordinator/in coordinator [kəʊ'ɔ:dɪneɪtə]
Kopf head [hed]
Kopfschmerzen haben have a headache ['hedeɪk]
Kopie copy ['kɒpi]
kopieren copy ['kɒpi]
Korb basket ['bɑ:skɪt]
Korbball netball ['netbɔ:l]
Körper body ['bɒdi]
Körperteil part of the body
korrekt correct [kə'rekt]
Korridor corridor ['kɒrɪdɔ:]
kosten 1. cost [kɒst] **Die Kamera kostet ...** The camera is ... **Die DVDs kosten ...** The DVDs are ... **Was/Wie viel kostet ...?** How much is ...? **Was/Wie viel kosten ...?** How much are ...? **2. etwas kosten** *(probieren)* taste sth. [teɪst]
kostenlos free; for free
köstlich delicious [dɪ'lɪʃəs]
Kostüm costume ['kɒstju:m]
Kraft *(Stärke)* power ['paʊə]; *(Energie)* energy ['enədʒi]
kräftig strong [strɒŋ]; *(mächtig)* powerful ['paʊəfl]; *(energisch)* vigorous ['vɪgərəs]
Kram stuff [stʌf] *(infml)*
krank sick [sɪk]; ill [ɪl]
Krankenhaus hospital ['hɒspɪtl]
Krankheit illness; sickness; *(ernsthaft; ansteckend)* disease [dɪ'zi:z]
Krebs *(Tier)* crab [kræb]
kreieren create [kri'eɪt]
Kreis circle ['sɜ:kl]
Kreisverkehr roundabout ['raʊndəbaʊt]
kreuzen *(überqueren)* cross [krɒs]
Kreuzotter adder ['ædə]
Kreuzung *(Straßenkreuzung)* junction ['dʒʌŋkʃn]
Kricket cricket ['krɪkɪt]
Kritik *(Rezension, Besprechung)* review [rɪ'vju:]
Krone crown [kraʊn]
Küche kitchen ['kɪtʃɪn]
Kuchen cake [keɪk]
Kugelschreiber pen [pen]
Kuh cow [kaʊ]
Kultur culture ['kʌltʃə]
kümmern: sich um jn. kümmern look after sb.
Kunst art [ɑ:t]
Künstler/in artist ['ɑ:tɪst]
künstlich man-made [ˌmæn'meɪd]
Kunststoff plastic ['plæstɪk]
Kunstwerk artwork ['ɑ:twɜ:k]; work of art
Kuppel dome [dəʊm]
Kürbis squash [skwɒʃ]
kurz short [ʃɔ:t] **kurz nachdem ...** just after ...
küssen; sich küssen kiss [kɪs]
Küste coast [kəʊst]

L

lächeln smile [smaɪl]
Lächeln smile [smaɪl]
lachen laugh [lɑ:f] **über jn./etwas lachen** laught at sb./sth.
laden *(Handy, Batterien)* charge ['tʃɑ:dʒ]
Laden shop [ʃɒp] **Laden an der Ecke** *(„Tante-Emma-Laden")* corner shop ['kɔ:nə ʃɒp]
Lage: in der Lage sein, etwas zu tun be able to do sth. ['eɪbl]
Lamm lamb [læm]
Lampe lamp [læmp]
Land country ['kʌntri]; land [lænd]

landen land [lænd]
Landkarte map ['mæp] **auf der Landkarte** on the map
Landschaft countryside ['kʌntrisaɪd]
Landungssteg landing ['lændɪŋ]
Landwirt/in farmer ['fɑːmə]
lang long [lɒŋ] **der/die/das längste ...; am längsten** (the) longest ... ['lɒŋgɪst] **lang aufbleiben** stay up late
Länge length [leŋθ]
langsam slow [sləʊ]
langweilen: sich langweilen be/feel bored [bɔːd]
langweilig boring ['bɔːrɪŋ]
Laptop *(tragbarer PC)* laptop ['læptɒp]
Lärm noise [nɔɪz] **voller Lärm** noisy ['nɔɪzi]
lärmend noisy ['nɔɪzi]
lassen: Lass mich dir ... zeigen. Let me show you ... **Lass(t) uns ...** Let's ... **Lass das!** Stop it! **etwas fallen lassen** drop sth. [drɒp] **etwas übrig lassen** leave sth. [liːv]
Lastwagen (LKW) truck [trʌk]; lorry ['lɒri] *(BE)*
laufen run [rʌn]
laut **1.** loud [laʊd]; *(voller Lärm)* noisy ['nɔɪzi] **laut (vor)lesen** read aloud [ə'laʊd] **etwas lauter stellen** turn sth. up [tɜːn]
2. laut ... *(... zufolge)* according to ... [ə'kɔːdɪŋ]
Laut sound [saʊnd]
läuten ring [rɪŋ]
Lautsprecher loudspeaker [ˌlaʊd'spiːkə]
Layout layout ['leɪaʊt]
leben *(am Leben sein)* be alive [ə'laɪv]; *(wohnen)* live [lɪv]
Leben life [laɪf], *pl* lives [laɪvz] **am Leben sein** be alive [ə'laɪv]
lecker delicious [dɪ'lɪʃəs]; tasty ['teɪsti]; yummy ['jʌmi] *(infml)*
Leder leather ['leðə]
ledig *(alleinstehend)* single ['sɪŋgl]
leer empty ['empti]
legen lay [leɪ]; *(hinlegen, ablegen)* put [pʊt]
legendär legendary ['ledʒəndri]
Legende legend ['ledʒənd]
lehnen: sich lehnen lean [liːn]
lehren teach [tiːtʃ] **jn. lehren, etwas zu tun** teach sb. to do sth.
Lehrer/in teacher ['tiːtʃə]
Lehrgang workshop ['wɜːkʃɒp]
Leiche body ['bɒdi]
leicht *(einfach)* easy ['iːzi]
leid: Es tut mir leid (wegen ...) I'm sorry (about ...)
leiden: nicht leiden können dislike [dɪs'laɪk]
Leine line [laɪn]
leise quiet ['kwaɪət]; silent ['saɪlənt] **mit leiser Stimme** in a soft voice **etwas leiser stellen** turn sth. down [tɜːn]
leiten *(führen)* lead [liːd]
Leiter/in leader ['liːdə]; director [də'rektə]
lenken steer [stɪə]
Lenkrad (steering) wheel ['stɪərɪŋ wiːl]
lernen learn [lɜːn]; *(untersuchen, beobachten)* study ['stʌdi]
lesen read [riːd] **laut (vor)lesen** read aloud [ə'laʊd]
letzte(r, s) last [lɑːst] **letztes Wochenende / letzten Freitag** last weekend/Friday **Wann hast du sie das letzte Mal gesehen?** When did you see them last?
leuchten shine [ʃaɪn]
leuchtend bright [braɪt]
Leute people ['piːpl]; guys *(pl)* [gaɪz]; folk *(pl)* [fəʊk] *(infml)*
Licht light [laɪt]
Lichtblitz flash [flæʃ]
Liebe: Alles Liebe, ... / Liebe Grüße, ... *(Briefschluss)* Love, ...
liebe(r, s) dear [dɪə]
lieben love [lʌv]
lieber: Ich sollte lieber ... I'd better ... (= I had better ...)
Lieblings-: mein Lieblingstag my favourite day ['feɪvərɪt]
Lied song [sɒŋ]
Lieferwagen van [væn]
liegen lie [laɪ] **Tiere liegen mir sehr am Herzen.** I really care about animals.
Lift elevator ['elɪveɪtə] *(bes. AE; BE auch: lift)*
lila purple ['pɜːpl]
Lineal ruler ['ruːlə]
Linie line [laɪn]
linke(r, s) left [left] **auf der linken Seite** on the left **nach links** left **(nach) links abbiegen** turn left
Lippe lip [lɪp]
Liste list [lɪst]
Literatur literature ['lɪtrətʃə]
Loch hole [həʊl]
Löffel spoon [spuːn]
Lokal- *(am/vom Ort)* local ['ləʊkl]
los: Los geht's. / Jetzt geht's los. Here we go. **Los mit euch jetzt!** Off you go now. **Was ist los?** What's the matter? ['mætə] **Was ist los mit Justin/dir?** What's wrong with Justin/you?
löschen *(streichen)* delete [dɪ'liːt]
Löwe lion ['laɪən]
Luft air [eə]
Luftballon balloon [bə'luːn]
lustig: sich über jn./etwas lustig machen make fun of sb./sth.
luxuriös luxurious [lʌg'ʒʊəriəs]

M

machen *(tun)* do [duː]; *(herstellen)*make [meɪk] **jn. zu etwas machen** make sb. sth. **einen Bootsausflug machen** go on a boat trip **einen Spaziergang machen** go for a walk [wɔːk] **Fotos machen** take photos **Hat es Spaß gemacht?** Was it fun? **sich über jn./etwas lustig machen** make fun of sb./sth.
Macht power ['paʊə]
mächtig *(kräftig, stark)* powerful ['paʊəfl]
Mädchen girl [gɜːl]
Magen stomach ['stʌmək]
mager *(dünn, dürr)* skinny ['skɪni]
magisch magic ['mædʒɪk]; magical ['mædʒɪkl]
Mahlzeit meal [miːl]
Mai May [meɪ]
Mais corn [kɔːn] *(AE, no pl)*
Mal time [taɪm] **dieses Mal** this time **zum ersten Mal** for the first time **Wann hast du sie das letzte Mal gesehen?** When did you see them last?
Malaria malaria [mə'leəriə]
malen paint [peɪnt]
Maler/in painter ['peɪntə]
Mama mum [mʌm]
man you
manchmal sometimes ['sʌmtaɪmz]
Mann man [mæn], *pl* men [men]
Mannschaft team [tiːm]
Mantel coat [kəʊt]
Marine navy ['neɪvi]
Marionette puppet ['pʌpɪt]
markieren: etwas markieren mark sth. up [ˌmɑːk‿'ʌp]; *(mit Textmarker)* highlight sth. ['haɪlaɪt]
Markt market ['mɑːkɪt]
Marmelade jam [dʒæm]; *(aus Zitrusfrüchten)* marmalade ['mɑːməleɪd]
Marschland swamp [swɒmp]
März March [mɑːtʃ]
Maschine machine [mə'ʃiːn]
Maske mask [mɑːsk]
Material material [mə'tɪəriəl]
Mathematik maths [mæθs]
Matsch mud [mʌd]
Mauer wall [wɔːl]
Maul mouth [maʊθ]
Medaille medal ['medl]
Medien media *(pl)* ['miːdiə] **soziale Medien** social media *(pl)* [ˌsəʊʃl 'miːdiə]
Medizin medicine ['medsn, 'medɪsn]
Meer sea [siː] **am Meer** by the sea
Meeresfrüchte seafood ['siːfuːd]
Meeresspiegel sea level ['siː levl]
Meerschweinchen guinea pig ['gɪni pɪg]
Megaphon loudspeaker [ˌlaʊd'spiːkə]
mehr more [mɔː] **nicht mehr** not ... any more
Mehrheit majority [mə'dʒɒrəti]
Meile mile [maɪl]
meilenweit for miles
mein(e) ... my ... [maɪ] **Meine Damen und Herren** Ladies and gentlemen [ˌleɪdiz‿ən 'dʒentlmən]
meinen *(sagen wollen)* mean [miːn]
meiner, meine, meins mine [maɪn]
Meinung opinion [ə'pɪnjən]; view [vjuː] **meiner Meinung nach** in my opinion/view

meisten: die meisten Menschen / die meisten von euch most people/most of you [məʊst]
meistens usually ['juːʒuəli]
Meister/in master ['mɑːstə]
Melodie tune [tjuːn]
Menge *(Menschenmenge)* crowd [kraʊd]
Mensa *(Kantine)* canteen [kæn'tiːn]
Mensch human ['hjuːmən]; human being
Menschen people ['piːpl]
Menschenmenge crowd [kraʊd]
menschlich human ['hjuːmən]
merken *(bemerken)* notice ['nəʊtɪs] **sich etwas merken** remember sth.
Merkzettel crib sheet ['krɪb ʃiːt] *(infml)*
Messer knife [naɪf], *pl* knives [naɪvz]
Metall metal ['metl]
Meter metre ['miːtə]
mich me [miː]; myself [maɪ'self]
Milch milk [mɪlk]
Million million ['mɪljən]
Minderheit minority [maɪ'nɒrəti]
Mine *(Bergwerk)* mine [maɪn]; *(Militär)* mine [maɪn]
Minute minute ['mɪnɪt] **ein zweiminütiger Vortrag** a two-minute talk
mir me [miː]; myself [maɪ'self]
Mischung mix [mɪks]
mit with [wɪð] **mit dem Bus/Auto fahren** go by bus/car
Mitfahrgelegenheit lift [lɪft]
mitkommen come along [ə'lɒŋ]
Mitlaut consonant ['kɒnsənənt]
mitmachen join in [ˌdʒɔɪn‿'ɪn]
mitnehmen: jn. mitnehmen give sb. a lift
Mitschüler/in classmate ['klɑːsmeɪt]
Mittag: zu Mittag essen have lunch [lʌntʃ]
Mittagessen lunch [lʌntʃ]
mittags at lunchtime ['lʌntʃtaɪm]
Mittagszeit lunchtime ['lʌntʃtaɪm]
Mitte middle ['mɪdl]; *(Zentrum)* centre ['sentə]
mittelgroß medium ['miːdiəm]
Mitternacht midnight ['mɪdnaɪt]
Mittwoch Wednesday ['wenzdeɪ, 'wenzdi]
Mitwirkende *(Theaterstück, Film)* cast [kɑːst]
Möbel furniture *(no pl)* ['fɜːnɪtʃə]
Mobiltelefon mobile phone [ˌməʊbaɪl 'fəʊn], *(kurz auch:)* mobile
möchte: Ich möchte … (haben) I'd like … [ˌaɪd 'laɪk] (= I would like …) **Ich möchte gehen.** I'd like to go. **Was möchtest du (haben)?** What would you like? [wʊd] **Was möchtest du essen?** What would you like to eat? **Ich möchte (gern), dass du …** I want you to … / I'd like you to …
Mode fashion ['fæʃn]
Modell model ['mɒdl]
Moderator/in host [həʊst]
modern modern ['mɒdən]
mögen like [laɪk] **Ich mag …** I like … **Ich mag Grün nicht. / Ich mag kein Grün.** I don't like green. **etwas mögen** *(auf etwas stehen)* be into sth. *(infml)* **etwas nicht mögen** dislike sth. [dɪs'laɪk]
möglich possible ['pɒsəbl]
Möglichkeit *(Gelegenheit, Chance)* chance [tʃɑːns]
Möhre carrot ['kærət]
mollig chubby ['tʃʌbi]
Moment moment ['məʊmənt] **im Moment** at the moment **genau in dem Moment** just then **Warte einen Moment. / Moment mal.** Wait a minute.
Monarch/in monarch ['mɒnək]
Monat month [mʌnθ]
monatlich monthly ['mʌnθli]
Mond moon [muːn]
Mondlicht moonlight ['muːnlaɪt]
Monster monster ['mɒnstə]
Montag Monday ['mʌndeɪ, 'mʌndi]
Morgen *(Vormittag)* morning ['mɔːnɪŋ] **am Morgen** in the morning
morgen tomorrow [tə'mɒrəʊ]
morgens in the morning ['mɔːnɪŋ]
Möwe seagull ['siːgʌl]
MP3-Player, MP3-Spieler MP3 player [ˌempiː'θriː ˌpleɪə]
müde tired ['taɪəd]
Mühe: sich (große) Mühe geben try hard
Müll rubbish ['rʌbɪʃ]; garbage ['gɑːbɪdʒ] *(AE)*
Mund mouth [maʊθ]
Mundharmonika harmonica [hɑː'mɒnɪkə]
Münze coin [kɔɪn]
murmeln: …, murmelte er. …, he said under his breath. [breθ]
Museum museum [mju'ziːəm]
Musik music ['mjuːzɪk]
Musiker/in musician [mju'zɪʃn]
müssen must [mʌst]; have to ['hæv tə]; need to ['niːd tə] **du musst es nicht tun** you needn't do it ['niːdnt] **Sie muss ihn gemocht haben.** She must have liked him.
Muster pattern ['pætn]
Mutter mother ['mʌðə]
Muttersprache native language
Muttersprachler/in native speaker
Mutti mum [mʌm]

N

Na: Na ja, … Well, … [wel] **Na los, Dad!** *(Komm, Dad!)* Come on, Dad. **Na und?** So? [səʊ]
nach **1.** *(örtlich)* to [tu], [tə] **einer nach dem anderen** one by one **nach draußen** outside [ˌaʊt'saɪd] **nach drinnen** inside [ˌɪn'saɪd] **nach Hause gehen** go home **nach Hause kommen** come home **nach oben** up; *(im Haus)* upstairs [ˌʌp'steəz] **nach unten** down; *(im Haus)* downstairs [ˌdaʊn'steəz] **nach vorn** to the front **2.** *(zeitlich)* after ['ɑːftə] **Viertel nach zehn (10.15 / 22.15)** quarter past ten ['kwɔːtə pɑːst]
Nachbar/in neighbour ['neɪbə]
nachdem after ['ɑːftə] **gleich nachdem …** just after …
nachdenken (über) think (about) [θɪŋk]
nachgehen *(Uhr)* be slow
Nachmittag afternoon [ˌɑːftə'nuːn] **am Nachmittag** in the afternoon
nachmittags in the afternoon [ˌɑːftə'nuːn]
Nachricht message ['mesɪdʒ] **eine Nachricht hinterlassen** leave a message [ˌliːv‿ə 'mesɪdʒ]
Nachrichten news *(no pl)* [njuːz]
nachschauen *(einen Blick werfen)* have a look
nachschlagen: etwas nachschlagen look sth. up
Nachspeise dessert [dɪ'zɜːt]
nächste(r, s) next [nekst] **das nächste Bild / die nächste Frage** the next picture/question **als Nächstes** next [nekst]
Nacht night [naɪt] **in der Nacht** at night **eines Nachts** one night **heute Nacht** tonight [tə'naɪt]
Nachtisch dessert [dɪ'zɜːt]
nachts at night [ət 'naɪt]
nachziehen *(spannen, festziehen)* tighten ['taɪtn]
Nähe: in der Nähe von near [nɪə] **hier in der Nähe** near here
nahe (bei) near [nɪə]; close (to) [kləʊs]
nahegelegen: eine nahegelegene Stadt a nearby town ['nɪəbaɪ]
nähern: sich nähern approach [ə'prəʊtʃ]
Name name [neɪm] **Mein Name ist Silky.** My name is Silky.
Nase nose [nəʊz]
nass wet [wet] **jn. nass spritzen** splash sb. [splæʃ]
Nation nation ['neɪʃn]
national, National- national ['næʃnəl]
Naturkunde natural history [ˌnætʃrəl 'hɪstri]
natürlich natural ['nætʃrəl]; *(selbstverständlich)* of course [əv 'kɔːs]
Naturwissenschaft science ['saɪəns]
Naturwissenschaftler/in scientist ['saɪəntɪst]
Nebel *(Dunstschleier)* mist [mɪst]
neben next to ['nekst tʊ]
Nebensatz sub-clause ['sʌbklɔːz] **Nebensatz mit *if*** if-clause
Neffe nephew ['nefjuː], ['nevjuː]
nehmen take [teɪk] **Ich nehme einen Tee/Hamburger/…** *(beim Essen, im Restaurant)* I'll have a tea/burger/… **etwas wichtig nehmen** care about sth. **Platz nehmen** *(sich setzen)* take a seat

nein no [nəʊ] **Nein, das ist falsch. / Nein, das stimmt nicht.** No, that's wrong.
nennen *(rufen, bezeichnen)* call [kɔːl]
nervös nervous ['nɜːvəs]
nett nice [naɪs]; kind [kaɪnd]
neu new [njuː] **etwas auf den neuesten Stand bringen** update sth. [ˌʌp'deɪt]
neugierig curious ['kjʊəriəs]
neun nine [naɪn]
nicht not [nɒt] **Geh nicht.** Don't go. [dəʊnt] **Ich mag Grün nicht.** I don't like green. **Ich weiß (es) nicht.** I don't know. **auch nicht** not … either ['aɪðə, 'iːðə] **nicht mehr** not … any more **nicht (mehr) da sein** be gone [gɒn] **nicht vor drei** not till three; not until three **…, nicht wahr?** …, right? **noch nicht** not … yet [jet] **(noch) nicht einmal** not even **nicht mögen** dislike [dɪs'laɪk]
Nichte niece [niːs]
nichts not … anything ['eniθɪŋ] **Nichts zu danken.** You're welcome. ['welkəm]
nicken nod [nɒd]
nie never ['nevə]
niederlassen: sich niederlassen *(sich ansiedeln)* settle ['setl]
niemals never ['nevə]
niemand no one ['nəʊ wʌn], nobody ['nəʊbədi]; not … anybody/anyone ['enibɒdi, 'eniwʌn]
niesen sneeze [sniːz]
nirgendwo(hin) nowhere ['nəʊweə]
noch: noch ein Foto one more photo; another photo [ə'nʌðə] **noch einmal** again [ə'gen] **noch nicht** not … yet [jet] **noch nicht einmal** not even **immer noch** still [stɪl]
Nomen noun
Norden; Nord- north [nɔːθ] **nach Norden** north **Richtung Norden** northbound ['nɔːθbaʊnd]
nördliche(r, s) northern ['nɔːðən]
Nordosten; nordöstlich north-east **nach Nordosten** north-east
Nordwesten; nordwestlich north-west **nach Nordwesten** north-west
normalerweise usually ['juːʒuəli]
Note *(Musik)* note [nəʊt]
nötig necessary ['nesəsəri]
Notiz note [nəʊt] **(sich) Notizen machen (über/zu etwas)** *(zur Vorbereitung)* make notes (on sth.); *(beim Lesen oder Zuhören)* take notes (on sth.)
notwendig necessary ['nesəsəri]
November November [nəʊ'vembə]
Null *(in Telefonnummern)* o [əʊ]
Nummer number
nun now [naʊ] **Nun, …** Well, … [wel] **Nun, da du …** Now that you …
nur only ['əʊnli]; *(einfach nur)* just [dʒʌst]

O

ob if; whether ['weðə] **als ob** as if; *(infml)* like **so tun, als ob** pretend [prɪ'tend]
oben *(im Haus)* upstairs [ˌʌp'steəz]; *(oberhalb)* above **nach oben** up; *(im Haus)* upstairs
Oberfläche surface ['sɜːfɪs]
oberhalb (von etwas) above sth. [ə'bʌv]
Oberhaupt head [hed]
Objekt object ['ɒbdʒɪkt]
Obst fruit [fruːt]
Obstkuchen pie [paɪ]
Obstsalat fruit salad [ˌfruːt 'sæləd]
obwohl although [ɔːl'ðəʊ]
oder or [ɔː] **entweder … oder …** either … or … ['aɪðə], ['iːðə]
offen open ['əʊpən]
öffentliche(r, s) public ['pʌblɪk]
öffnen; sich öffnen open ['əʊpən]
Öffnung opening
Öffnungszeiten opening times
oft often ['ɒfn], ['ɒftən]
ohne without [wɪ'ðaʊt]
Ohr ear [ɪə]
Ohrhörer earphones *(pl)* ['ɪəfəʊnz]
Ohrring earring ['ɪərɪŋ]
Oje! Oh dear! [dɪə]
okay OK [ˌəʊ'keɪ]; all right [ɔːl 'raɪt]
Oktober October [ɒk'təʊbə]
Öl oil [ɔɪl]
Oma grandma ['grænmɑː]
Onkel uncle ['ʌŋkl]
Opa grandpa ['grænpɑː]
Orange orange ['ɒrɪndʒ]
orange(farben) orange ['ɒrɪndʒ]
ordnen *(anordnen, organisieren)* organize ['ɔːgənaɪz]
Ordnung: in Ordnung *(okay)* all right [ɔːl 'raɪt]; OK [ˌəʊ'keɪ]; fine [faɪn]
organisieren organize ['ɔːgənaɪz]
Original- original [ə'rɪdʒənl]
Orkan hurricane ['hʌrɪkən, 'hʌrɪkeɪn]
Ort place [pleɪs]
örtlich *(Lokal-; am/vom Ort)* local ['ləʊkl]
Osten east [iːst] **nach Osten** east
östlich east [iːst]; eastern ['iːstən]
Ostern Easter ['iːstə]
oval oval ['əʊvl]
Ozean ocean ['əʊʃn]

P

paar: ein paar *(einige)* some [sʌm], [səm]; a few [ə 'fjuː]; a couple of ['kʌpl]
Paar pair [peə]; *(Ehe-, Liebespaar)* couple ['kʌpl]
Päckchen packet ['pækɪt]
packen pack [pæk]; *(schnappen)* grab [græb]
Packung packet ['pækɪt]
Palast palace ['pæləs]
Palme palm tree ['pɑːm triː]
Panik: in Panik geraten panic ['pænɪk]
Papa dad [dæd]
Papier paper ['peɪpə]
Papierhut paper hat ['peɪpə hæt]
Papst pope [pəʊp]
Parade *(Umzug)* parade [pə'reɪd]
Park park [pɑːk]
parken park [pɑːk]
Parlament parliament ['pɑːləmənt]
Partner/in partner ['pɑːtnə]
Party party ['pɑːti]
Pass *(Reisepass)* passport ['pɑːspɔːt]
Pass auf! *(Vorsicht!)* Watch out! [ˌwɒtʃ‿'aʊt]
Passagier/in passenger ['pæsɪndʒə]
passen: zu etwas passen match sth.; go with sth.
passieren (mit) happen (to) ['hæpən]
Passwort password ['pɑːswɜːd] **ein Passwort eingeben** enter a password
Pastete pie ['paɪ]
Pause break [breɪk] **eine Pause einlegen** pause [pɔːz]
pausieren pause [pɔːz]
peinlich embarrassing [ɪm'bærəsɪŋ]
Pence pence [pens]
perfekt perfect ['pɜːfɪkt]
Person person ['pɜːsn]; *(in Roman, Film, Theaterstück usw.)* character ['kærəktə]
Personalausweis ID card [ˌaɪ 'diː kɑːd]
Pfad path [pɑːθ]; trail [treɪl]
Pfannkuchen pancake ['pænkeɪk]
Pfeffer pepper ['pepə]
Pfeife *(Trillerpfeife)* whistle ['wɪsl]; *(Tabakspfeife)* pipe [paɪp]
pfeifen whistle ['wɪsl]; *(auf der Trillerpfeife)* blow the whistle [bləʊ]
Pferd horse [hɔːs]
Pflanze plant [plɑːnt]
pflanzen plant [plɑːnt]
Pflaster *(Heftpflaster)* plaster ['plɑːstə]
Pforte gate [geɪt]
Pfund *(britische Währung)* pound (£) [paʊnd]
Piano piano [pi'ænəʊ]
Picknick picnic ['pɪknɪk]
piepen beep [biːp]
Pilger/in pilgrim ['pɪlgrɪm]
pink pink [pɪŋk]
Pirat/in pirate ['paɪrət]
Pizza pizza ['piːtsə]
Plan plan [plæn]
planen plan [plæn]
Planet planet ['plænɪt]
Plastik plastic ['plæstɪk]
Platz place [pleɪs]; *(Raum)* space [speɪs]; *(in der Stadt)* square [skweə]; *(Sitz)* seat [siːt] **Platz nehmen** *(sich setzen)* take a seat
platzen burst [bɜːst]
Plätzchen *(Keks)* biscuit ['bɪskɪt]
plaudern chat [tʃæt]
plötzlich suddenly ['sʌdnli]
Pokal *(Trophäe)* trophy ['trəʊfi]
Politik politics ['pɒlətɪks]

Polizei police *(pl)* [pə'liːs]
Polizeiwache, -revier police station [pə'liːs steɪʃn]
Polizist/in police officer [pə'liːs‿ˌɒfɪsə]
Polnisch; polnisch Polish ['pəʊlɪʃ]
Pommes frites (French) fries *(pl)* [fraɪz] *(AE)*
Pony pony ['pəʊni]
populär popular ['pɒpjələ]
Porträt *(Personenbeschreibung)* profile ['prəʊfaɪl]
Postamt post office ['pəʊst‿ɒfɪs]
posten: etwas posten post sth. [pəʊst]
Poster poster ['pəʊstə]
Posting *(auf Blog)* post [pəʊst]
Postkarte postcard ['pəʊstkɑːd]
praktisch practical ['præktɪkl]
praktizieren practice ['præktɪs] *(AE)*
Praline chocolate ['tʃɒklət]
prallen: gegen etwas prallen hit sth. [hɪt]
Präsentation presentation [ˌprezn'teɪʃn]
präsentieren: (jm.) etwas präsentieren, vorstellen present sth. (to sb.) [prɪ'zent]
Präsident/in president ['prezɪdənt]
Preis **1.** *(Kaufpreis)* price [praɪs] **2.** *(Gewinn)* prize [praɪz]
preiswert *(billig)* cheap [tʃiːp]
Premierminister/in prime minister [ˌpraɪm 'mɪnɪstə]
prima fine [faɪn]
Prinz prince [prɪns]
Prinzessin princess [ˌprɪn'ses], ['prɪnses]
pro: … pro Tag/Woche/Jahr … a day/week/year; … per day/week/year [pə, pɜː]
probieren try [traɪ]
Problem problem ['prɒbləm]
Profil *(Personenbeschreibung, Porträt)* profile ['prəʊfaɪl]
Programm programme ['prəʊgræm]
Projekt project ['prɒdʒekt]
Prospekt *(Broschüre)* brochure ['brəʊʃə]
Protest protest ['prəʊtest]
Protestant/in Protestant ['prɒtɪstənt]
protestantisch Protestant ['prɒtɪstənt]
protestieren protest [prə'test]
Prozent per cent [pə'sent]
prüfen *(überprüfen)* check [tʃek]; *(testen)* test; *(untersuchen)* look into
Publikum audience ['ɔːdiəns]
Pullover pullover ['pʊləʊvə]
pummelig chubby ['tʃʌbi]
Punkt point [pɔɪnt]; *(Fleck)* spot [spɒt]
Puppe doll [dɒl]
Pute turkey ['tɜːki]
putzen clean [kliːn]
Puzzle jigsaw ['dʒɪgsɔː]
Pyjama-Party sleepover ['sliːpəʊvə]

Q

Quadrat square [skweə]
quadratisch square [skweə]
Quadratkilometer (km²) square kilometre (sq km) [ˌskweə 'kɪləmiːtə, kɪ'lɒmɪtə]
quer über das Moor/die Straße across the moor/the street [ə'krɒs]
Quiz quiz [kwɪz]

R

Rabe raven ['reɪvn]
Rad wheel [wiːl]; *(Fahrrad)* bike [baɪk]
Rad fahren ride a bike [ˌraɪd‿ə 'baɪk]
Radiergummi rubber ['rʌbə]
Radio radio ['reɪdiəʊ] **im Radio** on the radio
Rand *(Kante)* edge [edʒ]
Rasen lawn [lɔːn]
rasen race [reɪs]
Raster grid [grɪd]
Rat *(Stadtrat, Gemeinderat u.Ä.)* council ['kaʊnsl]
raten guess [ges]
Rätsel puzzle ['pʌzl]
Ratte rat [ræt]
rau rough [rʌf]
Rauch smoke [sməʊk]
rauchen smoke [sməʊk]
rauf und runter up and down [ˌʌp‿ən 'daʊn]
räumen clear [klɪə]
rausgehen: mit dem Hund rausgehen walk the dog
reagieren (auf) react (to) [ri'ækt]
Recherche research *(no pl)* ['riːsɜːtʃ]
Recht: jemand hat Recht someone is right [raɪt]
Rechte rights *(pl)* [raɪts]
rechte(r, s) right [raɪt] **auf der rechten Seite** on the right **nach rechts** right **nach rechts abbiegen** turn right
Rechtschreibung spelling ['spelɪŋ]
rechtzeitig zum Bus kommen *(den Bus erreichen)* be in time for the bus
Redakteur/in editor ['edɪtə]
Rede talk [tɔːk]; *(offiziell)* speech [spiːtʃ] **eine Rede halten (über)** give a talk (about)
reden (mit) talk (to) [tɔːk]
Referat talk [tɔːk] **ein Referat halten (über)** give a talk (about)
Refrain chorus ['kɔːrəs]
Regal shelf [ʃelf], *pl* shelves [ʃelvz]
Regel rule [ruːl]
regelmäßig regular ['regjələ]
Regen rain [reɪn]
Regenbogen rainbow ['reɪnbəʊ]
Regenschirm umbrella [ʌm'brelə]
Regenmantel raincoat ['reɪnkəʊt]
Regenwald rainforest ['reɪnfɒrɪst]
regieren govern ['gʌvən]
Regierung government ['gʌvənmənt]
Region region ['riːdʒən]
Regisseur/in director [də'rektə]
regnen rain [reɪn]
Reh deer [dɪə]
reich rich [rɪtʃ]
Reich *(Imperium)* empire ['empaɪə]
reichen: jm. etwas reichen hand sb. sth.
Reihe line [laɪn] **Ich bin an der Reihe.** (It's) my turn. [tɜːn]
Reihenfolge order ['ɔːdə]
Reim rhyme [raɪm]
Reise journey ['dʒɜːni]; trip [trɪp]
Reisekrankheit travel sickness ['trævl sɪknəs]
Reiseleiter/in guide [gaɪd]
reisen travel ['trævl]
Reisende(r) traveller ['trævələ]
Reisepass passport ['pɑːspɔːt]
Reisetasche *(Handgepäck)* carry-on bag ['kæri‿ɒn]
Reiten riding ['raɪdɪŋ]
Religion religion [rɪ'lɪdʒən]
rennen run [rʌn]
Rennen race [reɪs]
Reportage report [rɪ'pɔːt]
Republik republic [rɪ'pʌblɪk]
Reservat, Reservation reservation [ˌrezə'veɪʃn]
reservieren reserve [rɪ'zɜːv]
Rest rest
Restaurant restaurant ['restrɒnt]
Resultat result [rɪ'zʌlt]
retten save [seɪv]; rescue ['reskjuː]
Rettung rescue ['reskjuː]
Rezension review [rɪ'vjuː]
Rezept **1.** *(Kochrezept)* recipe ['resəpi] **2.** *(vom Arzt)* prescription [prɪ'skrɪpʃn]
Rhythmus rhythm ['rɪðəm]
richten: etwas auf jn. richten point sth. at sb. [pɔɪnt]
richtig right [raɪt]; correct [kə'rekt] **Ja, das ist richtig.** Yes, that's right.
Richtung: in die Richtung that way [weɪ] **Richtung Norden** northbound ['nɔːθbaʊnd] **in Richtung Bahnhof/Mr Bell** towards the station/Mr Bell [tə'wɔːdz]
riechen smell [smel] **an etwas riechen** smell sth.
Riegel *(Schokolade, Müsli)* bar [bɑː]
Riese giant ['dʒaɪənt]
Riesenhunger: einen Riesenhunger haben be starving ['stɑːvɪŋ]
Riesenrad big wheel [bɪg 'wiːl]
riesig huge [hjuːdʒ]
Rinderbraten roast beef [ˌrəʊst 'biːf]
Rindfleisch beef [biːf]
Ring ring [rɪŋ]
Risiko risk [rɪsk] **ein Risiko eingehen** take a risk
Ritt ride [raɪd]
Ritter knight [naɪt]
Robbe seal [siːl]
Robbenjunges baby seal ['beɪbi siːl]
Rock skirt [skɜːt]
Rock(musik) rock (music)
Rolle *(in einem Theaterstück, Film)* role [rəʊl]

rollen roll [rəʊl]
Roman novel ['nɒvl]
Römer/in Roman ['rəʊmən]
römisch Roman ['rəʊmən]
rosa pink [pɪŋk]
Rose rose [rəʊz]
rostig rusty ['rʌsti]
rot red [red] **rot werden** go red
Route route [ru:t]
Routine routine [ru:'ti:n]
Rücken back [bæk]
Rückfahrkarte return [rɪ'tɜ:n] *(kurz für: return ticket)*
Rückkehr return [rɪ'tɜ:n]
Rückmeldung feedback *(no pl)* ['fi:dbæk]
Rucksack backpack ['bækpæk]; *(BE auch:)* rucksack ['rʌksæk]
rufen call [kɔ:l]; shout [ʃaʊt]
Rugby rugby ['rʌgbi]
Rugby-Platz/-Spielfeld rugby ground ['rʌgbi graʊnd]
ruhen *(sich ausruhen)* rest [rest]
ruhig *(leise)* quiet ['kwaɪət]; *(Gemütszustand; Meer)* calm [kɑ:m]
Ruine ruin ['ru:ɪn]
rumhängen hang out [ˌhæŋ_'aʊt] *(infml)*
rund round [raʊnd]
Rundgang, Rundfahrt (durch) tour (of) ['tʊər_əv]
runter: rauf und runter up and down [ˌʌp_ən 'daʊn]
runzeln: die Stirn runzeln frown [fraʊn]
rutschig slippery ['slɪpəri]

S

Sache thing [θɪŋ]
Safari safari [sə'fɑ:ri]
Saft juice [dʒu:s]
Sage legend ['ledʒənd]
sagen say [seɪ] **jm. sagen, dass er/sie etwas (nicht) tun soll** tell sb. (not) to do sth.
Sahne cream [kri:m]
Saite string [strɪŋ]
Salat *(Gericht, Beilage)* salad ['sæləd]
Salz salt [sɔ:lt]
Samba samba ['sæmbə]
Samen seed [si:d]
sammeln collect [kə'lekt] **Geld sammeln (für)** raise money (for) [reɪz]
Samstag Saturday ['sætədeɪ, 'sætədi]
Sand sand [sænd]
Sandwich sandwich ['sænwɪtʃ], ['sænwɪdʒ]
sanft *(mit leiser Stimme)* in a soft voice
Satz **1.** sentence ['sentəns]
2. *(Set)* set [set]
Satzmelodie intonation [ˌɪntə'neɪʃn]
sauber machen clean [kli:n]
Säule column ['kɒləm]
Schach chess [tʃes]
schade: Es war schade, dass … It was a pity that … ['pɪti]
Schädel skull [skʌl]

Schaf sheep, *pl* sheep [ʃi:p]
schaffen: etwas schaffen *(zustande bringen)* manage sth. ['mænɪdʒ]
Schalter switch [swɪtʃ]
scharf *(Messer u.Ä.)* sharp [ʃɑ:p]
Schatten shadow ['ʃædəʊ]
Schatz *(infml, als Anrede)* honey ['hʌni]
schauen look [lʊk]
schaukeln *(Boot)* rock
Schauspiel *(darstellende Kunst)* drama ['drɑ:mə]
Schauspieler/in actor ['æktə]
Scheidung divorce [dɪ'vɔ:s]
scheinen **1.** *(Sonne)* shine [ʃaɪn]
2. (zu sein/zu tun) scheinen seem (to be/do) [si:m]
scheu shy [ʃaɪ]
Scheune barn [bɑ:n]
schicken: jm. etwas schicken send sth. to sb. [send] **einem Freund/einer Freundin eine SMS schicken** text a friend [tekst]
schieben push [pʊʃ]
schiefgehen go wrong
schießen shoot [ʃu:t] **ein Tor schießen** score [skɔ:]
Schiff ship [ʃɪp]
Schild sign [saɪn]; *(Etikett)* label
Schilderung narration [nə'reɪʃn]
Schildkröte *(Landschildkröte)* tortoise ['tɔ:təs]
Schinkenspeck bacon ['beɪkən]
Schirm umbrella [ʌm'brelə]
Schlacht battle ['bætl]
Schlaf sleep [sli:p]
schlafen sleep [sli:p]; *(nicht wach sein)* be asleep [ə'sli:p]
Schlafparty sleepover ['sli:pəʊvə]
schläfrig sleepy ['sli:pi]
Schlafzimmer bedroom ['bedru:m]
schlagen hit [hɪt]; *(besiegen)* beat [bi:t]; defeat [dɪ'fi:t]
Schlagzeug drums *(pl)* [drʌmz]
Schlagzeug spielen play the drums
Schlagzeuger/in drummer
Schlamm mud [mʌd]
Schlange **1.** *(Tier)* snake [sneɪk]
2. *(Reihe wartender Menschen)* queue [kju:] *(BE)*; line [laɪn] *(AE)* **Schlange stehen** queue [kju:] *(BE)*; be/stand/wait in line *(AE)*
schlau clever ['klevə]
Schlauchboot *(wildwassertauglich)* raft [rɑ:ft]
schlecht bad [bæd] **Mir ist schlecht.** I feel sick.
schließen close [kləʊz]
Schließfach *(Spind)* locker ['lɒkə]
schließlich at last [ət 'lɑ:st]; finally ['faɪnəli]
schlimm bad [bæd]
schlittern *(gleiten)* slither ['slɪðə]
Schlittschuhlaufen (ice) skating ['skeɪtɪŋ]
Schloss castle ['kɑ:sl]; *(Palast)* palace ['pæləs]

Schluss end [end]; ending ['endɪŋ]
Schlüssel key [ki:]
Schlüsselwort keyword ['ki:wɜ:d]
Schlussfolgerung conclusion [kən'klu:ʒn]
schmal narrow ['nærəʊ]
schmecken taste [teɪst]
schmelzen melt [melt]
schmerzen hurt [hɜ:t]
Schmetterling butterfly ['bʌtəflaɪ]
Schmuck jewellery *(BE)* / jewelry *(AE)* *(no pl)* ['dʒu:əlri]
Schmuggel; das Schmuggeln smuggling ['smʌglɪŋ]
schmuggeln smuggle ['smʌgl]
Schmuggler/in smuggler ['smʌglə]
schmutzig dirty ['dɜ:ti]
schnappen *(greifen, packen)* grab [græb]
Schnee snow [snəʊ]
schneiden cut [kʌt]; *(Film, Video bearbeiten)* edit ['edɪt]
schnell fast [fɑ:st]; quick [kwɪk]
Schnitt! *(beim Filmen)* Cut! [kʌt]
Schnur line [laɪn]
schockiert shocked [ʃɒkt]
Schokolade chocolate ['tʃɒklət]
schön beautiful ['bju:tɪfl]; nice [naɪs]; lovely ['lʌvli] **schöner als** more beautiful than **der/die/das schönste …; am schönsten** (the) most beautiful [məʊst]
schon already [ɔ:l'redi] **schon bald** before long **Hast du schon …?** Have you … yet? [jet]
Schotter gravel ['grævl]
Schrank cupboard ['kʌbəd]
schrecklich terrible ['terəbl], awful ['ɔ:fl]
schreiben write [raɪt]
Schreibtisch desk [desk]
Schreibweise spelling ['spelɪŋ]
schreien shout [ʃaʊt]; scream [skri:m]; yell [jel]; *(weinen)* cry [kraɪ]
Schriftsteller/in writer ['raɪtə]
Schritt step [step]
schüchtern shy [ʃaɪ]
Schuh shoe [ʃu:]
Schuld *(Fehler)* fault [fɔ:lt]
Schule school [sku:l] **in der Schule** at school
Schüler/in student ['stju:dənt]
Schulfach (school) subject ['sʌbdʒɪkt]
Schulheft *(Übungsheft)* exercise book ['eksəsaɪz bʊk]
Schulleiter/in head teacher [ˌhed 'ti:tʃə]
Schultasche school bag ['sku:l bæg]
Schulter shoulder ['ʃəʊldə]
Schüssel bowl [bəʊl]
schütteln shake [ʃeɪk]
Schutzgebiet reserve [rɪ'zɜ:v]
schwanken *(Boot)* rock
schwarz black [blæk]
schweigend silent ['saɪlənt]
Schwein pig [pɪg]
schwer *(schwierig)* difficult ['dɪfɪkəlt]; hard [hɑ:d]; *(von Gewicht)* heavy ['hevi]
Schwert sword [sɔ:d]
Schwester sister ['sɪstə]

schwierig difficult ['dɪfɪkəlt]; hard [hɑːd]
Schwierigkeit: in Schwierigkeiten geraten get into trouble
Schwimmbad, -becken (swimming) pool [puːl]
schwimmen swim [swɪm]
Schwimmer/in swimmer ['swɪmə]
Schwimmweste life jacket ['laɪf dʒækɪt]
schwindlig dizzy ['dɪzi]
sechs six [sɪks]
See 1. *(Binnensee)* lake [leɪk]
2. *(die See, das Meer)* sea [siː]
Segelboot sailing boat ['seɪlɪŋ bəʊt]
segeln sail [seɪl] **segeln gehen** go sailing ['seɪlɪŋ]
sehen see [siː]
Sehenswürdigkeiten sights *(pl)* [saɪts]
sehr very ['veri] **Das hat uns sehr geholfen.** That helped us a lot.
seidig silky ['sɪlki]
Seil rope [rəʊp]
sein *(Verb)* be [biː]
sein(e) ... *(vor Nomen; besitzanzeigend)*
1. *(zu „he")* his ... [hɪz]
2. *(zu „it")* its ... [ɪts]
seit 10 Uhr/letzter Woche/... since 10 o'clock/last week/... [sɪns] **seit Stunden/Wochen/...** for hours/weeks/...
Seite side [saɪd]
Seite 1. side [saɪd]
2. *(Buchseite)* page [peɪdʒ] **Auf welcher Seite sind wir?** What page are we on?
Sekunde second ['sekənd]
selber, selbst myself [maɪ'self]; yourself [jɔː'self]; himself [hɪm'self]; herself [hɜː'self]; itself [ɪt'self]; ourselves [ɑː'selvz], [aʊə'selvz]; yourselves [jɔː'selvz]; themselves [ðəm'selvz]
selbst wenn even if ['iːvn‿ɪf]
Selbstlaut vowel ['vaʊəl]
selbstverständlich of course [əv 'kɔːs]
seltsam strange [streɪndʒ]; weird [wɪəd]
senden: jm. etwas senden send sth. to sb. [send]
Sendung *(im Radio, Fernsehen)* programme ['prəʊgræm]
September September [sep'tembə]
Servus. Bye-bye.; Bye. [baɪ]
Sessel armchair ['ɑːmtʃeə]
setzen: sich setzen sit [sɪt]
seufzen sigh [saɪ]
Shorts *(kurze Hose)* shorts *(pl)* [ʃɔːts]
sich himself [hɪm'self]; herself [hɜː'self]; itself [ɪt'self]; *(Plural)* themselves [ðəm'selvz]; *(bei „Sie")* yourself [jɔː'self]/yourselves [jɔː'selvz]
sich gegenseitig *(einander)* each other [iːtʃ‿'ʌðə]; one another
sicher 1. *(gewiss)* sure [ʃʊə, ʃɔː]
2. *(in Sicherheit)* safe [seɪf]
sicherlich *(auf jeden Fall)* certainly ['sɜːtnli]
Sicht: aus meiner Sicht from my point of view [ˌpɔɪnt‿əv 'vjuː]

sie 1. *(Einzahl; weibliche Person)* she [ʃiː] **Frag sie.** Ask her. [hɜː]
2. *(Einzahl; Ding, Tier)* it [ɪt]
3. *(Mehrzahl)* they [ðeɪ] **Frag sie.** Ask them. [ðem, ðəm]
Sie *(höfliche Anrede)* you [juː, ju]
sieben seven ['sevn]
Siedler/in settler ['setlə]; *(Kolonist/in)* colonist ['kɒlənɪst]
Sieger/in winner ['wɪnə]
Signal signal ['sɪgnəl]
Silbe syllable ['sɪləbl]
Silvester New Year's Eve [ˌnjuː jɪəz‿'iːv]
singen sing [sɪŋ]
Sinn für Humor sense of humour [ˌsens‿əv 'hjuːmə]
Sirene siren ['saɪrən]
Situation situation [ˌsɪtʃu'eɪʃn]
Sitz seat [siːt]
sitzen sit [sɪt]
Smalltalk *(spontan geführtes Gespräch)* small talk
SMS text (message) ['tekst mesɪdʒ]
einem Freund/einer Freundin eine SMS schicken text a friend
Snack snack [snæk]
so 1. *(auf diese Weise)* like this / like that **so tun, als ob** pretend [prɪ'tend]
Und er so: „Stop ..." He was like: "Stopp ..." *(infml)*
2. **so ein/e ...** such a ... [sʌtʃ]
3. **so cool/nett/leise/...** so cool/ nice/quiet/... [səʊ]
4. **(nicht) so groß wie** (not) as big as [æz], [əz]
sobald as soon as [əz 'suːn‿əz]
Socke sock [sɒk]
sodass so that *(oft auch kurz:* so)
soeben just [dʒʌst]
Sofa sofa ['səʊfə]
sofort immediately [ɪ'miːdiətli]
sogar even ['iːvn]
Sohn son [sʌn]
solch ein/e ... such a ... [sʌtʃ]
Soldat/in soldier ['səʊldʒə]
sollen: Soll ich ...? Shall I ...? [ʃæl] **Du solltest .../Ihr solltet ...** You should ... [ʃʊd], [ʃəd]
Solo- solo ['səʊləʊ]
Sommer summer ['sʌmə]
Sonne sun [sʌn]
Sonnenbrille sunglasses *(pl)* ['sʌnglɑːsɪz]
sonnig sunny ['sʌni]
Sonntag Sunday ['sʌndeɪ, 'sʌndi]
Sorge: sich Sorgen machen (wegen, um) worry (about) ['wʌri]
sorgen: dafür sorgen, dass ... make sure that ...
sorgfältig carefully ['keəfəli]
Sorte (von) type (of) [taɪp]
Souvenir souvenir [ˌsuːvə'nɪə]
sowie as soon as [əz 'suːn‿əz]
sowohl ... als auch ... both ... and ... [bəʊθ]
soziale Medien social media *(pl)* [ˌsəʊʃl 'miːdiə]

Sozialwesen, soziale Dienste social services *(pl)* [ˌsəʊʃl 'sɜːvɪsɪz]
Spagetti spaghetti [spə'geti]
Spanisch; spanisch Spanish ['spænɪʃ]
spannen *(Saite u.Ä.)* tighten ['taɪtn]
spannend *(aufregend)* exciting [ɪk'saɪtɪŋ]
Spaß fun [fʌn] **Spaß haben** have fun
Das macht Spaß. That's fun. **Hat es Spaß gemacht?** Was it fun? **Viel Spaß!** *(Amüsiere dich gut!)* Enjoy yourself!
spät late [leɪt] **Du bist spät dran. / Du bist zu spät.** You're late. **Wie spät ist es?** What time is it?
später later ['leɪtə]
spazieren gehen go for a walk [wɔːk]; take a walk *(bes. AE)*
Spaziergang walk [wɔːk] **einen Spaziergang machen** go for a walk; take a walk *(bes. AE)*
spekulieren speculate ['spekjuleɪt]
sperren *(blockieren)* block [blɒk]
Spickzettel crib sheet ['krɪb ʃiːt] *(infml)*
Spiegel mirror ['mɪrə]
Spiel game [geɪm]; *(Wettkampf, Match)* match [mætʃ]
spielen play [pleɪ]; *(Geschichte, Handlung)* take place **gegen jn. spielen** play sb.; play against sb. **Gitarre spielen** play the guitar **Klavier spielen** play the piano **Schlagzeug spielen** play the drums
Spieler/in player ['pleɪə]
Spielzeug toy [tɔɪ]
Spind locker ['lɒkə]
Spinner/in weirdo ['wɪədəʊ] *(infml)*
Spitze *(oberes Ende)* top [tɒp]
Spitzer sharpener ['ʃɑːpnə]
Sport; Sportart sport [spɔːt] **Sport treiben** do sport
Sportunterricht PE [ˌpiː‿'iː] (Physical Education)
Sprache language ['læŋgwɪdʒ]
sprechen speak [spiːk]
Sprecher/in speaker ['spiːkə]; *(Erzähler/in)* narrator [nə'reɪtə]
springen jump [dʒʌmp]
spritzen: jn. nass spritzen splash sb. [splæʃ]
Sprung jump [dʒʌmp]
spülen: das Geschirr spülen wash the dishes *(pl)* [ˌwɒʃ ðə 'dɪʃɪz]
Spur: keine Spur von ... no sign of ... [saɪn]
Staat state [steɪt]
Stadel barn [bɑːn]
Stadt town [taʊn]; *(Großstadt)* city ['sɪti]
Stadtplan map [mæp] **auf dem Stadtplan** on the map
Stadtviertel quarter ['kwɔːtə]
Stahl steel [stiːl]
Stamm *(Volksstamm)* tribe [traɪb]
Stammbaum family tree ['fæməli triː]
stammen aus *(zeitlich)* date from

Stand 1. *(Marktstand)* stall [stɔ:l] **2. etwas auf den neuesten Stand bringen** update sth. [ˌʌp'deɪt]
Standard standard ['stændəd]
ständig: etwas ständig tun keep doing sth. [ki:p]
Standpunkt point of view [ˌpɔɪnt‿əv 'vju:]
Stapel pile [paɪl]
Star star [stɑ:]
stark strong [strɒŋ]; *(mächtig)* powerful ['paʊəfl] **starker Regen** heavy rain ['hevi]
Stärke *(Macht; Kraft)* power ['paʊə]
starren gaze [geɪz]
Station *(Haltestelle)* stop [stɒp]
statt *(anstelle von)* instead of [ɪn'sted‿əv]
stattdessen instead [ɪn'sted]
stattfinden take place
Statue statue ['stætʃu:]
Staub dust [dʌst]
stechen: etwas in etwas stechen stick sth. into sth. [stɪk]
stehen stand [stænd] **Schlange stehen** queue [kju:] *(BE)*; be/stand/wait in line *(AE)* **Hier steht: ...** It says here: ... **auf etwas stehen** be into sth. *(infml)*
steil steep [sti:p]
Stein stone [stəʊn]
steinig rocky ['rɒki]
Stelle place [pleɪs]; *(Job, Arbeitsstelle)* job [dʒɒb]
stellen *(hinstellen, abstellen)* put [pʊt] **sich (hin)stellen** stand [stænd] **eine Frage stellen** ask a question **etwas lauter/leiser stellen** turn sth. up/down [tɜ:n]
Stelzen stilts *(pl)* [stɪlts]
Stempel stamp [stæmp]
sterben die [daɪ]
Stern star [stɑ:]
steuern steer [stɪə]
Stichwort *(im Wörterbuch)* headword ['hedwɜ:d]
Stiefel boot [bu:t]
Stift *(zum Schreiben)* pen [pen]
Stil style [staɪl]
still quiet ['kwaɪət]; silent ['saɪlənt]; still [stɪl]
Stimme voice [vɔɪs] **mit leiser Stimme** in a soft voice
stimmen 1. *(Instrument)* tune [tju:n] **2. Ja, das stimmt.** Yes, that's right. [raɪt] **Nein, das stimmt nicht.** No, that's wrong. [rɒŋ]
Stimmung *(Atmosphäre)* atmosphere ['ætməsfɪə]
Stock stick [stɪk]
Stock, Stockwerk, Etage
Stock(werk) floor [flɔ:]; storey, *pl* storeys *(BE)*, story, *pl* stories *(AE)* ['stɔ:ri]
stöhnen groan [grəʊn]
Stöhnen groan [grəʊn]
stolz (auf) proud (of) [praʊd]

stoppen stop [stɒp]
stören: Stört es Sie, ...? Do you mind ...? [maɪnd]
stoßen push [pʊʃ] **gegen etwas stoßen** hit sth. [hɪt] **auf jn./etwas stoßen** *(zufällig treffen)* come across sb./sth.
Strafe *(Bestrafung)* punishment ['pʌnɪʃmənt]
strahlend *(leuchtend hell)* bright [braɪt]
Strand beach [bi:tʃ]; *(eines Sees)* shore [ʃɔ:]
Straße street [stri:t]; road [rəʊd]
Straßenkreuzung junction ['dʒʌŋkʃn]
Straßenkünstler/in street artist ['stri:t‿ˌɑ:tɪst]
Strauch shrub [ʃrʌb]
Strecke *(Route)* route [ru:t]
streichen 1. *(anstreichen)* paint [peɪnt] 2. *(löschen)* delete [dɪ'li:t]
Streit argument ['ɑ:gjumənt]
streiten; sich streiten argue ['ɑ:gju:]
streng strict [strɪkt]
Strom power ['paʊə]
strömen stream [stri:m]
Strophe verse [vɜ:s]
Struktur structure ['strʌktʃə]
Stück: ein Stück ... a piece of ... [pi:s]
Stückchen bit [bɪt]
Student/in student ['stju:dənt]
Studie *(Umfrage)* survey ['sɜ:veɪ]
studieren study ['stʌdi]
Studio studio ['stju:diəʊ]
Stufe step [step]
Stuhl chair [tʃeə]
Stunde hour ['aʊə]; *(Unterrichtsstunde)* lesson ['lesn] **eine halbe Stunde** half an hour
Stundenplan timetable ['taɪmteɪbl]
Sturm storm [stɔ:m]
stürzen *(eilen)* rush [rʌʃ]; *(hinfallen)* fall [fɔ:l]; *(die Regierung, das Staatsoberhaupt)* overthrow [ˌəʊvə'θrəʊ]
suchen: etwas suchen look for sth. ['lʊk fɔ:]
Süden south [saʊθ] **nach Süden** south
südlich south [saʊθ]; southern ['sʌðən]
Südosten south-east [ˌsaʊθ'i:st] **nach Südosten** south-east
südöstlich south-east [ˌsaʊθ'i:st]
Südwesten south-west [ˌsaʊθ'west] **nach Südwesten** south-west
südwestlich south-west [ˌsaʊθ'west]
summen hum [hʌm]
Sumpf *(Marschland)* swamp [swɒmp]
Supermarkt supermarket ['su:pəmɑ:kɪt]
Suppe soup [su:p]
surfen surf [sɜ:f]
süß sweet [swi:t]
Süßigkeiten sweets *(pl)* [swi:ts]
Symbol symbol ['sɪmbl]
Szene scene [si:n]; *(Film)* shot [ʃɒt]

T

Tabelle table ['teɪbl]
Tablette tablet ['tæblət] *(bes. BE)*
Tafel 1. *(Schultafel)* board [bɔ:d] 2. *(Schokolade)* bar [bɑ:]
Tag day [deɪ] **den ganzen Tag (lang)** all day **eines Tages** one day
Tagebuch diary ['daɪəri]
täglich daily ['deɪli]
Taille waist [weɪst]
Tal valley ['væli]
Talent talent ['tælənt]
talentiert talented ['tæləntɪd]
Tankstelle petrol station *(BE)*; gas station *(AE)*
Tante aunt [ɑ:nt]
Tante-Emma-Laden corner shop ['kɔ:nə ʃɒp]
Tanz dance [dɑ:ns]
tanzen dance [dɑ:ns]
Tasche bag [bæg]; *(Manteltasche, Hosentasche usw.)* pocket ['pɒkɪt]
Taschenlampe torch [tɔ:tʃ] *(BE)*; flashlight ['flæʃlaɪt] *(AE)*
Tasse: eine Tasse ... a cup of ... [kʌp]
Tatsache fact [fækt]
tatsächlich 1. *(adj)* actual ['æktʃuəl] 2. *(adv)* actually ['æktʃuəli]
tätscheln pat [pæt]
Taube *(Stadttaube)* pigeon ['pɪdʒɪn]
Tausend, tausend thousand ['θaʊznd]
Team team [ti:m]
Technik, Technologie technology [tek'nɒlədʒi]
Tee tea [ti:]
Teil part [pɑ:t]; bit [bɪt
teilnehmen: an etwas teilnehmen take part in sth.
Teilstück *(Abschnitt)* section ['sekʃn]
Telefon telephone ['telɪfəʊn], *(kurz auch:)* phone **ans Telefon gehen** answer the phone
Telefongespräch phone call ['fəʊn kɔ:l], *(kurz auch:)* call
Telefonzelle telephone box
Teller: ein Teller ... a plate of ... [pleɪt]
Temperatur temperature ['temprətʃə]
Tempus *(grammatische Zeit)* tense [tens]
Tennis tennis ['tenɪs]
Termin *(Verabredung)* appointment [ə'pɔɪntmənt]
Terrorist/in terrorist ['terərɪst]
terroristische(r, s) terrorist ['terərɪst]
Test test [test]
testen test
teuer expensive [ɪk'spensɪv]
Text text [tekst] **einen Text schnell nach bestimmten Wörtern/Informationen absuchen** scan a text [skæn]
Theater theatre ['θɪətə]
Theaterstück play [pleɪ]
Thema topic ['tɒpɪk]; theme [θi:m]
Thermometer thermometer [θə'mɒmɪtə]
tief deep [di:p]

tiefgekühlt frozen ['frəʊzn]
Tier animal ['ænɪml]
Tierarzt/-ärztin vet [vet]
Tipp tip [tɪp]
tippen *(vorsichtig klopfen)* tap [tæp]
Tisch table ['teɪbl]
Tischler/in carpenter ['kɑːpəntə]
Titel title ['taɪtl]
Toast(brot) toast [təʊst]
Tochter daughter ['dɔːtə]
Tod death [deθ]
Toilette toilet ['tɔɪlət]
Tomate tomato [tə'mɑːtəʊ], *pl* tomatoes
Top *(Oberteil)* top [tɒp]
Topf pot [pɒt]
Tor **1.** *(Pforte, Gatter)* gate [geɪt] **2.** *(Sport)* goal [gəʊl] **ein Tor schießen** score (a goal) [skɔː]
tosen roar [rɔː]
tot dead [ded]
total totally ['təʊtəli]
töten kill [kɪl]
Tourist/in tourist ['tʊərɪst]
Tradition tradition [trə'dɪʃn]
traditionell traditional [trə'dɪʃənl]
tragen carry ['kæri]; *(Kleidung)* wear [weə]
trainieren train [treɪn]; practise ['præktɪs]; practice ['præktɪs] *(AE)*
Training training ['treɪnɪŋ]
Trance trance [trɑːns]
Träne tear [tɪə]
Transport(wesen) transport ['trænspɔːt]
Transporter *(Lieferwagen)* van [væn]
Traum dream [driːm]
traurig sad [sæd]
Trauung wedding ['wedɪŋ]
treffen; sich treffen meet [miːt] **etwas treffen** hit sth. **jn./etwas zufällig treffen** *(auf jn./etwas stoßen)* come across sb./sth.
Treffer: einen Treffer erzielen score [skɔː]
Treppe stairs *(pl)* [steəz]
treten kick [kɪk]
Trikot jersey ['dʒɜːzi]
Trimester term [tɜːm]
trinken drink [drɪŋk]
trocken dry [draɪ]
Trommel drum [drʌm]
Trommler/in drummer
Trompete trumpet ['trʌmpɪt]
Trophäe trophy ['trəʊfi]
tropisch, Tropen- tropical ['trɒpɪkl]
Trottel jerk [dʒɜːk] *(infml)*
trotzdem still [stɪl]
Truthahn turkey ['tɜːki]
T-Shirt T-shirt ['tiːʃɜːt]
Tulpe tulip ['tjuːlɪp]
tun do [duː] **etwas tun müssen** have to do sth. **etwas tun wollen** want to do sth. [wɒnt] **etwas immer wieder/immer weiter tun; etwas ständig tun** keep doing sth. [kiːp] **so tun, als ob** pretend [prɪ'tend] **Tut mir leid.** (I'm) sorry. ['sɒri] **viel zu tun haben** be busy ['bɪzi]
Tunnel tunnel ['tʌnl]
Tür door [dɔː]
Türglocke, -klingel doorbell ['dɔːbel]
Turm tower ['taʊə]
Turnen gymnastics [dʒɪm'næstɪks]; *(Sportunterricht)* PE [ˌpiː‿'iː] (Physical Education)
Turnhalle gym [dʒɪm]
Turnschuh trainer ['treɪnə]
Typ *(Art, Sorte)* type [taɪp]; *(Kerl)* guy [gaɪ]; dude [djuːd] *(bes. AE, Slang)*
typisch (für) typical (of) ['tɪpɪkl]

U

U-Bahn subway ['sʌbweɪ] *(AE)*; *(in London)* the Tube *(no pl)* [tjuːb]
übel: Das ist echt übel! That sucks! [sʌks] *(infml)*
üben practise ['præktɪs]; practice *(AE)*
über **1.** *(räumlich)* over ['əʊvə]; *(oberhalb)* above [ə'bʌv] **(quer) über das Moor/die Straße** across the moor/the street [ə'krɒs] **2.** *(mehr als)* over ['əʊvə] **über 400 Jahre** over 400 years **3. über mich/dich/...** about me/you/... [ə'baʊt] **über dich selbst** about yourself [jɔː'self]
überall everywhere ['evriweə] **überall um sie herum** all around her
überarbeiten revise [rɪ'vaɪz]
übereinander on top of each other
überfliegen: einen Text überfliegen *(um den Inhalt grob zu erfassen)* skim a text [skɪm]
übergeben: Ich muss mich übergeben. I'm going to be sick.
überhaupt: Und überhaupt, ... And anyway, ... ['eniweɪ]
überleben survive [sə'vaɪv]
übernachten (in/bei) stay (at/with) [steɪ]
überprüfen check [tʃek]
Überprüfung check [tʃek]
überqueren cross [krɒs]
überrascht surprised [sə'praɪzd]
Überraschung surprise [sə'praɪz]
Überschrift title ['taɪtl]; heading ['hedɪŋ]
übersetzen translate [træns'leɪt]
Übersetzung translation [træns'leɪʃn]
üblich usual ['juːʒuəl]
übrig: etwas übrig lassen leave sth. [liːv] **übrig sein** be left [left]
übrigens by the way [ˌbaɪ ðə 'weɪ]; actually ['æktʃuəli]
Übung exercise ['eksəsaɪz]
Übungsheft exercise book ['eksəsaɪz bʊk]
Ufer *(eines Sees)* shore [ʃɔː]
Uhr **1.** *(Armbanduhr)* watch [wɒtʃ]; *(Wand-, Stand-, Turmuhr)* clock [klɒk] **2. 4 Uhr morgens** 4 am [ˌeɪ‿'em] **4 Uhr nachmittags / 16 Uhr** 4 pm [ˌpiː‿'em] **um 1 Uhr / 13 Uhr** at 1 o'clock [ə'klɒk]
Uhrzeit time [taɪm]
um **1.** *(räumlich)* **um ... (herum)** around ... [ə'raʊnd] **2.** *(zeitlich)* **um 1 Uhr / 13 Uhr** at 1 o'clock [ə'klɒk] **3. um zu** to [tu], [tə]
umarmen: jn. umarmen give sb. a hug [hʌg]; hug sb.
umdrehen *(wenden)* turn (a)round [ˌtɜːn‿ə'raʊnd] **sich umdrehen** turn (a)round
Umfrage survey ['sɜːveɪ]
umher: in der Bücherei / auf dem Strand umher around the library/the beach [ə'raʊnd]
Umsatz *(Verkäufe)* sales *(pl)* [seɪlz]
umschreiben *(mit anderen Worten sagen)* paraphrase ['pærəfreɪz]
Umschreibung paraphrase ['pærəfreɪz]
umsehen: sich (auf der Farm) umsehen look around (the farm)
umsonst *(kostenlos)* for free
umsteigen change [tʃeɪndʒ]
umtauschen *(Geld)* change [tʃeɪndʒ]
umwandeln: etwas in etwas umwandeln make sth. into sth.
umziehen (nach) move (to) [muːv]
unabhängig independent [ˌɪndɪ'pendənt]
Unabhängigkeit independence [ˌɪndɪ'pendəns] **die Unabhängigkeitserklärung** *(der Vereinigten Staaten im Jahr 1776)* the Declaration of Independence
unbequem uncomfortable [ʌn'kʌmftəbl]
und and [ænd, [ənd] **Und du? / Und was ist mit dir?** What about you? **Und? / Na und?** So? [səʊ] **Und überhaupt, ...** And anyway, ... ['eniweɪ]
Unentschieden draw) [drɔː] *(bes. BE)*
unfair unfair [ʌn'feə]
Unfall accident ['æksɪdənt]
unfreundlich unfriendly [ʌn'frendli]
ungeduldig impatient [ɪm'peɪʃnt]
ungefähr 30 Leute about 30 people
ungewöhnlich unusual [ʌn'juːʒuəl]
unglaublich incredible [ɪn'kredəbl]; *(erstaunlich)* amazing [ə'meɪzɪŋ]
unglücklich unhappy [ʌn'hæpi]
unheimlich scary ['skeəri]
unhöflich impolite [ˌɪmpə'laɪt]; *(unverschämt)* rude [ruːd]
Uniform uniform ['juːnɪfɔːm]
Universität university [ˌjuːnɪ'vɜːsəti]
unmöglich impossible [ɪm'pɒsəbl]
Unrecht: jemand hat Unrecht someone is wrong [rɒŋ]
unregelmäßig irregular [ɪ'regjələ]

uns us [ʌs], [əs]; ourselves [ɑːˈselvz], [aʊəˈselvz]
unser(e) … our … [ˈaʊə]
unserer, unsere, unseres ours [ˈaʊəz]
unten *(am unteren Ende von)* at the bottom (of) [ˈbɒtəm]; *(im Haus)* downstairs [ˌdaʊnˈsteəz]; *(unter etwas)* below [bɪˈləʊ] **nach unten** down; *(im Haus)* downstairs
unter under [ˈʌndə]; *(unterhalb von)* below [bɪˈləʊ]
Unterarm forearm [ˈfɔːrɑːm]
unterhalb (von) below [bɪˈləʊ]
unterbrechen interrupt [ˌɪntəˈrʌpt]
untergehen *(Sonne)* set; go down [daʊn]
unterhalten: sich unterhalten (mit) talk (to) [tɔːk]
Unterhaltung *(Gespräch)* conversation [ˌkɒnvəˈseɪʃn]
unterirdisch underground [ˌʌndəˈgraʊnd]
Unterkunft shelter [ˈʃeltə]
unterrichten teach [tiːtʃ]
Unterschied difference [ˈdɪfrəns]
unterschiedlich sein be different; vary [ˈveəri]
unterstreichen underline [ˌʌndəˈlaɪn]
untersuchen *(beobachten, studieren)* study [ˈstʌdi]
Untertitel subtitle [ˈsʌbtaɪtl]
unterwegs out and about
Unwetter *(Gewitter)* storm [stɔːm]
Urgroßvater great-grandfather
Urgroßmutter great-grandmother
Urlaub holiday [ˈhɒlədeɪ] *(BE)*; vacation [vəˈkeɪʃn] *(AE)* **in Urlaub sein/fahren** be/go on holiday
ursprüngliche(r, s) original [əˈrɪdʒənl]
usw. (und so weiter) etc. (et cetera) [etˈsetərə]

V

Vater father [ˈfɑːðə]
Vati dad [dæd]
Vegetarier/in vegetarian [ˌvedʒəˈteəriən]
vegetarisch vegetarian [ˌvedʒəˈteəriən]
Verabredung date [deɪt]; *(Termin)* appointment [əˈpɔɪntmənt]
Veranda *(USA)* porch [pɔːtʃ]
verändern: (sich) verändern change [tʃeɪndʒ]
verängstigt scared [skeəd]
verantwortlich responsible [rɪˈspɒnsəbl]
Verb verb [vɜːb]
verbessern; sich verbessern improve [ɪmˈpruːv]
Verbesserung improvement [ɪmˈpruːvmənt]
verbleiben remain [rɪˈmeɪn]
verbeugen: sich verbeugen bow [baʊ]
verbinden link [lɪŋk]; join [dʒɔɪn]
Verbindung: sich (mit jm.) in Verbindung setzen get in touch (with sb.) [tʌtʃ] **(mit jm.) in Verbindung bleiben** stay in touch (with sb.)
verbreiten: (sich) verbreiten spread [spred]
verbreitet: weit verbreitet common [ˈkɒmən]
verbringen: Zeit verbringen (mit) spend time (on) [spend]
verbunden sein be connected [kəˈnektɪd]
vereinigt united [juˈnaɪtɪd] **das Vereinigte Königreich** the United Kingdom (UK) [juˌnaɪtɪd ˈkɪŋdəm] **die Vereinigten Staaten** *(von Amerika)* the United States (US)
verfügbar *(erhältlich)* available [əˈveɪləbl]
Vergangenheit past [pɑːst]
vergehen *(Zeit)* go by; pass [pɑːs]
vergessen forget [fəˈget]
vergewissern: sich vergewissern, dass … make sure that …
vergleichen compare [kəmˈpeə] **verglichen mit …** compared to …
Vergnügungspark fun park [ˈfʌn pɑːk]
verhaften arrest [əˈrest]
verhalten: sich verhalten behave [bɪˈheɪv]
Verhältnis *(Beziehung)* relationship [rɪˈleɪʃnʃɪp]
verheiratet (mit) married (to) [ˈmærɪd]
verirren: sich verirren get lost [lɒst]
Verkauf *(Umsatz, Absatz)* sales *(pl)* [seɪlz]
verkaufen sell [sel]
Verkäufer/in shop assistant [ˈʃɒp‿əˌsɪstənt] *(kurz auch: assistant)*
Verkehr traffic [ˈtræfɪk]
Verkehrsampel traffic light [ˈtræfɪk laɪt] *(oft auch:* traffic lights *(pl))*
Verkehrsmittel transport [ˈtrænspɔːt]
verkehrt wrong [rɒŋ]
verkleiden: sich verkleiden dress up [ˌdres‿ˈʌp]
Verkleidung costume [ˈkɒstjuːm]
verknüpfen link [lɪŋk]
Verkündung *(Erklärung)* declaration [ˌdekləˈreɪʃn]
verlassen leave [liːv]
verlaufen *(Straße; Grenze)* run **sich verlaufen** get lost [lɒst]
verletzen hurt [hɜːt]
verletzt hurt [hɜːt]
verlieren lose [luːz]
vermissen miss [mɪs]
Vermutungen anstellen speculate [ˈspekjuleɪt]
verneigen: sich verneigen bow [baʊ]
verpassen miss [mɪs]
verrostet rusty [ˈrʌsti]
verrückt mad [mæd]; crazy [ˈkreɪzi]
Vers rhyme [raɪm]; *(Strophe)* verse [vɜːs]
verschieden different [ˈdɪfrənt] **verschieden sein** be different; vary [ˈveəri]
verschwinden disappear [ˌdɪsəˈpɪə]
Versehen: aus Versehen by mistake
versprechen promise [ˈprɒmɪs]
Verständigung *(Kommunikation)* communication [kəˌmjuːnɪˈkeɪʃn]
verstecken; sich verstecken hide [haɪd]
verstehen understand [ˌʌndəˈstænd] **Hast du es verstanden?** Did you get it? *(infml)* **Verstehe.** I see.
Versuch try [traɪ]
versuchen try [traɪ] **Versuch's mal.** Have a go.
verteidigen: jn./etwas verteidigen (gegen jn./etwas) defend sb./sth. (against sb./sth.) [dɪˈfend]
verwenden use [juːz]
Vibration vibration [vaɪˈbreɪʃn]
Video video [ˈvɪdiəʊ]
Videokamera video camera [ˈvɪdiəʊ kæmrə]
viel a lot (of); lots (of); much [mʌtʃ] **Viel Glück!** Good luck! [lʌk] **Viel Spaß!** *(Amüsiere dich gut!)* Enjoy yourself! **viel zu tun haben** be busy [ˈbɪzi] **viel zu gut/clever/…** way too good/clever/… *(bes. AE)* **Wie viel kosten …?** How much are …? **Wie viel kostet …?** How much is …?
viele a lot (of); lots (of); many [ˈmeni]
vielleicht maybe [ˈmeɪbi] **sie sind vielleicht daheim** they may be at home
vier four [fɔː]
Viertel **1.** *(Stadtviertel)* quarter [ˈkwɔːtə]
2. *(Uhrzeiten)* **Viertel nach zehn (10.15/22.15)** quarter past ten [ˈkwɔːtə pɑːst] **Viertel vor elf (10.45/22.45)** quarter to eleven [ˈkwɔːtə tʊ]
violett purple [ˈpɜːpl]
Visum visa [ˈviːzə]
Vogel bird [bɜːd]
Vokal vowel [ˈvaʊəl]
voll (von/mit) full (of) [fʊl] **voller Menschen** crowded [ˈkraʊdɪd]
Volleyball volleyball [ˈvɒlibɔːl]
völlig totally [ˈtəʊtəli]
von of [ɒv], [əv]; from [frɒm], [frəm] **ein Lied von** a song by **von … bis …** from … to … **von … herunter** off … **von hinten** from behind
vor **1.** *(örtlich)* in front of [ɪn ˈfrʌnt‿əv] **vor der Schule** *(vor dem Schulgebäude)* in front of the school; *(außerhalb der Schule)* outside the school [ˌaʊtˈsaɪd]
2. *(zeitlich)* before [bɪˈfɔː] **vor zwei Tagen** two days ago [əˈgəʊ] **vor der Schule** *(vor Schulbeginn)* before school **vorm Unterricht** before lessons **Viertel vor elf (10.45/22.45)** quarter to eleven [ˈkwɔːtə tʊ] **nicht vor drei** *(erst um drei)* not till/not until three

3. vor allem *(insbesondere)* especially [ɪ'speʃli]
vorankommen *(zurechtkommen)* get on [ˌget_'ɒn]
Voraussage *(Vorhersage)* prediction [prɪ'dɪkʃn]
vorbei (an) past [pɑːst]
vorbei sein *(zu Ende sein)* be over ['əʊvə]
vorbei-: an etwas/jm. vorbeigehen/vorbeifahren pass sth./sb. [pɑːs]
vorbeikommen (bei) come over (to)
vorbereiten: etwas vorbereiten prepare sth. [prɪ'peə] **sich vorbereiten (auf)** prepare (for); get ready (for)
Vordergrund foreground ['fɔːgraʊnd]
Vorderseite front [frʌnt]
Vorfahr/in ancestor ['ænsestə]
Vorführung *(Demonstration)* demonstration [ˌdemən'streɪʃn]
vorgehen *(Uhr)* be fast
Vorhersage prediction [prɪ'dɪkʃn]
vorlesen: laut vorlesen read aloud [ə'laʊd]
Vorlieben und Abneigungen likes and dislikes *(pl)* [ˌlaɪks_ən 'dɪslaɪks]
Vormittag morning ['mɔːnɪŋ]
Vorschlag suggestion [sə'dʒestʃən]
vorschlagen: (jm.) etwas vorschlagen suggest sth. (to sb.) [sə'dʒest]
Vorschrift *(Regel)* rule [ruːl]
Vorsicht! *(Pass auf!)* Watch out! [ˌwɒtʃ_'aʊt]
vorsichtig careful ['keəfl]
vorspielen: etwas vorspielen act sth. out [ˌækt_'aʊt]
Vorspielen *(Theater)* audition [ɔː'dɪʃn]
Vorsprechen *(Theater)* audition [ɔː'dɪʃn]
vorstellen **1. sich etwas vorstellen** imagine sth. [ɪ'mædʒɪn] **Stell dir vor, Dad …** Guess what, Dad …
2. jn. jm. vorstellen introduce sb. to sb. [ˌɪntrə'djuːs]
3. jm. etwas vorstellen present sth. to sb. [prɪ'zent]
Vorstellung **1.** *(Idee)* idea [aɪ'dɪə]
2. *(Präsentation)* presentation [ˌprezn'teɪʃn]
3. *(Auftritt)* performance [pə'fɔːməns]
Vortrag talk [tɔːk] **einen Vortrag halten (über)** give a talk (about)
vorüber (an) past [pɑːst]
vorübergehen *(Zeit)* go by; pass [pɑːs]

W

Wache, Wachposten guard [gɑːd]
wachsen grow [grəʊ]
wählen *(aussuchen)* choose [tʃuːz]
wahr true [truː] **…, nicht wahr?** …, right?
während **1. während des Spiels** during the match ['djʊərɪŋ]
2. während wir spielten while we were playing [waɪl]; as we were playing
Wahrheit truth [truːθ]
wahrscheinlich **1.** *(adj)* probable ['prɒbəbl]
2. *(adv)* probably ['prɒbəbli]
Währung currency ['kʌrənsi]
Wal whale [weɪl]
Wald forest ['fɒrɪst]
Walisisch; walisisch Welsh [welʃ]
Wand wall [wɔːl]
Wandschrank *(oft begehbar)* closet ['klɒzɪt] *(bes. AE)*
wann? when? [wen] **Wann hast du Geburtstag?** When's your birthday.
Wappentier state animal [ˌsteɪt_'ænɪml]
wäre: es wäre … it would be … [wʊd]
Waren *(Güter)* goods *(pl)* [gʊdz]
warm warm [wɔːm]
Warnung warning ['wɔːnɪŋ]
warten (auf) wait (for) [weɪt] **Warte einen Moment.** Wait a minute.
warum? why? [waɪ]
was? what? [wɒt] **Was gibt es zum Mittagessen?** What's for lunch? **Was gibt's? / Was ist los?** What's up? **Was haben wir als Hausaufgabe auf?** What's for homework? **Was hättest du gern? / Was möchtest du?** What would you like? **Was ist denn? / Was ist los?** What's the matter? **Und was ist mit dir?** What about you? **Was könnte besser sein?** What could be better? [kʊd], [kəd] **was (auch) immer** whatever [ˌwɒt'evə]
waschen wash [wɒʃ]
Wasser water ['wɔːtə]
Wasserfall waterfall ['wɔːtəfɔːl]
Website website ['websaɪt]
Wechselgeld change [tʃeɪndʒ]
wechseln change [tʃeɪndʒ]
wecken: jn. (auf)wecken wake sb. up [ˌweɪk_'ʌp]
weg away [ə'weɪ] **weg sein** *(nicht mehr da sein)* be gone [gɒn]
Weg way [weɪ]; *(Pfad)* path [pɑːθ]; trail [treɪl] **auf dem Weg zu/nach …** on the way to … **jm. den Weg (nach …) beschreiben** tell sb. the way (to …) **jn. nach dem Weg fragen** ask sb. the way
wegen: Es tut mir leid wegen … I'm sorry about …
weggehen leave [liːv]
weglassen: etwas weglassen leave sth. out [ˌliːv_'aʊt]
wegrennen run off
wehtun hurt [hɜːt]
weich soft [sɒft]
Weide field [fiːld]
Weihnachten Christmas ['krɪsməs] **Frohe Weihnachten!** Merry Christmas! **1. Weihnachtstag** *(25. Dezember)* Christmas Day **2. Weihnachtstag** *(26. Dezember)* Boxing Day
weil because [bɪ'kɒz]; as [æz, əz]
Weile: eine Weile a while [waɪl]; for a while
weinen cry [kraɪ]
weise wise [waɪz]
Weise: Art und Weise way [weɪ] **auf diese Weise** in this way
weiß white [waɪt]
weit (entfernt) far [fɑː] **weit verbreitet** common ['kɒmən] **weiter** further ['fɜːðə] **geradeaus weiter** straight on [streɪt_'ɒn]
weiter-: weitergehen/-laufen/-segeln/… walk/run/sail/… on
weitermachen go on [ˌgəʊ_'ɒn]
weiterreden go on [ˌgəʊ_'ɒn]
welche(r, s) **1. Auf welcher Seite sind wir?** What page are we on? **Welche Farbe …?** What colour …?
2. *(aus einer begrenzten Anzahl)* which [wɪtʃ] **Welche(r, s)?** Which one? **Welche Wörter …?** *(= Welche von diesen Wörtern …?)* Which words …?
Welle wave [weɪv]
Welt world [wɜːld] **auf der Welt** in the world
Weltraum space [speɪs]
wem? who? **Wem hast du es erzählt?** Who did you tell?
wen? who? **Wen kennt Sam?** Who does Sam know?
wenden *(umkehren)* turn around [ˌtɜːn_ə'raʊnd] **sich an jn. wenden** turn to sb.
wenig *(ein bisschen, etwas)* a little
weniger (als) less (than) [les]
wenigstens *(zumindest)* at least [ət 'liːst]
wenn when [wen]; *(falls)* if [ɪf]
wer? who? [huː]
werben: für etwas werben *(etwas fördern)* promote sth. [prə'məʊt]; *(Werbung machen)* advertise sth. ['ædvətaɪz]
Werbespot advertisement [əd'vɜːtɪsmənt] *(kurz auch:* advert ['ædvɜːt], ad [æd])
Werbung advertising ['ædvətaɪzɪŋ] **Werbung machen (für etwas)** advertise (sth.) ['ædvətaɪz]
werden become [bɪ'kʌm] **rot werden** *(erröten)* go red **hart/schlecht/verrückt werden** go hard/bad/mad **rot/braun/… werden** turn red/brown/… [tɜːn] **wütend/kalt werden** get angry/cold **(allmählich) dunkler/alt/… werden** grow darker/old/…
werfen throw [θrəʊ] **einen Blick auf etwas werfen** have a look at sth.
Werkstatt workshop ['wɜːkʃɒp]
wert worth [wɜːθ]
wessen? whose? [huːz]

Westen west [west] **nach Westen** west
westlich, West- western ['westən]
wetten bet [bet]
Wetter weather ['weðə]
Wettbewerb competition [ˌkɒmpə'tɪʃn]
Wettkampf *(Match)* match [mætʃ]
wichtig important [ɪm'pɔːtnt] **etwas wichtig nehmen** care about sth. [keə] **Tiere sind mir sehr wichtig.** I really care about animals.
widerlich disgusting [dɪs'gʌstɪŋ]
wie 1. *(Fragewort)* how [haʊ] **Wie alt bist du?** How old are you? **Wie findest du …? / Wie gefällt dir …?** How do you like …? **Wie geht's? / Wie geht es dir/euch?** How are you? **Wie heißt du?** What's your name? **Wie ist sie (so)?** What's she like? **Wie spät ist es?** What time is it? **Wie viel kosten …?** How much are …? **Wie viel kostet …?** How much is …? **Wie war es?** What was it like?
2. wie Buben like boys [laɪk] **genau wie …** just like … ['dʒʌst laɪk] **Wie dem auch sei, …** Anyway, … ['eniweɪ]
3. der-/die-/dasselbe wie … the same as … **(nicht) so groß wie …** (not) as big as … [æz], [əz]
wieder again [ə'gen] **immer wieder** again and again
wiederaufbauen rebuild [ˌriː'bɪld]
wiederholen repeat [rɪ'piːt]; *(Lernstoff)* revise [rɪ'vaɪz]
Wiederholung *(des Lernstoffs)* revision [rɪ'vɪʒn]
wiegen weigh [weɪ]
wild wild [waɪld]; *(heftig)* fierce [fɪəs] **wild auf etwas sein** be keen on sth. [kiːn] **wild darauf sein, etwas zu tun** be keen on doing sth.
Wildwasser whitewater ['waɪtwɔːtə]
Wildwasserfahren *(im Schlauchboot)* whitewater rafting [ˌwaɪtwɔːtə 'rɑːftɪŋ]
Willkommen in Plymouth. Welcome to Plymouth. ['welkəm]
Wind wind [wɪnd]
windig windy ['wɪndi]
winken wave [weɪv]
Winter winter ['wɪntə]
winzig tiny ['taɪni]
wir we [wiː]
wirklich 1. *(adj)* real ['riːəl]; actual ['æktʃuəl]
2. *(adv)* really *(adv)* ['rɪəli]; actually ['æktʃuəli]
Wirklichkeit: in Wirklichkeit in fact [ɪn 'fækt]
wischen *(Fußboden)* mop [mɒp]
Wischmopp mop [mɒp]
wissbegierig curious ['kjʊəriəs]
wissen know [nəʊ] **über etwas Bescheid wissen** know about sth. **…, weißt du./…, wissen Sie.** …, you know./…, you see. **Weißt du was, Dad …** Guess what, Dad … **Woher weißt du …?** How do you know …? **gern wissen wollen** *(sich fragen)* wonder ['wʌndə]
Witz joke [dʒəʊk]
witzig funny ['fʌni]
wo? where? [weə]
Woche week [wiːk]
Wochenende weekend [ˌwiːk'end] **am Wochenende** at the weekend
Wochentag day of the week
wöchentlich week ['wiːkli]
Woher kommst du? Where are you from?
wohin? where? [weə]
Wohlfahrtsorganisation charity ['tʃærəti]
Wohltätigkeit *(wohltätige Zwecke)* charity ['tʃærəti]
wohnen *(leben)* live [lɪv]; *(vorübergehend)* stay [steɪ]
Wohnheim hostel ['hɒstl]
Wohnung flat [flæt]; apartment [ə'pɑːtmənt]
Wohnwagen caravan ['kærəvæn]
Wohnzimmer living room ['lɪvɪŋ ruːm]
Wolke cloud [klaʊd]
Wolkenkratzer skyscraper ['skaɪskreɪpə]
wollen: etwas haben wollen want sth. [wɒnt] **etwas tun wollen** want to do sth. **sagen wollen** *(meinen)* mean [miːn]
Workshop workshop ['wɜːkʃɒp]
Wort word [wɜːd]
Wortart part of speech [ˌpɑːt‿əv 'spiːtʃ]
Wortstellung word order ['wɜːd‿ɔːdə]
Wovon handelt die Geschichte? What is the story about?
wund sore [sɔː]
wunderbar wonderful ['wʌndəfəl]
wundervoll *(zauberhaft)* magical ['mædʒɪkl]
Wunsch wish [wɪʃ]
wünschen wish [wɪʃ] **sich etwas wünschen** make a wish
würde: Ich würde gern … I'd like to … **Ich würde sehr gern …** I'd love to …
wütend angry ['æŋgri]

Y

Yoga yoga ['jəʊgə]

Z

Zahl number ['nʌmbə]; *(Ziffer)* figure ['fɪgə]
zählen count [kaʊnt]
Zahn tooth [tuːθ], *pl* teeth [tiːθ]
Zahnarzt/-ärztin dentist ['dentɪst]
Zahnschmerzen haben have a toothache ['tuːθeɪk]
Zauber- magic ['mædʒɪk]
zauberhaft magical ['mædʒɪkl]
Zaun fence [fens]
z.B. (zum Beispiel) e.g. [ˌiː 'dʒiː]
Zeh toe [təʊ]
zehn ten [ten]
Zeichen sign [saɪn]; *(Signal)* signal ['sɪgnəl]
zeichnen draw [drɔː]
Zeichnung drawing ['drɔːɪŋ]
zeigen show [ʃəʊ] **auf etwas zeigen** point to sth. [pɔɪnt] **es zeigt, dass …** it shows that …
Zeile line [laɪn]
Zeit 1. time [taɪm] **aller Zeiten** of all time **einige Zeit** a while **eine Zeit lang** for a while
2. *(grammatische Zeit, Tempus)* tense [tens]
Zeitalter age [eɪdʒ]
Zeitleiste timeline ['taɪmlaɪn]
Zeitmesser timer ['taɪmə]
Zeitschrift magazine [ˌmægə'ziːn]
Zeitstrahl timeline ['taɪmlaɪn]
Zeitung newspaper ['njuːspeɪpə], *(kurz auch:)* paper
Zelt tent [tent]
Zelten camping ['kæmpɪŋ]
Zeltplatz campsite ['kæmpsaɪt]
Zentimeter centimetre (cm) ['sentɪmiːtə]
zentral central ['sentrəl]
Zentrum centre ['sentə] **im Zentrum von Albuquerque** in downtown Albuquerque ['daʊntaʊn] *(AE)*
zerbrechen break [breɪk]
zerbrochen broken ['brəʊkən]
zerstören destroy [dɪ'strɔɪ]
Zeug stuff [stʌf] *(infml)*
Ziege goat [gəʊt]
ziehen pull [pʊl]
ziemlich quite [kwaɪt]
Ziffer number ['nʌmbə]; figure ['fɪgə]
Zimmer mit Frühstück bed & breakfast
Zimmerer/Zimmerin carpenter ['kɑːpəntə]
zischen hiss [hɪs]; *(in der Pfanne, auf dem Grill)* sizzle ['sɪzl]
Zoll *(Längenmaß; 2,54 cm)* inch [ɪntʃ]
Zoo zoo [zuː]
zu 1. *(örtlich)* to [tu], [tə]
2. zu spät/kalt/groß/… too late/cold/big/… [tuː] **viel zu gut/clever/ …** way too good/clever/… *(bes. AE)*
3. Es ist Zeit zu gehen. It's time to go. **Nice to meet you.** Freut mich, dich/euch/Sie kennenzulernen.
zudecken cover ['kʌvə]
zueinander passen go together
zuerst first [fɜːst]; at first
zufällig by accident ['æksɪdənt]
zufolge according to [ə'kɔːdɪŋ]
Zug 1. train [treɪn]
2. *(bei Brettspielen)* move [muːv]

Dictionary

Zugabe encore ['ɒŋkɔː]
Zugang (zu) access (to) ['ækses]
Zügel reins *(pl)* [reɪnz]
Zuhause home [həʊm]
zuhören listen ['lɪsn] **Hör(t) mir zu.** Listen to me.
Zuhörer/innen *(Publikum)* audience ['ɔːdiəns]
Zukunft future ['fjuːtʃə]
zukünftige(r, s) future ['fjuːtʃə]
zulassen *(erlauben)* allow [ə'laʊ]
zuletzt: Wann hast du sie das zuletzt gesehen? When did you see them last?
zum Beispiel for example [ɪg'zɑːmpl]
zumachen *(schließen)* close [kləʊz]
Zunge tongue [tʌŋ]
Zungenbrecher tongue-twister ['tʌŋˌtwɪstə]
zurechtkommen *(vorankommen)* get on [ˌget‿'ɒn]
zurück back [bæk]
zurücklassen leave [liːv]
zusammen together [tə'geðə]
zusammenbrechen collapse [kə'læps]
zusammenfassen sum sth. up [ˌsʌm‿'ʌp]
zusammenpassen *(zueinander passen)* go together
Zuschauer/innen *(Publikum)* audience ['ɔːdiəns]
zustimmen: jm. zustimmen agree with sb. [ə'griː]
Zusammenhang *(Text-, Satzzusammenhang)* context ['kɒntekst]
Zutritt access ['ækses]; entry ['entri]
zuvor: besser als je zuvor better than ever
zuwenden: sich jm. zuwenden turn to sb. [tɜːn]
zuwinken: jm. zuwinken wave at sb. [weɪv]
zwei two [tuː]
zweimal twice [twaɪs]
zweisprachig bilingual [baɪ'lɪŋgwəl]
zweite(r, s) second ['sekənd] **Zweitens, ...** Second, ...
Zwiebel onion ['ʌnjən]
Zwillinge twins *(pl)* [twɪnz]
zwischen between [bɪ'twiːn]
Zwischenüberschrift sub-heading ['sʌbˌhedɪŋ]
zwölf twelve [twelv]

English sounds

[iː] green, he, sea
[i] happy, monkey
[ɪ] big, in, expensive
[e] red, yes, again, breakfast
[æ] cat, animal, apple, black
[ɑː] class, ask, car, park
[ɒ] song, on, dog, what
[ɔː] door, or, ball, four, morning
[uː] blue, ruler, too, two, you
[ʊ] book, good, pullover
[ʌ] mum, bus, colour
[ɜː] girl, early, her, work, T-shirt
[ə] a partner, again, today

[eɪ] name, eight, play, great
[aɪ] time, right, my, I
[ɔɪ] boy, toilet, noise
[əʊ] old, no, road, yellow
[aʊ] town, now, house
[ɪə] here, year, idea
[eə] where, pair, share, their
[ʊə] tour
[b] boat, table, verb
[p] pool, paper, shop
[d] dad, window, good
[t] ten, letter, at

[g] good, again, bag
[k] cat, kitchen, back
[m] mum, man, remember
[n] no, one, ten
[ŋ] song, young, uncle, thanks
[l] hello, like, old, small
[r] red, ruler, friend, sorry
[w] we, where, one
[j] you, yes, uniform
[f] family, after, laugh
[v] river, very, seven, have
[s] sister, poster, yes
[z] please, zoo, quiz, his, music
[ʃ] shop, station, English
[ʒ] television, usually
[tʃ] teacher, child, watch
[dʒ] Germany, job, project, orange

[θ] thanks, three, bathroom
[ð] the, this, father, with
[h] here, who, behind
[x] loch

Am besten kannst du dir die Aussprache der einzelnen Lautzeichen einprägen, wenn du dir zu jedem Zeichen ein einfaches Wort merkst – das [iː] ist der **green**-Laut, das [eɪ] ist der **name**-Laut usw.

Unit 1

6 Everyday English Small talk

p. 13

c) Partner B:
You're from Britain. At a tourist sight in London (your partner will tell you which sight) you meet a visitor from Germany.
You start talking to him/her and have a nice conversation.

Unit 5

5 Something went wrong

p. 121

Partner B:
Read the text and make notes on the key points.

Use your notes to tell your partner what happened.

"My text is about someone who ..."
...
"I bet Emma wishes she had/hadn't ..."

A group of kids had taken their kayaks out on a small river in the hills in the north of the country. Emma was slow, so she was behind the rest of the group. She hated being alone and tried hard to get to the others. In front of her, she saw a little bridge. The water was high and there wasn't enough room to go under the bridge, so she decided to stop and carry her kayak around it. "I'll get as close as I can before I get out," she thought. But "as close as I can" was too close. The river was very fast here and it carried her kayak under the bridge. The kayak turned over and the girl's head was under the water. She got out of the kayak as quickly as she could. On the other side of the bridge she swam to the shore and watched as her kayak disappeared downstream.

How did you do? / How can you do better?

How did you do?	Tips
Content	
Did you give enough information about the objects you presented?	• Check your notes. Think about important facts you may have left out and write them down.
Were you able to explain words your classmates didn't understand?	• Think of two words and practise paraphrasing them.
Could you answer your classmates' questions?	• When you prepare your talk, think of questions people might ask and how to answer them.
Structure	
Did you lead your audience through your talk?	• Think of phrases you could use, e.g. – *Today, I'm going to talk about …* – *The first/next/… thing I'd like to show you…*
Did you sum up your talk at the end?	• Summing up helps your audience to remember your main ideas. Think of how to put these ideas in one or two sentences, e.g. *Well, I've shown you three things altogether. They show different things about my life / how important sport is in our family / …*
Did you ask for questions?	• Answering questions helps your audience to understand your ideas better. Try to remember to ask for questions after you've summed up.
Delivery	
Was the speed of your talk OK?	• Record your talk while you're practising to check your speed and how clearly you speak.
Did you speak clearly?	• We often speak too quickly or unclearly when we're nervous. Remember, you needn't feel nervous if you have prepared well. Tell yourself that before you start. Taking a deep breath before you speak can also help you to relax.
Did you look at your classmates while you were speaking?	• Practise moving your head slowly from one side of your audience to the other. Make eye contact with different people for two seconds.
Did you show them the objects as you spoke?	• Remember that a talk is easier to understand if the speaker uses both pictures and words.

➔ *SF 16: Giving a good presentation (p. 165)*

First names (Vornamen)

Abraham ['eɪbrəhæm]
Adam ['ædəm]
Adrian ['eidriən]
Albert ['ælbət]
Alex ['ælɪgz]
Amelia [ə'mi:liə]
Angus ['æŋgəs]
Ben [ˌben]
Beth [beθ]
Beyoncé [bɪ'jɒnseɪ]
Brian ['braɪən]
Callum ['kæləm]
Cate [keɪt]
Charles [tʃɑ:lz]
Charlie ['tʃɑ:li]
Chloe ['kləʊi]
Christopher ['krɪstəfə]
Clementine ['kleməntaɪn]
Dan [dæn]
Dave ['deɪv]
Dean ['di:n]
Dylan ['dɪlən]
Edward ['edwəd]
Emily ['eməli]
Eugene [ju: 'dʒi:n]
Frank [fræŋk]
Gareth ['gærəθ]
Gemima [dʒə'meɪmə]
George [dʒɔ:dʒ]
Giles [dʒaɪlz]
Gordon ['gɔ:dn]
Grace [greɪs]
Gwen [gwen]
Hadrian ['heɪdriən]
Harry ['hæri]
Iain ['i:ən]
Jack [dʒæk]
James [dʒeɪmz]
Jasmine/Jaz [dʒ]
Jerry ['dʒeri]
Jill ['dʒil]
Jimmy ['dʒɪmi]
John [dʒɒn]
Kaylee ['keɪli]
Katie ['keɪti]
Khan [kɑ:n]
Knuckles ['nʌkəlz]
Luke [lu:k]
Mary ['meəri]
Maxine [mæk'si:n]
Mishal ['mɪʃəl]
Mo [məʊ]
Morgan ['mɔ:gən]
Norman ['nɔ:mən]
Oliver ['ɒlɪvə]
Oonagh ['u:nə]
Paige [peɪdʒ]
Paul [pɔ:l]
Philip ['fɪlɪp]
Ray [reɪ]
Ringo ['rɪŋgeʊ]
Robert ['rɒbət]
Roger ['rɒdʒə]
Ronald ['rɒnəld]
Ruscaire ['rʌskərə]
Sandra ['sændrə], ['sɑ:ndrə]
Sam [sæm]
Sandy ['sændi]
Sherlock ['ʃɜ:lɒk]
Skye [skaɪ]
Susan ['su:zən]
Tiffany ['tifəni]
Tyler ['taɪlə]
William ['wɪliəm]
Willy ['wɪli]

Family names / Surnames (Familiennamen)

Abrams ['eibrəmz]
Baden-Powell [ˌbeɪdn'pəʊəl]
Barnes [bɑ:nz]
Bates [beɪts]
Beedle ['bi:dl]
Blanchett ['blɑ:ntʃət]
Boyd [bɔɪd]
Clarke [klɑ:k]
Carson ['kɑ:sən]
Davis ['deɪvɪz]
Dickens ['dɪkɪnz]
Edwards ['edwədz]
Evans ['evənz]
Ferguson ['fɜ:gəsən]
Foster ['fɒstə]
Fraser ['freɪzə]
Grant [grɑ:nt]
Grimble ['grɪmbl]
Hammerstein ['hæməstaɪn]
Harrison ['hærɪsən]
Henri ['henri]
Hill [hɪl]
Holmes [həʊmz]
Hunter ['hʌntə]
Jezzard ['dʒezɑ:d]
Kirk [kɜ:k]
Lennon ['lenən]
Lincoln ['lɪnkln]
Lopez ['lɒpez]
Nash [næʃ]
Nobel [nəʊ'bel]
Oscar ['ɒskə]
O'Shea ['əʊʃi:]
Patten ['pætən]
Potter ['pɒtə]
Reid [ri:d]
Rogers ['rɒdʒəz]
Ross [rɒs]
Scott [skɒt]
Seeger ['si:gə]
Sims [sɪmz]
Skeefe [ski:f]
Smart [smɑ:t]
Smith [smɪθ]
Starr [stɑ:]
Twist [twɪst]
Washington ['wɒʃɪŋtən]

Place names (Ortsnamen)

Albuquerque ['ælbəkɜ:ki]
Arizona [ˌærɪ'zəʊnə]
Bangor ['bæŋgə]
Bannockburn ['bænəkbɜ:n]
the **Beat Museum** ['bi:t]
Blackfriars [ˌblæk'fraɪəz]
Boston ['bɒstən]
Brandenburg ['brændnbɜ:g]
Buckingham Palace [ˌbʌkɪŋəm 'pæləs]
the **Burren** ['bʌrən]
Caerdydd [kaɪə'di:ð]
Caernarfon [kə'nɑ:vən]
California [ˌkælə'fɔ:niə]
Cardiff ['kɑ:dɪf]
Carlingford ['kɑ:lɪŋfəd]
Castlebay [ˌkɑ:sl'beɪ]
the **Cavern Club** ['kæven]
Chelsea ['tʃelsi]
Colorado [ˌkɒlə'rɑ:dəʊ]
Dublin ['dʌblɪn]
Euston ['ju:stən]
Everton ['evətən]
Fulham ['fʊləm]
Georgetown ['dʒɔ:dʒtaʊn]
Grand Canyon [ˌgrænd'kenjən]
Great Homer Street [ˌgreɪt 'həʊmə stri:t]
Hamburg ['hæmbɜ:g]
Hammersmith ['hæməsmɪθ]
Hampstead Heath [ˌhæmpstɪd 'hi:θ]
Hyde Park [ˌhaid 'pɑ:k]
Isle of Barra [ˌaɪl‿əv 'bærə]
King's Cross [ˌkɪŋz 'krɒs]
Lambeth ['læmbəθ]
Las Vegas [læs 'veɪgəs]
Liverpool ['lɪvəpu:l]
London ['lʌndən]
Los Angeles [lɒs‿'ændʒələz]
Marble Arch [ˌmɑ:bl‿'ɑ:tʃ]
Mathew Street ['mæθju:]
Merseyside ['mɜ:zisaɪd]
Moscow ['mɒskəʊ]
Nevada [nə'vɑ:də]
New Mexico [ˌnju: 'meksɪkəʊ]
New Orleans [ˌnu: 'ɔ:lənz], [ˌnju: 'ɔ:liənz]
New York [ˌnju: 'jɔ:k]
Notting Hill [ˌnɒtɪŋ 'hɪl]
Normandy ['nɔ:məndɪ]
One New Change [ˌwʌn nju: 'tʃeɪndʒ]
Oxford Street ['ɒksfəd stri:t]
Philadelphia [fɪlə'delfiə]
Phoenix ['fi: nɪks]
Pueblo ['pwebləʊ]
Richmond ['rɪtʃmənd]
the **Rio Grande** [ˌriəʊ 'grændə]
the **River Mersey** ['mɜ:zi]
the **River Thames** ['temz]
Russell Square [ˌrʌsl 'skweə]
Saint Patrick's Cathedral [sənt ˌpætrɪks kə'θi:drəl]
Saint Paul's Cathedral [sənt ˌpɔ:lz kə'θi:drəl]
Santa Fe [ˌsæntə 'feɪ]
the **Shard** [ʃɑ:d]
Slidell [slaɪ'del]
Snowdon ['snəʊdn]
Snowdonia [snəʊ'dəʊniə]
Southampton [ˌsaʊθ'hæmptən]
Taos [taʊs]
Texas ['teksəs]
Utah ['ju:tɑ:]
Vauxhall ['vɒksɔ:l]
the **Watkin Path** ['wɒtkɪn]
Wavertree ['weɪvətri:]
Westbourne Grove [ˌwestbɔ:n 'grəʊv]
Westminster ['westmɪnstə]
Wimbledon ['wɪmbldən]

Other names

Angles, Saxons, Anglo-Saxons [ˌæŋglo'sæksons]
Beatle ['bi:tl]
Big Ben [ˌbɪg 'ben]
Britons ['britons]
Igbo ['i:bəʊ]
the **Jubilee line** ['dʒu:bəli]
Navajo ['nævəhəʊ]
Ogoni [əʊ'gəʊni]
Raven ['reɪvn]
the **Rosetta Stone** [rəʊ'zetə]
Shadow ['ʃædəʊ]
Shoshone [ʃəʊ'ʃəʊni]
UNESCO [ju:'neskəʊ]

Country/Continent	Adjective	Person	People
*Marco is from **Italy**.*	*Pizza is **Italian**.*	*Marco is **an Italian**.*	***The Italians** invented pizza.*
Africa ['æfrɪkə] *Afrika*	African ['æfrɪkən]	an African	the Africans
Albania [æl'beɪniə] *Albanien*	Albanian [æl'beɪniən]	an Albanian	the Albanians
Asia ['eɪʒə, 'eɪʃə] *Asien*	Asian ['eɪʃn, 'eɪʒn]	an Asian	the Asians
Australia [ɒ'streɪliə] *Australien*	Australian [ɒ'streɪliən]	an Australian	the Australians
Austria ['ɒstriə] *Österreich*	Austrian ['ɒstriən]	an Austrian	the Austrians
Belarus [ˌbel'ruːs] *Weißrussland*	Belarusian [ˌbel'ruːsiən]	a Belarusian	the Belarusians
Belgium ['beldʒəm] *Belgien*	Belgian ['beldʒən]	a Belgian	the Belgians
Bosnia and Herzegovina ['bɒzniə ən ˌhɜːtsəgə'viːnə] *Bosnien und Herzegowina*	Bosnian ['bɒzniən]; Herzegovinian [ˌhɜːtsəgə'vɪniən]	a Bosnian; a Herzegovinian	the Bosnians; the Herzegovinians
Bulgaria [bʌl'geəriə] *Bulgarien*	Bulgarian [bʌl'geəriən]	a Bulgarian	the Bulgarians
China ['tʃaɪnə] *China*	Chinese [ˌtʃaɪ'niːz]	a Chinese	the Chinese
Croatia [krəʊ'eɪʃə] *Kroatien*	Croatian [krəʊ'eɪʃn]	a Croatian	the Croatians
Cyprus ['saɪprəs] *Zypern*	Cypriot ['sɪpriət]	a Cypriot	the Cypriots
the **Czech Republic** [ˌtʃek rɪ'pʌblɪk] *Tschechien, die Tschechische Republik*	Czech [tʃek]	a Czech	the Czechs
Denmark ['denmɑːk] *Dänemark*	Danish ['deɪnɪʃ]	a Dane [deɪn]	the Danes
England ['ɪŋglənd] *England*	English ['ɪŋglɪʃ]	an Englishman / an Englishwoman	the English
Estonia [e'stəʊniə] *Estland*	Estonian [e'stəʊniən]	an Estonian	the Estonians
Europe ['jʊərəp] *Europa*	European [ˌjʊərə'piːən]	a European	the Europeans
Finland ['fɪnlənd] *Finnland*	Finnish ['fɪnɪʃ]	a Finn [fɪn]	the Finns
France [frɑːns] *Frankreich*	French [frentʃ]	a Frenchman / a Frenchwoman	the French
Germany ['dʒɜːməni] *Deutschland*	German ['dʒɜːmən]	a German	the Germans
(Great) Britain ['brɪtn] *Großbritannien*	British ['brɪtɪʃ]	a Briton ['brɪtn]	the British
Greece [griːs] *Griechenland*	Greek [griːk]	a Greek	the Greeks
Greenland ['griːnlənd]	Greenlandic [griːn'lændɪk]	a Greenlander ['griːnləndə]	the Greenlanders
Guyana [gaɪ'ænə] *Guyana (früher: British Guyana)*	Guyanese [gaɪ'əniːz]	a Guyanese	the Guyanese
Hungary ['hʌŋgəri] *Ungarn*	Hungarian [hʌŋ'geəriən]	a Hungarian	the Hungarians
Iceland ['aɪslənd] *Island*	Icelandic [aɪs'lændɪk]	an Icelander ['aɪsləndə]	the Icelanders
India ['ɪndiə] *Indien*	Indian ['ɪndiən]	an Indian	the Indians
Ireland ['aɪələnd] *Irland*	Irish ['aɪrɪʃ]	an Irishman / an Irishwoman	the Irish
Italy ['ɪtəli] *Italien*	Italian [ɪ'tæliən]	an Italian	the Italians
Kosovo ['kɒsəvəʊ] *Kosovo*	Kosovan ['kɒsəvən]	a Kosovan	the Kosovans

Country/Continent	Adjective	Person	People
Marco is from ***Italy.***	*Pizza is* ***Italian.***	*Marco is* ***an Italian.***	***The Italians*** *invented pizza.*
Latvia ['lætviə] *Lettland*	Latvian ['lætviən]	a Latvian	the Latvians
Lithuania [ˌlɪθju'eɪniə] *Litauen*	Lithuanian [ˌlɪθju'eɪniə]	a Lithuanian	the Lithuanians
Luxembourg ['lʌksəmbɜːg] *Luxemburg*	Luxembourg	a Luxembourger ['lʌksəmbɜːgə]	the Luxembourgers
Macedonia [ˌmæsə'dəʊniə] *Mazedonien*	Macedonian [ˌmæsə'dəʊniən]	a Macedonian	the Macedonians
Malta ['mɔːltə] *Malta*	Maltese [mɔːl'tiːz]	a Maltese	the Maltese
Moldova [mɒl'dəʊvə] *Moldawien*	Moldovan [mɒl'dəʊvən]	a Moldovan	the Moldovans
Montenegro [ˌmɒntɪ'niːgrəʊ] *Montenegro*	Montenegrin [ˌmɒntɪ'niːgrɪn]	a Montenegrin	the Montenegrins
the **Netherlands** ['neðələndz] *die Niederlande*	Dutch [dʌtʃ]	a Dutchman / a Dutchwoman	the Dutch
Nigeria [naɪ'dʒɪəriə] *Nigeria*	Nigerian [naɪ'dʒɪəriən]	a Nigerian	the Nigerians
North America [ˌnɔːθ‿ə'merɪkə] *Nordamerika*	North American [ˌnɔːθ‿ə'merɪkən]	a North American	the North Americans
Northern Ireland [ˌnɔːðən‿'aɪələnd] *Nordirland*	Northern Irish [ˌnɔːðən‿'aɪrɪʃ]	a Northern Irishman / a Northern Irishwoman	the Northern Irish
Norway ['nɔːweɪ] *Norwegen*	Norwegian [nɔː'wiːdʒən]	a Norwegian	the Norwegians
Poland ['pəʊlənd] *Polen*	Polish ['pəʊlɪʃ]	a Pole [pəʊl]	the Poles
Portugal ['pɔːtʃʊgl] *Portugal*	Portuguese [ˌpɔːtʃu'giːz]	a Portuguese	the Portuguese
Romania [ru'meɪniə] *Rumänien*	Romanian [ru'meɪniən]	a Romanian	the Romanians
Russia ['rʌʃə] *Russland*	Russian ['rʌʃn]	a Russian	the Russians
Scotland ['skɒtlənd] *Schottland*	Scottish ['skɒtɪʃ]	a Scot [skɒt]; a Scotsman / a Scotswoman	the Scots, the Scottish
Serbia ['sɜːbiə] *Serbien*	Serbian ['sɜːbiən]	a Serbian	the Serbians
Slovakia [sləʊ'vækiə] *die Slowakei*	Slovak ['sləʊvæk]	a Slovak	the Slovaks
Slovenia [sləʊ'viːniə] *Slowenien*	Slovenian [sləʊ'viːniən]	a Slovenian	the Slovenians
South America [ˌsaʊθ‿ə'merɪkə] *Südamerika*	South American [ˌsaʊθ‿ə'merɪkən]	a South American	the South Americans
Spain [speɪn] *Spanien*	Spanish ['spænɪʃ]	a Spaniard ['spænɪəd]	the Spanish
Sweden ['swiːdn] *Schweden*	Swedish ['swiːdɪʃ]	a Swede [swiːd]	the Swedes
Switzerland ['swɪtsələnd] *die Schweiz*	Swiss [swɪs]	a Swiss	the Swiss
Turkey ['tɜːki] *die Türkei*	Turkish ['tɜːkɪʃ]	a Turk [tɜːk]	the Turks
Ukraine [juː'kreɪn] *die Ukraine*	Ukrainian [juː'kreɪniən]	a Ukrainian	the Ukrainians
the **United Kingdom** [juˌnaɪtɪd 'kɪŋdəm] *das Vereinigte Königreich*	British ['brɪtɪʃ]	a Briton ['brɪtn]	the British
the **United States of America** [juˌnaɪtɪd ˌsteɪts‿əv‿ə'merɪkə] *die Vereinigten Staaten von Amerika*	American [ə'merɪkən]	an American	the Americans
Wales [weɪlz] *Wales*	Welsh [welʃ]	a Welshman/-woman	the Welsh

Irregular verbs

infinitive	simple past form	past participle	
(to) **be**	*I/he/she/it* **was**; *you/we/you/they* **were**	**been**	sein
(to) **beat** [iː]	**beat** [iː]	**beaten** [iː]	schlagen; besiegen
(to) **become**	**became**	**become**	werden
(to) **begin**	**began**	**begun**	beginnen, anfangen
(to) **bend down**	**bent down**	**bent down**	sich hinunterbeugen, sich bücken
(to) **bet**	**bet**	**bet**	wetten
(to) **bite** [aɪ]	**bit** [ɪ]	**bitten**	beißen
(to) **blow** [əʊ]	**blew**	**blown** [əʊ]	pusten, blasen
(to) **break** [eɪ]	**broke**	**broken**	brechen; zerbrechen
(to) **bring**	**brought**	**brought**	(mit-, her)bringen
(to) **build**	**built**	**built**	bauen
(to) **burst**	**burst**	**burst**	platzen
(to) **buy**	**bought**	**bought**	kaufen
(to) **catch**	**caught**	**caught**	fangen
(to) **choose** [uː]	**chose** [əʊ]	**chosen** [əʊ]	aussuchen, (aus)wählen; sich aussuchen
(to) **come**	**came**	**come**	kommen
(to) **cost**	**cost**	**cost**	kosten
(to) **cut**	**cut**	**cut**	schneiden
(to) **do** [uː]	**did**	**done** [ʌ]	tun, machen
(to) **draw**	**drew**	**drawn**	zeichnen
(to) **drink**	**drank**	**drunk**	trinken
(to) **drive** [aɪ]	**drove** [əʊ]	**driven** [ɪ]	fahren *(ein Auto/mit dem Auto)*
(to) **eat**	**ate** [et, eɪt]	**eaten**	essen
(to) **fall**	**fell**	**fallen**	fallen, stürzen; hinfallen
(to) **feed**	**fed**	**fed**	füttern
(to) **feel**	**felt**	**felt**	fühlen; sich fühlen
(to) **fight**	**fought**	**fought**	kämpfen; bekämpfen
(to) **find**	**found**	**found**	finden
(to) **fly**	**flew**	**flown** [əʊ]	fliegen
(to) **forget**	**forgot**	**forgotten**	vergessen
(to) **get**	**got**	**got**	bekommen; besorgen, holen; werden; gelangen, (hin)kommen
(to) **give**	**gave**	**given**	geben, schenken
(to) **go** [əʊ]	**went**	**gone** [ɒ]	gehen; werden
(to) **grow** [əʊ]	**grew**	**grown** [əʊ]	wachsen; anbauen, anpflanzen; werden
(to) **hang**	**hung**	**hung**	hängen
(to) **have**	**had**	**had**	haben
(to) **hear** [ɪə]	**heard** [ɜː]	**heard**	hören
(to) **hide** [aɪ]	**hid** [ɪ]	**hidden**	verstecken; sich verstecken
(to) **hit**	**hit**	**hit**	schlagen; prallen gegen, stoßen gegen
(to) **hold**	**held**	**held**	halten
(to) **hurt**	**hurt**	**hurt**	schmerzen, wehtun; verletzen
(to) **keep**	**kept**	**kept**	halten; behalten; aufbewahren
(to) **kneel** [niː]	**knelt** [nelt]	**knelt** [nelt]	knien
(to) **know** [nəʊ]	**knew** [njuː]	**known** [nəʊn]	wissen; kennen
(to) **lay**	**laid**	**laid**	legen
(to) **lead** [iː]	**led**	**led**	führen, leiten

infinitive	simple past form	past participle	
(to) **leave** [iː]	**left**	**left**	lassen; zurücklassen; verlassen; (ab)fahren; (weg)gehen
(to) **let**	**let**	**let**	lassen
(to) **lie**	**lay**	**lain**	liegen
(to) **light**	**lit**	**lit**	anzünden
(to) **lose** [uː]	**lost** [ɒ]	**lost** [ɒ]	verlieren
(to) **make**	**made**	**made**	machen; herstellen
(to) **mean** [iː]	**meant** [e]	**meant** [e]	bedeuten; meinen, sagen wollen
(to) **meet** [iː]	**met** [e]	**met**	treffen; sich treffen; kennenlernen
(to) **pay (for)**	**paid**	**paid**	bezahlen
(to) **put**	**put**	**put**	*(etwas wohin)* tun, legen, stellen
(to) **read** [iː]	**read** [e]	**read** [e]	lesen
(to) **ride** [aɪ]	**rode** a bike	**ridden**	reiten; *(Rad)* fahren
(to) **ring**	**rang**	**rung**	klingeln, läuten
(to) **rise up**	**rose up**	**risen up**	aufragen, emporragen *(Berge, Türme, ...)*
(to) **run**	**ran**	**run**	rennen, laufen
(to) **say** [eɪ]	**said** [e]	**said**	sagen
(to) **see**	**saw**	**seen**	sehen
(to) **sell**	**sold**	**sold**	verkaufen
(to) **send**	**sent**	**sent**	schicken, senden
(to) **set**	**set**	**set**	untergehen *(Sonne)*
(to) **set up**	**set up**	**set up**	aufstellen, aufbauen, errichten, einrichten
(to) **shake**	**shook**	**shaken**	schütteln
(to) **shine**	**shone** [ɒ]	**shone** [ɒ]	leuchten; scheinen *(Sonne)*
(to) **shoot**	**shot** [ɒ]	**shot** [ɒ]	(er)schießen
(to) **show**	**showed**	**shown**	zeigen
(to) **sing**	**sang**	**sung**	singen
(to) **sit**	**sat**	**sat**	sitzen; sich setzen
(to) **sleep**	**slept**	**slept**	schlafen
(to) **speak** [iː]	**spoke**	**spoken**	sprechen
(to) **spend**	**spent**	**spent**	*(Zeit)* verbringen; *(Geld)* ausgeben
(to) **spin around**	**spun around**	**spun around**	sich (im Kreis) drehen; herumwirbeln
(to) **spread** [e]	**spread** [e]	**spread** [e]	(sich) ausbreiten, verbreiten
(to) **stand**	**stood**	**stood**	stehen; sich (hin)stellen
(to) **stick**	**stuck**	**stuck**	stechen, stecken
(to) **swim**	**swam**	**swum**	schwimmen
(to) **take**	**took**	**taken**	nehmen, mitnehmen; (weg-, hin)bringen; *(Zeit)* brauchen; dauern
(to) **teach** [iː]	**taught**	**taught**	unterrichten, lehren
(to) **tear down** [eə]	**tore down**	**torn down**	abreißen *(Gebäude)*
(to) **tell**	**told**	**told**	erzählen, berichten
(to) **think**	**thought**	**thought**	denken, glauben
(to) **throw**	**threw**	**thrown**	werfen
(to) **understand**	**understood**	**understood**	verstehen
(to) **wake up**	**woke up**	**woken up**	aufwachen; wecken
(to) **wear** [eə]	**wore** [ɔː]	**worn**	tragen *(Kleidung)*
(to) **win**	**won** [ʌ]	**won**	gewinnen
(to) **write**	**wrote**	**written**	schreiben

Unit 1

a)

1	B	E	G	A	N
2	C	H	O	S	E
3	D	R	O	V	E
4	H	E	A	R	D
5	T	H	R	E	W

BEGAN
CHOSE
DROVE
HEARD
THREW

Famous London building

SHARD

b)

1	A	G	R	E	E	D
2	B	E	C	O	M	E
3	C	H	O	S	E	N
4	D	R	I	V	E	N
5	J	U	M	P	E	D
6	P	L	A	Y	E	D

AGREED
BECOME
CHOSEN
DRIVEN
JUMPED
PLAYED

Game

MEMORY

1 a) *False. Our neighbours have been living here since 2011.*
b) *True.*
c) *False. Our neighbours have been living here for xx years. (In 2015 xx = 4 years. In 2016 xx = 5 years, etc.)*

2 a) *False. It's been raining for just under 7 hours.*
b) *False. It's been raining since just after 8 o'clock.*
c) *True.*

3 a) *True.*
b) *False. Mrs Bell has been waiting since 10:05.*
c) False. Mrs Crown has been waiting for 20 minutes.

Unit 2

a) 1 *scientist* 2 *furniture* 3 *rock*
4 *school* 5 *fly* 6 *painter*
7 *dentist* 8 *autumn* 9 *glove*

b) *a, I*
an, in
air, all, ill, lip, paw, ran, win
fair, fall, fill, pair, plan, rain, will, wall

Unit 3

1 *in*, 2 *in*, 3 *in*, 4 *on*, 5 *on*, 6 *at*, 7 *on*, 8 *on*, 9 *on*, 10 *at*, 11 *in*, 12 *at*, 13 *at*, 14 *in*, 15 *on*
Tina's birthday is on the 6th June.

Unit 4

1 a) candy	2 b) trash can	3 c) restroom	4 a) streetcar	5 b) apartment
6 c) yard	7 a) sneakers	8 c) flashlight	9 b) schedule	10 a) eraser

Unit 5

What would you do … (Suggestions)

2 if an old woman got on the bus and there were no free seats?
A: I'd stand up and offer her my seat.

3 if you broke a neighbour's window while you were playing ball?
A: I'd go to the neighbours and say sorry. *B: I'd run away and laugh.*

4 if you didn't like the birthday present your best friend gave you?
A: I'd smile and say thank you anyway. *B:* I'd ask for something else.

5 if you saw a friend stealing something in a shop?
A: I'd tell him/her not to steal, or I'd phone the police. B: I'd ask him/her to steal something for me too.

Classroom English

Zu Beginn und am Ende des Unterrichts

Guten Morgen, Frau …	**Good morning, Mrs/Miss …** *(bis 12 Uhr)*
Guten Tag, Herr …	**Good afternoon, Mr …** *(ab 12 Uhr)*
Entschuldigung, dass ich zu spät komme.	**Sorry I'm late.**
Auf Wiedersehen! / Bis morgen.	**Goodbye. / See you tomorrow.**

Du brauchst Hilfe

Können Sie/Kannst du mir bitte helfen?	**Can you help me, please?**
Auf welcher Seite sind wir, bitte?	**What page are we on, please?**
Was heißt … auf Englisch/Deutsch?	**What's … in English/German?**
Können Sie/Kannst du mir bitte … buchstabieren?	**Can you spell …, please?**
Können Sie es bitte an die Tafel schreiben?	**Can you write it on the board, please?**

Hausaufgaben und Übungen

Tut mir leid, ich habe mein Schulheft nicht dabei.	**Sorry, I don't have my exercise book.**
Kann ich bitte vorlesen?	**Can I read, please?**
Ich verstehe diese Übung nicht.	**I don't understand this exercise.**
Ich kann Nummer 3 nicht lösen.	**I can't do number 3.**
Entschuldigung, ich bin noch nicht fertig.	**Sorry, I haven't finished.**
Ich habe … Ist das auch richtig?	**I have … Is that right too?**
Tut mir leid, das weiß ich nicht.	**Sorry, I don't know.**
Was haben wir (als Hausaufgabe) auf?	**What's for homework?**

Wenn es Probleme gibt

Kann ich es auf Deutsch sagen?	**Can I say it in German?**
Können Sie/Kannst du bitte lauter sprechen?	**Can you speak louder, please?**
Können Sie/Kannst du das bitte noch mal sagen?	**Can you say that again, please?**
Kann ich bitte das Fenster öffnen/zumachen?	**Can I open/close the window, please?**
Kann ich bitte zur Toilette gehen?	**Can I go to the toilet, please?**

Partnerarbeit

Kann ich mit Julian arbeiten?	**Can I work with Julian?**
Kann ich bitte dein Lineal/deinen Filzstift/… haben?	**Can I have your ruler/felt tip/…, please?**
Danke. / Vielen Dank.	**Thank you. / Thanks a lot.**
Du bist dran.	**It's your turn.**

Diese Arbeitsanweisungen findest du häufig im Schülerbuch.

Act out the song.	Spiele das Lied vor.
Add more words to the table.	Füge weitere Wörter zur Tabelle hinzu.
Ask/Answer the questions.	Stelle/Beantworte die Fragen.
Check/Compare with a partner.	Prüfe/Vergleiche mit einem Partner/einer Partnerin.
Choose the correct/right words.	Wähle die richtigen Wörter.
Copy the words from the box.	Schreibe die Wörter aus dem Kästchen ab.
Correct the sentences.	Verbessere/Korrigiere die Sätze.
Find this information.	Finde/Suche diese Informationen.
Find out about cities in Britain.	Informiere dich über Großstädte in Großbritannien.
Finish/Complete the table below.	Vervollständige die Tabelle unten.
Get more words from page 44.	Hole zusätzliche Wörter von Seite 44.
Give reasons.	Gib Gründe an.
Give your text to another pair.	Gebt euren Text einem anderen Paar.
Go on with new ideas.	Mache weiter mit neuen Ideen.
Hang the poster up in your classroom.	Hänge das Poster im Klassenzimmer auf.
Hold up the card.	Halte die Karte hoch.
Imagine you're Silky.	Stelle dir vor, du bist Silky.
Label your drawing.	Beschrifte deine Zeichnung.
Learn the rhyme.	Lerne den Reim/Vers auswendig.
Leave space for your answers.	Lasse Platz für deine Antworten.
Listen to Morph.	Höre Morph zu.
Look at page 10.	Siehe auf Seite 10 nach. / Siehe dir Seite 10 an.
Look at the picture.	Schaue dir das Bild an.
Look up the word if you don't understand it.	Schlage das Wort nach, wenn du es nicht verstehst.
Make appointments with three partners.	Verabrede dich mit drei Partnern/Partnerinnen.
Make groups of three.	Bildet Dreiergruppen.
Match the words to the pictures.	Ordne die Wörter den Bildern zu.
Practise the words.	Übe die Wörter.
Put all the verbs in the right place.	Setze alle Verben an der richtigen Stelle ein.
Put the card into your MyBook.	Lege die Karte in dein MyBook.
Put up your hand.	Melde dich.
Read the dialogue out loud to your group.	Lies deiner Gruppe den Dialog laut vor.
Rewrite the text.	Schreibe den Text neu.
Scan the text to find these words.	Überfliege den Text und versuche, diese Wörter zu finden.
Sing along with the chorus.	Singe den Refrain mit.
Start a profile for Sam.	Fange ein Profil für Sam an.
Swap cards with another team.	Tauscht Karten mit einem anderen Team.
Take turns.	Wechselt euch ab.
Talk to different partners about the photo.	Rede mit verschiedenen Partnern/Partnerinnen über das Foto.
Talk to your partner like this: …	Rede so mit deinem Partner/deiner Partnerin: …
Think of a sentence.	Denke dir einen Satz aus.
Use these words: …	Verwende diese Wörter: …
Walk around the classroom.	Gehe im Klassenzimmer herum.
Write down the letters in the right order.	Schreibe die Buchstaben in der richtigen Reihenfolge auf.

Titelbild

Carlos Borrell Eiköter (S. I-Introseiten); **Mauritius** (S. I Leuchtturm: Alamy /GeoStills); **Shutterstock** (S.I Flagge: Luis Santos; S.I Wanderer: marino bocelli)

Illustrationen

Stefan Bachmann (S. 115; S. 135; S. 136; S. 146); **Christian Bartz** (S. 132; S. 133); **Roland Beier**, Berlin (S. 156; S. 160; S. 161; S. 162 Mi.; S. 166 ob.; S. 172 Mi. li.; S. 172 un. (1-3); S. 174 Mi. (1-4); S. 177 un.; S. 182 ob.; S. 182 Mi. (1-4); S. 190; S. 192; S. 193 Mi.; S. 194 re.; S. 196 re.; S. 198; S. 199 ob.; S. 200; S. 201; S. 203 Mi.; S. 206 ob.; S. 208); **Volkhard Bindner** (S. 108 re.; S. 109 Mi.); **Tobias Dahmen**, Utrecht (S. 12; S. 19; S. 26; S. 28 un.; S. 41; S. 42; S. 43 Mi.; S. 50; S. 52; S. 63; S. 68; S. 78 un.; S. 80; S. 92; S. 93; S. 114; S. 121; S. 140; S. 143; S. 144; S. 147; S. 149; S. 169; S. 171; S. 172 un. li.; S. 172 Mi. re.; S. 173; S. 174 Mi. li.; S. 175; S. 176; S. 177 ob.; S. 178; S. 180; S. 181; S. 182 Mi. li.; S. 184; S. 185); **Carlos Borrell Eiköter, Berlin** (S. 5 Hintergrund; S. 8 Hintergrund; S. 56 un.; S. 57; S. 168); **Michael Fleischmann**, Waldegg (S. 189; S. 211 ob.; S. 211 un.; S. 212; S. 217 un.) **Eric Gira** (S. 30, un. li.; S. 91 Mi.; S. 105 un.; S. 131 un.; S. 134; S. 137 Mi.: Zweiband) **Bonnie Glänzer** (S. 158; S. 159); **Jeongsook Lee** (S. 188); M. B. Schulz, Düsseldorf (S. 60; S. 77; S. 88 un.; S. 118 ob.; S. 138); **Michael Teßmer** (S. 108 li.).

Fotos

Adam Roach (S. 39 ob.); **Adobe** (S. 4 Unit 3: ronnybas; S. 6 Unit 4: MarcelS; S. 9 L: cla'; S. 9 F: zefart; S. 15 (4): ian woolcock; S. 22 (2): pauws99; S. 22 (3): mohsinjamil; S. 27 B: daliu; S. 27 E: Dmitry Naumov; S. 28 ob.: okorokovanatalya; S. 56 (5): Fred; S. 56 (6): Nejron Photo; S. 59 B: ronnybas; S. 64 (1): batman6794; S. 64 (4): Silvy K.; S. 65 ob.: Darla Hallmark; S. 86 B: Tupungato; S. 86 C: MarcelS; S. 98: alon; S. 104: MarcelS; S. 105 Mi.: ras-slava; S. 106: Tupungato; S. 111 un. li.: virtua73; S. 111 un. Mi.: Kletr; S. 111 un. re.: Gabriele Rohde; S. 128 v. li. n. re. (1): dianamower; S. 128 (2): lizascotty; S. 128 (4): Constantinos; S. 128 (6): teomakla; S. 128 (7): robootb; S. 128 (9): virtua73; S. 128 (10): Kletr; S. 128 (11): Gabriele Rohde; S. 128 (13): matthias21; S. 128 (15): Scisetti Alfio); **akg** (S. 15 (2): Heritage-Images/The Print Collector; S. 30 un. re.: SCIENCE PHOTO LIBRARY; S. 32 re.: WHA/World History Archive; S. 33 un. North Wind Picture Archives; S. 56 (3): Album); **bpk** (S. 32 li.: Alinari Archives/ Vasari Alessandro; S. 109 ob.: Coll. Marc Walter/ adoc-photos); **Bridgeman Images** (S. 30 Mi.: Look and Learn; S. 32 Mi.: Philip Mould Ltd, London); **Cecile Niemitz-Rossant** (S. 88 ob.: S. 112 ob. li. hinten); **Chuck Lewis** (S. 112 Mi. li.); **ClipDealer** (S. 54 (2): Andres Rodriguez; S. 78 (3): ArTo; S. 128 (5): hadot; S. 163: © Robert Kneschke); **Courtesy of AELTC** (S. 9 A: Bob Martin); **Crooked Letter Films** (S. 85 ob.; S. 86 Mi.; S. 86 un.; S. 87 D; S. 87 un.; S. 125); **DPA** (S. 13: EPA; S. 78 (2): Wolfgang Kumm; S. 78 (7): chromorange; S. 85 un.: REUTERS; S. 110 A: Leemage/Luisa Ricciar; S. 110 D: dpaweb; S. 111 C: AP/AP Photo); **Guardian News and Media Ltd.** (S.61); **interfoto** (S. 14 ob. li.: Mary Evans/ Natural History Museum; S. 14 ob. re.: Mary Evans/Natural History Museum); **Mauritius** (S. 4 Unit 2: alamy stock photo/Alan Novelli; S. 9 D: alamy stock photo/Andy Myatt; S. 9 I: Carlos Sánchez Pereyra; S. 9 N: alamy stock photo/Greg Balfour Evans; S. 15 (3): Simon Montgomery; S. 34: alamy stock photo/Alan Novelli; S. 54 (3): alamy stock photo/Jeff Morgan 01; S. 55 Mi. re.: Bernd Brueggemann/Alamy; S. 55 un. re.: alamy stock photo/RugbyUnionWales; S. 56 (1): Rick Strange; S. 65 un.: alamy stock photo/FLPA; S. 66 ob.: Julie Quarry; S. 66 un.: Nikreates; S. 78 (6): Steffen Beuthan; S. 83 un.: alamy stock photo/Conner Flecks; S. 83 ob.: alamy stock photo/Joseph Reid; S. 86 A: alamy stock photo/Kevin Foy; S. 87 E: mauritius images / Richard Ellis / Alamy; S. 88: alamy stock photo/Melvyn Longhurst; S. 111 F: alamy stock photo/RSBPhoto; S. 112 Mi.re.: alamy stock photo/Irene Abdou; S. 113: alamy stock photo/Irene Abdou; S. 126 ob.: alamy stock photo/James Davis Photography; S. 153 un.: Barry Lewis); **Network Rail** (S. 27 C: Copyright © 2017 Network Rail); **Nigel Wilson Photography**, Bristol (S. 4 Mo; S. 4 Emily; S. 4 Philip; S. 5 Dylan; S. 7 Tyler; S. 7 Jasmine; S. 10: M. B. Schulz/Nigel Wilson; S. 11 ob.; S. 20: M. B. Schulz/Nigel Wilson; S. 21; S. 24: M. B. Schulz, Düsseldorf/Nigel Wilson; S. 36: M. B. Schulz/Nigel Wilson; S. 40: M. B. Schulz/Nigel Wilson/Stefan Höhne; S. 47: M.B. Schulz/Nigel Wilson; S. 48; S. 58 li.; S. 66 Emily, Philip, Dylan; S. 67 Emily, Philip, Dylan; S. 70 Philip u. Emily; S. 71; S. 112 ob. li.; S. 141); **Panther Media GmbH** (S. 78 8: Daniel Kühne/Daniel Kühne); **Rockfinch/Claire Cunningham** (S. 23; S. 97 re.); **Sapna Richter** (S. 17 ob. li.; S. 17 un. re.; S. 39 Mi.; S. 43 ob.; S. 69 1; S. 69 4; S. 69 3; S. 69 2; S. 99 un.; S. 117; S. 120; S. 162 un.; S. 164; S. 165); **Shutterstock** (S. 4 Unit 1: pisaphotography; S. 6 Unit 5: torm; S. 9 B: Jaco van Rensburg; S. 9 E: Tupungato; S. 9 G: Monkey Business Images; S. 9 H: Kiev.Victor; S. 9 J: AdStock RF; S. 9 K: Cedric Weber; S. 9 M: Chris Jenner; S. 9 O: RTimages; S. 9 P: Peter Nadolski; S. 9 Q: Nigel Jarvis; S. 11 Mi.: Cornelsen/Algol/Zoltan Gabor/ Bonnie Glänze; S. 11 un.: DavidYoung;S. 14 un. li.: lullabi; S. 15 ob. li.: anshar; S. 15 ob. re.: pptara; S. 15 un. (1): Anna Kucherova; S. 22 v. ob. n. un. (1): Natalya Okorokova; S. 22 (4): Dinko G Kyuchukov; S. 27 A: anshar; S. 27 D: Peter Nadolski; S. 27 F: Cedric Weber; S. 29 A: Photobank gallery; S. 29 B: Risto Puranen; S. 29 C: Giorgio Rossi; S. 29 D: Michael Smith ITWP; S. 32 ob.: jennyt; S. 44: Luminis; S. 54 (4): Helen Hotson; S. 54 ob. li.: image4stock; S. 54 ob. re.: Rainer Lesniewski; S. 55 ob. re.: Mike Charles; S. 56 (2): Jaco van Rensburg; S. 56 (4): kenkistler; S. 58 A: Tomasz Wozniak; S. 59 C: Andriy Blokhin; S. 59 D: Traveller70; S. 64 (2): Mavrick; S. 64 (3): Mr_ seng; S. 65 Mi.: Joseph Sohm; S. 66 Mi.: Jimack; S. 67 ob.: Patrick Civello; S. 67 un.: LizCoughlan; S. 69 Mi. li.: Barbara Ash; S. 69 Mi. Mi.: Bill Florence; S. 69 Mi. re.: Piotr Kalinowski Photos; S. 74: Raymond Thill; S. 78 v. li. n. re. (1): Tupungato; S. 78 (4): piaharrisphotography; S. 78 (5): Pelfophoto; S. 81: TwentyFiveOctober; S. 89: American Spirit; S. 95: kryzhov; S. 96 ob.: Cynthia Farmer; S. 96 Mi. re.: Jessica B. Kirk; S. 96 Mi. li.: Stephen Coburn; S. 96 un.: mooremedia; S. 97 li.: Monkey Business Images; S. 99 ob.: altanaka; S. 100: Christian Mueller; S. 107: Yevgenia Gorbulsky; S. 110 E: Pierre Jean Durieu; S. 111 B: torm; S. 111 ob.: Richard A. McGuirk; S. 112 ob. re.: alexandre zveiger; S. 118 un.: Brocreative; S. 119 ob.: Danny E Hooks; S. 119 un.: B. Franklin; S. 122: travelview; S. 124: holbox; S. 126 un.: HSSphoto; S. 127: Judy M Darby; S. 128 (3): Gavran333; S. 128 (8): focal point;S. 128 (12): Andre Bonn; S. 128 (14): Elena Schweitzer; S. 128 (16): Nenov Brothers Images; S. 131 ob.: Aimee M Lee; S. 137 ob.: pio3; S. 152: Sam Spicer; S. 153 ob.: Bonnie Taylor Barry; S. 155: sarahdesign; S. 191: Anna Kucherova; S. 193 un.: optimarc; S. 194 li.: spline_x; S. 197 ob.: Zentangle; S. 197 Mi.: pupahava; S. 199 Mi. li.: omphoto; S. 199 Mi. re.: Roman Samokhin; S. 199 un.: Sergey Furtaev; S. 202 ob.: Ammit Jack; S. 202 Mi.: Stokkete; S. 202 un.: sergua; S. 203 ob. li.: gresei; S. 203 ob. re.: design56; S. 205 ob.: Gary James Calder; S. 205 un. re.: GraphicsRF; S. 205 un. li.: LineTale; S. 206 Mi. li.: Laurentlesax; S. 206 Mi. re.: optimarc; S. 210: James Steidl; S. 211 Mi.: Anne Kitzman; S. 213 ob.: Gallinago_media; S. 213 un.: Maly Designer; S. 214 v. ob. n. un. (1): DrMadra; S. 214 (2): Hurst Photo; S. 214 (3): Marcio Jose Bastos Silva; S. 214 (4): 1000 Words; S. 214 (5):

Singkham; S. 215 ob. v. li. n. re. (1): Mr.Teerapong Kunkaeo; S. 215 ob. (2): Lifestyle Graphic; S. 215 ob. (3): Iasha; S. 215 ob. (4): Sanit Fuangnakhon; S. 215 gravel: Gunnerchu; S. 215 bits of glass: Runrun2; S. 215 bits of wood: xpixel; S. 215 un.: Sergei Kardashev; S. 216 ob.: boitano; S. 216 Mi. re.: flight of imagination; S. 216 Mi. li.: Angel_AMX; S. 216 un.: browndogstudios; S. 217 ob. li.: All for you friend; S. 217 ob. Mi.: Leena Robinson; S. 217 ob. re.: Kerdkanno; S. 218 ob.: napocska; S. 218 un.: stockcreations; S. 220 ob.: Elena Elisseeva; S. 220 Mi. re.: Jarp2; S. 220 Mi. li.: tommaso lizzul; S. 220 un. re.: mubus7; S. 220 un. li.: Kunal Mehta); **Stefanie Gira**, Berlin (S. 37); **Telluvision** (S. 55 un. li.); **Timothy Vogel** (S. 102); **Transport for London** (S. 18); **Ungermeyer, Rosemeyer + Unger GbR** (S. 30 un. li.: Eric Gira).

TEXT — PRESENTATION

✓ Choose criteria[1] for your feedback.

✎ Add other criteria you need, e.g. for feedback on a story.

	CONTENT
✓	You covered the important points in the task.
	The information was interesting/new.
	You gave examples/details.
	You gave your opinion.
	You gave arguments for your opinion.
✎	Your story had a plot.[2]
	You described the characters.
	...

TEXT

	STRUCTURE
	Your introduction said what the text is about.
	You used paragraphs.
	Each paragraph had a new idea.
	You had a conclusion.
✎	...

	LANGUAGE
	You used different adjectives and adverbs.
	You joined sentences with linking words.
	You used special vocabulary for the topic.
	Your spelling was correct.
	Your grammar was correct.
✎	...

PRESENTATION

	STRUCTURE
	You introduced the topic.
	Your presentation had a clear structure.
	You showed your main points on a poster/...
	You summed up at the end.
	You invited us to ask questions.
✎	...

	DELIVERY
	You seemed relaxed.
	You made eye contact.
	You used notes.
	You spoke clearly.
	You explained your pictures.
✎	...

TIPS

1 Use the criteria you chose to assess your classmate's work.

2 Give details when you say what a classmate did/didn't do well.
Always start with something positive.

Where	What
In the first paragraph you	wrote a good introduction ....
At the end of your presentation you	didn't ask if we had questions /...

3 Suggest how the classmate could do better.
You could try to use more linking words like **and** or **because** /use more pictures / ...

[1] **criteria** *(pl)* [kraɪˈtɪəriə] Kriterien [2]**plot** [plɒt] Handlung

Giving feedback to your classmates: Phrases

You can use emoticons (😃 …) when you assess a classmate's work.

CONTENT	😃	🙂	😐	☹️
You covered the important points in the task.	✓			
The information was interesting/new/…			✓	
You gave examples/details/…				

The phrases below can help you when you give feedback and make suggestions.

😃

Your	introduction ideas pictures …	was were	brilliant! clever! interesting! …

I really liked the way you	structured your text. summed up at the end. explained your pictures ….

Here's an example of what I liked.

🙂

Your	introduction ideas pictures …	was were	quite good. quite interesting. mostly OK. …

You	structured your text explained your pictures summed up …	quite well.

Here's an example of what you	did well. could improve.

😐

Some of your	ideas examples pictures …	were	quite good. interesting. all right. …

Your	introduction grammar …	was OK, but …

You didn't (always)	use linking words. speak very clearly. …

I don't think you	checked your text very carefully. gave very good examples. used enough adjectives. …

Maybe you could	join up these sentences. use captions under your pictures. …

☹️

You forgot to You didn't	cover the important points. use paragraphs. introduce your subject. sum up at the end. …

You almost never	used linking words. gave examples. made eye contact with us. …

I don't think you	did enough research. spent much time on your text. had a good conclusion. …

If I were you I would	start a new paragraph here. write the conclusion again. …